1,000,000 Books

are available to read at

www.ForgottenBooks.com

Read online
Download PDF
Purchase in print

ISBN 978-1-5281-6017-9
PIBN 10925425

This book is a reproduction of an important historical work. Forgotten Books uses state-of-the-art technology to digitally reconstruct the work, preserving the original format whilst repairing imperfections present in the aged copy. In rare cases, an imperfection in the original, such as a blemish or missing page, may be replicated in our edition. We do, however, repair the vast majority of imperfections successfully; any imperfections that remain are intentionally left to preserve the state of such historical works.

Forgotten Books is a registered trademark of FB &c Ltd.
Copyright © 2018 FB &c Ltd.
FB &c Ltd, Dalton House, 60 Windsor Avenue, London, SW19 2RR.
Company number 08720141. Registered in England and Wales.

For support please visit www.forgottenbooks.com

1 MONTH OF FREE READING

at

www.ForgottenBooks.com

By purchasing this book you are eligible for one month membership to ForgottenBooks.com, giving you unlimited access to our entire collection of over 1,000,000 titles via our web site and mobile apps.

To claim your free month visit: www.forgottenbooks.com/free925425

* Offer is valid for 45 days from date of purchase. Terms and conditions apply.

English
Français
Deutsche
Italiano
Español
Português

www.forgottenbooks.com

Mythology Photography **Fiction**
Fishing Christianity **Art** Cooking
Essays Buddhism Freemasonry
Medicine **Biology** Music **Ancient Egypt** Evolution Carpentry Physics
Dance Geology **Mathematics** Fitness
Shakespeare **Folklore** Yoga Marketing
Confidence Immortality Biographies
Poetry **Psychology** Witchcraft
Electronics Chemistry History **Law**
Accounting **Philosophy** Anthropology
Alchemy Drama Quantum Mechanics
Atheism Sexual Health **Ancient History**
Entrepreneurship Languages Sport
Paleontology Needlework Islam
Metaphysics Investment Archaeology
Parenting Statistics Criminology
Motivational

Progress Report
on
State Planning
for
Massachusetts

1936

MASSACHUSETTS STATE PLANNING BOARD

ELISABETH M. HERLIHY, CHAIRMAN.

CLARENCE J. BILADEAU. WILLIAM TRUFANT FOSTER.
FREDERIC H. FAY. HENRY I. HARRIMAN.
WILLIAM STANLEY PARKER.
COMMISSIONER OF CONSERVATION.
COMMISSIONER OF PUBLIC HEALTH.
COMMISSIONER OF PUBLIC WORKS.

ARTHUR W. DEAN, CHIEF ENGINEER.
ARTHUR C. COMEY, CONSULTANT.
DAVID ROZMAN, ASSOCIATE CONSULTANT.
ASSISTED BY W. P. A. STATE PLANNING BOARD PROJECTS

The Commonwealth of Massachusetts
State Planning Board
Room 24, State House
Boston

MEMBERS
ELISABETH M. HERLIHY, C
CLARENCE J. BILADEAU
FREDERIC H. FAY
WILLIAM TRUFANT FOSTER
HENRY I. HARRIMAN
WILLIAM STANLEY PARKER

COMMISSIONER OF CONSER
COMMISSIONER OF PUBLIC
COMMISSIONER OF PUBLIC

ARTHUR W. DEAN, Chief E

—also, Authorized by Chapter 278 of the Acts of 1936 to act jointly with commissions or individuals designated by other New England States and New York in formulating compacts for the development and improvement of natural waterways common to any two or more of said states.

FOREWORD

The Massachusetts State Planning Board has received from Arthur C. Comey, Consultant, addressed to the Board and to the National Resources Committee as coöperating sponsors, the following staff progress report on State Planning for Massachusetts, embodying the major activities of the department for the first year of its existence.

The Board has accepted the report in accordance with the following vote unanimously adopted December 17, 1936:

> VOTED: That the Massachusetts State Planning Board accepts and orders released for public distribution the Staff Progress Report on State Planning for Massachusetts, received from Arthur C. Comey, Consultant, under date of November 30, 1936.

It is, of course, obvious that this report can represent but the first step on the part of the Board toward carrying out the provisions of the Legislative Act under which it was created, which Act declares it shall be the function and duty of the Board "(a) to prepare and from time to time revise and perfect a master plan for the physical development of the Commonwealth."

Such master plan must be a living vital thing. It must, in the first place, possess a background of stability through being reared upon a solid factual basis, such as here presented, complete as far as circumstances permit, and accurate within the limits of records available and field studies possible. It must, in the second place, lend itself to further analysis and development, as here indicated, capable of adaptation to meet changing needs and conditions. Finally, and eventually, it must reach into the future in order that the words of the Act may be fulfilled: "Said master plan shall be made with the general purpose of guiding and accomplishing a coordinated, adjusted, efficient and economic development of the Commonwealth."

With all of these conditions in mind, the Massachusetts State Planning Board is pleased to accept this progress report, and extends to all who had a share in making it possible its most sincere thanks. The Board acknowledges with pleasure its indebtedness to national, regional, state and local officials, to private agencies, and particularly to the able, efficient and loyal service rendered by its consultants, by the members of its permanent staff, by its temporary employees and by its W.P.A. workers. With a continuance of this same cooperation, and of this same splendid type of public service, combined with the criticisms and suggestions which it is hoped will result from a distribution of this present volume, the Massachusetts State Planning Board approaches with confidence the further steps necessary to achieve the final mandate of the Legislative Act to "plan and assist in planning better housing, national, regional and municipal planning and zoning and the better distribution of population and industry."

                                          Massachusetts State Planning Board

                                                          Elisabeth M.

                                                                   Chairman

LETTER OF TRANSMITTAL

November 30, 1936

To the Massachusetts State Planning Board
and the National Resources Committee

Gentlemen:

      I submit herewith a staff progress report on State planning for Massachusetts embodying the results of the first year's work to date. It is particularly gratifying to record here the keen loyal spirit of all members of the various State and Federal staffs that have worked together, without whose combined efforts no such comprehensive presentation of the many diverse facts involved in developing a State plan could have been remotely approached. This report is a truly coöperative undertaking and while it has seemed impractical to set down opposite each chapter or special section the name or names of persons directly responsible for its production, general recognition is here rendered to each of those supervisors and other project leaders who have had charge of the preparation of some specific part of the report.

      This spirit of coöperation has likewise been notable among the various agencies and officials contacted, especially those under whose sponsorship and direction the staffs have been set up and are operating. Thanks are particularly due the State Department of Public Health for making the findings of Works Progress Administration staffs engaged on projects under their supervision an integral part of the water-basin or valley studies covering the entire State. Their general supervision and guidance on water-resource studies, especially in relation to supply and pollution, have been invaluable and have resulted in this section of the report being far more authoritative and complete than could otherwise have been the case.

      Finally, cordial appreciation should be recorded of the friendly help furnished by WPA officials in keeping the WPA staffs operating at the maximum efficiency possible under the limiting circumstances. A large part of the present report is the work of members of these WPA staffs working under general supervision. Furthermore, in those sections of the report that have been in the direct charge of a member of the State Planning Board's own staff a large part of the investigations, drafting, and other work has been performed by WPA people. Since it obviously would be impossible to separate out the work of the WPA staffs from the composite work of all staffs, this progress report constitutes a report of the results of the various WPA projects concerned with State planning, and as such is transmitted to the coöperating sponsors of these projects.

      Respectfully submitted,

Arthur C. Comey
Arthur C. Comey
Consultant

TABLE OF CONTENTS

		Page
Index of Tables		viii
Index of Maps and Charts		xi
Personnel		xvii
Summary		xxi
Chapter I	Introduction	1
Chapter II	Land	9
Chapter III	Water	39
Chapter IV	Power	75
Chapter V	Industry	101
	Part I	102
	Part II	160
Chapter VI	Social Conditions	163
	Population	167
	Employment	179
	Housing	191
	Education	221
	Welfare	229
	Correction	243
Chapter VII	Recreation	261
Chapter VIII	Transport	333
	Highways	334
	Railroads	346
	Water Transport	350
	Aviation	357
Chapter IX	Public Works	377
Chapter X	Community Planning	409
Appendix	Maps and Charts (Prepared, but Not Presented in This Report)	437

INDEX OF TABLES

Table Number		Page
1.	U.S. Agricultural Census Figures for Massachusetts	16
2.	Location of Electric Generating Plants in Massachusetts	77
3.	Installed Capacities of Central-Station Generators in Massachusetts	80
4.	Installed Central-Station Generating Capacities in New England	80
5.	Potential Hydroelectric Power	81
6.	Electric Companies Operating in Massachusetts, and the Areas They Serve	82
7.	Potential Water Power in New England and Adjoining Regions	86
8.	Potential Water Power in Massachusetts 60% of Time	87
9.	Annual KWH Demand in Massachusetts for Selected Areas of Intensive Usage and Companies Serving Each	89
10.	Central-Station Power Produced Annually in Massachusetts	92
11.	Central-Station Kilowatt Hours Sold and Used Annually in Massachusetts	93
12.	Estimated Breakdown of Costs By Operating Power Companies	97
13.	State Planning Board Index of Massachusetts Business	103
14.	Principal Massachusetts Industries	111
15.	Total Industrial Production	149
16.	Total Spendable Income in Massachusetts and Fifteen Other Leading Industrial States	155
17.	Per Capita Spendable Income in Massachusetts and Fifteen Other Leading Industrial States	155
18.	Individual Income Tax Returns By Net Income Classes in Massachusetts and Fifteen Other Leading Industrial States	156
19.	Density of Population, 1930	154
20.	Average Hardness of Water from Large Public Supplies in Each State	158
21.	Future State Population Estimates	171
22.	Distribution of Employment in Massachusetts, New England, and the United States in 1920 and 1930	181
23.	Manufacturing Employment in Massachusetts	183
24.	Employment for All Manufacturing Industries in the United States, New England, and Massachusetts, and for Twelve Important Massachusetts Industries, 1919-1935	184

Table Number		Page
25.	Average Number of Persons Employed in Manufacturing in Ten Important Cities of Massachusetts, 1925-1934	185
26.	Employment in Manufacturing by Counties	186
27.	Percentage Trends in the Number of One-Family, Two-Family, and Multi-Family Houses for Ten Massachusetts Cities, 1900 and 1930	201
28.	Population, Families, and Dwellings in Massachusetts 1910, 1920, 1930	203
29.	Number of Foreclosures, and Percentage Increases Or Decreases in Massachusetts, 1913-1934	205
30.	Tabulation of Facts Revealed by Real Property Inventories of Seven Cities in Massachusetts, 1934	207
31.	Tenure of Homes, Farm and Non-Farm, for Massachusetts, 1890-1930	209
32.	Farms and Farm Property in Massachusetts, 1900-1930	210
33.	Rural Housing Conditions in Part-Time Farming Areas Near Lowell and Taunton, Massachusetts, 1930	211
34.	President's Conference on Home Building and Home Ownership Survey of Rural Housing in U.S. 1932	213
35.	Rural Housing Conditions in Franklin, Hampshire, and Worcester Counties, 1934	214
36.	Use of Two Educational Systems	223
37.	Roman Catholic Schools - Data by Dioceses	224
38.	Persons Given Relief and Relief Expenditures by the State and by Cities and Towns	238
39.	Expenditures of the Department of Public Welfare, 1920-1935	239
40.	Private Incorporated Charitable Organizations in Massachusetts	240
41.	Capacity and Daily Inmate Average of Massachusetts Correction Institutions, 1935	246
42.	Total Number of Arrests, by Cities and Towns, 1920-1935	249
43.	Total Arrests and Number Per 1000 Population by Cities of Over 25,000 Population in Massachusetts, 1935	251
44.	Probation Figures for Massachusetts, 1920-1935	252
45.	Parole Statistics for Massachusetts, 1922-1935	254
46.	Social Status of Prisoners Sentenced to State Adult Penal Institutions and County Jails and Houses of Correction, 1920-1935	255
47.	Annual Per Capita Costs of State and County Penal Institutions, 1920-1935	257
48.	Reported Number of People Who Can Be Served by Vacational Shelters in Massachusetts, 1936	265

Table Number		Page
49.	Capacity of Hotels, Boarding Houses, and Tourist Homes in Massachusetts	267
50.	Overnight Tourist Cabins in Massachusetts	269
51.	Public Campgrounds, Tent and Trailer Sites, and Cabins and Open Shelters in Massachusetts	271
52.	Juvenile and Adult Camps in Massachusetts	273
53.	Youth Hostels in Massachusetts	274
54.	Classification of Golf Courses in Massachusetts	279
55.	Yacht, Boat, and Canoe Clubs, Canoe Trips, and Boat Liveries in Massachusetts	283
56.	Picnic Grounds and Facilities in Massachusetts, 1936	297
57.	Horse and Dog Race Track Activities in Massachusetts, 1935	299
58.	Massachusetts Winter Sports, 1935-1936	304
59.	Hunting In Massachusetts, 1935	315
60.	Game Distribution in Massachusetts, 1934-1935	318
61.	Fishing Facilities in Massachusetts, 1936	319
62.	Stocked Waters in Massachusetts, 1933-1935	321
63.	Stocked Fish Distribution in Massachusetts, 1934-1935	322
64.	Open Space Lands in Massachusetts, 1936	325
65.	Reliability of Air Transportation Service, 1935	359
66.	Statistics of Scheduled and Miscellaneous Flying Operations	362
67.	Public Works Administration 1935 Projects	382
68.	Works Progress Administration Projects	384
69.	State Departments Making Substantial Capital Improvement Expenditures	385
70.	County Expenditures for Capital Improvements in 1935	405
71.	Planning Boards in Massachusetts	418
72.	Suggested Forms for Current Reports of Action by Zoning Appeal Boards and for Zoning District Changes	431

INDEX OF MAPS AND CHARTS

Number		Following Page
50-C3	Organization of Massachusetts State Planning	xvi
50-C4	WPA State Planning Projects	xvi
71-2	Topographical Map Showing Altitudes	10
71-6	Reconnaissance Soil Erosion Survey	12
51-12	Average Winter Temperature	12
51-19	Average Annual Snowfall	12
51-18	Average Annual Precipitation	12
51-22	Average Annual Runoff	12
51-25	Type of Farming Areas in Massachusetts	12
61-C2	Land Utilization in Massachusetts, 1880-1935	18
51-6	Percentages of Farm Areas in Woodland by Towns and Cities, 1935	18
51-C1	Average Size of Farms and Improved Land per Farm in Massachusetts, 1880-1935	20
51-C2	Total Farm Acreage and Improved Farm Land in Massachusetts, 1880-1935	20
51-C3	Total Number of Farms in Massachusetts, 1880-1935	20
71-10	Distribution of Farms	20
51-5	Average Value per Acre of Farm Land and Buildings by Towns and Cities, 1935	22
51-7	Farm Population per Square Mile in the Towns and Cities of Massachusetts, 1935	22
51-8	Percentages of Improved Land in Farms by Towns and Cities, 1935	22
51-9	Percentages of Town and City Areas in Farms, 1935	22
51-C4A	Symbols for Land Utilization Map (Sheet 1)	24
51-C4B	Symbols for Land Utilization Map (Sheet 2)	24
51-C5	Symbols for Road and Building Map	24
51-C6	Symbols for Soil Classification Map	24
51-84B	Roads and Buildings - Town of Chester	24
51-84E	Roads and Waterways - Town of Chester	24
51-84C	Land Utilization - Town of Chester	24
51-84D	Soil Classification - Town of Chester	24
51-84A	Topography - Town of Chester	24
51-C7	Chester - Land Cover; Soil Adaptability for Agriculture	24
51-261B	Roads and Buildings - Town of Peru	26
51-261C	Land Utilization - Town of Peru	26
51-175B	Roads and Buildings - Town of Lancaster	28
51-175C	Land Utilization - Town of Lancaster	28
51-175D	Soil Classification - Town of Lancaster	28

MASSACHUSETTS STATE PLANNING BOARD

Number		Following Page
51-175A	Topography - Town of Lancaster	28
51-C8	Lancaster - Land Cover; Soil Adaptability for Agriculture	28
51-56B	Roads and Buildings - Town of Billerica	30
51-56C	Land Utilization - Town of Billerica	32
51-333B	Roads and Buildings - Town of Uxbridge	34
51-333C	Land Utilization - Town of Uxbridge	34
51-159B	Roads and Buildings - Town of Hingham	36
51-159C	Land Utilization - Town of Hingham	36
72-2	Water Supply and Treatment	42
72-15	Municipalities Discharging Untreated Domestic Sewage	42
72-3	Sewage Disposal Works	42
72-7	Municipalities Without Sewerage Systems	42
72-5	Flood Damage - March 1936	42
72-6	Water Resources Composite Data Map	46
52-C20	Precipitation - Nashua River Watershed at Fitchburg Station	48
52-C15	Precipitation - Chicopee River Watershed at Hardwick Station	48
52-C18	Precipitation - Blackstone River Watershed at Worcester Station	48
52-C17	Precipitation - Connecticut River Watershed in Massachusetts at Amherst Station	48
52-C13	Precipitation - Housatonic River Watershed at Pittsfield Station	48
52-C12	Precipitation - Deerfield River Watershed at Heath Station	48
52-C16	Precipitation - Westfield River Watershed at Chesterfield Station	48
52-C14	Precipitation - Millers River Watershed at Winchendon Station	48
72-8	Nashua River Water Resources Data	52
72-9	Nashua River Water Supply	54
72-10	Nashua River Sewage Disposal	54
72-12	Nashua River Flood Areas & Damages	56
72-13	Nashua River Flood Control	58
52-18	Sample Study for Detention Basin	58
73-1	Transmission Lines and Power Plants in Massachusetts	78
83-1	Generating Stations and Transmission Lines in New England	80
53-C6	Installed Capacity of Central Station Electric Generators in Massachusetts	80
73-5	Developed and Potential Water Power	82

MASSACHUSETTS STATE PLANNING BOARD

Number		Following Page
83-2	Principal Sources of Undeveloped Water Power in New England and Adjoining Regions	82
73-4	Areas Served by Operating Power Companies in Massachusetts	82
73-3	Principal Centers of Electric Power Demand in Massachusetts	88
53-C1	Central Station Power Produced Annually in Massachusetts	88
53-C2	Central Station Power Consumed Annually in Massachusetts	88
73-2	Proposed Rural Electrification Extensions	94
53-C5	Composite Graph Showing Typical Costs of Production, Transmission and Distribution of Electric Power	96
53-C4	Estimated Decrease in Domestic Power Rates Through Increased Usage	98
54-C15	Massachusetts Business Index - Physical Volume of Business	104
54-C13	Business Activity in Massachusetts and United States	106
74-7	Value Added in Manufacture	110
54-C1	Index of Value Added by Manufacture in Massachusetts and United States, All Industries, 1849-1933	110
54-C3G	Percentage of the Value of Products in Each Main Industrial Group in Massachusetts to the Value of Products of all Massachusetts Industry, 1909-1933	110
54-C47	Thirty-two States Which are Important Producers in One or More of Massachusetts' Leading Industries	111
54-C2	Value of all Manufactured Products in Massachusetts and Fifteen Competing States, 1909-1935	112
54-C4	Value of Woolen and Worsted Goods Manufactured in Massachusetts and Six Competing States, 1909-1933	114
54-C3	Value of Boots and Shoes (other than rubber) Manufactured in Massachusetts and Eight Competing States, 1909-1935	116
54-C5	Value of Cotton Goods Manufactured in Massachusetts and Fifteen Competing States, 1909-1933	118
54-C11	Value of Dyeing and Finishing Textiles in Massachusetts and Eight Competing States, 1909-1933	120
54-C23	Value of Leather, Tanned, Curried and Finished in Massachusetts and Twelve Competing States, 1909-1933	122
54-C30	Value of Newspapers and Periodicals Printing and Publishing in Massachusetts and Seven Competing States, 1914-1933	124

MASSACHUSETTS STATE PLANNING BOARD

Number		Following Page
54-C7	Value of Electrical Machinery, Apparatus and Supplies Manufactured in Massachusetts and Twelve Competing States, 1909-1933	126
54-C10	Value of Pulp and Paper Manufactured in Massachusetts and Seven Competing States, 1909-1933	128
54-C8	Value of Foundry and Machine Shop Products Manufactured in Massachusetts and Twelve Competing States, 1909-1933	130
54-C31	Value of Book, Job, Music Printing and Publishing in Massachusetts and Seven Competing States, 1914-1933	132
54-C14A	Value of Meat Packing in Massachusetts and Twenty-one Competing States, 1909-1933	134
54-C14B	Value of Meat Packing in Massachusetts and Twenty-one Competing States, 1909-1933	134
54-C12A	Value of Knit Goods Manufactured in Massachusetts and Fifteen Competing States, 1909-1933	136
54-C12B	Value of Knit Goods Manufactured in Massachusetts and Fifteen Competing States, 1909-1933	136
54-C27	Value of Textile Machinery and Parts Manufactured in Massachusetts and Four Competing States, 1919-1933	138
54-C29	Value of Silk and Rayon Goods Manufactured in Massachusetts and Six Competing States, 1909-1933	140
54-C25	Value of Women's Clothing Manufactured in Massachusetts and Eight Competing States, 1909-1933	142
54-C24	Value of Confectionery Manufactured in Massachusetts and Eight Competing States, 1909-1935	144
54-C28	Value of Rubber Boots and Shoes Manufactured in Massachusetts with Total for All Other States, 1909-1933	146
54-C26A	Value of Furniture Manufactured in Massachusetts and Fifteen Competing States, 1909-1933	148
54-C26B	Value of Furniture Manufactured in Massachusetts and Fifteen Competing States, 1909-1933	148
54-C6	Ratio of State and Municipal Taxes to Spendable Income, 1932-1933	152
54-C9	Massachusetts Tax Receipts, 1924-1935	152
54-C32	Number of Industrial Strikes and Lockouts per Establishment in Nineteen Leading Industrial States Compared with Strikes in Massachusetts	154
54A-C1	a. Percentage Rate of Increase in Population of Massachusetts; b. Population of Massachusetts 1850-1935, at five year intervals	170

MASSACHUSETTS STATE PLANNING BOARD

Number		Following Page
54A-C2	Births, Deaths and Net Immigration in Massachusetts, 1880-1935	170
54A-C3A	Population of Massachusetts 1880-1935, with various estimates for 1935-1960	170
54A-C3B	Estimates for Future Population of Massachusetts, 1940-1960	170
54A-C4	a. Births and Deaths per Thousand Population in Massachusetts, 1910-1935; b. Births and Deaths in Massachusetts, 1910-1935	172
54A-C5	Cumulative Births, Deaths, and Net Immigration in Massachusetts, 1880-1935	172
74-3	Population Distribution, 1860	172
74-2	Population Distribution, 1910	174
74-4	Population Distribution, 1935	174
74-5	Population Density, 1935	174
74-6	Population Changes, 1910-1935	174
54A-C14	Percentage Rate of Change for Municipalities of Various Size Classes in Massachusetts, 1880-1935	174
54A-C30	Percentage Distribution in Special Age Groups of Population of Massachusetts, 1880-1935, with Projections to 1960	176
54A-C12	Population of Massachusetts in 1930 by Sex, Origin, and Five-Year Age Groups	176
54A-C22	Population of Massachusetts at Ten-Year Intervals, 1880-1930, by Sex, and Five-Year Age Groups	176
54A-C32	Trend of Occupational Composition in Massachusetts, 1830-1930	178
54D-C3	Employment in Manufacturing in Seven Massachusetts Industries	184
54D-C4	Employment in Manufacturing in Ten Massachusetts Industries	184
54D-C2	Employment in Manufacturing in Ten Massachusetts Cities	188
54D-C1	Employment in Manufacturing by Counties	188
54B-C1	Relative Variation in the Total Population, Families and Dwellings, 1900-1930	202
54B-C2	Relative Variation in Rents, Costs of Living and Buildings, 1916-1936	202
54B-C3	Average Housing Conditions in Seven Massachusetts Cities - 1934	206
77-10	Public School Systems and State Educational Institutions, 1935	224
54E-C1	Illiterate Minors, 16-21 Years of Age	226

MASSACHUSETTS STATE PLANNING BOARD

Number		Following Page
54E-C2	a. Total Cost of Education in Public Schools of Massachusetts, 1925-1935; b. Average Costs per Pupil in Public Schools of Massachusetts, 1925-1935	228
77-8	Public Institutions - 1935 - State Hospitals	232
77-9	Public Institutions - 1935 - Correctional	244
75-4	Capacity of Vacational Shelters	264
75-1	Juvenile and Adult Camps	272
75-3	Distribution of Golf Courses	278
75-2	Yacht, Boat and Canoe Clubs, and Canoe Trips	282
55-1	Existing and Proposed State Ocean Beaches	286
75-7	Public Picnic Sites, Beaches and Camp Grounds	296
75-10	Winter Sports Areas	302
75-8	Distribution of Wildlife Areas	312
75-6	Distribution of Public Recreational Lands	324
75-9	Distribution of Public Lands	326
76-10	Registration of Motor Vehicles	336
76-11	Routes of Common Carrier Truck Companies	338
76-1	Common Carrier Bus Routes	338
76-2	Railroad Freight Service Map	348
76-4	Railroad Passenger Service Map	348
56-C1	a. Air Express Revenue and Pounds Carried; b. Passenger Revenue and Passenger Miles; c. Pound Miles and Mail, Total Cost of Mail and Average Cost per Mile	358
56-1	Number of Flights Daily in Northeastern United States	358
56-2	Volume of Airmail Monthly in Northeastern United States	358
76-12	Tentative Plan for Airways and Airports	364
77-C1	Advance Planning - Programming of Public Works	388
58-2	Planning Boards and Zoning	422

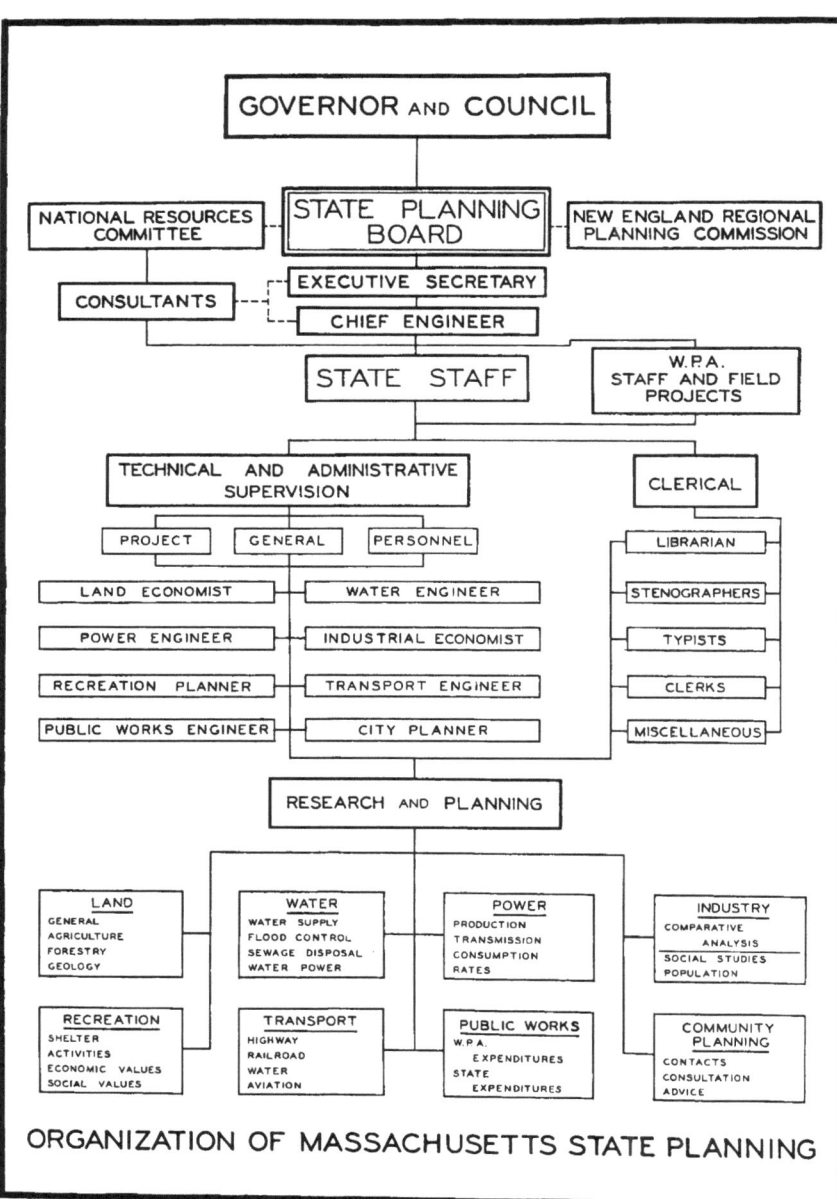

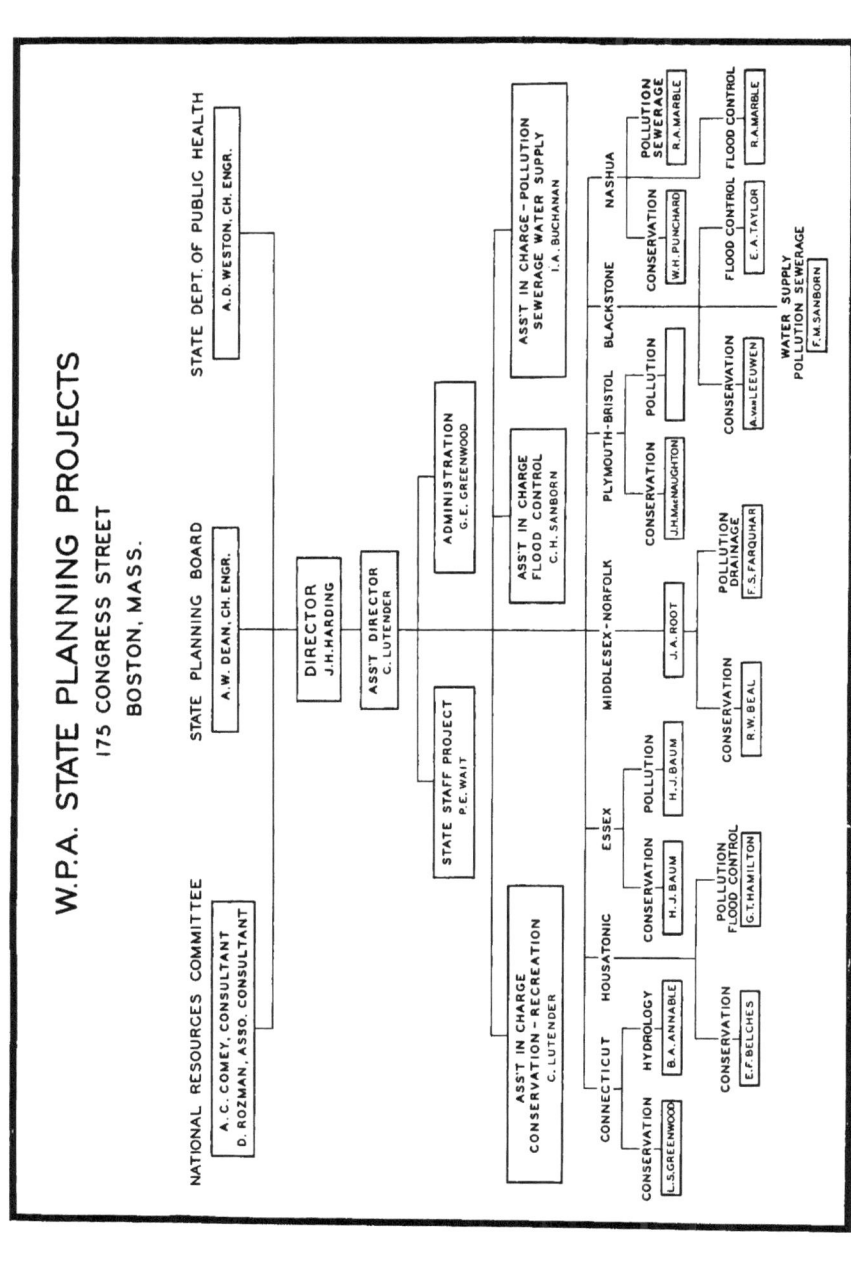

P E R S O N N E L

October 23, 1936

MEMBERS OF THE STATE PLANNING BOARD

Elisabeth M. Herlihy, Chairman
Clarence J. Biladeau
Frederick H. Fay
    Commissioner of Conservation
    Commissioner of Public Health
    Commissioner of Public Works

William Trufant Foster
Henry I. Harriman
William Stanley Parker

CONSULTANTS

Arthur C. Comey, Consultant, National Resources Committee
David Rozman, Associate Consultant, National Resources Committee
William Stanley Parker, Special Consultant, Urbanism Committee of the National Resources Committee

STATE PLANNING BOARD STAFF

Draveaux Bender, 1st Planning Assistant
Agnes C. Conroy, Head Clerk
John H. Dardis, Head Planning Draftsman
Arthur W. Dean, Chief Engineer
Elisabeth M. Herlihy, Executive Secretary
Margaret Monahan, Senior Clerk
Melvin L. Morse, Director of Business, Economic, and Industrial Survey
Theodore R. Rose, Storeroom Helper
Violet M. Thompson, Librarian
Elizabeth V. Tobin, Principal Clerk
Karl M. Tomfohrde, 2nd Planning Assistant

Temporary and Emergency Employees

  Frederick J. Adams, Technical Adviser
  Agnes Boodro, Stenographer
  Edwin S. Burdell, Technical Adviser
  Philomena R. Caputo, Research Clerk
*Arthur C. Conley, Research Clerk

---

    *Services terminated

MASSACHUSETTS STATE PLANNING BOARD

Temporary and Emergency Employees - Continued

William J. Coughlin, Draftsman
David P. Erlick, Research Clerk
Margaret M. Gallagher, Stenographer
Albert Hayes, Designing Artist
Frances Iovine, Clerk-Stenographer
*Dorothy M. Judge, Typist-Clerk
*William L. Little, Draftsman
*George N. Lykos, Draftsman
Thomas W. Mackesey, Statistical Clerk
Fred A. McDonald, Draftsman
*James G. McGinley, Draftsman
Catherine McGrath, Stenographer
Henry McLaren, Draftsman
Howard K. Menhinick, Technical Adviser
Harry H. Pulsifer, Statistical Clerk
Carm E. Rihbany, Draftsman
Walter P. Rowe, Planning Draftsman
Chester N. Russell, Planning Draftsman
*Edward N. Smith, Draftsman
Oscar Sutermeister, Draftsman
*George L. Thompson, Draftsman
Howard A. Tonsager, Draftsman
Roger R. Wallace, Designing Artist
J. Thomas C. Waram, 3rd Planning Assistant
Fred A. Wilson, Technical Adviser
F. Paul Zuffante, Asst. Chemist

WPA PERSONNEL

All State Planning Projects

  John H. Harding, Director
  Carl Lutender, Assistant Director
**Carl H. Sanborn, Coördinator, Water Resources
  Ivan A. Buchanan, Coördinator, Pollution and Sanitation
  George E. Greenwood, Supervisor, Administration
  Edward F. Kelley, Supervisor, Finance
  Gilbert Simpson, Supervisor, Soil Classification

State Staff Project

  Philip E. Wait, Supervisor
  David Geer, Assistant Supervisor

---

*Services terminated
**On project sponsored by State Department of Public Health

MASSACHUSETTS STATE PLANNING BOARD

State Staff Project - Continued

   Asadour Topalian, Assistant Supervisor
   Arnold H. Engberg, Senior Technician, Water-Basin Studies
   Edward S. Brown, Senior Technician Water-Basin Studies
   Frederick N. Fowler, Supervisor, Water-Basin Studies

   Jerome Shanahan, State Field Project Auditor
   Harold Ferdinand, Senior Engineer
   Ralph H. Morton, Senior Engineer
   Hollis O. Walsh, Senior Engineer
   Prentiss E. Thomas, Office Manager
   Grace E. Herlihy, Secretary
   Mary McManus, Secretary
   F. Tyler Carlton, Junior Engineer
   Felix S. Casipit, Junior Engineer
   Arthur L. Grout, Junior Engineer
   John C. Koomas, Junior Engineer
   Rose D. Arsenault, Draftsman
   Edward L. Bell, Draftsman
   Leon K. Riganess, Draftsman
   James Calderwood, Draftsman
   Harold F. Fisher, Draftsman
   Fred Flieger, Draftsman
   William F. Meyers, Draftsman
   Joseph Milano, Draftsman
   Bernard J. Parker, Draftsman
   James F. Pierce, Draftsman
   Leslie E. Sparrow, Draftsman
   Walter E. Burbank, Technician
   George Tripp, Technician
   James H. McFarland, Clerk-Payroll
   Margaret App, Stenographer
   Rosalie C. Dolan, Stenographer
   Margaret L. Jackson, Stenographer
   Eleanor J. Ferri, Typist
   Marion E. Lund, Typist

Supervisory Personnel of District Projects
   (Including Projects Sponsored by State Department of Public Health, see p. 6)

Supervisors

   Burleigh A. Annable, Connecticut, Water Resources and Pollution
   Lee S. Greenwood, Connecticut, Conservation

MASSACHUSETTS STATE PLANNING BOARD

Supervisory Personnel of District Projects - Continued

Supervisors - Continued

**Edwin A. Taylor, Blackstone, Water Resources
**Fred M. Sanborn, Blackstone, Pollution
Adrian van Leeuwen, Blackstone, Conservation
**George T. Hamilton, Housatonic, Water Resources and Pollution
**Ralph A. Marble, Nashua, Water Resources and Pollution
**William H. Punchard, Nashua, Conservation
John A. Root, Middlesex - Norfolk, Pollution and Conservation
Horace J. Baum, Essex, Pollution and Conservation
James H. MacNaughton, Plymouth - Bristol, Pollution and Conservation

Assistant Supervisors

Robert M. Sears, Connecticut, Conservation
Llewellyn Smith, Connecticut, Conservation
**Francis B. Thompson, Blackstone, Water Resources
**Edward F. Belches, Housatonic, Conservation
**Nelson E. Frissell, Nashua, Conservation
**Berton L. Blanchard, Nashua, Pollution
Bertrand H. Hale, Nashua, Water Resources
Warren H. Manning, Essex, Conservation
Robert W. Beal, Middlesex - Norfolk, Conservation
Carl A. Held, Middlesex - Norfolk, Pollution and Conservation
Robert H. Dods, Middlesex - Norfolk, Pollution and Conservation

---

**On projects sponsored by State Department of Public Health

SUMMARY

"Massachusetts, there she stands!" The people of this Commonwealth are proud of that salutation. It affirms, from the past, an abiding strength. It summons, for the future, a picture of power enduring. But what can be done, beyond the terms of that familiar phrase, to keep Massachusetts moving ahead? How shall the Commonwealth not only stand, preserving every useful element of its present position, but also forge onward to greater prosperity? How, in any sound way, can the State so advance that its motto hereafter will be, "Massachusetts, there she grows!"

The active steps, the decisions making progress toward that goal, are for the Legislature to choose and determine. But at every stage of such determination the Legislature needs a broad supply of facts, logically arranged and truly interpreted. After several years of debate in appropriate legislative committee, the State Planning Board was instituted and specifically instructed by the General Court to find all the available facts as to this State's present position, outlook, and needs, and to report these facts in as clear and expressive a manner as possible, as an integral step in a master plan for the beneficial development of the State.

A complete statement of the Commonwealth's existing conditions is obviously required for any wise choice of means to improve present deficiencies. The State must fully understand and correct, as far as possible, whatever factors are operating to retard its progress. It also must develop certain underdeveloped assets which it clearly possesses and which may well be made the basis of great advance in the public welfare.

Fortunately, the State Planning Board came into operation at a time when large staffs of WPA relief workers were being enrolled, and close cooperation between State and Federal Government was made possible by the allotment of substantial Federal grants to projects which the Planning Board proposed and sponsored. The work of the State Planning Board was greatly advanced thereby, and, on the other hand, the supervision which it supplied has directed a large amount of relief labor to work of enduring benefit.

A year ago the National Resources Committee assigned consultants and secured an allotment for a staff project, and a larger amount was allocated by the WPA to supply workers for surveys needed in planning (under the sponsorships of the State Planning Board and the Department of Public Health) for flood control, elimination of excessive pollution of rivers, and a study of land uses within

MASSACHUSETTS STATE PLANNING BOARD

the State all of which is meeting with marked success. Certainly the accomplishment of the Board in the past year is far greater than could have been possible except for the Federal assistance given, and it probably is equally true that the results obtained by workers on relief, have been far more valuable than would have been possible without the State's direction and supervision.

In the several ensuing chapters of this report and in the brief divisions of this summary is outlined the work accomplished during the year under the following headings: Land, Water, Power, Industry, Recreation, Transport, Public Works, and Community Planning. While some of the studies presented are of more immediate interest and usefulness than others, all of them are essential in a comprehensive plan for the full development of the State's resources.

Under the heading of Land, a survey of immediate value is nearing completion. For the first time the quality of land is being classified in each town, together with the use to which it is now being put, road and other transportation facilities by which it is served, and the types of buildings in its rural areas. Only last year the General Court approved a reforestation program under which 500,000 acres of forest land are to be acquired by the State during the next twenty years. The first yearly appropriation for such purpose is to be made during the coming legislative session. On the basis of the studies above referred to, areas which may well be returned to forestation may be shown very clearly. These studies also reveal some tracts of good farming land which apparently are not being used to the fullest extent and still other land that is being farmed which might well be devoted to different uses. A third application of these studies may well be made in the promotion of part-time industry, agriculture, and recreational service.

Under the heading of Water, the research conducted by the State Planning Board staff, directing WPA projects, furnishes valuable material in solving the problem of flood control, and a companion project, sponsored by the Department of Public Health deals with that of excessive pollution in some of our rivers and streams. As to water supply, the Commonwealth is fortunate: few communities have any serious problem in this regard, although in some of them the natural water supplies have not been properly developed.

A significant feature of the survey of power resources is its indication that the present development of plant and distribution systems is sufficient to supply all current needs, and that prospective demand for some time into the future can be easily taken care of by additions already contemplated.

MASSACHUSETTS STATE PLANNING BOARD

In the industrial field, the State Planning Board's objective has been mainly to supply factual information which will reveal (1) the advantages that Massachusetts offers to business concerns, and (2) the disadvantages which, as far and as quickly as possible, should be corrected. It also has organized in convenient form the best available series of business records, from which it is possible to see rather accurately the current trend of trade and industry within the State.

Recreation has been given extended attention for it represents perhaps the second largest industry of the State, and surely it has a very direct bearing upon the health and happiness of all classes of people. Of most immediate use may be the careful study which has been made of ocean beaches which can be acquired by the Commonwealth for public use. The facts in this regard are available for the consideration of the coming session of the General Court. Other phases of the study of recreational activities are equally interesting. All the recreational sites that are open to the public have been mapped and studies have been made of various opportunities for developing outdoor sports.

Transportation facilities have been considered as an essential means to other activities. An important part of the study in this division has been devoted to the problem of keeping the main through highways free from unnecessary interference, and the State Planning Board has filed for the consideration of the coming session of the General Court, specific bills which will operate to this end.

The financial survey of public works in the state, including all Federal, State and municipal projects, has thrown a new light on these activities, since it has produced, apparently for the first time, an accurate compilation of projects carried out and permits a comparison of the present total expenditures with those of preceding years.

In its efforts to forward the practice of community planning the State Planning Board has made definite headway. Its work is primarily educational and consequently requires time, but many of the meetings held with the planning groups of individual cities and towns have resulted in definite action on their part to employ sound, advance planning in the development of their communities.

The new magazine, A PLANNING FORUM, to be published monthly by the State Planning Board, is helping to coordinate the activities of the 136 local planning boards of the State by furnishing a medium for the regular interchange of sound information and ideas regarding planning work.

MASSACHUSETTS STATE PLANNING BOARD

The foregoing are only a few of the highlights in this report, of the first year's activity of the State Planning Board, but they serve to show some of the practical uses to which its findings will be put immediately as well as to indicate longer term benefits to be derived from sound, advance planning.

LAND

At the beginning of this year, the State Planning Board organized and sponsored, through WPA, a project for a detailed land-use survey of the entire State, and is presenting the results for each town on four separate maps. The first of these shows present land use and cover, depicting types of agricultural enterprises and forests, recreational uses, and industrial, commercial, and residential uses. The second map shows the location of roads and buildings, differentiating between various types and conditions of farm buildings, private and public buildings, parks, reservoirs, and similar features. The third shows soil classifications; and the fourth, topography, by means of contours at twenty-foot intervals.

An analysis and correlation of these maps with available statistics make it possible to indicate the desirable developments in land use in individual towns.

The land study of Massachusetts has been carried out in terms of: (a) its natural physical characteristics; (b) the man-made changes resulting from the development of the State; (c) present uses of the land and the problems they present; and (d) an approach to careful planning for the best future uses of land.

The State is as diversified in its soil types as it is in its general and local topography. Knowledge of these soil types and other physical factors, together with understanding of economic and social conditions of individual areas, is fundamental to a consideration of wise development of the State's natural resources. Areas not well adapted to farming might well be considered for development of forests and recreational sites where the topography is favorable. Areas not farmed at all should be examined for development as part-time farming in connection with industry. A complete knowledge of all natural resources in individual areas of the State will help to determine whether some new industries could not be developed in declining rural towns, and thus bring about the strengthening of the whole social and economic structure of the communities.

There are five major uses of land: agricultural, industrial, residential, forestry, and recreational, the last two in some degree related.

Agriculture in Massachusetts has undergone a radical evolution. In the past, when the land areas of the State were taken up for farming, conditions were different from those prevailing now, in two respects: (1) the competitive status of agriculture; and (2) the general character of farming, which was then primarily self-sufficient. Depending little upon outside markets, and with a labor resource both at home and in small industries flourishing in rural towns, it was possible for early agriculturists to make a living on poor land areas not well adapted to modern farming. A number of factors have contributed to the change. Rural industry has suffered at the hands of centralization. Farming has become competitive and specialized. As a result of these influences, much land was released from agricultural use. Not all of it has remained idle. Much land has been taken for urban uses, either directly, for housing, or indirectly, as for reservoirs. Part-time farming in areas adjacent to large centers has become important, even though carried on chiefly for family needs. Much land in certain scenic areas has been diverted to recreational uses.

Thus, from these and other influences, the total amount of land in farms in this State has declined from 3,360,000 acres in 1880 to about 2,200,000 acres in 1935. In other words, more than 20 per cent of the total area of the State has changed its functions in fifty years. According to the last census, 90 towns, or over one-fourth of the total number in the Commonwealth, have less than 25 per cent of their area in farming, with most of the remaining area in unplanned wood and brush land in various stages of growth.

In the general agricultural change, some good land went out of use, along with land poorly adapted for agriculture. Therefore, it is possible that the revival of some communities may be brought about by returning this land to cultivation. But, in the absence of accurate information, it is impossible to approach, in any adequate way, the pressing problems of land utilization in the problem areas. The first step is to take a complete inventory of the land resources of the Commonwealth and subject it to a searching analysis.

The diversity of soil types and of topography is almost equalled by variations in climate, which is affected by altitude and distance from the sea. Accordingly, individual farms in the same area may have entirely different problems. Nevertheless, allowing for this and for local market conditions which may produce exceptions, it is possible to indicate broad areas of the State where specific types of farming enterprises are predominant.

Dairying contributes the largest share to the farming income of the State. Production of milk per cow in Massachusetts and percentage of whole milk sold are among the highest in the country.

MASSACHUSETTS STATE PLANNING BOARD

Milk production and number of cows have remained almost stable for the last twenty-five years. The largest concentration of dairy farms is in the four western counties, where a large amount of home-grown feed is available and where individual farms average larger than in any other part of the State, although some fifty per cent of the area is in woodland.

Adjoining this area is the dairy-fruit section, with large orchards and the highest milk production per farm of any part of the State. Next, to the eastward, is the Connecticut Valley, with mixed farming, most notably tobacco, onions, and market gardens. The central dairying section includes also a few commercial orchards and market gardens near Worcester and Fitchburg. The Nashoba Valley has made notable progress in specialized apple orchards, and shows some development of market gardens and poultry farms.

The eastern dairy-poultry-fruit area, including the valley of the Merrimack River, has one of the highest percentage of tillable land per farm and the highest value of land and buildings per farm. Part-time farming is an important factor here. The Bristol County region produces dairy products, poultry and eggs, and market-garden crops, though showing high expenditures for feed and fertilizer.

The Plymouth region carries on poultry raising more intensively than any other region, in addition to raising small fruits, market crops, and dairy products. Cape Cod has a limited farming territory. Its most notable crop is cranberries, with an output of about 22 million quarts annually.

While dairying produces the largest item of farm income in Massachusetts, there are certain other outstanding phases of agriculture in this State. From the standpoint of acreage, hay is the most important crop, occupying more than three-fourths of the total crop area. Of the grains, corn is the most important, oats, rye, and wheat being grown in very small quantities. The production of corn per acre is one of the highest in the United States.

Tobacco acreage has decreased sharply in ten years, due to over-production and crop control. In 1934, only about $5\frac{1}{2}$ million pounds were produced, as compared with about 14 million pounds in 1924. Poultry are found on most Massachusetts farms and are an important source of income.

The total value of the State's agricultural output in 1930 was $80,400,492, as compared with $47,001,196 in 1910.

Of other land uses, forestry is of perhaps the most pressing economic importance. The major part of the area of the State is covered by woodland, totaling some three million acres. The greater portion of this is undeveloped and represents a considerable waste of natural resources. Better use of these woodlands is essential, and could provide important additional income to agriculture, as well as open up valuable development in scientific forestry, and provide for the rapidly expanding recreational and game-preservation needs. At least two million acres lie outside of farms, and any future policy for utilizing this area will inevitably consider the possibility of developing a large portion of this land into well-managed forests under public or semi-public ownership. At present, the State has some 170,000 acres in forests, parks, and reservations, and the last legislature authorized purchase of another 500,000 acres during the next twenty years. All of this land is to be developed under careful plans for recreational facilities, fish and game preservation, and scientific forestry.

WATER

The water resources of the State are vital, their proper conservation and use being fundamental to the social and economic welfare of Massachusetts. To plan the most effective development calls for consideration of water supply, sewage disposal, flood control, hydroelectric power, irrigation, and navigation. More important is the problem of integrating all these factors into a comprehensive water-resources program, not only on a local but on a State-wide, basis.

The supply of water for domestic purposes is fairly well taken care of, although there is need for thought and action on the matter of future requirements. Water for industrial purposes is a matter of increasingly serious concern. Pollution of streams has reached the point at which industries, are compelled to install expensive water-treating apparatus, and may reach a further point at which certain industries will no longer find it economically feasible to stay in Massachusetts. Pollution has an important bearing also on health and on recreational uses of water, especially in regard to bathing and fishing. In all of these aspects, much study is needed.

Flood control is of great importance. The flood of March 1936 caused damage of between 35 and 45 million dollars in Massachusetts alone. It is apparent, from recent experience and from investigations by various authorities, that a large part of possible flood damage is beyond the State's individual control, many of our important streams having their headwaters, where most effective control is possible, in other States. Excessive rainfall, thaws, failure of dams, and so forth cause floods. These can be guarded against, so far as Massachusetts is concerned, by interstate coöperation. Such coöperation is now in an effective stage among certain of the New England States. The cost of methods of prevention

MASSACHUSETTS STATE PLANNING BOARD

and control must be weighed against the value of the benefits to be gained, such as protection from damage, increased power production, greater dilution of pollution, and enhanced recreational values.

Hydroelectric power resources within the State itself are not of commanding importance. However, important potential resources lie within a useful radius of the Massachusetts markets and should be considered in the logical development of interstate streams.

Recreational uses are manifold, but their economic value must be balanced against the costs of achieving and maintaining a suitable condition of the various streams.

Detailed studies of these various water-resources problems have been carried out for various streams by WPA projects sponsored by the State Planning Board and the Department of Public Health. These projects have had the benefit of the cooperation of many Federal and State agencies. Preliminary progress reports have already been made for several of the inland river valleys.

POWER

Massachusetts is well served by electric power facilities. Hydro-generating plants in the western part of the State and steam plants in the eastern provide substantial amounts of locally produced power, and, in addition, there are abundant facilities within practical transmission distance elsewhere in New England. (By law, Maine does not import or export power).

Since the present feasible transmission distance of 200 miles is likely to be extended, a survey has been made of undeveloped hydro-power within a radius of 500 miles of Boston. An element of this survey is the work now being done by the United States Army engineers in connection with proposed storage reservoirs in flood-control projects. In all, there is estimated to be in excess of eight million undeveloped horsepower within 500 miles of Boston. The survey indicates that large amounts of yet undeveloped power exist in this State, Vermont, and New Hampshire, which may be utilized in providing for future demands.

In the matter of electric power consumption, there are many variables to be considered. New sociological factors, inventions, rates, and other elements will affect any attempt at forecast. Outstanding in this connection is the proposed rural electrification program. Federal authorities propose extensions of 1168.22 miles of aerial electrical plant at an estimated cost of $2,024,549, bringing central-station power to 5474 new rural customers, with an initial estimated revenue of $215,847 per year.

MASSACHUSETTS STATE PLANNING BOARD

The benefits to the farm and to the State from such a program are measurable and satisfactory. It is continually being demonstrated that such development is an important sociological factor, that the advent of power has changed the entire complexion of a locality, bringing about the modernization of homes and property and generally benefiting the mode of life. Utility companies indicate their belief that the procedure is feasible.

There has been a steady increase of about ten per cent a year in electric-power demand during the last ten years, and this rate of increase may possibly continue for another decade. But since power companies were generally over-built in the last decade, little addition to capacity has been made during the depression. The resumption of the upward trend in power consumption however will soon force the building of new capacity.

No single factor is looked for to give an abnormal impetus to power consumption. Probably the greatest increase in domestic usage will come from electric stoves, water heaters, and refrigerators. Electric house heating is still too remote economically to be an important factor. New devices will undoubtedly appear and be popular, but their increased efficiency tends to counterbalance the increase in units in use.

Consumer costs in Massachusetts are a vital field for further study. Marked differentials appear as between even closely adjacent regions, and the question of municipal versus privately owned plants needs further consideration. It is suggested that more exhaustive study, with mutual cooperation of State officials and power companies, would demonstrate the practicability of drawing up a program of rate equalization for Massachusetts that could be inaugurated in the near future. The adoption of such equalized standards would probably result in sufficient rate decreases to increase the amount of power used, increase the sale of appliances, and make a momentous contribution to social and economic well-being.

INDUSTRY

Part I

The order of the General Court, contained in Chapter 475 of the Acts of 1935, directed the State Planning Board, along with its other duties, to make such studies and plans as would best promote the trade and industry of the Commonwealth. In accordance with this instruction, the Board's staff made a careful survey of the problem, aided by helpful counsel from numerous business leaders in widely diversified industries, and during the past year has completed certain work to accomplish the following ends:

MASSACHUSETTS STATE PLANNING BOARD

1. To establish and maintain reliable measures which will show the current trend of Massachusetts trade and industry as a whole, compared with preceding periods and also with the trend of business in other parts of the United States.

2. To gather and arrange in convenient form all available data which will truly show the advantages and disadvantages of Massachusetts as an industrial or commercial site, in relation to those of other competing States.

Under the first division, the State Planning Board compiled and charted the records of such business series as were available, and combined five of the more important of these into a composite monthly index of Massachusetts business extending back through 1928. This apparently was the first time that such an index of Massachusetts has been made. The number of series it contains is necessarily limited, but careful tests show that the composite index figure, nevertheless, is fairly indicative of the trend of general business in the State. It is published each month in the daily newspapers.

In its original survey to determine what industrial and commercial research would be of most practical value to the Commonwealth, the State Planning Board found a widespread misconception regarding the condition of industry within the State. Many persons, otherwise well informed in business matters, were under the impression that the long-swing trend of industry in Massachusetts was unfavorable. "On the down grade" was an expression frequently heard. "No future except as a playground", and "Geographical location too big an obstacle for industry", others said. From these and similar pessimistic opinions, it became evident that at least one of the greatest needs in this State was the facts regarding the true condition and outlook; in short, and unbiased accurate appraisal, as far as possible, of the advantages and disadvantages of Massachusetts an industrial site, compared with other industrial States with which the Commonwealth is in competition.

One outstanding misconception is that failure of Massachusetts to maintain a given percentage of the total production of the nation, indicates decline. It is true that in the early days, when there were only thirteen States, Massachusetts produced a large share of all the manufactures used in the United States, and, even up to 1849, the date of the first census, the Bay State was manufacturing $16\frac{1}{2}$ per cent of all the country's production. At that time, there were thirty States in the Union, with a population of about 23,000,000 people.

Many people overlook the fact that, as the country expands, the need for industry in other sections increases, and, consequently, new industrial States develop. It is only natural, therefore, that now, in a nation of forty-eight States with a population of 128,000,000 people, Massachusetts should not be able to hold the same proportion of the national output that it originally controlled. Obviously, any long-term comparison of the industrial gain or loss in the Commonwealth should be made, not with the country as a whole, but with the individual States principally competitive with this State, that is, States which are engaged primarily in types of industrial production for which Massachusetts is adapted. This calls for an analysis of the different kinds of business in the Commonwealth.

In the total industrial output of Massachusetts, there are about eighteen groups of industries which individually are of outstanding importance to the State, all together producing about 52 per cent of Massachusetts' manufactures. The value of production of each of these industries has been charted, by census years, from 1909 to the date of the latest census report, either 1933 or 1935. On the same charts are presented also curves of the production of the industry in each of the other States where it has reached important size or where its rate of growth is found to be unusually rapid. This series of charts enables one to see very quickly the States which are most highly competitive with Massachusetts and those which should be studied especially from this standpoint.

No attempt has been made in this report to present reasons for the growth or decline of a given industry, either in Massachusetts or in competing States. The study turns instead to a consideration of the general advantages and disadvantages of Massachusetts as an industrial site, in comparison with those of the Commonwealth's principal competitors, among which fifteen States have been selected especially for study.

In this division of the work, the first subjects considered have been taxation and cost of government, cost of labor, and industrial water supply. At least, a good start has been made to bring to light essential facts from which the management of a business concern that is seeking a new location, may fairly judge the relative merits of Massachusetts as against certain other States. It is the purpose of the Planning Board staff, to continue research along these lines, seeking to determine the assets and liabilities of the State from an industrial standpoint, so that the disadvantages which exist may possibly be corrected and the advantages may be properly recognized.

MASSACHUSETTS STATE PLANNING BOARD

Part II

A special study of Massachusetts industry, to appraise the economic relations of an industry to its community and to guide community officials in any efforts they may see fit to make toward developing local industrial activity, has been made by Mr. W. Stanley Parker, Special Consultant to the Urbanism Committee of the National Resources Committee. It is apparently the first survey of its kind, and endeavors to bring out clearly the factors which should determine the desirability of a given industry in a given community.

SOCIAL CONDITIONS

Population

Extensive statistical studies of the population of Massachusetts have been made under the three major headings of growth, distribution, and composition.

Charts and tables representing the growth of population have been made, based upon thorough studies of births, deaths, immigration, and emigration. These present, as nearly as it is possible on the basis of available information, the general trend of the basic factors affecting population. From an analytical study of these, various future population estimates have been made, based upon (a) mathematical projections of past curves of total populations without references to the individual factors; and (b) rational projections from a study of the various basic factors: birth rates, death rates, immigration, and emigration, individually. In each case the projection has been carried to 1960.

The distribution of population is a simpler study, arrived at through "spot maps", covering the years 1860 to 1935, in 25-year periods. These maps show a change from a relatively even distribution in rural areas, and small metropolitan concentrations, to sparser rural population and greater concentration around the large cities. Density of population in the State ranges from fewer than 50 per square mile to more than 30,000. A study of distribution in municipalities of various sizes shows a remarkable similarity in the rate of growth in the different groups, except the smallest.

The composition of the population of the State has been considered from the standpoints of: (a) age groups; (b) sex; (c) nativity; and (d) occupation. All of these are interrelated, even as separate studies, and more complexly so in any attempt at prediction of future population growth. Typically important reasons for such studies as those of the age groups are (1) provision of educational facilities, and (2) achieving an index of old-age assistance requirements. The conclusion from the studies of sex composition of population, is that for more than fifty years Massachusetts has had a relatively well-balanced distribution of males and females, in all age groups. Nativity studies showed that, due to a falling off of immigration from foreign countries, there is not only a decrease in the number of foreign-born whites, but a greater than proportional decrease in the number of first-generation whites of foreign-born parents. It is to be inferred from various well-defined factors that the birth rate will continue to decrease.

An occupational study of population is not entirely satisfactory, due to changes in classification at various times from 1880 to 1930 and within the several brackets, but the data show a gradual increase in the number of persons engaged in all commercial activities except manufacturing and mechanical industries, which now show a pronounced decrease from 1920 to 1930.

Employment

Reliable unemployment statistics for Massachusetts are lacking, and estimates vary widely. Annual reports of the State Department of Labor and Industries show that, for the nine-year period of 1926-1934, the peak of industrial employment in Massachusetts occurred in 1926. There was a gradual decrease through 1928, a slight increase in 1929, then a sharp decline to a new low point in 1932, with an upturn in 1933 and 1934. It appears doubtful that the 1926 figure of 602,343 will soon be attained again.

A clear estimate of the industrial condition of the State is difficult to obtain. There is undoubted recovery from the depths of 1932. A significant development lies in the fact that in normal times the four major manufacturing industries (cotton, leather, wool, and metal products) provide employment for more than 40 per cent of the total number of wage earners in all manufacturing industries in the State, but in 1934, the number employed in these major industries was only approximately 28 per cent of the wage earners in manufacturing.

There is every indication of improvement in industry, but its future extent is problematical. It is evident the State has lost its initial advantage of a head start in industry. It now appears that the development of new industries is essential to the welfare of the Commonwealth.

Housing

Despite a long history of interest in improved housing, the Commonwealth of Massachusetts must still confess to sore conditions.

MASSACHUSETTS STATE PLANNING BOARD

Nearly fifty years ago the first studies of slum conditions were made, and from these scattered and particularized efforts there has been a steady increase of interest and activity. In 1912 and 1913, the first Tenement House Laws were enacted; in 1913, the Legislature authorized Town Planning Boards; in 1916, the First Homestead Commission, a State agency, was authorized to undertake an experiment in suburban housing, the first State housing enterprise in continental North America. The war interfered with completion of the project, but twelve houses were completed at Lowell, to rent within the means of men earning $15 to $25 a week. They have proved a financial success. Practically the entire capital spent by the Commonwealth, together with interest, has been paid back. The State Board of Housing was created in 1933.

Just before the war, there had been a great amount of overbuilding, making real estate loans unattractive. But suspension of building during the war and high costs of labor and materials thereafter reversed the situation. Rents went up, in the face of an exaggerated shortage, and there was much speculation. For many, who had enjoyed war-time prosperity, there was no hardship, but for others, the situation was pitiful. In 1923, building was resumed. Much of it was speculative and shoddy in suburban developments, with mostly higher-priced apartments in congested areas. Rising construction costs halted this boom in 1926, with still no new housing at rentals of $35 a month or less.

From 1927 to 1933, real estate was considered a desirable investment for savings. Home ownership increased but so did foreclosures, reaching a total of 12,171 in 1933.

Rentals from 1920 to 1929 went through varying phases, but the lowest group suffered most of the time. Prosperity advanced rents generally and hard times caused greater demand for lower rent dwellings. Since 1929, rents have been fairly stationary. For fifteen years there has been an increasing tendency toward home ownership.

Since its creation, the State Board of Housing has been instrumental in obtaining Federal funds for housing projects now under way in Cambridge and South Boston, and has been carrying on fact-finding investigations into housing throughout the State. To date, analyses of sub-standard areas in six cities have been made. The Board has also assisted in the realization of a rehabilitation project in Chicopee Falls, through a limited-dividend company; has worked in close cooperation with local planning boards; and has maintained close connection with the various local and Federal housing authorities.

MASSACHUSETTS STATE PLANNING BOARD

Studies have been made of trends in building, as among one-, two-, and multi-family dwellings; in comparative changes in cost of living and foreclosures; and in the present physical condition of urban houses. This last investigation, based on an inventory taken in the seven cities of Boston, Cambridge, Newton, Everett, Springfield, Worcester, and Haverhill has lead to the following conclusions:

1. By far the greatest percentage of structures is built of wood.

2. Approximately one structure in every hundred is unfit for human habitation.

3. The largest percentage of structures is under 25 years of age.

4. Only one third of the dwellings is owner-occupied. Of the total dwelling units, one out of twelve is vacant.

5. Approximately 24 per cent of the dwelling units are overcrowded.

6. 2.5 dwelling units out of every one hundred are without indoor water closets, and 11 are without tubs or showers.

7. One out of every ten has neither gas nor electricity for cooking, and one out of 78 has neither for lighting.

There is but limited information at present on rural housing, but it is interesting to note that from 1900-1930 the average value of land and buildings per farm increased, as did the average mortgage debt.

It appears, from various statistical studies, that accommodations are sufficient in the best and medium classes of dwellings, but there is a great lack in rentals of $35 and below. The one-family house is still predominant in the urban areas, but is decreasing in proportion to other types. Owner-occupancy is increasing. The cost of building has doubled since the war, and the cost of shelter in the family budget has increased 45 per cent, as against a 22.3 per cent increase for food. There is still a great deal of crowding and doubling up.

The demand for low-cost housing cannot be met by private enterprise alone. Suitable houses can not be built to rent, at a profit, for fifteen or even twenty dollars a month. New houses in slum areas, or even thorough modernization of old ones in these sections, will not pay. Yet several surveys have shown conclusively that city income from sub-standard areas is far below the cost of maintaining them and providing them with fire and police protection, schools, and so on. In many instances, the cost is 300 per cent in excess of the income.

At present, there are no provisions for State or municipal financing of housing projects, although both political units have the legal power to engage in such projects. Two bills which were before the last Legislature would have given authorization for such financial participation.

The only limited dividend company operating, so far, is that at Chicopee Falls, a project sponsored by the State Housing Board.

Education

Massachusetts has 53 educational institutions granting degrees. Eleven of these institutions are State-supported: Massachusetts State College and ten State Teachers' Colleges. In addition, there are seventeen private schools of higher education which do not grant degrees.

In the academic year 1934-35, the public day schools had an enrollment of 770,653 pupils, with faculties totalling 26,252 persons.

In private schools, for the year 1934-1935, there were 159,044 pupils, of whom 153,485 were in schools maintained by the Roman Catholic Church.

An important educational activity of the State is the maintenance of special schools or the provision of instruction for such people as the physically handicapped, and inmates of State institutions. There are three State textile schools, at Fall River, New Bedford, and Lowell, the latter granting a degree.

University Extension courses last year enrolled 30,784, and operated at a per pupil cost of $0.355. Adult alien education courses enrolled 11,488, the result of a steady decline from 23,903 in 1925, due largely to reduced immigration.

Illiteracy among people ten years old and over has decreased from 5.9 per cent in 1900, to 3.5 in 1930. The decrease of immigration accounts for some of this reduction, but the educational system of the State has played an important part in this progress.

A serious condition exists in the educational plant of the

Commonwealth. In the period from 1918 to 1933, 490 new school buildings were constructed, but the educational plant is still inadequate, with instances of school populations nearly twice the preper normal capacity.

Curtailments necessitated by the depression have reduced the total expenditures for public schools in the State from $82,593,749, in 1930, to $68,661,141, in 1935. The per capita cost of education has decreased from $107.80 in 1925 to $93.74 in 1935.

Welfare

The Commonwealth of Massachusetts has been a leader in taking measures for the public welfare, through legislative action and by private effort. Moreover, it has for a considerable period been spending proportionately large amounts of money for its many welfare activities. These expenditures have increased very rapidly in the last few years. Where the cost to the State stood at about thirteen million dollars in 1930, it reached more than thirty-seven million in 1935. This expenditure by the State was actually surpassed by private welfare activities to the extent of ten million dollars in 1935. Increasing grants of Federal funds in the last few years have extended and will continue to extend the amount of relief expenditures within the State.

Established legislation is now providing for State participation in welfare activities for the aged; for the crippled, blind, diseased, or insane; for the poor; for dependent or neglected children; for mothers' aid; for the unemployed; and in various public-health activities.

Private welfare agencies are supervised by the State to the extent that they must have charters, must report annually, and must submit to an examination of their records.

Local municipal welfare activities are in varying degrees related to State welfare agencies, through collection and allocation of funds, determination of responsibility under the settlement laws, and through general coördination and coöperation.

There is increasing indication of closer coöperation between public and private relief agencies, a development which is valuable not only because of possible financial savings but also because of a possible enhancement of the total effort toward public welfare.

Correction

In the correction of offenders against society, Massachusetts is credited with several pioneering moves, and is still noted for its advanced penal methods and for its unique statistical records.

Correctional institutions range from county training schools for habitual truants and schools for juvenile delinquents through the cottage type of adult correctional institutions, to maximum-security prisons and reformatories.

These are all under the coördinating authority of the State Commissioner of Correction. As has been indicated, the methods applied are generally of the most modern approved order. Case work is carefully pursued; medical care is provided; educational facilities are numerous; and provision for prison work is satisfactory.

The physical plant for the various types of institution is such as to require immediate attention and action, except in the case of the juveniles. There is almost universal overcrowding, juxtaposition of widely different types of inmates, inadequate housing for officers, and generally unhealthful conditions.

Studies of probation and parole, fields in which the Commonwealth has claim to pioneering effort, show clearly that there is urgent need for increased personnel. The case-load is far too high for a continued good showing, and serious failure of the whole system may well be a result of continued understaffing.

Detailed studies have been made in many special divisions of the correctional problem. These include such studies as those of total arrests over a 15-year period; capacity and daily inmate average for each institution; per capita costs for correction; and percentage graphs of probationers in terms of results obtained.

RECREATION

Recreation is the second largest industry in the State, second only to textiles. In itself, it comprises many elements and it touches upon many other phases of the life of the Commonwealth.

The recreational studies have been carried out with the objective of preparing a State-wide plan (a) to provide an ample and coördinated program of activities and facilities; and (b) to promote the recreational industry in this State.

The first step in the Planning Board's year of activity has been the taking of an inventory, in order that the citizens' needs and the extent to which they are fulfilled may be determined. The social importance of recreation rather than its economic value has been stressed, although the latter has been considered throughout. There is still need for a complete survey of the economic phase, and for more study as to existing conditions in certain recreational activities.

Vacational Shelter

Important for many reasons is a thorough knowledge and careful interpretation of the needs and present provision for vacational shelter. New developments in the past few years--notably autocamping, trailers, hiking, and bicycling--have seriously changed the traditional understanding of vacation shelter, in as much as "shelter" may now mean no more than camp and trailer sites, with attendant new problems of policing and sanitation.

As far as "permanent" shelter is concerned, Massachusetts is well favored with hotels, and has adequate facilities; 903 hotels, accommodating 75,000 people. There are approximately 2800 rooms in 497 tourist homes, housing 4500 people, a marked increase during recent years, due to their convenience and economy for the tourist and for their added income to residents. Upon the basis of 1936, this State is not as fully served as it might be with this type of shelter, especially in recreational centers, and local civic organizations might well foster this kind of enterprise. Overnight cabins number 1990, housing 5552 persons, again a recent and marked development and one which may be encouraged under careful safeguards.

Tent and trailer sites and open shelters on public lands will accommodate more than 2000 people; others, on private lands, would possibly increase this figure several hundred per cent. These are of growing importance in the general picture, and at present such sites on public lands are poorly distributed, most of them being in the four western counties. Without competing with private enterprise, it is desirable that this facility be provided more generally in State forests and reservations.

Private shelter includes juvenile and adult camps, clubs, and the new youth hostels. There were, in 1935, 211 camps, with a capacity of 13,033 people, and, assuming an average turnover of two persons per season, an enrollment of 25,000 is indicated, placing the State in a leading position. No data are available at present on individual vacation cottages, farms, and houses. The youth hostels now number 22, with a capacity of 404, and, due to short stays, some 9000 accommodations have been provided in two years. They are open the year-round and enjoy strong patronage in winter.

MASSACHUSETTS STATE PLANNING BOARD

Proper promotion might well encourage the utilization of abandoned farms for vacation homes, aiding rehabilitation of certain areas of the State.

Recreational Activities

Recreational activities are numerous in Massachusetts. Many of them are local in nature, such as golf, baseball, and tennis. Others are seasonal and grouped about certain centers, such as winter sports, water sports, and hunting and fishing. Still others involve continued travel, as in hiking, bicycling, motor touring, and horseback riding. Other interests are scenic, scientific, and historical.

In most of these, the State has exceptionally fine provision for present and near-future demands, warranting efforts by State and local agencies to publicize their further use. Certain others of them, however, demand immediate attention for further development under careful planning.

Perhaps most notably pressing is the matter of ocean beaches. One of the most valuable of the State's assets is its 1000 miles of ocean front. But the public has access to only a small mileage of it. Private owners or local communities tend to restrict general use of beaches more and more each year. The State is developing Salisbury Beach, and the Metropolitan District Commission has five sea beaches, but these are far from adequate for existing and potential demands. The State should acquire and develop as rapidly as possible more ocean beaches: to relieve pressure on other public beaches, to protect private property, to help increase the tourist trade, to escape steadily rising land costs, and to furnish employment.

This matter has been the subject of study several times in the past. In 1935, six ocean beaches were proposed for acquisition by the State by 1940. A 1936 Legislative resolve provides for a study of Horse Neck Beach in the Town of Westport. The State Planning Board has drawn up analyses of six beaches and three alternate sites, considering ocean and shore conditions, present development, accessibility, and demand, and recommends their acquisition.

Winter sports is another activity which must loom large in any adequate plan for serving the public needs in recreation. Much work has been done in providing trails and other facilities, the State Department of Conservation working in conjunction with the National Park Service and the CCC, and other work is in progress.

There are two important centers of this activity, the Berkshires and the Wachusett region, with secondary areas not unworthy of attention. An outstanding sport is skiing, with a variety of activity within this category which calls for special types of facility, ranging from epen slopes for beginners to downhill racing courses and jumps. At present, approximately 75 per cent of the facilities which have been provided are in the Berkshire Hills; most of the rest are in the Wachusett region, with but three or four ski trails near Boston. Considering the centers of population, the winter sports facilities should be located as near as possible to the eastern part of the State but it is clear that topographical and climatic conditions dictate in large measure what can be done. Nevertheless, more should be done in the eastern and central parts of the State, and, in all areas, effort should be made to acquire more epen slopes for the novice skiers, who are in the majority.

Other winter sports are fairly well provided for, except that the rivers and ponds which lie in State or local parks should be more generally available to skaters, through keeping the ice clear and providing shelters.

Bicycling has developed so fast that there is not proper provision for the convenience and safety of its enthusiasts. A State-wide system of paths should be surveyed and mapped, preferably in conjunction with the Massachusetts Bridle Trails systems; and some means of control of bicycle traffic in Metropolitan areas should be achieved.

Within the other spheres of activity there are needed, but less commanding, improvements to be made. There should be more picnicking grounds along main highways; fresh-water bodies should be freed from pollution and debris so that swimming and boating may be improved; points of geologic interest might well be made more familiar; access to reservations and parks needs the improvement of trails and markers. There is continuous and pressing need for more work in the establishment, or development, of game sanctuaries and the breeding and stocking of fish and game. Provision should be made, also, for more shooting and fishing areas.

Recreation Areas

State forests are important woodlands for public use, comprising as they do the three-point program of forestry, wildlife management, and recreation. Under the Massachusetts Plan of 1934, 26 tentative purchase areas were designated. Twenty-one of these are now being acquired, and the others await appropriations. The forests, with eleven State reservations and two State parks, now total some 182,000 acres. Of these, some 37 per cent are located in Berkshire County. Future acquisitions should be located in relation to population.

MASSACHUSETTS STATE PLANNING BOARD

The Metropolitan District Commission now holds 15 reservations and 19 parkways, with an area of approximately 12,600 acres. Despite an admirable achievement in development, there is still opportunity for further recreational facilities, notably in winter sports. There are about 100 municipal forests in the State, totaling 27,500 acres, and more than 1300 municipal parks.

The Trustees of Public Reservations, the principal quasi-public organization holding public lands, has secured 28 sites, totaling 9883 acres, of historic, scenic, geological, and botanic interest, and wildlife sanctuaries, many of which have been turned over to the State. These have been developed to a limited extent for picnicking, camping, and hiking.

Social Aspects

An inventory of the 200 or more semi-public or private agencies which are interested in advancing recreational facilities in this State is being made.

The social values of recreation, as a profitable use of leisure and as a constructive force in society, are well recognized and are furthered by other groups or organizations.

The Recreation Industry

Estimates place the annual income from recreation in Massachusetts at $200,000,000, derived through taxes, rents, retail sales, amusements, licenses, and services. The State Planning Board has not yet attempted an estimate.

Publicity and other promotional efforts for the recreation industry in Massachusetts are carried on by the New England Council, by the Recreation Publicity Division of the office of the Secretary of State, and by many local and regional organizations. These efforts include paid advertising in newspapers and magazines, outdoor advertising, booklets, and special articles and photographs in various publications.

The general trend in recreational activity is definitely upward, due to better economic conditions and a new appreciation of the use of leisure time. Two special activities in this trend are motor camping and winter sports, strongly indicating the need of acquiring more public lands, and their wise development under a State plan.

MASSACHUSETTS STATE PLANNING BOARD

TRANSPORTATION

Highways

Highways within the State should be considered in terms of present and probable future demands made upon them. These demands are of three significant origins: private vehicles, busses, and trucks.

Private vehicles constituted, in 1935, 87 per cent of the total motor-vehicle registration. To the great majority of owners, the motor vehicle has economic advantages. In addition to being a tool of dollars and cents value, there are factors of recreational use, most important of which is pleasure driving. This is but poorly provided for at present. Provision of special pleasure driveways would be difficult and expensive, but all-purpose highways, parkways, and freeways can be and should be built attractively. Facilitating travel to recreational areas is an important problem, not only as it applies to residents of the Commonwealth but in its connection with developing interest in Massachusetts as a recreational center for out-of-State motorists.

From various indices, it is apparent that the use of passenger cars is still increasing, but not at so fast a rate as previously. The saturation point may be reached within twenty years.

Just as recent improvements in the operative qualities and power of automobiles have altered the highway requirements of the State, so may further technical advances and variations in real incomes make other changes.

Motor trucks have increased in use during the past thirty years. Approximately 100,000 are now registered in Massachusetts, of which about 80 per cent are privately owned, 15 per cent are common carriers. The three groups are highly competitive and reasonable public control is imperative. Trucks have certain intrinsic advantages over railroads, notably door-to-door service, lower terminal costs, and greater flexibility. The railroads have recognized this and have entered the trucking field. From numerous sources, it has been possible to define the major channels of highway freight traffic within the State, and also to indicate an approximation of the useful radius of freight-truck operations.

Busses have found an increasing patronage in the last few years, but there is no reason to believe that the rate of increase will maintain its curve. Here again railroads have met competition voluntarily by providing better equipment and improved schedules, and involuntarily by the new mileage rates. Thus the inherent advantages of rail travel -- namely, safety, sureness of schedule, more room per passenger, smoothness of ride, and comforts en route -- are brought again into the actively competitive field. Still, there are definite needs which the bus provides which the railroad cannot, on an economically justifiable basis. Short-haul traffic of light volume, more frequent service, and greater range of operation are among the undeniable assets of bus service.

The design and construction of highways must comprise study of these factors from many viewpoints, economic, engineering, and social. Highway congestion and highway accidents have been the subjects of several studies; each of them requires more extensive research. Immediate objectives are a trunk highway system for through travel which, by careful selection and planning of routes which are free from hazards and congestion, will carry over 50 per cent of the vehicle-miles of inter-city traffic. On the whole, Massachusetts has a serviceable system of primary intrastate and secondary highways. Many settled rural areas imperatively need land-service roads. The economic justification for all such improvement is being given careful and comprehensive study. For all types of highways a study should be made of the economic aspects of a long-term highway program, making sure that the benefits of such activity are being shared equitably by the various groups of taxpayers.

Three bills which would facilitate action on a program of highway development have been drawn up by the State Planning Board in the light of the State's condition and needs, and in the light of experience elsewhere. Recommendations are made for legislation as to freeways and other means of protecting roadsides.

Railroads

Numerous factors, new within the last ten years, have brought about what was until quite recently a decidedly unfavorable picture in railroad transportation. Automotive development is perhaps the most considerable, comprising private vehicles, busses, and trucks, all of which have tended to take freight and passenger traffic from the railroads. The depression reduced the volume of travel generally. Heavy debt burdens and complex financial structures have been further handicaps.

Nevertheless, there are fundamental functions of transportation which the railroads will still carry under favored circumstances. They provide the best service in long-haul operations, both passenger and freight. Short-haul freight is comparatively unprofitable. Short-haul passenger service has been largely lost to busses and

MASSACHUSETTS STATE PLANNING BOARD

private motors, except for urban-suburban commuting, in which the railroads are still the most important agency, due to motor traffic congestion in metropolitan areas. In short-hauls outside these areas, the Boston and Maine and the New Haven roads have met motor-bus competition by establishing similar services of their own. Rate reductions and the introduction of new equipment have also improved traffic volume.

Further endeavors to improve the circumstances of railroads may well take the forms of: more economical equipment, greater comfort, abandonment of unprofitable trackage, reduced costs of terminal operations, greater coordination of local with outside services, and assurance of opportunity to develop such subsidiary operations as busses, truck, airlines, and steamship services.

Waterways

There are no inland waterways of importance in Massachusetts, and, accordingly, examination of water-borne transportation must chiefly concern coastal ports. There are three major ones: Boston, Fall River, and New Bedford. Their harbors and facilities, especially Boston's are excellent.

It is important that seaways and shipping facilities be maintained, since they constitute valuable services to many industries in providing efficient and low-cost transportation of incoming raw materials and outgoing manufactures.

Boston's geographical location and its fine harbor justify strong efforts to develop express connections inland for transatlantic steamship services handling passengers, mail, and express, and resulting in important time savings.

An important study of port administration is being made by a recess commission of the General Court. Among other things the advisability of transferring the waterfront terminals of the Commonwealth to the Boston Port Authority is being considered.

Aviation

As an established transportation medium of great existing and potential value to the State, aviation may be considered from the three standpoints indicated below. The general aspect of aviation as a developing utility and as a means of recreation is fairly clearly understood. The special application of this development in regard to Massachusetts appears as follows:

Scheduled Common-Carrier Air Transport Operations. This as the most important commercial phase of aviation, is well developed in the State, with full and integrated airline schedules serving most of New England and tieing into national and international services via the New York (Newark) and the Boston-Springfield-Albany routes. Important possibilities for airways development in the near future are (a) an east-west route across Massachusetts via Greenfield, on a direct line to Buffalo; (b) between Boston and some centrally located point on Cape Cod; (c) from Providence via Fall River and New Bedford to Cape Cod; and (d) a north-south route along the Connecticut Valley. The development of existing and future airways calls for provision of such navigational aids as radio beams, beacon lights, air markers, and intermediate landing fields. In the location and construction of airports (since many of them serve as emergency fields for air-transport lines of a public utility importance), the State has a definite function in helping the city or town evaluate the needs, the desirability of the site, and other factors.

Private Flying and Miscellaneous Commercial Aviation. An emergency port for scheduled airlines may, at the same time, serve as a home port for the other activities. Under these circumstances, additional facilities for private flying and miscellaneous commercial aviation will be needed in only a few cases.

Special State Airport Problems. Consideration should be given to the development of a Transatlantic air base in Massachusetts. The geographical advantages are obvious, and adequate facilities could be easily provided.

A dirigible base, if one were to be provided, should certainly not be at East Boston.

A study should be made of the utility of a regular seaplane service to vessels at sea, to expedite passenger travel, mail, and express.

PUBLIC WORKS

Public works are the translation of planning into physical counterparts. Under State planning, public works would find expression in a coördinated program comprehending expenditure of public money on Federal, State, district, county, and municipal projects.

The State Planning Board has had to confine its study to the coördination of the public-works programs of the various political subdivisions. Such coördination is necessary for reasons of economy and of assurance that the greatest utility will be provided. Long-range plans, drawn from all available information, are essential, although it is recognized that changing social conditions may require modifications. Complete and continuing contact among all interested agencies will clarify such problems. The State Planning Board acts as a medium for gathering and studying information on the future capital expenditure needs of all these agencies.

An interim report has been prepared, summarizing a complete report, which will include charts and graphs.

There are some eleven Federal agencies which make expenditures for public works in Massachusetts, but there has been no coördinated planning. Certain of them do not have large programs of new construction, but such agencies as the Federal Bureau of Public Roads, the Emergency Administration of Public Works, the War Department Corps of Engineers, and the Works Progress Administration have made and are making expenditures running into many millions of dollars. Among them, they make many important contributions to the resources of the State, and the need for coördinated planning is apparent.

The State itself makes large expenditures through its various departments, seven of them furnishing the bulk of capital improvements. The Department of Public Works spends more on new construction than all other departments combined, with the Department of Mental Diseases second, though expending only one third as much. Then follow in order the Department of Correction, Metropolitan District Commission (boulevards), Department of Public Health, Department of Public Welfare, Department of Education. Outlines of the functions of each of these departments, with reference to expenditures in recent years for new construction and future programs, have been drawn up. In each of them, there is careful presentation of the pressing needs, of opportunities for realignment of plant uses, of cost estimates, and of reports on programs in progress.

The Metropolitan District Commission comprises Parks, Water, and Sewerage Divisions, and these three divisions plan and control the construction of new works. They have long-term plans and close estimates of needs and costs. Their operations are necessarily closely coördinated with Federal, State, county, and municipal work.

The counties of the Commonwealth make most of their public expenditures for inter-town road improvements, and coöperate closely with the State and towns, both as to plans and provision of and use of funds. Other expenditures are made for county courts, prisons, hospitals, and schools.

MASSACHUSETTS STATE PLANNING BOARD

Municipalities make large total capital expenditures on schools and libraries, municipal buildings, roads and sidewalks, water-supply and sewerage systems, and parks and playgrounds. To bring such construction into agreement with the public-works programs of the other agencies will require a complete survey with a view to creating a master plan.

The State Planning Board, at the suggestion of the National Resources Committee, has communicated with city and town officials and members of planning boards to obtain information on projects recommended for construction in the six-year period beginning Jan. 1, 1937. Replies have been slow in coming in, and a number of the officials, for various reasons, been unable to supply the information. The State Planning Board may have to make personal contact and assist the officials in filling out the forms distributed.

COMMUNITY PLANNING

Historically, community planning in Massachusetts dates from earliest Colonial times, when planning was a fairly simple problem. Some of the best traditions of town and village planning are to be found in New England. Charlestown was planned by Thomas Graves, of Kent, England, in 1629, for the Massachusetts Company.

The first important modern manifestation of community planning in Massachusetts was the development of industrial villages in the latter part of the 19th and early 20th centuries, notably Hopedale, Whitinsville, and Ludlow.

Legislation covering planning is even more recent, but the State is credited with pointing the way by establishing the Metropolitan Park Commission and the Water Supply and Sewerage Board of 1890, the Homestead Commission in 1911, and by enacting the Planning Laws of 1913 and 1936. There were earlier State and local building regulations, chiefly aimed at protection of health and elimination of fire risks.

The Homestead Commission was created to investigate methods of providing suburban cottages for families in the lower-income groups. Its reports are still noteworthy, and show a grasp of the relation of housing to city planning that was unusual in that period. The Commission preposed that planning boards be instituted in each city and in each town of more than 10,000 population. The Acts of 1913 provided for this, and also enlarged the duties of the Commission. In 1917, initial funds were provided and twelve houses constructed in Lowell, but as no further funds were voted the project developed no further.

MASSACHUSETTS STATE PLANNING BOARD

Each year since 1914, has seen increasing activity by planning boards of cities and towns throughout the State, variously concerning parks, highways, zoning, and housing. Springfield had the distinction of having its plan adopted as an official document by the city.

Since 1930, there has been a universal lessening of municipal construction, and planning boards have tended to be inactive or have been largely employed in directing projects under CWA, ERA, and WPA auspices, Boston being particularly active. A number of other municipalities have undertaken planning projects in the nature of surveys of social, economic, and physical resources.

A general view of local planning boards indicates that many of them, optional as well as required, are clearly inactive. Lack of funds, failure of interest, and absence of incentive are apparent reasons. On the other hand, there have been signs of remarkable activity, even in smaller communities. In an effort to clarify the functions and relationships which brought about this disparity, regional meetings, letters, and questionnaires have been employed.

The problems of the local boards have been recorded and direct contacts gained with nearly half the local boards in the State. The functions appropriate to the State Planning Board and to the local boards have been clearly established, and a program of coöperation has been developed, including a means by which the State Planning Board can keep the local boards informed on current developments in this field of community planning.

INTRODUCTION

Courtesy of Secretary of the Commonwealth

CHAPTER I

INTRODUCTION

Summary Outline

I. The Scope of State Planning

II. Principal Divisions of a State Plan

III. A Progress Report

IV. Methods of Procedure

    A. Fact-Finding Studies
    B. Graphic Presentations
    C. Progress along a Broad Front
    D. Building up of Reference Files

V. Staff Organization

VI. Financing

MASSACHUSETTS STATE PLANNING BOARD

INTRODUCTION

Planning for a State seeks to accomplish results similar to those sought in the planning for a city, for a school system, or for private enterprise. Among the objectives are the economic use of land, the conservation of natural resources, better sanitation, greater use of power, stimulation of appropriate industry, improved social conditions, development of recreation, integrated transportation, and efficient public works. Foresight and a broad, comprehensive viewpoint applied to guiding the orderly development of Massachusetts should bring about cumulative benefits and avoidance of waste worth many times the cost of the effort. Thus, each phase of human activity in the State should be studied, first, with a view to developing a long-time program for its own greatest advantage and, second, with a view to correlating this program with each other phase so that all may fit into a single integrated scheme with a minimum of overlap and conflict. Many of these activities are already the concern of a State department, but others, some of them of prime importance, fall outside the field of any existing agency. The greater the interest of State departments the more successful will be the combined plan.

The Scope of State Planning

The State Planning Board's major interest is the State Plan for Massachusetts. While conceivably such a plan might embrace all human institutions, a greater degree of success is likely to be achieved if its scope is confined at the outset fairly closely to the physical world, where the durability of man's constructions forces him to plan for the future if they are not to become obsolete long before they wear out. Those activities most dependent on efficient physical facilities will in the largest degree repay planning in advance. This is not at all to say that social and economic factors should be ignored. They motivate the entire plan by indicating the objectives to be sought. At the other end of the process, government, administration, and finance provide the means of carrying the plan into effect.

While the physical plan for the State is naturally to be expressed in terms of areas on maps and plans for structures, the key approach to the successful plan is the study of man's activities. No area and no construction is of any value except insofar as it provides facilities for some human activity.

MASSACHUSETTS STATE PLANNING BOARD

Principal Divisions of a State Plan

In order to attain the ultimate goal of a comprehensive State plan, the undertaking must be broken into manageable divisions, their subsequent recombination into the integrated plan being kept constantly in mind. Each division should relate to one of the prime classes of the inhabitants' activities, and in it may be grouped comparatively minor activities of similar nature. Foremost come problems of use of land and the natural resources on and under its surface, — agriculture, forestry, geologic resources, urban uses, and so forth. Scarcely less important are water problems, — supply, flow, sanitation, and so on. Power is vital to the conduct of modern civilization. Industry is the leading activity of the citizens of Massachusetts, and with it may be classed trade, men's other private activities, and social problems, which arise in large measure therefrom. Recreation may be considered as a land use or as an industry, but it is so important in Massachusetts that it may better be handled in a class by itself. Transport — by highway, rail, air and water — is an essential means to the success of the activities already mentioned.

While these six divisions of land, water, power, industry, recreation, and transport constitute the central structure of the studies for the State plan of Massachusetts, certain additional interests appropriate to State planning are of sufficient importance to warrant a coordinate status in the program. Since much of its accomplishment depends upon the carrying out of projects by public authorities, a public works program should be developed to facilitate their financing. Since planning should proceed at various levels of government, the promotion of community planning and correlation of local and State plans is an important function of the State Planning Board. Similar coöperative efforts with agencies outside or larger than the State are likewise essential.

A Progress Report

The present report sets forth the results of the work of the combined staffs on State planning for Massachusetts during the approximately twelve months that the work of the State Planning Board has been under way. Since in practically every part of the work the forces of the Works Progress Administration staffs sponsored by the Massachusetts State Planning Board and by the National Resources Committee have participated in one way or another, this report likewise incorporates the results of the respective WPA projects directly concerned. Other activities of the State Planning Board, such as its work as an Interstate Compact Commission, are outside the scope of this report and will be alluded to only inci-

MASSACHUSETTS STATE PLANNING BOARD

dentally in their relation to specific parts of the State plan.

At the outset a tentative program of work was drawn up as a guide for the ensuing year, it being felt that this was the shortest time within which a reasonably rounded schedule could be completed. While a variety of unforeseen circumstances has curtailed the effective forces both in numbers and in individual training and ability below that originally contemplated, the major part of the program has been carried through, with such modifications as experience has proved to be beneficial, or in some cases necessary owing to lack of data. Moreover, with the further continuation of the work, there is every expectation of completing a number of studies either not included herein, or thus far reported on only in a preliminary way.

Methods of Procedure

Fact-Finding Studies

The normal first step in attacking problems of the nature of those susceptible to solution through planning is to survey the existing situation so as to provide a solid basis for the plan. These fact-finding surveys and the presentation of the facts in graphic form are particularly important for such a ramifying field as State planning. Furthermore, the natural inclination first to secure as many as possible relevant facts was in the present case emphasized by the unusual opportunity to gather such data afforded by the large WPA staffs available for this work and not for the most part especially trained for making actual planning studies. In this respect success has been noteworthy, the land use and water resources data secured in particular being far superior in extent and detail to what could otherwise have been secured by the Planning Board. Moreover, in many subjects, adequate relevant data could be quickly abstracted from the vast amount of information in reports and files that has been gathered for years by various State departments and others, making new field studies and lengthy reporting of conditions unnecessary.

While the work thus far, as reported herein, is chiefly of a fact-finding nature, every effort has been made to confine the surveys and presentations to those which should be directly useful in actual planning. No data have been gathered merely for general information. To aid in assuring this result, all activities have been grouped under their appropriate divisions in the integrated State planning program. These divisions were selected with this end, among others, definitely in view.

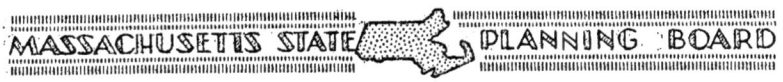

Graphic Presentations

To facilitate the rapid grasp and application of data to the many related problems involved, graphic methods have been used wherever possible in their presentation. A "key series" of maps embodies the principal relevant facts having a significant bearing on the State plan. The majority of those contemplated are now drafted and most of these are reproduced in this report, as listed above. In addition, a number of maps prepared by other agencies are included in the complete file.

Progress along a Broad Front

The opportunity to make a general attack on all the major elements of the physical plan for Massachusetts has been utilized, thus keeping to the fore the essential idea of the comprehensive, inter-related plan, as contrasted with special studies in limited fields. While progress along such a broad front will naturally be comparatively slow and uneven, many conclusions and abstract recommendations have been reached and are incorporated later in this report. It has also been possible to push in a few directions to the point of preparing concrete tentative plans. These are already proving useful for study purposes with the State department most directly concerned and with the New England Regional Planning Commission. The active co-operation of several of the State departments is of inestimable value in testing and perfecting the plans. The activities of the Regional Commission and interstate conferences with consultants of neighboring States are indispensable to a perfect fitting of Massachusetts plans at the State's borders with those of the States adjacent.

As each successive tentative plan is adopted, it is correlated with those previously adopted and they in turn are adjusted to meet the requirements of the most recent plan. In this way, a comprehensive State plan can gradually be built up.

Building up of Reference Files

An important adjunct to the technical work of the office is the reference file comprising library and map files. These have been organized under a classification scheme developed in collaboration with the Harvard Graduate School of City Planning based on the State Planning Classification issued by the National Resources Committee, April 8, 1935. The library bibliography alone already includes over 800 titles.

MASSACHUSETTS STATE  PLANNING BOARD

Staff Organization

Each of the divisions of the planning program was placed in the immediate charge of a division head and for each there was appointed a sub-committee of the State Planning Board. For each division a project outline was prepared as a guide to procedure, and served as a background for the corresponding chapter of this report. In order to secure the maximum of efficiency, the personnel of the several staffs available was pooled and organized according to the special abilities of the various men.

The State Planning Board has financed the nucleus staff of the central office from its annual State appropriation. The National Resources Committee has provided the Consultant, Associate Consultant, and also the Special Consultant working through its Urbanism Committee on industrial and community planning studies in Massachusetts and elsewhere. The State Planning Board and the National Resources Committee have acted as co-sponsors for a WPA staff for the Board. Also the Board has sponsored five, and the State Department of Health six, valley projects for land use and water resources studies on various watersheds of the State. The personnel of these combined staffs now numbers 445, as follows (For details, see "Personnel"):

State-financed staff — 35 persons, 24 of these being employed on temporary assignments.

National Resources Committee — 3 persons.

WPA State Planning Board staff project, No. 265-6905 — 38 persons.

WPA 11 valley or field projects, as listed below — 369 persons.

Sponsor -- State Planning Board

Connecticut Valley Hydrology	No. 65-14-6133
Connecticut Valley Conservation	" 65-14-1159
Essex County	" 65-14-1160
Bristol-Plymouth Counties	" 65-14-1161
Middlesex-Norfolk Counties	" 65-14-1162

Sponsor -- State Department of Public Health

Nashua Valley Water Supply and Sewerage	No. 65-14-7603
Blackstone Valley Flood Control	" 65-14-7604

MASSACHUSETTS STATE PLANNING BOARD

Nashua Valley Flood Control No. 65-14-7605
Housatonic Valley " 65-14-8070
Blackstone Valley Water Supply and
    Sewerage " 65-14-8071
Nashua Valley Conservation " 65-14-9613

Financing

Funds for operating the Massachusetts State Planning Board's activities (exclusive of National Resources Committee Consultants) are as follows:

	Spent Prior to Nov. 1, 1936	Unexpended Balance as of Nov. 1, 1936
State Appropriation		
(Sept. 18, 1935 - Nov. 30, 1935)-	6,891.11	---
Salaries	2,014.55	---
Expenses	4,876.56	---
State Appropriation		
(Dec. 1, 1935 - Nov. 30, 1936)---	36,127.73	7,872.27
Salaries	28,714.28	4,285.72
Expenses	7,413.45	3,586.55
WPA State Staff Project (Federal #3)		
(Nov. 20, 1935-about Nov. 15, 1936)	41,576.69	4,369.80
Salaries	38,575.05	2,543.64
Expenses	3,001.64	1,826.16
WPA 11 valley projects, combined		
(Nov. 18, 1935-about Dec. 15, 1936)	282,599.54	95,826.46
Salaries	252,268.15	87,013.61
Expenses	30,331.39	8,812.85

LAND

Courtesy of Secretary of the Commonwealth

CHAPTER II

L A N D

Summary Outline

I. Physical Characteristics

    A. Topography
    B. Soils
    C. Climate

II. Agriculture

    A. Types of Farming Areas
    B. Trends in Agricultural Production

III. Forestry, Recreation, and Wildlife Preservation

IV. Land-Utilization Problems in Massachusetts

V. Land-Use Survey As Applied to Individual Communities

    A. Information and Methods of Presentation
    B. Chester — Forestry and Recreational Uses
    C. Peru — Forestry Uses
    D. Lancaster — Agricultural Uses
    E. Billerica and Uxbridge — Part-Time Farming Uses
    F. Hingham — Residential and Recreational Uses

    Conclusion

MASSACHUSETTS STATE PLANNING BOARD

LAND

Physical Characteristics

Topography

    The surface of Massachusetts is greatly diversified, both as to the different sections in the State and as to the small individual areas. A general examination of the topographic map (Map 71-2) indicates that the surface has the highest elevation in the western part, where it is rough and mountainous as compared with the eastern and southeastern parts of undulating to level character. The central section of the State is mostly hilly and broken. In general the land rises and becomes rougher toward the west, interrupted by the important level valleys of the Connecticut and Housatonic Rivers. The coast is mostly rough and irregular in the north, but around Boston and to the south extending around Cape Cod, it is largely gravelly and sandy with numerous beaches and salt marshes.

    The Connecticut, which crosses Massachusetts, is the longest river. The Merrimack, Blackstone, and Housatonic come next in size. There are numerous other streams throughout the State, mostly small and short, useful primarily for power and water-supply purposes. Lakes and ponds are also found throughout the State, most of them being small in size. In the southeastern section a considerable area is covered by fresh-water marshes and peat bogs.

Soils

    The diversified topography in Massachusetts is accompanied by an even greater diversification of soil types arising not only from the effect of water action on rough topography but from former very active glacial action as well. Generally speaking the hilly areas are characterized by stony soils; those of finer texture, such as gravelly loams, sandy loams, and the fine silty types, are found on the valley floor and lower foothill regions. Throughout the western counties, ending with the western edge of the Connecticut Valley, soils are improved by the presence of limestone although even here much of this stone is too far below the surface to exert much natural influence on the soil.

    Many areas covered with chemically fertile soils are rendered useless for cultivation by the presence of numerous large stones, while in other places stones have been cleared from soils not especially fertile and such areas thrown into a mediocre type of

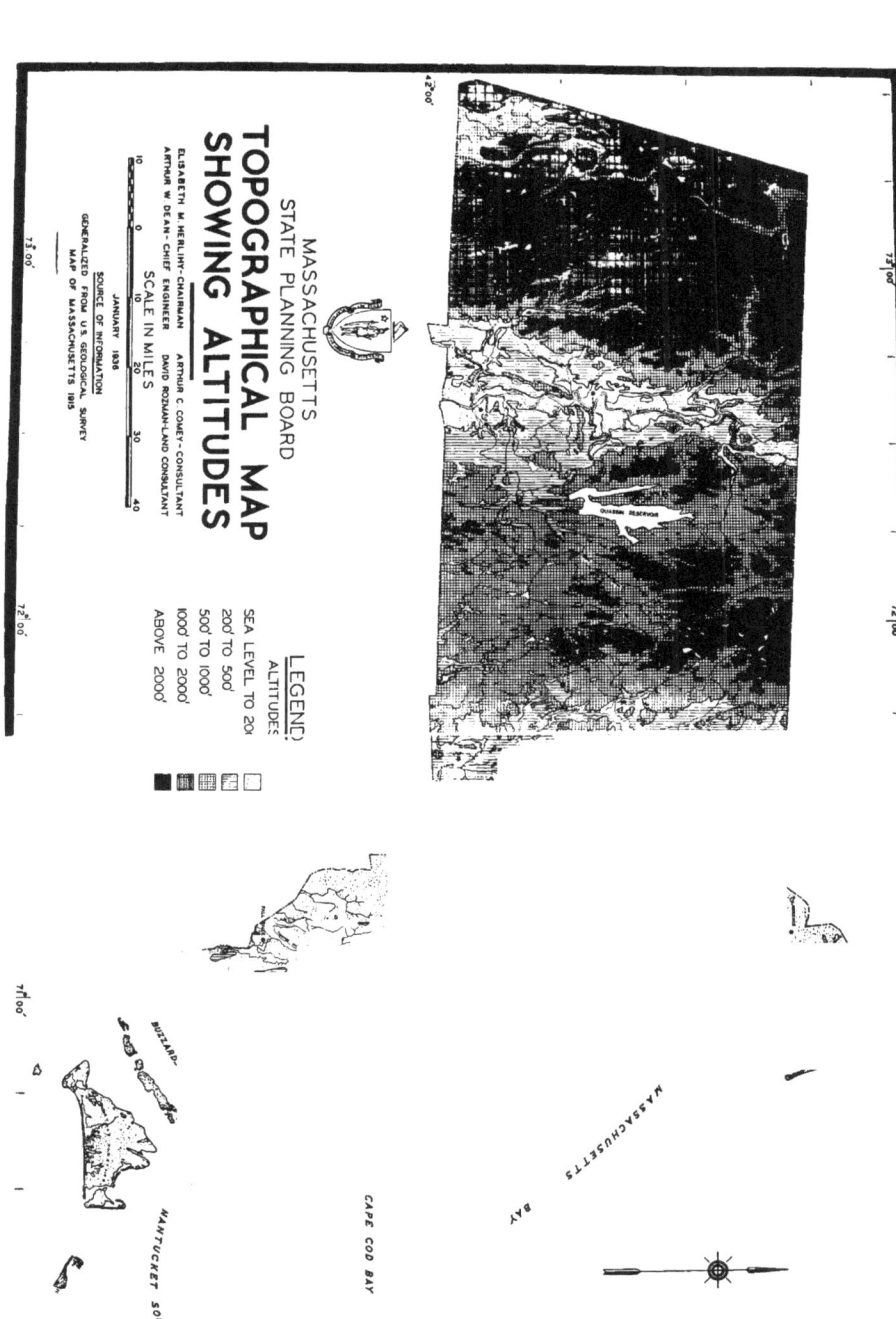

cultivated land.

Important Types of Well-Textured Soils. In the level river valleys and rolling lower foothills are found ideally textured soils of three types, all useful for cultivation under proper treatment.

The first type consists of the moist soils of generally loamy consistency. These soils are naturally rich in plant food, and are droughty or over-moist only in the most abnormal seasons. On these soils grow most of the ordinary farm crops of the State: hay, corn, potatoes, and the better pastures, together with considerable market-garden and specialty crops.

The second type consists of the soils equally ideal in texture but inclined to be leachy and therefore droughty and poor in natural fertility. On these soils, reinforced with large quantities of fertilizer, are grown most of the tobacco and onions produced in the State.

The third type of the well-textured soils is the muck and peat type. In the western end of the State much of this rich land has been left in its natural cover and used either as meadow, hay land, swamp, or swamp pasture. In the east, however, it has been developed into some of the most valuable market-garden land in the State, while on Cape Cod its use for cranberries is responsible for the present leadership of Massachusetts in the growth of this product.

Scattered throughout the State, but broadly located in two main sections mentioned below, are the soils best adapted to the growing of orchard fruits. Usually these soils belong to the stonier groups, quite fertile, but hard to cultivate; and they occur on the low ridge and drumlin formations so essential for providing the air drainage necessary for a successful orchard.

Climate and Length of Growing Season

The climate of Massachusetts is affected considerably by the variations in altitude and distance from the shore. The temperate climate of the State is often punctuated by severe winter days and hot summer days. However, very great extremes in temperature, both in winter and summer, seldom occur for more than a few successive days. On the average, there is from 40 to 50 inches of rainfall during the year. (See accompanying maps.)

The average length of growing season is from 160 to 180 days, depending mostly on local conditions such as elevation, air drainage, proximity to the shore, and the direction of the prevailing winds. In the areas with higher elevation and in the hilly sections the season is shorter. A very uneven topography interspersed with hills and adjacent valleys makes it very difficult to indicate the length of growing season for any large area. In fact, individual farms in the same locality have their own climatic problems which must be closely studied in order to obtain the best results from farming operations.

Agriculture

Types of Farming Areas

Except for a few specific localities it is extremely difficult to separate the State into distinct types of farming areas. On individual farms are usually found several types of farming enterprises, and, within small areas, owing to the natural and economic conditions and especially local markets, farmers specialize in different types of agricultural production. Nevertheless, after allowance for these exceptions, it is possible to indicate broad areas where specific types of farming enterprises are predominant or where some type of farming is distinguished by a difference in the general setup of the farms (See Map 51-25). In as much as dairying is the most important type of farming in Massachusetts and is found in all sections, some areas can be divided on the basis of differences in the general setup of dairying farms. In general, as we go from the western to the eastern part of the State the average size of a farm becomes smaller, the percentage of tillable land increases, and the amount of available pasture declines. More land in the eastern part of the State is devoted to vegetable gardening, the average value of farm land and buildings becomes higher, and the raising of poultry and the production of eggs become more prominent. As compared with the western part of the State the amount expended for feed and fertilizers is much greater. Part-time farming, found throughout the State, is especially prevalent in the eastern, more industrialized sections.

Western Dairy Section. This includes all of Berkshire County, portions of Hampden and Hampshire Counties, and a few towns in Franklin County. In the Berkshire highlands the land is very rough and hilly with narrow fertile valleys. The Housatonic Valley, which is included in this area, is a rolling plain surrounded by high, steep ridges. The majority of soils in this area are derived from glacial drift with considerable deposits of lime in the Housatonic Valley. The western dairy area differs from other sections in that it has a larger amount of home-grown feed available, and large areas of pasture on the farms. The average size of farm is larger than in any other section, but usually more than about fifty per cent of

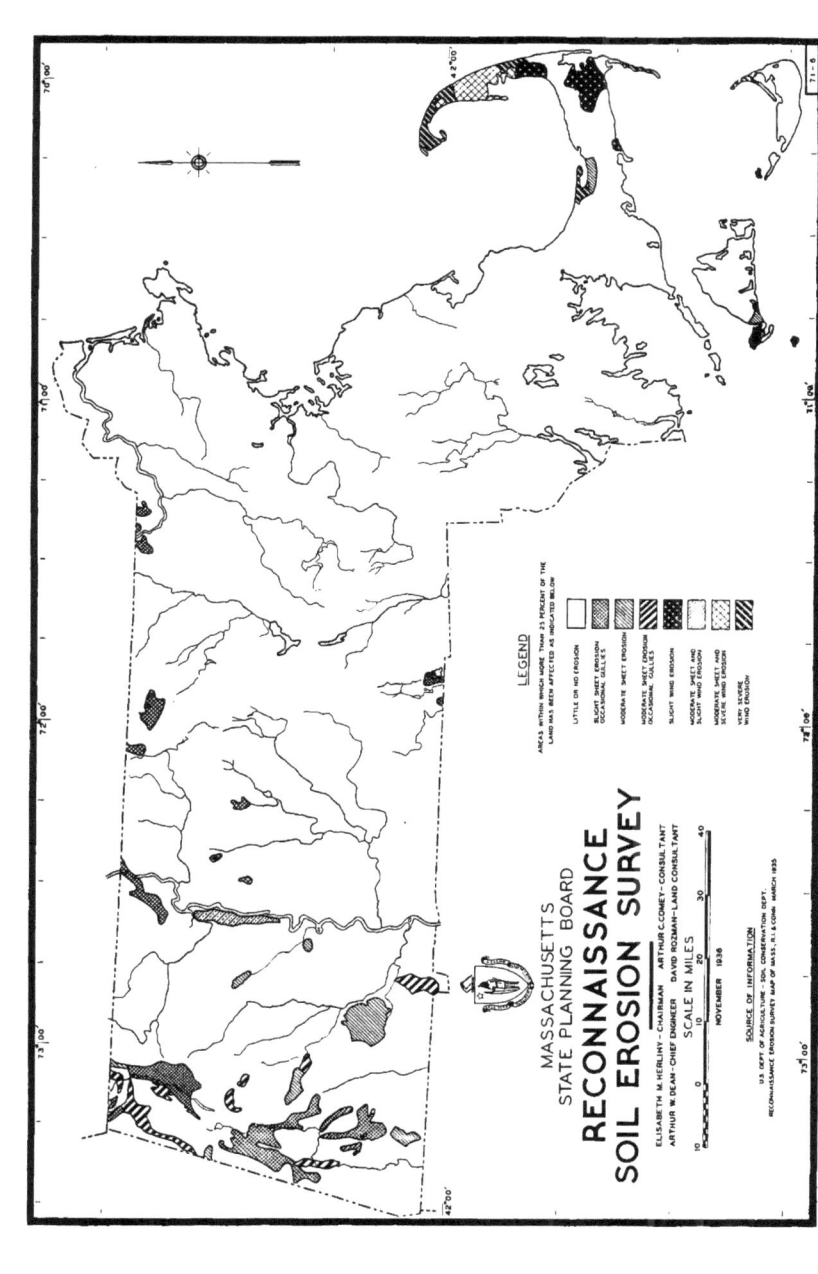

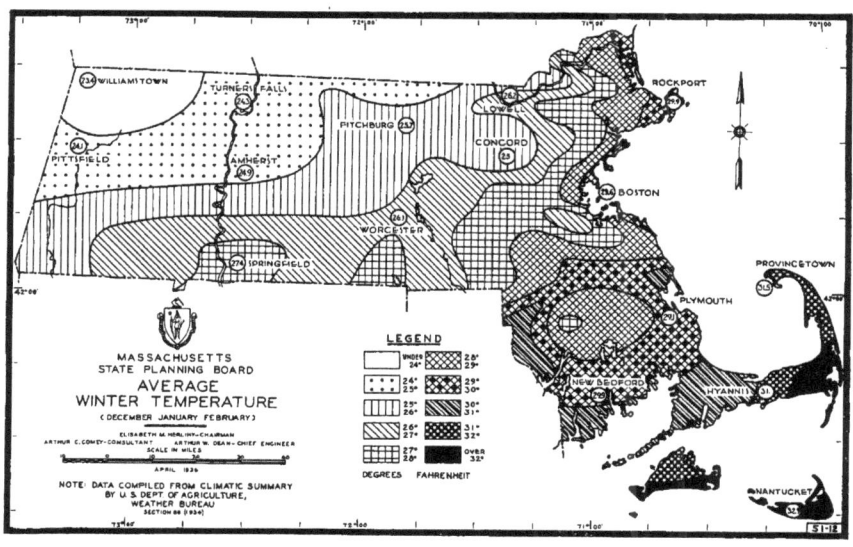

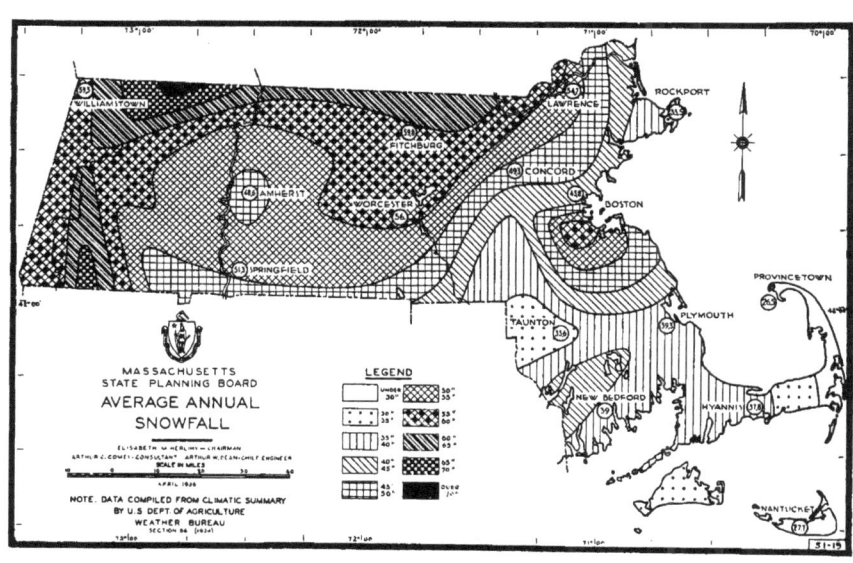

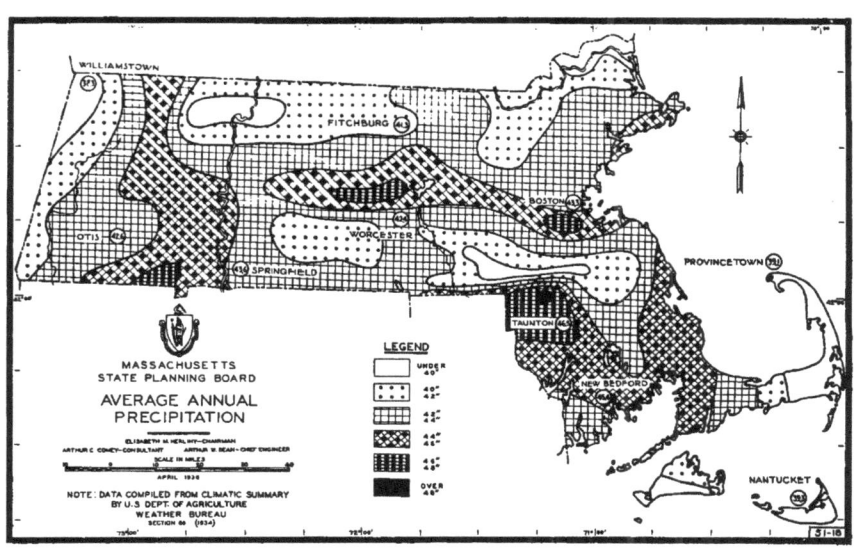

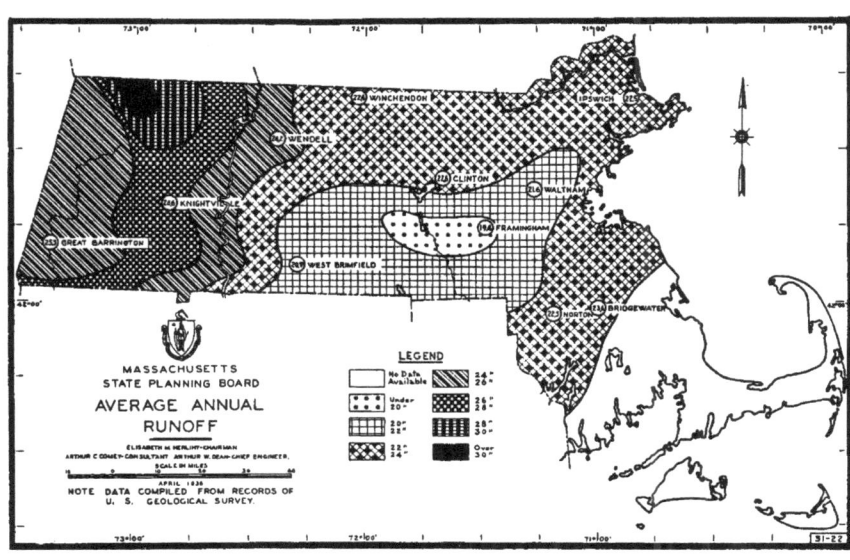

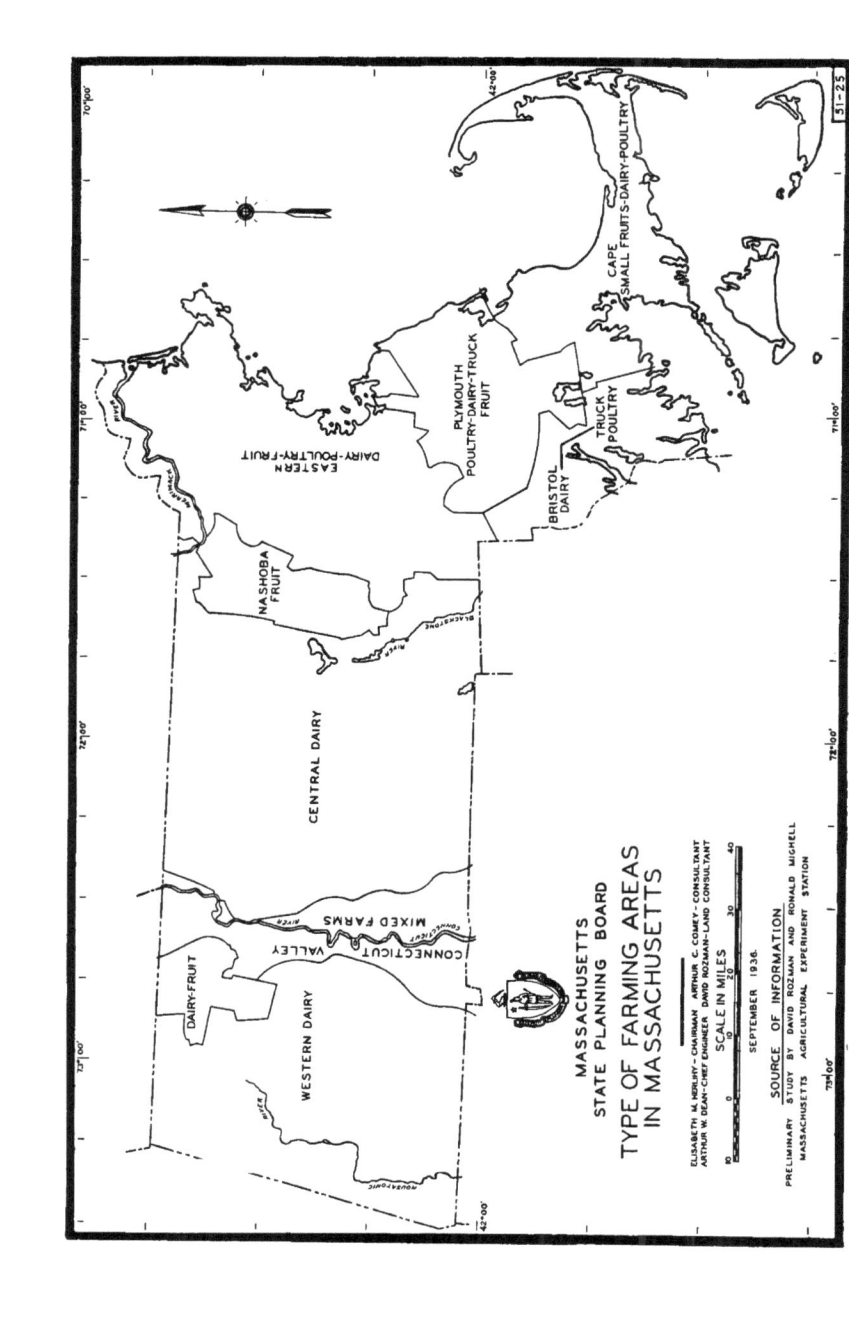

it is in woodland. Except for the adjoining dairy-fruit area, the percentage of tillable farm land is lower than in any other section. A greater self-sufficiency in feed results in lower expenditures for outside purchases of feed as well as fertilizers.

<u>Dairy-Fruit Area</u>. The dairy-fruit area is located in the western part of Franklin County. In addition to important dairy farms there are located here most of the commercial orchards of the western part of Massachusetts. The topography of the area is largely rough in contrast to the adjoining valley of the Deerfield River. This area also grows a considerable amount of hay, and the average size of farms is second only to the western dairy area, with the same large percentage of the total acreage in woodland. The average number of apple trees per farm is the highest in the State. The percentage of tillable land, however, is the lowest in the State. This area produces the greatest amount of milk per farm, while it has a low expenditure for feed and fertilizer.

<u>Connecticut Valley-Mixed Farms</u>. The soil here is mostly sandy loam with some silt and sand. This farming area comprises a narrow strip of land on both sides of the Connecticut River and is a fertile section. Farms of different types are encountered; of especial significance are onions, tobacco, and market-garden crops. The percentage of tillable land in farms and the average value of land and buildings per farm are among the highest in the State. The area has the highest number of acres of vegetables per farm and exceeds others in the output of corn and potatoes. It stands low in the amount of purchased feed, but greatly exceeds all other sections in the amount of purchased fertilizer per farm.

<u>Central Dairying Section</u>. The central dairying area consists of two sections somewhat distinct in natural make-up. The north central upland contains a large amount of very rough, unproductive land. The soil is chiefly gravelly, frequently mixed with granite boulders. In the section south of Worcester the elevation is lower, the topography is not as rough, and the soil is better adapted for agricultural cultivation. Several large valleys and a number of smaller valleys intersect this section. The general type of farming is mixed, but throughout the area dairying is the predominant type of enterprise. Market-garden areas are located near the cities of Worcester and Fitchburg, and a few commercial orchards are found near Worcester. South of this latter city there is an abundance of roughage, hay, and silage and fodder corn, as compared with the northern part of the area. The average size of farms in this central dairying area is lower than in the two western areas, but is higher than in the Connecticut Valley and all the sections lying to the east. In the matter of available tillable land and expenditures

13

for feed and fertilizers this area keeps an intermediate position between the western and eastern part of the State.

Nashoba Fruit Area. In addition to a combination of dairying and apple growing there are many specialized apple orchards in this section. It extends over several towns in Worcester and Middlesex Counties. Market-garden areas and poultry raising are being developed for the Boston market. The average size of farms is smaller than in any area lying to the west.

Eastern Dairy-Poultry-Fruit Area. This general farming area includes a combination of dairying, fruit growing, poultry raising, and market gardening. There are a number of specialized farms, especially market gardens near Concord, Lawrence, Boston, and other cities. The soil is rather gravelly, often interspersed with areas of muck, and outside of the coastal region is of a hilly character. The area includes the valley of the Merrimack River. The average size of farms is only about fifty acres, and the amount of pasturage available is very small. The percentage of tillable land in farms is one of the highest in the State, while the value of farm land and buildings per farm is the highest. As in other eastern sections of the State, part-time farming here is wide-spread and accounts for a considerable amount of agriculture. The expenditures for fertilizers are very high as well as the expenditure for purchased feed.

Bristol Dairy-Truck-Poultry Area. This is a region of low elevation, mostly below 200 feet, with low, rounded hills. Considerable sandy areas extending over the region are often adaptable for truck gardens. Poultry raising and egg production form another prominent enterprise. This region exceeds all other areas in the amount of milk produced per farm, but the expenditures for feed and fertilizers run very high.

Plymouth Poultry-Dairy-Truck-Fruit Area. Poultry raising is conducted here on a more intensive basis than in any other section. The nearness of Boston and other cities makes profitable the raising of market-garden crops and small fruits, especially strawberries. The size of farms is the smallest in the State with the least amount of pasture land available. However, the proportion of farm land tillable is one of the highest in the State. As in other eastern sections the expenditures for feed and fertilizers are very high.

Cape Cod Small Fruit-Dairy-Poultry Area. The soil is mostly sandy, with peat bogs located both on the Cape and in several Plymouth County towns. On the Cape itself farms are found only on a limited territory. The area produces a large cranberry crop, and also strawberries. Recreational facilities and uses provide an additional income to many farmers. Next to small fruit, dairying and poultry raising are important types of farming. The average size of farms is larger than in other eastern areas, but the proportion of tillable land is small. With very little hay and pasture available the dairying is conducted on a limited basis. As contrasted with other eastern areas the expenditures for feed and fertilizers are low.

Trends in Massachusetts Agricultural Production and Livestock on Farms

Hay. From the standpoint of crop acreage, hay is the most important crop in Massachusetts, occupying more than three-fourths of the total crop area. Since the end of the last century there has been some decline in total hay production in line with the general decrease of land in farms, but not to the same extent as in the production of grain crops.

Grain. Of the grains, corn is the most important in Massachusetts. Oats, rye, and wheat are grown in very small quantities. As compared with the quantity of corn grown several decades ago the present production of grain shows a considerable decline, although the total acreage of corn for all purposes is about the same. A more severe decline has occurred in the production of oats, as well as of rye and wheat. The production of corn per acre is one of the highest in the country.

Potatoes. Potatoes as a supplementary crop are grown on many farms throughout the State, mostly for farm use. They are an important crop in total production in Massachusetts agriculture, and have been on the increase in recent years. The total acreage at present, however, is somewhat lower than in 1900.

Other Vegetables. Vegetables other than potatoes are grown throughout the State, but specialized vegetable farms are located mostly in the Connecticut Valley and the eastern part of the State, especially near cities. Onions, grown primarily in the Connecticut Valley, are the most important vegetable crop. The vegetable crops next in importance are sweet corn followed by cabbage, lettuce, tomatoes, celery, and asparagus. Since 1900 the total acreage in vegetables has shown a slight increase, amounting to over 33,000 acres in 1934, according to the last Agricultural Census.

Tobacco. The acreage and total production of tobacco have been increasing since the beginning of the century and the highest

Table 1

U. S. AGRICULTURAL CENSUS FIGURES FOR MASSACHUSETTS

	1800	1900	1935
Number of farms	38,406	37,715	35,094
Land in farms (acres)	3,359,079	3,147,064	2,195,714
% of State area	65.3	61.2	42.7
% of farm land improved	63.4	41.1	34.5
Average acreage per farm	87.5	83.4	62.6
Value of farm land and buildings	$146,197,415	$158,019,290	$255,676,839
Average value per acre	$43.52	$50.21	$116.44
Livestock on Farms			
Horses	59,629	71,937	26,770
Dairy Cattle	150,435	184,562	137,884
Sheep	67,979	33,869	8,216
Swine	80,123	78,925	90,238
Poultry	962,968	1,680,693	2,517,778
Dairy and Poultry Products			
Milk sold (gallons)	29,662,953	68,180,759	54,886,363
Eggs produced (dozens)	6,571,553	12,928,630	24,079,913
Some Leading Crops			
Corn (bushels)	1,797,768	1,539,980	357,329
Hay, cultivated (tons)	684,679	848,950	458,525
Potatoes, white (bushels)	3,070,389	3,346,590	2,584,184
Tobacco (pounds)	5,369,436	6,406,570	5,411,107

Note: The total value of agricultural output, according to the Agricultural Census, was, for 1880, $24,158,881; for 1910, $47,001,198; and for 1930, $80,400,492.

16

acreage was reported by the Census of 1925. In the last few years, owing to general overproduction and also to production control, the tobacco acreage has been brought to a much lower figure. In 1934 only about 5 1/2 million pounds were produced as compared with about 14 million pounds in 1924.

Orchard Fruits. Apples are the most important of orchard fruits, the number of trees and production showing slight changes in the last few years, although in general some decline in production is registered. The production of peaches is next in importance, with production in general showing a slight increase.

Small Fruits. Of the small fruits cranberries are the most important, with production concentrated on Cape Cod and in near-by sections. The acreage in cranberries has been more or less constant for a number of years, over 6,000 acres being cultivated in 1930 with an output of about 22 million quarts. Strawberries raised in the eastern part of the State come next in importance with about 1,500 acres in 1930.

Dairying. Dairying contributes the largest share to the farm income in the State. Production of milk per cow and percentage of whole milk sold are among the highest in the country. The total production of milk and number of cows show a slight decline since 1900, but have been almost stable for the last twenty-five years.

Poultry. Poultry is found on most of the farms in Massachusetts and is a very important source of farm income. The total number of poultry on farms has increased about 50 per cent since 1900, but through modern practices in poultry keeping, over three times as many chickens are now raised annually. As a result of the same improved methods the production of eggs has increased at a more rapid rate than the total number of mature birds kept.

Forestry, Recreation, and Wildlife Preservation

The major part of the land area in Massachusetts is now covered by forests, including under that term all types of woodland, cut-over land, and old fields reverting to brush and trees. Of the estimated woodland area of three million acres, a little over one million acres, or about one-third, are included in farms (See Chart 61-C2). With the exception of some land in State forests, town forests, and other small areas under control of various institutions and private individuals, the major part of woodland both on the farms and outside of them remains undeveloped and represents a considerable waste of natural resources.

Need for Better Utilization of Woodland

Better utilization of the wooded area in farms will go a long way toward influencing income return from Massachusetts agriculture. By developing his woodlot, the farmer will obtain many advantages and make it an asset to the farm enterprise instead of a burden, as it frequently is. This will increase the production of material consumed on the farm in the form of fuel, fencing, and lumber, and furnish employment to farm labor in slack seasons. In addition, it will bring cash revenue, obtained from periodical cutting, systematically arranged. There is also the possibility of creating local markets for farm products, and of bringing other advantages to the rural communities and farming population through the development of local wood-working industries because of the presence of a greater supply of the essential raw materials.

The major part of the woodland, about two million acres, however, lies outside of the farms and is the main reservoir to be drawn upon to supply land for scientific forestry and for the rapidly expanding recreational and game-preservation needs. Any future land policy dealing with the problem of utilizing this area will inevitably take into consideration the possibility of developing a considerable portion of this land into well-managed forests under public or semi-public ownership.

Forests and Parks under Public or Semi-Public Ownership

The beginning in this direction has already been made by an orderly utilization of land areas for the cultivation of trees in State forests, town forests, various public reservations, and public parks.

At the end of 1935 the total area in State forests, parks, and reservations amounted to almost 170,000 acres. During the last session of the State legislature a bill* was passed to purchase an additional 500,000 acres for the State forests and parks over the period of the next twenty years.

Until 1934, few recreational facilities had been provided in the State forests. At the present time the Department of Conservation has developed a general policy in connection with the development of State forests, providing for recreational facilities and the restoration of wildlife.

---

*Chap. 415, Act of 1936.

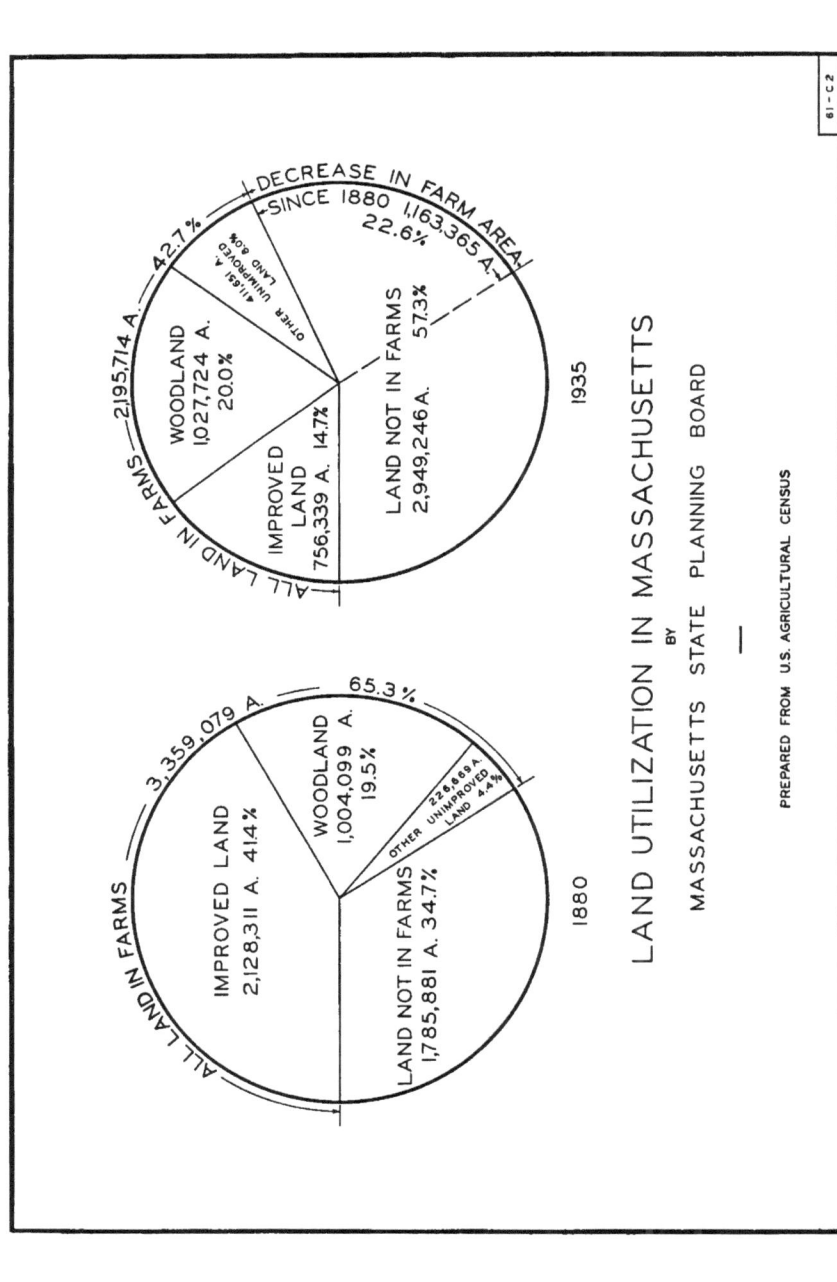

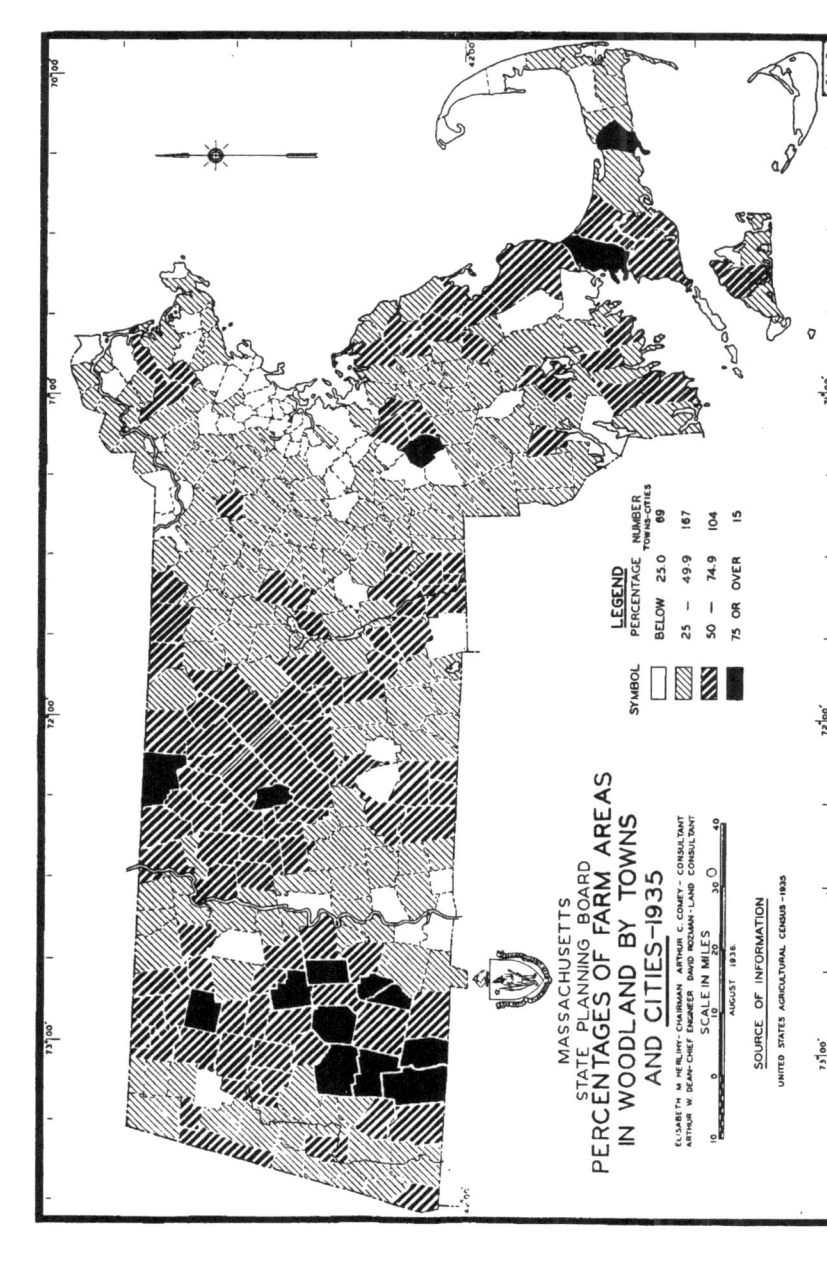

MASSACHUSETTS STATE PLANNING BOARD

With the addition of new areas to the State forests detailed plans are drawn for recreational facilities, including such items as picnic groves with fireplaces and tables, tent sites, cabins, and trails. Where possible, an effort is made to dam streams or flood swamps to create ponds to be stocked with fish for the sportsmen, and to be used for swimming, boating, or skating.

In providing for wildlife restoration, a certain portion of the State forest is set aside as a sanctuary and treated so as to provide year-round food and protection for desirable species of game animals and birds.

The forest area under public control is further augmented by the existence in Massachusetts of town forests established within recent years by over 100 towns largely due to the efforts of the Massachusetts Forest and Park Association.

Recreational aspects of land use are treated in detail in Chapter VII.

Forests under Private Ownership

To provide for forest development of the land held by private individuals the legislature passed, in 1922, the Forest Classification Act*, under which "forest land, coming within the terms of eligibility, can be separately classified and thereafter pays a tax on land value only, with a products tax payable at the time the timber is cut". When the timber on such land is cut, a yield tax of 6 per cent is assessed on the stumpage value of the material cut.

By providing further measures facilitating public or private reforestation of present idle acres great possibilities will be open for the development of recreational facilities, preservation of wildlife, and elimination of poor areas from agricultural land utilization.

Land Utilization Problems in Massachusetts

During the last few decades a very significant change has occurred in the general picture of land utilization in Massachusetts. The total amount of land in farms registered a pronounced drop, declining from 3,360,000 acres in 1880 to about 2,200,000 acres in 1935. In other words over one million acres, representing more than 20 per cent of the total area of the State formerly held in farms, has been released for other uses (See Chart 51-C2).

---

*Chap. 360, Acts of 1922.

MASSACHUSETTS STATE PLANNING BOARD

A Period of Change

In the past, when the Massachusetts land areas were taken up for farming, the conditions were different from those prevailing now, not only in reference to the competitive status of agriculture, but also in the general character of farming, which had been primarily self-sufficient. With little dependence on outside markets and with subsidiary employment available both at home and in small industries flourishing in rural towns, it was possible for early agriculturists to eke out a living on poor land areas not well adapted to modern farming. In the course of time, owing to the changed conditions of living and greater specialization, many things formerly produced and manufactured on the farm had to be purchased by the farmer from outside markets.

Declining Rural Industries.

Likewise, technical changes in the methods of production favored the development of large industrial centers and contributed to the decline of small rural industries. The subsidiary employment on which many Massachusetts farmers had depended so much in the past became very limited and farming itself in Massachusetts as well as throughout the country became a highly competitive business. Under these conditions the Massachusetts producers had to concentrate their operations on the best land, and the areas poorly adapted for cultivation have been gradually going out of this use.

Increasing Use of Land for Urban Needs

A certain portion of the land released from agriculture was taken up within recent times for uses connected largely with the needs of our large cities and towns. With the growth of population and especially of large centers there is a necessity of keeping a greater amount of land for present or prospective water reservoirs. Thus, the Metropolitan Water Commission supplying the Boston area has under its control an area of over 80,000 acres.

Extension of Part-Time Farming

Still more important within recent years has been extension of part-time farming, especially in the areas adjacent to industrial cities and towns. The development of good roads and automobile transportation enabled many people from congested urban areas to settle on the land not only in the immediate vicinity but sometimes at a considerable distance from the place of their work. Much of the land formerly in commercial farms is now being cultivated on a small scale as part-time farms. The production here is being

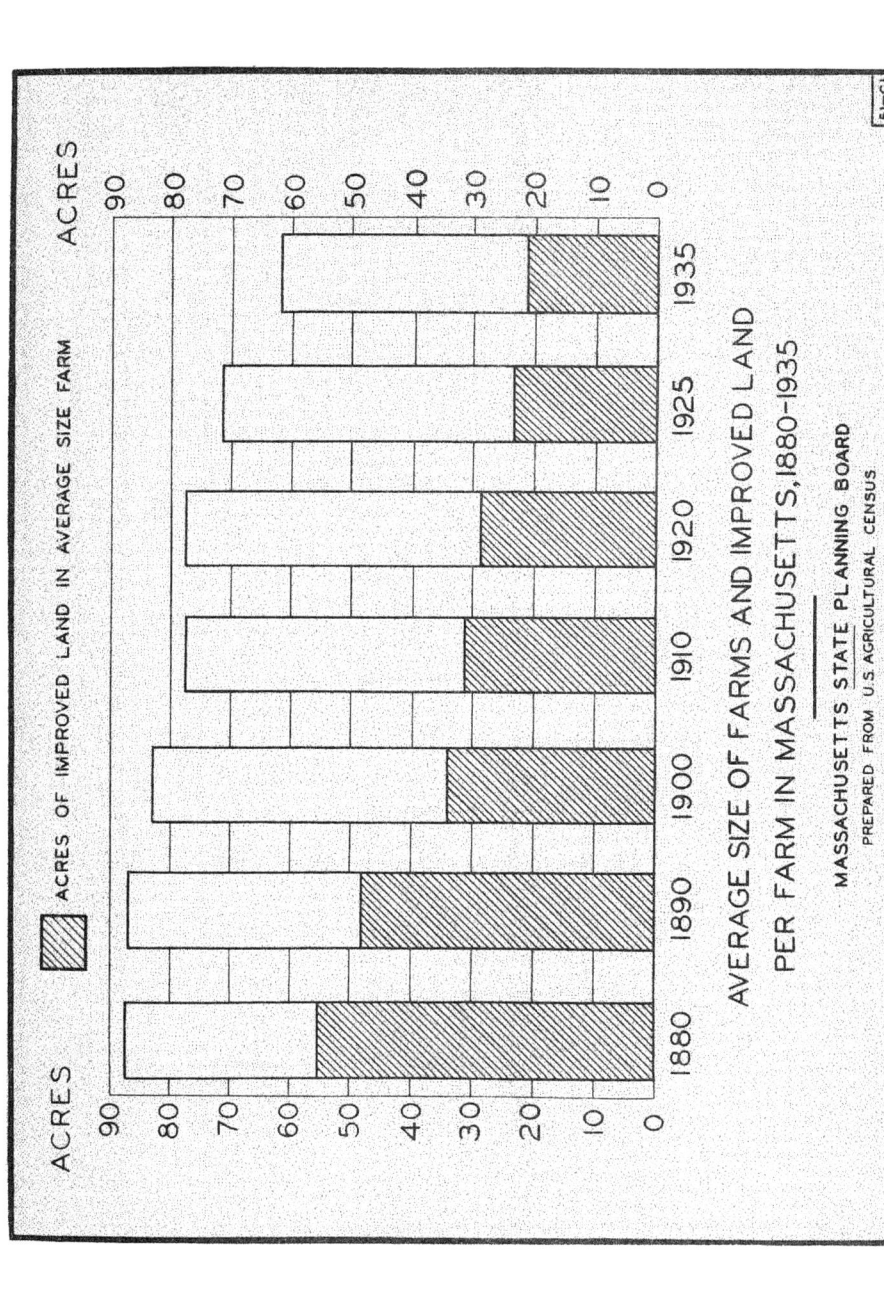

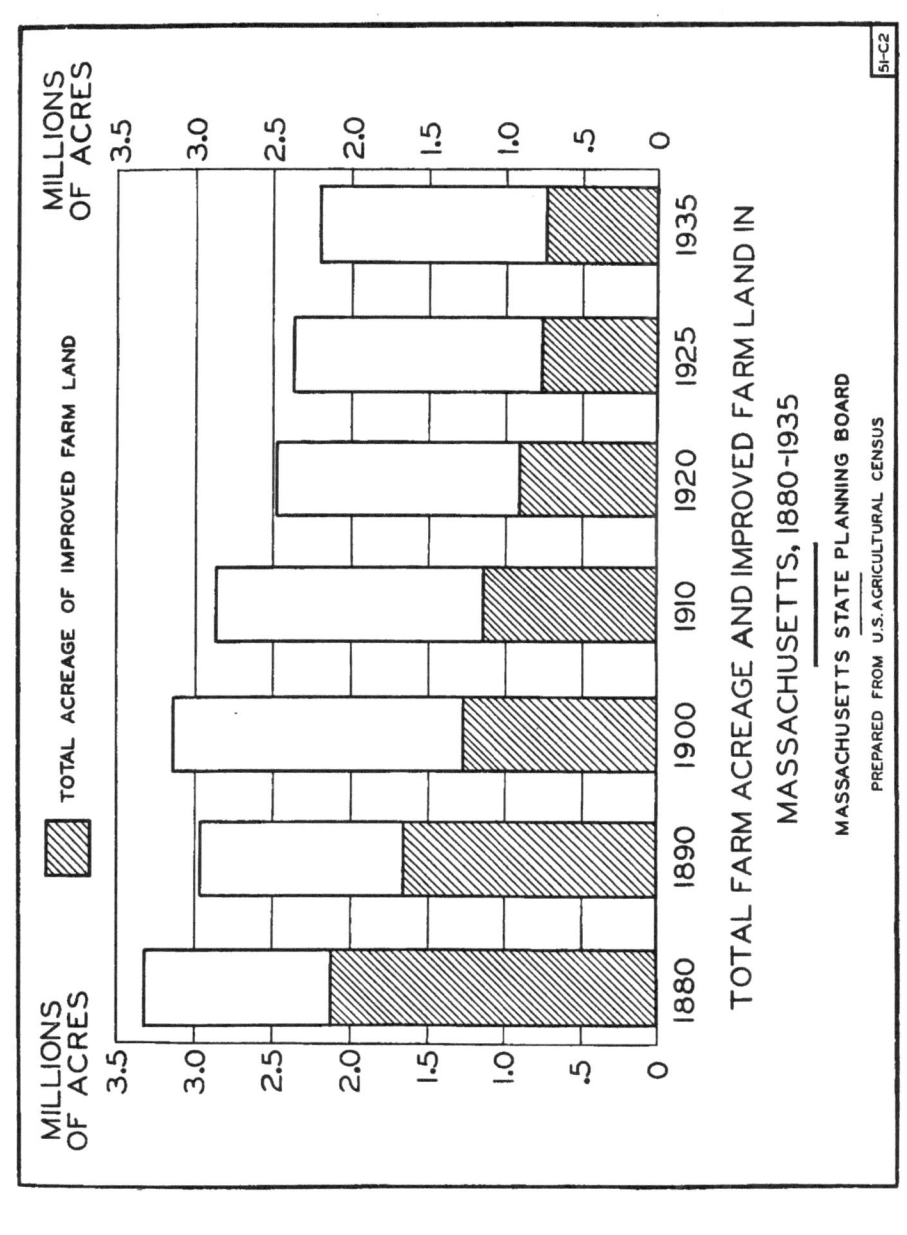

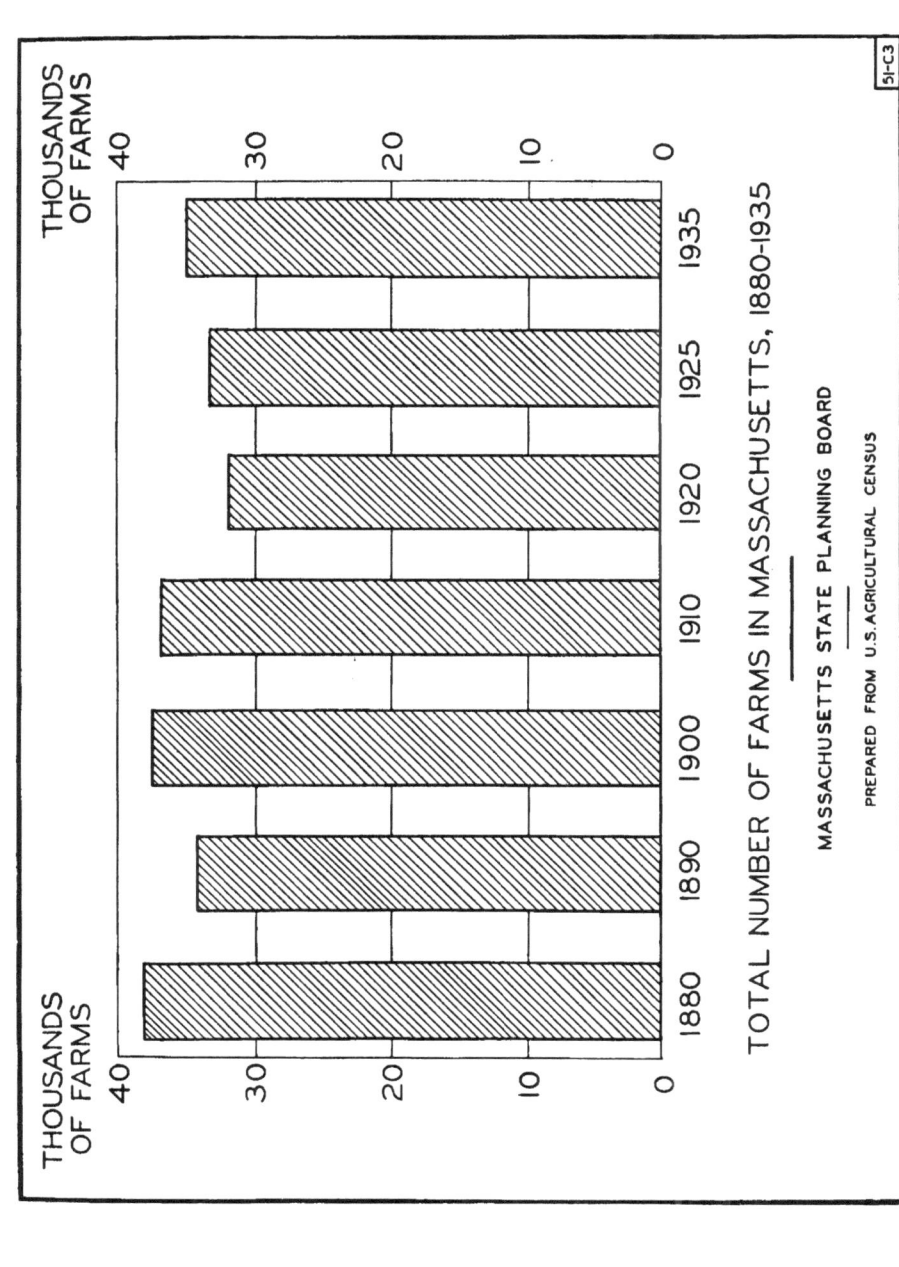

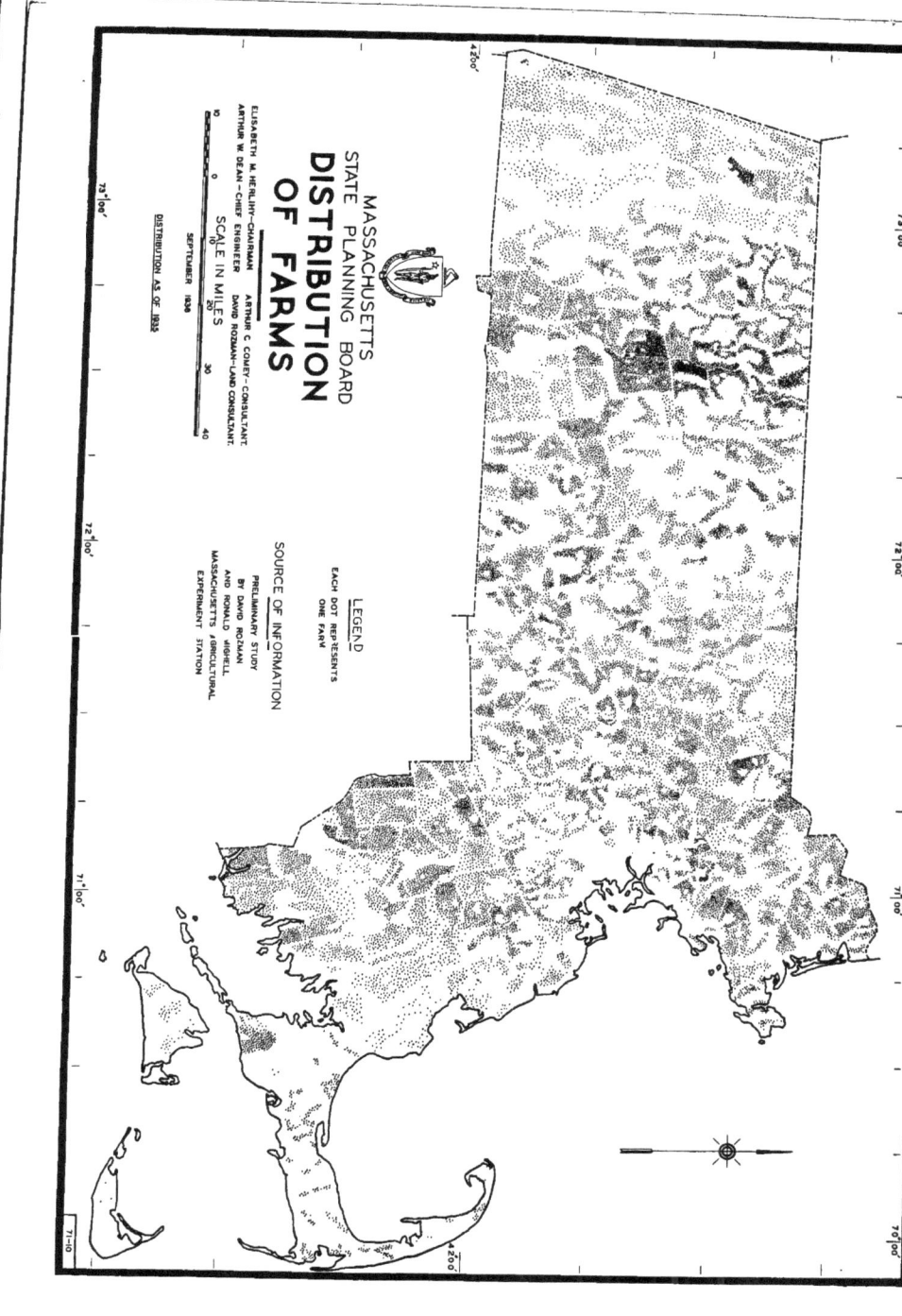

carried on mostly for the family needs, but in the aggregate contributes considerably to the total agricultural production.

Increasing Recreational Uses.

In some sections distinguished by their scenery and natural beauty, or in the vicinity of the lakes, ponds, and rivers a considerable amount of land was taken up for such recreational developments as country estates, summer homes, or camps. The necessity of conserving our land resources and putting to systematic uses many idle acres has resulted in the reservation of over 200,000 acres of land, which is now held in State forests, and parks, town forests, and other public and semi-public areas devoted to the systematic development of forestry, recreation, and game preservation.

Problems of Idle Land

Nevertheless, even with these new developments the fact remains that large areas of land formerly in agriculture still remain idle and have no productive use. Thus, according to the latest census, 90 towns, or over one-fourth of the total number in the Commonwealth, have less than 25 per cent of their area in farming, with most of the remaining area in unplanned wood and brush land in various stages of growth. (See Maps 51-8 and 51-9.)

This large acreage of unused land causes depopulation of the towns, with the result that in 92 towns an average of less than 50 persons are now found on a square mile. In these towns the expenditures for schools, roads, and other improvements are greater than the return in taxes, and the treasury of the Commonwealth is burdened with the necessity of covering the deficit.

The examination of economic and social forces operating within recent times indicates the possibility of revival in abandoned rural areas through development of new uses like recreational, residential, industrial, and part-time farming. A complete knowledge of all natural resources in individual areas of the State will help to determine whether some new industries could not be developed in declining rural towns and thus bring about the strengthening of the entire social and economic structure of the communities. Areas which by their natural conditions and locations promise no other utilization than the growth of trees and the preservation of wildlife should be devoted to scientific forestry. This in itself may contribute eventually to the welfare of local populations by creating subsidiary employment both in the forests and in the woodworking industries associated with the systematic development of forest areas.

MASSACHUSETTS STATE PLANNING BOARD

In process of general decline in agricultural areas in Massachusetts some good land went out of use along with the land poorly adapted for agricultural utilization. It is possible, therefore, that the revival of some communities may be brought about by bringing this good land back into cultivation, with the result that the total area in farms in the Commonwealth may become greater rather than smaller in comparison with the present. But in the absence of accurate scientific information it is impossible to approach in any adequate way the pressing problems of land utilization in our problem areas. The first step in achieving the final purpose of providing a definite basis for an orderly development of our land resources to the advantage of the Commonwealth and local areas is to take a complete inventory of these resources and subject it to a searching analysis.

The Land-Use Survey as Applied to Individual Communities

Kinds of Information and Method of Presentation

Realizing the importance of a land-use survey, the State Planning Board, at the beginning of this year, organized and sponsored through the Works Progress Administration a project for a detailed land survey of the entire Commonwealth. The results of this study are being presented for each town on four separate maps, drawn to the scale of two inches to the mile. The first map shows the existing land use and cover for individual tracts of land, indicating areas devoted to various agricultural uses, types of forests, and recreational uses, as well as industrial, commercial, and residential uses.

The second set of information obtained in the field survey and presented on a separate map for each town indicates exact location of roads and buildings by their type and condition, differentiating between various types of farms, part-time farms, residential, commercial, and industrial buildings, schools, hospitals, churches, and other types of private and public and semi-public developments, such as parks, playgrounds, golf courses, aviation fields, cemeteries, and water-supply reservoirs.

The third map for each town indicates the character of the soil, classified in several groups on the basis of productivity and adaptability for agriculture.

To complete the picture the topography of each town is presented on a separate map by means of contours with 20 feet intervals.

By correlating and analyzing the basic factors presented on

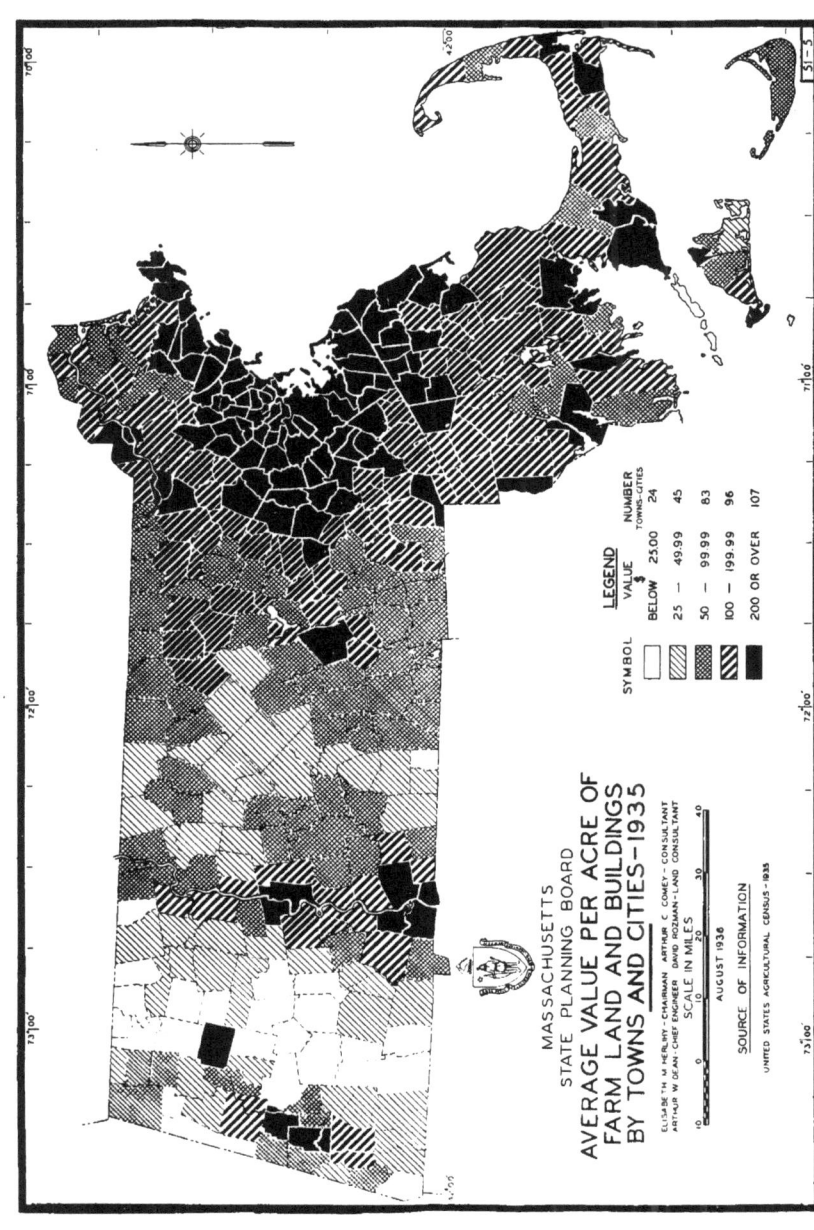

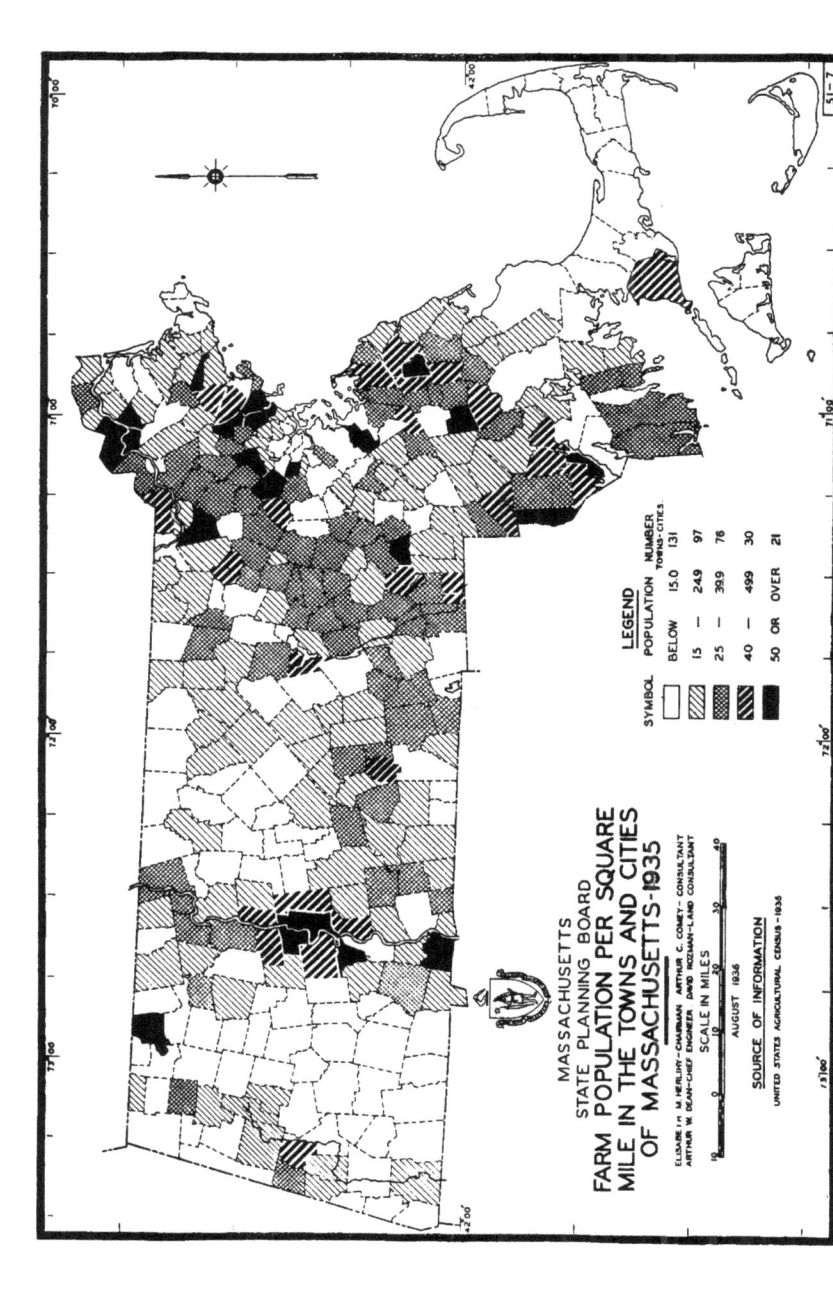

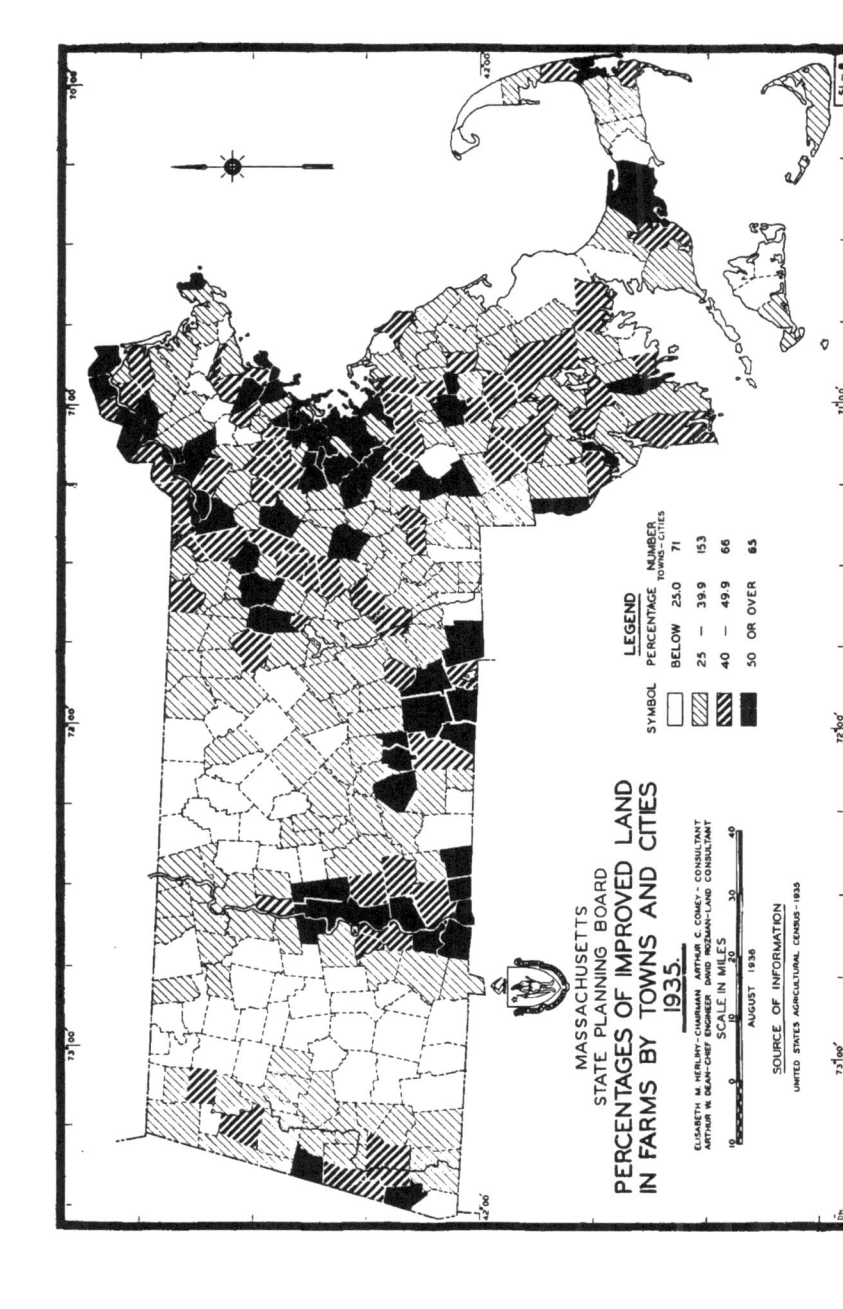

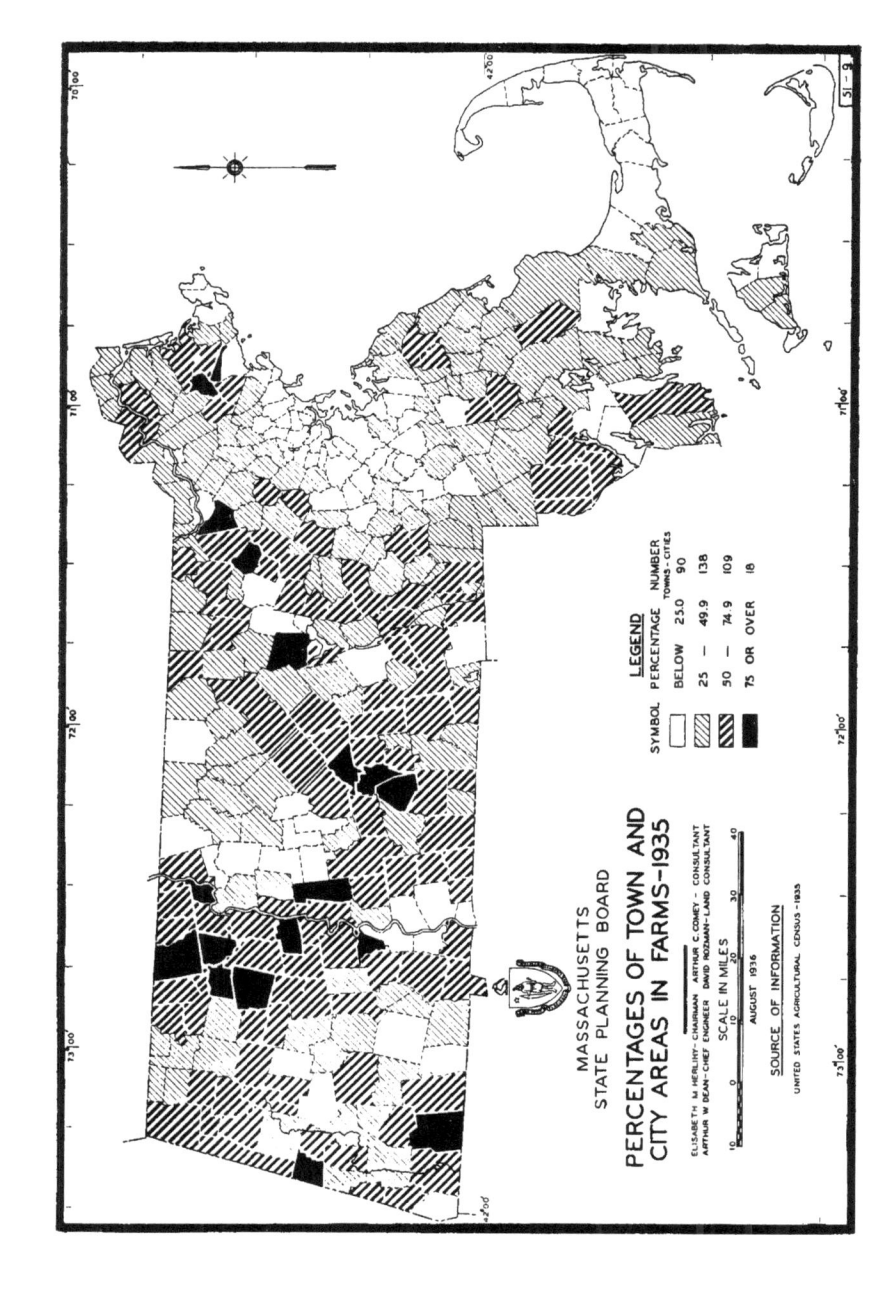

these maps and interpreting them in conjunction with available statistics for the towns it will be possible to outline the most desirable developments in land utilization for individual towns. As an illustration of the type of material collected by the State Planning Board in its study of natural resources of the Commonwealth, several towns have been selected for the discussion of their present and prospective land uses.

CHESTER — Forestry and Recreational Uses

The town of Chester, situated on the eastern slope of the Berkshire Hills, offers many problems for a study that may be typical of a number of declining hilltowns of western Massachusetts. A glance at the soil map of Chester (Map 51-84D) quickly establishes the fact that a major proportion of this town is covered by soils not suited to the growing of crops. This indication is further borne out by a perusal of the topographic map (Map 51-84A), which establishes very definitely the exceptionally rugged topography of this town. Practically all of the better land is found in three narrow diagonal strips running from northeast to southeast through the length of the town. This condition precludes the possibility of any extensive development of agriculture in this town under modern conditions. The areas suitable for farming may be easily detected from the soil and topographic picture as presented on the maps.

Abandoned Farms. In the past, the town of Chester had been supporting a considerable number of farm families. At the height of sheep raising 3,700 sheep were listed in the town, and, as late as 1865, there were 137 farms which kept a total of over 700 cattle. In the eighties of the last century there were several flourishing local industries, of which the working of an emery mine was the most important. This industry is still an important factor in the town, but agriculture has declined until only 50 farms are found, located mostly on the land of better quality.

Through the process of trial and error the cultivation of poor lands has been abandoned. From the map indicating roads and buildings (Map 51-84B) it will be seen that over 18 miles of roads have been abandoned, and 36 cellar holes found in this town are evidences of vanished farms which could not persist on the poor land. In addition to that it will be observed from the roads and buildings map that there are several roads in the town on which only a few farms and other buildings remain, and, judging by their poor condition, it is only a matter of a short time before these too will be abandoned. As a result of depopulation in the eastern part of the town the schoolhouse which served this territory is now vacant, and the only

MASSACHUSETTS STATE PLANNING BOARD

schools available are in the western part, not easily accessible to the rest of the town, from which school children have to be transported over long distances. With the existence of sparsely populated areas and considerable mileage of roads used only by a few people the expense of town maintenance per person is extremely high, calling for high taxes on the townspeople and requiring additional subsidies from the State.

A Town of Picturesque and Beautiful Scenery. While lacking in richness of natural resources for agricultural development the town of Chester possesses picturesque and beautiful scenery which should make it attractive as a place of residence and certain types of recreational development. In fact, there are at the present time in Chester two sizable camps, one of the Springfield Y.M.C.A., and the other of the Holyoke Boy Scouts Council. There are a few summer homes, six private houses with tourist accommodations, and two small hotels. In this town, the State forest occupies an area of about 1,500 acres, in which have been provided 36 stone fireplaces and many picnic tables. Taking into consideration the scenic beauty of this town, it might be expected that more people will be attracted to enjoy its recreational advantages.

The population of the town has remained practically stable for almost one hundred years, although there has been a decline from 1464 people in 1930 to 1362 in 1935. What was lost over a long period in agricultural population is almost compensated by additional industrial employment provided by the local granite and emery industry and by a greater number of people selecting the town for residence.

Preliminary Analysis. A preliminary analysis of basic information on natural resources in Chester indicates the following:

1. The major portion of the town formerly in agriculture is now in woodland which, except for a very small portion occupied by the State forest, is not being systematically developed.

2. In view of its picturesque scenery, the town presents a good opportunity for recreational developments such as summer homes, camps, and tourist accommodations.

3. With a possibility of further development of local industries some of the land will be utilized by the added population.

4. Every effort should be made to discourage an attempt by uninformed people to farm poor areas.

SYMBOLS FOR LAND UTILIZATION MAP

CROPLAND

    ORCHARDS

    HAY

    MARKET GARDEN

    OTHER CULTIVATED CROPS

PASTURE

    PLOWABLE PASTURE

    STONY PASTURE

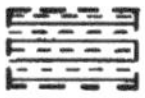

    WOODLAND PASTURE

FORESTS

    MERCHANTABLE TIMBER

    POTENTIALLY MERCHANTABLE TIMBER

    BRUSH LAND

    H = DOMINANTLY HARDWOOD
    C = DOMINANTLY CONIFEROUS
    M = MIXED HARDWOOD AND CONIFEROUS

        o = OPEN (NOT MORE THAN 20 % OF COVER)
        t = THIN (FROM 20 TO 50% OF COVER)
        d = DENSE (50% OR OVER)

51 – C4A

PUBLIC AND QUASI-PUBLIC AREAS

- PARKS
- PLAYGROUNDS, BALL FIELDS, ETC.
- BATHING BEACHES
- SKI GROUNDS
- GOLF COURSES AND COUNTRY CLUBS
- AVIATION FIELDS
- CEMETERIES
- WATER SUPPLY - RESERVOIRS

  - STATE OWNERSHIP
  - COUNTY OWNERSHIP
  - TOWN OWNERSHIP RESERVED FOR FOREST

OTHER AREAS

- LAKES
- SWAMPS
- SANDY WASTE LAND

THICKLY SETTLED AREAS

INDUSTRIAL AND COMMERCIAL AREAS

TOWN BOUNDARIES

- STATE LINE
- COUNTY LINE
- TOWN LINE

SYMBOLS FOR ROAD AND BUILDING MAP

THICKLY SETTLED AREAS
INDUSTRIAL AND COMMERCIAL AREAS
PRIVATE ESTATES
BUILDINGS IN RURAL AREAS
- RESIDENTIAL (INCLUDING SUMMER HOMES)
- CELLAR HOLES
- SEMI-AGRICULTURAL
- FARMSTEADS

d – DAIRY   P – POULTRY
LETTER APPEARS UNDER SYMBOLS

CHURCHES   OTHER RELIGIOUS INSTITUTIONS
SCHOOL HOUSES   OTHER EDUCATIONAL INSTITUTIONS
HOSPITALS
CORRECTIONAL INSTITUTIONS
OTHER PUBLIC AND QUASI-PUBLIC BUILDINGS
COMMERCIAL BUILDINGS (GAS STATIONS, ETC.)
COMMERCIAL GREENHOUSES AND NURSERIES
TOURIST ACCOMMODATIONS   HOTEL OR INN

OCCUPIED GOOD CONDITION   VACANT GOOD CONDITION   ABANDONED
OCCUPIED POOR CONDITION   VACANT POOR CONDITION

ROADS
- HARD SURFACED
- GRAVEL
- DIRT
- ABANDONED

HIGH TENSION LINES

51–C5

SYMBOLS FOR SOIL CLASSIFICATION MAP

GROUP   I — VERY DROUGHTY SOILS
             (PRINCIPALLY COASTAL AND DUNE SANDS)

GROUP   II — DROUGHTY SOILS
             (USUALLY SOILS OF THE SANDY LOAM AND
             LOAMY SAND SERIES)

GROUP   III — SOILS BOTH MOIST AND OF GOOD TEXTURE
              (WELL-WATERED LOAMS AND THE BETTER
              SOILS OF THE ABOVE TEXTURED GROUP)

GROUP   IV — SOILS MOIST BUT SOMEWHAT ROUGH AND
             STONY (STONY SOILS OF VALLEYS AND
             LOWER FOOTHILLS)

GROUP   V — ROUGH AND STONY SOILS
            (ROUGH STONY AND OTHER OF THE VERY
            STONY AND STONY LOAM GROUP)

GROUP   VI — WET SOILS
             (ALL SOILS MORE OR LESS SATURATED
             YEAR ROUND, WITHOUT STONES)

GROUP   VII — WET STONY SOILS

GROUP   VIII— WATER BODIES

GROUP   IX — THICKLY SETTLED AREAS

51-C6

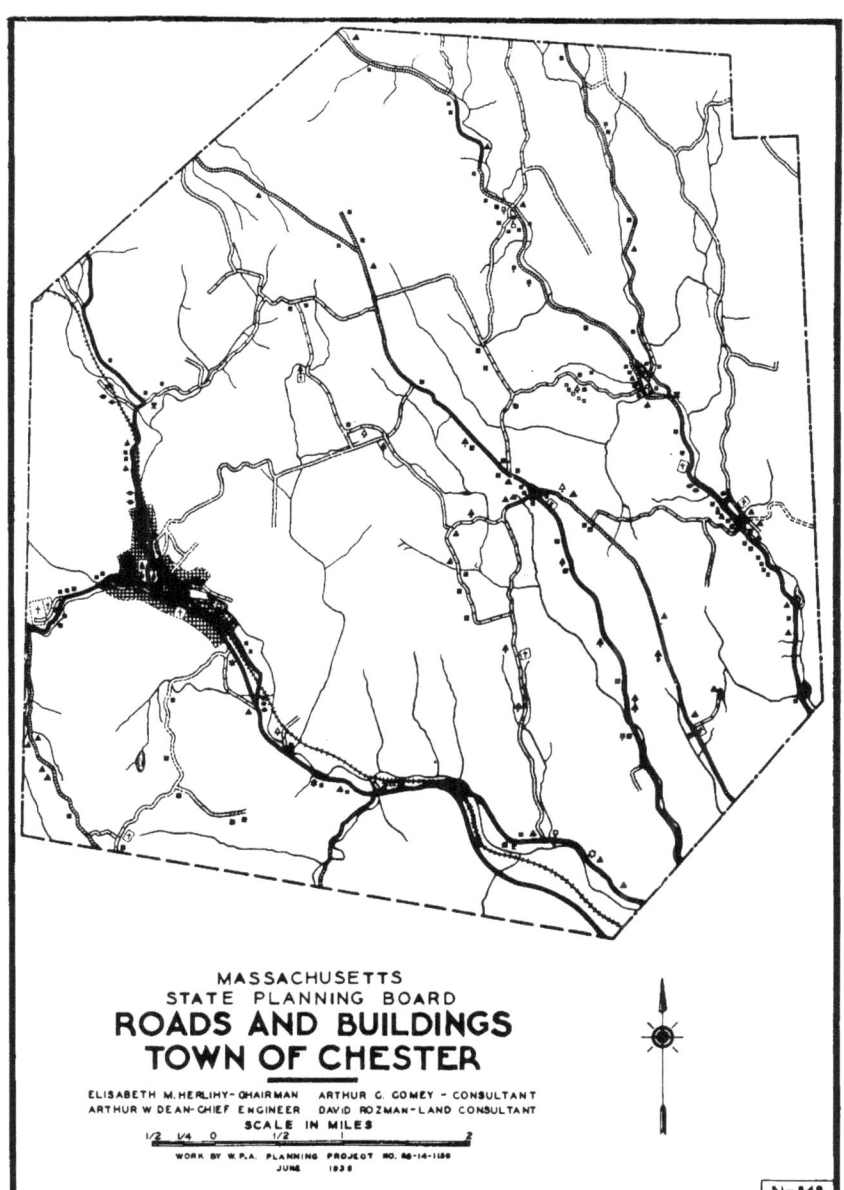

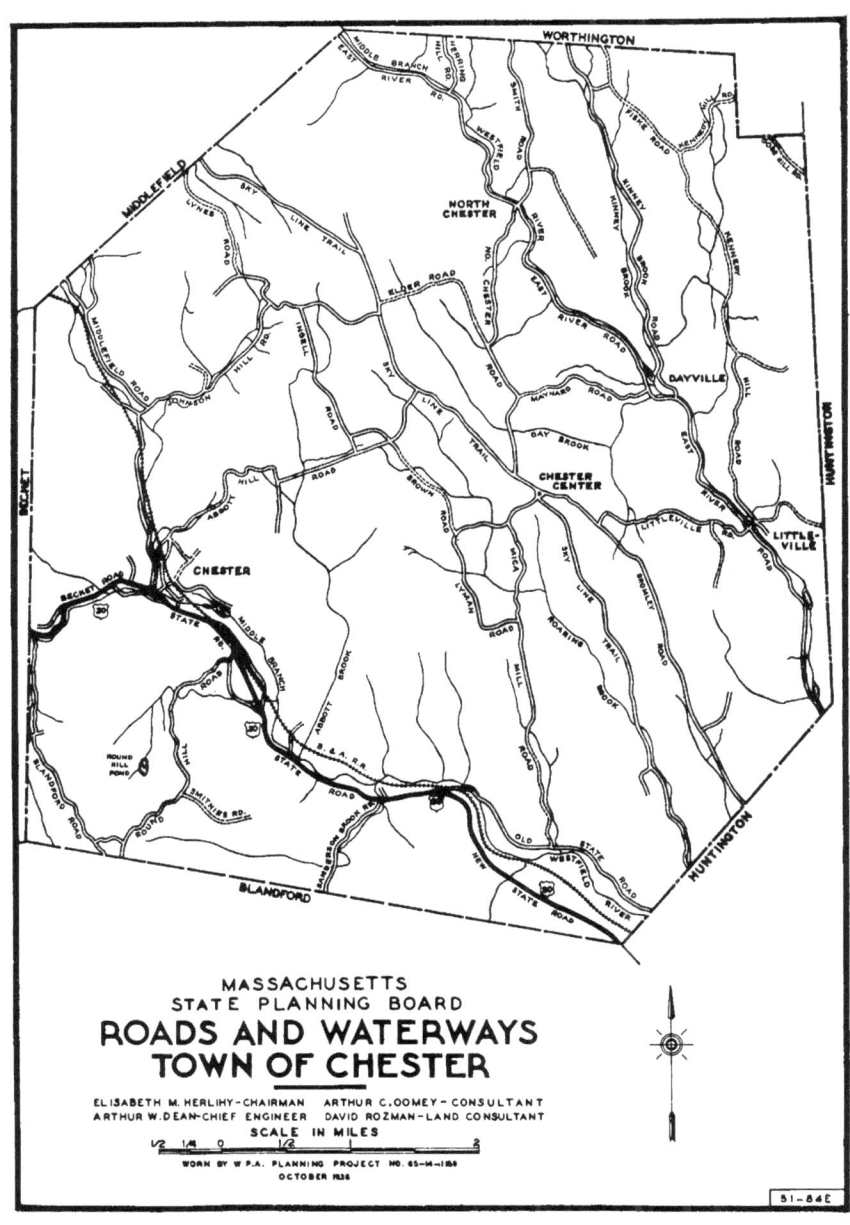

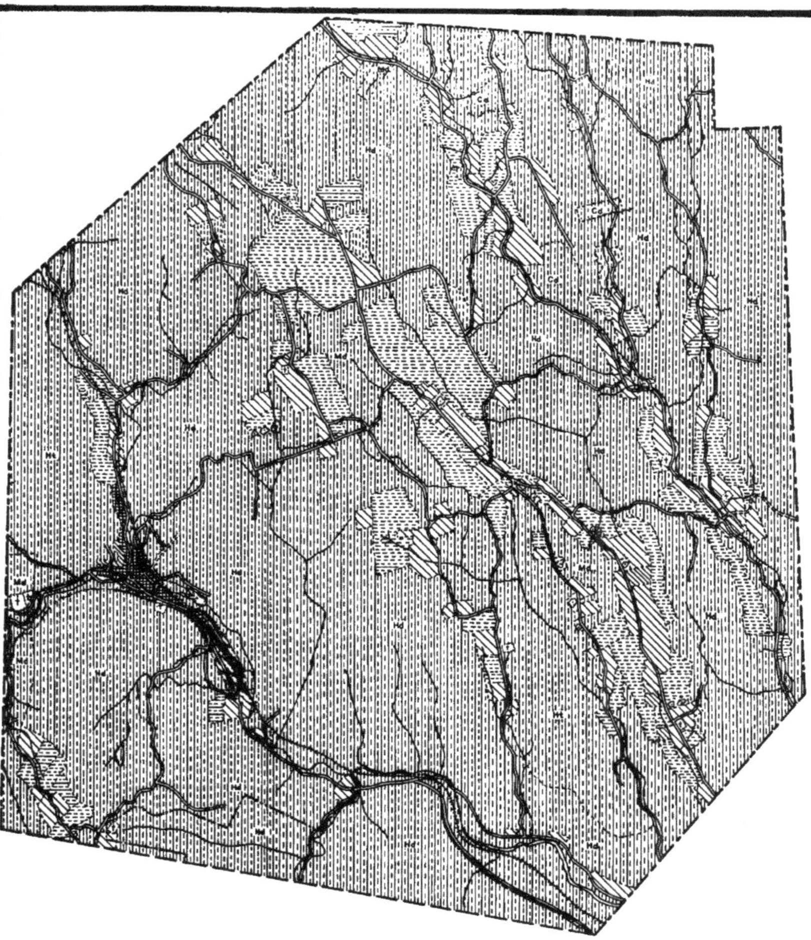

MASSACHUSETTS
STATE PLANNING BOARD

LAND UTILIZATION
TOWN OF CHESTER

ELISABETH M. HERLIHY-CHAIRMAN ARTHUR C. COMEY - CONSULTANT
ARTHUR W. DEAN-CHIEF ENGINEER DAVID ROZMAN-LAND CONSULTANT

SCALE IN MILES

1/2 1/4 0 1/2 1 2

WORK BY W.P.A. PLANNING PROJECT NO. 65-14-1159
JUNE 1936

51-84C

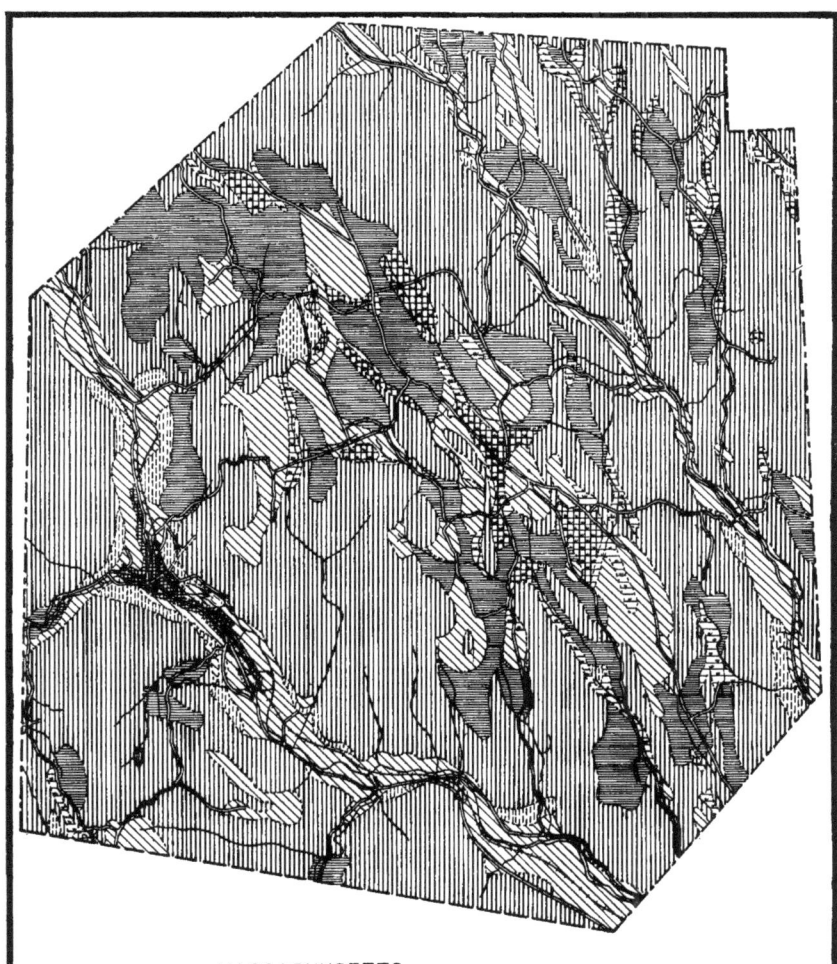

MASSACHUSETTS
STATE PLANNING BOARD
SOIL CLASSIFICATION
TOWN OF CHESTER

ELISABETH M. HERLIHY-CHAIRMAN   ARTHUR C. COMEY-CONSULTANT
ARTHUR W. DEAN-CHIEF ENGINEER   DAVID ROZMAN-LAND CONSULTANT
SCALE IN MILES

WORK BY W.P.A. PLANNING PROJECT NO. 65-14-1158
AUGUST 1936
BASED ON U.S.D.A. SOIL SURVEY

51-84D

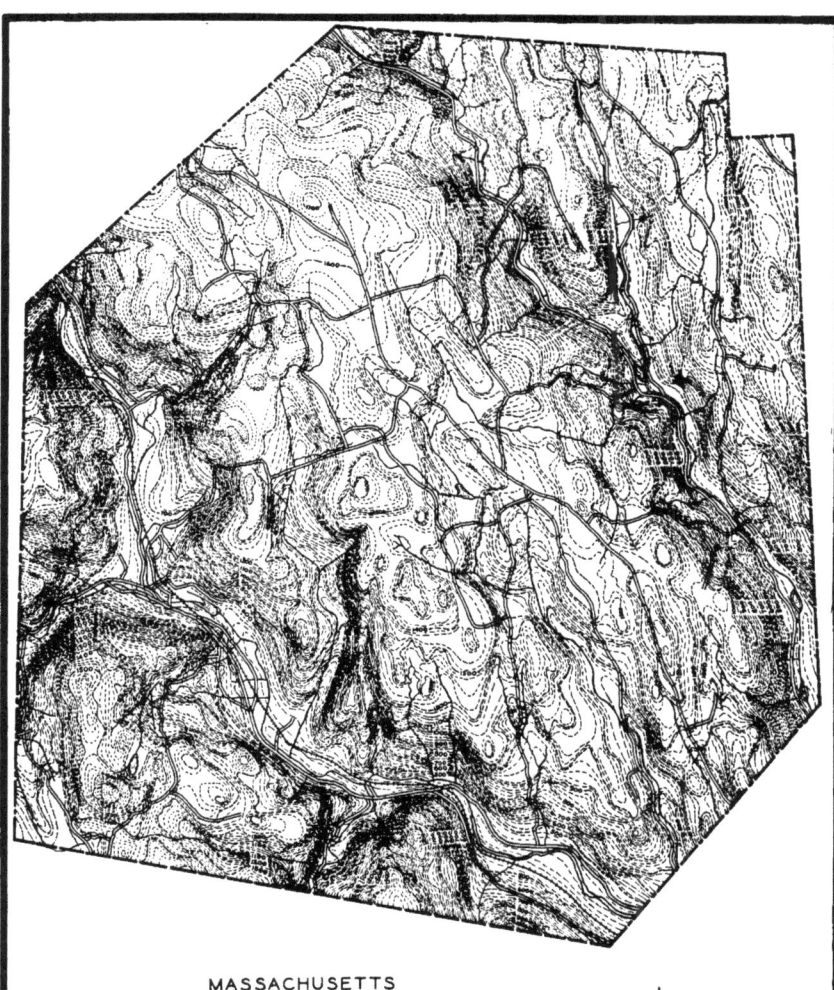

CHESTER
TOTAL ACREAGE — 23,745.0
POPULATION — 1,362 — (1935)

6/36

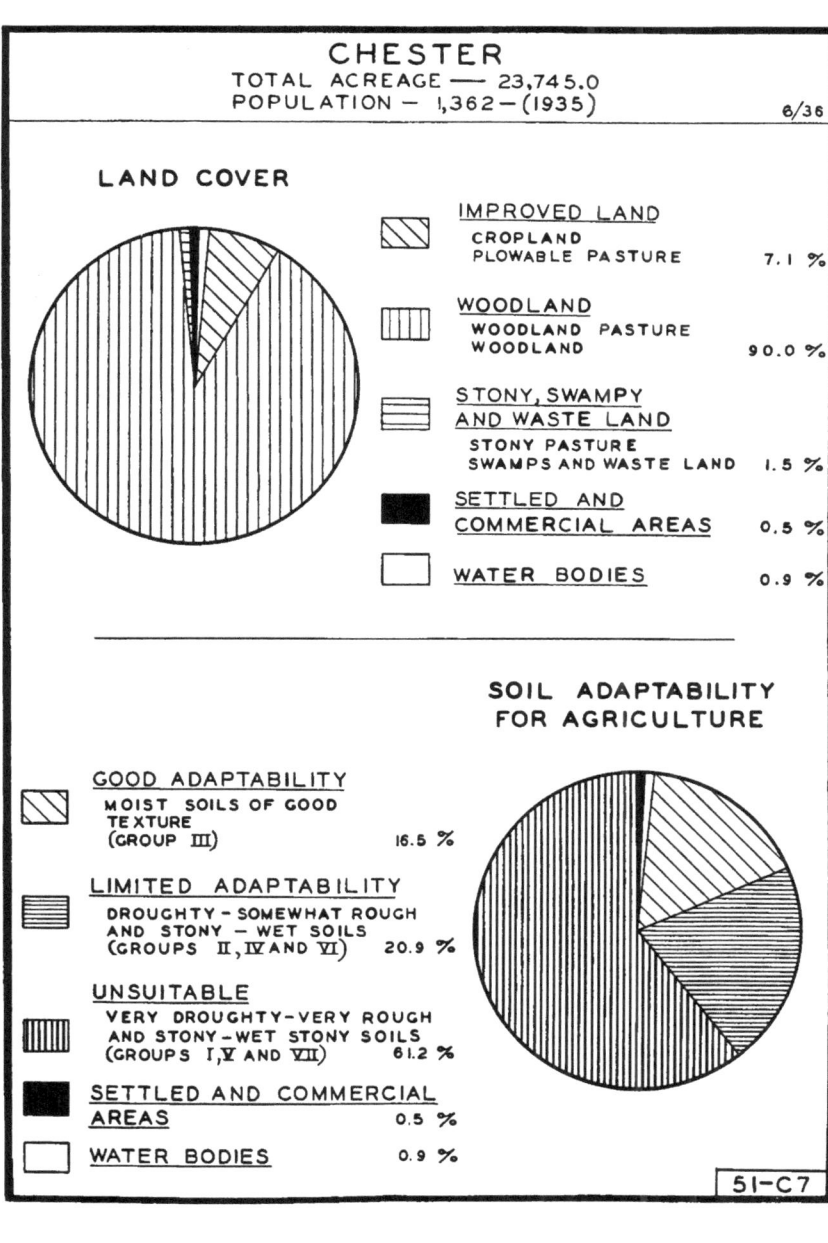

LAND COVER

IMPROVED LAND
CROPLAND
PLOWABLE PASTURE — 7.1 %

WOODLAND
WOODLAND PASTURE
WOODLAND — 90.0 %

STONY, SWAMPY AND WASTE LAND
STONY PASTURE
SWAMPS AND WASTE LAND — 1.5 %

SETTLED AND COMMERCIAL AREAS — 0.5 %

WATER BODIES — 0.9 %

SOIL ADAPTABILITY FOR AGRICULTURE

GOOD ADAPTABILITY
MOIST SOILS OF GOOD TEXTURE
(GROUP III) — 16.5 %

LIMITED ADAPTABILITY
DROUGHTY — SOMEWHAT ROUGH AND STONY — WET SOILS
(GROUPS II, IV AND VI) — 20.9 %

UNSUITABLE
VERY DROUGHTY — VERY ROUGH AND STONY — WET STONY SOILS
(GROUPS I, V AND VII) — 61.2 %

SETTLED AND COMMERCIAL AREAS — 0.5 %

WATER BODIES — 0.9 %

51-C7

5. Several areas of abandoned farm land are likely to remain idle unless they are used for State forests or are devoted to systematic tree culture by other public agencies or private individuals.

6. The town organization and finances should be revised in terms of prospective development of the town and adjustments made in the interests of local inhabitants and the best utilization of the natural resources of the Commonwealth.

PERU — Forestry Uses

Peru, in the heart of the highest part of the Berkshire hills, has gone through the process of agricultural decline of an even more accentuated nature than that of the town of Chester. The cover map (Map 51-261C) shows that the same huge proportion of forest cover and insignificant amount of crop-land cover exists here as in the latter town, while the high, rugged topography and stony soils point to the general impossibility of agricultural development in this town.

A further limitation to land-use development in Peru is the complete absence of large streams or water bodies with their attendant possibilities for development of industrial or recreational factors. Unlike most of the towns in the Berkshire region, Peru cannot offer the pleasure seeker or camper much in the way of fishing, canoeing, or other water sports; neither can it offer to the prospective summer resident the charming combination of lake and woodland views.

Serious Economic and Social Problems. An inspection of the roads-and-buildings map (Map 51-261B) presents a striking picture of semi-abandonment. To the total of 61 of all sorts of standing dwellings in Peru, there are observed 49 cellar holes, mournful remnants of former farm homesteads. The town contains a total of 44.89 miles of roads, a truly enormous mileage for a population of 151 persons to maintain. Of these, 8.37 miles are already abandoned, while another 8 miles are simply dirt roads of the ordinary sort.

It will be further observed that many of the present gravel and other cared-for roads serve very few homes and form a very large part of the serious maintenance problem of this town. This is especially true in the northern and central portions of the town. The village now consists of a town hall and a church but contains no store or village homes. With very little improved land or buildings available in the town, the tax rate is necessarily high.

MASSACHUSETTS STATE PLANNING BOARD

and the remaining property owners are called upon to carry a higher burden with the general progress of decline.

A Possible Solution of the Problems. Over 80 per cent of the town area has already reverted to woodland and the presence of a State forest on 1550 acres points the way to the most logical course for the future development of this town. The inclusion of the entire town area under State forest control will provide for the most desirable use of the land resources and put an end to the economic and social problems which beset this community.

LANCASTER -- Agricultural Uses

In the towns like Chester and Peru the operation of economic and social forces over a period of time has brought about a condition where the land utilization pattern has adjusted itself to the physical background as presented on the above maps. The future of these communities has only a limited place for agricultural development, and has to be built on a combination of other land uses. On the other hand, it is possible to indicate in Massachusetts a number of communities whose physical background justifies a greater amount of agricultural land utilization than is found at present.

A Town of Large Estates. The study of obtained information for the town of Lancaster will serve as an illustration of this condition. At a time when most of the towns in eastern Massachusetts were deserting their former interests in self-sufficient agriculture in favor of either commercialized farming or manufacturing, the pleasant scenery, convenient location, and rich land of Lancaster attracted numerous wealthy business men from Boston, Worcester, and other places. These persons set about the establishment of large, permanent, and carefully landscaped estates to serve as their country residences and, up until recent times, this sort of development has progressed and has dominated the land utilization of this town.

This type of development, continued over a long period, has had the effect of bringing into being a rather definite land-use program. Desirous of keeping the tranquil beauty of the town intact, the older estate owners, together owning a large proportion of the land, have exercised their control to keep Lancaster as a town made up largely of estates with their extensive wooded surroundings, little industry, and few small farms.

This program accounts for the picture presented when the soil map (Map 51-175D) is compared with the cover map (Map 51-175C). This comparison brings out the fact that large areas of the best

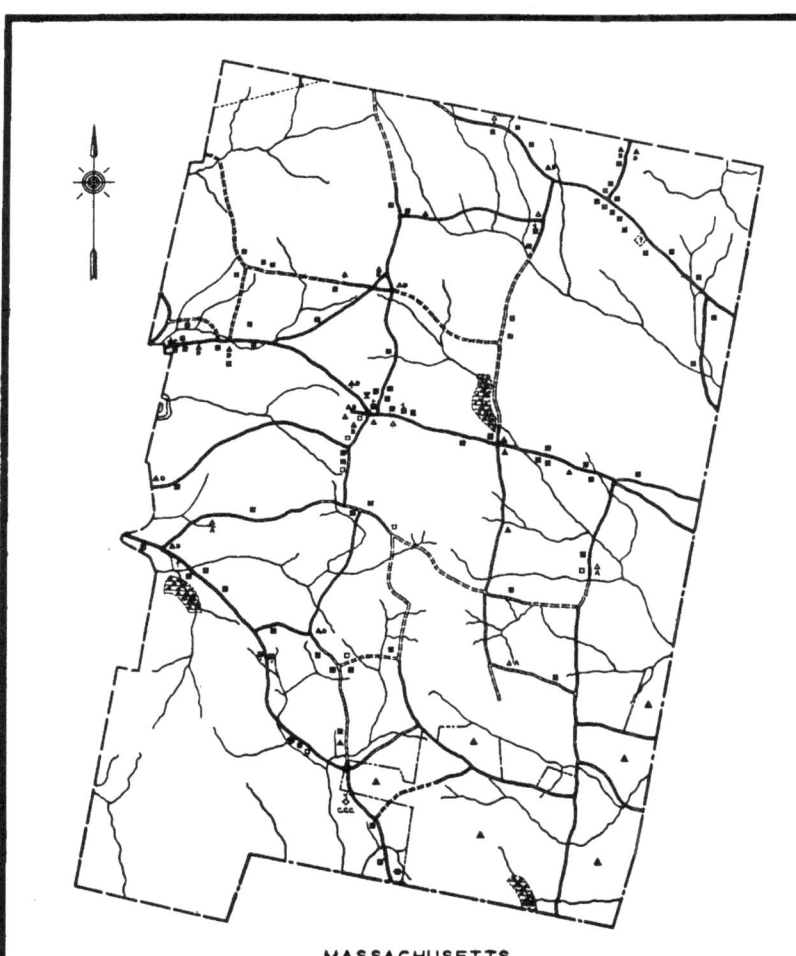

MASSACHUSETTS
W.P.A. PROJECT No. 65-14-8070
ROADS AND BUILDINGS
TOWN OF PERU

SPONSORED BY
STATE DEPARTMENT OF PUBLIC HEALTH
SCALE IN MILES

WORK DIRECTED BY STATE PLANNING BOARD
AUGUST 1936

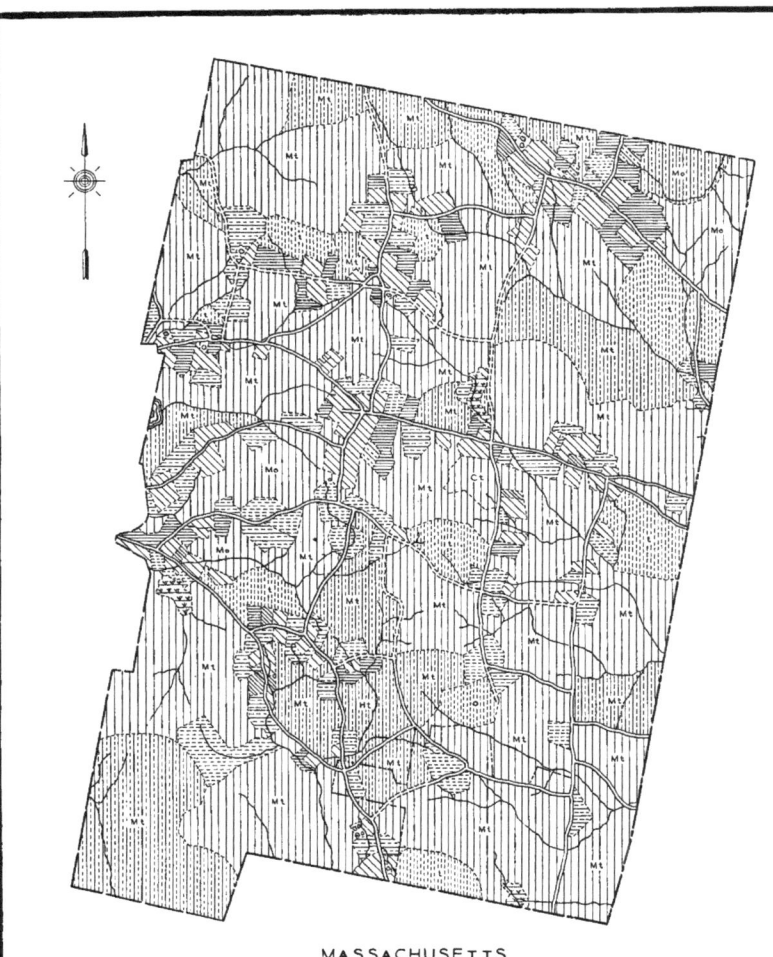

MASSACHUSETTS STATE PLANNING BOARD

soils are covered with woods and other non-agricultural cover, especially in the north-central part and in a very large area occupying practically the entire southwest quarter of the town. The topographic map (Map 51-175A) indicates that only a very small part of these areas might logically be excluded from cultivation for topographic reasons, yet the roads-and-buildings map (Map 51-175B) proves that these sections are left in woodland cover and are not settled. Left to their own forces land uses ordinarily adjust themselves in any community or larger area on a competitive basis, with that use gaining supremacy which can bring the greatest return. At the period of transition the town of Lancaster evidently offered a greater attraction as a region for country-estate settlement, which use won over agriculture by bidding higher prices. Whether this condition still prevails in problematical. In fact some evidences indicate a movement under way to release much of the land previously held in country residences.

The Changes in the Estates. In Lancaster the effect of two factors is now being felt by the estates. The first of these is psychological and is concerned with the unwillingness of the younger generation to maintain the ponderous elegance of these large establishments; the other is economic and is concerned with the inability of many owners to keep up the huge expenses necessary to run these places. Furthermore, the increasing ease of travel and the development elsewhere of more scenic and otherwise desirable summer-home sites has aided in undermining the hold of the estates in Lancaster.

The Return to Agriculture. Evidence that this change is taking effect is found in the abandonment and demolition of several places and the physical neglect and desertion of others. There is no reason to doubt that this trend, already started, will continue, with the result that much good land, artificially held out of production for many years, may again become available for purchase by the small land holder and be used for agricultural cultivation, for which it is best suited. This process, however, may take some time before its final completion. In Massachusetts agricultural land not used in cultivation for a long period of time reverts to woodland, and to bring it back to use a considerable expenditure is required in clearing it from this growth. While this may slow down the process of transition it will not prevent an eventual utilization of land for the highest needs for which it is best adapted.

Flood Control. The recent studies of flood-control measures in the Nashua River basin indicate that it may be desirable to build a detention reservoir over a strip of land on both sides of the river. This will take up a tract of land of about 1600 acres which

MASSACHUSETTS STATE PLANNING BOARD

contains very little good agricultural land. To determine the areas which are best suited for flood control measures, prospective developments of agriculture, and other uses, it is necessary to refer again to the four basic maps presented in connection with this discussion. The topographic map in itself is especially useful in designating areas best suited for future crop-land and water-body locations. Combined with the roads-and-buildings map it may be used in discovering areas in which land might be acquired with the least amount of disturbance to established homes and institutions.

Discovering Areas Suited to Agriculture and Forestry. The soil and the cover maps are indispensable in the discovery of areas best suited for the differing requirements of agriculture and forestry. For example, the large area on both sides of the abandoned road in the upper half of the southwest quarter of town is a stretch of land bordered by estates, at present entirely uninhabited yet covered with agriculturally useful soils over reasonably even topography. Another similar area is noted in the upper northwestern quarter, where a very sparse population along excellent roads and in a section covered by fertile soil suggests that some factor aside from natural conditions influences the use of land here. Two other areas uncovered by these maps point toward the development of a land-use program in another direction. The first of these lies about the pond adjoining the upper western boundary of the town. It includes an abandoned road and one farmstead in poor condition, and is covered by a type of soil eminently suited to forest cover. The second lies directly south of the Government reservation along the town's eastern boundary and runs as far as the first east-and-west road below. Here the presence of a small hill and good but somewhat stony soil suggests that this site could be used for a small forest reserve, a logical addition to the adjoining Federal reservation, or even an orchard site. Still other areas of good land, suitable for either agricultural, forest, or recreational developments, are to be found in and around the central portion of the town, just south and west of the Federal reservation.

All of these areas of good land, served by good roads, may quite definitely be considered as useful for either part or full-time farming especially when the close proximity of Lancaster to two thriving industrial centers, Clinton and Leominster, is considered. As for the areas less desirable in soil type and topography, the need for forest and recreational reservations in a densely populated section so near to Worcester, Fitchburg and other population centers is evident.

Conclusions from an Analysis of the Maps. A preliminary analysis of the basic information on natural resources presented on these

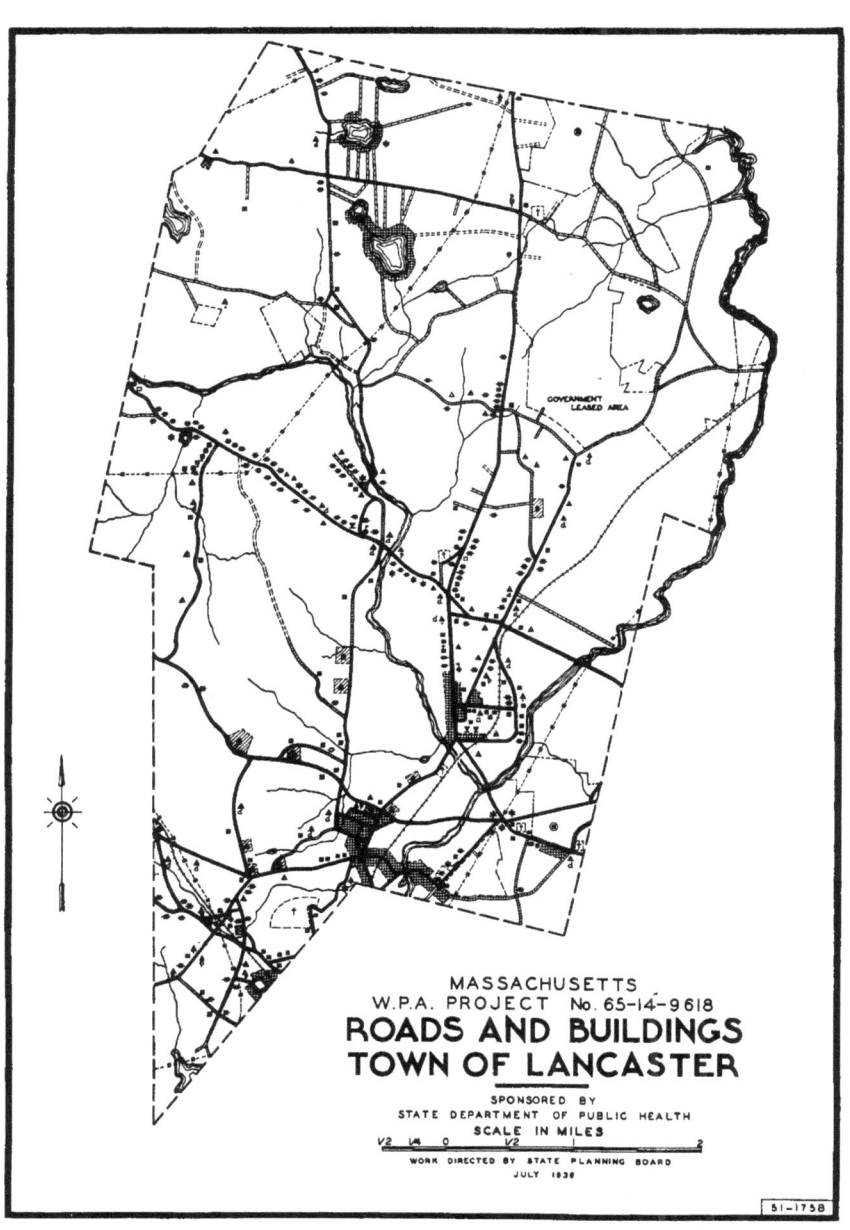

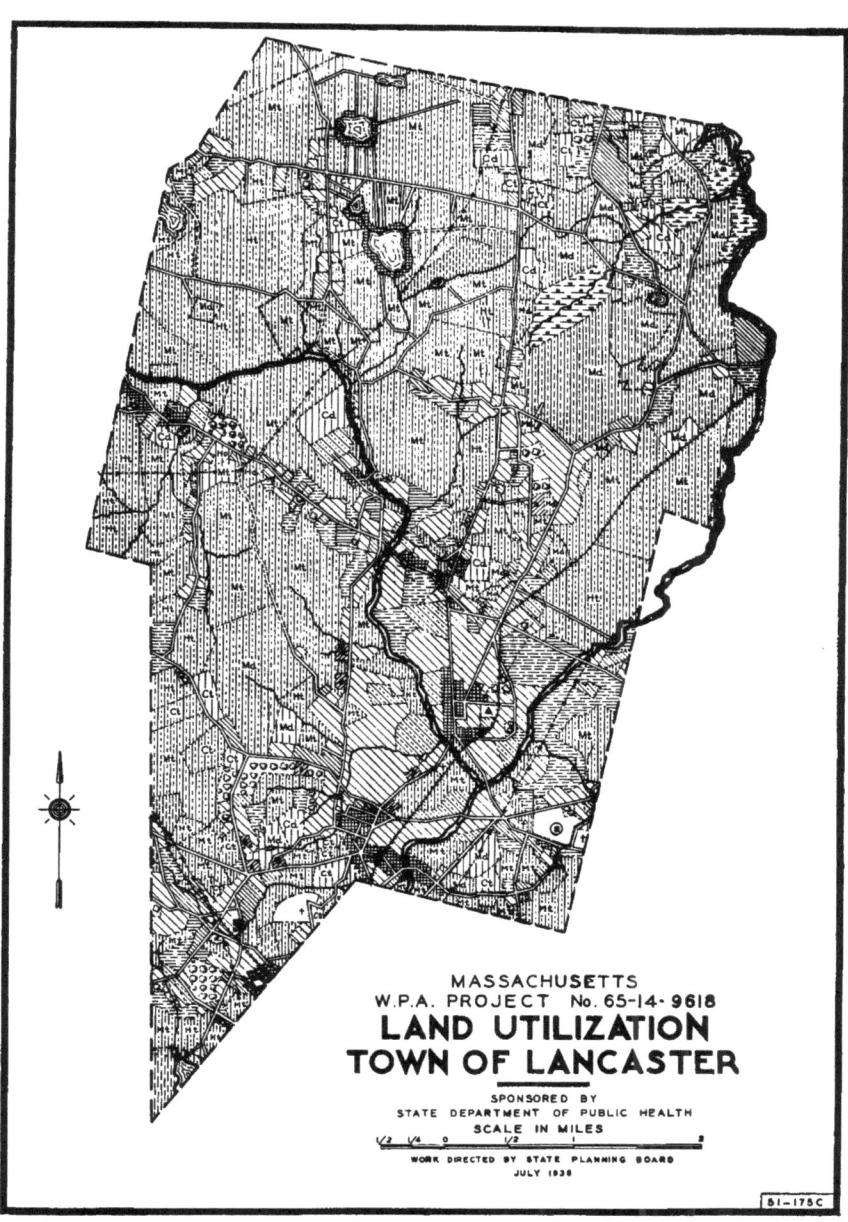

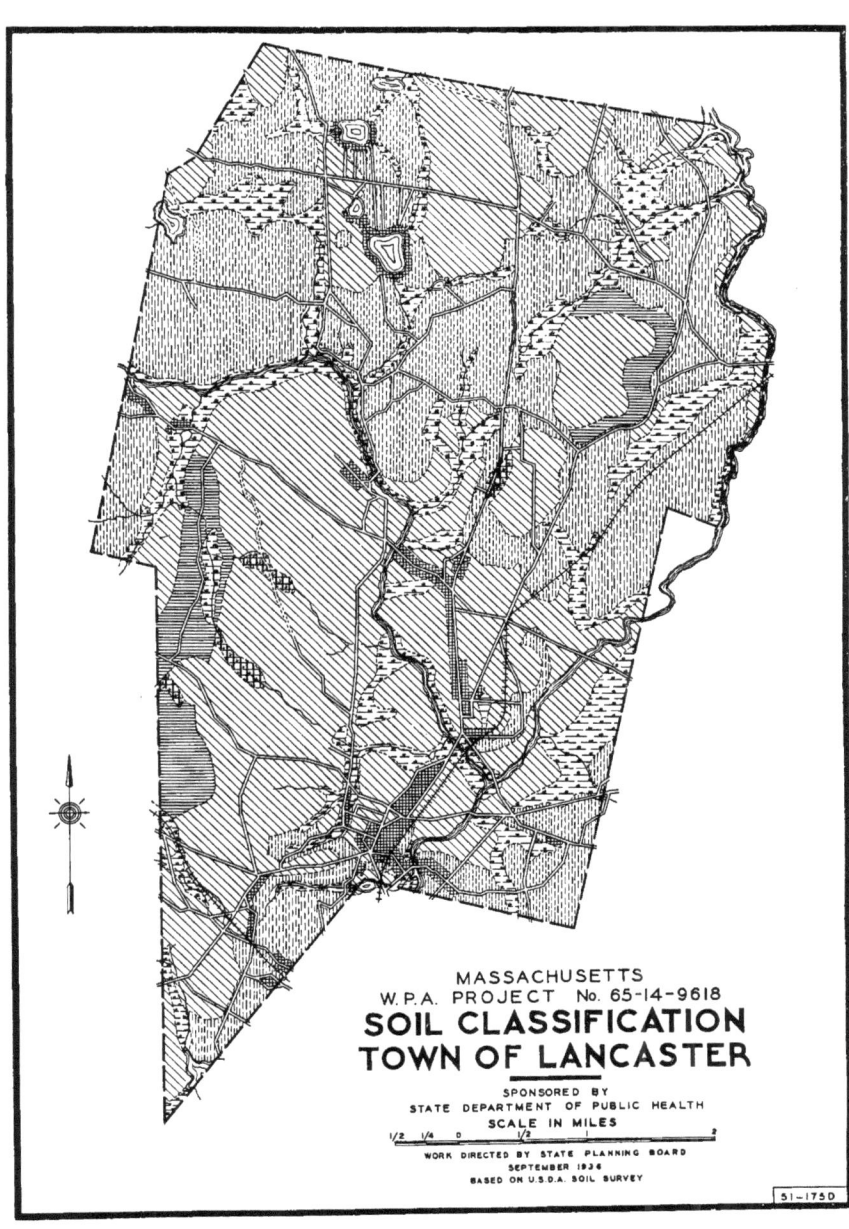

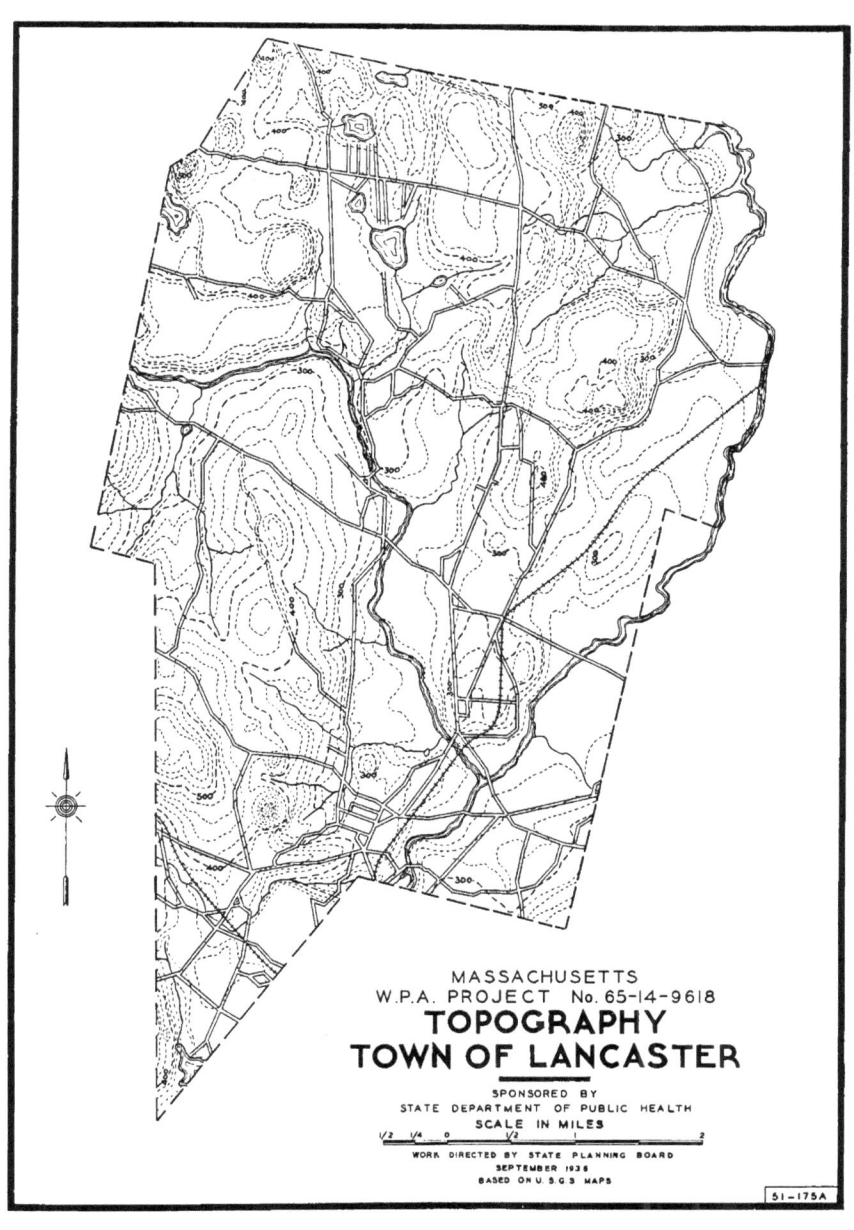

LANCASTER
TOTAL ACREAGE — 17,877.0
POPULATION — 2,590 — (1935)

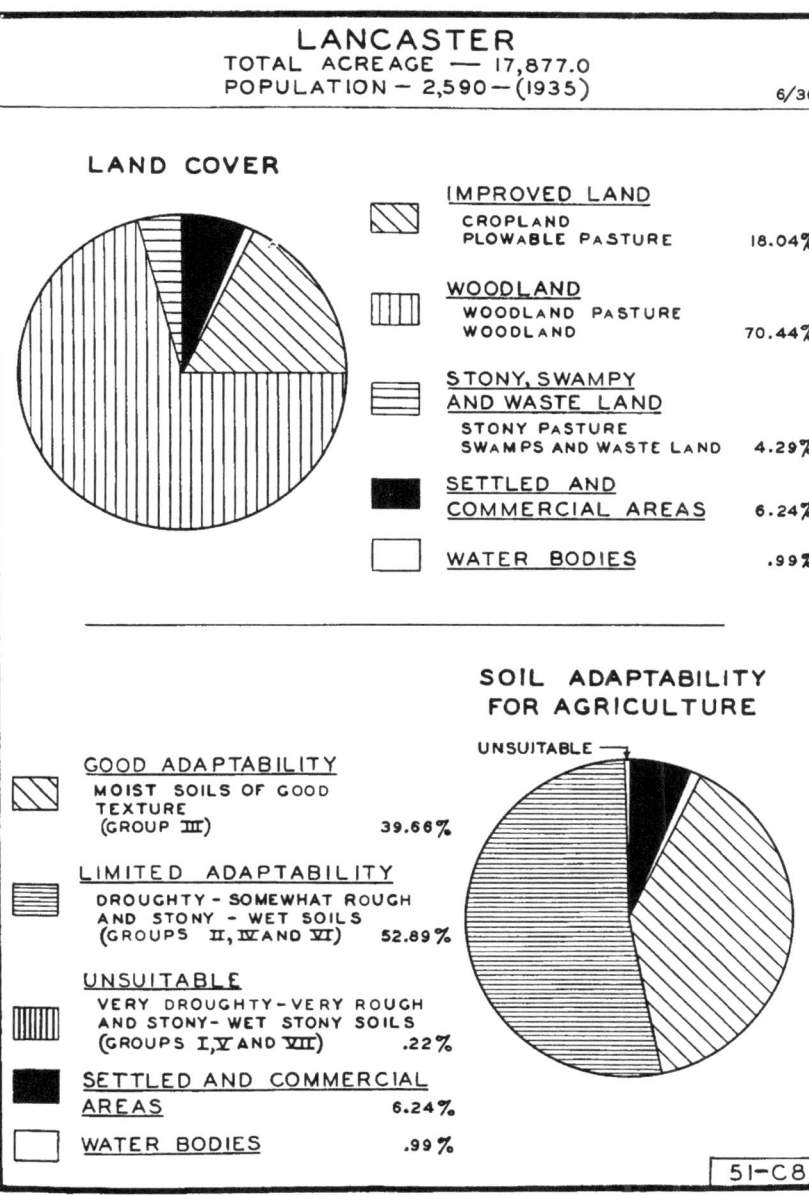

LAND COVER

- IMPROVED LAND
  - CROPLAND
  - PLOWABLE PASTURE — 18.04%
- WOODLAND
  - WOODLAND PASTURE
  - WOODLAND — 70.44%
- STONY, SWAMPY AND WASTE LAND
  - STONY PASTURE
  - SWAMPS AND WASTE LAND — 4.29%
- SETTLED AND COMMERCIAL AREAS — 6.24%
- WATER BODIES — .99%

SOIL ADAPTABILITY FOR AGRICULTURE

- GOOD ADAPTABILITY
  - MOIST SOILS OF GOOD TEXTURE (GROUP III) — 39.66%
- LIMITED ADAPTABILITY
  - DROUGHTY - SOMEWHAT ROUGH AND STONY - WET SOILS (GROUPS II, IV AND VI) — 52.89%
- UNSUITABLE
  - VERY DROUGHTY - VERY ROUGH AND STONY - WET STONY SOILS (GROUPS I, V AND VII) — .22%
- SETTLED AND COMMERCIAL AREAS — 6.24%
- WATER BODIES — .99%

51-C8

maps in Lancaster indicates:

1. That this is a town containing large areas of soils acceptable for agricultural use.

2. That much of this good land formerly in farms has been held out of production by its inclusion in large estates.

3. That the present trend is away from large estate occupancy with no definite indications as to the new direction of land use.

4. That the condition and direction of the roads, their proximity to the areas of undeveloped good land, together with the nearness of the town to the growing industrial centers indicate that a possible and logical development of part-time farming could take place in this town.

BILLERICA and UXBRIDGE — Part-Time Farming Uses

The Importance of Part-Time Farming. The general decline in land area use for farming in Massachusetts over the period of several decadesd has taken place in the eastern as well as in the western part of the State. In most of the eastern communities, however, the loss in commercial farming has been accompanied with the development of part-time farming on the same or adjacent areas. Many factors present in our modern industrial, social, and economic conditions point out that part-time farming already wide-spread in the State is likely to grow to greater proportions. The movement is prompted and facilitated by good roads, better means of transportation, shorter working hours, and a general tendency of people to get away from congested urban conditions, and a desire to obtain cheaper and better living by raising some of the products on the land. Likewise a forced retirement of middle-aged workers from modern industrial organizations forms a considerable group of people looking for some suitable part or full-time employment. Those who have some savings and also agricultural background or inclinations often prefer to settle on the land and carry on a small scale agriculture to obtain some income and cut down their living expenses.

Part-time farming practiced by these different groups of people is rapidly gaining in practically all the areas of the State, but especially in the eastern, more populous sections. In fact, judging by present indications, commercial farming is likely to become unprofitable and be replaced by part-time farming in the eastern part of the State and in the proximity to urban centers.

Comparative Advantages of Part-Time Farming. There are many factors which make it possible for the part-time farmer to thrive where commercial agriculture becomes unprofitable. In the densely settled areas land values are high and call for large payments in taxes. By controlling only a small area the part-time farmer may more easily meet expenses than the regular farmer who needs large areas for his operations. Furthermore, a part-time farmer does not depend on the land exclusively for his living, and often may carry on his farming business under conditions which would be considered unprofitable from the standpoint of a commercial farmer. An additional factor is that the part-time farmer is ordinarily better adjusted in the matter of location and available time to selling his product at retail prices, thus obtaining advantage in the cost of distribution.

In view of these tendencies and conditions part-time farming is becoming an important factor in the land utilization pattern of many communities of the State. For the purposes of illustration the information on two towns, Billerica and Uxbridge, is here presented and discussed.

The first town is indicative of developments in land use and part-time farming in a community situated in the neighborhood of an industrial city. The town of Uxbridge, on the other hand, presents a picture of land utilization and part-time farming which is primarily dependent upon its own industries.

BILLERICA — Part-Time Farming Uses

Billerica has been often referred to as the "bedroom of Lowell". Within its boundaries live many persons who work in the latter city and travel daily to and from it. It is a populous little town and has shown a steady and very rapid growth from only 2,789 in 1910 to 6,650 in 1935. Because this rapid growth has taken place without any definite plan, the people who have poured into this town during the last twenty-five years have distributed themselves over its surface in an unplanned manner, causing many difficulties in the community adjustments, and land utilization problems in certain areas.

The consideration of the buildings-and-roads map (Map 51-56B) in connection with the maps portraying the physical background of this town will indicate the most salient facts necessary for the foundation of its land-use programs.

A Town Served by Excellent Roads. The former map shows

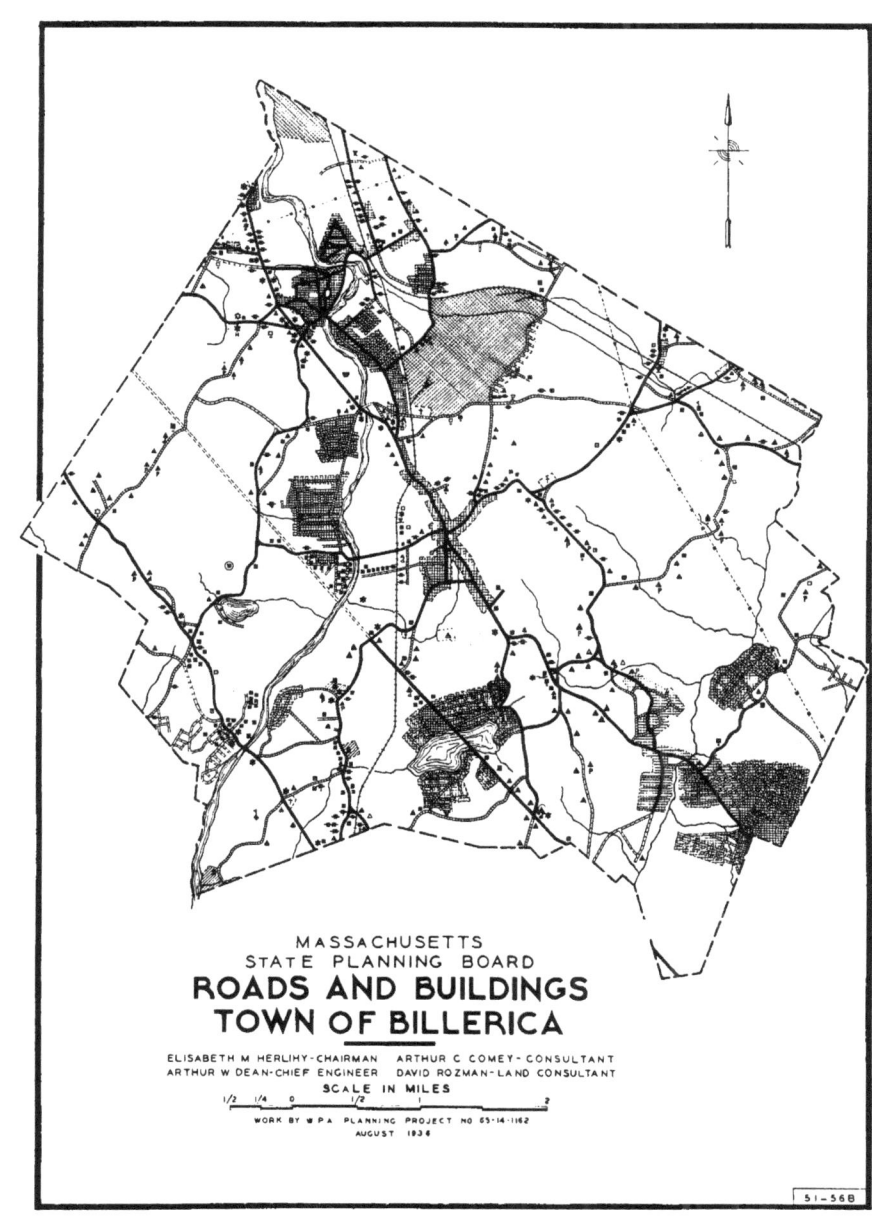

Billerica to be on the whole quite thickly settled, the more open areas covered with a close network of excellent roads, bordered with numerous residences and both semi-agricultural and commercial farm properties. This condition indicates the present existence of a large amount of part-time farming. The good roads are especially important in a town in which a large proportion of the inhabitants are employed elsewhere. The presence of numerous poultry farms is also significant in as much as this type of farming lends itself very easily to a part-time farming program. The cover map (Map 51-56C) shows large areas of unused land, already well served by good roads. Much of this land, although not well adapted to full-time commercial farming, could be profitably utilized for the less exacting requirements of the home-garden-with-poultry type of farming usually characteristic of part-time farms.

The Problems of Haphazard Settlement. All of the above facts are significant when one considers Billerica's present land-use problems, which are concerned chiefly with the proper absorption of a large and rapidly growing population already located outside of the thickly settled areas.

Previous to 1929, high-pressure land speculation schemes forced the development of much land, especially around the lake shores, as summer property. The more difficult times experienced since that date have caused many families to occupy these temporary structures the year round. The soil of this resort section, which is by no means of the best quality, and the dense cover of mixed coniferous and hardwood trees combine to make the cultivation of this land highly undesirable even for part-time farmers. Therefore, a land-use program could logically propose that this section be returned to its former recreational use.

The result of this haphazard settlement is that numerous families are, at present, more or less stranded on the land, dependent upon the soil and casual labor or relief funds for their income, and greatly in need of better houses and more land for their comfort and well-being. It throws also a tremendous burden on the town in the provision of schools, transportation of pupils, road improvements, police, and public utilities.

A judicious use of basic information obtained in the land-use survey can be of immense aid in presenting the facts concerning soil, cover, topography, and present man-made improvements so necessary to the correct selection of areas where future development along both forestry and recreation, or part-time and full-time farming might proceed, with the maximum chances for their respective success.

MASSACHUSETTS STATE PLANNING BOARD

Areas Suitable for Part-Time Farming. From the soil and the cover maps (Maps 51-56D and 51-56C) it will be seen that considerable areas lie near-by this lake property, especially on the west, extending up along a first-class road to the northwest boundary of the town. Much excellent soil on gently rolling topography exists here, at present occupied only at its northern extremity by a few small farms and along the rest of its extent by rather widely spaced dwellings. Another section of good soil at present undeveloped is found just northeast of the five corners in the center of town. Here a large area of mixed dense woodland now only partially invaded by semi-agricultural dwellings would seem to offer a good opportunity for the further development of part-time farming. Still another area is found directly north of this, bordering on the mid-section of the northern boundary of the town, where a dirt road with several branches penetrates a very thickly settled area of mostly brush land on good soil.

Areas Suitable for Forestry and Recreational Developments. The basic facts presented on the maps also point out a logical start for the development of a practical forest and recreational program for Billerica. The topographic map indicates that the surface of this town is dotted by several small hills or "knobs" which rise rather abruptly from the surrounding terrain. The two most prominent western ones are quite near the settled area of the town and are served by a good road which passes by the foot of each. These soils are not suited to agricultural use, and no dwellings or other human occupancy are in the immediate vicinity. It would seem therefore that these "knobs" might well be transformed from their present unused condition to a small forest reservation with picnic and other recreational advantages. A similar area also exists just west of the angle in the high-tension electric line. This hill, the second highest in town, lies in the northwest corner of its most extensive wooded area. The cover map fails to show much real farming development on the small farms in this area and the poor soil indicates that this entire section would stand investigation in regard to its present value to the town as compared with its ultimate returns as a supervised forest or recreational place.

Conclusions. A preliminary analysis of the basic information presented by these maps in Billerica would indicate:

1. That Billerica has the soil, topography, and road conditions suitable for greater development as a part-time farming town serving as a residence for persons working in local industries, in Lowell, and elsewhere.

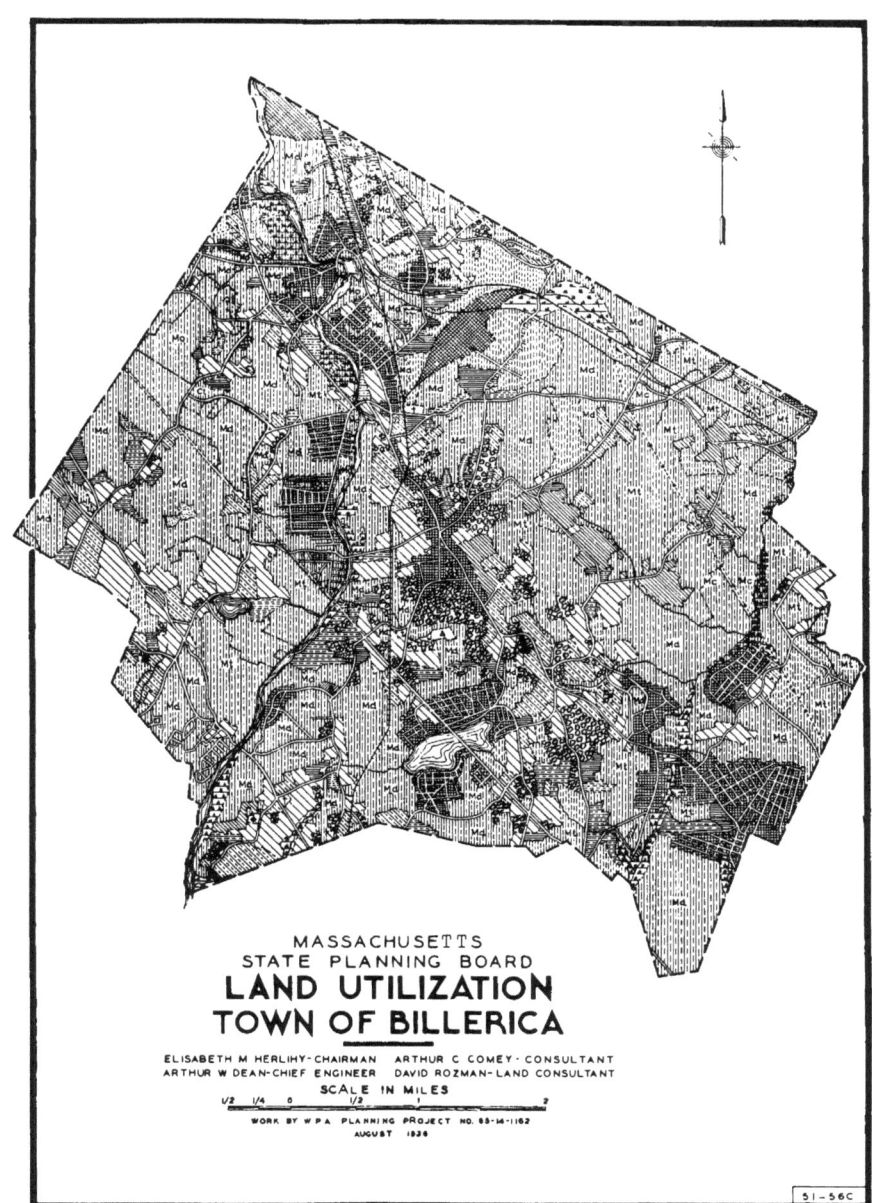

MASSACHUSETTS STATE PLANNING BOARD

2. That at present, especially around the lakes, conditions exist which could be best alleviated by the reversion of these areas to the recreational uses for which they are best suited.

3. That several sites, at present neglected, could serve very well as starting points for a useful forest and recreational program.

4. That certain areas at present used for a rather unsuccessful type of part-time farming might better be transformed into other, non-agricultural uses.

UXBRIDGE — Part-Time Farming Uses

In common with most of the older Massachusetts towns Uxbridge was at one time a prosperous and important agricultural community. In 1832, for example, local estimates gave the town a crop-land acreage of 4,199 acres; pasture, 4,612 acres; and woodland only 4,000 acres. Present-day figures indicate crop land shrunken to about one half (2320 acres), pasture less than one fourth (1160 acres), while woodland has more than doubled, increasing to about 9,000 acres.

Numbers of Farms in Uxbridge. In spite of this great decrease in cultivated area, the total number of farms, including part-time farms, has actually increased. Credited with 165 farms in 1855 this town now contains 105 places classified as farmsteads and an additional 91 classed as semi-agricultural occupancy. This means that at least 196 land occupants carry on some form of agricultural activities, although individually this is done on a much smaller scale than formerly.

The Woolen-Weaving Industry. Industrially, Uxbridge has enjoyed a long and progressive growth. As early as 1835 this town was beginning to be known as a center of the woolen-weaving industry, and, at present, has within its borders five large mills. All of these mills have continued to run rather steadily throughout the depression, and at present all but one are running full time. The splendid record of these mills in providing steady work has made it possible for a good many workers to purchase their own homes and often to develop farming operations on a part-time basis.

Location of Residences. The roads-and-buildings map (Map 51-333B) shows that by far the largest proportion of the homes in this town are to be found in the northeast quarter, immediately surrounding the industrial center, which lies just north and east of the

33

town's geographical center. The southwest corner is very thinly settled and has no hard-surfaced roads. It will be noticed that most of the semi-agricultural dwellings are located near the mills and almost always border on hard-surfaced roads.

Under present conditions in Uxbridge a very high percentage of the workers living in the town also work there. Because of this, commuting has not developed to any great extent as a customary way of living. This probably accounts for the much higher degree of concentration of the dwellings in this town than in Billerica, where a considerable number of people have been accustomed to working in the adjoining city of Lowell. The early establishment and continuing activity of the mills near the northeast quarter of town doubtless started this growth, since there is no special soil or topographic features making this area especially desirable as compared with several other places in town.

The Wooded Areas. The cover map (Map 51-333C) shows the usual large wooded areas so common over much of the State. A rather larger proportion of hardwood forests are found here than in other places, and the generally sturdy appearances of the cover, together with the low, rolling topography, indicate that large areas of good soils are under woods cover. This fact is further brought out by reference to the soil and the topographic maps. As usual the woods cover has grown with little or no supervision and has suffered from the numerous forest fires so prevalent in unrestricted areas. Many weed trees and undesirable underbrush conditions exist, all of which retard the growth of useful trees and prevent the best use of the land in these sections.

Quite large areas of desirable crop-land soils are under woods cover in this town. Their condition indicates that about 26 per cent of the soils are adaptable for crops, while another 58 per cent offer possibilities for useful development for hay, orchard, or pasture. At present, however, only about 16.7 per cent of the town's area is under any kind of agricultural use, including even woodland pasture, while only 12 per cent of the whole area is cultivated.

Areas Suitable for Part-Time Farming. The soil map shows that some farms exist on every area of good soil; yet the roads and buildings map (Map 51-333B) indicates a very uneven distribution, with much good land neglected. It would seem that the presence of good roads, the generally prosperous condition of the industries in this town, and the growing interest in country living might encourage under proper guidance better use of the good land in this town by a greater participation in part-time farming. Areas in which

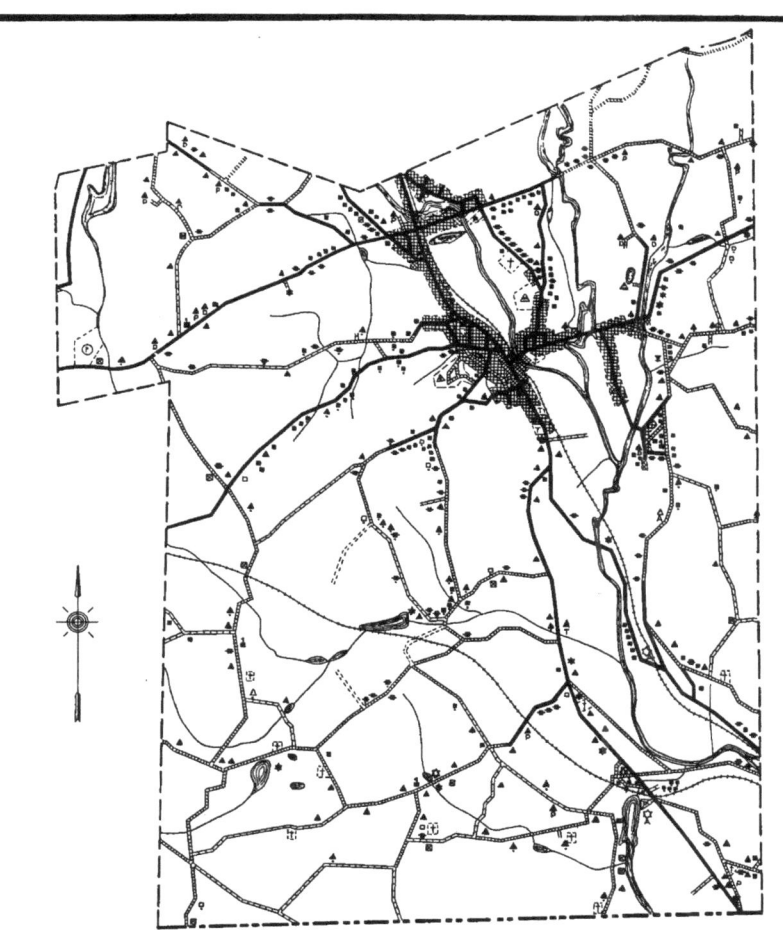

MASSACHUSETTS
E.R.A.M. PROJECT No. S-A1-U43
**ROADS AND BUILDINGS
TOWN OF UXBRIDGE**

SPONSORED BY
STATE DEPARTMENT OF PUBLIC HEALTH
SCALE IN MILES

WORK DIRECTED BY STATE PLANNING BOARD
JUNE 1938

51-3338

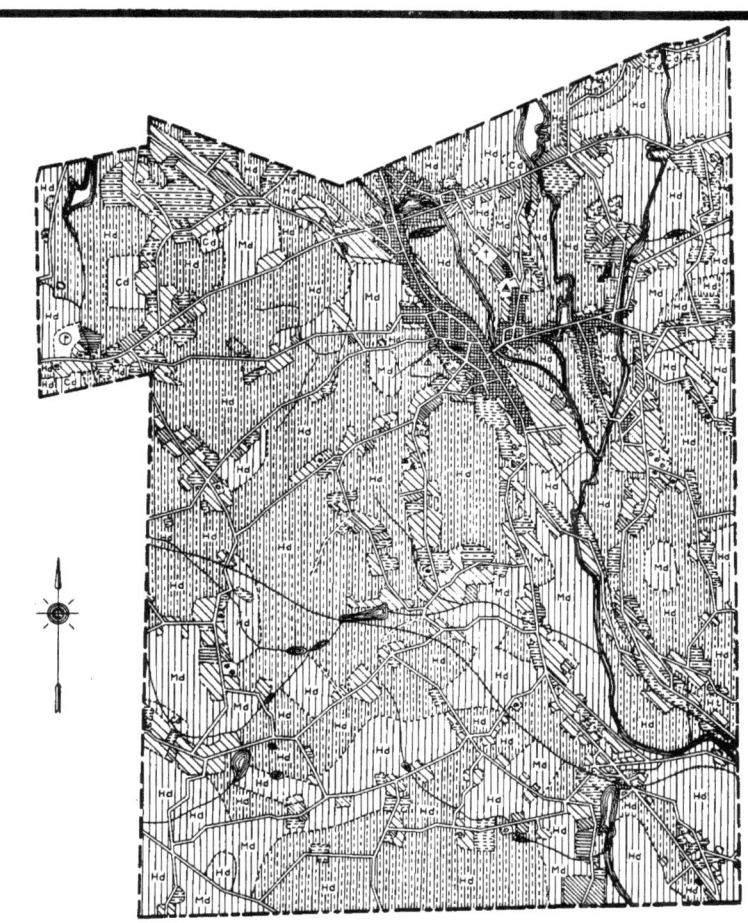

MASSACHUSETTS
E.R.A.M. PROJECT No. S-A1-U43
LAND UTILIZATION
TOWN OF UXBRIDGE

SPONSORED BY
STATE DEPARTMENT OF PUBLIC HEALTH
SCALE IN MILES

WORK DIRECTED BY STATE PLANNING BOARD
JUNE 1938

51-333C

MASSACHUSETTS STATE PLANNING BOARD

this sort of development might be desirable are indicated by a study of the maps. One such area borders on the long, well-paved road extending from the extreme southeast corner of the town. This road runs directly into the main industrial portion of town and is bordered along most of its length by good crop-land soils, at present occupied by a few widely spaced farms, dwellings, and semi-agricultural occupancies. Another very similar area is found bordering the road which runs north and south in the northwest corner of the town. This road lies within easy commuting distance of the mills, runs through an area of good soil, and, although not as level in topography as the southern section just referred to, is by no means rough enough to interfere seriously with either transportation or crop-raising. Still other areas of good soil not at present developed are found in the southwest quarter. This section is more remote than the others from the center of town, and is somewhat rougher in topography. Its future, especially in the extreme southern part, will probably be identified more with forestry than with agriculture, yet the amount of good land present warrants some consideration of its possibility for the development of part-time farming.

Conclusions. In conclusion a consideration of the basic information revealed by the map would indicate:

1. That this town has large areas, at present neglected, suitable for agricultural uses.

2. That present road and soil conditions in this town are such that a more decentralized distribution of homes, especially part-time farms, could easily take place.

3. That certain areas in the southeast and northwest are better equipped for part-time farming development than areas in the rest of the town.

4. That the southwest corner of the town is at present indicated as the best site for any forestry or recreational development.

HINGHAM — Residential and Recreational Uses

Hingham is a town in which agricultural land areas have been displaced to a considerable extent by residential and recreational uses of land. The land-use pattern in this town is determined predominantly by its proximity to the Boston area and its location at the seashore. Woods cover is found now on considerable areas characterized by good soil adaptable for agricultural use. It is not

MASSACHUSETTS STATE PLANNING BOARD

to be expected however that this land will be utilized for commercial farming. The land values are generally high and are determined by present or prospective uses capable of commanding higher prices for the use of land than can be expected from agricultural cultivation. The most that is likely to develop in the way of agriculture will be part-time farming in connection with residential uses which are now so prominent. In fact, part-time farming is already quite widespread in the town and accounts for a large portion of the agricultural activities found in this community.

Industry Not of Great Importance. Industry has likewise ceased to be of any great importance in the town. Hingham reached the peak in its industrial activity shortly before the Civil War, when about 60 manufacturing establishments gave employment to almost 800 persons. At the present only a score of workers are employed in several small industries.

From the soil map (Map 51-159D) it will be seen that practically all of the better soil areas are found in the northern and southwestern parts of the town, while the southeastern section is covered mostly with stony types.

Residential Advantages. The topographic map (Map 51-159A) shows the town to contain many gentle slopes with numerous low knolls and ridges which provide ample opportunities for the scenic locations so greatly valued for residential purposes. The shore line is extensive and highly irregular, with numerous coves and other sheltered indentations. It faces on Boston Bay and is ideal for all sorts of salt-water activities.

The quality of its seacoast as a summer resort is shown by the dense settlement along most of the shore and the presence of a number of estates which border on much of the remaining area. The permanence and quality of this occupancy is further attested by the presence of two good-sized golf courses within easy distance of both shore and urban settlements.

Conclusions. The basic evidence presented by the maps indicates:

1. That land use in Hingham has been definitely tending away from industrial and commercial agricultural uses.

2. That a definite trend toward recreational and residential developments is taking place.

3. That this movement has already resulted in a good develop-

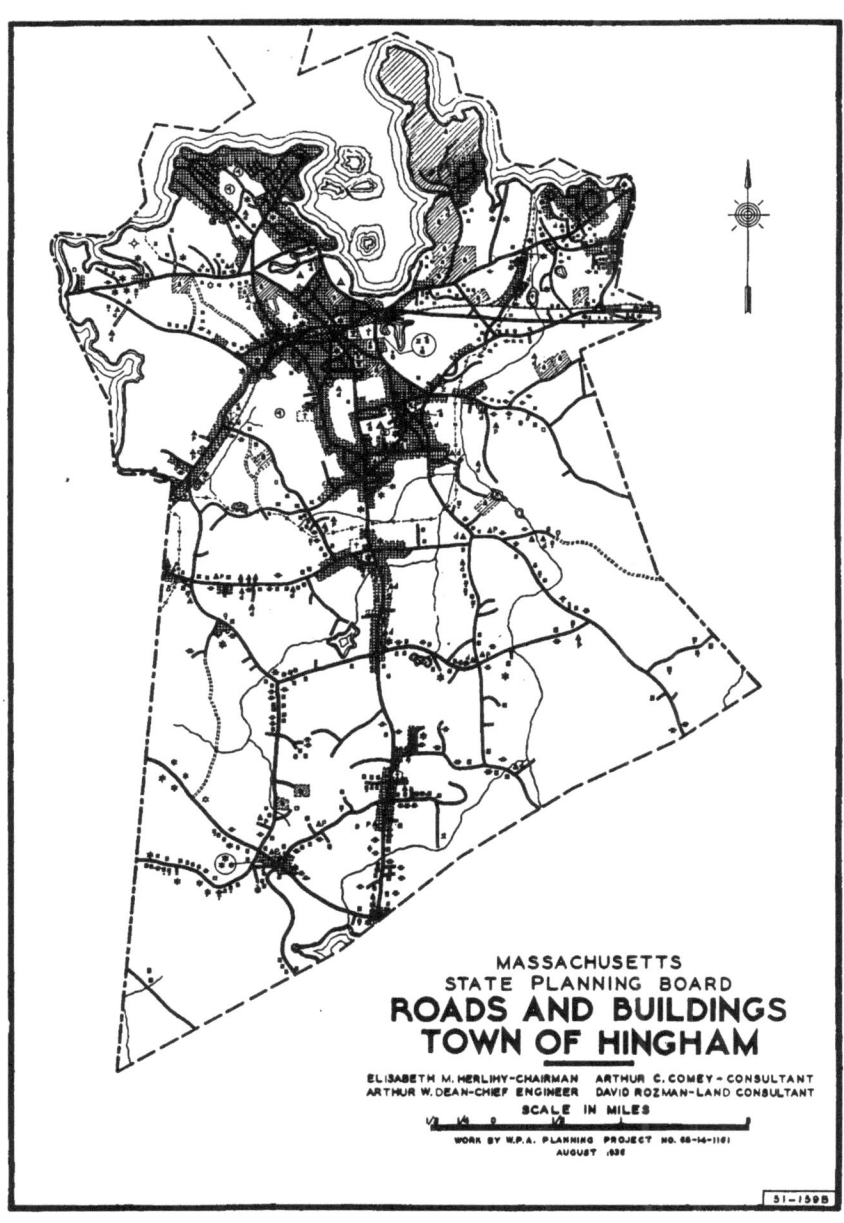

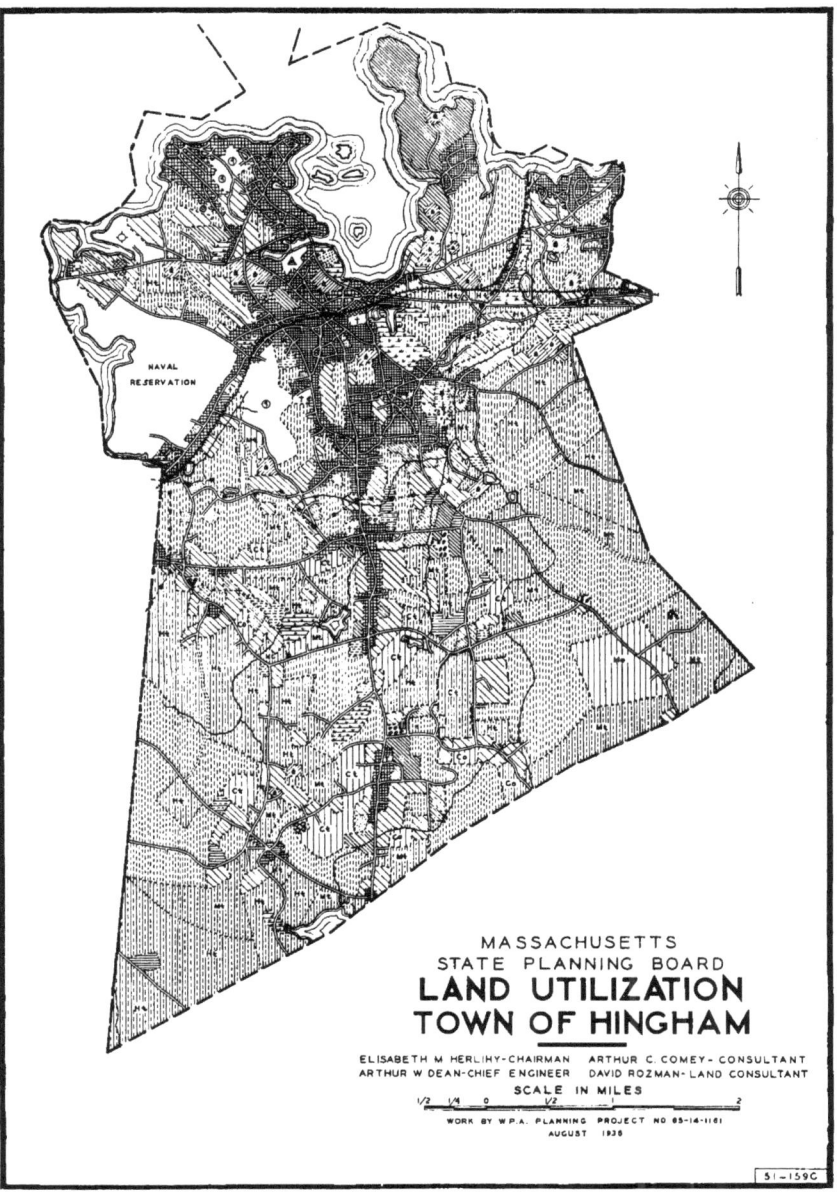

ment of the physical equipment, such as good roads and recreational features, which are necessary to the expansion of such recreational and residential uses.

4. That, because of the above conditions, Hingham should be more concerned with the orderly development of the present trends than with the projection of any major changes in land uses now in existence.

Conclusion

In the preceding discussion of land-use problems in several towns the fundamental idea has been to point out the diversity of land problems existing in individual communities of the Commonwealth and the importance of the land-use survey undertaken by the State Planning Board in providing basic information essential to the solution of these problems. The recommendations made are tentative in nature, pending the completion of the survey and the analysis of all the pertinent facts.

With further progress of the land-use survey it will be possible to project the desirable sectional and regional developments in the State which should be taken into consideration in formulating land-use programs for individual communities. Keeping in mind the general objective of developing in the most adequate way the natural resources of the State for the benefit of both rural and urban population, the proposed land-utilization program in Massachusetts will cover primarily the following:

1. Delineation of the areas most desirable for acquisition for State forests and game preserves as well as for State parks and other recreational purposes. With the State legislature having already passed a bill for the purchase and reforestation of an additional 500,000 acres of land, this part of the program (the selection and recommendation of suitable areas for State acquisition) becomes of immediate practical significance and will receive the first consideration.

2. Consideration of areas subject to overflow, with a view to land utilization measures preventing further destruction from floods, and selection of the most suitable sites for location of reservoirs and other improvements required for flood control.

3. Land-utilization programs and governmental reforms for communities having serious problems of tax delinquency and difficulty in maintaining local economic and social institutions.

MASSACHUSETTS STATE PLANNING BOARD

4. Locating agricultural areas best adapted to furnish farm population with a higher income and a better standard of living.

5. Working out a series of economic and social patterns for different groups of communities on the basis of combining the predominant land use with other opportunities, such as:

    a. Residential and recreational
    b. Residential, part-time farming, and recreational
    c. Farming, forestry, and recreational
    d. Farming, forestry, industrial and so on.

The means whereby the recommended measures in a land program will be put into actual operation will vary, depending on the nature of the problem and the extent of necessary changes. In some cases the mere existence of systematically developed information, as provided in the above mentioned land-use survey, will work for more desirable land-use developments. This will take place, for instance, when the agricultural county and State extension workers, chambers of commerce, and other public and semi-public institutions will be able by means of available information to direct, in a more adequate way, agricultural land settlement, and indicate the most desirable locations for residential, industrial, commercial, and other land uses. The same service will be accomplished by providing the necessary information for the selection and development of suitable areas in fulfilment of adopted public-land purchase measures, as in the selection of areas for public forests or the location of sites for water-supply and flood-control improvements.

In other cases the desired ends of an adequate land-utilization program will not be accomplished unless more direct action is undertaken by the State or local public authority. In the settled areas of our cities and towns the principles of zoning have been generally recognized and widely applied. To extend the same principle to the orderly development of rural areas it may be necessary either to give a broader interpretation to the existing urban zoning laws or to pass new legislation to accomplish the same end.

WATER

Courtesy of Secretary of the Commonwealth

CHAPTER III

W A T E R

Summary Outline

I. Water-Resources Problems
    A. Water Supply
    B. Sewage Disposal and Stream Pollution
    C. Flood Control
    D. Hydroelectric Power
    E. Water Recreation
    F. Problems of Integration

II. State Water-Resources Studies
    A. Hydrology
    B. Sanitation
    C. Flood Control
    D. Hydroelectric Power
    E. Water Recreation

III. Coöperating Agencies

IV. Nashua River Valley Study

V. Preliminary Progress Report
    A. Hoosic River Valley
    B. Housatonic River Valley
    C. Connecticut River - Main Stream
    D. Deerfield River Valley
    E. Westfield River Valley
    F. Millers River Valley
    G. Chicopee River Valley
    H. Blackstone River Valley
    I. Merrimack River Valley
    J. Massachusetts Bay River Valleys

MASSACHUSETTS STATE PLANNING BOARD

WATER

Introduction

Planning for the use and control of water involves consideration of many other elements: land, agriculture, forestry, industry, power, recreation, and so forth. When any one factor is altered, adjustments must be made in the others. If a State plans a storage reservoir for flood control, it may also have to plan a new community to replace the old, destroyed by the reservoir. If it plans to develop power in connection with the reservoir, it may also have to plan a new industrial life for the community.

Although these complex interrelations with the problem of planning for water resources are of paramount importance, this chapter of necessity confines itself principally to problems of the planning of water resources, as such, and treats the overlapping interrelations only incidentally.

Even in a narrow sense, planning for the development of water resources involves planning of a highly complex nature, not only for water supply, sewage disposal, flood control, hydroelectric power, irrigation, and navigation but also for the integration of each of these into one comprehensive water-resources program. The relationships and the importance of each of these elements of the program vary widely in the different watersheds of the State. For example, in a watershed having a heavy concentration of population, water supply and sewage disposal might be the most important considerations; in another, they might be those of navigation; while in still another, they might be almost entirely problems of flood control. Each watershed must be treated as an individual case.

Water-Resources Problems

What are the more important water-resources problems confronting the State? They may be grouped into six categories: (1) water supply; (2) sewage disposal and stream pollution; (3) flood control; (4) hydroelectric power; (5) water recreation; and (6) problems of integration.

Water Supply

Domestic. Most of the major problems of domestic water supply have been solved. Although 243 out of the 355 municipalities of

MASSACHUSETTS STATE PLANNING BOARD

the Commonwealth have public water-supply systems, they are not all served throughout their entire areas. Those municipalities with no public water-supply systems are, for the most part, small or sparsely populated. Only a few have a population of more than 10,000 persons. (See Map 72-2.)

A substantial proportion of the State's area is reserved for water-supply purposes. The most recent large addition to these lands is Quabbin Reservoir, with a watershed area of about 186 square miles. This large reservation will take care of the water-supply needs of the Boston Metropolitan District, with a population of about two million people, or half the population of the State, for many years unless there develops some unforeseen change in population growth or in the use of water. There still remain ample available lands to care for possible future surface-water needs in the State, without seriously interfering with existing land uses, but these lands should be reserved and protected as soon as possible.

In the western part of the State, most municipalities use surface waters which can be delivered by gravity, because the topography offers excellent opportunities for storage reservoirs at convenient elevations. In the eastern part of the State, a majority of the municipalities, with the exception of the communities of the Boston Metropolitan District, utilize ground waters taken from shallow wells.

Industrial. Problems of industrial water supply are often interwoven with problems of sewage disposal. Many industries originally established themselves in Massachusetts because of the availability of a dependable supply of clean water. In the early days, before the heavy concentrations of population in the river valleys, these industries could utilize the water from the river without treatment. Today, with municipalities and industries discharging untreated sewage and industrial wastes into the streams, it is becoming increasingly difficult to find a good industrial water supply. Industries are forced to install water-treatment plants. Since suitable industrial supply is a matter of considerable economic importance, those rivers receiving considerable pollution, as the Blackstone and parts of the Nashua, Merrimack, Housatonic, and Connecticut Rivers, should be given immediate attention.

Sewage Disposal and Stream Pollution

Preper sewage disposal and elimination of stream pollution will help protect the public against contagious diseases, will make the streams once more suitable for such recreational purposes as

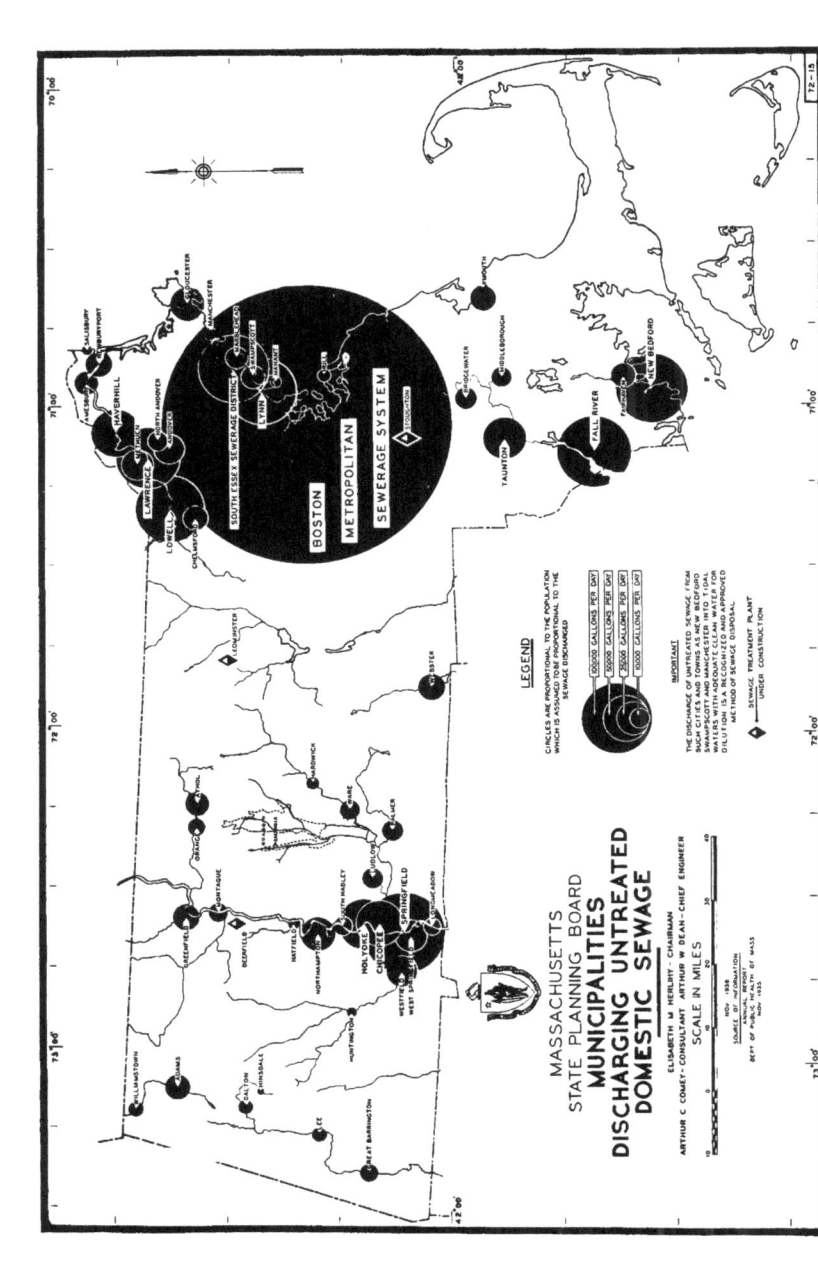

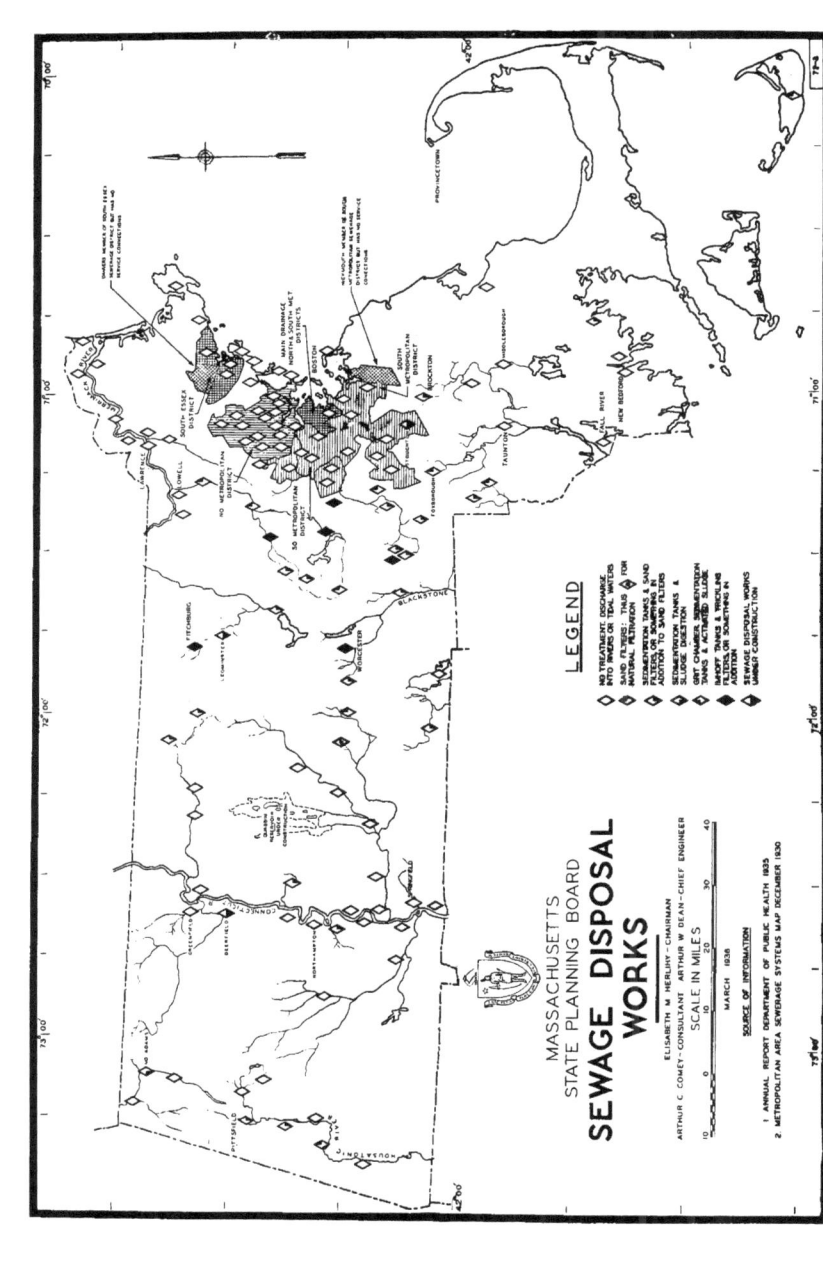

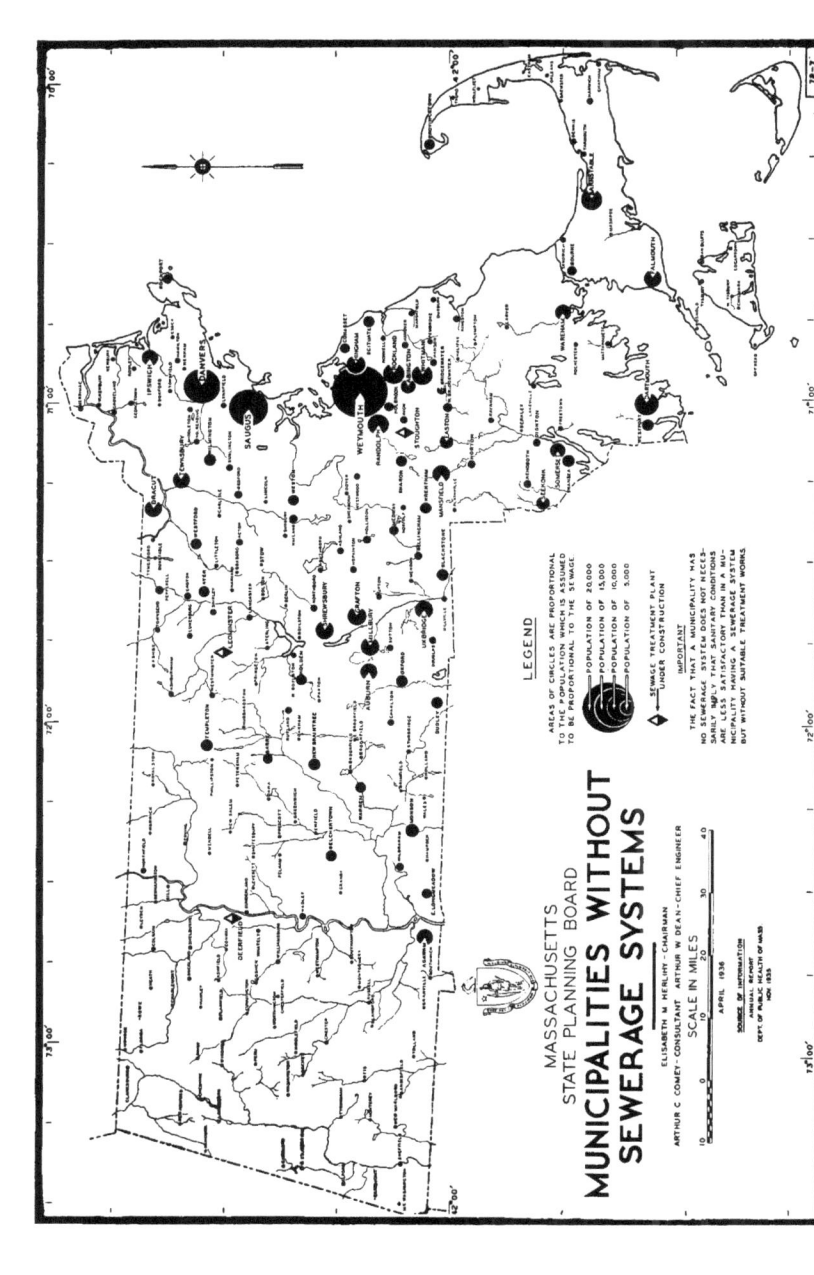

MASSACHUSETTS STATE PLANNING BOARD

Floods are due chiefly to:

1. Excessive rainfall
2. Excessive runoff, resulting from melting snow and excessive rainfall
3. Failure of dams
4. Formation and break-up of ice jams

Past floods have been of two general types: (1) those caused by excessive rainfall, and usually occurring in the fall months, and (2) those caused by excessive runoff resulting from a combination of excessive rainfall and the melting of large accumulations of snow, and usually occurring in the spring months. The 1927 flood was an example of the first type, and the 1936 flood an example of the second type.

A brief description of the 1936 flood is given in the Weather Bureau's Climatological Data for March 1936, by G. H. Noyes, of the Boston Weather Bureau, as follows:

"The early days of March were, generally speaking, normal. There was one moderately hard freeze, and one moderate snowstorm. Temperatures rose somewhat above normal on Monday, the 9th, and continued almost without exception somewhat above normal during the remainder of the month. This resulted in the situation of but little nighttime freezing except in the higher elevations, and northern portions of the region, and rather regular daytime thawing. Snow or rain began on the 9th, with a rise in temperature, and continued into the 10th. Without important interruption, rain began again on the 11th and was very heavy, amounts of 3 inches being frequently recorded in many of the upper reaches of the river's drainage basins, and an extreme of over 7 inches at Pinkham Notch. During the nighttime at this period, temperatures were not enough below freezing to check daytime thawing and runoff. On the 14th, 15th, and 16th temperature minima moved generally below freezing in the three northern States, and about to freezing in the three southern States, and there was but little precipitation, the runoff was briefly halted. On the 16th rain began again in Maine, New Hampshire, and Vermont, and continued with unimportant cessations through the 22nd. During the entire period from the 9th through the 21st temperatures in Maine and New Hampshire average at $39°$, in Vermont about $41°$, and in Massachusetts about $45°$. The volume of rain on the 18-19th was unprecedented in volume, accumulating a 48-hour total of over ten inches at Pinkham Notch. This vast quantity of rain, accompanied by continuously thawing temperatures depleted the snow cover approximately 20 inches in the three northern States. Density measurements of this snow were made at representative localities, and a percentage of 28 was approximated to indicate the water equivalent of the snow cover.

"The fall of heavy and recurring rains was the dominating factor which caused the floods. Since average monthly rainfall for New England as a unit area was first computed, there have been but two other months with greater amounts than this, namely, September 1888, with 8.29 inches, and June 1922, with 8.11 inches, but in neither of those months was there a snow cover to melt and augment the flood of rain. During September 1888, several stations reported monthly amounts of ten inches, and the greatest station record was 13.43 inches at Northampton, Mass., while in March of 1936, several stations reported precipitation in excess of twelve and thirteen inches for the month, and Pinkham Notch, N. H., recorded 23.86. A search, not entirely thorough, seems to show that this occurrence, and a record of 23.90 inches on Mt. Washington, N. H., in July 1884, are probably the records for all time since settling of the country.

"No protection can be advanced against such storms, but engineering skill can overcome such disastrous consequences."

Consideration of the 1936 and other important floods leads to the following summary of desirable methods of control:

1. Use of every method possible, either palliative or preventive, that can be economically justified, giving due consideration to both direct and indirect benefits, such as direct damage prevented, increased power production, increased or improved industrial water supply, increased dilution of pollution, increased use of the stream for recreational purposes, and general better appearances of the river and welfare of the residents.

2. Use of reforestation, detention basins, storage reservoirs, channel improvements, diking, riprapping, widening, straightening, and so forth.

3. Use of partial control to reduce abnormal stages of the river wherever the channel is fixed so that the remaining overloads do not cause excessive damage.

4. Use of some program of land control or zoning to prevent or limit unnecessary occupation of land subject to damaging inundation.

Only by a consideration of all the above methods and their interrelation can Massachusetts hope to alleviate the present flood difficulties. With regard to interstate rivers, only by the application of the same methods through coöperative action of the State, after detailed study of the rivers, can difficulties such as have been encountered in the lower Connecticut be eliminated.

Hydroelectric Power

The undeveloped hydroelectric power in the State is not of great importance. Early in the history of the Commonwealth, most of the large power sites were developed, and almost all of the economically available water power is being utilized.

Undeveloped hydroelectric power in Massachusetts has been estimated at 100,000 to 150,000 horsepower, distributed approximately as follows: 50,000 horsepower on the Deerfield; 30,000 horsepower on the Westfield; 16,000 horsepower on the Millers; 7,500 horsepower on the Hoosic; 3,000 horsepower on the Chicopee; 2,000 horsepower on the Farmington; and 1,000 horsepower on the Nashua. Preliminary surveys indicate that the development of most of this power would be difficult to justify economically.

Water Recreation

There is steadily increasing sentiment for the elimination of pollution in the streams of the State in order that they may be used for recreational purposes. This has been especially true in the Connecticut and Housatonic river valleys, where the local organizations and the newspapers have aroused public interest in this problem. In all cases, the advantages of clean water for recreation and other purposes must be weighed against the costs of treating domestic and industrial wastes before discharging them into the stream. This aspect is dealt with further in Chapter VII.

Problems of Integration

In the preceding discussion, the five types of water problems have been considered individually. It is also necessary to consider them in relation to each other. For example, in the solution of a flood-control problem, it might be found advisable to create several large storage reservoirs in the upper headwaters of a river, but it might be impossible to justify their cost on the basis of flood protection alone. However, if hydroelectric power could be developed at these sites and used, part of the expense of the reservoir might be charged against power production. Furthermore, it might also be discovered that a large number of the communities were discharging domestic and industrial wastes into this river in quantities which seriously polluted the stream at times of low flow. It might be discovered that the water in the reservoirs could be used to increase low flows of the river and so improve the dilution ratio that only simple treatment of the wastes would be necessary, thus

MASSACHUSETTS STATE PLANNING BOARD

eliminating the high cost of installing complete treatment plants. If these secondary benefits were charged against the cost of the original flood-control storage reservoirs, the remaining cost might be entirely justifiable for flood prevention. The program has thus secured the combined benefits of flood control, hydroelectric power development, and the elimination of objectionable pollution during periods of low water. This is integration.

The studies carried on thus far have shown conclusively the need for considering together all the related water problems. The difficulties produced by a non-comprehensive treatment are illustrated by the following example. A Massachusetts city has recently invested about one million dollars in a sewage-disposal plant that is placed at an elevation which reduces the effectiveness of a possible detention reservoir downstream by limiting the possible elevation of the impounded water. If there had been a coördinated study, it might have been possible to place the sewage-disposal works at a higher elevation, allowing a twenty- or thirty-foot increase in the height of the detention dam and thus securing a reservoir with about twice as much storage capacity.

As previously stated, the water from any stream may be needed for a number of more or less competing purposes, which, in Massachusetts, rank in approximately the following order of importance:

1. Water supply for domestic purposes
2. Water supply for industrial purposes
3. Disposal of domestic and industrial wastes
4. Recreational uses
5. Irrigation and Navigation

State Water-Resources Studies

A series of WPA water-resources survey projects have been set up, each covering one of the principal drainage areas of the State. The Department of Public Health sponsored projects in the basins of the Housatonic and Hoosic, the Nashua, and the Blackstone Rivers. The State Planning Board sponsored similar projects for the Massachusetts portion of the basin of the Connecticut River, and for streams in the counties of Middlesex and Norfolk, Essex, and Bristol and Plymouth. These projects are carrying out parallel investigations in each area, so far as available personnel permits, and are under the direct control of the WPA. The Department of Public Health is primarily interested in the sanitary, water-supply, and sewage-disposal studies, while the Planning Board is primarily concerned with flood control and hydroelectric power, though, of

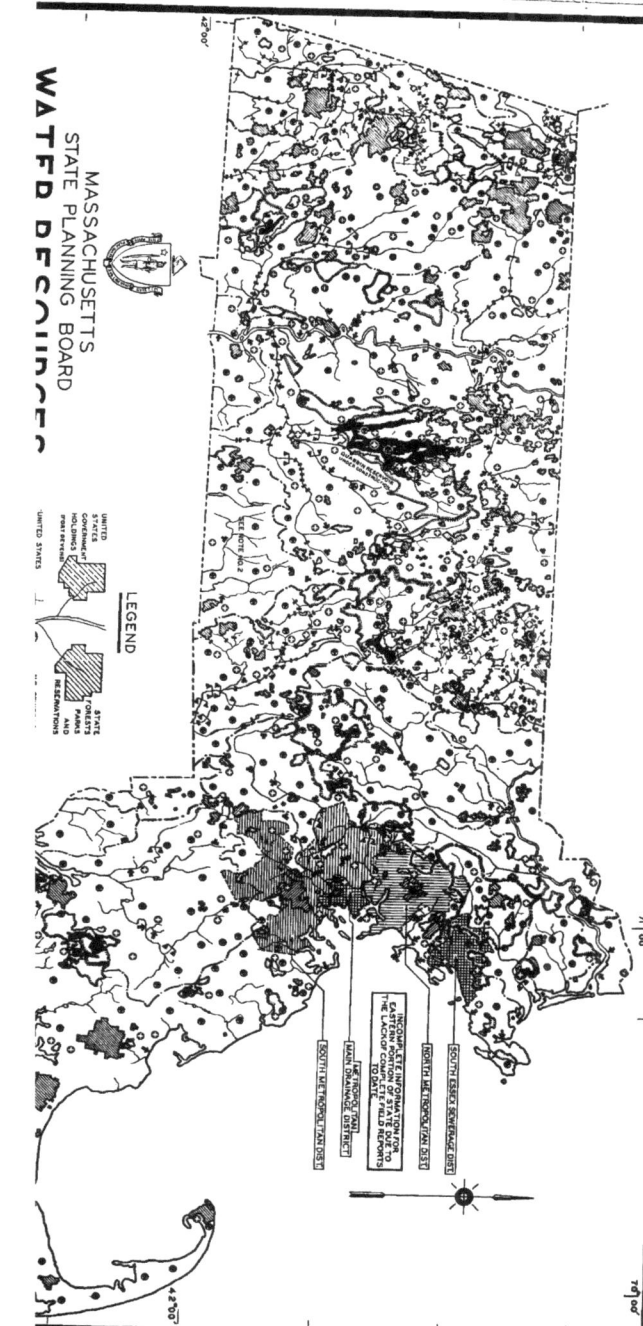

course, it is vitally interested in the other three. Coöperating with these two State offices are the WPA directors and their coördinators, one for sanitation and one for flood control.

In carrying out the process of coördination, the State Planning Board, through its State WPA staff, supplements the work done on the individual projects, and ties together the State-wide analysis and the individual results of the studies of the different watershed or county projects.

The program of study of water resources was divided into the five parts of: (1) Hydrology; (2) Sanitation; (3) Flood control; (4) Hydroelectric power; and (5) Recreation.

Hydrology

The hydrologic studies consisted primarily of the various records of the precipitation stations located in each of the valleys, and the relation of those records to runoff as recorded at the various stream-gauging stations in the valleys. An effort was made in every case to arrive at some correlation between precipitation and resultant runoff so that information on rainfall for a definite area could be correlated with the stream flow in that area. (See Maps 51-18 and 51-22 and the accompanying Precipitation Charts.)

A study of the principal causes of flood with particular reference to large storms of the past, to determine whether the cause was primarily lack of sufficient cover, severe rain, melting of snow and ice, or a combination of all three, is in progress. Preliminary studies of the 1936 flood and its causes, as compared with the 1927 flood and its causes, have led to many valuable conclusions.

Sanitation

The program for the study of water supply and sewage disposal was prepared by the Department of Public Health and used as a basis for studies in the projects sponsored by them; namely, the Housatonic and Hoosic, and the Nashua and Blackstone WPA Projects. The following is a typical river-basin study outline:

Water Supply

1. Study of water supply in municipalities to determine adequacy

2. Preliminary design of supply system where the system is either non-existent or inadequate

47

MASSACHUSETTS STATE PLANNING BOARD

  3. Estimate of cost for new and supplementary supplies

Pollution

  4. Preliminary survey of the river to locate the principal industrial plants to determine the approximate amount of industrial waste discharged into the stream

  5. Preliminary survey of the river to locate all sewer outlets and to determine the approximate number of people served by each

  6. Study of character and quantity of industrial wastes in order to devise methods of treatment

  7. Survey of towns having no collection works in order to design sewerage systems

  8. Design of sewerage systems and treatment plants

  9. Cost estimates of sewerage systems and treatment plants

  The same type of analysis is now being pursued in the various tributaries of the Connecticut River, such as the Westfield, Chicopee, Millers, and Deerfield Rivers.

Flood Control

  An outline for the study of flood control was prepared by WPA engineers on the staff of the State Planning Board, and submitted for criticism to the Water Resources Division of the Nation Resources Committee and to the Boston office of the Flood-Control Division of the United States Army Engineers.

  The present flood study was formulated subsequent to the experience of the 1936 flood, although basic hydrologic information is a matter of long years of record. The 1936 flood, which caused losses in the State aggregating over thirty-five millions of dollars, presented sufficiently serious conditions to warrant development of plans to prevent losses from a flood of similar or even greater magnitude.

  <u>Precipitation, Runoff, and Stream Flow.</u> The flood-control investigations deal first with hydrologic studies of precipitation and runoff, mentioned above.

(STORM RECORD NOT NECESSARILY INCLUDED IN AVERAGES)

PRECIPITATION
NASHUA RIVER WATERSHED
AT FITCHBURG STATION
RECORD PERIOD 1865 TO JUNE 1936 INCLUSIVE

MASSACHUSETTS STATE PLANNING BOARD
PREPARED FROM W.P.A. FIELD PROJECT DATA
OCT. 1936

52-C20

(STORM RECORD NOT NECESSARILY INCLUDED IN AVERAGES)

PRECIPITATION
CHICOPEE RIVER WATERSHED
AT HARDWICK STATION
RECORD PERIOD 1920 TO 1935 INCLUSIVE

MASSACHUSETTS STATE PLANNING BOARD
PREPARED FROM W.P.A. FIELD PROJECT DATA
OCT. 1936

52-C15

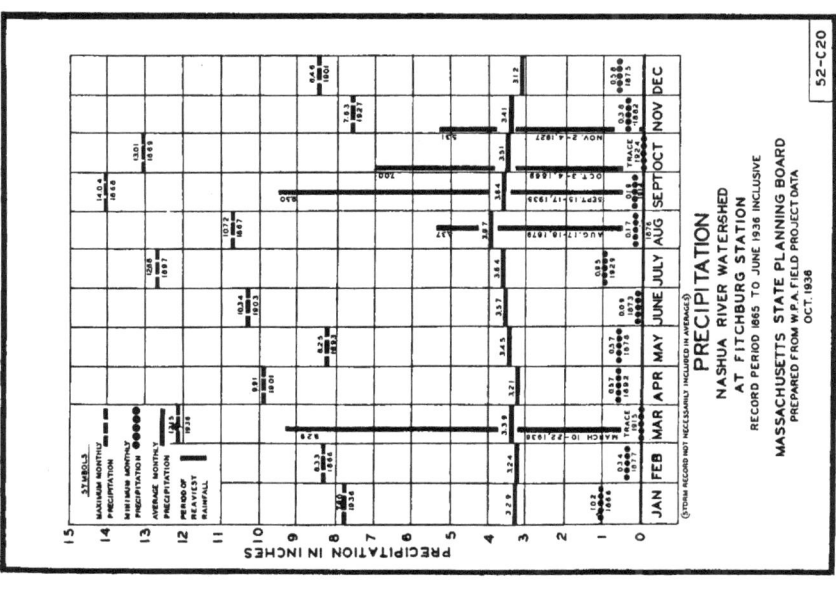

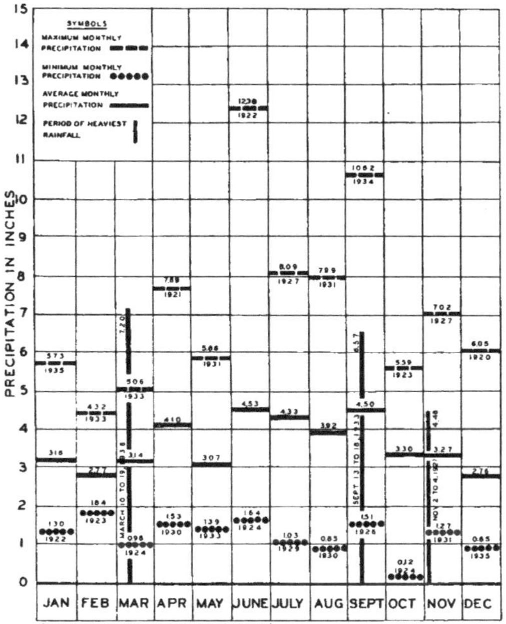

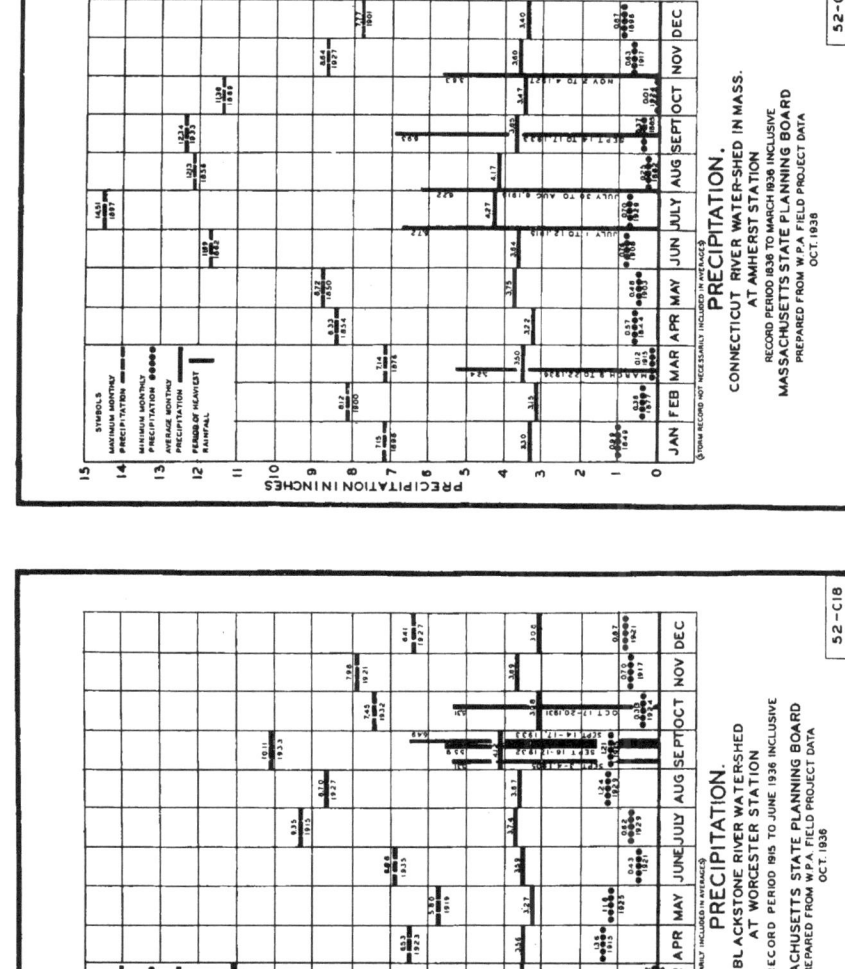

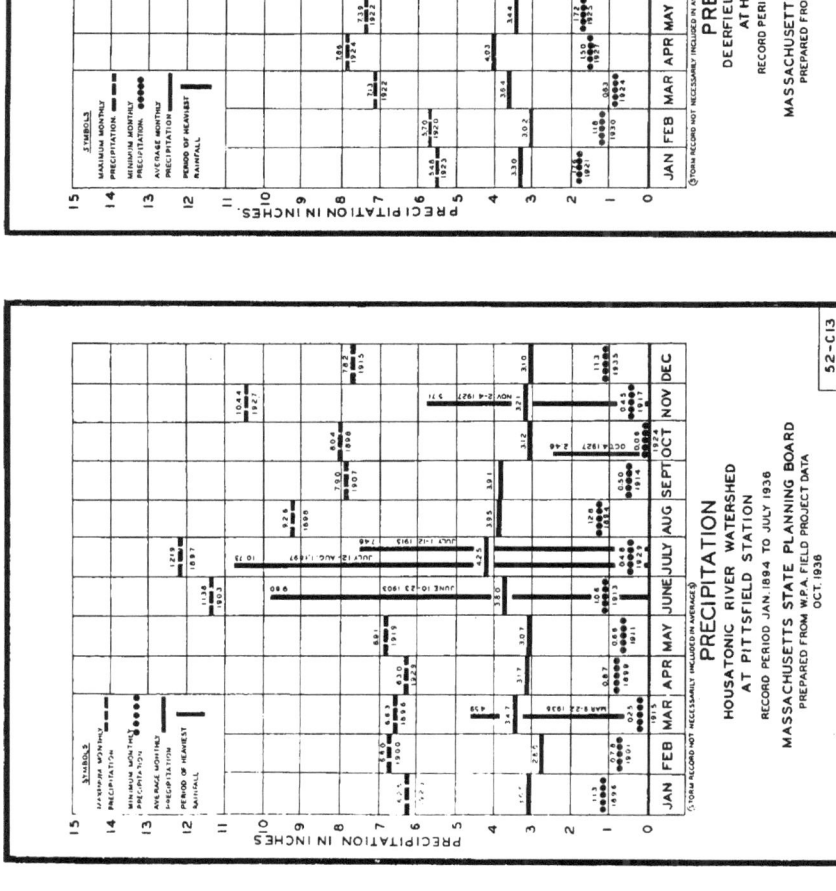

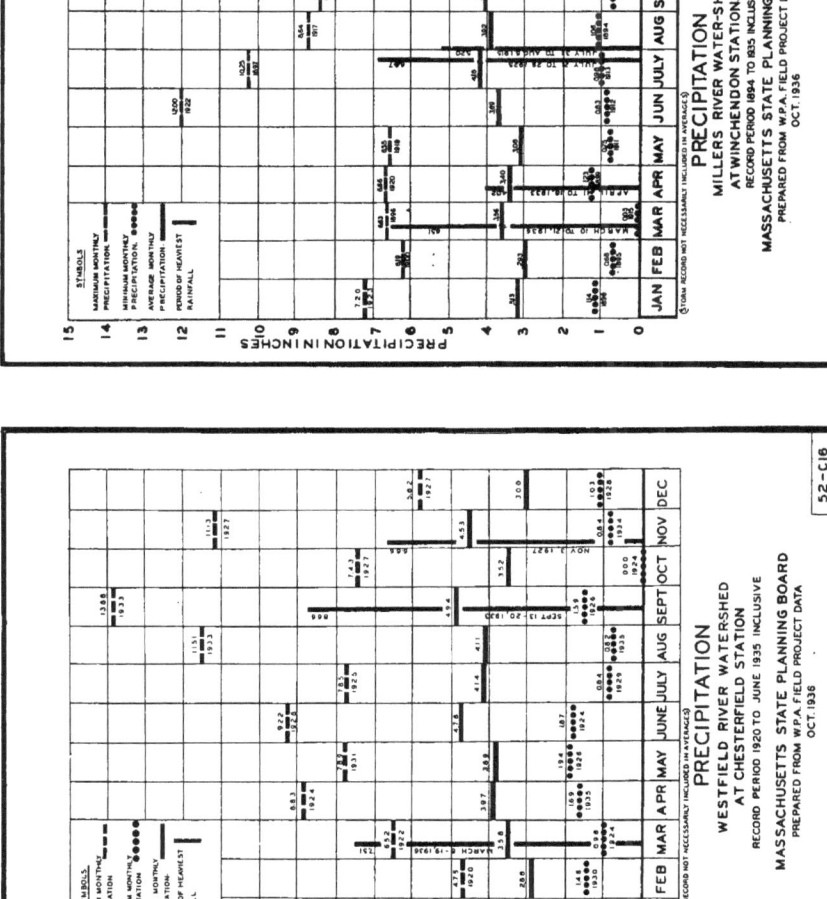

Flood Damage. Detailed studies have been made of the damage from the 1936 flood to highways, railways, farmlands, and residences.

Theoretical Floods. Following this basic study of recorded floods, precipitation, runoff, and damage, studies were made of a theoretical flood assuming that there was an occasion when there was a rainfall during a 48-hour period of six inches over the entire watershed of the stream. Calculations of stream flow are made at important points along the river, showing the estimated height of water. A comparison of known elevations of land and property with estimated flood heights indicates the possible extent of area in which damage may be caused. It is then possible to consider measures of various kinds to protect the potentially endangered areas.

Methods of Flood Control. Methods of retaining part of the water in upstream areas in impounding reservoirs or behind detention dams, methods of channel widening or straightening to enable streams to handle greater flows with safety, and methods of diking and riprapping to confine the stream to safe channels have been studied. Studies were next undertaken to determine the probable frequency of occurrence of floods of a given magnitude. In correlating the frequency studies of storms and ensuing floods of given magnitude against the damage produced, it is possible to arrive at a theoretical answer to the amount of money which might be justifiably spent for flood control. Having once obtained the theoretical economic justification, a reconsideration of flood-control measures can then be made in light of the amount of money available for control. A program of flood control based upon damage incurred, frequency of flood, and funds available is then prepared.

Hydroelectric Power

The study of hydroelectric power consists of three parts: (1) an estimate of the total potential power on the stream; (2) a survey of existing developments; and (3) a comparison of the first and second to determine the potential power yet undeveloped.

In estimating the total potential power on the stream, an analysis is made of the available head, together with the flow of the stream. The first determination of potential power may be modified by introducing various assumptions as to storage reservoirs. The second step, the inventory of existing developments, will disclose the location of power plants, water-storage facilities, installed capacities, power developed, and so forth.

From a comparison of these two studies, it is possible to make approximate estimates of the physically potential power still undeveloped. The staff has confined itself to physical potentiality only, and has not attempted to study in any detail the economic possibilities of power development on the various sites. However, it is probable that a large proportion of the remaining undeveloped power could not be justified economically under present conditions of power cost, supply, and demand.

Water Recreation

The study of opportunities for water recreation has been an important part of the water-resources studies. Recreational uses of the streams are particularly important in the western part of the State, especially of the streams in the Berkshire Hills. In this section of the State, studies are being made of the possibilities of reserving strips of land along the streams for public access, recreation, and control.

The benefits of water recreation, made possible by the elimination from the streams of polluting domestic and industrial wastes, can be secured only at a price. The cost of sewage-disposal facilities and the economic effects produced upon industries and municipalities by the requirement of the construction of these facilities merit careful study.

Cooperating Agencies

In carrying out the program of water-resources studies, a number of different agencies aided and cooperated. The following is a brief outline of these agencies, their activities, and their relation to the study:

1. <u>United States Army Engineers</u>. The Flood Control Division of the United States Army Engineers is making extensive flood-control studies of the Connecticut, Merrimack, and Blackstone Rivers. They have also contributed valuable information and criticisms.

2. <u>Works Progress Administration</u>. In addition to being the main source of personnel, WPA gave the State Planning Board much important information, especially from studies already in existence at the time of the creation of the Board.

3. <u>New England Regional Planning Commission</u>. The New England Regional Planning Commission, through its staff and its reports on the various interstate watersheds, served as an important source of general or supplementary material and background for more detailed studies.

4. <u>Weather Bureau</u>. The cooperation of the Weather Bureau was

an absolute necessity. From them the State Planning Board obtained basic hydrologic data on rainfall, snow cover, and temperature.

5. United States Geological Survey, Water Resources Division. Again, as in the case of the Weather Bureau, it would have been impossible to proceed without the generous assistance of the United States Geological Survey, especially the Boston office. From this office the State Planning Board obtained detailed analyses of runoff at each of the forty-three gauging stations in Massachusetts, and data and analysis of records of private mills.

6. Department of Public Health. The Department of Public Health, in addition to its function as sponsor of several of the WPA projects, prepared the main program for the sanitary studies, and contributed information and suggestions regarding water supply and sewage disposal throughout the State.

7. Public Works Department. The Department of Public Werks has made available essential information relative to highways, bridges, and other structures.

8. Department of Conservation. This department has furnished valuable aid, particularly in supplying copies of the individual town maps prepared by it.

Nashua River Valley Study

A description of the Nashua River Valley investigation is here presented as a typical example of the water-resources studies in progress in most of the river valleys of the State. It is the furthest advanced of the studies and affords an excellent example of the interrelation of land studies and water studies. The Nashua study is not entirely completed; the findings and recommendations are here presented as possible solutions rather than as definite proposals.

Organization of the Study

The Nashua River Valley Survey is divided into three parts, each sponsored by the State Department of Public Health, as follows: (1) a Land Project (No. 9618), with the local office in Leominster; (2) a Flood Control Project (No. 7605), with the local office in Leominster; and (3) a Sanitary Project (No. 7603) with

MASSACHUSETTS STATE PLANNING BOARD

the local office in Fitchburg. The Department of Public Health, as sponsor, advises the Fitchburg office, while the State Planning Board guides the Leominster offices. The Sanitary and Flood Control Surveys were initiated by local interests and formulated into definite projects about one year before the State Planning Board was formed. The Land Study was begun in the late summer of 1936. The accomplishments of the early project operations under the Department of Public Health direction have made possible the subsequent progress of these projects, cooperatively directed by the State Planning Board and the Department of Public Health. The especial interest of the State Planning Board in these studies has been to suggest those aspects which will dovetail into a comprehensive State-wide scheme of development.

Description of the River Valley

The Nashua River Basin (See Map 72-8) is a tributary of the Merrimack, with sources in Worcester and Middlesex counties. It has a total drainage area of about 532 square miles, of which 448 lie in Massachusetts. The general direction of flow of the main stream is north by a little east, crossing the Massachusetts - New Hampshire line at Dunstable and then emptying into the Merrimack at Nashua, New Hampshire. The length of the main stream in Massachusetts is approximately 24 miles, and the length of the north branch, its principal tributary, on which most of the problems arise, is about 16 miles. The drainage area of the south branch is largely controlled by the Wachusett Reservoir, a part of the water-supply system of the Metropolitan District.

The river may be described generally as a main stream flowing northward through level land at a low hydraulic gradient. Coming in from the northwest are three principal tributaries: the south branch, draining through the Wachusett Reservoir; the north branch, coming down from the highlands around Fitchburg and entering at Lancaster; and the Squannacook, entering at Ayer.

The Nashua River and its tributaries flow through rolling topography, from which runoff is severe in the spring. The flood waters of the tributaries discharge into the main stream at approximately the same time. This situation, coupled with the fact that the main stream has a low hydraulic gradient, makes inundation along the banks of the main stream an almost annual occurrence, and in times of heavy flood a considerable area is covered.

Principal Problems in the Nashua River Valley

The principal problems in the Nashua River Valley occur in and

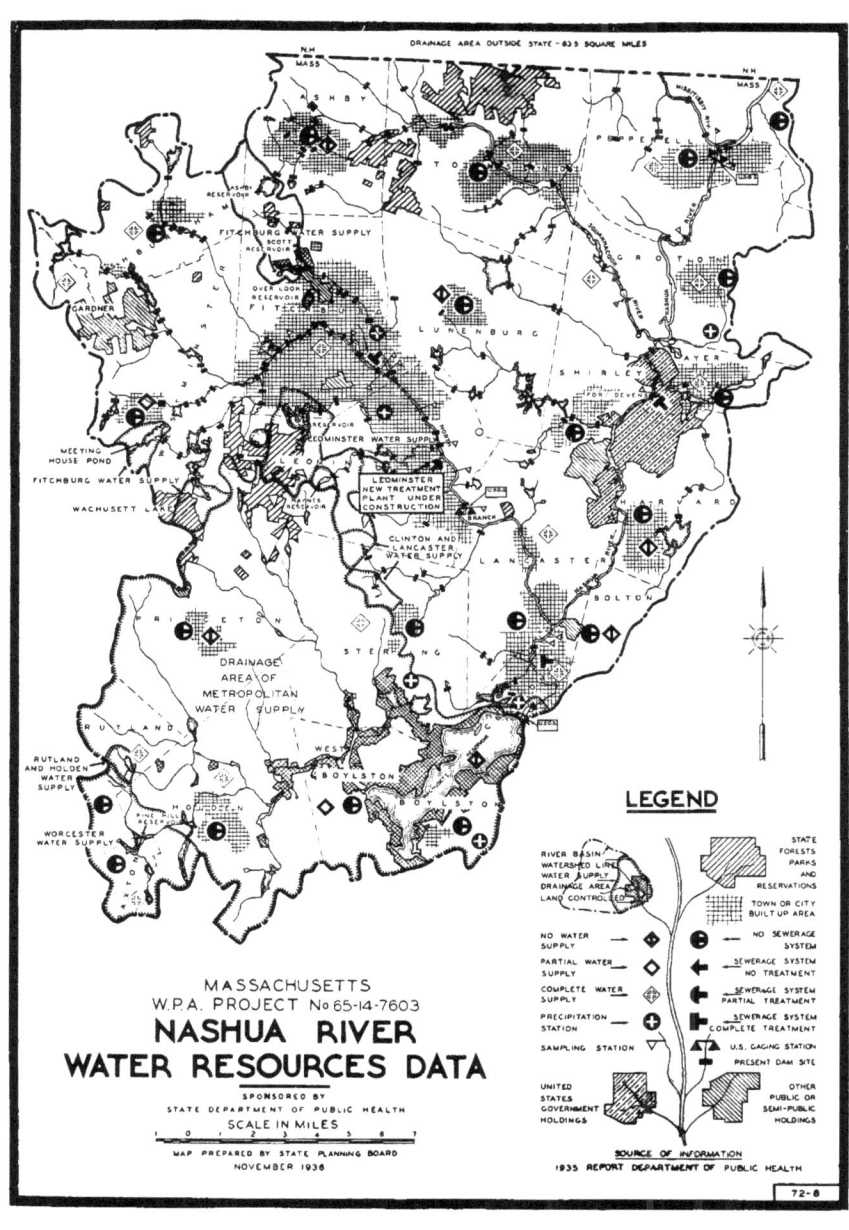

near the two largest cities in the valley, Fitchburg and Leominster, both located on the north branch. Of the total of approximately three million dollars flood damages for the whole valley in 1936, 1,600,000 dollars of damage were concentrated on the north branch at Fitchburg, due principally to restricted channels, which were unable to carry the tremendous volumes of water contributed from the hills upstream. Fitchburg and Leominster discharge (including recirculation) a total of about fifteen million gallons of domestic and industrial wastes daily, of which about ten million gallons are untreated. These ten million gallons of untreated wastes are a terrific load, and at times of low flow in the summer and early autumn render the stream not only unfit for water supply but also for fishing, bathing, and recreation. At these times it is usually unsightly and disagreeable to the sense of smell. Although there are several small hydroelectric power plants on the river, there are no large potential power sites, owing to the low flow of the river and to the fact that adequate storage reservoirs for power purposes would be too expensive. The duties of the Water-Resources Projects were: (1) to segregate, locate, and evaluate the factors contributing to the above problems, and (2) to suggest remedial measures.

Water Supply and Sewage Disposal. The studies of water supply and sewage disposal were carried on under the guidance of the Department of Public Health. From studies of population and its probable future trend, and the probable increased water demand, it was found that no serious shortage of water existed. Map 72-9 shows that all of the large cities and towns in the valley have adequate water supplies. Problems of industrial water supply facing certain industries located on the river are problems of pollution rather than of supply.

The next step in the studies was to determine the location of all river outlets for domestic and industrial wastes. Quantitative studies were then made to determine, in the case of domestic discharges, the approximate number of people served and the daily discharge and, in the case of the industrial discharges, the quantity and character of the wastes and their periods of discharge. Each type of waste was analyzed, chemically and physically, as a basis for later recommendations for treatment.

Surveys were made of towns where there were no domestic sewerage systems, to determine the most desirable locations for possible sewer lines and treatment plants. Preliminary designs and cost estimates were made for sewerage systems for several of these areas.

53

MASSACHUSETTS STATE PLANNING BOARD

Studies of the treatment of the various kinds of wastes, both domestic or industrial, were carried on. Possibilities of reclaiming portions of the industrial wastes were investigated. A detailed presentation of the findings will be found in a report of the Department of Public Health on sanitary conditions in the Nashua River Valley.

Since the southern portion of the Nashua watershed, and the area tributary to the south branch, supply water for the Boston Metropolitan District, these lands are regulated as to the disposal of domestic and industrial wastes by the Metropolitan District Commission. The substantial pollution of the Nashua River with both industrial and domestic wastes comes largely from the cities of Fitchburg and Leominster on the north branch, from the towns of Pepperell and Groton on the main stream, and from Clinton on the south branch just below Wachusett Dam. Map 72-10 illustrates graphically the discharges of wastes.

Fitchburg discharges daily approximately 15,000,000 gallons of industrial and domestic wastes. Although most of the domestic wastes pass through the city treatment plant, the domestic wastes from industries employing about four thousand people are discharged directly into the stream. About 6,000,000 gallons of industrial wastes are discharged untreated. Domestic wastes from some houses located at a low elevation along the river are discharged directly into the stream. Furthermore, during periods of high runoff the combined sewage and surface-runoff flow directly into the river.

Leominster, the second largest source of pollution, discharges daily approximately 1,500,000 gallons of untreated domestic sewage and more than 2,000,000 gallons of untreated industrial wastes. However, a large new sewage-disposal plant, which is now under construction, will eliminate this pollution.

Clinton has an inadequate sewage-treatment plant. A new plant of modern design and construction would be of great value in relieving the objectionable pollution of the south branch. The remaining towns on the watershed discharge between three and four million gallons of industrial wastes daily. Of these four million gallons, about three million are wastes from the manufacture of paper.

Rubbish and other debris are also dumped into the streams. Although municipal ordinances prohibit this, they are poorly enforced and ineffective.

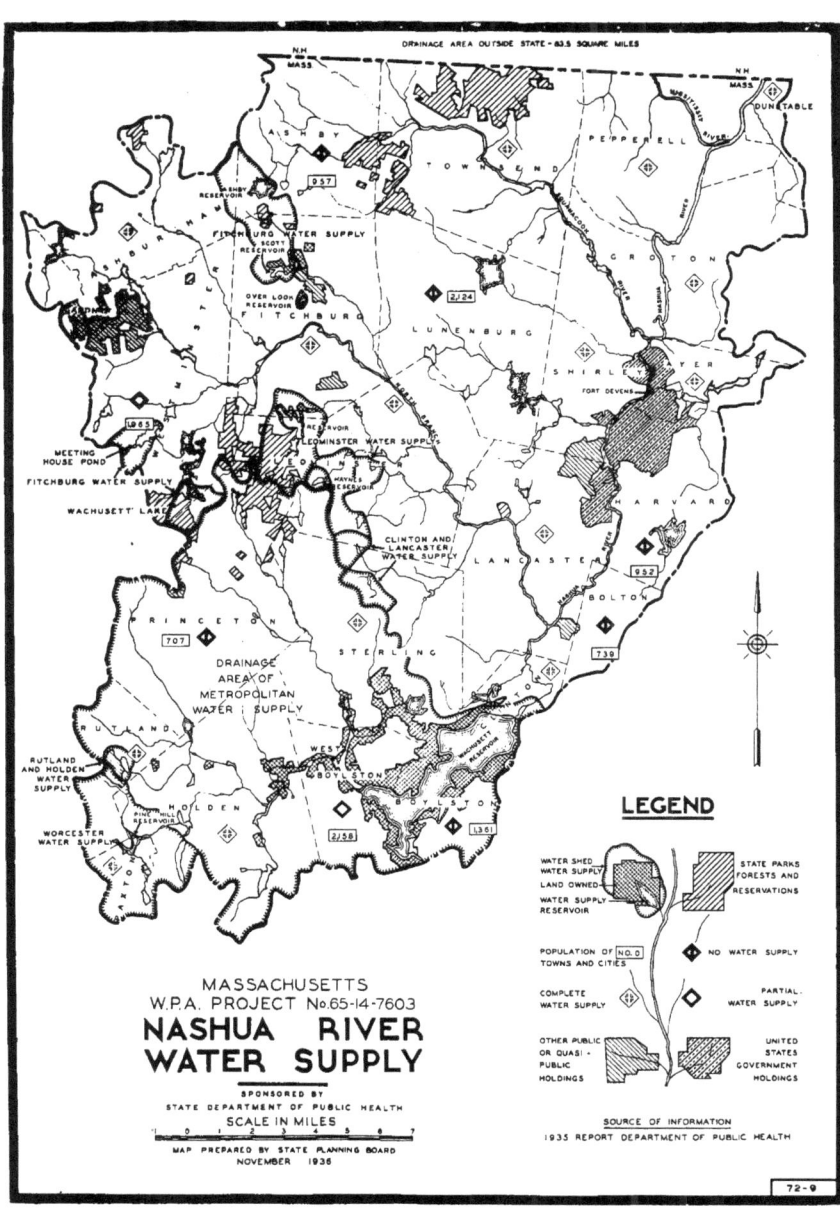

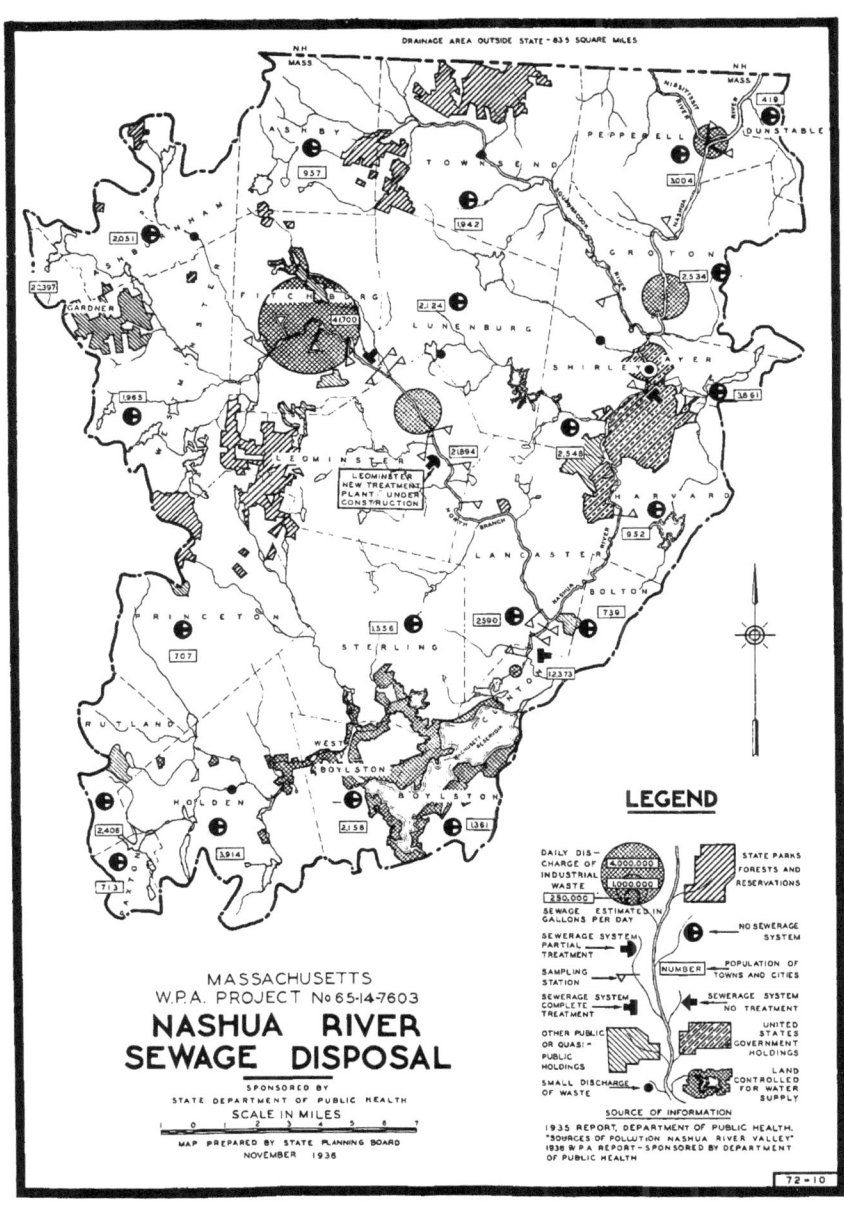

Power. New hydroelectric power in the Nashua River Valley is relatively unimportant. A number of small developments and several large ones now exist. Although there are several minor power sites that are as yet undeveloped, the chances of their being utilized are small because of the low flow of the river. Storage reservoirs, to supplement the flow during dry periods, are not feasible because communities have been built in the suitable sites. Hydroelectric power, therefore, need be given only incidental consideration.

Flood Control. Preliminary studies for flood control were instigated and carried on by local public interests. With these as a beginning, further studies were undertaken by Project No. 7604, which cooperated with an independent project directed by the Flood Control Division of the United States Army Engineers. The first step was a study of all precipitation records in the basin. Then a study was made of the data collected at the various stream-gauging stations. Early in the project it was discovered that at several important points on the river no measurements were being made. The Department of Public Health, cooperating with the Water Resources Division of the United States Geological Survey, succeeded in securing the establishment of two automatic gauging stations: one in Leominster at the old Worcester Traction Company Dam, and another downstream in the town of Pepperell. Without these two important additions, vital runoff information for the 1936 flood would probably not have been obtained.

A detailed study of the stream-gauging stations in the river, considering the total discharges, the rates of discharge, and the time element, showed the progress of the flood waters downstream. The next step was a study of a theoretical flood such as would be caused by a six-inch runoff. From this study a determination was made of the amount of discharge likely to be encountered, the time-factors, the quantity of water at the various stations on the river, and the resultant stages of the river.

The next step was to determine the location and magnitude of the flood damages at the various river stages.

An estimate could then be made of the amount of money which it is necessary to spend on flood-control measures.

The United States Army's method of establishing basic economic justification for flood-control construction is to determine the probability of occurrence of various flood stages by means of the Slade skew probability function and to determine the damages corresponding to each river stage by actual field appraisal of damages incurred during the March 1936 flood. Hydraulic designs, routing

MASSACHUSETTS STATE PLANNING BOARD

computations, and cost estimates are then prepared to determine the effectiveness of the various elements of a flood-control system in reducing flood-crest heights at the principal critical damage centers and the corresponding construction costs. With data on the hydraulic effectiveness and damages available, it is possible to estimate the benefits of various alternative flood-control projects. That combination of reservoirs is finally selected which gives the highest ratio of average annual flood benefits to average annual fixed carrying charges.

The following is a discussion of the principal findings of the Nashua River Valley study and of the tentative proposals for flood control.

The problem of flood control divides itself into three principal phases:

1. Regional aspects, involving the relation of the Nashua River Valley to the Merrimack Valley and the States of Massachusetts and New Hampshire.
2. The watershed problem of the Nashua River itself.
3. The local problem of the north branch of the Nashua River.

From a comparison of the relative size of the drainage area of the Nashua River (about 500 square miles) with that of the Merrimack (approximately 5000 square miles), it appears that the contribution of the Nashua River to the flood conditions on the main stream of the Merrimack was about 10 per cent of the total. Hence, about 10 per cent of the flood damage of the lower Merrimack could justly be attributed to the Nashua River.

The total damage in the Nashua River watershed, itself, was probably four or five million dollars, of which about three million dollars occurred in Massachusetts. Of this three million, $1,600,000 were concentrated at Fitchburg.

The flood-damage map (Map 72-12) shows the distribution of losses throughout the valley. In general, the drainage area of the Wachusett Reservoir was least affected, although Princeton and Holden were damaged to the extent of thirty-five thousand and fifty-three thousand dollars, respectively. The Wachusett Reservoir in a large measure controls the drainage area of the south branch. Therefore, any damage on the main stream above the confluence of the north and south branches can be attributed almost entirely to the water from the north branch, until the confluence of the main stream with the Squannacook is reached.

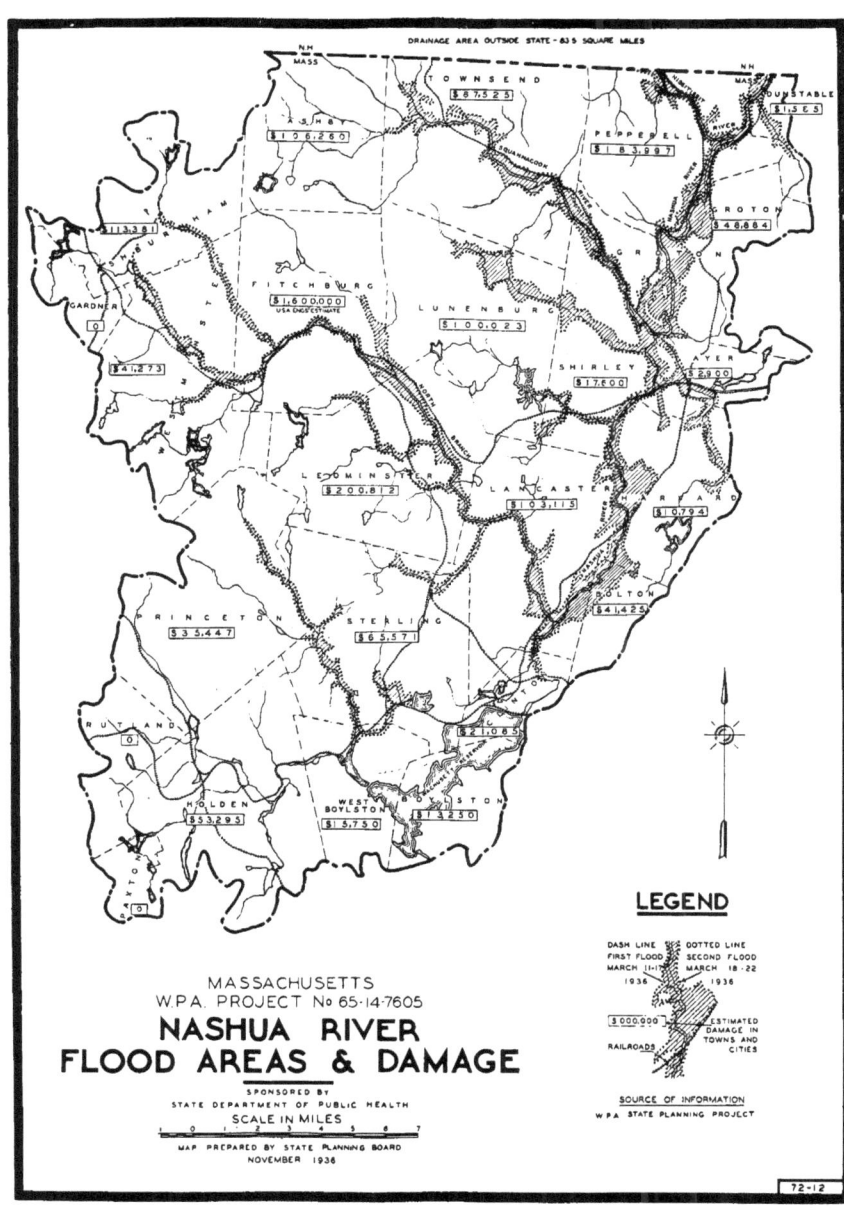

MASSACHUSETTS STATE PLANNING BOARD

On the main stream, the principal losses occurred in Groton and Pepperell, which were damaged to the extent of forty-nine thousand and one hundred and eighty-four thousand dollars, respectively. The principal losses on the Squannacook were one hundred and six thousand dollars and eighty-seven thousand dollars in the towns of Ashby and Townsend, respectively. Lunenburg, in Mulpus Brook basin, suffered damage of about one hundred thousand dollars.

The flood problem in the Nashua Valley in Massachusetts occurs almost entirely at Fitchburg, on the north branch.

From a consideration of the technical studies of precipitation and runoff and the resultant floods, together with the regional, the valley, and the local flood problems (especially the assignment of damage burdens), the Flood Control Division of the United States Army Engineers has prepared a program for flood control, and has begun construction work.

There are in general two methods of approaching the solution of any flood-control problem: the application of (1) preventive measures, and (2) palliative measures. In the first group are normally included storage reservoirs or detention basins, which tend to reduce flood flows by the actual storage of water, lengthening the time of discharge and reducing the severity at any one moment. The second group, the palliative measures, includes channel widening, straightening, diking, riprapping, or any other method of carrying off the water more rapidly, once it has reached the river.

In preparing a program of flood control for the Nashua River Valley, both preventive and palliative methods have been utilized. (See Map 72-13.)

Probably the most effective method of successfully coping with the difficulties at Lowell, Lawrence, and Haverhill is the building of storage or detention reservoirs in the headwaters of the Merrimack River, thus checking the discharge of the river. It would be almost impossible to provide channel capacity for the tremendous quantity of water contributed by the 5000-square-mile drainage area. Only a channel many times as big as now exists would carry off the discharge. Such a channel would probably involve the destruction of large portions of the towns.

As mentioned previously, Fitchburg's $1,600,000 damages were caused largely by the restricted river channel. Hence, the solution is almost self-evident. It is necessary to provide:

MASSACHUSETTS STATE PLANNING BOARD

1. Larger channel capacity by widening and deepening the existing channel.
2. A lower hydraulic gradient to reduce velocity in order to obviate the necessity for extensive riprapping to resist erosion from the high channel velocities occurring during flood periods.
3. The elimination of obstructions which restrict the channel and cause flooding backwaters.

These are essentially palliative measures of control.

The flow in the Fitchburg section reached 12,000 cubic feet per second during the peak of the 1936 flood, and for a period of five days averaged approximately 8000 cubic feet per second. The proposed channel improvements will not entirely protect the city. The improved channel would be able to carry a much higher rate of flow than is now possible, but not enough to care for certain maximum discharges. Hence, consideration of the preventive methods of storage reservoirs and detention dams is necessary.

On the headwaters of the north branch (Flag Brook, Whitman River, and Nookagee River) small dams, regulating and controlling the flow of those rivers, are proposed. With several of these dams, properly regulated in the spring and during times of flood to permit alternate discharges from the different rivers, the flood flow might be lowered enough so that the improved channel could care for it. This might successfully protect Fitchburg. Theoretically, in the very act of improving the Fitchburg condition, the conditions downstream might be made worse, for the discharge through the Fitchburg channel, and therefore the flow in the channel near Leominster and elsewhere downstream will be increased by reason of elimination of existing valley storage. However, the valley between the steep hills at Fitchburg is so narrow that the magnitude of the storage so lost is, for all practical purposes, negligible.

The WPA engineers, on the basis of a six-inch storm, tentatively calculate that a storage of 40,000 acre-feet is necessary for complete control of the north branch. A special study is, therefore, being made of the desirability of constructing a dam at Lancaster and flooding adjacent lands as shown on the accompanying map (Map 52-18) in the towns of Lancaster and Leominster. A dam could be built just above North Village, storing about 20,000 acre-feet. This storage, combined with the storage above Fitchburg, would materially aid in controlling the north branch. It is doubtful, however, whether a dam would be economically feasible at this point.

The Army Engineers are considering further sites on the main

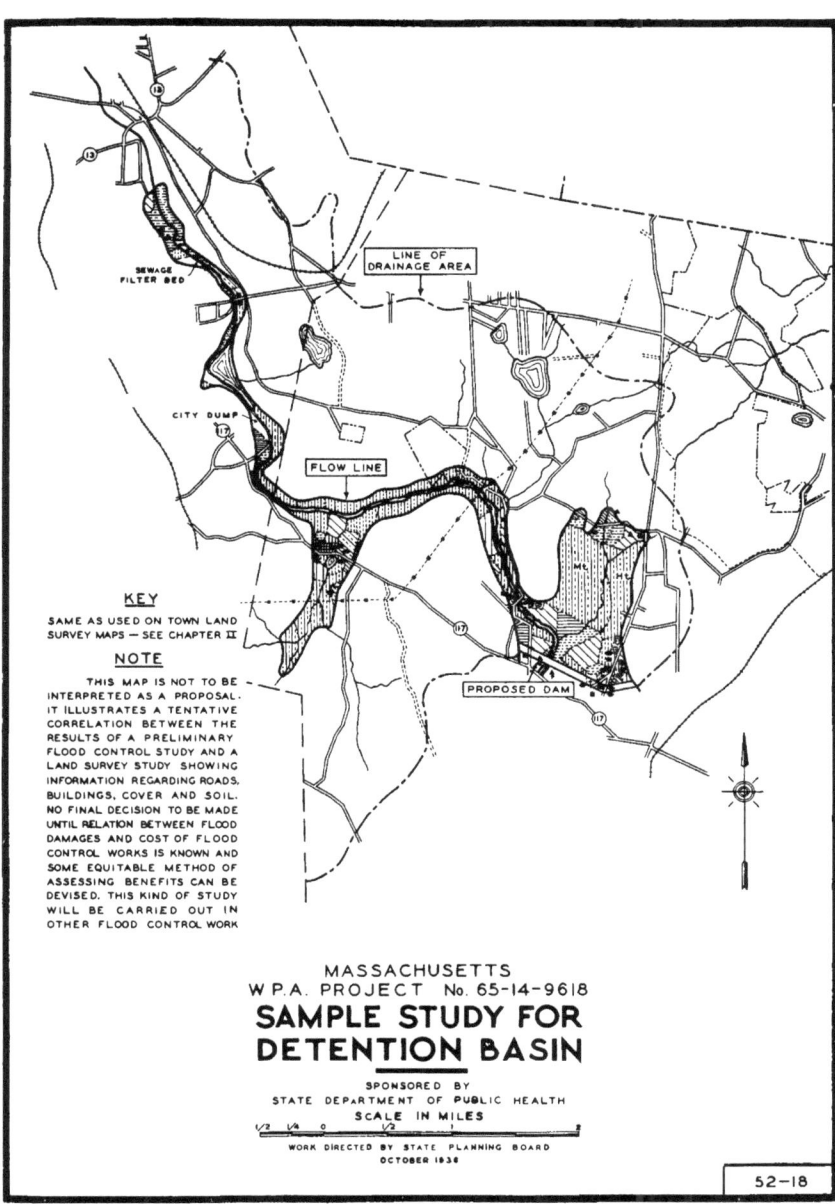

stream, where there exists, at present, considerable natural storage. Along this part of the river above Pepperell, the land is so level that a large area can be flooded, and, if the water level over the area which now is inundated every spring could be raised but slightly, the additional storage, because of the very extensive area, would be considerable.

The Army Engineers have considered other control measures on the Squannacook, the Mulpus, and the Nissitissit, but now look with more favor upon the one large reservoir at Pepperell than upon a series of smaller reservoirs on the tributaries.

Preliminary Progress Report

The following is a preliminary report of the progress to date of the WPA water-resources projects sponsored by the State Planning Board and the Department of Public Health.

Seven water-supply and stream-pollution projects were undertaken, as follows:

    1. The Housatonic and Hoosic Project, covering also the Farmington River. Sponsored by the Department of Public Health.
    2. The Connecticut Hydrology Project, covering the main stream of the Connecticut, the Deerfield, Westfield, and Chicopee Rivers. Sponsored by the State Planning Board.
    3. The Blackstone Project, covering also the French and Quinebaug Rivers. Sponsored by the Department of Public Health.
    4. The Nashua Project, covering also the Millers, Assabet, and Concord Rivers. Sponsored by the Department of Public Health.
    5. The Essex Project, covering the Merrimack, Ipswich, and Parker Rivers. Sponsored by the State Planning Board.
    6. The Middlesex-Norfolk Project, covering the Charles and Neponset Rivers and other minor streams. Sponsored by the State Planning Board.
    7. The Bristol-Plymouth Project, covering the Taunton River and several minor tidal streams. Sponsored by the State Planning Board.

The Nashua, Blackstone, and Housatonic projects are the furthest advanced.

Seven flood-control projects were set up in the foregoing watersheds and counties. The Nashua and Blackstone projects were set up as separate projects, whereas the other five are separate divisions of the same project. From the above outline of the projects it may be seen that the coverage was State-wide.

The following is a presentation of the progress and findings by watersheds. (The Nashua findings are set forth in the preceding pages of this chapter.)

Hoosic River Valley

"The Hoosic River drains the northwestern corner of Massachusetts and is formed at North Adams by the union of the north and south branches. From this point it flows in a northwesterly direction past Williamstown to the Massachusetts-Vermont borderline and after crossing the southeastern corner it continues in New York State and becomes one of the most important tributaries of the Hudson. Its total drainage area is 710 square miles and that portion in Massachusetts is about 174 square miles."*

The mean annual rainfall is about 44 inches, which is slightly higher than the average for the State.

Sewage Disposal. Sewage-disposal problems are concentrated at Adams, North Adams, and Williamstown. During 1935, works for partial treatment of sewage in North Adams were installed near the Williamstown line.

Flood Damage. The total flood damage in the watershed in 1936 was $446,000.

Hydroelectric Power. Preliminary estimates indicate that there are about 7,500 hydroelectric horsepower still undeveloped on the river. Army engineers have reported on a potential storage site above North Adams near Clarksburg. Two storage reservoirs already exist: one at the Clarksburg, and the other at Cheshire, at the head of the south branch, providing a certain amount of flood control.

Housatonic River Valley

The Housatonic River Valley contains 498 square miles in Massachusetts, comprising a large part of the Berkshire County. The length of the stream from the Connecticut State line upstream to the source in Hinsdale is approximately 65 miles.

Precipitation is fairly well distributed throughout the year,

---

*Senate Document 289 — 1918.

with the minimum varying from 2.8 inches in February to 4.25 inches in July. The maximum recorded precipitation for months was in June 1903, with 11.38 inches, and in July 1897, with 12.19 inches.

Stream Pollution and Sewage Disposal. Problems of sewage disposal demand immediate attention. The loads of domestic and industrial wastes placed in this stream are so heavy that the treatment of sewage should be made compulsory. Conditions are particularly bad in the towns of Hinsdale, Dalton, Lee, Great Barrington, and Sheffield. The city of Pittsfield is at present discharging a considerable amount of sewage into the river, because of the insufficient capacity of its treatment plant. This condition will be somewhat alleviated in the near future as the city is now installing trickling filters, which should be in operation early in the spring of 1937, to replace the present sand filters. The town of Stockbridge has a treatment plant, and the sewage in the town is discharged to this plant, except for one pipe which discharges directly into the river. The sewage carried by this pipe could easily be pumped into a line leading to the sewage-treatment plant. Although the treatment plant is well operated, it has insufficient capacity. An addition should be made in the near future to prevent further pollution of the river. Although the town of Lenox has a sewage system and treatment plant, certain parts of the village, such as Lenox Station and Lenoxdale, have outlets that discharge directly into the river. The sewage from these outlets should be treated. Preliminary plans have been prepared by the Housatonic Project for sewerage systems and treatment plants for the towns of Hinsdale and Dalton. Studies are also being made for the towns of Lee and Great Barrington.

The industrial wastes within the Housatonic River watershed are of particular importance. The towns in which industrial wastes should be given attention are Pittsfield, Lee, Great Barrington, Lenox, and Dalton. A large portion of the wastes result from the manufacture of paper. At the present time analyses are being made and experiments conducted to determine the most efficient method of disposing of these wastes. It is the opinion of the engineers that detention basins for floods would not be of any particular value in solving the pollution problem. The only sound method of clearing the stream is to build disposal systems to care for domestic wastes and, in towns within which industries are discharging wastes into the stream, to treat such wastes in municipal treatment plants after the wastes have received preliminary treatment at the individual industrial plants.

The Department of Public Health, the sponsor for the Housatonic Sanitation Project, is publishing a detailed tentative report giv-

MASSACHUSETTS STATE PLANNING BOARD

ing the types and volumes of industrial wastes, location of each plant and outlet, and sanitary conditions in the various communities.

Flood Damage and Control. Although the major portion of the watershed is still forested, there are areas in which, owing to excessive cutting of timber, natural snow retention has been materially lessened. From these areas the first heavy flood discharges come. Within this watershed, 1936 flood losses have been estimated at $725,000, divided as follows: damages to public works, highways, and highway bridges, $239,000; to water-supply and sewage-disposal systems, $12,000; to railroads, $18,000; to industries, $75,000; to crop land, $195,000; to dams, $30,000; and to private property, $183,000.

Certain flood-control measures appear at present to offer possibilities worthy of serious consideration. Control of headwaters may be possible in the town of Hinsdale. Studies are in progress to determine the possibility of a detention basin. There is a considerable acreage of land which is normally flooded annually. It may be possible to provide a comparatively low dam behind which an accumulation of water could be held for a period of six weeks. The gradual release of this impounded water would not exceed the safe channel capacity of the river below. Comparatively large numbers of dams have been constructed along the river for power purposes, but since the usual commercial procedure is to accumulate back of each dam as much water as possible, no storage capacity is available at times of flood. If arrangements could be made to provide storage space, either by lowering the water levels of the reservoirs before heavy rainfalls begin, or by providing increased height of dams with properly gauged flood-water outlets, some additional control could be obtained. In the city of Pittsfield certain comparatively low lands have been occupied for residential purposes, and when the river rises three to five feet, large areas become inundated. In such areas, the construction of dikes might afford protection against rising water. It should be noted, however, that these dikes should not be constructed directly at the river bank, but sufficiently far back on each side so that a flood channel is provided. Downstream from Pittsfield desirable corrective measures include channel dredging, widening, and diking until the more level lands below the town of Great Barrington are reached. In this area it might be possible to provide emergency channels protected by dikes that would afford increased flowage volume and yet confine the stream within much smaller areas than were submerged in 1936.

Damage on the tributaries of the Housatonic in the 1936 flood resulted largely from the scouring action of rapidly flowing water. In some instances, protection against this scouring action can be given by planting along the banks, willows or other trees with an extensive root system, or by laying rubble walls or heavy stone riprapping.

Owing to the fact that the lower portion of the Housatonic River lies in the State of Connecticut, cooperation with that State in the development of a program for control of floods should be undertaken, for it is not equitable to develop a program within the State which will merely pass excessive volumes of flood water downstream to Connecticut.

Hydroelectric Power. The present installed hydroelectric power capacity, according to the WPA project report, is about 11,000 horsepower, distributed among twenty-one plants. Power development might be aided by the development of reservoirs. It has been estimated that there is additional available storage at Richmond Pond and Monterey of 45,000,000 and 225,000,000 cubic feet, respectively. However, the following statement from Senate Document 289, of 1918, still is true.

"While the large amount of developed and undeveloped fall on the Housatonic River makes any increase of the storage of the basin highly desirable, the natural topography of the basin is such that when considered in connection with the location of towns and railroads, the creation of this storage becomes too costly to be feasible. It might be that a small amount of storage can be created at various places that would be of considerable benefit to the power located directly below them, and when it comes to the creation of a comprehensive system of storage reservoirs large enough materially to affect the flow of the main river, one is forced to the conclusion that the cost would be too great."

Connecticut River — Main Stream

The Connecticut Hydrology Project, sponsored by the State Planning Board, has confined itself to a study of the hydrology of the tributaries of the Connecticut River: namely, the Deerfield, Westfield, Millers, and Chicopee. The problems of the Connecticut River are interstate or regional in character, and should be studied by a regional organization. Flood-control problems of the entire river valley are being studied by the United States Army Engineers.

Deerfield River Valley

The Deerfield River, the second largest tributary of the Connecticut in Massachusetts, has a total drainage area of 665 square miles, of which 348 lie in Massachusetts. The stream rises in central Vermont, flows southerly into Massachusetts, and then turns sharply to the east and empties into the Connecticut. The length of the river in Massachusetts is about forty miles. The shape of the basin is long and narrow. The topography is rough and very steep and there is considerable fall. There are several large power developments along the stream. The basin has a few lakes but only a small amount of actual storage capacity. Much of the basin is wooded and only a small portion is devoted to agriculture. Although annual precipitation has averaged 44 inches, the runoff is high. The principal cities in the area are Greenfield, Deerfield, Shelburne, and Colrain.

Water Supply. Problems of water supply in the basin are relatively simple. The towns in the watershed are comparatively small, and their water-supply problems are not complex.

Sewage Disposal. Problems of sewage disposal are likewise relatively simple, for the river is not highly industrialized, and the largest single city is Greenfield, which treats its sewage by dilution. Furthermore, the main stream of the river, owing to the series of large power plants on it, has a well-sustained flow.

Hydroelectric Power. The Deerfield River has several large public-utility power installations. It has potential undeveloped power of about 50,000 horsepower located at two sites now owned by private interests.

Flood Control. Total flood damage in the town of Greenfield in 1936 was approximately $1,112,000. This damage, however, was due more to the flood waters of the Green River than to those of the Deerfield, for the Deerfield is substantially controlled by the large storage reservoirs of the power interests.

Westfield River Valley

The Westfield River and its four main branches drain a watershed of approximately 515 square miles on the eastern slopes of the Berkshires, lying principally in Hampshire and Hampden counties. The lower reach of the river is sometimes known as the Agawam. The rough topography and steep slopes, with only a small amount of natural storage, produce a very rapid runoff, which more than once has caused disastrous floods. The principal municipalities on the Westfield River are Westfield, West Springfield, Huntington, and Chester. With the exception of a few industries concentrated principally in West Springfield, Westfield, Huntington, and one or two other small towns, the area is primarily agricultural.

Water Supply. A considerable preportion of the watershed has already been appropriated for municipal water supply by the cities of Springfield and Westfield.

Sewage Disposal. Pollution of the Westfield River consists of the domestic wastes discharged without treatment by the various towns in the watershed and industrial wastes discharged by manufacturing establishments located on the banks of the river. The greatest discharge of domestic waste occurs in the city of Westfield, where approximately two million gallons of untreated sewage enter the river daily. Sewerage systems in the towns of Agawam and West Springfield also discharge untreated domestic wastes. In the town of Huntington, seven outlets of the sewerage system and about forty private outlets discharge domestic waste directly into the river. The remaining sources of domestic wastes are private outlets in the towns of Becket, Chester, Plainfield, Chesterfield, and Russell, and those of twenty industrial establishments located on the banks of the river and its tributaries.

Industrial wastes discharged into the river and its tributaries consist chiefly of the effluent from paper-making operations. There are seven paper mills in the valley, contributing approximately seven million gallons of waste liquors per day. In addition to this there are two textile mills, one gas works, two plants engaged in the washing of emery and carborundum, and one factory doing electroplating work, discharging a total of approximately 200,000 gallons of waste liquors daily. There is need for more detailed study of the character of the wastes and for methods of treating both the domestic and the industrial discharges. These studies are now being carried forward.

Hydroelectric Power. The potential undeveloped horsepower on the Westfield River is somewhere between 30,000 and 35,000, based on installations developing the mean flow of the river.

Flood Control. Direct flood damage along the Westfield River in the 1936 flood was approximately $3,500,000 at West Springfield, $290,000 at Westfield, $140,000 at Cummington, and $80,000 at Huntington. Damage in the towns of West Springfield and Agawam, bordering on the Westfield River, was about $3,575,000, due probably to the backwaters of the Connecticut River. In the upstream area some storage capacity is available behind dams, but investigations so far have not disclosed opportunities of providing increased flood-storage capacities by increasing the height of these dams. Some relief from floods in the upper sections of the river may be obtained by clearing the channel. Present indications are that runoff is so rapid that rubble walls or riprap protection could be utilized along the stream to good advantage in a number of localities.

There are instances where projections into the stream caused some backing up of flood waters, but it will be necessary to determine whether greater benefits will result from the removal of these obstructions, to facilitate stream flow, or from their continuance, to detain flood waters.

The Westfield Little River is almost entirely controlled by the Springfield water-supply structures located at Borden Brook and Cobble Mountain.

Millers River Valley

Millers River is the smallest of the four main tributaries of the Connecticut River in the State of Massachusetts. The drainage area in Massachusetts is approximately 312 square miles, lying in the northwestern part of Franklin County and the northern part of Worcester County. The length along the main stream from the confluence with the Connecticut to the Massachusetts - New Hampshire line is approximately 39 miles. Its two main tributaries from the south are the Otter River, with a drainage area of 59 square miles, and the Eagleville, with a drainage area of 20.2 square miles.

The watershed is relatively flat, with considerable natural storage, together with favorable opportunities for increasing it. The land is largely unimproved, the soil being sandy and not particularly adapted to farming purposes. The principal cities of the basin are Gardner, Athol, Montague, Winchendon, Templeton, and Orange.

Water Supply. The population of the towns in this watershed is so small that the provision of water for municipal and manufacturing purposes is not a serious problem.

The principal city without a public water supply is Montague, which has a population of about 8000 persons.

Sewage Disposal. The towns of Athol, Erving, and Orange discharge untreated sewage. Millers Falls, Templeton, and Erving, and twenty-eight industrial establishments located on the banks of the river and its tributaries have private sewerage outlets discharging untreated domestic wastes.

Four paper mills in the basin contribute approximately 1,400,000 gallons of waste liquors per day. In addition to these, there are four factories doing metal plating, one textile mill, and one artificial-leather plant discharging approximately 392,000 gallons of waste liquors daily. Other important sources of industrial pollution are the following: in the town of Templeton, 172,000 gallons of waste water per day are discharged; in the town of Erving, 1,310,000 gallons; in the town of Athol, 310,000 gallons per day of waste liquors containing dye and salts, and liquors from the rinsing and washing of artificial leather; and in the town of Winchendon, 35,000 gallons per day of waste liquors from the dye settling tanks.

Flood Control. The total damage on the Millers River from the 1936 flood was approximately $2,500,000. The principal destruction occurred at Winchendon, with about $620,000 damage; Erving, with $250,000; Athol, with $480,000; and Orange, with $365,000.

The river basin affords opportunities for the construction of a number of small detention basins. Fortunately, the major part of the basin is fairly well wooded, which tends to reduce the runoff from both rain and melting snow. If this land is cleared in the future, the steep slopes should not be denuded because, without the protective vegetation, the resulting heavy runoff would produce floods even more destructive than have yet been experienced.

A large part of the damage in this area was due to the formation and break-up of ice jams. In some cases, large sheets of ice actually battered down sections of buildings near the river. Ice-breaking and ice-protection barriers are needed. There may be opportunities for several smaller detention basins to be located in the headwaters, and it may also be possible to supply increased channel capacity.

In the towns of Winchendon, Athol, Orange, and Erving there are dams constructed for power use, which form reservoirs that at present have little available flood-detention capacity. If it were possible to increase the height of these dams and to provide properly throttled outlets, it would appear possible to mitigate to a large extent future flood losses.

In studying and solving the problems of the river valley, co-operation with the State of New Hampshire, in which some of the headwaters rise, will be necessary.

Chicopee River Valley

The Chicopee River, having a total drainage area of 720 square miles, the Quaboag, 210, the Ware, 221, and the Swift, 216, drain a large section of central Massachusetts, comprising portions of Worcester, Franklin, Hampshire, and Hampden counties.

The principal municipalities in the valley are Chicopee, Palmer, Ware, Ludlow, Monson, and Warren. The watershed has a mean annual rainfall of about 44 inches. The river flow is well sustained throughout the year, because the basin contains much natural storage in its many lakes, ponds, and flat, swampy regions.

Water Supply. The largest municipality without a substantial public water supply is Palmer. In this watershed, extensive water-supply activities of the Metropolitan District Water Supply Commission are under way. A considerable amount of water for water-supply purposes is now diverted from the Ware River. The Quabbin Reservoir, controlling the Swift River, its east branch, middle branch, and west branch, will be completed shortly.

Hydroelectric Power. Water power on this river was developed at an early date, and by far the greater part is used directly by manufacturing industries. About 3000 undeveloped horsepower are found on the Quaboag.

Flood Control. The diversion of flow from the Ware River and the control of the Swift, when the Quabbin Reservoir is completed, will probably greatly minimize the damage from flood in this river. If coupled with some system of control on the Quaboag, these measures might entirely eliminate serious floods in the lower reaches of the Chicopee.

Recreation. No particular study of possible water recreation on this river has been made. Because of the large area controlled by the Metropolitan District Water Supply Commission for their new water supply, a large portion of the Swift River, including its east, middle, and west branches, will be under strict control and therefore probably eliminated from the possibility of active recreational use.

Blackstone River Valley

The Blackstone River drainage basin, located in the southeastern section of Worcester County, has a total area of about 475

MASSACHUSETTS STATE PLANNING BOARD

square miles, of which 311 square miles are in the State of Massachusetts. The river flows southeastward, and crosses the Massachusetts - Rhode Island line at Woonsocket, eventually emptying into Narragansett Bay. The length northward upstream from the State line to the principal headwaters in the towns of Holden and Paxton is about 43 miles. The principal cities in the valley are Worcester, Northbridge, Grafton, Uxbridge, Blackstone, and Millbury. The valley is highly industrialized.

Although the watershed is far from level, the region is well suited for farming, and a large portion of the farm land is now devoted to truck gardening and part-time farming. The headwater section is comparatively hilly, and is composed largely of agricultural land, with a lesser proportion of wooded area.

Below the city of Worcester the hilly condition continues, at some distance away from the river. The profile of the river, itself, is rather flat. Along it are some of the earliest developed waterpower sites in the United States, many of which have been abandoned. Owing to the age of the dams and ordinary low velocity of flow, it is very common to find reservoirs heavily silted, with the result that, although water levels and hydraulic heads have been maintained, storage capacities have been very materially reduced.

There is throughout the basin an annual rainfall varying from about 44 inches, in Worcester, to as much as 46 inches or 48 inches, in the lower portion of the valley.

Water Supply. A preliminary survey and design for a water-supply system for the town of Blackstone, which now has inadequate water supply for both domestic and fire-protection purposes, has been made by the Blackstone project. The town of Millville has no water supply for domestic purposes, and only a partial supply for fire protection. A preliminary design has been made for water-supply protection in this town. A preliminary design has also been made for the village of Manchaug, in the town of Sutton, which at present is using a water supply that has been condemned by the Department of Public Health, and which is inadequate both for domestic purposes and for fire protection. The project is now developing two water-supply-system designs for the Linhill district of the town of Auburn: one, a low-pressure system; and the other, a high-pressure system. The choice will depend upon which of the two systems in Worcester that city will sell water from.

Sewage Disposal. A detailed study of pollution and sewage disposal in the Blackstone River Valley has been made, and a report has been published by the Department of Public Health. The Blackstone River is in a polluted condition from its source to the Massachusetts - Rhode Island line, due to the extensive discharges of both industrial and domestic wastes. Some of the tributaries of the river, namely, Kettle Brook, Middle River, and Singletary Brook, are highly polluted. Millbrook Canal, which joins Middle River about two miles above the Worcester sewage-treatment plant, is highly polluted by industrial wastes, and during periods of rainfall this canal receives a considerable amount of domestic sewage from by-passes of Worcester's combined sewerage system. A considerable amount of domestic sewage is discharged into the Blackstone River and its tributaries, without treatment, from the towns of Millbury, Leicester, Auburn, Sutton, Grafton, Douglas, Uxbridge, Millville, and Blackstone.

Both the cities of Worcester and Northbridge have treatment plants which, although designed for domestic sewage, also care for a considerable amount of industrial waste. Both are well maintained, and, in the case of the Worcester plant, the discharge is well nitrified and the effluent is stable.

The project has made preliminary surveys and designs for sewerage systems and sewage-treatment plants for the following towns: Blackstone, Millville, Uxbridge, and Douglas, and for the village of Manchaug in Sutton. At the present time, surveys are being made for the towns of Millbury, Leicester, Auburn, Grafton, and Shrewsbury. Plans and estimates are on file in the engineering division of the Department of Public Health and in the office of the WPA.

A possible solution to the problem of eliminating pollution from the Blackstone River is that of collecting all the domestic wastes by an intercepting sewer, and treating them before discharging them into the river. In many cases it might be possible to treat certain industrial wastes along with the domestic sewage. However, many of the industrial plants would have to pre-treat their wastes in order that they might not be injurious to the natural bacterial action of decomposition.

Hydroelectric Power. Most of the potential hydroelectric power on the Blackstone River has already been developed, and the only possible increases in power, small at best, would be obtained by improvement of existing facilities. The size of the mills is such that in most cases the demand for power is greater than the capacity of the stream.

Flood Control. Lake Quinsigamond has storage capacity for excessive runoff in the twenty-six square miles of territory tributary to it. Hence this portion of the basin is least in need of attention from the flood-control standpoint.

In the headwaters of the town of Leicester and adjacent area, the hilly country, with very little retention of accumulated snow, has been the cause of extensive washouts and other damages usually associated with heavy rainfall. It should be noted, however, that flood damage per se (due directly to an increase in water level above normal stream flow) is not large, and that the principal problem is that of providing better drainage facilities.

Through the city of Worcester, encroachments on the natural course of the stream and the construction of various culverts and bridges have so lessened the capacity for flood flows that excessive runoff, such as was experienced in the 1936 flood, has resulted in the inundation of comparatively large areas.

Below Worcester, the heavily silted reservoirs should be studied to determine whether the demolition of the dams and the clearing of the waterway are required. . Toward the southeast end of the valley, the possibility of increasing the height of dams to provide additional flood detention capacity is being studied, but, as it appears likely that any considerable increase of water elevation might necessitate reconstruction of highways, sewage disposal works, or other utilities in which an appreciable investment has already been made, definite recommendations cannot be offered until more engineering study has been applied to all the elements of the problem.

Studies are being carried on at present to determine how many relatively small detention basins could be developed in the headwaters of the Blackstone and its tributaries. It appears that nowhere will there be space available for a basin of even 500-acre-foot capacity, but it may be possible to provide a large number of sites in which flood waters can be detained and then released in such a manner that the peak flows from all of them would not result at the same time.

This river is interstate in character, and flows through part of the State of Rhode Island. The use of corrective measures in Massachusetts, such as clearing the channel and removing obstructions, might, if sufficiently extensive, appreciably increase the volume and velocity of the river through Rhode Island. Cooperation between the two States is obviously required.

Recreation. There is little opportunity for recreational uses in the highly industrialized valley of the Blackstone River, although the demand for recreational facilities is extensive. On one or

MASSACHUSETTS STATE PLANNING BOARD

two of the tributaries and smaller lakes, several minor recreational developments might be possible, but no extensive program can be developed on the main stream.

Integration. There seems to be little possibility of coordinating flood control proposals with water supply or sewage disposal, owing to the fact that the primary problem is pollution and sewage disposal, and that flood control in the valley, although desirable in some respects, will be difficult of attainment. Certainly the problem will not be solved by the use of large storage reservoirs whose summer flow would increase the dilution of sewage.

Merrimack River Valley

The Merrimack, the second largest river passing through Massachusetts, is formed at Franklin, N.H., by union of the Pemigewassett and Winnepesaukee. From thence it pursues its southerly course for about 60 miles, passing into Massachusetts. As it approaches the city of Lowell, it makes a sharp turn to the east, and then flows north by northeast for 40 miles, entering the Atlantic Ocean at Newburyport. Its length in Massachusetts is 47 1/2 miles. The total drainage area is about 5000 square miles, of which about 1200 square miles are in Massachusetts. Its main tributaries in Massachusetts are the Powow, with a drainage area of 60 square miles; the Shawsheen, 75 square miles; the Concord, 402 square miles; and the Nashua, 531 square miles. The mouth of the Nashua is in New Hampshire, but the greater part of its watershed is in Massachusetts.

The principal cities in the basin in Massachusetts are Lowell, Lawrence, Haverhill, and Newburyport, all having very important manufacturing industries.

The Merrimack Valley has not been studied in detail by either the State Planning Board or the Department of Public Health, owing to the fact that a detailed study of sanitary conditions was made several years ago by the Department of Public Health, and that the United States Army Engineers are studying flood control throughout the entire valley, both in Massachusetts and in New Hampshire. The Department of Public Health recommended that a sanitary intercepting sewer be built along the lower reaches of the river from Lowell to Lawrence through Haverhill, thus eliminating the heavy pollution from these three cities.

Flood Control. The enormous damages inflicted by the 1936 flood demonstrate that the problem of flood control is paramount. The method of prevention is primarily one of detention basins located in the headwaters, nearly all of which, except that of the Nashua, lie in New Hampshire. Again, as in the case of the Connecticut, this is a problem demanding interstate coöperation.

The problem of undeveloped power on the river is closely associated with flood-control measures, for nearly all of the potential power is developed. The amount of power might be increased by redevelopments and by increased flow from detention basins.

Massachusetts Bay River Valleys

The area referred to generally as Massachusetts Bay Basin was originally set up to be studied by the Essex, Middlesex-Norfolk and Bristol-Plymouth Projects. This area is composed of the several small river basins draining into Massachusetts Bay on the east, and also includes Cape Cod. It has a total area of about 2000 square miles. Streams included are the Parker, Ipswich, Mystic, Charles, Neponset, Weymouth Fore, and Weymouth Back Rivers. The entire area is fairly flat, with a few undulating hills ranging in elevation from 100 to 200 feet, and with the area flattening out toward the Cape. The area around Massachusetts Bay is the highly industrialized Metropolitan Boston. Around the outskirts of the metropolitan area much of the fertile land is used for part-time farming and the cultivation of food products for local consumption. The average annual rainfall is about 42 inches.

Water Supply. Problems of water supply are principally those of extending existing works or reinforcing present distribution works, and providing additional storage facilities. The supplies are adequate and the development of new sources is not a serious problem. The Boston Metropolitan District Commission water supply, which consists of the Cochituate, Wachusett, Sudbury, and new Quabbin developments, appears to be adequate to meet the demands of the metropolitan district for a long time to come. Water power in the region is almost negligible, since the hydraulic gradients of the rivers are very slight and the river flows are not great.

Sewage Disposal. Metropolitan Boston, including the area tributary to Boston Harbor and Quincy Bay, and the Mystic, Charles, and Neponset Rivers, is served by a system of sewers in the city of Boston and by the facilities of the Metropolitan District Water Supply Commission. Some of the sewers are old and inadequate, and enlarged or additional sewers must be installed to relieve the load now placed on the existing systems. The method of disposal is by outfall into the waters of the harbor, without treatment, except screening and natural dilution. This system is not entirely

satisfactory, often causing annoyance and unsightliness along the beaches near the outfalls. Since the Boston Harbor and its beaches are so vital a recreational asset to the two million people living in the district, this problem is of paramount importance. Some of the suburban areas, towns of considerable size, are without sewerage systems, and pollute the rivers draining into the ocean. Conditions like these could be solved by the establishments of several sanitary districts similar to the Salem, Peabody, Beverly, and Danvers district.

Recreation. The problem of recreational development of the several lakes and streams in the area along the coast is almost entirely a problem of eliminating pollution. This does not mean that all the beaches are contaminated so that they cannot be used for swimming, but, in many instances, the general aspect and appearance of the water would be considerably improved by more careful treatment of wastes.

POWER

Courtesy of TECHNOLOGY REVIEW.
Photographed by H. Armstrong Roberts, Philadelphia

CHAPTER IV

P O W E R

Summary Outline

I. Objectives

II. Scope of Power Studies
    A. Production and Transmission
    B. Consumption
    C. Costs

III. Production and Transmission
    A. General
    B. Potential Power

IV. Consumption
    A. General
    B. Present Demand
    C. Rural Electrification
    D. Future Utilization

V. Costs
    A. Special-Cost Analysis
    B. Cost Differentials

VI. Sources of Information

MASSACHUSETTS STATE PLANNING BOARD

POWER

Objectives

The ultimate objective of a State power plan is the development and coordination of all existing and potential economic sources of power to serve most effectively both present and anticipated future needs and to produce the most desirable social results.

Because it is possible, even today, to transmit power economically for long distances, the problem of power transcends State lines and becomes one which can be solved only in terms of a larger region. Under favorable conditions, large hydroelectric plants, with substantial and dependable supplies of water, can transmit power for two hundred miles and still compete successfully with modern steam plants.

This means that the region within which Massachusetts may find potential power extends at least two hundred miles beyond the State boundaries. Furthermore, with improvements in methods of transmission, which are now apparently possible, line losses may be so reduced that the transportation of power for much greater distances may become economically feasible. If this is accomplished, the power situation in Massachusetts and elsewhere may be greatly changed. For example, vast new sources of hydroelectric power, now too far removed from demand centers for economical development, may be opened up and the carboelectric power which is now dominant almost everywhere along the Atlantic seaboard might meet serious competition.

Scope of Power Studies

The power studies undertaken by the State Planning Board are of three principal types, as follows:

1. Production and Transmission

The study of production and transmission involves the location, capacity, and output of both carboelectric and hydroelectric plants in Massachusetts and in the larger region from which the State may draw power. It also includes a study of local, State, and regional transmission lines.

MASSACHUSETTS STATE PLANNING BOARD

2. Consumption

Consumption requires a study of both the present and probable future use of power.

Table 2

LOCATION OF ELECTRIC GENERATING PLANTS IN MASSACHUSETTS

NO.*	LOCATION	OWNERSHIP	TYPE	INSTALLED CAPACITY (KW)
1.	Turners Falls	Turners Falls Pr.&Elec. Co.	Hydro	50,000
2.	Granville	City of Springfield	"	23,000
3.	Turners Falls	Turners Falls Pr. & Elec.Co.	"	5,000
4.	Indian Orchard	United Elec. Lt. Co.	"	4,900
5.	Buckland	Western Mass. Elec. Co.	"	4,000
6.	Chicopee	The Quinnebtuk Co.	"	2,100
7.	Indian Orchard	" " "	"	700
8.	Ipswich	Municipal	Diesel	1,073
9.	Hudson	"	"	2,500
10.	Springfield	United Elec. Lt. Co.	Steam	35,000
11.	Chicopee	Turners Falls Pr. & Elec. Co.	"	25,000
12.	Pittsfield	Pittsfield Elec. Co.	"	2,000
13.	Lawrence	Lawrence Gas & Elec. Co.	Hydro-steam	14,300
14.	Conway	New England Power Co.	Hydro	7,000
15.	Buckland	" " " "	"	6,000
16.	Buckland	" " " "	"	6,000
17.	Florida	" " " "	"	15,000
18.	Rowe	" " " "	"	6,000
19.	Beverly	Beverly Gas & Elec. Co.	Steam	1,500
20.	Fall River	Fall River Elec. Lt. Co.	"	14,300
21.	Gloucester	Gloucester Elec. Co.	"	3,600
22.	Haverhill	Haverhill Elec. Co.	"	13,100
23.	Newburyport	" " "	"	7,000
24.	Weymouth	E.E.I. Co. of Boston	"	140,000
25.	Lowell	The Lowell Elec. Lt. Corp.	"	32,700
26.	Malden	Malden Elec. Co.		2,250
27.	Uxbridge	New England Power Co.		17,900
28.	Salem	Salem Elec. Ltg. Co.		27,500
29.	Revere	Suburban Gas & Elec. Co.		1,000
30.	Webster	Webster & Southbridge Gas & Elec.		7,200
31.	Worcester	The Worcester Elec. Lt. Co.	"	57,000

*The numbers on this table refer to the accompanying Map 75-1, entitled, "Transmission Lines and Power Plants in Massachusetts".

MASSACHUSETTS STATE PLANNING BOARD

Table 2 - Continued

NO.	LOCATION	OWNERSHIP	TYPE	INSTALLED CAPACITY(KW)
32.	Amesbury	Amesbury Elec. Lt. Co.	Hydro	800
33.	Amesbury	" " " "	"	360
34.	Clinton	Metropolitan Water Supply	"	3,200
35.	Wendell	Athol Gas & Elec. Co.	..	1,100
36.	Erving	" " " "	"	400
37.	Palmer	Central Mass. Elec. Co.	"	900
38.	Rockdale	So. Berkshire Pr. & Elec. Co.	"	400
39.	W.Stockbridge	" " " " "	"	30
40.	Sudbury Dam	Metropolitan Water Supply	"	1,000
41.	Winchendon	Winchendon Elec.Lt. & Pr.Co.	"	250
42.	East Weymouth	Weymouth Lt. & Pr. Co.	"	200
43.	Taunton	Municipal	Steam	15,200
44.	Middleboro	Municipal	Hydro	280
45.	Somerset	Montaup Elec. Co.	Steam	70,800
46.	New Bedford	New Bedford Gas & Elec. Co.	"	92,000
47.	East Bridgewater	E.E.I. Co. of Brockton	"	18,960
48.	Braintree	Municipal	..	8,000
49.	Fitchburg	Fitchburg Gas & Lt. Co.	"	16,000
50.	Provincetown	Provincetown Lt. & Pr. Co.	Diesel	1,015
51.	Nantucket	Nantucket Gas & Elec. Co.	Steam	1,600
52.	Marthas Vineyard	Cape & Vineyard Elec. Co.	Diesel	1,200
53.	Boston	E.E.I. Co. of Boston	Steam	198,000
54.	Lynn	Lynn Gas & Elec. Co.	"	40,000
55.	Cambridge	Cambridge Elec. Co.	"	23,950
56.	Stockbridge	Monument Mills	Hydro	500
57.	Great Barrington	" "	Steam	300
58.	Great Barrington	So.Berkshire Pr.& Elec.Co.	Hydro	500
59.	Holyoke	Holyoke Water Pr. Co.	Hydro-steam	24,000
60.	Reading	Reading Municipal Lt.Dept.	Steam	1,200
61.	Holyoke	City of Holyoke G.&E.Dept.	Hydro	19,000
62.	Amesbury	Amesbury Light Co.		150

(Last two plants not shown on map)

3. Cost

This factor of power involves an analysis of the typical cost of carboelectric and hydroelectric production, of transmission, and

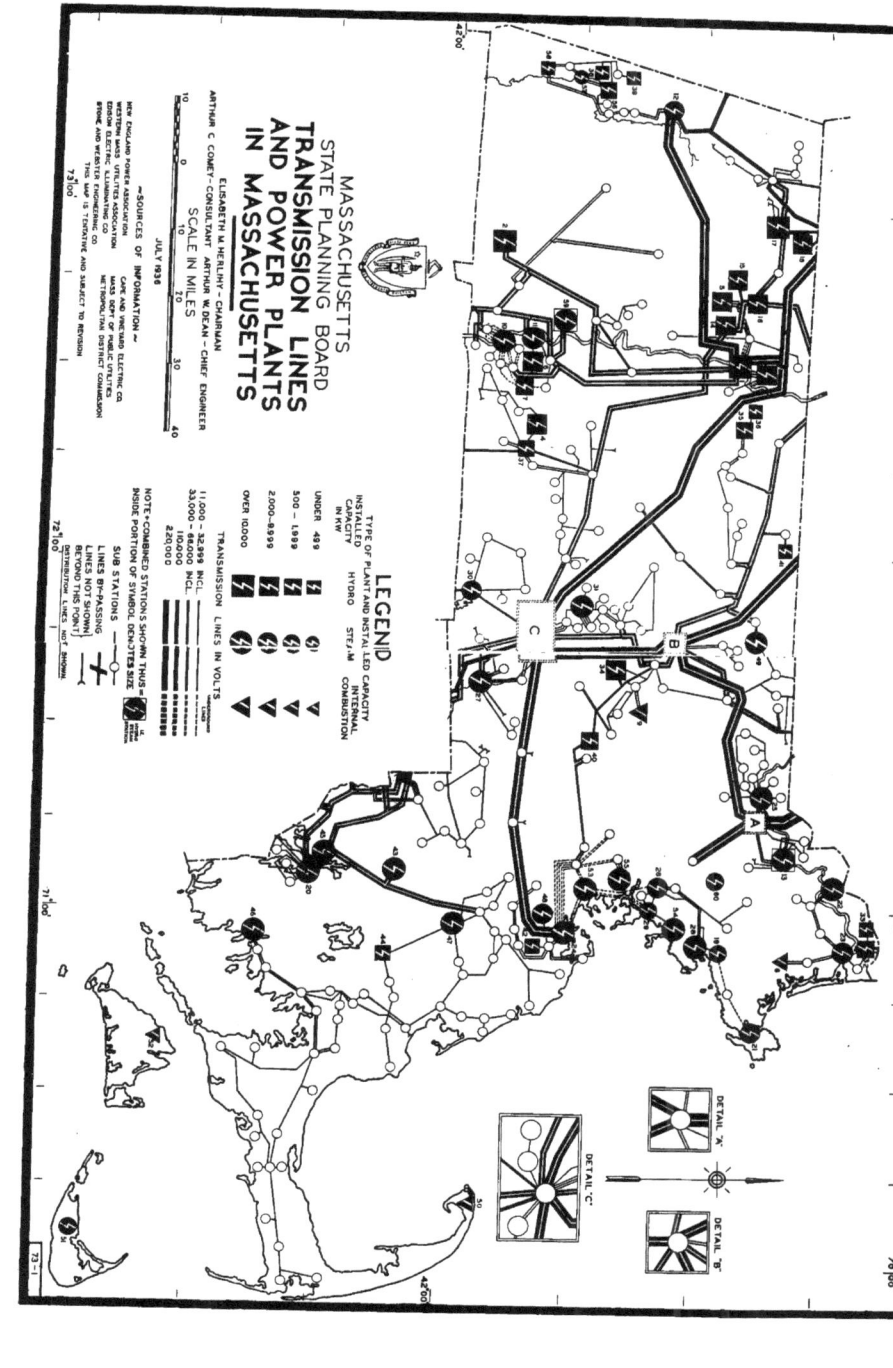

of distribution. Each of these different aspects affects the others and has important repercussions upon industry, population distribution, transportation, and countless other economic and social elements.

Production and Transmission

General

In order to indicate trends or to form conclusions about power production and usage, existing conditions must be accurately depicted. This is done principally through the medium of maps and graphs, a summary of the data being as follows:

Central-station generators produced during 1935 about 2,884,173,000 kilowatt hours, of which 338,000,000 kilowatt hours were exported. This power was produced from about 60 central-station generating plants, having a combined installed capacity of 1,075,923 kilowatts.

Anything more than a brief summary of the facts contained in the following maps and graphs would be superfluous. We may note, however, from the map of transmission lines and generating stations, that Massachusetts is well served by power facilities, the concentration of which may be noted in the industrial areas. The preponderance of steam plants along the eastern portion of the State and of hydro plants in the western part are noteworthy. The use of internal-combustion generator stations is limited as yet, there being only four in the State, these serving more or less isolated communities.

In addition to its own plants, Massachusetts has abundant power facilities in out-of-state areas indicated on the map of New England showing generating stations and transmission lines (Map 83-1). This map shows that the area comprising the New England states is one which may be called a power zone, within which the concentration of power facilities makes it, in a way, self-sufficient, at least at the present time. Owing to local regulations, however, the State of Maine does not import or export power to and from the rest of New England.

MASSACHUSETTS STATE PLANNING BOARD

Table 3*

INSTALLED CAPACITIES OF CENTRAL-
STATION GENERATORS IN MASSACHUSETTS
(KW—1926 to 1935, Inclusive)

YEAR	HYDRO	STEAM	INTERNAL COMBUSTION	TOTAL
1926	152,036	807,639	**	959,675
1927	151,944	946,543	**	1,098,487
1928	154,201	917,468	2840	1,074,509
1929	145,760	973,485	3065	1,122,310
1930	153,160	978,185	3065	1,134,410
1931	143,085	976,120	3659	1,122,864
1932	173,100	974,850	3500	1,151,450
1933	175,700	975,850	3500	1,155,050
1934	169,675	951,280	5009	1,125,964
1935	171,070	899,060	5793	1,075,923

*Sources of Information: Edison Electric Institute; Massachusetts Department of Public Utilities.
**Included in Steam Figures prior to 1928.

A comparison of the installed central-station generating capacities in New England is given on the following table:

Table 4

INSTALLED CENTRAL-STATION GENERATING CAPACITIES IN NEW ENGLAND

STATE	INSTALLED CAPACITIES			
	Steam	Hydro	Internal Comb.	Total
Maine	50,480	205,037	1124	256,641
New Hampshire	60,871	204,255	140	265,266
Vermont	12,360	177,478	-	189,838
Massachusetts	899,060	171,070	5793	1,075,923
Rhode Island	201,000	1,750	-	202,750
Connecticut	441,749	94,470		536,219
New England Total	1,665,520	854,060	7057	2,526,637

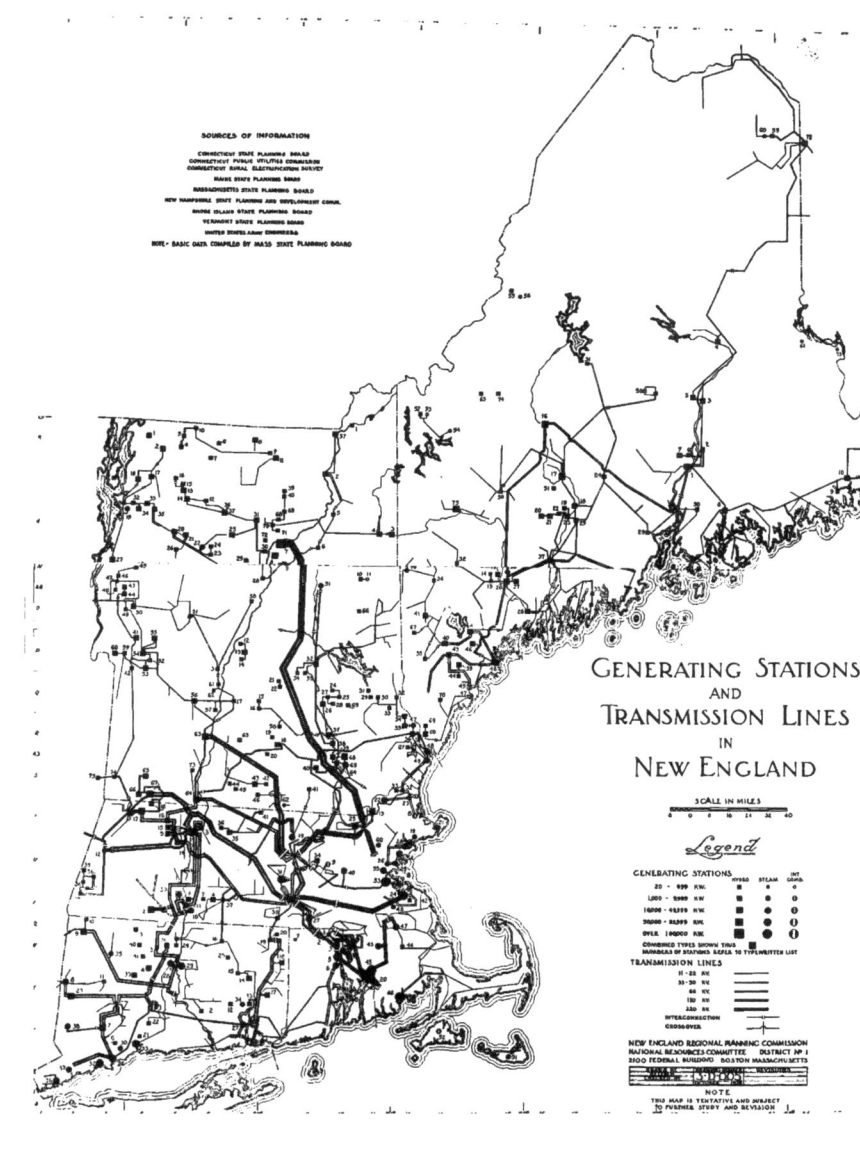

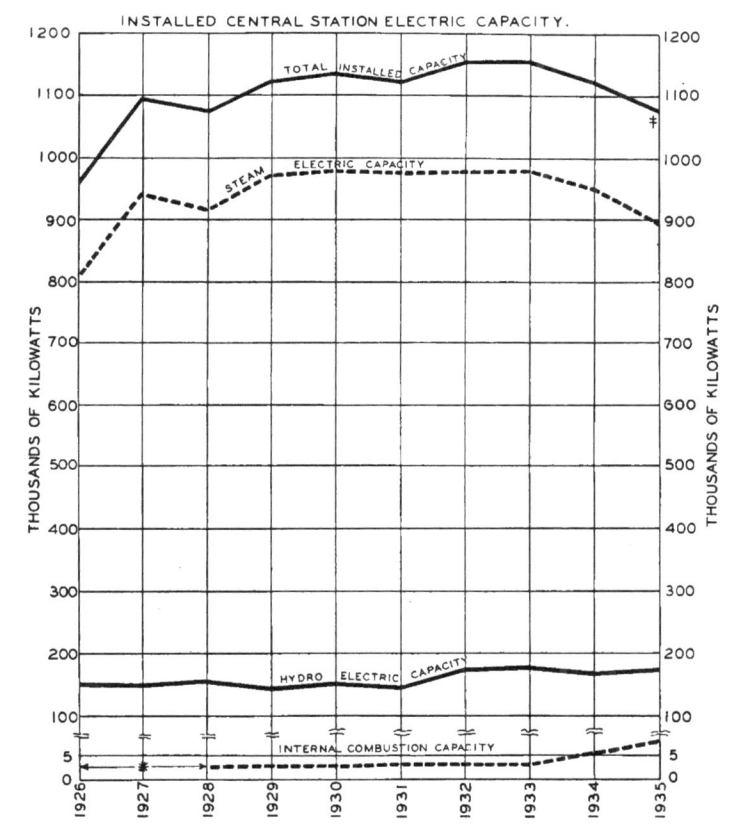

INSTALLED CAPACITY OF CENTRAL STATION ELECTRIC GENERATORS IN MASS.

NOTE FIGURES ARE SHOWN AS OF DEC. 31 OF YEARS INDICATED.
* INTERNAL COMBUSTION INCLUDED IN STEAM FIGURES PRIOR TO 1928.
‡ DROP IN 1935 DUE TO A FEW MFG. PLANTS NOT NOW DEFINED AS CENTRAL STATION GENERATORS.
SOURCES OF INFORMATION – EDISON ELECTRIC INSTITUTE BULLETINS

**MASSACHUSETTS
STATE PLANNING BOARD**

OCTOBER 1936

53-C6

MASSACHUSETTS STATE PLANNING BOARD

Potential Power

On the assumption that it is now economically feasible to transmit power for at least two hundred miles, and that in the near future it may be transported for even greater distances, an attempt has been made to show the principal sources of undeveloped water power within a radius of five hundred miles of Boston. This study is purely hypothetical insofar as it disregards the factor of adverse legislation prohibiting interstate transfer of power, or the existence of treaties governing apportionment of power between the United States and Canada.

For this purpose, two maps have been prepared: one for the State of Massachusetts, showing the principal sources of developed and potential water power (Map 73-5), and another for the region, showing the location of large blocks of undeveloped power outside of Massachusetts (Map 83-2). A summary of data shown on these maps is given in the following table:

Table 5

POTENTIAL HYDROELECTRIC POWER

(Horsepower 60 Per Cent of the Time)

MILEAGE FROM BOSTON	UNDEVELOPED HYDRO POWER*	
	Within Area	Cumulative
0-100 Miles	230,500	230,500
100-200 "	863,900	1,094,400
200-300 "	5,411,300	6,505,700
300-400 "	1,638,900	8,144,600
400-500 "	257,300	8,401,900
TOTAL	8,401,900	8,401,900

*These figures are approximate, and subject to change after further field surveys.

MASSACHUSETTS STATE PLANNING BOARD

Table 6

ELECTRIC COMPANIES OPERATING IN MASSACHUSETTS, AND THE AREAS THEY SERVE

NEW ENGLAND POWER ASSOCIATION

*1. ATTLEBORO STEAM & ELECTRIC CO.
    Attleboro   Rehoboth
    Seekonk

2. DEERFIELD RIVER ELECTRIC CO.
    Florida   Heath
    Rowe

3. FALL RIVER ELECTRIC LIGHT CO.
    Dighton   Somerset
    Fall River   Swansea
    Westport (part)

4. GARDNER ELECTRIC LIGHT CO.
    Athol (part)   Oakham
    Barre   Petersham(part)
    Dana   Phillipston
    Gardner   Royalston
    Hubbardston   Rutland
    New Braintree   Shutesbury
    New Salem   Warwick(part)
    Westminster

5. BEVERLY GAS & ELECTRIC CO.
    Beverly   Topsfield
    Hamilton   Wenham

6. GLOUCESTER ELECTRIC CO.
    Essex   Gloucester
    Rockport

7. SALEM ELECTRIC LIGHTING CO.
    Salem

8. LAWRENCE GAS & ELECTRIC CO.
    Andover   Lawrence
    Boxford   Methuen
    North Andover

9. LOWELL ELECTRIC LIGHT CORP.
    Billerica   Lowell
    Chelmsford   Tewksbury
    Dracut   Tyngsboro (part)
    Westford

10. QUINCY ELECTRIC LIGHT & POWER CO.
    Quincy

11. WEBSTER & SOUTHBRIDGE GAS & ELECTRIC CO.
    Brimfield(part)   Oxford
    Charlton   Southbridge
    Dudley   Sturbridge
    Holland   Wales
    Webster

12. WORCESTER ELECTRIC LIGHT CO.
    Leicester   Worcester

13. HAVERHILL ELECTRIC CO.
    Haverhill   Newburyport
    Newbury   West Newbury

14. MALDEN ELECTRIC CO.
    Everett   Medford
    Malden   Melrose

15. SUBURBAN GAS & ELECTRIC CO.
    Revere   Winthrop

MASSACHUSETTS UTILITIES ASSOCIATES

16. AMESBURY ELECTRIC CO.
    Amesbury   Salisbury

17. ATHOL GAS & ELECTRIC CO.
    Athol(part)   Petersham(part)
    Erving(part)   Warwick (part)
    Orange   Wendell

*The numbers on this table refer to the accompanying Map 73-4, entitled, "Areas Served by Operating Power Companies in Massachusetts".

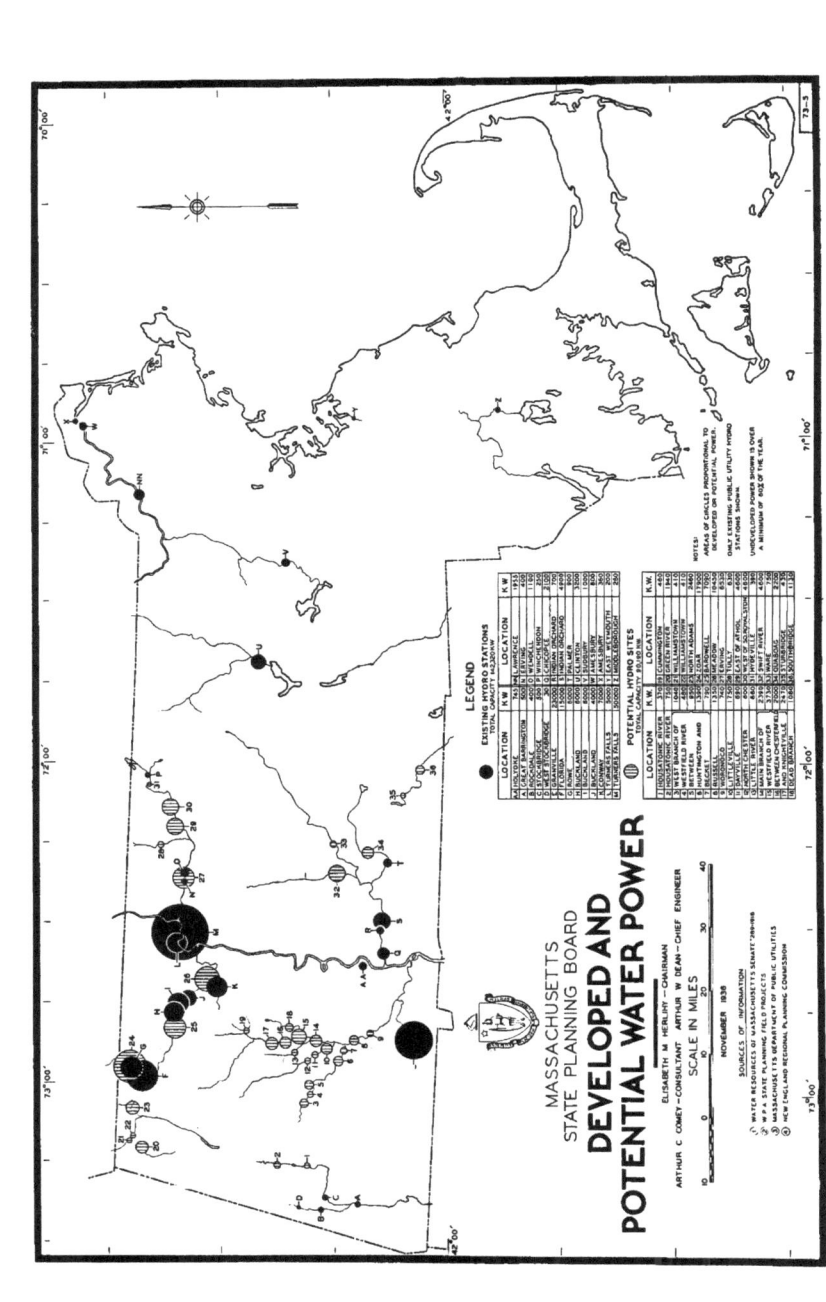

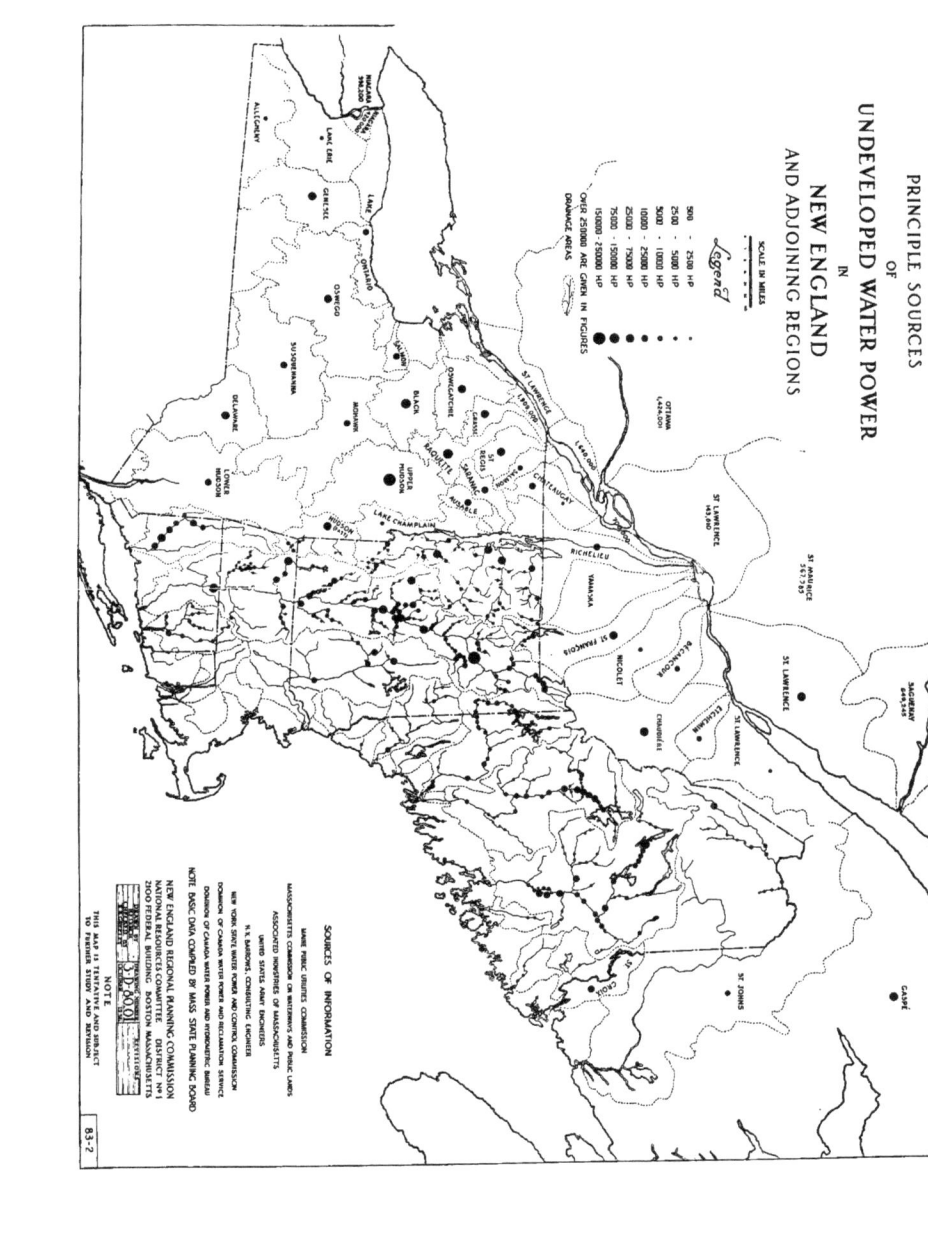

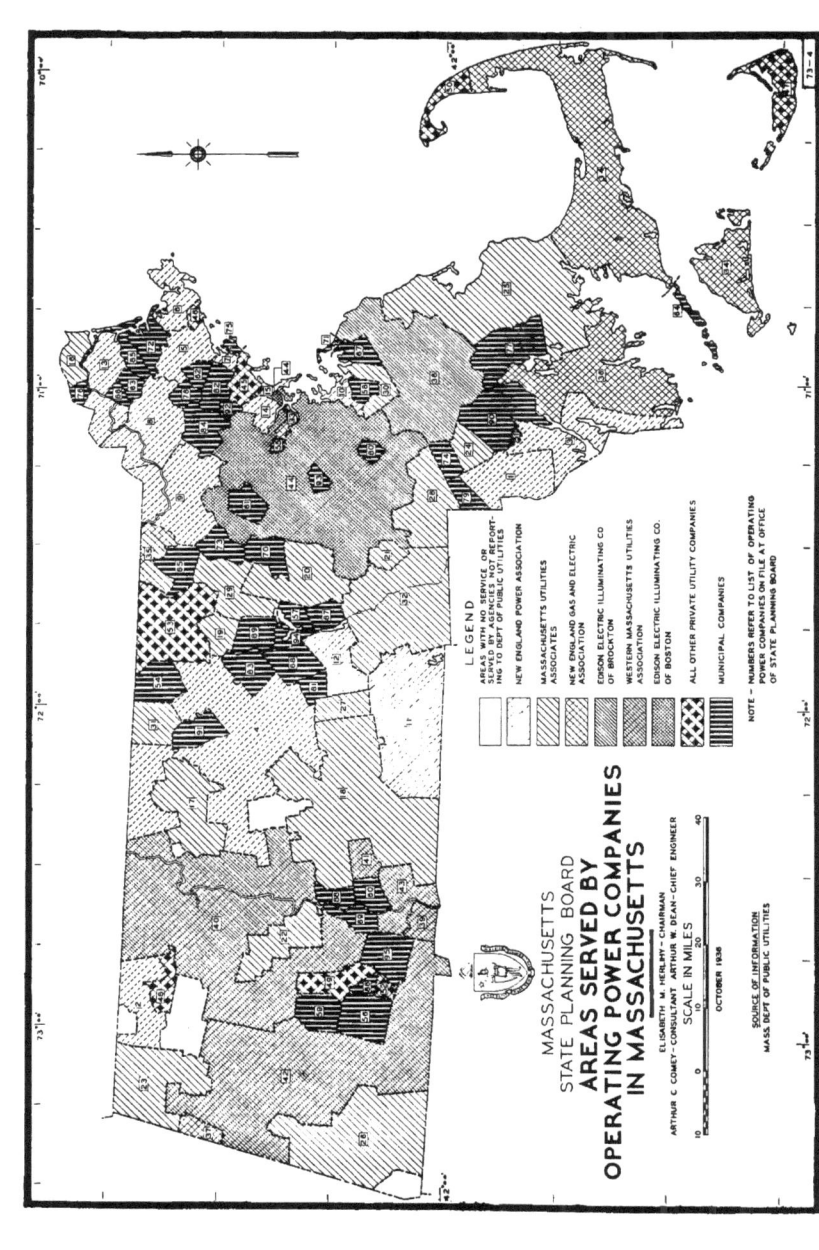

Table 6 - Continued

MASSACHUSETTS UTILITIES ASSOCIATES - CONTINUED

18. CENTRAL MASSACHUSETTS ELEC-
    TRIC CO.
    Belchertown   Hardwick
    Brimfield(part) Ludlow(part)
    Brookfield   Monson
    E.Brookfield   N.Brookfield
    E.Longmeadow   Palmer
    Enfield   Ware
    Granby   Warren
    Hampden   W.Brookfield
    Wilbraham
19. LEOMINSTER ELECTRIC LIGHT &
    POWER CO.
    Leominster
20. MARLBOROUGH ELECTRIC CO.
    Berlin   Northborough
    Bolton   Southborough
    Marlborough   Westborough
21. MILFORD ELECTRIC LIGHT &
    POWER CO.
    Hopedale   Milford
22. NORTHAMPTON ELECTRIC LIGHT-
    ING CO.
    Goshen   Northampton
    Williamsburg
23. NORTHERN BERKSHIRE GAS CO.
    Adams   Hancock(part)
    Cheshire(part) No. Adams
    Clarksburg   Williamstown
24. NORTON POWER & ELECTRIC CO.
    Norton
25. PLYMOUTH COUNTY ELECTRIC CO.
    Bourne(part)   Marion
    Carver   Marshfield
    Duxbury   Pembroke(part)
    Kingston   Plymouth

25. PLYMOUTH COUNTY ELECTRIC CO.
    (cont.)
    Plympton   Scituate(part)
    Rochester   Wareham
26. SOUTHERN BERKSHIRE POWER &
    ELECTRIC CO.
    Alford   Monterey
    Egremont   New Marlboro
    Gt.Barrington Sheffield
    Lenox (part)   Stockbridge
    W. Stockbridge
27. SPENCER GAS CO., THE
    Spencer
28. UNION LIGHT & POWER CO.
    Bellingham(part) Franklin
    Foxborough   Plainville
    Wrentham
29. WACHUSETT ELECTRIC CO.
    Ayer   Harvard
    Clinton   Lancaster
30. WEYMOUTH LIGHT & POWER CO.
    Holbrook   Randolph
    Weymouth
31. WINCHENDON ELECTRIC LIGHT &
    POWER CO.
    Winchendon
32. WORCESTER SUBURBAN ELECTRIC
    CO.
    Auburn   Millbury
    Blackstone   Millville
    Douglas   Northbridge
    Grafton   Sutton
    Mendon   Upton
    Uxbridge

NEW ENGLAND GAS & ELECTRIC ASSOCIATION

33. CAMBRIDGE ELECTRIC LIGHT CO.
    Cambridge
34. CAPE & VINEYARD ELECTRIC CO.
    Barnstable   Brewster
    Bourne (part) Chatham

34. CAPE & VINEYARD ELECTRIC CO.
    (cont.)
    Chilmark   Edgartown
    Dennis   Falmouth
    Eastham   Gay Head

MASSACHUSETTS STATE PLANNING BOARD

Table 6 - Continued

NEW ENGLAND GAS & ELECTRIC ASSOCIATION - CONTINUED

34. **CAPE & VINEYARD ELECTRIC CO.** (cont.)
    Harwich   Sandwich
    Mashpee   Tisbury
    Oak Bluffs   Wellfleet
    Orleans   W. Tisbury
    Yarmouth

35. **MIDDLESEX COUNTY ELECTRIC CO.**
    Dunstable   Pepperell (part)
    Tyngsboro (part)

36. **NEW BEDFORD GAS & EDISON LIGHT CO.**
    Acushnet   Freetown
    Berkley   Lakeville
    Dartmouth   Mattapoisett
    Fairhaven   New Bedford
    Westport (part)

37. **WESTERN HANCOCK ELECTRIC CO.**
    Hancock (part)

STONE & WEBSTER

38. **EDISON ELECTRIC ILLUMINATING CO. OF BROCKTON**
    Abington   Hanover
    Avon   Hanson
    Brockton   Norwell
    Bridgewater   Pembroke (part)
    Cohasset   Rockland
    E. Bridgewater   Scituate
    Easton   Stoughton
    Halifax   W. Bridgewater
    Whitman

WESTERN MASSACHUSETTS COMPANIES

39. **AGAWAM ELECTRIC CO., THE**
    Agawam

40. **WESTERN MASSACHUSETTS ELECTRIC CO.**
    Amherst   Greenfield
    Ashfield   Hadley
    Bernardston   Hatfield
    Buckland   Leverett
    Chesterfield   Leyden
    Colrain   Montague
    Conway   Northfield
    Cummington   Pelham
    Deerfield   Plainfield
    Easthampton   Shelburne
    Erving (part)   Southampton
    Gill   Sunderland

40. **WESTERN MASSACHUSETTS ELECTRIC CO.** (cont.)
    Westhampton   Whately
                    Worthington

41. **LUDLOW ELECTRIC LIGHT CO.**
    Ludlow (part)

42. **PITTSFIELD ELECTRIC CO.**
    Becket   Middlefield
    Cheshire (part)   New Ashford
    Dalton   Otis
    Granville   Pittsfield
    Hancock (part)   Peru
    Hinsdale   Richmond
    Lanesboro   Sandisfield
    Lee   Southwick
    Lenox (part)   Tolland
    Tyringham

MASSACHUSETTS STATE PLANNING BOARD

Table 6 - Continued

WESTERN MASSACHUSETTS COMPANIES - CONTINUED

42. **PITTSFIELD ELECTRIC CO.**
    (cont.)
    Washington   Windsor

43. **UNITED ELECTRIC LIGHT CO.**
    Longmeadow   Springfield
    W. Springfield

MISCELLANEOUS

44. **EDISON ELECTRIC ILLUMINATING CO. OF BOSTON, THE**

Acton	Medway
Arlington	Millis
Ashland	Milton
Bedford	Natick
Bellingham(part)	Needham
Boston	Newton
Brookline	Norfolk
Burlington	Sharon
Canton	Sherborn
Carlisle	Somerville
Chelsea	Stoneham
Dedham	Sudbury
Dover	Walpole
Framingham	Waltham
Holliston	Watertown
Hopkinton	Wayland
Lexington	Weston
Lincoln	Westwood
Maynard	Winchester
Medfield	Woburn

45. **LYNN GAS & ELECTRIC CO.**
    Lynn   Saugus
    Nahant   Swampscott

46. **MANCHESTER ELECTRIC CO.**
    Manchester

47. **NANTUCKET GAS & ELECTRIC CO.**
    Nantucket

48. **CHARLEMONT ELECTRIC LIGHT & POWER CO.**
    Charlemont

49. **HUNTINGTON ELECTRIC LIGHT CO.**
    Huntington   Montgomery

50. **PROVINCETOWN LIGHT & POWER CO.**
    Provincetown   Truro

51. **MOUNT HOPE FINISHING CO.**
    Dighton (part)

52. **STRATHMORE PAPER CO.**
    Worcnoco, Town of Russell
    (part)

53. **FITCHBURG GAS & ELECTRIC CO.**
    Ashby   Pepperell (part)
    Fitchburg   Shirley
    Lunenburg   Townsend

MUNICIPAL LIGHTING PLANTS

54. Ashburnham
55. Belmont
56. Blandford
57. Boylston
58. Braintree
59. Chester
60. Chicopee
61. Concord
62. Danvers
63. Georgetown
64. Gosnold
    (Serves Gosnold Islands)
65. Groton
66. Groveland
67. Hingham
68. Holden
69. Holyoke
70. Hudson
    (Serves Stow also)
71. Hull
72. Ipswich
73. Littleton
    (Serves Boxborough also)
74. Mansfield
75. Marblehead
76. Merrimac
77. Middleborough
78. Middleton
79. No. Attleborough
80. Norwood

MASSACHUSETTS STATE PLANNING BOARD

Table 6 - Continued

MUNICIPAL LIGHTING PLANTS - CONTINUED

81. Paxton
82. Peabody
    (Serves Lynnfield also)
83. Princeton
84. Reading
    (Serves No. Reading and Wilmington, also)
85. Rowley
86. Russell
    (Serves part of Russell)
87. Shrewsbury
88. So. Hadley
89. Sterling
90. Taunton
    (Serves Raynham also)
91. Templeton
92. Wakefield
93. Wellesley
94. W. Boylston
95. Westfield

TOWNS NOT SERVED

The following towns are not served by electric companies in Massachusetts reporting to the Department of Public Utilities:

Savoy
Hawley
Prescott

Greenwich
Mt. Washington
Monroe

Table 7

POTENTIAL WATER POWER IN NEW ENGLAND AND ADJOINING REGIONS

LOCATION	UNDEVELOPED WATER POWER (Horsepower 60% of time)
Maine	625,608
New Hampshire	541,090
Vermont	483,920
Massachusetts	108,208
Rhode Island	none
Connecticut	170,170
New England Total	1,928,996
New York	958,000
Canada	7,695,586
*International	3,327,200
New York and Canada Total	11,930,786
Regional Total	13,909,782

Note 1: See New England Regional Planning Commission Map.
Note 2: The above figures include estimated potential water power to be created by construction of storage reservoirs now being planned for flood control. Detailed figures, by drainage area or sites, are on file at office of Massachusetts State Planning Board.
*Apportioned between United States and Canada by treaties.

Table 8

POTENTIAL WATER POWER IN MASSACHUSETTS 60% OF TIME

STREAM	SITE NO.	OVER 500 CAPACITY	SITE NO.	UNDER 500 CAPACITY	AGGREGATE CAPACITY
Thames (Mass. only)	2	2,963	-	-	2,963
Connecticut (Mass. only)	26	96,795	-	-	96,795
Millers	5	16,261	-	-	-
Deerfield	3	47,500	-	-	-
Chicopee	1	2,960	-	-	-
Westfield	17	30,074	-	-	-
Hoosic (Mass. only)	4	7,000	1	450	7,450
TOTAL (MASSACHUSETTS)	32	107,758	1	450	108,208

Closely associated with the study of potential power is work now being conducted by the United States Army Engineers in connection with flood control. Naturally, the planning and creation of huge storage reservoirs have an important bearing on potential power. Although these reservoirs are designed primarily to check the flow of water during periods of excessive discharge, and, therefore, do not have their full storage capacity available for power purposes during most of the year, they may add appreciably to the store of potential hydroelectric power.

At the present time, these dams and reservoirs are being planned to insure the future economical installation of hydroelectric plants by public or private enterprise, without detracting from the basic purpose, which is flood control.

Outside of New England, but still within the radius of five hundred miles of Boston, tremendous amounts of developed and undeveloped water power are available, perhaps in excess of 10,000,000 horsepower. This power lies chiefly in Canada, and while not economically usable in Boston under normal conditions, it should be considered in a study of potential power. Along the St. Lawrence and Saguenay Rivers, hydroelectric power has been almost hopelessly overdeveloped. These installations have been made chiefly by large paper companies who built in anticipation of business which did not materialize, owing to economic disturbances. Because of this condition, these companies are willing to sell large blocks of surplus power at a ridiculously small figure. In view of the probable short duration of these low prices, however, and because of the almost prohibitive cost of line construction, and excessive transmission losses between Massachusetts and Canada, it is doubtful whether any public-utility company in Massachusetts will avail itself of this power.

The next largest sources of power in this area lie in Maine and New York. As has been previously stated, adverse legislation prohibits the interstate transfer of power from Maine; however, on the assumption that these laws could readily be repealed if their repeal would prove of benefit to the state of Maine, Massachusetts would be the logical consumer of this power.

The reverse of this is probably true in regard to the power in New York State. No existing laws prevent the import of power from New York to Massachusetts, but the bulk of it will find markets within New York State.

The net result from all these legislative and economic barriers to the transfer of power is that within the greater zone there is a secondary area composed of Vermont, New Hampshire, Massachusetts, Rhode Island, and Connecticut which functions more or less as a unit. Broadly speaking, Vermont and New Hampshire are the great producing centers, while Massachusetts and Rhode Island are essentially the consumers. Insofar as there is enough power available within this smaller zone to take care of the estimated future requirements for the next decade, it is fair to assume that this condition will prevail, without much change, during that period.

Consumption

General

In contrast to the foregoing discussion of production, which is almost a purely physical study, consumption leads to the realm of conjecture based largely on past utilization. However, future demand estimates cannot be based entirely on the trends of the past ten or twenty years. New sociological factors, inventions, rates, and other variables must be considered in order to provide a reasonably accurate forecast. For this purpose, two maps have been prepared: one showing the principal centers of electric power demand in Massachusetts (Map 73-3), and another showing the proposed rural electrification extension (Map 73-2), both of which will be discussed in greater detail in the following paragraphs. Supplementing these maps, two charts (Charts 53-C1 and 53-C2) show the central-station power produced and consumed annually in Massachusetts.

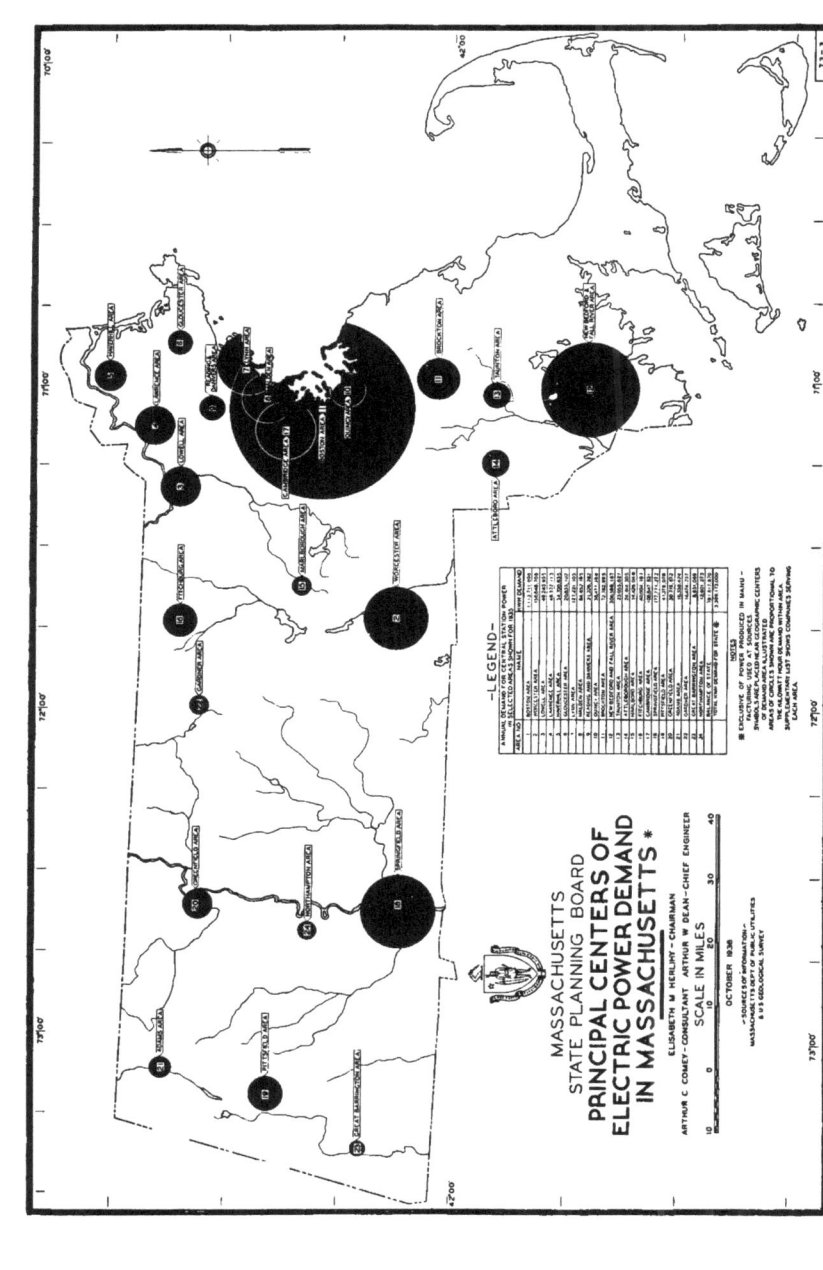

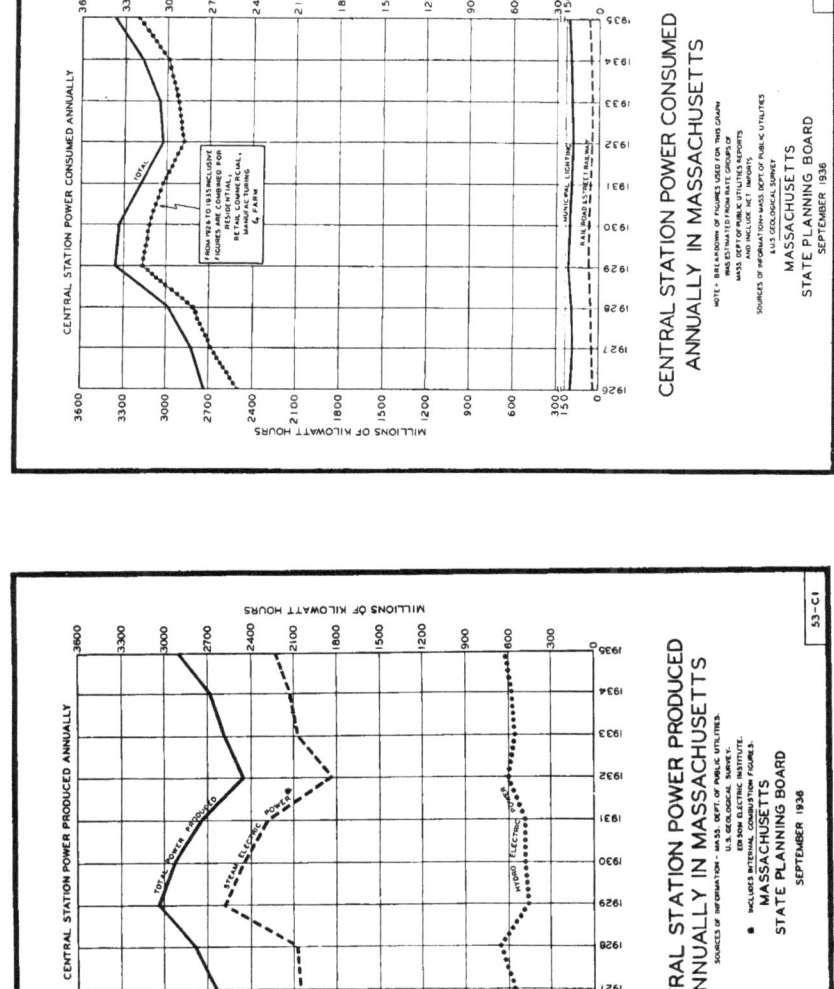

Table 9

ANNUAL KWH DEMAND IN MASSACHUSETTS FOR
SELECTED AREAS OF INTENSIVE USAGE
AND COMPANIES SERVING EACH

(Municipal companies are marked with an asterisk)

LOCATION OF COMPANY	TOTAL KILOWATT HOUR DEMAND FOR 1935
I Boston	
E.E.I. Co. of Boston	1,094,865,363
*Concord	3,489,940
*Wellesley	6,977,154
*Norwood	8,379,241
Total	1,113,711,698
II Worcester	
Worcester Suburban Electric	32,617,056
Worcester Electric Light Co.	124,031,650
Total	156,648,706
III Lowell	
Lowell Electric Light Corp.	49,245,955
Total	49,245,955
IV Lawrence	
Lawrence Gas & Electric Co.	48,372,713
Total	48,372,713
V Haverhill	
Haverhill Electric Co.	25,665,333
*Merrimac	646,531
*Groveland	303,873
*Georgetown	420,349
*Rowley	253,127
Amesbury Electric Light Co.	7,411,622
Total	34,700,835
VI Gloucester	
Gloucester Electric Co.	9,037,458
Beverly Gas & Electric Co.	10,685,713
Manchester Electric Co.	1,109,931
Total	20,833,102
VII Lynn	
Salem Electric Lighting Co.	54,299,679
Lynn Gas & Electric Co.	69,555,326
*Marblehead	3,366,100
Total	127,221,105
Total Carried Forward	1,550,734,114

Table 9 - Continued

	LOCATION OF COMPANY	TOTAL KILOWATT HOUR DEMAND FOR 1935
	Total Brought Forward	1,550,734,114
VIII	Malden	
	Malden Electric Co.	72,081,821
	Suburban Gas & Electric Co.	12,570,364
	Total	84,652,185
IX	Reading-Danvers Area	
	*Reading	6,926,745
	*Middleton	627,985
	*Peabody	9,625,768
	*Danvers	4,047,764
	Total	21,228,262
X	Quincy	
	Quincy Electric Light & Power Co.	38,477,386
	Total	38,477,386
XI	Brockton	
	E.E.I. Co. of Brockton	72,782,995
	Total	72,782,995
XII	Fall River - New Bedford Area	
	Fall River Electric Light Co.	125,205,821
	New Bedford Gas & Edison Light Co.	181,183,550
	Mt. Hope Finishing Co.	208,796
	Total	306,598,137
XIII	Taunton	
	*Taunton	20,407,294
	*Middleborough	2,648,533
	Total	23,055,827
XIV	Attleborough	
	Attleborough Steam & Electric Co.	15,048,831
	*North Attleborough	3,869,050
	*Mansfield	3,992,715
	Norton Power & Electric Co.	1,703,709
	Total	24,614,305
XV	Marlborough	
	Marlborough Electric Co.	8,574,859
	*Hudson	5,853,187
	Total	14,428,046
XVI	Fitchburg	
	Leominster Electric Light & Power Co.	14,750,618
	Fitchburg Gas & Electric Co.	25,253,569
	Total	40,004,187
	Total Carried Forward	2,176,575,474

MASSACHUSETTS STATE PLANNING BOARD

Table 9 - Continued

	LOCATION OF COMPANY		TOTAL KILOWATT HOUR DEMAND FOR 1935
	Total Brought Forward		2,176,575,474
XVII	Cambridge		
	Cambridge Electric Co.		100,791,288
	*Belmont		8,056,343
		Total	108,847,631
XVIII	Springfield		
	United Electric Light Co.		120,872,428
	*Westfield		9,832,045
	*Chicopee		14,705,150
	*Holyoke		30,991,937
	The Agawam Electric Co.		1,369,712
		Total	177,771,272
XIX	Pittsfield		
	Pittsfield Electric Co.		41,378,078
		Total	41,378,078
XX	Greenfield		
	Western Mass. Electric Co.		30,719,672
		Total	30,719,672
XXI	Adams		
	Northern Berkshire Gas Co.		16,336,424
		Total	16,336,424
XXII	Gardner		
	Gardner Electric Light Co.		14,474,237
		Total	14,474,237
XXIII	Great Barrington		
	Southern Berkshire Power & Elec. Co.		8,651,069
		Total	8,651,069
XXIV	Northampton		
	Northampton Electric Lighting Co.		12,601,273
		Total	12,601,273
	Balance of State		781,817,870
	TOTAL KWH DEMAND FOR STATE		3,369,173,000

Note: Since this table includes some inter-company transfers and uses, it does not exactly equal net demand.

Table 10*

CENTRAL-STATION POWER PRODUCED ANNUALLY
IN MASSACHUSETTS

(1000's KWH —1926 to 1935, Inclusive)

YEAR	HYDRO	STEAM	INTERNAL COMBUSTION	TOTAL
1926	478,896	2,020,019	**	2,498,915
1927	565,043	2,044,084	**	2,609,127
1928	656,653	2,094,815	**	2,751,468
1929	467,651	2,558,775	**	3,026,426
1930	484,375	2,423,181	**	2,907,556
1931	479,323	2,258,600	**	2,737,923
1932	605,937	1,835,397	**	2,441,334
1933	552,426	2,042,329	**	2,594,755
1934	554,224	2,118,280	**	2,672,504
1935	620,190	2,250,761	13,222	2,884,173

*Sources of information: Massachusetts Department of Public Utilities; U.S. Geological Survey; Edison Electric Institute.
**Included in Steam figures, 1926 to 1934, inclusive.

Table 11*

CENTRAL STATION KILOWATT HOURS SOLD AND USED
ANNUALLY IN MASSACHUSETTS

(1000's of Kilowatt Hours — 1926 to 1935, Inclusive)

YEAR	RESIDENTIAL	RETAIL COMMERCIAL	MANUFACTURING	FARM	MUNICIPAL LIGHTING	RAILROAD & STREET RY.	TOTAL
1926	----	----	2,582,300	----	123,326	27,289	2,732,915
1927	----	----	2,697,000	----	117,436	28,391	2,842,827
1928	----	----	2,836,198	----	119,456	29,814	2,985,468
1929	----	----	3,190,506	----	134,336	33,584	3,358,426
1930	----	----	3,147,881	----	132,540	33,135	3,313,556
1931	----	----	3,023,778	----	127,316	31,829	3,182,923
1932	----	----	2,869,319	----	120,812	30,203	3,020,334
1933	----	----	2,898,420	----	122,028	30,507	3,050,955
1934	----	----	2,999,629	----	126,300	31,575	3,157,504
1935	----	----	3,200,718	----	134,764	33,691	3,369,173

Note: Figures include net imports.
*Sources of information: U.S. Geological Survey and Massachusetts Department of Public Utilities.

MASSACHUSETTS STATE PLANNING BOARD

Present Demand

As might be expected, the greatest demand is found in Boston and in the Metropolitan area around Boston. Other large industrial areas, such as Fall River, New Bedford, Worcester, and Springfield, show a heavy demand concentration, as indicated on the above-mentioned demand map. Outside of the principal centers of demand, a fairly uniform distribution is noted for the balance of the State. The chief exceptions to this are found in the Berkshire Hills, the Central Highland section, east of the Connecticut River, and on Cape Cod, where the requirements are obviously not great.

It is interesting to note from the demand map that after subtracting the gross demand of all the selected principal centers, the balance of the State has an annual requirement of less than the Boston area alone.

Rural Electrification

A rather complete survey of Massachusetts Rural Electrification was made by the Federal Emergency Relief Administration of Massachusetts, the findings of which were published in July 1935.

The maps accompanying the above study show by counties the proposed line extensions and a certain portion of the adjacent existing power lines. For the purpose of the State Planning Board report, a single map has been prepared, showing all of these extensions and other pertinent data (Map 73-2).

The Federal Rural Electrification authorities propose that extensions of 1168.22 miles of aerial plant be erected at an estimated cost of $2,024,549. This construction would make central-station power available to about 5475 rural customers who now have no power facilities or who rely on small generators of their own. From these potential customers would be derived an initial estimated annual revenue of $215,847 and an annual demand of 3,237,825 kilowatt hours.

The benefits to the farm and to the State from such a program are measurable and satisfactory. A fact continually being demonstrated is that the availability of electricity in the country is an important sociological benefit. There are proven cases in which the advent of power has changed the entire complexion of a locality, bringing about the modernization of homes and property and creating a more contented class of rural dwellers.

The actual uses of electricity on the farm are too numerous to

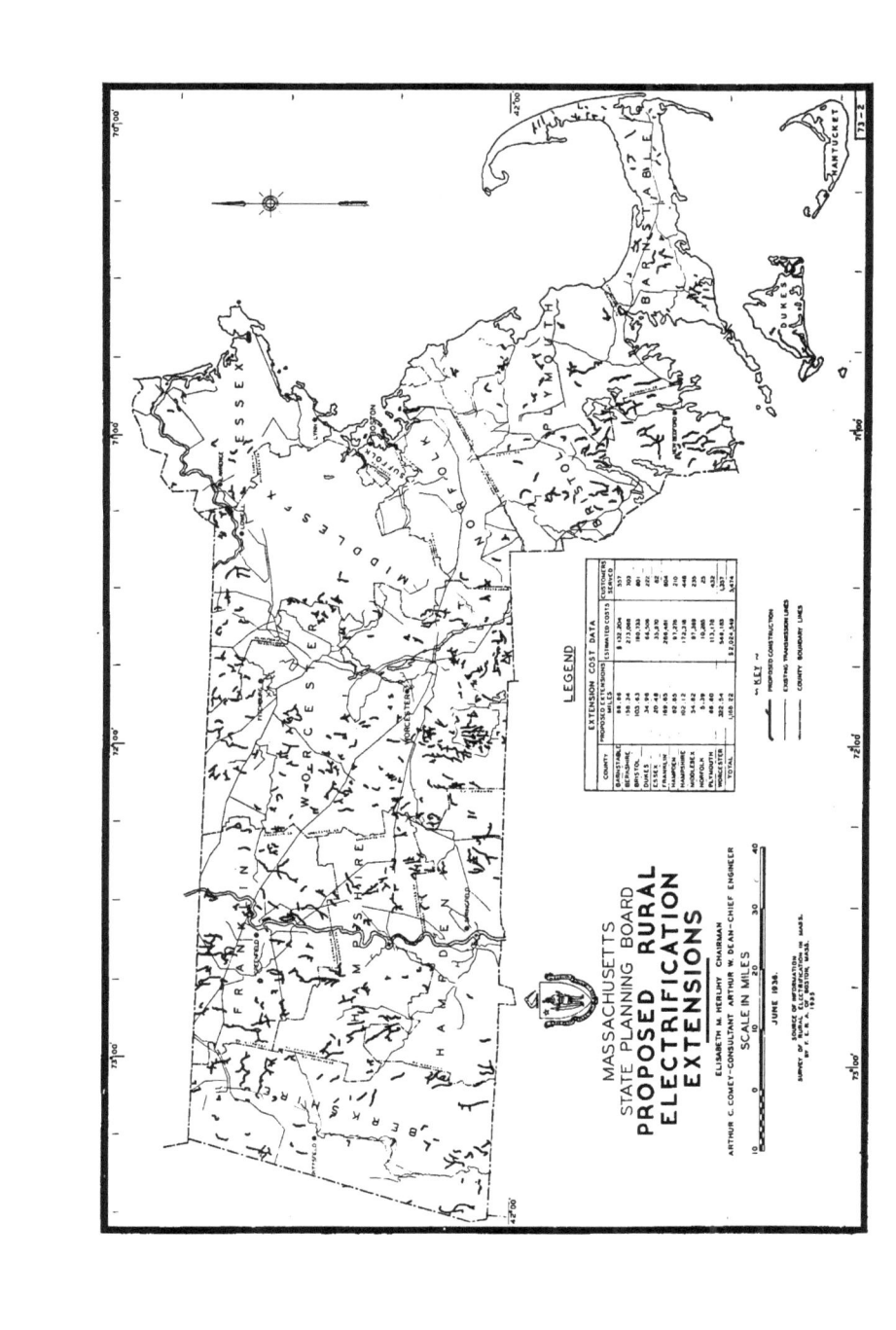

list here, but one might readily say that all the benefits of power to the urban citizen would accrue to the farmer, plus the benefit which results from a medium which can do a large part of his work.

The question of the practicability of utility companies making these extensions is an important one. Inquiries into the policies of the companies in this regard indicate that such a procedure is entirely feasible. Prospects are required to use sufficient electricity to equal 20 per cent of the capital cost, for four or five years, or to guarantee income equal to the same percentage for the same period. Experience shows, in most cases, that the use will exceed the required demand.

From the nature of the proposed extensions it would seem that the rates for this service would not be in excess of those now prevailing in the areas served by existing feeders. It is also probable that farms may enjoy lower rates because of the nature of their equipment and their larger use of off-peak power.

Future Utilization

Despite unusual economic conditions in the last ten years, there has been a steady increase in electric power demand. Roughly speaking, an increase of about 10 per cent annually has occurred.

Like many other industries, however, the power companies were greatly overbuilt. For this reason, little added capacity has been required during these ten years, and while not yet approaching the saturation point, a healthy upward trend is expected in power utilization, and plans are under way for large plant extensions.

From reliable sources it is estimated that the percentage increase in the next ten years will not exceed that of the last decade. It is not expected that any single factor will provide a sudden impetus to distort this rather normal increase.

Probably the greatest increase in usage will come from electric stoves, water heaters, and refrigerators. Undoubtedly, many new appliances will be put into general use, and these time- and labor-saving devices in the home will probably be tremendously popular. The use of electric accessories to central-heating plants will perhaps have a steadying influence in the use of off-peak power. It is generally conceded, however, that the use of electricity for actual house heating is remote. Present costs make it prohibitive at the moment.

MASSACHUSETTS STATE PLANNING BOARD

Although a substantial increase in the use of appliances is expected, the power demand will not increase proportionally, because of the greater efficiency of the devices. For instance, a modern refrigerator takes about half the power required three or four years ago. When this factor is applied to the whole domestic picture, it can readily be seen that a check is applied to power consumption. Adding to this the fact that greater efficiency may be expected from generating, transmission, and distribution of power, we may conclude that great benefits will accrue to the user with relatively small increase in costs.

Costs

Special Cost Analysis

The main object in a study of costs and rates for electric power is to create a standard by which production and distribution costs of power may be measured at any given time or place. After limited research on the matter, however, it is evident that a common yardstick cannot be applied.

There are three main categories to consider in a study of power costs,— production, tranmission, and distribution. In each are contained so many variables that it is practically impossible to provide a hard and fast average that can apply to any given case.

Therefore, in an analysis of these three spheres of costs, there have been selected, for the purpose of the accompanying chart and graph, three sources whose cost data probably come as close to being typical as any utility company that might have been chosen. The results of studies by the Federal Power Commission, the Detroit Edison Company, and the New York Power Authority, for their respective areas, are presented. (See Chart 53-C5.)

To clarify the appended chart, it may be well to indicate the physical dividing line between the three groups in the following manner:

1. **Production.** Cost of producing power until ready to leave the generating plant. This includes:
    a. Operating expenses
    b. Purchased current
    c. Pro-rated share of general expense

2. **Transmission.** Cost of transmitting high-voltage power from the generating station to and including the sub-station.
    a. Operating expense
    b. Pro-rated share of general expense

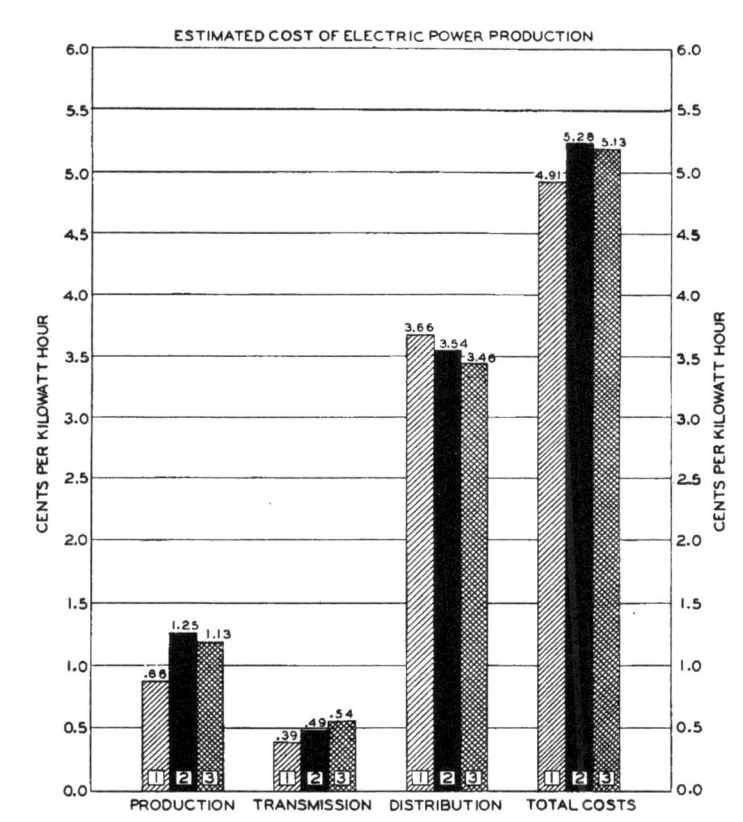

COMPOSITE GRAPH SHOWING TYPICAL COSTS OF PRODUCTION, TRANSMISSION & DISTRIBUTION OF ELECTRIC POWER

~LEGEND~
1- NEW YORK CITY- SURVEY BY POWER AUTHORITY
2- DETROIT   -   "   " DETROIT EDISON CO
3- COMPOSITE -   "   " FEDERAL POWER COMMISSION FOR
              BOSTON MASS.-GREENFIELD MASS.-NEW YORK CITY

MASSACHUSETTS
STATE PLANNING BOARD
OCTOBER 1936

53-C5

3. Distribution. Cost of distributing electricity from the sub-station to the customer's meter:

    a. Operating expenses
    b. Utilization
    c. Commercial expense
    d. New business
    e. Pro-rated share of general expense

Included in the operating expenses are fixed charges which cover taxes, insurance, depreciation, and return on investment. Since distribution expense generally comprises more than one half of the total costs and because of the great number of variables contained in it, it is worthy of further analysis. The major part of so-called utilization expenses cover operation and maintenance of the street lighting systems with only a very small part of this expense being applicable to the other classes of customers. Commercial expense is composed of meter reading and billing. New business takes care of appliance sales and customer solicitation.

Table 12

ESTIMATED BREAKDOWN OF COSTS BY OPERATING POWER COMPANIES

(Cents Per Kilowatt Hour)

TYPE OF EXPENSE	*	DETROIT	NEW YORK
Production - Operating Expense	.63	.47	.42
Fixed Charge	.56	.78	.44
Transmission - Operating Expense	.10	.16	.13
Fixed Charge	.44	.33	.26
Distribution - Fixed Charge	1.58	1.45	1.49
Operating Expense	.47	.29	.43
Utilization	.14	.30	.24
Commercial	.53	1.26	.61
New Business	.34	.24	.15
General Expenses	.40	-	.31
Duct Rentals	-	-	.43
TOTAL	5.19	5.28	4.91

*Composite data by Federal Power Commission for Boston and Greenfield, Massachusetts, and New York City.

MASSACHUSETTS STATE PLANNING BOARD

Cost Differentials

One of the paradoxical features of power costs particularly apparent to the lay person is that sometimes radical differences in consumer costs exist between different sections of the State, and also between small adjacent areas. From a survey of rate schedules it would seem that municipally operated companies can deliver power to the consumer at a much lower rate than the private utility company. However, this may not be particularly significant as municipal companies do often times enjoy favorable conditions which are not always available to private companies.

To be more specific, some municipal companies are almost entirely free from local taxation. In some cases low rates prevail, but deficits in operating expenses must be made up through other methods of taxation. Furthermore, these organizations are sometimes able to purchase surplus power and off-peak power from public-utility companies at a lower rate than they could produce it themselves. It may also be true that some municipal companies do not set aside funds for plant replacements to the same degree as do private companies, which would tend to reduce costs to a large extent.

A factor which municipal companies generally do not have to consider, as part of their operating costs, is that of dividends to stockholders, or similar returns on money invested. It is also fair to assume that some small companies, not necessarily municipal, but functioning similarly to municipal companies, do not have the burden of extremely high-paid officials, nor do they have to maintain a large technical staff for the purpose of research. In justice to the large operating power companies or associations, it may be said that results of research and invention ultimately accrue to the smaller companies who do not share this particular burden.

A comparison of the average domestic rate (for a demand of 100 kilowatt hours monthly) of the municipal companies in Massachusetts with a like average of the other electric public utilities within the State indicates the following as shown by a Federal Electric Rate Summary (Rate Series No. 2 State Report No. 1):

    Municipal --------------------4.76 cents per kilowatt hour
    Other Utilities --------------5.72 cents per kilowatt hour

To indicate further the rate differential, the lowest and the highest average rate for all residential sales, for a demand of 100 kilowatt hours, is herewith shown. The lowest rate, 2.93 cents

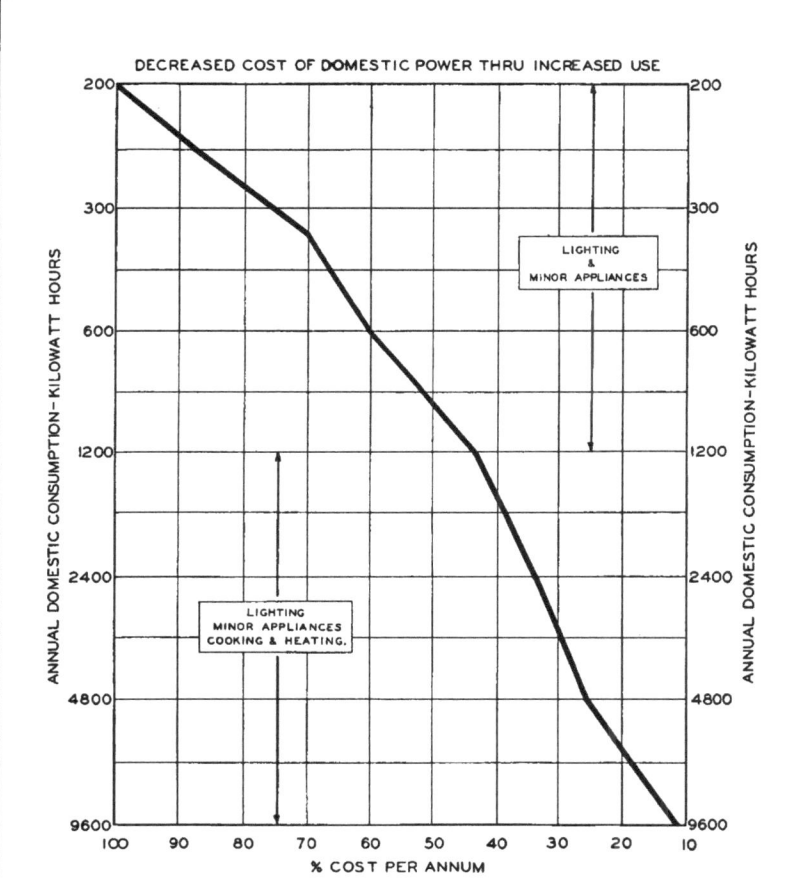

ESTIMATED DECREASE IN DOMESTIC POWER RATES THROUGH INCREASED USAGE.

NOTE-THIS ESTIMATE IS BASED ON SURVEYS BY NEW YORK STATE POWER AUTHORITY & DETROIT EDISON CO. BEING TYPICAL IT COULD BE APPLICABLE TO MASSACHUSETTS.

MASSACHUSETTS
STATE PLANNING BOARD
SEPT. 1936.

53-C4

per kilowatt hour, is that of the Braintree Municipal Light Department, a municipal company located in Braintree and serving that town solely. The highest rate, 13.3 cents per kilowatt hour, is that of the Nantucket Gas & Electric Co., a private utility company, located on Nantucket Island, and serving only that island. Although having the highest rate, the Nantucket Company is not a good subject for comparison, because its revenue is derived chiefly from a large summer population. The next highest rate, 8.12 cents per kilowatt hour, is that of Barnstable, a town served by the Cape & Vineyard Electric Company.

Having established the fact that large differentials exist throughout the State, it might not be presumptuous to suggest that further study, with the mutual coöperation of State authorities and power companies, would demonstrate the practicability of drawing up a program of rate equalization for Massachusetts that could be inaugurated in the near future. It is also reasonable to conclude that the adoption of such equalized standards would result in sufficient rate decreases to bring about increased utilization, an increase in the sale of electric appliances, and a momentous contribution to the social and economic well-being of Massachusetts citizens.

As indicated by the accompanying Chart 53-C4, wherever utilization can be sufficiently increased by a decrease in rates, no net financial loss need be involved.

Sources of Information

ABSTRACT OF THE UNITED STATES CENSUS (1934)
Associated Industries, Park Square Building, Boston, Mass.
Cape & Vineyard Electric Co., Cambridge, Mass.
Connecticut Planning Board, Hartford, Conn.
Department of Lands & Forests, Province of Quebec, Canada
Department of Surveys, Province of Ontario, Canada
Edison Electric Illuminating Co., 182 Tremont St., Boston, Mass.
Federal Power Commission, Washington, D. C.
HANDBOOK OF POWER PLANTS IN THE UNITED STATES, McGraw-Hill Book
  Company, New York, N.Y.
Maine Public Utilities Commission, Augusta, Maine
Maine State Planning Board, Augusta, Maine
Massachusetts Department of Public Utilities, 100 Nashua St.,
  Boston, Mass.
Massachusetts Utilities Associates, 89 Broad St., Boston, Mass.
Metropolitan District Commission, Boston, Mass.
New England Council, Park Square Building, Boston, Mass.

MASSACHUSETTS STATE PLANNING BOARD

New England Power Association, 89 Broad St., Boston, Mass.
New England Regional Planning Board, 2100 Federal Building,
    Post Office Square, Boston, Mass.
New Hampshire Planning Board, Concord, N.H.
New York State Water Power Survey, Albany, N. Y.
Professor H. K. Barrows, Boston, Mass.
Rhode Island Planning Board, Providence, R. I.
Stone & Webster Engineering Corporation, Inc., Boston, Mass.
SURVEY OF RURAL ELECTRIFICATION IN MASSACHUSETTS, (1935)
    by Federal Emergency Relief Administration of Mass.
United States Army Engineers, War Department, Washington, D. C.
United States Geological Survey, Room 935 Federal Building,
    Post Office Square, Boston, Mass.
Vermont Planning Board, Montpelier, Vt.
Western Utilities, Springfield, Mass.

INDUSTRY

Courtesy of TECHNOLOGY REVIEW

CHAPTER V

INDUSTRY

Summary Outline

PART I

A. Massachusetts Business Index
B. Comparison of Massachusetts Business with that of the United States
C. Notes Regarding the Individual Business Series
D. Industrial Production in Massachusetts
E. Principal Massachusetts Industries
F. Fifteen Principal Competing States
G. Advantages and Disadvantages of Massachusetts as Compared with Competing States

PART II

A. Basis of Investigation
B. Types of Analysis
C. A Balance Sheet
D. Are New Industries Always Community Assets?

MASSACHUSETTS STATE PLANNING BOARD

INDUSTRY - PART I

The order of the General Court, contained in Chapter 475 of the Acts of 1935, directed the State Planning Board, along with its other duties, to make such studies and plans as would best promote the trade and industry of the Commonwealth. In accordance with this instruction, the Planning Board staff made a careful survey of the problem, aided by helpful counsel from numerous business leaders in widely diversified industries, and during the past year has completed certain work to accomplish the following ends:

1. To establish and maintain reliable measures which will show the current trend of Massachusetts trade and industry as a whole, compared with preceding periods and also with the trend of business in other parts of the United States.

2. To gather and arrange in convenient form all available data which will truly show the advantages and disadvantages of Massachusetts as an industrial or commercial site, in relation to those of other competing States.

Massachusetts Business Index

Under the first division, the State Planning Board compiled and charted the records of such business series as were available, and combined five of the more important of these into a composite monthly index of Massachusetts business extending back through 1928. This is apparently the first time that such an index for Massachusetts has been made. While the number of series it contains is necessarily limited, the Composite index figure seems to be fairly indicative of the trend of general business in the State.

While everyone should recognize the limitations of any composite index, it is interesting to note that the index of Massachusetts business showed a gain in September 1936, of 17 per cent, compared with the same month a year ago, and 57 per cent over the depression low in the summer of 1932. It also indicates that the recovery of business in this State has been steady from year to year, and apparently compares well with the gains in many of the other eastern industrial States, although it has not been so rapid as that for the United States as a whole.

Massachusetts experienced less drop from the peak years before the depression than the average of other States, but the Bay State's peak came in 1923, rather than in 1929, which the national indexes show as the year of greatest volume for the total country. From the Planning Board's index it is apparent that, in Massachusetts, both the years 1928 and 1929 registered lower than the average of the three years, 1925-1927, which was taken as the base, 100. These business-index figures refer only to the physical volume of business and not to its dollar value, which is affected by the inflation of prices.

In the period of recovery, since 1932, Massachusetts business has been subject to approximately the same fluctuations as that of the total United States, except for the break in September 1934, when the textile strike in Massachusetts gave business a bad setback. The net gain in business during the first nine months of 1936 over the same period of 1935 is considerably better than the gain of 1935 over 1934, and points to an average for the current year which may well exceed that of any year since 1930.

The wide seasonal fluctuations to which Massachusetts industry is subject are clearly pictured in the index curve. In general, these show as pronounced peaks in the spring and fall; with deep recessions in the summer and winter. Exceptions to this typical trend occurred during the banking crisis in the spring of 1933 and during the textile strike in the fall of 1934. It also should be noted that last winter the seasonal slump took place in January, instead of in November, as in most other years. All the factors in the index accounted for this high winter level, showing that most lines of industrial activity benefited.

The figures of the State Planning Board index of Massachusetts business are as follows:

Table 13

STATE PLANNING BOARD INDEX OF MASSACHUSETTS BUSINESS*

	1928	1929	1930	1931	1932	1933	1934	1935	1936
Jan.	93.3	96.9	86.7	74.6	69.2	62.0	66.5	71.7	75.5
Feb.	95.1	92.4	86.1	71.5	69.6	59.5	68.5	68.1	71.0
Mar.	104.4	100.9	93.9	78.6	70.5	58.8	73.6	73.1	73.7
Apr.	96.2	102.0	93.6	81.4	61.9	57.6	72.6	72.0	77.8
May	98.6	103.7	89.4	87.3	58.1	65.4	72.6	70.0	76.3
June	92.1	95.3	83.1	75.5	55.8	67.9	66.7	68.5	73.3
July	87.1	95.6	77.5	76.4	51.8	68.1	63.1	68.2	76.2
Aug.	91.3	95.0	77.9	76.7	62.1	72.3	66.4	70.7	83.8
Sept.	93.5	97.0	83.7	77.6	65.8	70.3	57.4	70.0	81.6
Oct.	109.1	105.9	83.1	77.0	67.0	73.0	71.0	76.5	
Nov.	99.4	88.5	79.1	69.1	62.7	69.7	67.2	74.2	
Dec.	97.2	84.7	73.1	71.9	61.3	66.8	68.7	79.8	
AVERAGE	96.4	96.5	84.4	76.4	63.1	65.9	67.8	71.9	78.4

*Based on physical volume, not on dollar value

MASSACHUSETTS STATE PLANNING BOARD

Construction of Massachusetts Business Index

The State Planning Board's index of business in Massachusetts is a composite of five series of Massachusetts business subjects, figures for which are available monthly and which are believed to be the most reliable indicators available of the volume of business in this State. No correction has been made to eliminate either seasonal fluctuations or secular trend.

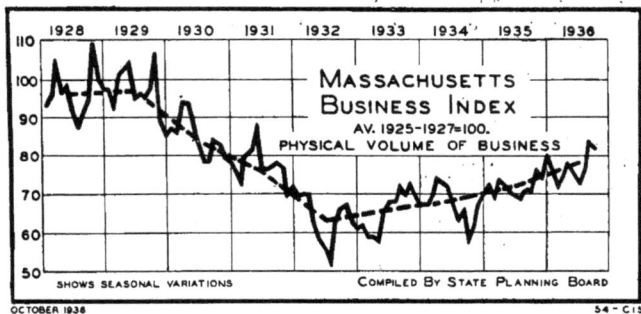

The five series making up the business index, together with weights assigned to each, are as follows:

	Weight
Industrial employment in all manufacturing, as reported by the Department of Labor and Industries.	40
Electric-power consumption, as reported by the Federal Power Commission, plus the net imports of power from other States, as reported by the New England Power Association.	25
Total square feet of floor area of new building contracts awarded, as reported by the F.W. Dodge Corporation.	25
Shoe production, in number of pairs, as reported by the United States Bureau of Census.	5
Cotton-spindle hour activity, as reported by the United States Bureau of Census.	5

MASSACHUSETTS STATE PLANNING BOARD

The base period used as 100 is the average of the three years, 1925-1927. The dash line running through the chart shows the average for each year, plotted in the center of the year space.

Comparison of Massachusetts Business with that of the United States

To compare accurately the commercial and industrial activity of Massachusetts with that of the whole country, many different factors must be considered. In a general way, the series of business statistics, plotted on Chart 54-C13, furnish a reasonable basis of comparison. Unfortunately, it is not possible to secure for the State of Massachusetts more than a few of the business series that are currently made available for the nation.

The eight individual series presented on the above-mentioned chart are the most reliable Massachusetts business indicators for which monthly reports can be secured at present. Some of these are being presented for the first time, in this report. Five of the individual series indicate physical volume of production, and these are the subjects combined in the composite index. Three of the subjects, Bank Debits, Department-Store Sales, and Value of New Building Construction, are based on value in terms of dollars.

Plotted with each of these series is the corresponding series representing the entire United States. It will be noted that, from the low point of 1932 to 1935, the recovery in Massachusetts business was somewhat slower than in that of the country as a whole; but during the past year, in certain industrial divisions, the pace of recovery in the Commonwealth has quickened, so that at present its showing in comparison with the total country is much improved.

Better conditions in the Bay State during the present year are indicated by the index of Industrial Employment. Throughout 1934 and 1935, employment in certain sections of the nation increased much more rapidly than in Massachusetts; but so far in 1936, the gain in the number of people employed by industry in Massachusetts exceeds that in the rest of the nation as a whole.

Shoe Production and Value of New Building Construction are two of the series in which Massachusetts appears at the moment to be progressing more rapidly than the nation as a whole. Some of the other series give a less favorable picture, notably those of Electric Power Consumption, the Actual Floor Area of New Building Construction, Cotton Textile Output, Bank Debits, and Department-Store Sales.

MASSACHUSETTS STATE PLANNING BOARD

Notes Regarding the Individual Business Series

The Index of Industrial Employment in Massachusetts represents the number of persons employed by manufacturing industry in this State, as recorded by the Bureau of Labor and Industries. The index figures show the increase or decrease in employed, as compared with the base years, 1925-1927. The Employment Index for the United States is the one recorded by the Bureau of Labor Statistics, the index having been converted to the 1925-1927 base.

The Index of Electric-Power Consumption in Massachusetts presents power production, as recorded by the Federal Power Commission, to which are added the net imports of electric power into Massachusetts as recorded by the New England Power Association. This Association imports approximately 90 per cent of all out-of-State power that is used in Massachusetts. The Power-Consumption Index for the United States is made from the records of total power production, as recorded by the Federal Power Commission, to which are added the net imports of power recorded by the Edison Electric Institute. Neither of these two indices has been adjusted to eliminate the seasonal or secular trend. It will be noted that the seasonal variation in electric-power consumption in Massachusetts is much more pronounced than in the country as a whole. This must be taken into account when comparing the Massachusetts curve with that of the entire United States.

The Index of Building Construction, both for Massachusetts and for the United States as a whole, is based upon the monthly reports of the F.W. Dodge Corporation, and includes all types of construction except such public utilities and public engineering works as do not create floor space. The F.W. Dodge Corporation reports, representing the country as a whole, actually cover thirty-seven States, and record new contracts awarded. On the chart are plotted these records, based on series both in terms of square feet of floor area and in terms of the dollar value of new contracts. It will be noted that whereas Massachusetts appears to be lagging behind the rest of the country in the actual floor area of construction, it has apparently been gaining more rapidly in recent months than the total United States in the value of new building. The explanation of this difference in the two indices is not wholly clear, but suggests that the building taking place in Massachusetts is of more expensive quality than that in some other sections.

The Index of Shoe Production is based upon the actual figures supplied monthly by the Bureau of the Census, both for Massachusetts and for the country as a whole. It represents all production of boots, shoes, and slippers, except those made of rubber. The chart

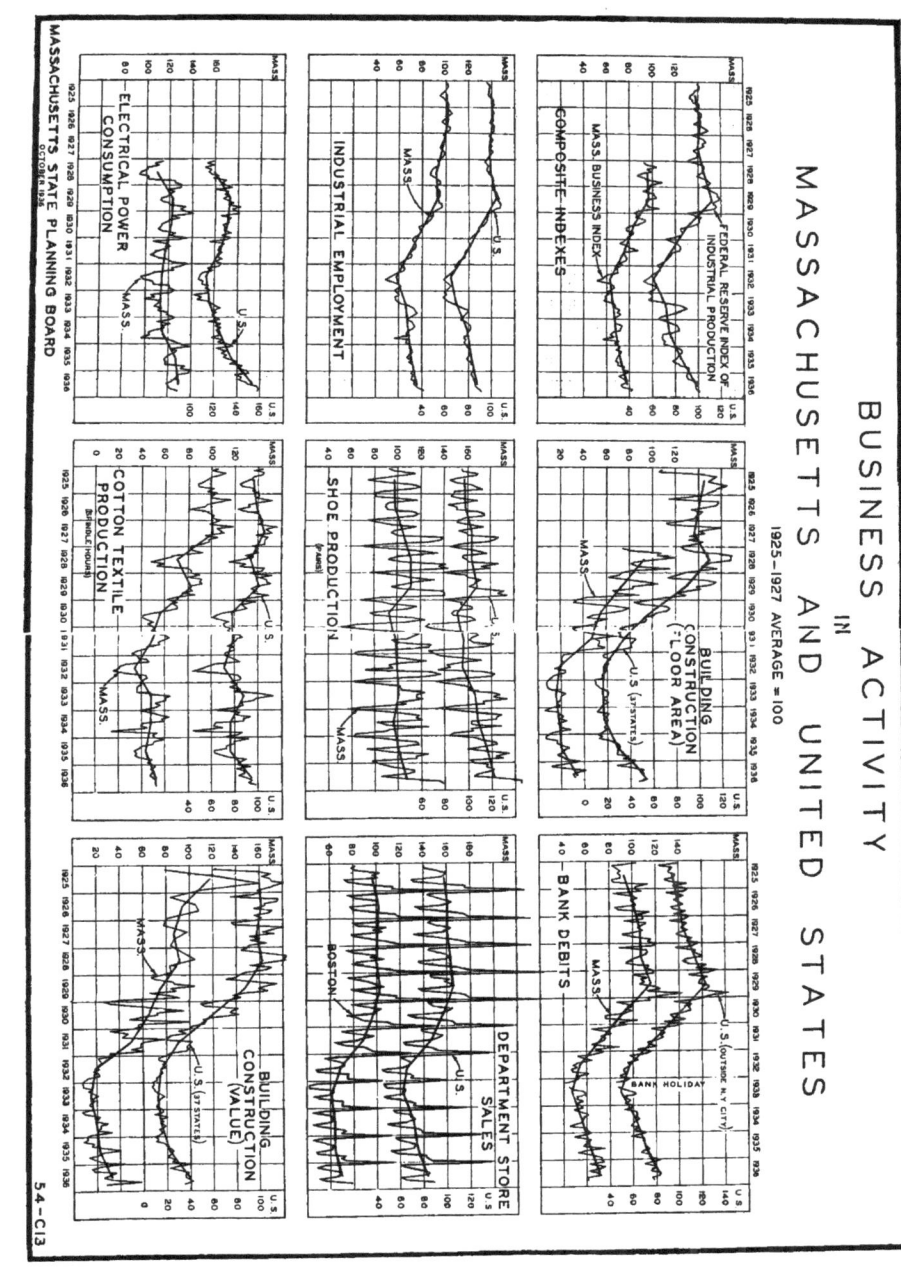

shows the wide seasonal fluctuations to which this industry is subject. From 1932 up to the current year, Massachusetts shoe output did not increase as did that of the entire United States; but, during the current year, production in Massachusetts has made more rapid headway than that in the rest of the country, and is one of the industries responsible for the sharp upturn in the Massachusetts Employment Index.

The Index of Cotton Textiles is based upon the monthly reports of the number of spindle hours of operation, as recorded each month by the Bureau of the Census. From 1927 to 1932, the Massachusetts share of this business suffered a severe decline. During later years, however, the trend of this State's production has been much more nearly parallel to that of the total country.

The Index of Bank Debits is based upon reports of the Federal Reserve Board, and is, perhaps, the best measure, in terms of dollars, of the total amount of all kinds of business transacted. In the index for the entire United States, the bank debits of New York City have been subtracted because of the preponderant weight in them of investment transactions.

In a general way, the curve of bank debits in Massachusetts may be used as a check on the accuracy of the composite index of business, compiled by the State Planning Board. These bank debits include all payments which are made by check. The annual average figures show that Massachusetts bank debits have advanced 26 per cent from 1932 to 1936, using the first nine-months' average to represent 1936. During this period, the average increase in general commodity prices, balancing wholesale with consumer prices, is estimated to have been about 15 per cent, so that if the Index of Bank Debits is corrected to eliminate the rise due to increasing prices, the present average would stand 17 per cent over 1933. In this same period, the composite index, which includes only subjects measuring physical volume of production, increased 22 per cent. Considering the widely different bases of these two calculations, and having in mind also that the conclusions to be derived from any business index must be only approximate, it seems apparent that the picture shown by the State Planning Board's' composite index of Massachusetts business, checks rather well with that indicated by the entirely independent measure of bank debits.

The Index of Department-Store Sales is based upon reports from the Federal Reserve Board, applying to the entire United States. For Massachusetts, the record is that of twelve leading Boston department stores, compiled monthly by the Federal Reserve Bank in Boston. This record is significant in that it presents one important division of retail merchandising, but should not be taken as a complete measure of all consumer buying, first, because it does not include certain important lines, such as automobiles and real estate, and second, because it does not take into account the rapidly growing business done by chain and certain types of independent stores scattered throughout the State. A more complete report on this subject will be made by the State Planning Board at a later date.

Industrial Production in Massachusetts

In its original survey to determine what industrial and commercial research would be of most practical value to the Commonwealth, the State Planning Board found a widespread misconception regarding the condition of industry within the State. Many persons, otherwise well informed in business matters, were under the impression that the long-swing trend of industry in Massachusetts was very unfavorable. "On the down grade" was an expression frequently heard. "No future except as a playground", and "Geographical location too big an obstacle for industry", others said. From these and similar pessimistic opinions, it became evident that at least one of the greatest needs in this State was the facts regarding the true condition and outlook; in short, an unbiased, accurate appraisal, as far as possible, of the advantages and disadvantages of Massachusetts as an industrial site, compared with other industrial States with which this State is in competition.

A Popular Fallacy

One outstanding misconception is that failure of Massachusetts to maintain a given percentage of the total production of the nation indicates decline. It is true that in the early days, when there were only thirteen States, Massachusetts produced a large share of all the manufactures used in the United States, and, even up to 1849, the date of the first census, the Bay State was manufacturing 15 1/2 per cent of all the country's production. At that time, there were thirty States in the Union, with a population of about 23,000,000 people. (The measure of manufacturing activity used is the value added by manufacture, as recorded in the United States Census).

Many people overlook the fact that, as the country expands, the need for industry in other sections increases, and, consequently, new industrial States develop. It is only natural, therefore, that now, in a nation of forty-eight States with a population of 128,000,000 people, Massachusetts should not be able to hold the same proportion of the national output that it originally controlled. In fact, such an accomplishment would be impossible for any one State, over a long period of time, in a nation the size of this, and it is entirely wrong to count as decline any reasonable loss in the ratio between Massachusetts production and that of the nation as a whole.

The Trend Since 1849

The accompanying Chart 54-C1, shows what actually has happened. On this chart is pictured the total value added by manufacture to all industrial products made in Massachusetts, compared with those made in the country as a whole, during each of the census years since 1849. On this chart, the dash line represents the percentage of Massachusetts' output to that of the entire United States. At the foot of the chart is indicated, in figures, the percentage of Massachusetts' output to that of the entire United States during each of the census years.

The significant point presented by this chart is the growth of Massachusetts industry, and its ability to withstand economic depression. Viewed from this standpoint, the Bay State presents a fairly satisfactory picture; certainly not one in keeping with the gloomy forebodings so often expressed.

Trends of Major Industrial Groups

Obviously, any long-term comparison of the industrial gain or loss in the Commonwealth should be made, not with the country as a whole, but with the individual States principally competitive with this State, that is, with States which are engaged primarily in industrial production. This calls for an analysis of the different kinds of business in the Commonwealth.

A study is here presented showing the trend of all Massachusetts industrial activity, divided into seventeen major classifications. The trend of each of these groups, in comparison with that of the same group for the entire United States, and also in comparison with the total of all Massachusetts production, is shown on Chart 54-C36. In the upper half of this chart is indicated the proportion of these classifications in Massachusetts to the totals of the same classifications in the entire United States, by census years, back to 1909. The industry of the State engaged in the production of worsted and woolen goods produced the largest proportion of the total value of these goods in the United States, accounting for nearly one third of all the nation's output. It will be noted, also, that this industry in Massachusetts during the twenty-five year period held its own against the rest of the country.

The leather industries of Massachusetts have also the largest share of the nation's production. In 1933, they produced about 23 per cent of the total output. Cotton textiles, rubber goods, and jewelry, with approximately 10 per cent each, rank about equal in the proportion which they represent of the total nation's production of these commodities. Electrical machinery is another important group, as are other textiles and paper production.

In the lower half of the chart are shown the same seventeen classifications in the proportion which the Massachusetts output of each bears to the total Massachusetts industrial output. Measured in terms of the value of the product, leather goods is the largest single group; woolen goods, food products, other textiles, iron and steel, and printing industries also hold important places.

Most significant of all, probably, is the group entitled, "All Other Industries", for in these are included the myriad little companies which produce, in the aggregate, such an important part of this State's industrial output. Many of those are new industries, products of Yankee ingenuity. It will be noted that all through the depression, in fact since 1923, these smaller groups have continued to increase in their relative importance in the State's total business, furnishing a valuable back-log which provided steady employment to thousands of people whom some of the larger industries were forced to discharge. In any endeavor which is made to stimulate the industrial development of the Commonwealth, this group of miscellaneous business concerns should receive most careful attention, for it is, perhaps, the cradle from which will emerge some of the foremost industries of the future.

Principal Massachusetts Industries

In the foregoing analysis, the entire industrial production of Massachusetts is presented. For the more detailed studies of the individual industries, it naturally is necessary to consider finer industrial divisions than the broad classifications employed above. For example, the group of industries included under leather goods is made up of those engaged in leather production, boot and shoe production, and the production of other goods made of leather. From this point on, the boot-and-shoe industry and leather production are considered as individual units.

In the total industrial output of Massachusetts, there are about eighteen groups of industries which individually are of outstanding

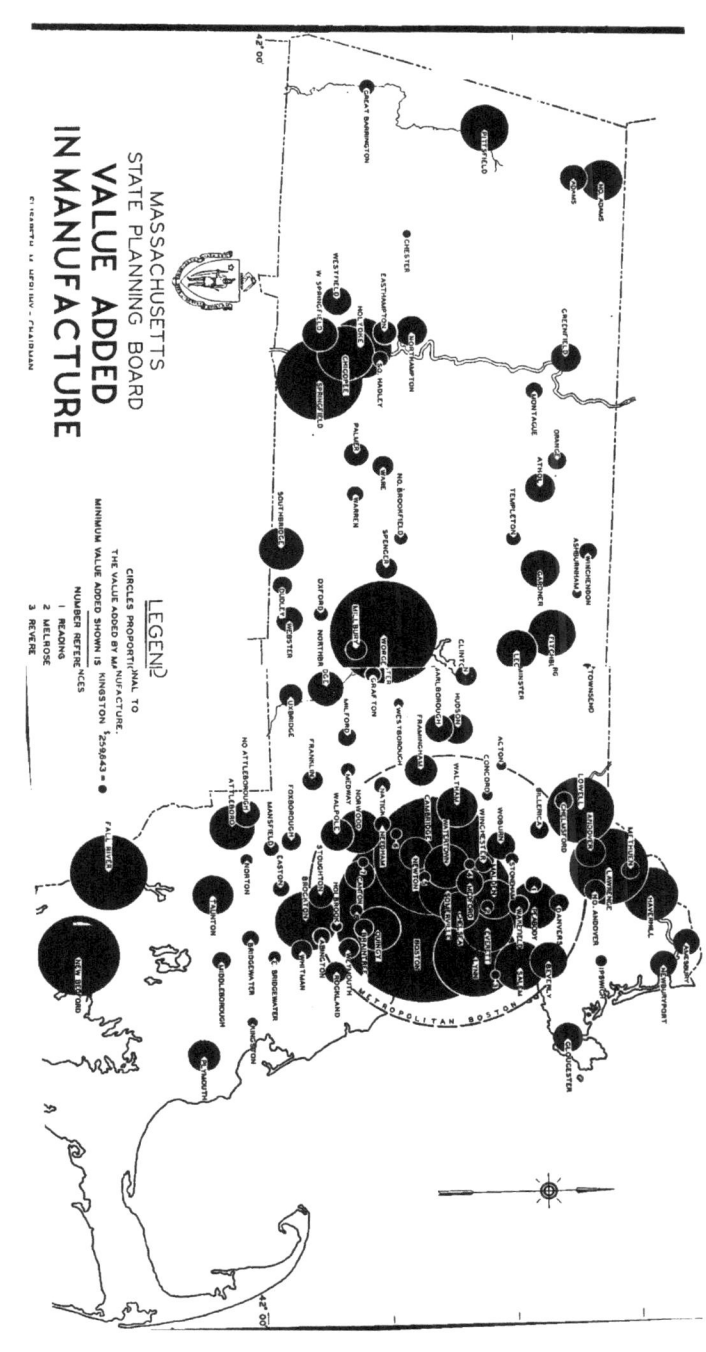

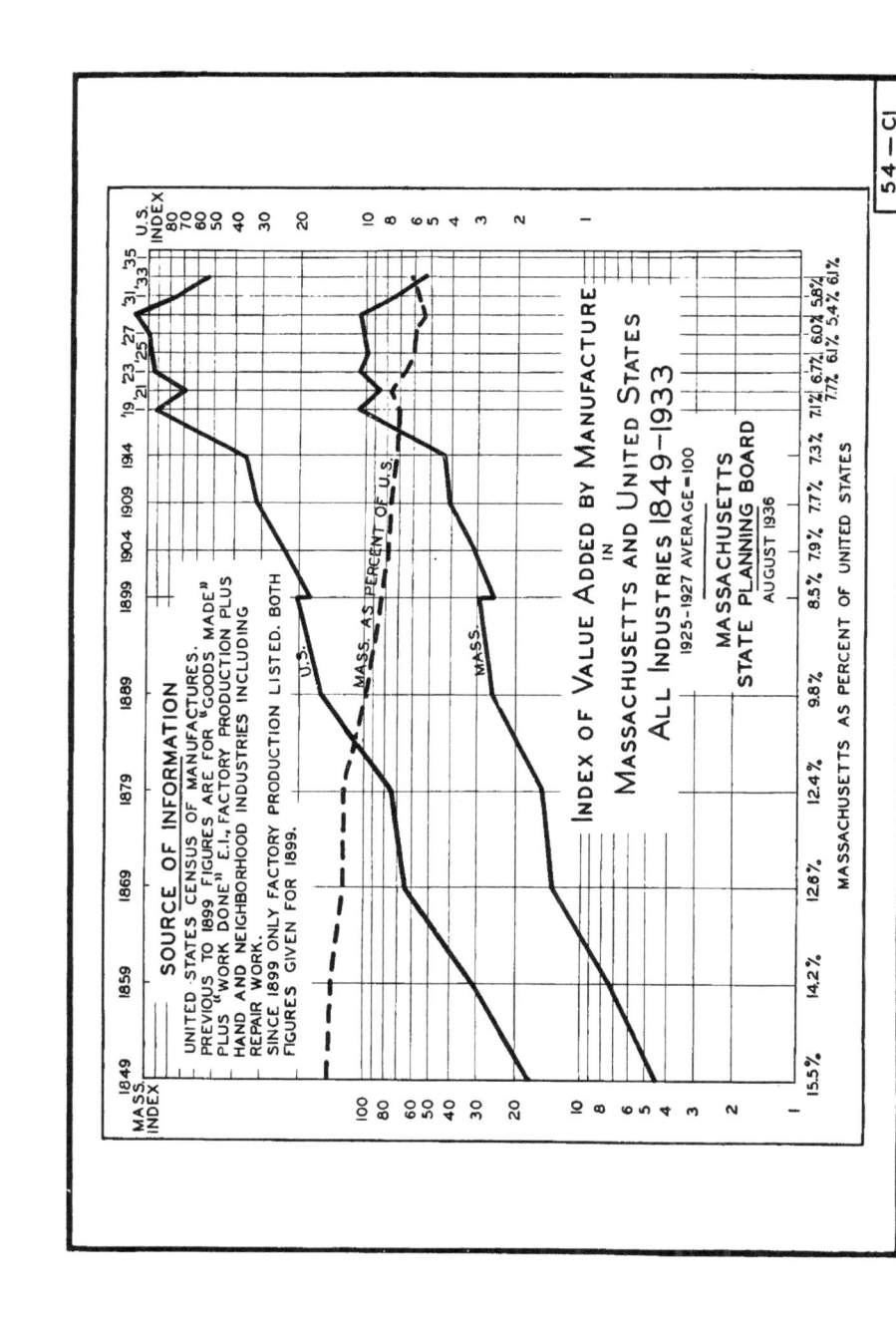

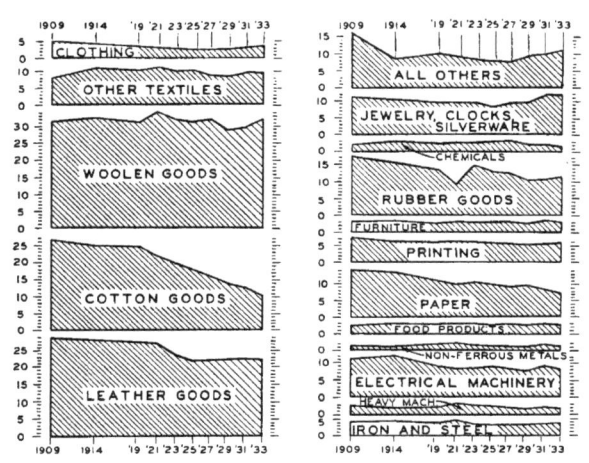

PERCENTAGE OF MASSACHUSETTS PRODUCTION TO UNITED STATES PRODUCTION BY MAIN INDUSTRIAL GROUPS — BASED ON VALUE OF PRODUCTS

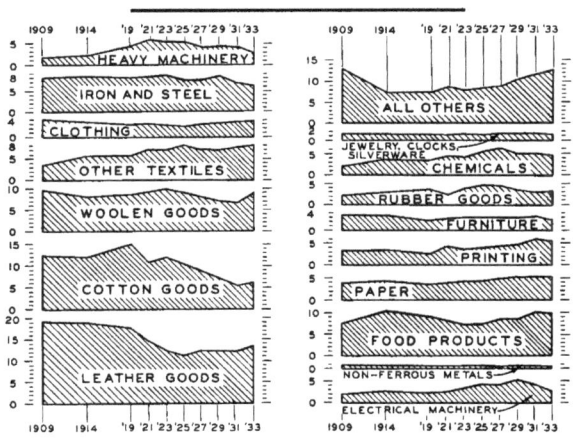

PERCENTAGE OF THE VALUE OF PRODUCTS IN EACH MAIN INDUSTRIAL GROUP IN MASSACHUSETTS TO THE VALUE OF PRODUCTS OF ALL MASSACHUSETTS INDUSTRY
1909–1933

MASSACHUSETTS STATE PLANNING BOARD
NOVEMBER 1936

54-C36

importance to the State, producing all together about 52 per cent of Massachusetts manufactures. These industries, arranged in the order of the value of their output according to the 1933 Census, are as follows:

Table 14

PRINCIPAL MASSACHUSETTS INDUSTRIES

	Industry	Value of Output 1933 (1000 Dollars)
1.	Woolen and Worsted Goods	148,799
2.	Boots and Shoes -- Other Than Rubber	128,074
3.	Cotton Goods	98,603
4.	Dyeing and Finishing Textiles	54,715
5.	Leather -- Tanned, Curried, and Finished	48,630
6.	Printing and Publishing -- Newspapers and Periodicals	48,579
7.	Electrical Machinery, Apparatus, and Supplies	47,959
8.	Pulp and Paper	40,064
9.	Foundry and Machine-Shop Products (Not elsewhere classified)	38,524
10.	Printing and Publishing -- Book, Music, and Job	32,586
11.	Meat Packing	30,181
12.	Knit Goods	25,550
13.	Textile Machinery and Parts	25,143
14.	Silk and Rayon Goods	23,937
15.	Clothing, Womens, Not elsewhere classified	23,659
16.	Confectionery	20,960
17.	Boots and Shoes, Rubber	18,292
18.	Furniture, Including Store and Office Fixtures	15,497

Whatever industrial competition is offered to the Commonwealth by other States usually can be measured by its effect upon one or more of these leading industries. Examination of the census figures shows that there are only about twenty other States in which any of these industries have attained important size, and, of this list of twenty competing States, about fifteen command special attention.

Semi-logarithmic Scale.

It should be noted that in the preceding charts, Nos. 54-C1 and 54-C36, and also in most of the following charts, the semi-logarithmic or percentage scale is used, in order to depict clearly the rate of movement in the individual curves and to make easier the comparison of one curve with another. The rise or fall of the curve represents the percentage rather than the actual amount of change.

Thirty-Two States Which Are Important Producers in One or More of Massachusetts' Leading Industries

INDUSTRY	ALA.	CALIF.	COL.	CONN.	DEL.	GA.	ILL.	IND.	IOWA	KAN.	KY.	ME.	MD.	MICH.	MINN.	MO.	NEB.	N.H.	N.J.	N.Y.	N.C.	OHIO	ORE.	PENN.	R.I.	S.C.	TENN.	TEX.	VA.	WASH.	W.VA.	WIS.
ALL MANUFACTURED PRODUCTS		x		x			x	x						x		x			x	x	x	x		x	x			x				x
1. WOOLEN GOODS AND WORSTED GOODS				x								x						x	x	x				x	x							x
2. BOOTS AND SHOES, OTHER THAN RUBBER				x			x					x				x		x		x		x		x								x
3. COTTON GOODS	x			x		x						x						x	x	x	x			x	x	x	x					
4. DYEING AND FINISHING TEXTILES				x															x	x				x	x	x	x					
5. LEATHER, TANNED, CURRIED AND FINISHED		x			x		x							x				x	x	x		x		x			x					x
6. PRINTING AND PUBLISHING — NEWSPAPER AND PERIODICALS		x					x									x			x	x		x		x				x				
7. ELECTRICAL MACHINERY APPARATUS AND SUPPLIES				x			x							x					x	x		x		x								x
8. PULP AND PAPER												x		x				x		x		x		x						x		x
9. FOUNDRY AND MACHINE SHOP PRODUCTS, NOT ELSEWHERE CLASSIFIED		x		x			x							x					x	x		x		x				x				x
10. PRINTING AND PUBLISHING, BOOK, MUSIC AND JOB		x					x							x					x	x		x		x								
11. MEAT PACKING		x	x				x		x	x				x	x	x	x		x	x		x						x				x
12. KNIT GOODS		x	x				x		x					x				x	x	x	x			x	x		x					x
13. TEXTILE MACHINERY AND PARTS				x														x	x	x	x			x	x	x						
14. SILK AND RAYON GOODS				x															x	x	x			x								
15. CLOTHING, WOMEN'S, NOT ELSEWHERE CLASSIFIED		x					x						x			x			x	x		x		x								x
16. CONFECTIONERY		x					x									x			x	x		x		x								
17. BOOTS AND SHOES, RUBBER				x			x							x				x	x	x		x		x	x							x
18. FURNITURE, INCLUDING STORE AND OFFICE FIXTURES	x						x							x						x	x	x		x			x		x		x	x

MASSACHUSETTS STATE PLANNING BOARD
NOVEMBER 1936
SOURCE: U.S. CENSUS OF MANUFACTURES

54—C47

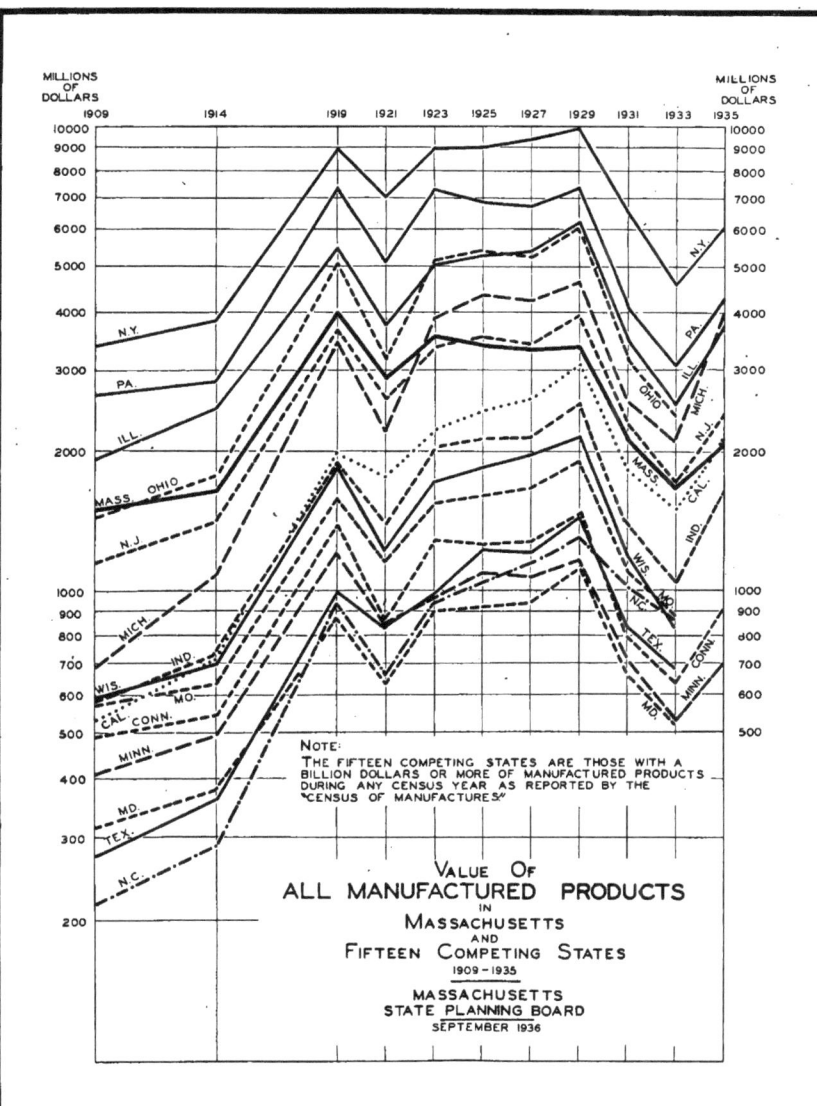

WOOLEN AND WORSTED GOODS

Based on 1933 Census reports, Massachusetts is the largest producing State, in this industry. The total value of production in Massachusetts and six other leading woolen- and worsted-goods manufacturing States in 1933 was as follows:

Massachusetts	$148,799,000	Maine	$28,554,000
Rhode Island	82,511,000	New Jersey	27,497,000
Pennsylvania	52,085,000	Connecticut	24,685,000
		New York	13,581,000

The woolen- and worsted-goods industry is the second largest industry in Massachusetts. This State is the largest producer of woolen and worsted goods in the United States. In 1933, its output amounted to 33 per cent of the country's total production. During the period shown on the accompanying chart, Rhode Island moved from third to second place and Maine from seventh to fourth place. Massachusetts has shared the growth of this industry with other industrial States, but still holds by a good margin its position of supremacy.

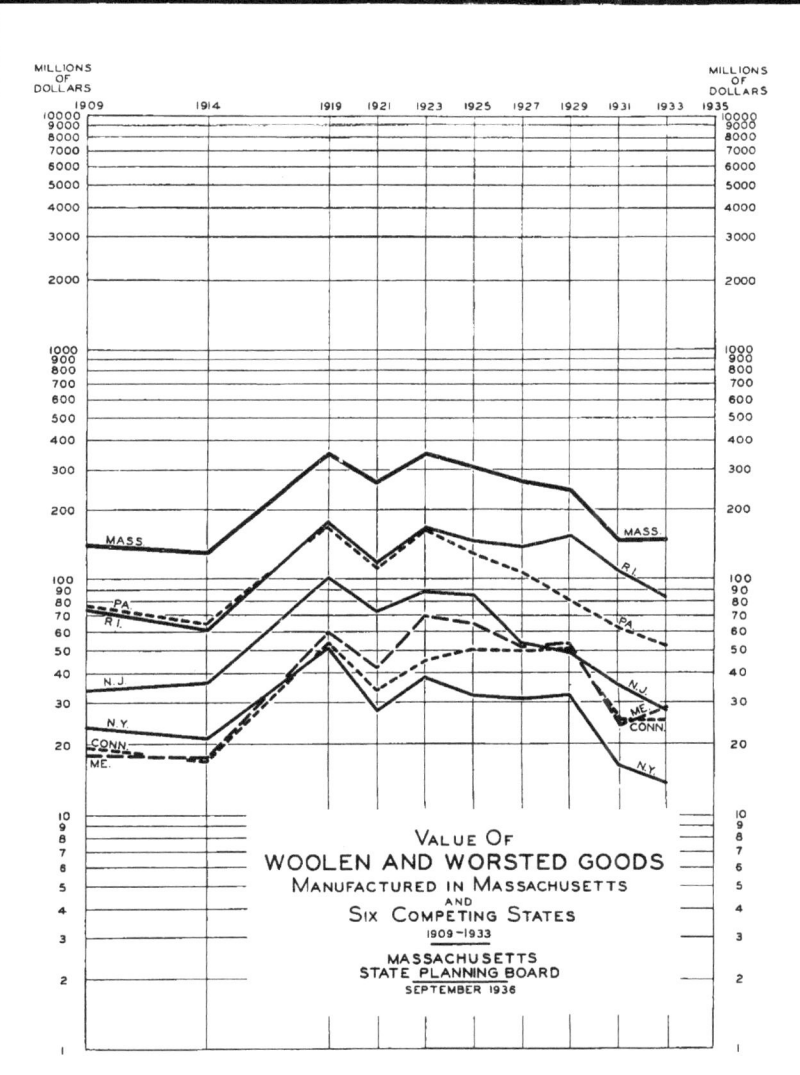

BOOTS AND SHOES -- OTHER THAN RUBBER

This is an industry in which, for various reasons, **Massachusetts** has had to share its business with other States. In part, this may have been the fault of Massachusetts, but certainly it is only natural that an essential industry such as boot-and-shoe production should develop in the newer manufacturing centers of the country. It would be unreasonable to expect any State to maintain a monopoly in the output of a product which can be made anywhere, and which is used in every State of the Union.

The nine leading shoe-producing States, together with the value of their production in 1935, are indicated below. These values for 1935 are estimated in accordance with the monthly reports of boot-and-shoe production, issued by the Bureau of the Census. They are not the results of the complete Census taken for 1935 and may be subject to some revision when the final census figures are available.

Massachusetts	$128,161,000	Illinois	$46,911,000
New York	107,607,000	Maine	38,763,000
Missouri	73,280,000	Ohio	37,705,000
New Hampshire	49,653,000	Wisconsin	32,316,000
		Pennsylvania	30,929,000

From 1909 to 1929, the States which gained most in shoe production were New York, Wisconsin, Illinois, and Missouri. During the depression, between 1929 and 1933, all States lost to some extent. Massachusetts, New Hampshire, Missouri, and New York lost more heavily than the others.

Between 1933 and 1935, the States showing the largest percentage of gain were New Hampshire, Maine, Ohio, and Pennsylvania. New York and Illinois made some advance; Massachusetts and Missouri were stationary; Wisconsin showed a slight decline.

As in some other industries, it appears that the showing for Massachusetts in shoe output during 1936 has been much better, as compared with that of the other States, than was indicated in the figures of 1935. This is apparent in the chart of Business Activity, which reveals a recent improvement in Massachusetts shoe production as compared with that of the entire United States.

Everyone who is acquainted with the shoe industry will realize that other bases of measurement beside that of the value of production may well be considered. In this report, however, it is impossible to go into further detail, although it is the Board's intention to present more complete data in a future report.

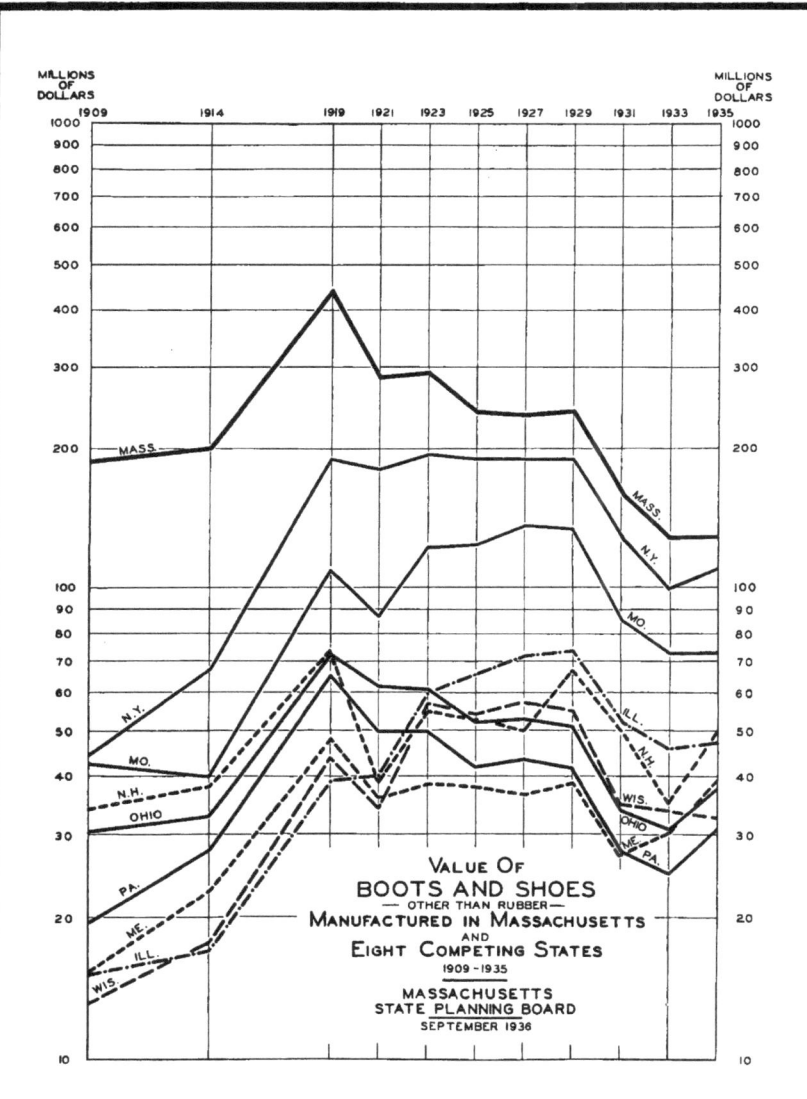

COTTON GOODS

According to the Census of 1933, Massachusetts was the fourth largest cotton-textile producing State in the Union, being preceded by North Carolina, South Carolina, and Georgia. The leading cotton-goods producing States, with the value of their production in 1933, are as follows:

North Carolina	$189,751,000	Connecticut	$20,141,000
South Carolina	162,411,000	Virginia	19,949,000
Georgia	126,301,000	Pennsylvania	16,543,000
Massachusetts	98,603,000	Tennessee	12,779,000
Alabama	66,939,000	New Jersey	11,990,000
Rhode Island	34,714,000	New York	9,730,000
Maine	28,979,000	Texas	8,715,000
New Hampshire	25,595,000	Maryland	3,219,000

Taking the figures of production at their face value, it seems evident that, in the last decade, cotton textile production has definitely become an industry of the South. Of the sixteen cotton-manufacturing States, there is not a single northern State which has maintained its 1923 production. Texas, followed by Alabama, has been making the most rapid growth. A composite curve of seven southern States is added to this chart to indicate the progress in the South in this industry, as against the decline in the northern States.

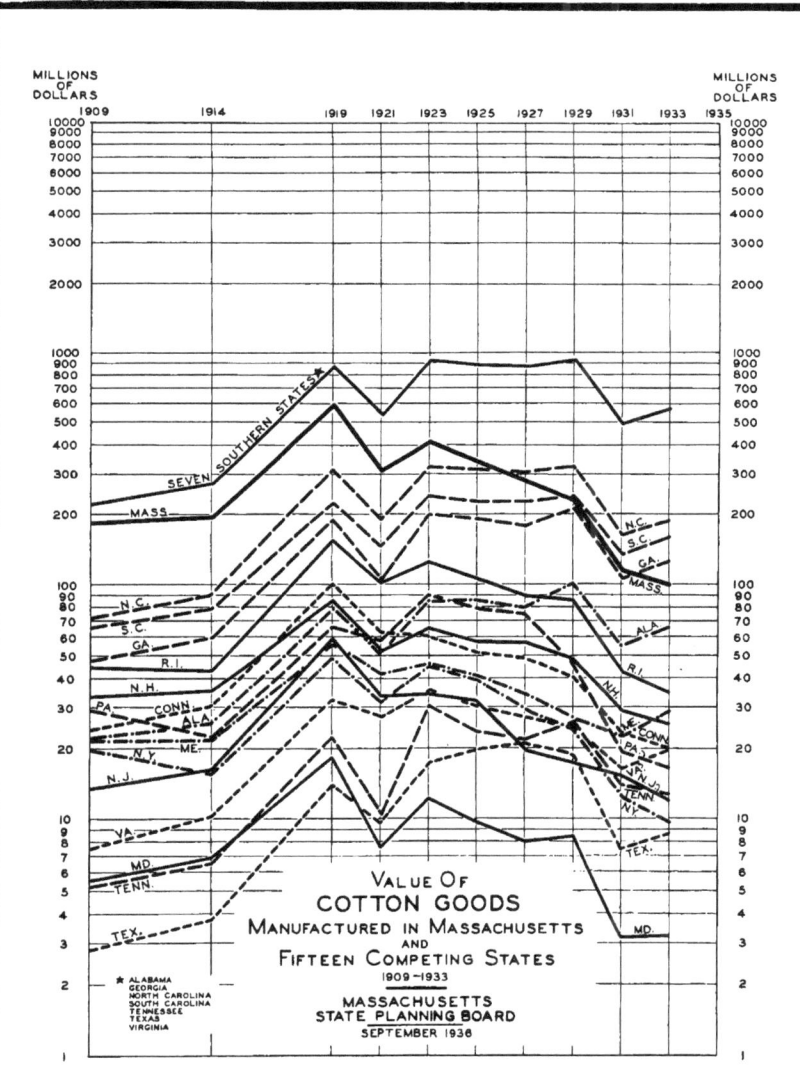

DYEING AND FINISHING TEXTILES

Massachusetts holds second place in this industry, according to the Census of 1933. It is interesting to note that, within recent years, the State has been exchanging first and second places with New Jersey. The leading States in this industry, with the value of their production in 1933, are as follows:

New Jersey	$57,898,000	Pennsylvania	$26,379,000
Massachusetts	54,715,000	New York	20,391,000
Rhode Island	33,659,000	North Carolina	12,297,000
South Carolina	27,894,000	Connecticut	8,923,000
		Tennessee	7,374,000

The outstanding feature shown on the accompanying chart is growth of this industry in North Carolina and South Carolina. Of the remaining seven States, New Jersey, Pennsylvania, Rhode Island, and Connecticut form a group in which the industry shows a rising trend; in Massachusetts and New York it has been declining. The tendency of this industry in the State of Tennessee is not clear.

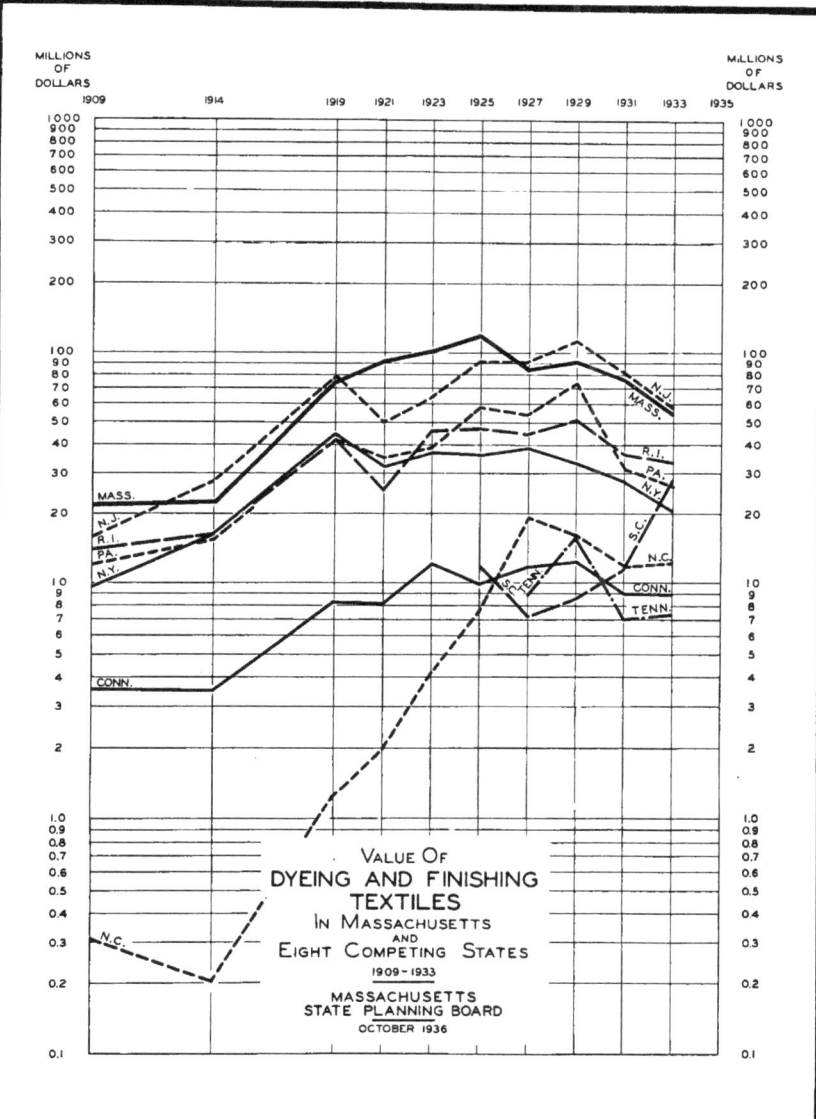

LEATHER -- TANNED, CURRIED, AND FINISHED

Massachusetts holds first place in the manufacture of leather, according to the Census of 1933. The twelve leading States in this industry, with the value of their production in 1933, are as follows:

Massachusetts	$48,630,000	Delaware (1931)	$10,860,000
Pennsylvania	43,523,000	Michigan	10,116,000
New York	29,510,000	Ohio	8,750,000
Illinois	20,586,000	North Carolina	6,562,000
Wisconsin	15,653,000	West Virginia	5,291,000
New Jersey	13,335,000	Virginia	2,978,000
		California	2,971,000

The outstanding points shown on this chart are the lack of severe decline of the industry during the depression, and the fact that Massachusetts changed from second to first place during the industrial decline. The industry, as a whole, has shown no spectacular gains or losses in any of the other thirteen States which are engaged in leather tanning.

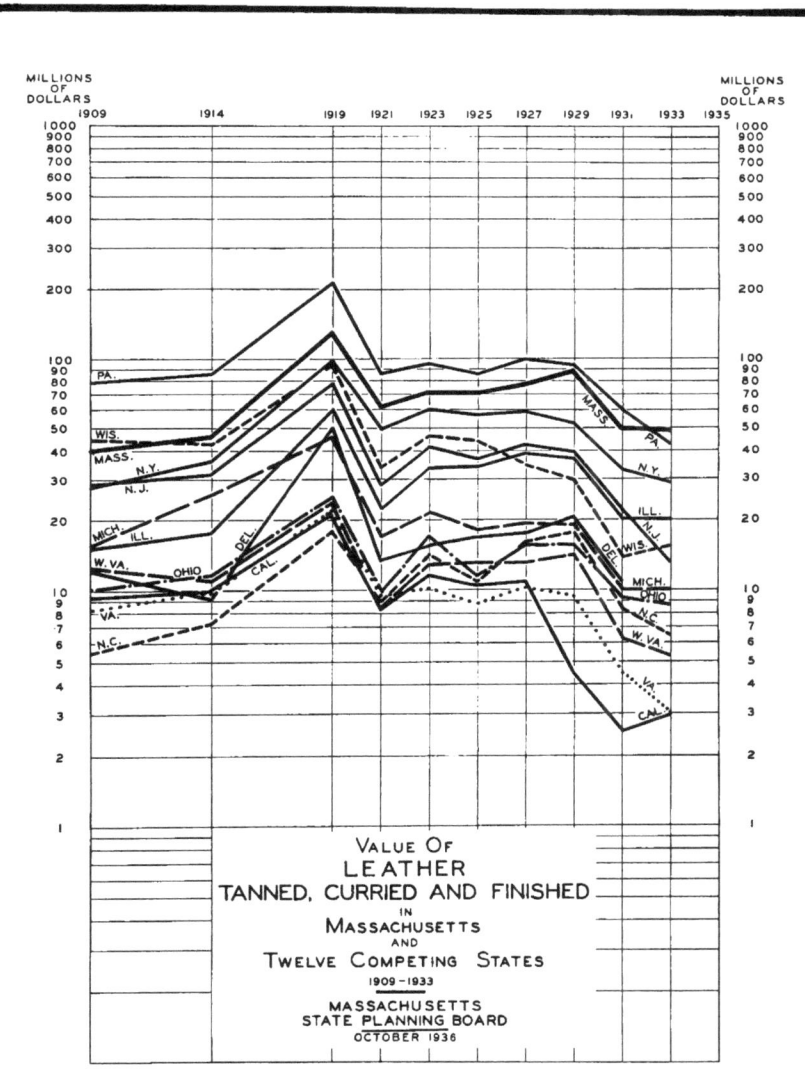

PRINTING AND PUBLISHING -- NEWSPAPERS AND PERIODICALS

The United States Bureau of Census divides the printing and publishing industry into two groups: one, consisting of newspapers and periodicals; a second, consisting of book, music, and job printing.

According to the Census of 1933, the leading newspaper and periodical publishing States, with the value of their production for that year, are as follows:

New York	$266,412,000	California	$59,051,000
Pennsylvania	105,286,000	Massachusetts	48,579,000
Illinois	93,386,000	Michigan	29,531,000
Ohio	76,504,000	Missouri	28,749,000

The printing and publishing of newspapers and periodicals is one of the industries which show a strong secular trend throughout the period covered by the accompanying chart. This industry, unlike many others, has not experienced much decline during the recent depression. Massachusetts, which occupied fifth place in 1914, the beginning of the period for which there are available data, lost its place to California in 1921. Since then, however, it has maintained its place, and it has substantially shared in the growth of the industry.

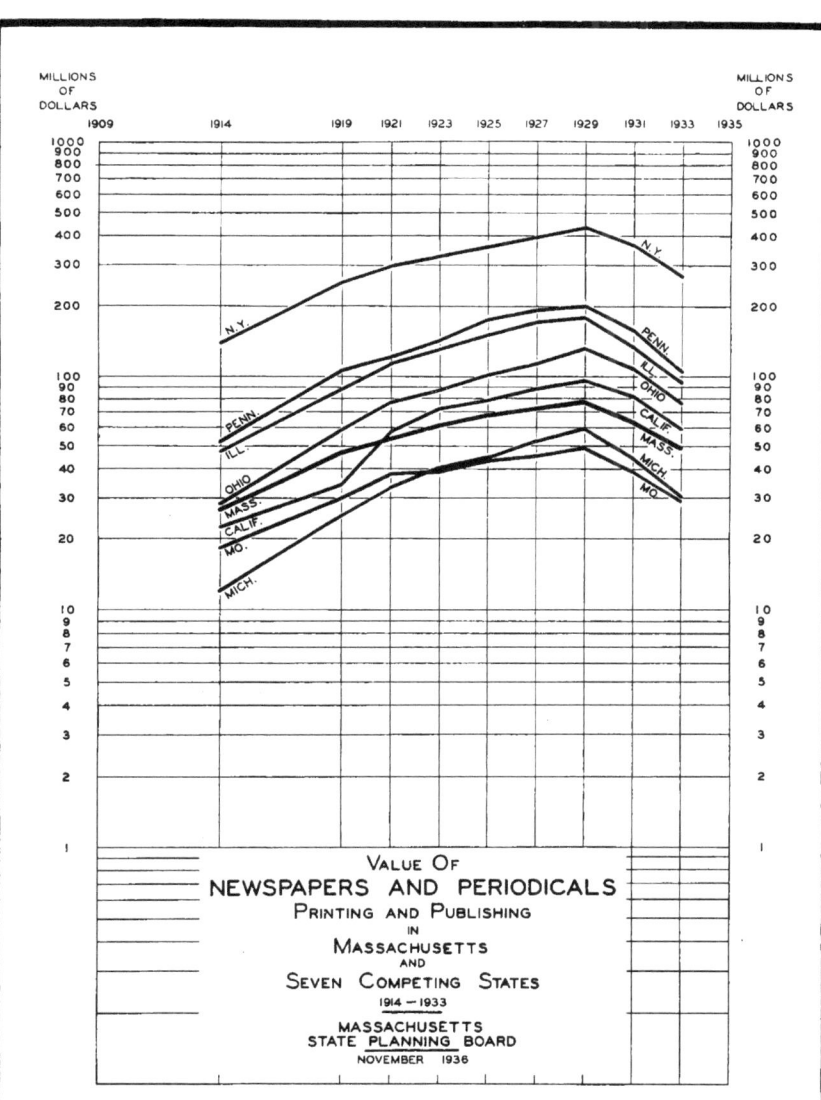

ELECTRICAL MACHINERY, APPARATUS, AND SUPPLIES

According to 1933 Census reports, Massachusetts holds seventh place in this industry. The leading electrical-machinery manufacturing States, with the value of their production in 1933, are as follows:

Ohio	$99,308,000	Massachusetts	$47,959,000
New York	63,735,000	Connecticut	30,123,000
Pennsylvania	62,634,000	Missouri	18,943,000
New Jersey	61,299,000	Wisconsin	17,923,000
Illinois	55,977,000	Michigan	10,450,000
Indiana	50,380,000	California	10,267,000
		Rhode Island	4,932,000

A strong secular growth for this industry is indicated by the accompanying chart. Massachusetts, in common with the other leading States, has shared the growth of the industry. Michigan and California seem to have made the most rapid advance.

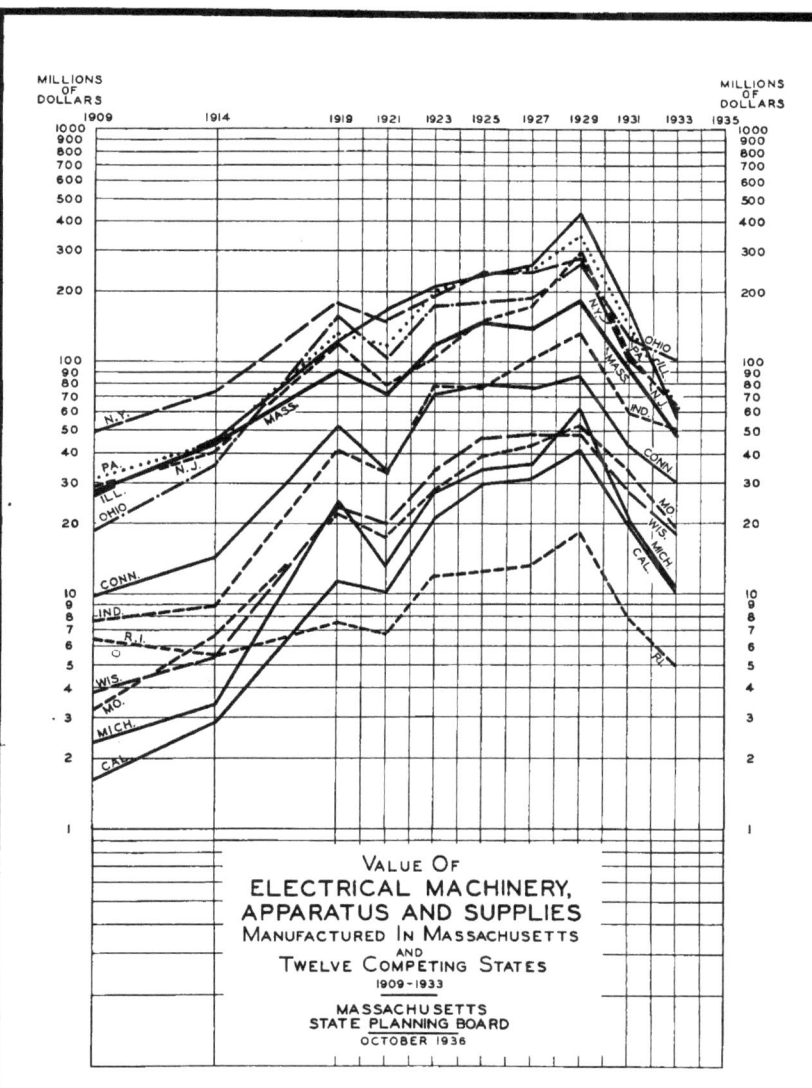

PULP AND PAPER

According to the 1933 Census, Massachusetts holds eighth place among the eleven leading pulp- and paper-manufacturing States. The eleven States, with the value of their production for 1933, are as follows:

New York	$77,981,000	Ohio	$47,563,000*
Wisconsin	77,001,000	Washington	40,657,000
Maine	63,025,000	Massachusetts	40,577,000
Michigan	61,607,000	New Jersey	23,746,000*
Pennsylvania	52,546,000	Illinois	18,388,000*
		New Hampshire	11,641,000*

As the accompanying chart indicates, Massachusetts has dropped from second place, in 1909, to eighth place, in 1933, yielding its place, first to Wisconsin, and then to Michigan, Ohio, Pennsylvania, and Maine.

*Figures for Pulp Wood are not given for these States individually.

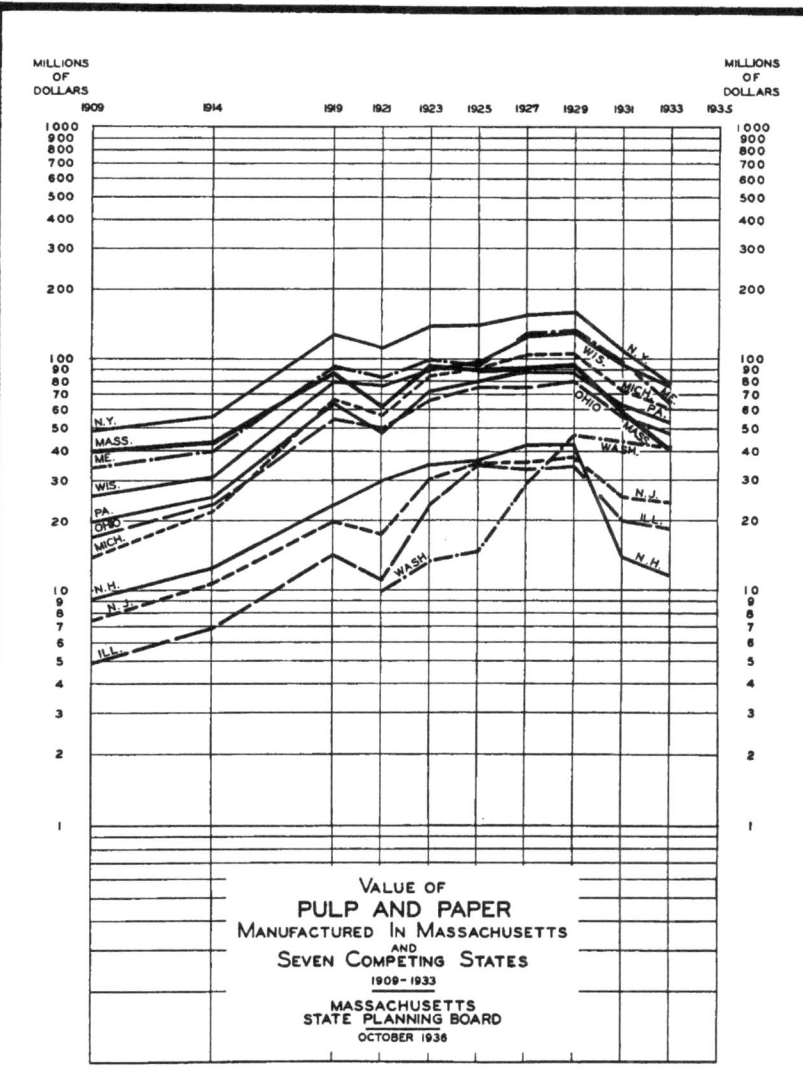

FOUNDRY AND MACHINE-SHOP PRODUCTS

According to 1933 Census, Massachusetts holds seventh place in the manufacturing of foundry and machine-shop products. The leading States in the industry, with value of their products in 1933, are as follows:

Ohio	$106,782,000	Massachusetts	$38,524,000
Pennsylvania	91,539,000	New Jersey	38,170,000
Michigan	90,189,000	Wisconsin	37,086,000
Illinois	79,267,000	Connecticut	34,272,000
New York	77,643,000	California	28,805,000
Indiana	42,288,000	Missouri	16,383,000
		Texas	15,893,000

This industry, like the electrical-machinery and supplies industry, shows a rising secular trend, although not so pronounced. Massachusetts has shared in the growth of this industry, but not to the extent of some of the other States. Texas and California seem to have had the fastest growth.

The figures here presented do not include operation of steel foundries or boiler-shop, foundry, and machine-shop departments of establishments engaged primarily in the manufacture of specific classes of products assigned to other industries.

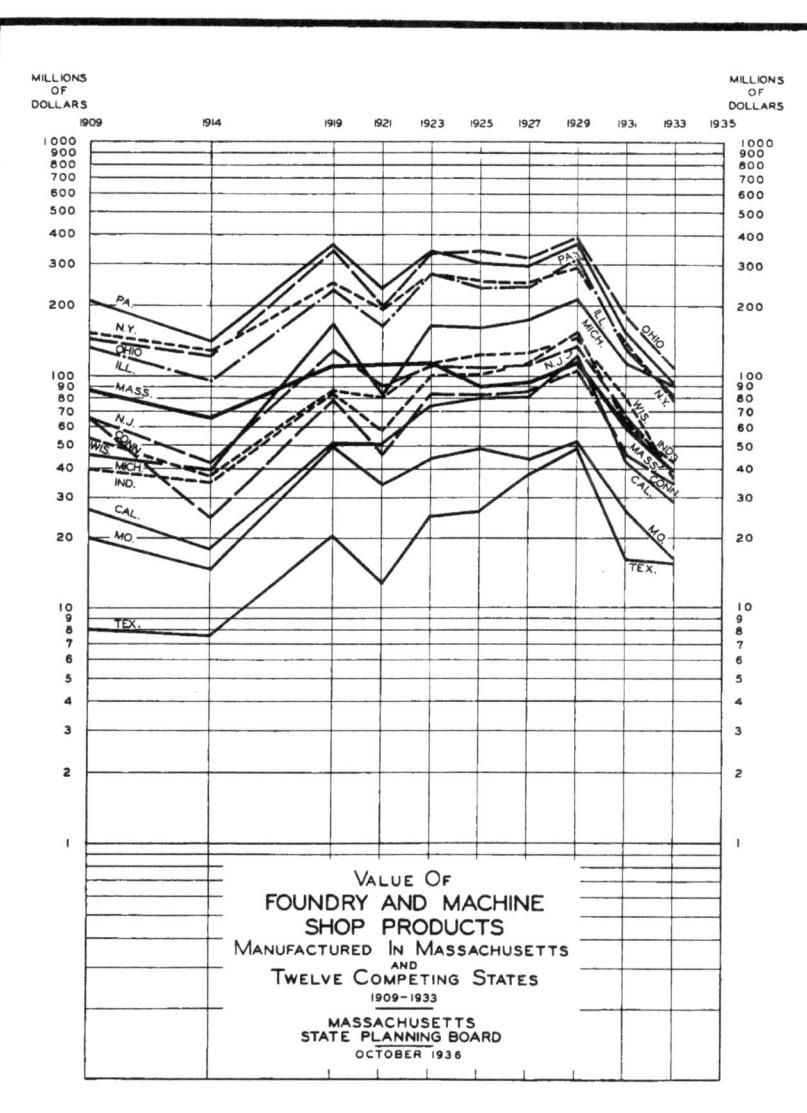

PRINTING AND PUBLISHING -- BOOK, MUSIC, AND JOB

This is the second of the two charts of the printing and publishing industry. According to the Census report of 1933, there are eight States which are leaders in this branch of the printing and publishing industry. These States, with the value of their products in 1933, are as follows:

New York	$138,410,000	Massachusetts	$32,586,000
Illinois	81,865,000	California	24,986,000
Ohio	40,045,000	Missouri	16,483,000
Pennsylvania	36,418,000	Michigan	15,174,000

This branch of the printing and publishing industry, and newspaper and periodical publishing, seem to have had very similar secular trends, and to have declined little during the recent depression. Massachusetts, which occupied fourth place in this industry in 1914, has lost that place to Pennsylvania, and now occupies fifth place. As in many other industries, California seems to be the fastest growing State, followed by Michigan and New York.

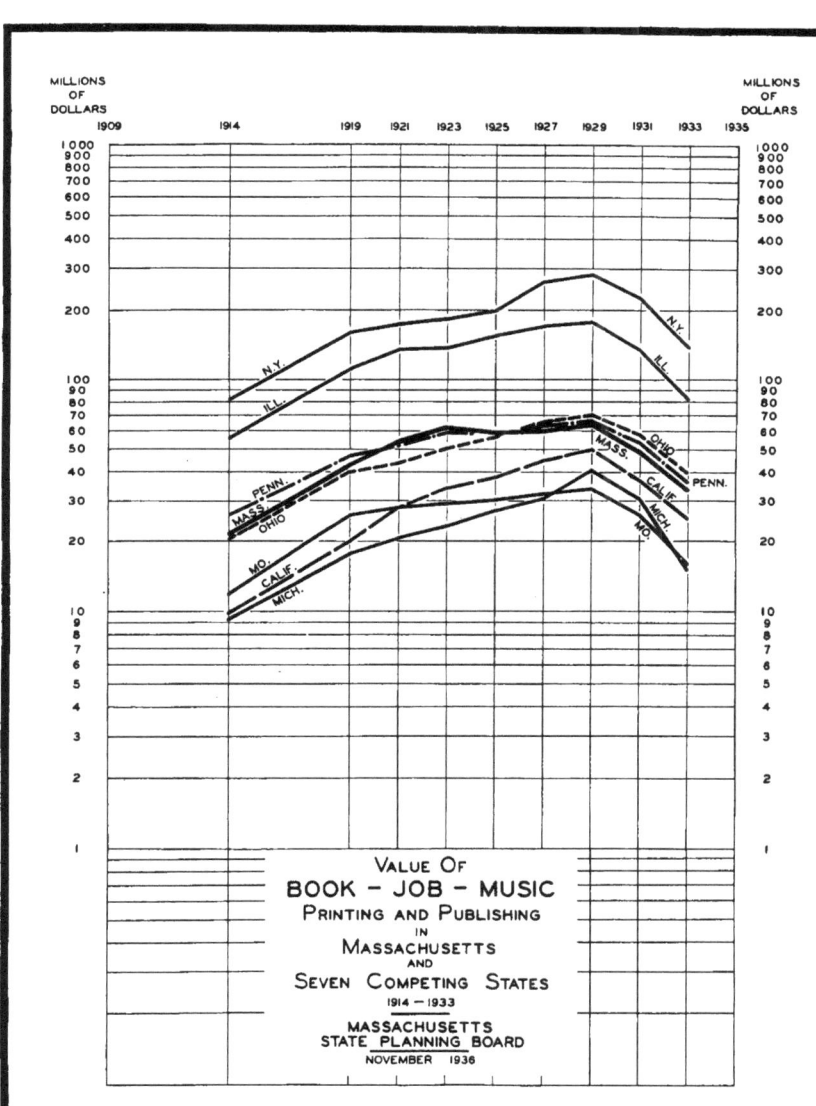

MEAT PACKING

Massachusetts holds fifteenth place in this industry. The leading meat-packing States, with the value of their production in 1933, are as follows:

Illinois	$310,160,000	Wisconsin	$37,910,000
Iowa	119,585,000	Texas	34,868,000
New York	115,255,000	Massachusetts	30,181,000
Kansas	97,404,000	South Dakota	25,124,000
Minnesota	87,255,000	Michigan	22,145,000
Nebraska	83,218,000	Maryland	18,956,000
California	76,575,000	Colorado	16,021,000
Ohio	75,851,000	Washington	15,755,000
Missouri	73,587,000	Kentucky	10,332,000
Pennsylvania	63,709,000	Tennessee	8,838,000
New Jersey	47,305,000	Oregon	7,694,000
Indiana	44,136,000		

With hardly a single exception, the industry has had a slowly rising trend in all twenty-one States. There seem to be no outstanding gains or losses on the party of any of the States which have been leaders in this industry during the period covered. The individual States are shown on two separate charts to avoid confusion of the curves.

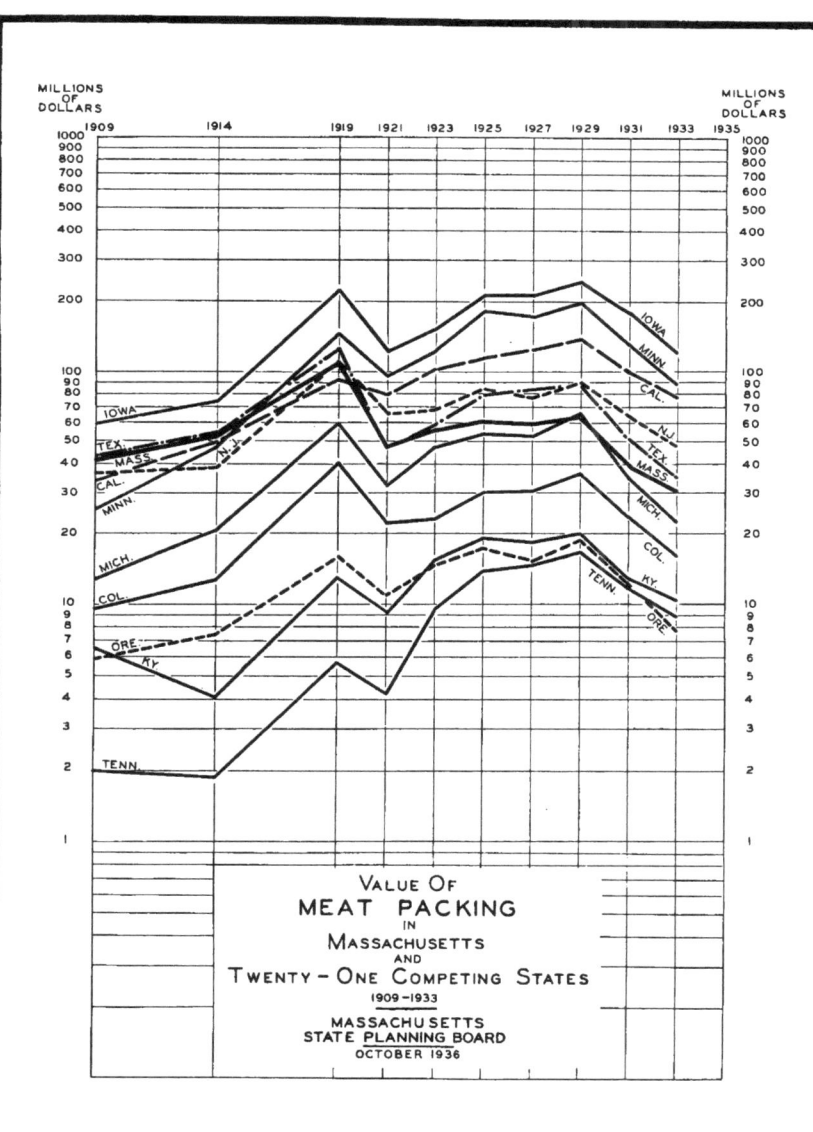

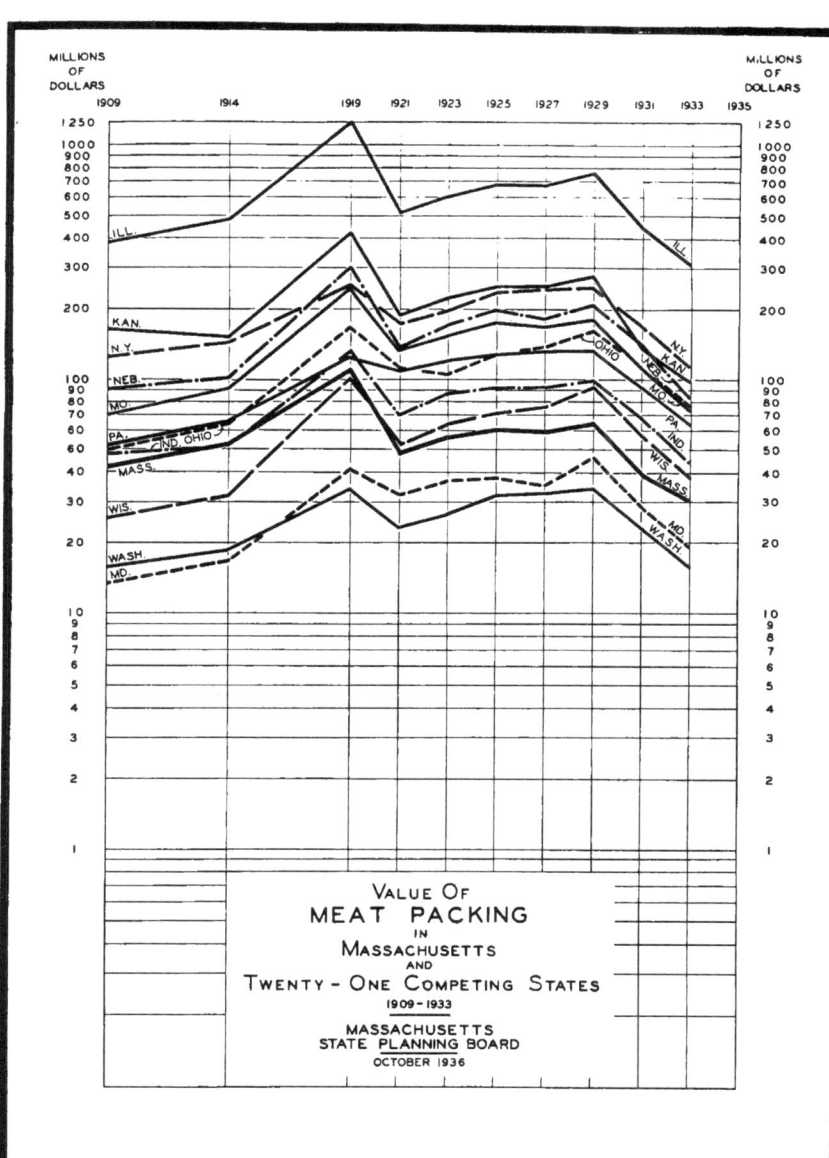

KNIT GOODS

According to the 1933 Census, Massachusetts is fifth in a group of sixteen leading knit-goods manufacturing States. The sixteen States, with the value of their production in 1933, are as follows:

Pennsylvania	$133,766,000	Georgia	$14,468,000
New York	79,882,000	Indiana	13,336,000
North Carolina	64,092,000	Illinois	11,595,000
Tennessee	33,477,000	Virginia	9,058,000
Massachusetts	25,550,000	Minnesota	7,235,000
New Jersey	21,594,000	Michigan	5,510,000
Wisconsin	20,424,000	California	5,415,000
Ohio	14,799,000	Rhode Island	4,382,000

This industry has shown a strong upward secular trend, but examination of the two accompanying charts indicates that not all of the States have shared in its growth. North Carolina, Indiana, and California seem to be leading. Massachusetts appears to be holding its own, and New York, Ohio, and Illinois have shown a downward tendency.

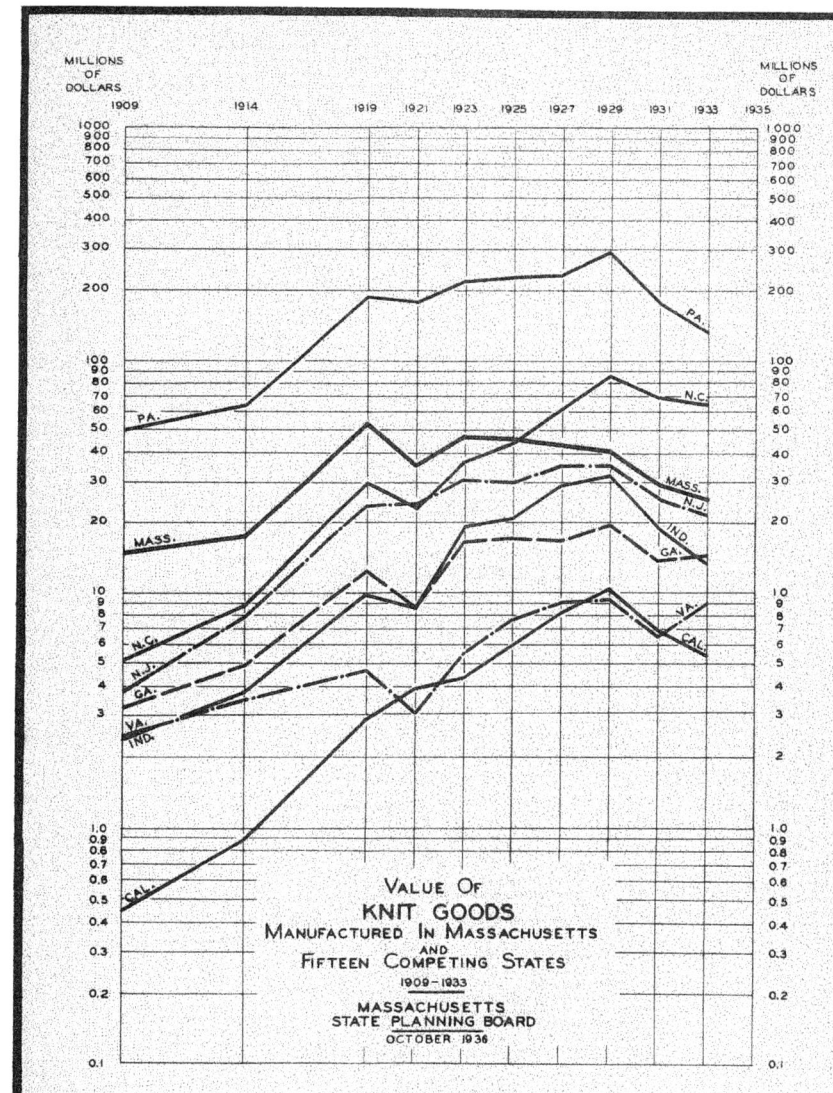

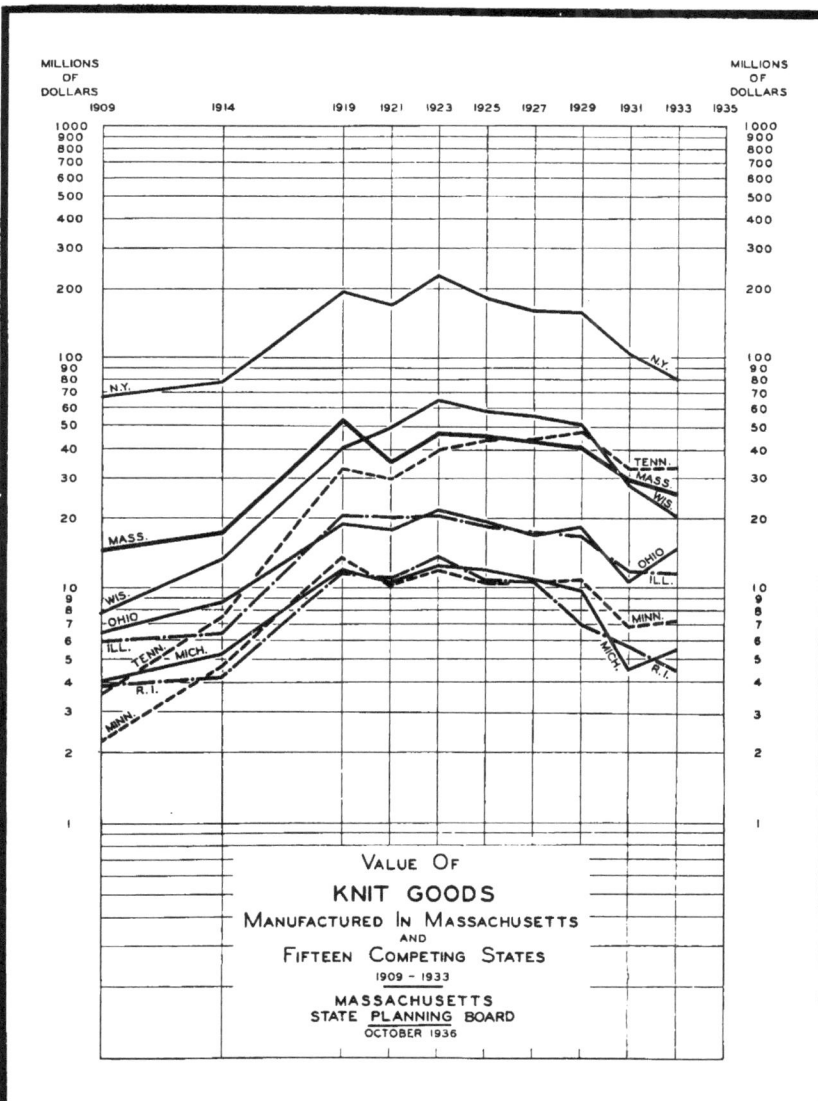

TEXTILE MACHINERY AND PARTS

Data on this industry for the years prior to 1919 are not available. From 1919 to 1933 Massachusetts was the leader. Five States are engaged in the manufacture of textile machinery and parts. These States, with the value of their production in 1933, are as follows:

Massachusetts	$25,143,000	Rhode Island	$6,594,000
Pennsylvania	12,108,000	New Hampshire	2,951,000
		New Jersey	2,574,000

The accompanying chart indicates that Pennsylvania has made the greatest gain during the period for which data are available. Massachusetts showed a rising trend between 1931 and 1933, when all other States were declining, following the general trend of industry.

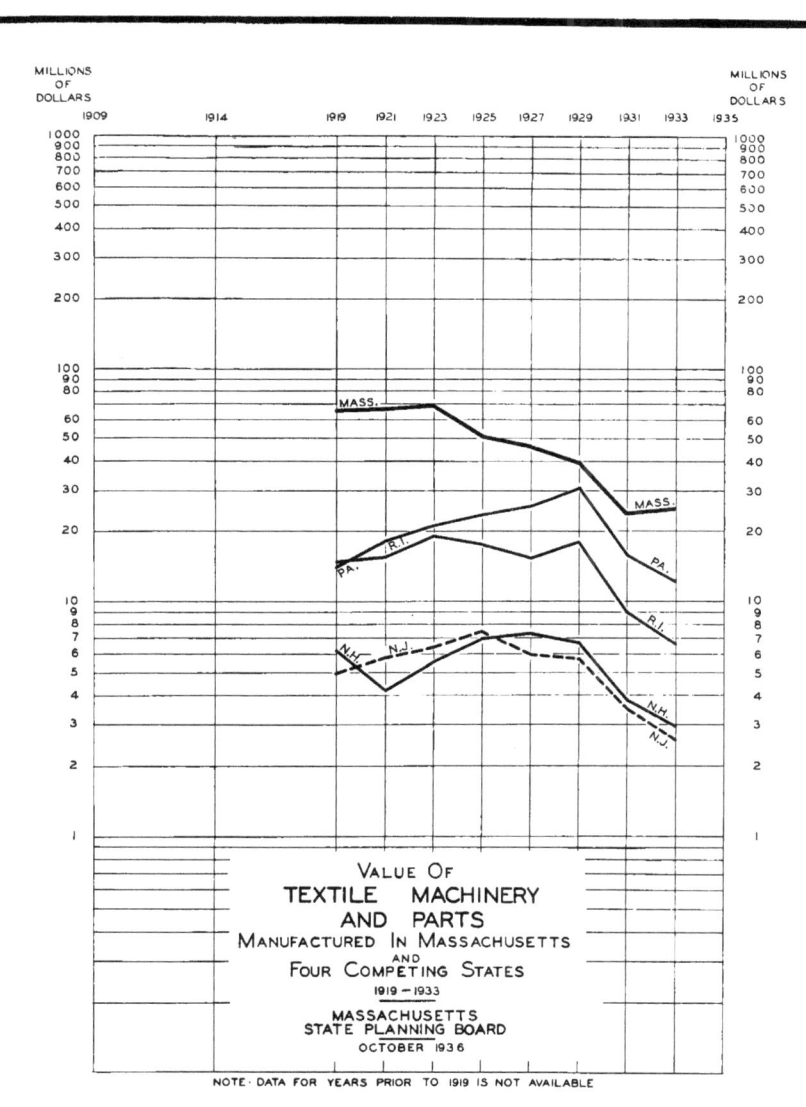

SILK AND RAYON GOODS

The seven States which are leaders in the manufacture of silk and rayon goods, with the value of their production in 1933, are as follows:

Pennsylvania	$109,925,000	Rhode Island	$24,965,000
New Jersey	31,533,000	New York	23,966,000
North Carolina	31,289,000	Massachusetts	23,937,000
		Connecticut	23,243,000

As is often stated, this industry seems to be gaining at least some of the market that has been lost by cotton textiles. Massachusetts, while one of the lesser States in the production of silk and rayon goods, has shared in their growth. North Carolina, in the short period for which there are available data, has made a notable start. Of the other States, Pennsylvania has made the best showing in this particular industry.

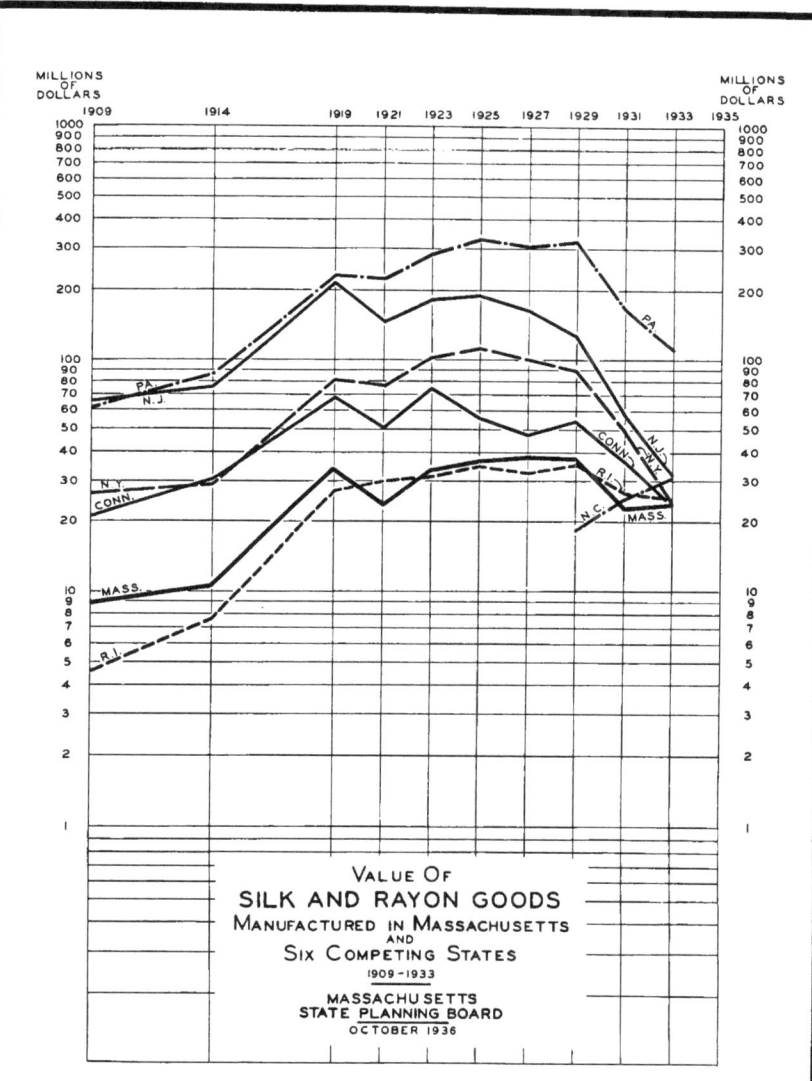

WOMEN'S CLOTHING

According to the Census of 1933, Massachusetts holds fifth place in this industry. The nine leading women's-clothing manufacturing States, with the value of their production in 1933, are as follows:

New York	$619,073,000	Massachusetts	$23,659,000
Illinois	38,565,000	New Jersey	19,263,000
Pennsylvania	38,050,000	Missouri	17,339,000
California	23,790,000	Ohio	15,978,000
		Maryland	8,319,000

New York State holds a commanding position in this industry, producing more than twice as much as all other States combined. The industry has shown a decided upward trend in all the nine States which are leaders in this field. Apparently, Massachusetts has been getting its full share of growth. It is interesting to note also the progress of this industry in California. During the period covered by this chart, California has jumped from ninth to fifth place.

The figures given here do not include the manufacture of underwear and outerwear in knitting mills.

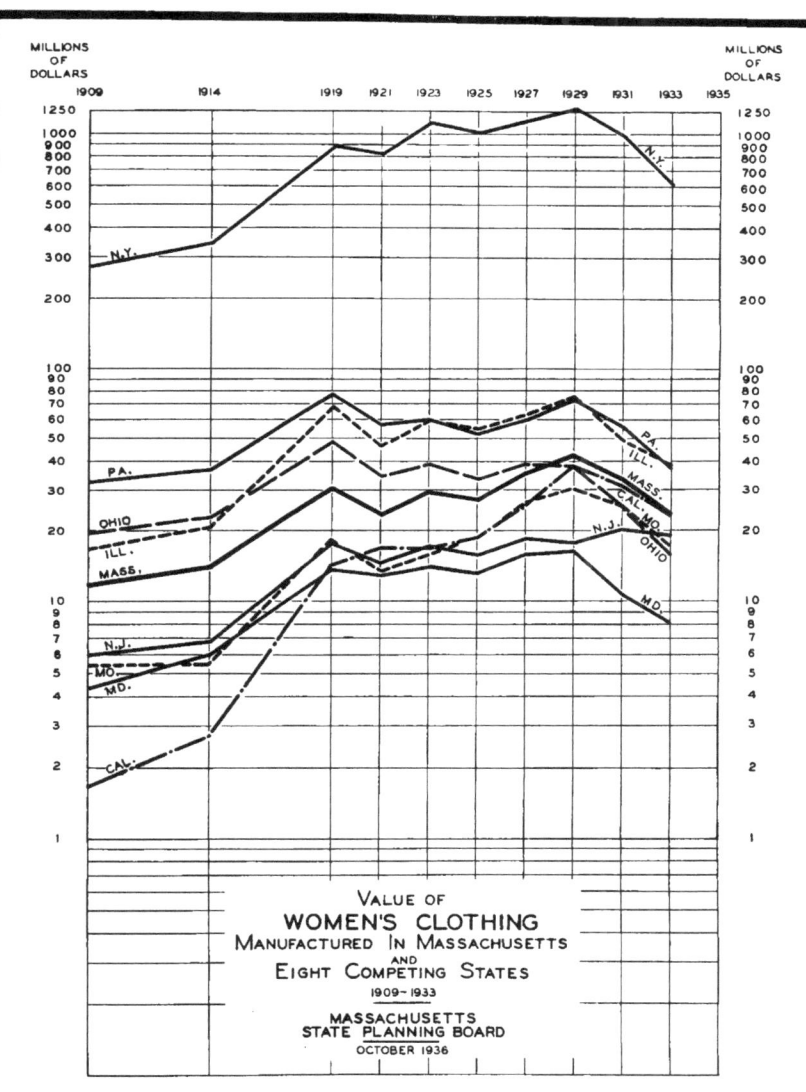

CONFECTIONERY

According to the 1933 Census, Massachusetts holds fourth place in this industry, in a group of nine foremost confectionery-manufacturing States. The leading States, with the value of their production for 1933, are as follows:

Illinois	$64,192,000	California	$9,692,000
New York	30,447,000	Missouri	9,273,000
Pennsylvania	22,266,000	Ohio	8,881,000
Massachusetts	20,960,000	Wisconsin	4,594,000
		Virginia	3,545,000

The accompanying chart shows Illinois and Virginia as the two States in which the best growth has occurred in the confectionery industry. All other States, including Massachusetts, seem to be nearly parallel in trend although, during the period covered by the chart, Massachusetts has dropped from second to fourth place. Illinois and Pennsylvania have taken second and third places, respectively.

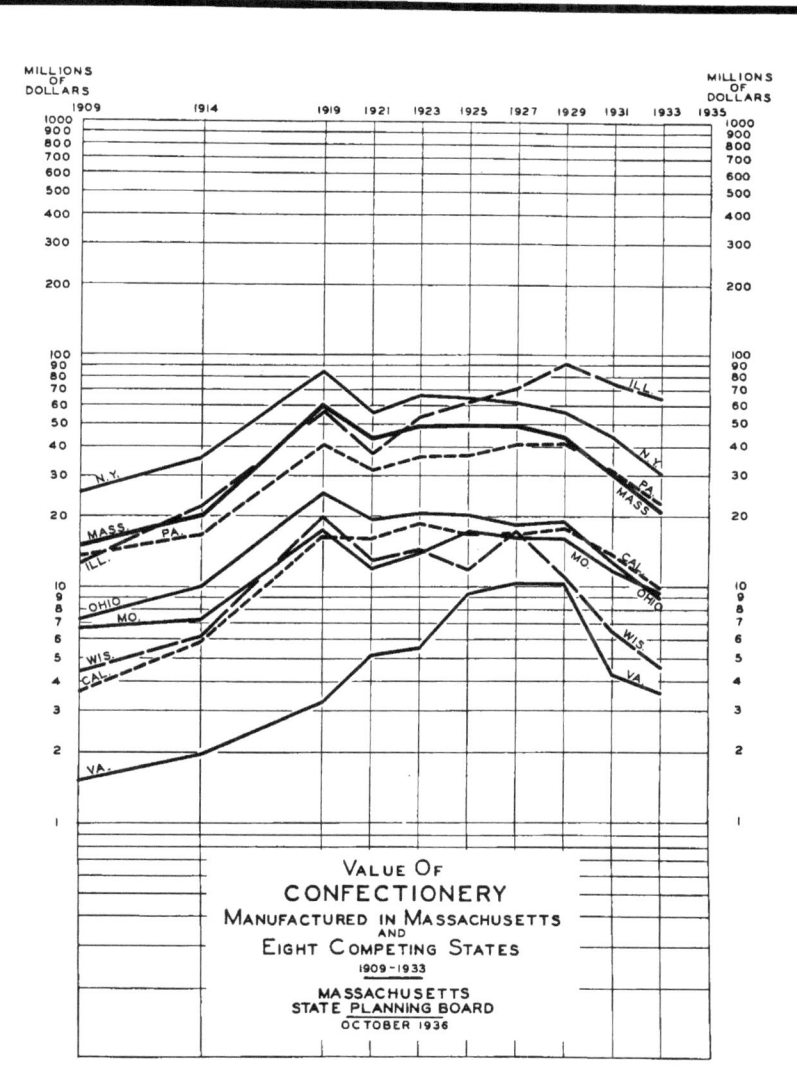

BOOTS AND SHOES -- RUBBER

Massachusetts is the only State in the Union for which the Bureau of Census gives separate data for this industry. All other States engaged in the manufacture of rubber boots and shoes are combined into one composite, as is indicated on the accompanying chart. In 1933, Massachusetts produced $18,292,000 worth of goods, as against $23,727,000 produced by all other States.

The following are listed by the Census Bureau under "All Other States": Connecticut, Illinois, Indiana, New Jersey, Pennsylvania, Rhode Island, and Wisconsin.

It is quite obvious from the chart that the curve for Massachusetts and the composite curve for all other States show about the same trend for the 1909-1933 period covered by the chart. Evidently Massachusetts is getting its full share of the growth of this industry.

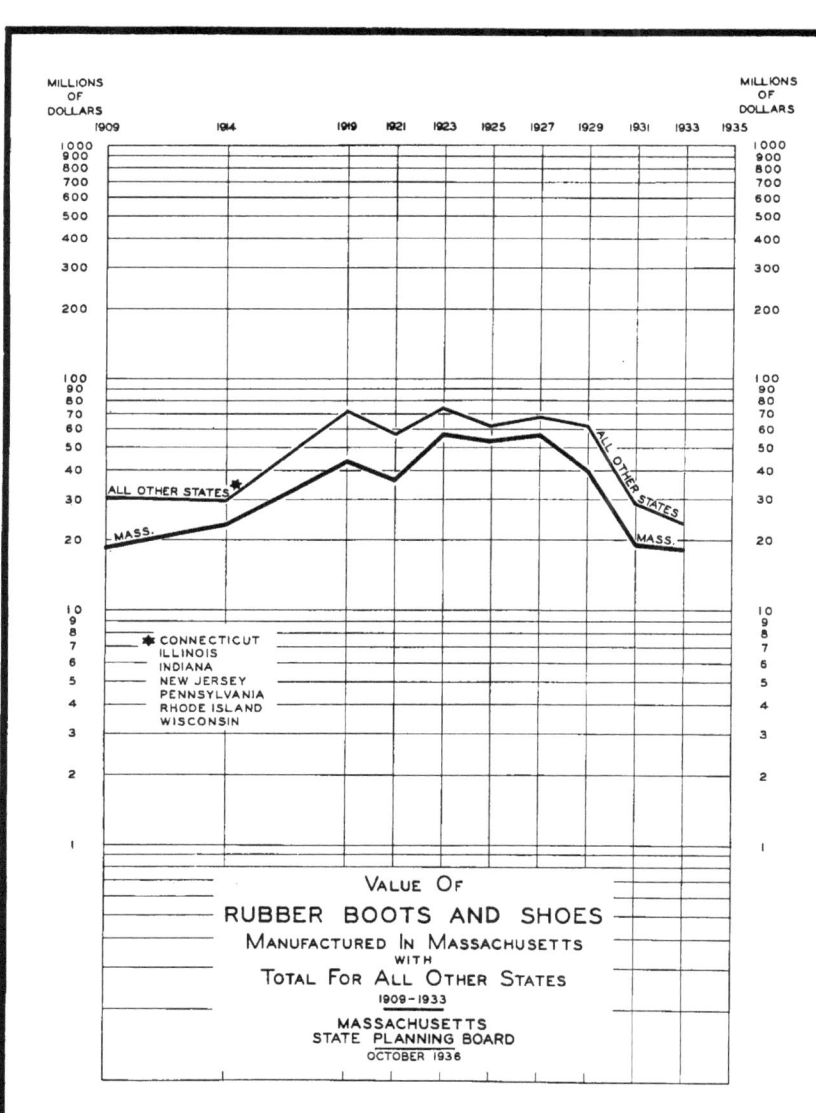

FURNITURE, INCLUDING STORE AND OFFICE FIXTURES

The Census of manufacture for 1933 shows Massachusetts in ninth place in a group of sixteen leading furniture-manufacturing States. The States, with the value of their manufactured products in 1933, are as follows:

New York	$50,363,000	Massachusetts	$15,497,000
Illinois	28,782,000	California	13,188,000
North Carolina	26,625,000	Wisconsin	11,803,000
Michigan	23,330,000	Missouri	5,380,000
Indiana	21,269,000	New Jersey	5,269,000
Pennsylvania	19,280,000	Tennessee	3,335,000
Ohio	18,332,000	Maryland	3,322,000
Virginia	16,281,000	Minnesota	3,236,000

This industry seems to have a pronounced upward secular trend in the sixteen States where its volume is important. The most pronounced growth is indicated in the State of Virginia. The curve for Massachusetts indicates that the State has shared better than some of the others in the growth of this industry.

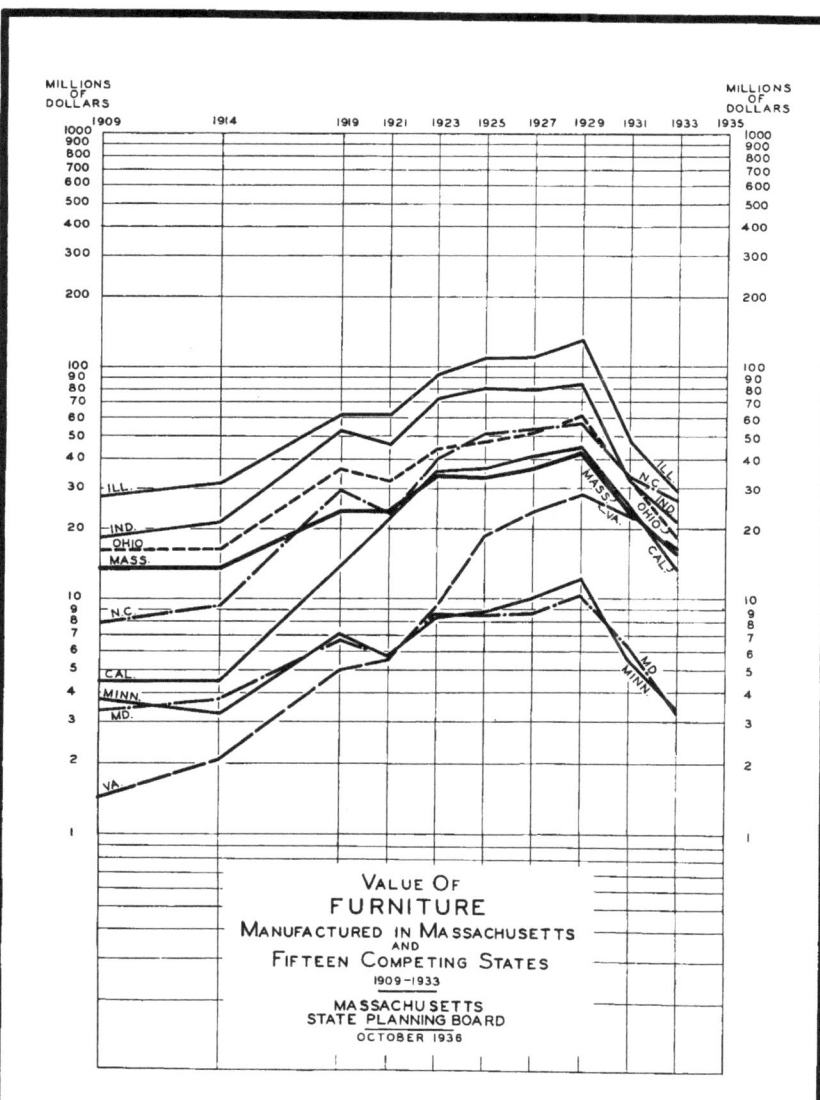

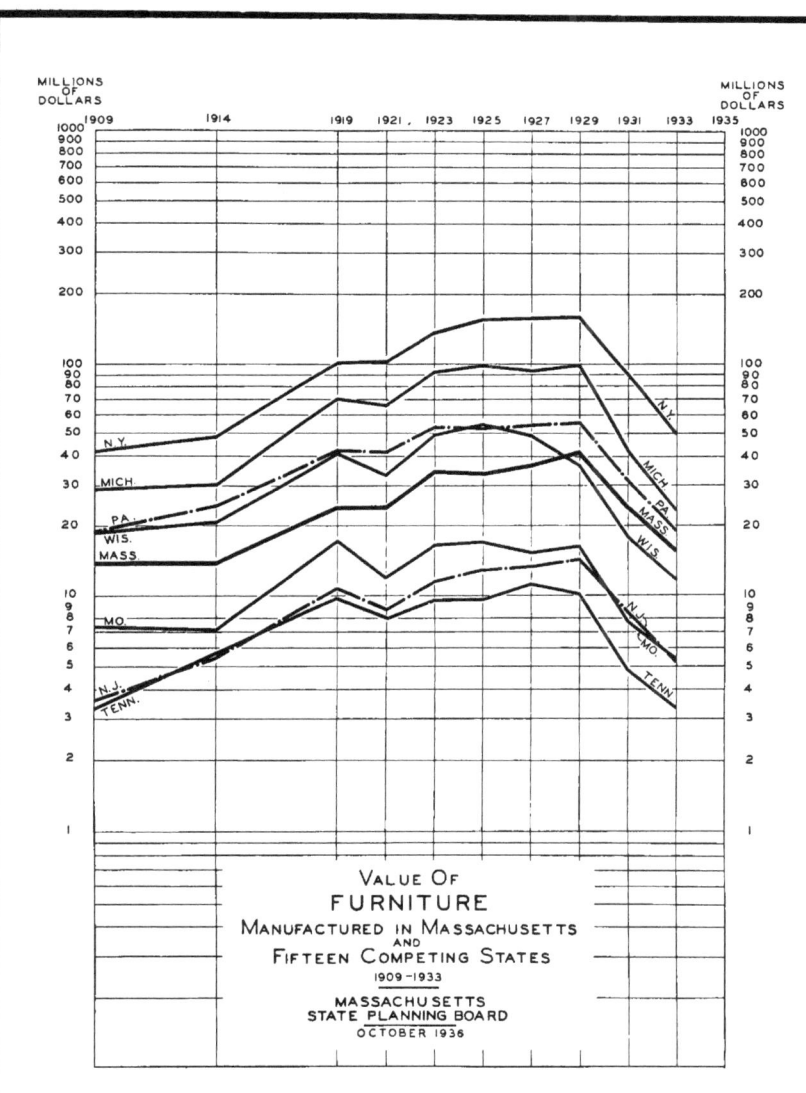

Fifteen Principal Competing States

It will be noted that in the foregoing charts of the eighteen principal industries, there are thirty-two different States involved. Some of these States have only one of the industries that are most important to Massachusetts, while other States are more generally competitive.

In order to simplify the task of comparing the advantages and disadvantages of Massachusetts with those of other States, we have taken fifteen States (of the 32 above mentioned) which, apparently, are the largest industrial competitors. In making such a selection we have had to leave out certain States which may be highly competitive with Massachusetts in some one industry. New Hampshire and Maine, for example, are not in the list of fifteen States, although both merit most careful study by reason of the competition they offer in certain lines of business.

The fifteen States are listed in the table below in the order of their total industrial production, according to the 1935 Census. At the time this report is being written, the census figures for six of these States have not been reported for 1935, but the census figures for 1933 probably indicate their present relative importance.

Table 15

TOTAL INDUSTRIAL PRODUCTION

	1933	1935
New York	$4,596,258,000	$6,022,173,000
Pennsylvania	3,051,579,000	4,249,041,000
Michigan	2,104,105,000	3,970,037,000
Illinois	2,502,175,000	3,765,502,000
Ohio	2,374,653,000	----
New Jersey	1,686,129,000	2,420,836,000
California	1,488,181,000	2,126,429,000
Massachusetts	1,668,733,000	2,065,491,000
Indiana	1,040,148,000	1,657,792,000
Missouri	881,184,000	----
North Carolina	887,853,000	----
Wisconsin	824,040,000	----
Texas	686,752,000	----
Connecticut	634,705,000	905,436,000
Minnesota	529,733,000	698,828,000
Maryland	518,707,000	----

MASSACHUSETTS STATE PLANNING BOARD

The accompanying chart gives a clear comparison of Massachusetts' manufacturing output with that of the other States. The only period of serious divergence from the general trend occurred between 1923 and 1929. In that period, the value of industrial production in nearly all the industrial States showed a net upward trend, whereas the value of industrial production in Massachusetts suffered a loss, due primarily, as indicated in the foregoing studies, to a loss in the production of textile mills and shoe factories. During that period, both Michigan and New Jersey passed Massachusetts, putting the State into the position of seventh largest industrial producer.

From 1929 to 1933, Massachusetts showed more stability than nearly all of the other States. In fact, only one of the fifteen competing States withstood the shock of depression so well as did Massachusetts.

Between 1933 and 1935, all States for which the figures have been received show a vigorous upward trend. Apparently, the recovery in Massachusetts during this period was not so great as in most of the other States. California, in which industry has been making phenomenal gains, has finally risen to seventh place among industrial producers. Massachusetts now is eighth, by a close margin.

Apparently, Massachusetts was slower in participating in the recovery than were most other States, but on the monthly chart of business activity, presented earlier in this report, the trend of business in Massachusetts during 1936 shows considerable acceleration and some narrowing of the spread between business in this State and business in the entire United States. This suggests, therefore, that the next census period of 1937 may reveal a more favorable comparative position for the Commonwealth than was shown by the 1935 Census.

It is interesting to note the extent to which all these States apparently are affected by nation-wide changes in economic conditions. Although, in the present survey, attention is directed entirely to the competitive position of the different States, it should be clearly borne in mind that conditions affecting the nation as a whole have a most profound influence on the growth and prosperity of all the States, and practically all industries.

Still another important point is that the most vigorous growth among these foremost industrial States has occurred in relatively new manufacturing States, as, for example, California, which appears to be capturing the business of the Pacific Coast, and

MASSACHUSETTS STATE PLANNING BOARD

North Carolina and Texas, whose rapid advance is traceable primarily to the migration of textile producers. Michigan is the only mature industrial State that is forging ahead at unusual pace, and its advance apparently is due chiefly to the boom in the automobile industry.

From the above, it should be apparent that conclusions regarding interstate competition require much more basis than simply the study of total-production records. It is necessary at least to consider each industry by itself, noting the trends shown in the various States where it has gained a significant foothold.

Advantages and Disadvantages of Massachusetts as Compared with Competing States.

In considering ways and means of increasing the attractiveness of the Commonwealth as a site for industrial and commercial concerns, the first step is obviously to determine exactly how the State stands in comparison with its chief competitors in assets which are most important to business. The following pages present some of the facts. These data are by no means complete. Much additional information is desired; but the facts here given seem to disprove, rather definitely, the popular impression that Massachusetts is generally outclassed in the advantages which it offers to industrial and commercial concerns.

Taxes and Cost of Government. A matter of primary importance in interstate competition appears to be that of the relative tax load, and the statement is often heard that Massachusetts is the most heavily taxed State in the Union. There is no question that taxes here -- both State and municipal -- are high, but there are ten other States which apparently have higher taxes than Massachusetts. Among them are two foremost competitors, New York and New Jersey.

Naturally, there are various bases upon which the burden of taxes of a State can be calculated, but perhaps the most accurate is the ratio which the total tax assessments bear to the total income of the people. In the study herein presented, the State Planning Board has used the tax reports compiled by the Tax Research Foundation, under the direction of the New York State Tax Commission, and published in the sixth edition of "Tax Systems of the World". It is practically impossible to obtain for a large group of States comparative tax figures that are more recent than 1933. The calculations herein referred to are based upon figures for 1932 and 1933. The estimates of spendable income refer to the total

151

income actually realized by all individuals in each State. They do not include corporate income. The estimates made by Brookmire Bulletins, Inc., have been used.

The following Chart 54-C6 shows the ratio of State, county, and municipal taxes to spendable income for each State in the Union, calculated as above described. It will be noted that although Massachusetts is well up on the list, its ratio of 14.8 per cent of taxes to spendable income is less than that in ten other States, among which are included three prominent industrial States, namely, New York with a ratio of 16.3 per cent, New Jersey with 15.2 per cent, and Minnesota with 15 per cent. Some of the other competing States have a much lower ratio of tax load than Massachusetts. For certain industries this doubtless gives these States an advantage, but in making such comparisons it is always necessary to measure the benefits which accrue to business through the public services provided by a State. The question, for example, of available highways, police and fire protection, provision for public welfare of employees, and similar items all have a bearing upon the facility of doing business.

The treatment here given does not assume to uphold a theory of taxation from any standpoint, but is presented simply to show at least that Massachusetts is not the most heavily taxed of the important industrial States, and to furnish as accurate a basis as possible by which to measure the bare tax cost in the various States with which this Commonwealth is competing.

Analysis of Massachusetts Taxes. If one wishes to make a further analysis of taxes in Massachusetts, the following Chart 54-C9, which is self-explanatory, supplies important information. The total tax receipts indicated include all State, county, and municipal taxes paid by the people of Massachusetts each year from 1924 to 1935, inclusive. These figures were obtained from reports of the Commissioner of Corporations and Taxation.

Cost of Labor in Massachusetts and Competing States. For various reasons, it is difficult to secure accurate data showing the actual average cost of industrial labor in the various industrial States. The subject naturally is much involved, since not only actual wage rates but also the productivity of labor must be calculated. The latter, in turn, is dependent in part upon union restrictions, legislative restrictions, and the prevalence of labor troubles. The State Planning Board's present report deals with only one of these phases, namely, labor troubles.

In Massachusetts, as in all other older industrial States, la-

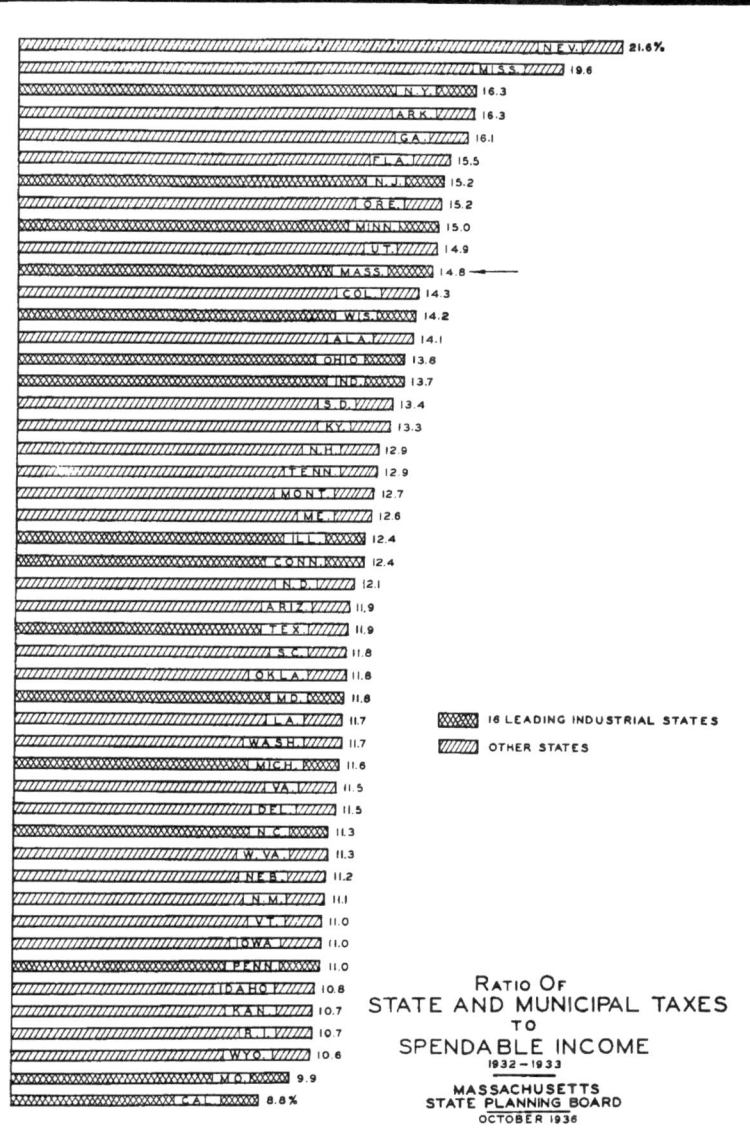

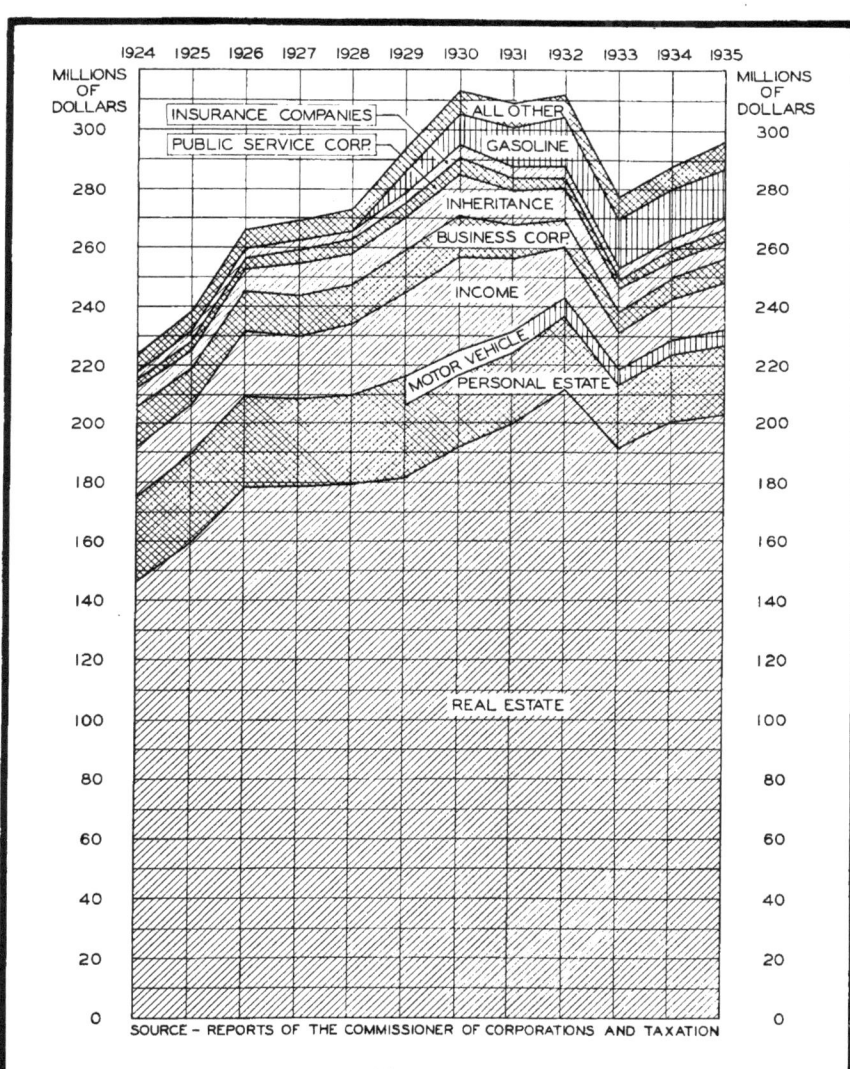

bor is rather fully organized. During past years, the State had the reputation of suffering from more than the usual amount of strikes and lockouts. That this reputation was earned is indicated by Chart 54-C32, which shows the comparison of labor troubles in other competing States, with those in Massachusetts. In this chart, the factor used is the ratio of industrial strikes and lockouts to the number of industrial establishments. In each instance, the record of Massachusetts is plotted as the base, 100, against which the records of the other respective States are plotted.

For example, in the section referring to California, the chart shows that, in 1919, California had only about 25 per cent as many strikes and lockouts, in proportion to the number of establishments, as did Massachusetts; in 1928, it had only about 16 per cent as many as Massachusetts; but, in 1935, the proportion of such labor troubles in California became almost exactly the same as in Massachusetts. Note that a semi-logarithmic, or percentage, scale is used in the chart; also that figures for 1935 have so far been received for only some of the States.

Up to the time of the depression, the only one of nineteen other industrial States which seemed to match Massachusetts in the amount of labor troubles was Rhode Island. Connecticut was perhaps second. In 1929 and the early part of the depression, New Jersey and Pennsylvania had considerably more labor difficulties than Massachusetts, but these subsided. In 1933, the only States of these nineteen having a higher proportion of labor troubles than Massachusetts were Rhode Island, New Hampshire, and Pennsylvania.

In 1934, the general picture changed. Other prominent industrial States, which previously had enjoyed much less labor trouble than Massachusetts, suddenly showed a reverse trend. During 1934 and 1935, Ohio, New Jersey, Maine, Wisconsin, and Connecticut rose above Massachusetts in the ratio of their strikes and lockouts, and California, Missouri, Michigan, Minnesota, Illinois, Indiana, North Carolina, and New York showed marked increases which brought them close to the same relative labor situation as existed in Massachusetts.

It seems apparent from these figures that the long-cited disadvantage of labor difficulties formerly laid at the door of the Bay State has become about equally pronounced in most of the States which are its principal competitors. What the future holds, is, of course, impossible to predict, but it seems reasonable to believe that other States which formerly advertised their low labor costs, are now reaping the natural reaction, and that Massachusetts in the coming years will have a more stable labor situation than many of

MASSACHUSETTS STATE PLANNING BOARD

its competitors.

Comparison of Local Markets. Although modern industry finds its markets in all parts of the world, it must take into account the advantage of placing its producing centers as near as practicable to good markets. From this standpoint, Massachusetts compares rather favorably with most of its principal competitors, as shown in the following tables. The total spendable income, which is estimated at $2,179,000,000 in Massachusetts for 1935 was approximately $503 per capita, putting the State in ninth place among the sixteen leading States.

In order to judge the relative distribution of spending power in Massachusetts, as compared with other industrial states, the above Table 18, presenting individual tax returns, is submitted. Massachusetts ranks fifth in total number of persons making Federal tax returns, the highest proportion of which report net incomes of between $2,000 and $5,000 per year. The second largest group in the State has net incomes of between $1,000 and $2,000. The proportion of persons in Massachusetts receiving less than $1,000 (about 13 per cent) is unfavorably higher than that of most other industrial States, but the proportion receiving $10,000 or more net income is considerably better than that for most other States.

Density of Population. Massachusetts ranks second among the sixteen leading industrial States in number of inhabitants per square mile of area, showing a high degree of concentration in its consumer market. Detailed figures are as follows:

Table 19

DENSITY OF POPULATION, 1930

STATE	POPULATION	DENSITY PER SQ.MI.	STATE	POPULATION	DENSITY PER SQ.MI.
New Jersey	4,041,334	537.8	Indiana	3,238,503	89.8
Mass.	4,249,614	528.6	Michigan	4,842,325	84.2
Conn.	1,606,903	333.4	No. Carolina	3,170,276	65.0
New York	12,588,066	264.2	Wisconsin	2,939,006	53.2
Penn.	9,631,526	214.8	Missouri	3,629,367	52.8
Maryland	1,631,526	164.1	California	5,677,251	36.5
Ohio	6,646,697	163.1	Minnesota	2,563,953	31.7
Illinois	7,630,654	136.2	Texas	5,824,715	22.2

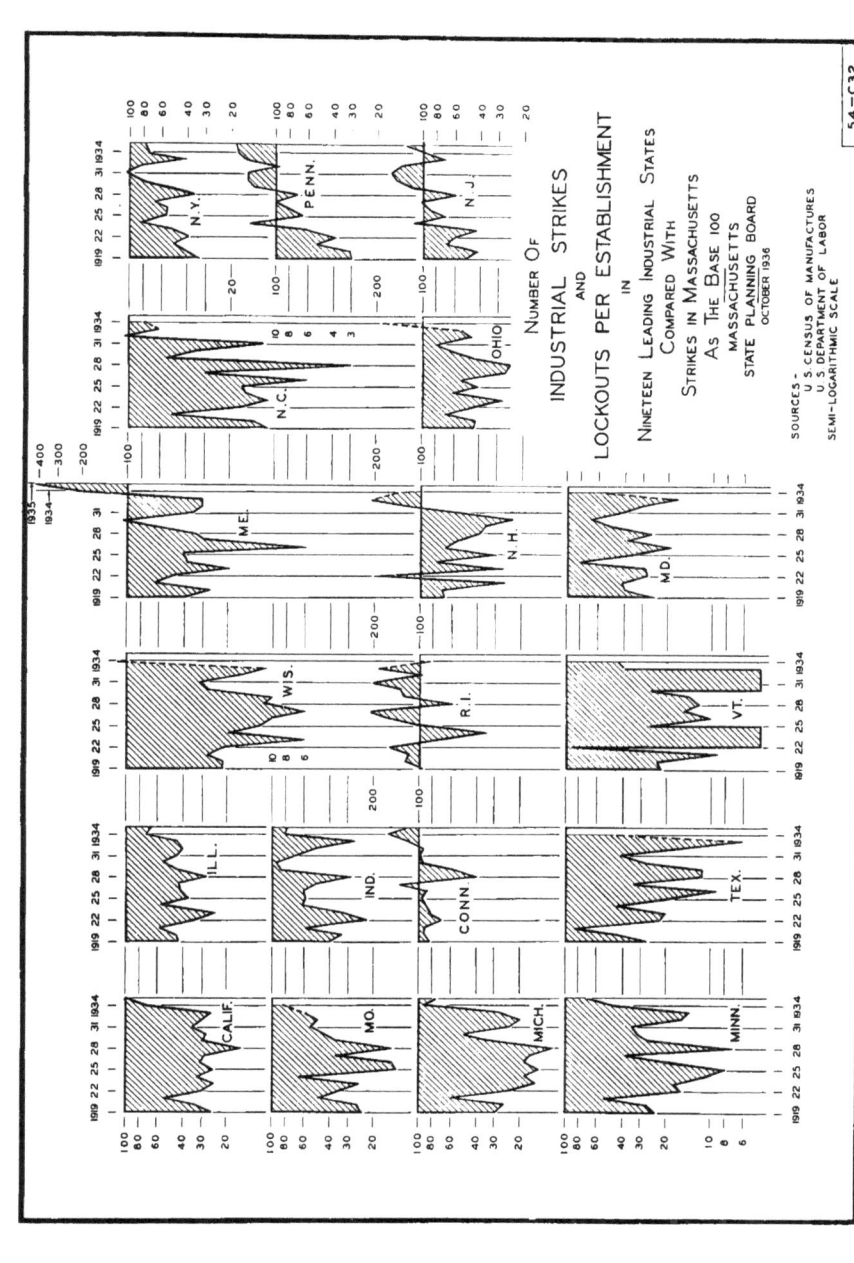

MASSACHUSETTS STATE PLANNING BOARD

Table 16

TOTAL SPENDABLE INCOME IN MASSACHUSETTS
AND
FIFTEEN OTHER LEADING INDUSTRIAL STATES*

1935

STATE	INCOME IN MILLIONS OF DOLLARS	STATE	INCOME IN MILLIONS OF DOLLARS
1. New York	$6,993	9. Texas	$1,906
2. Pennsylvania	4,819	10. Indiana	1,852
3. Illinois	4,262	11. Wisconsin	1,491
4. Ohio	3,783	12. Missouri	1,482
5. California	3,689	13. Minnesota	1,114
6. Michigan	3,278	14. Connecticut	1,033
7. Massachusetts	2,179	15. North Carolina	873
8. New Jersey	2,159	16. Maryland	753

*Source of information: Brookmire Bulletins, Inc.

Table 17

PER CAPITA SPENDABLE INCOME IN MASSACHUSETTS
AND
FIFTEEN OTHER LEADING INDUSTRIAL STATES*

1935

STATE	INCOME	STATE	INCOME
1. Michigan	$644	9. Massachusetts	$503
2. Connecticut	624	10. Wisconsin	496
3. California	599	11. Pennsylvania	490
4. Indiana	561	12. Maryland	451
5. Ohio	553	13. Minnesota	428
6. Illinois	541	14. Missouri	403
7. New York	513	15. Texas	327
8. New Jersey	510	16. North Carolina	234

*Source of information: Brookmire Bulletins, Inc.

Table 18

INDIVIDUAL INCOME TAX RETURNS BY NET INCOME CLASSES
IN
MASSACHUSETTS AND FIFTEEN OTHER LEADING INDUSTRIAL STATES*

STATE	TOTAL NUMBER OF RETURNS	UNDER $1000		$1000-$2000		$2000-5000		$5000-$10,000		$10,000-$25,000		$25,000 & OVER	
		Number	Per Cent	Number	Per Cent	Number	Per Cent	Number	Per Cent	Number	Per Cent	Number	Per Cent
1. N.Y.	748,054	76,437	10.22	294,903	39.42	292,763	39.14	53,267	7.12	21,122	2.82	9,559	1.28
2. Penn.	323,960	33,160	10.24	131,431	40.57	130,060	40.15	19,772	6.10	7,036	2.17	2,501	0.77
3. Calif.	286,580	29,447	10.28	122,459	42.73	111,419	38.88	17,162	5.99	4,528	1.58	1,565	0.55
4. Ill.	282,360	24,322	8.79	119,205	42.23	111,582	39.53	18,675	6.62	6,062	2.15	2,014	0.71
5. Mass.	231,960	29,935	12.91	87,990	37.93	92,527	39.89	14,209	6.12	5,431	2.34	1,868	0.80
6. N.J.	202,190	16,420	8.12	79,035	39.09	86,908	42.98	14,126	6.99	4,374	2.16	1,327	0.66
7. Ohio	181,212	16,763	9.25	74,629	41.18	74,663	41.20	10,730	5.92	3,417	1.89	1,010	0.56
8. Mich.	112,053	17,811	15.90	40,491	36.14	46,413	41.42	5,326	4.75	1,557	1.38	455	0.39
9. Tex.	105,950	11,804	11.14	35,852	33.84	49,481	46.70	6,752	6.37	1,663	1.57	398	0.36
10. Mo.	93,308	6,872	7.36	40,019	42.89	37,658	40.36	6,087	6.52	2,086	2.24	586	0.64
11. Conn	81,850	8,603	10.51	33,413	40.82	31,135	38.04	5,900	7.21	2,072	2.53	727	0.83
12. Md.	76,409	7,625	9.98	26,325	34.45	34,613	45.30	5,596	7.32	1,727	2.26	523	0.68
13. Ind.	61,675	6,635	10.00	24,831	40.26	25,876	41.96	3,154	5.11	966	1.57	213	0.33
14. Minn.	59,803	6,092	10.19	25,855	43.23	22,787	38.10	3,607	6.03	1,118	1.87	344	0.57
15. Wis.	89,739	23,418	26.10	36,026	40.15	26,148	29.14	3,101	3.46	809	0.90	237	0.25
16. N.C.	29,462	3,095	10.51	9,420	31.97	14,584	49.50	1,619	5.50	567	1.92	177	0.60

*Source: Statistics of Income, Bureau of Internal Revenue

Climate. With mean summer temperatures of about 68 degrees, winter temperatures of about 27 degrees, and an annual average temperature of 48 degrees Fahrenheit, the Commonwealth provides one of the most healthful, invigorating climates in the country. Numerous experiments indicate that the most mental energy is developed in a mean day and night temperature of about 40 degrees. As the temperature rises above that point, mental energy falls off gradually until the temperature reaches about 70 degrees. Above that point, the drop in mental energy is abrupt. Physical energy, as shown by resistance to death and diseases, goes up gradually to a mean temperature of 64 degrees, above which the drop is abrupt. These two factors, when combined, give between 40 and 65 degrees as the most favorable temperature for mental and physical activity. This is further borne out by a study of efficiency in textile mills, where the productive peak for both men and women was found to occur at 60 degrees. Further study in industrial plants shows that fewest accidents occur at a temperature of 68 degrees. Ellsworth Huntington's research, covering the United States, shows the most favorable climatic conditions, as far as energy is concerned, to be in the northeast quadrant extending from the central prairie States and east and north of the Ohio River. Health, as reflected by life insurance statistics, also favors this northeast quadrant.

Industrial Water Supply. The natural water supply of Massachusetts is rated by the United States Geological Survey as the best for industrial purposes of any of the leading manufacturing States of the Union. The average supplies, both surface and ground, show only fourteen parts of $CaCO_3$ per million, as against a much larger preportion of hardness in the waters of all other large industrial States. Comparative analyses are shown in the following Table 20, as reported in "Water Supply Paper 496", of the United States Geological Survey.

All manufacturing plants using steam power are affected by the quality of the water supply. A high content of scale-producing agents makes it necessary to treat all the water used in boilers. Certain industrial processes are particularly dependent upon a suitable quality of water, the principal factor of which is a low content of $CaCO_3$, which determines the water's relative softness. In a general way, it may be said that the softer the water, the better, especially for use in industries such as the following: chemicals; cotton manufactures; druggists' preparations, patent medicines and compounds, perfumery and cosmetics; dyeing and finishing textiles, exclusive of that done in textile mills; knit goods; leather, tanned, curried, and finished; liquors, distilled; paper and wood pulp; silk manufactures; wool manufactures.

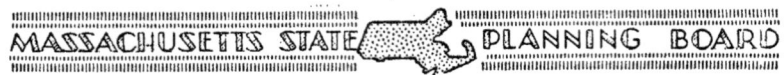

Table 20

AVERAGE HARDNESS OF WATER FROM LARGE PUBLIC
SUPPLIES IN EACH STATE

(As measured by parts of $CaCO_3$ Per Million)

STATE	SURFACE SUPPLIES	GROUND SUP-PLIES	ALL SUPPLIES	STATE	SURFACE SUPPLIES	GROUND SUP-PLIES	ALL SUP-PLIES
Oreg.	9	19	9.6	Ida.		91	91
N. H.	6	20	9.7	Mont.	91		91
R. I.	12		12	Wyo.	119		119
*Mass.	13	29	14	N.Mex.	20	177	126
Miss.	14		14	Ill.[1]	131		131
Me.	18		18	*Mich.	114	267	134
N. C.	22		22	*Tex.	100	166	130
*Conn.	25		25	N.Dak.	141		141
Ga.	14	82	27	Col.	144		144
S. C.	31		31	*Wis.	132	205	145
Vt.	39		39	*Mo.	147	195	148
Wash.	22	125	41	Ark.	149		149
Va.	45		45	*Ohio	125	341	153
*N. Y.	46	120	47	*Ill.[3]	136	350	156
*N. J.	46	65	48	*Minn.	158		158
Del.	49	115	51	Utah	172	109	158
Ala.	59	20	53	*Calif.	156	243	172
*Md.	53		53	Ariz.		221	221
La.	54		54	Neb.	244	221	239
Tenn.	64	46	57	*Ind.	244	330	264
*Penn.	67	188	69	Ill.[2]	184	350	274
Nev.	36	185	74	Fla.		296	296
W. Va.	76		76	Ia.	181	357	298
D. C.	80		80	Kan.	255	543	316
Ky.	90		90	Okla.	400		400
				S. Dak.		503	503

*One of the sixteen leading industrial States.
[1]Supplied from Lake Michigan.
[2]Not supplied from Lake Michigan.
[3]Average for the State.

Massachusetts apparently ranks very near the top of all States in the softness of its water supplies, both surface and underground, and, according to the 1933 Census, produced $467,000,000 of goods in the industries above mentioned, the largest output of any State except Pennsylvania, which produced $521,507,000. The total output of all States in these "soft-water" industries, in 1933, was $4,145,228,000. It is interesting to note that, in 1919, the twenty-six States which have natural water supplies averaging less than 100 parts per million of $CaCO_3$ produced 64 per cent of all the output in these special industries, but, in 1933, they produced 85 per cent of the total output. It also should be noted that of the fifteen other leading industrial States with which Massachusetts is especially in competition, only six have natural water supplies containing less than 100 parts of $CaCO_3$ per million.

Certainly the industrial water supply of Massachusetts is an asset that should be thoroughly advertised. Also, every reasonable step should be taken to protect it against waste and pollution.

MASSACHUSETTS STATE PLANNING BOARD

INDUSTRY - PART II

A special study of industry has been carried on under the direction of Mr. William Stanley Parker, Special Consultant to the Urbanism Committee of the National Resources Committee. The research attempts to establish a definite method for the appraisal of the economic relations of an industry to its community, to make such an appraisal, and to guide community officials in any efforts they may make toward developing local industrial activity. No similar research has apparently ever been made elsewhere.

Basis of Investigation

The investigation is based upon two reports issued by the Boston City Planning Board: the "Real Property Inventory" and the "Income and Cost Survey", both issued in 1935 as the result of ERA projects. These reports provide the unit values needed in applying to Boston the findings of the later investigations. For other cities, it is at present necessary to make assumptions based upon the Boston reports.

The study assumes the city or town to be a corporate body providing essential municipal services, and the industry and its employees a joint group buying such services. It develops a balance sheet of taxes and service costs to show whether taxes paid are adequate to cover the cost of municipal services. In addition, the study seeks to appraise the indirect taxes developed from the accumulated spendable income of the community, created by the money spent in the community by the industry for payroll and other items.

Types of Analysis

The study analyzes industrial statistics in order to determine approximately the maximum and minimum amounts for the following:

1. Assessed value of plant per employee
2. Average yearly wage per employee
3. Other local expenditures per employee

An investigation of municipal expenses has made possible a determination of approximate values for the following items in cities of different size and character:

1. Cost of all services per capita
2. Cost of services of industrial districts

3. Cost of services of residential districts having different median rentals

4. Taxes paid to the city from each type of district

All items are reduced to the amount per employee.

The undertaking has been aided by the cordial coöperation of Mr. Roswell Phelps of the Division of Statistics of the Department of Labor and Industries, who has made available and helped in the interpretation of the statistics of forty-two leading industries of Massachusetts.

A Balance Sheet

The balance sheet, as described, is not a complete measure of the desirability of a given industry for a given community. Many factors, such as power, transportation, raw materials, labor, and markets will affect the final decision. The social desirability of the industry and its appropriateness to the general character of the community must be considered. The balance sheet relates merely to those factors measurable in monetary values, and thus supplies a further guide, not heretofore available, to the appropriate location of industry.

Are New Industries Always Community Assets?

In the past it has often been assumed that any industry is an asset anywhere. This idea still persists, but some communities have learned by experience that this is not the case. The results of their experience have not been made generally available, nor have they been, it is believed, completely analyzed. The "Income and Cost" studies in Boston have presented a new analysis of community conditions having a direct bearing on this problem. The further studies, above reported, should prove useful to all communities, both in the Commonwealth and elsewhere, and to all industries seeking a desirable location.

SOCIAL CONDITIONS

Courtesy of Secretary of the Commonwealth

CHAPTER VI

SOCIAL CONDITIONS

Summary Outline

Introduction

I. Population

II. Employment

III. Housing

IV. Education

V. Welfare

VI. Correction

Note: Summary outlines are presented at the beginning of each of the above numbered sections.

MASSACHUSETTS STATE PLANNING BOARD

SOCIAL CONDITIONS

Introduction

This chapter on Social Conditions is composed of several divisions, each treating a separate but related part of the subject. The chapter deals primarily with the functional aspects and results of man's activities, as opposed to the emphasis on his physical environment, which characterizes the other chapters. It seemed desirable to group these discussions of man's activities under one heading, even though they are not, in all cases, closely related. Brief summaries of the sections follow:

Population

This study has for its objective the preparation of an estimate of the future State population, its physical distribution among the various cities and regions, and its composition.

Amount. The future State population has been estimated on the basis of studies of births, deaths, immigration, emigration, and internal migration, recognizing the fact that the algebraic sum of the first four determines the change in the population of the State.

Distribution. The distribution of population throughout the various regions of the State has been determined for different years, and presented on a series of maps. Population distribution has been studied, further, by analyzing the rates of growth of cities in the different population groups.

Composition. The composition of population has been studied by age groups, sex, nativity, and occupation during the past fifty years.

Employment

The analysis of employment in all occupations covers the period from 1920 to 1930. However, most of the attention was devoted to a study of employment in manufacturing industries. Because so large a proportion of all wage earners are so employed, these latter studies provided a valuable key to an understanding of the fluctuations in employment in Massachusetts.

Housing

This study presents a cross-section of housing conditions in Massachusetts. The historical survey of pre-war and post-war housing is followed by an analysis of present-day conditions, and brief discussions of such special aspects as the financing of housing projects and cooperation between different housing agencies operating within the State.

Education

A bird's-eye picture of present educational facilities in Massachusetts is presented. A more complete study of the State educational system, including significant recommendations, is being reviewed by the State Planning Board.

Welfare

This section presents a brief outline of the organization and functions of the welfare agencies in Massachusetts, including provisions for social security.

Correction

This final section of the chapter deals with juvenile and adult correctional institutions in Massachusetts. Data on types of institutions and their administration, arrests, probation, parole, social status of prisoners, and other correctional problems are presented. The section concludes with recommendations based upon the twenty-five-year plan adopted by the State Department of Correction, and upon the findings of the State Planning Board.

POPULATION

Summary Outline

I. Introduction
   A. Population Studies

II. Population Growth
   A. Past Records
   B. Future Estimates

III. Population Distribution
   A. Past Records
   B. Predictions of Future Distribution

IV. Population Composition
   A. Age Groups
   B. Sex
   C. Nativity
   D. Occupation

MASSACHUSETTS STATE PLANNING BOARD

POPULATION

Introduction

The study of population is fundamental and basic to many forms of planning. For example, it is impossible to order man's physical environment without knowing something of man, himself.

The accuracy and validity of population estimating are limited, first, by the quantity and accuracy of available past-experience data, and second, by the fact that the future can never be exactly predicated. Furthermore, a study of population pattern is merely an analysis of the end product of the physical and economic activities of people,--a study not of causes but of effects. Population curves are simply reflections of results of many inter-related biological, social, and economic factors. In using population figures of the past to predict those of the future, these limitations should be kept in mind.

To predict future population, it is necessary to discover the causes which have produced past population and its distribution, and to predict the trend of the causes. From these data, the trend of population can be predicted. If no casual analysis is made, the resulting population curve will be merely a mathematical projection of the past curve, which implies that the same causes will operate with the same power in the future, as in the past. Such an assumption is likely to be fallacious; hence, the primary objective of this study has been to analyze the causes of past population growth, distribution, and composition, and to determine their probable effects in the future.

Population Studies

Future population growth has been predicted on the basis of studies of births, deaths, immigration, and emigration.

Predictions as to future distribution of population within the State are based upon studies of the probable future growth of cities of different sizes, and of rural areas. Special attention has been given to studies of the probable future growth of metropolitan regions, in total population, in area, and in population density.

The future composition of population has been predicted on the bases of studies of population age-groups, sex, and nativity. The

probable future number of people in the different age-groups is
particularly important in preparing programs for public education,
old-age benefits, and so forth. Additional studies of population
composition from the standpoints of income, ownership of property,
housing, and so on would be interesting but of little immediate use
in preparing plans for the physical development of the State.

Population Growth

Past Records

The record of population growth over a reasonable period in
the past has been studied for the State as a whole, taking into consideration both the magnitude and rate of growth.

The lower portion of Chart 54A-C1 presents the growth of Massachusetts population from a little less than one million persons,
in 1850, to almost four and one half million, in 1935. The curve
of population growth is in the form of a reverse S-curve, starting
out relatively flat, rising sharply during the period from 1885 to
1900, and then leveling off to 1935. This trend is further emphasized in the upper portion of the chart, "Percentage Rate of Increase," which portrays the rate of growth by five-year periods.
This chart indicates that the rate of population growth has been
falling gradually from about 17 per cent for the five-year period,
1850-1855, to about 2 1/2 per cent for the period, 1930-1935. Although the rate-of-growth curve has been very uneven from one five-year period to the next, the general trend has been a depression
during the Civil War, then a period of relatively high rate of increase, followed by a period of very low rate of increase starting
about 1915 and continuing to the present time.

Chart 54A-C2, "Births, Deaths, and Net Immigration," portrays
the general trend of these factors in the population growth of
Massachusetts from 1880 to 1935. The chart shows that the number
of births increased gradually from approximately 44,000, in 1880,
to a maximum of about 96,000, in 1917, leveled off to 1924, and then
dropped sharply to a low of approximately 63,000, in 1933. On the
contrary, the annual number of deaths, during the past twenty-five
years, has remained at the fairly constant figure of between 50,000
and 52,000, except for the years of 1917 and 1918.

A determination of the annual State immigration and emigration
is difficult to make, for there are no direct statistics. This as-

pect of State population change has been studied by using the Federal ten-year Census figures. (State Census figures have been eliminated because of inconsistencies.) By subtracting from the total State population growth for any ten-year period, the excess of births over deaths for the same period, the excess of immigration over emigration is obtained. This figure was then divided by ten to obtain an average yearly figure, which was plotted on the chart in the form of a bar.

It will be noted that, during the period covered by the study, the net annual State immigration reached a maximum during the decade, 1890-1900 (with an average of approximately 36,000 persons per year) and has since fallen off rapidly, the 1930-1935 average being less than 2,000 persons per year. It seems probable, because of existing Federal immigration laws, that immigration will continue to equal emigration, and thus produce a net resulting figure of approximately zero.

Chart 54A-C5, entitled "Cumulative Births, Deaths, and Net Immigration," presents the same data, but in cumulative relationship, so that the total effects due to trends of births, deaths, immigration, and emigration may be studied.

The year 1880, with a population of 1,783,085, has been adopted as the base year. The total population for each year, to 1935, has been plotted. In the middle portion of the graph has been plotted the cumulative result of births, deaths, and immigration.

Future Estimates.

Future population may be predicted, first, by mathematical projections based entirely upon an analysis of past curves of total population, without reference to the individual factors making up the total; and, second, by rational projections, based upon detailed studies and projections of the basic factors of births, deaths, immigration, and emigration, of which the population total is the algebraic sum.

Mathematical Projections of Past Total Population Curve. Charts 54A-C3A and 54A-C3B and Table 21 present Massachusetts population estimates, to 1960, as obtained by arithmetic, geometric, straight-line, and parabolic projections of the past curve of total population. The estimates for the year 1960 range from a low of 4,367,242 persons, for the parabolic projection, to a high of 5,595,070 persons, for the straight-line projection.

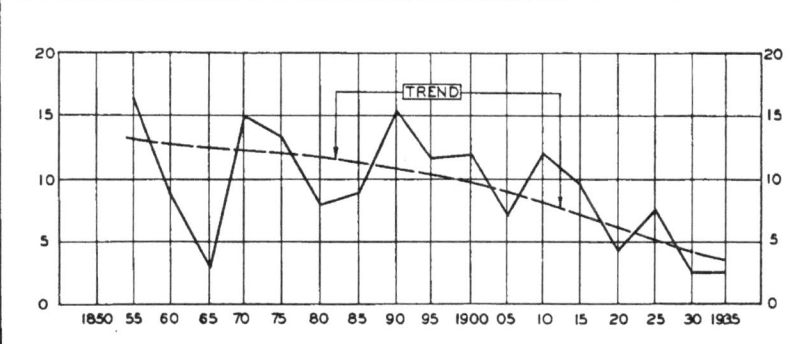

PERCENTAGE RATE OF INCREASE IN POPULATION OF MASSACHUSETTS
EVERY FIFTH YEAR OVER PRECEDING FIFTH YEAR, 1850-1935

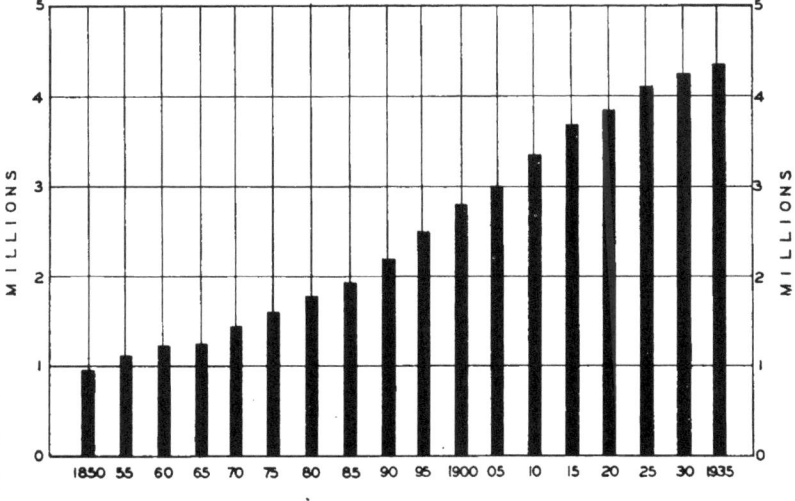

POPULATION OF MASSACHUSETTS, 1850-1935
AT FIVE YEAR INTERVALS

MASSACHUSETTS
STATE PLANNING BOARD
OCTOBER 1936

SOURCE: MASS. AND U.S. CENSUSES

54A-C1

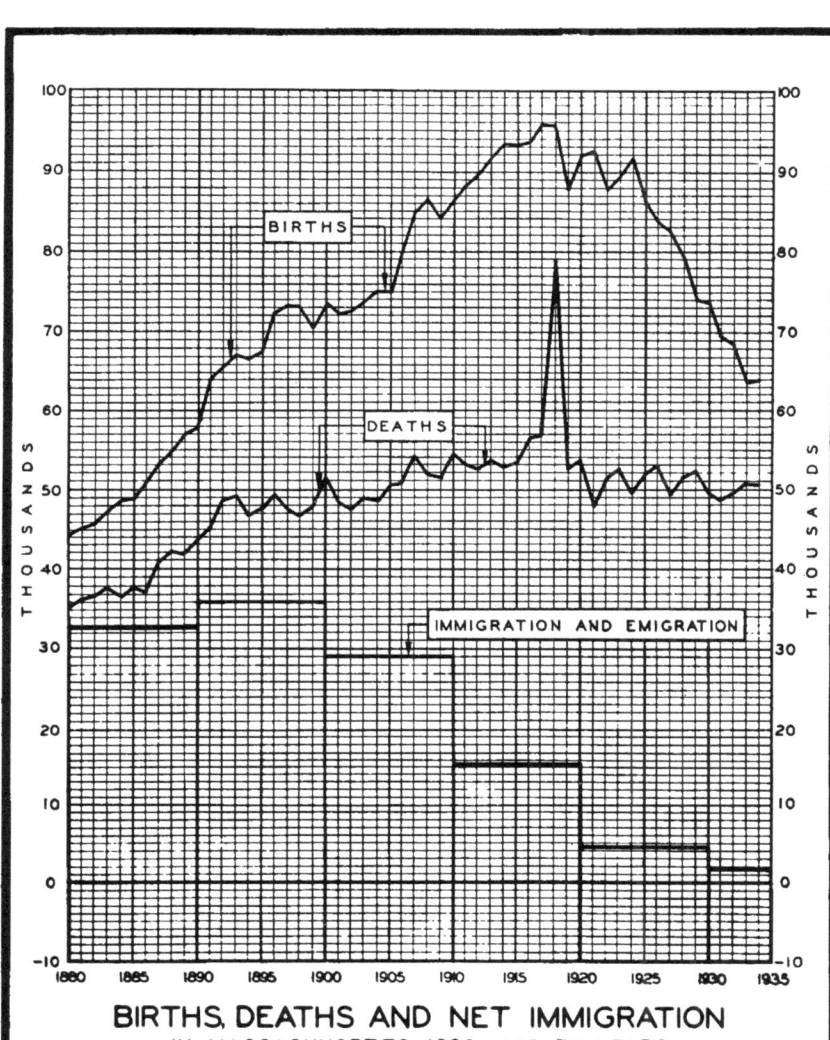

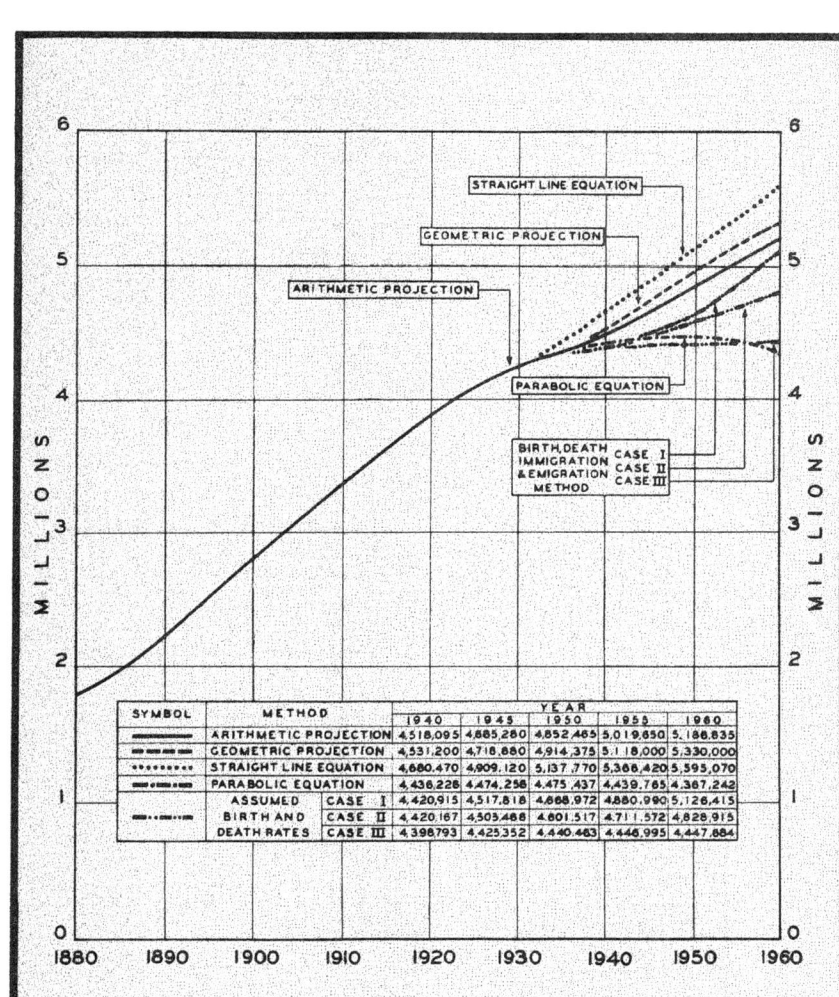

POPULATION OF MASSACHUSETTS, 1880-1935
WITH VARIOUS ESTIMATES FOR 1935-1960

MASSACHUSETTS
STATE PLANNING BOARD
OCTOBER 1936

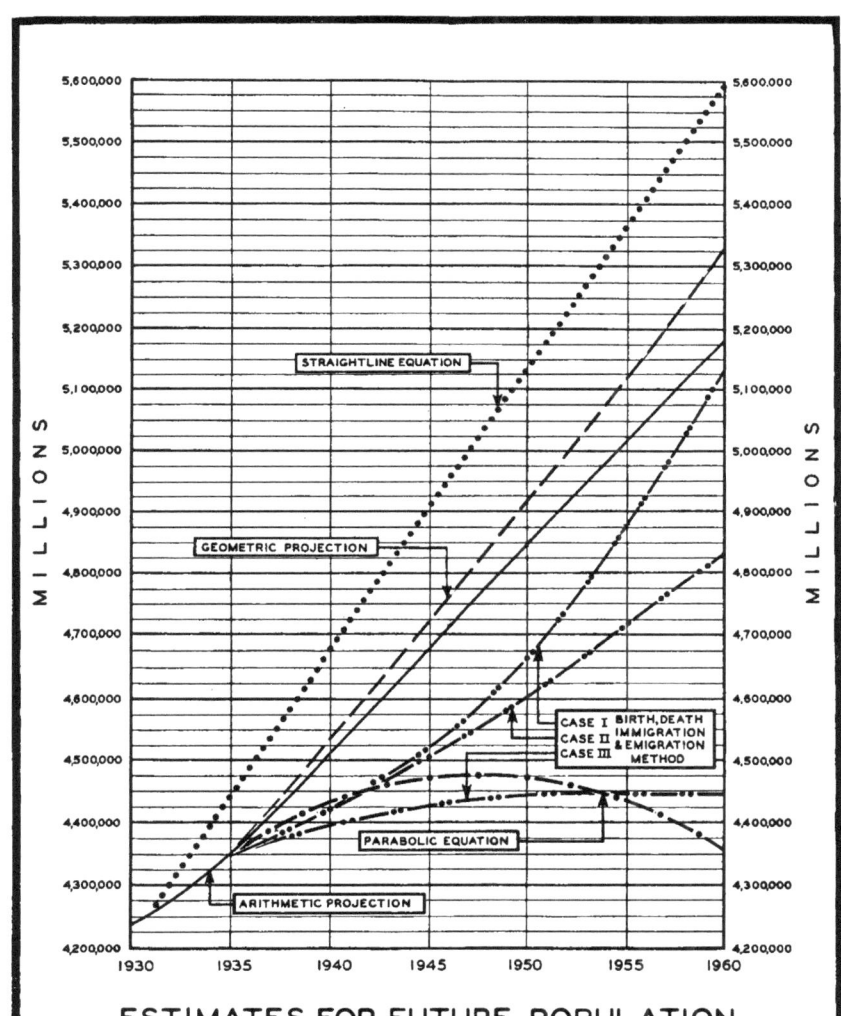

MASSACHUSETTS STATE PLANNING BOARD

Table 21

FUTURE STATE POPULATION ESTIMATES

YEAR	BY ARITHMETICAL PROJECTION	BY GEOMETRICAL PROJECTION	BY STRAIGHT-LINE PROJECTION	BY PARABOLIC PROJECTION
1940	4,518,095	4,531,200	4,680,470	4,436,228
1945	4,684,280	4,718,380	4,909,120	4,474,258
1950	4,850,565	4,914,375	5,137,770	4,475,457
1955	5,016,750	5,118,000	5,366,420	4,439,765
1960	5,182,935	5,330,000	5,595,070	4,367,242

Estimates Based on Predictions as to Future Births, Deaths, Immigration, and Emigration. Charts 54A-C4 and 54A-C5 present future-population estimates based upon separate assumptions as to future births, deaths, immigration, and emigration.

Birth Rates. Birth rates for each of the last twenty-five years were plotted and connected by a line to portray past trends. The line, starting somewhat above twenty-five births per thousand, remains fairly level for nine years, then begins a decline which continues, at a fairly uniform rate, to 1935.

Because of the obvious impossibility of estimating exactly the future birth rate, three different assumptions, as shown on Chart 54A-C4, for the birth rate at 1960 were made. The first assumption was that the birth rate will rise in a gradual S-curve from approximately fourteen, in 1935, to twenty, in 1960. The second assumption was that it will rise only to fifteen, in 1960. The third assumption was that it will continue to fall in the future at approximately the same rate that it has in the past, and will reach a low point of ten, in 1960. In all three cases, the curve from 1935 to the assumed point is so drawn as to become horizontal by 1960, thus representing the achievement of a stationary rate at that time.

Calculations were made, to illustrate the possible effect upon total population of each of the assumptions as to the future birth rate.

Death Rate. The assumption was made that the death rate would fall to ten, by 1960. A smooth curve, connecting this point on the graph with the plot of the 1935 death rate, continues fairly accurately the general trend of the annual death rates for the preceding twenty-five years.

171

MASSACHUSETTS STATE PLANNING BOARD

Chart 54A-C4 illustrates the assumptions as to birth and death rates, and their effects on population.

Immigration and Emigration. The assumption has been made that, on the average, over the next twenty-five years, immigration and emigration will be about equal. Supporting this assumption is the past record of decline in net immigration described previously.

Resultant Population. Yearly estimates of future population are then made by computing births and deaths during each year, according to the assumed rates. The difference between 1935 births and 1935 deaths, as recorded by the Massachusetts Bureau of Vital Statistics, represents the natural increase of population during 1935, and, added to the population of January 1, 1935, gives the computed population for January 1, 1936.

Chart 54A-C5 contains the cumulative records of births and deaths. The three different assumptions as to future birth rates naturally produce different future total population estimates. On the basis of the first assumption, population will rise to 5,126,415, by 1960, and will continue its rise thereafter; on the basis of the second assumption, it will rise to 4,828,915, by 1960, and will continue to rise; and on the basis of the third assumption, it will rise to 4,447,684, by 1960, at which point it will become stable.

Population Distribution

Population distribution has been studied from the standpoints of: (1) distribution throughout the State; and (2) distribution in municipalities of various sizes. Records of past distribution form one basis for predictions as to the future distributions.

Past Records

Distribution throughout the State. The simplest method of studying population distribution is by population spot maps. Changes in population distribution have been studied by twenty-five-year periods from 1860 to 1935.

Map 74-3 illustrates the distribution of population in Massachusetts in 1860. At that time, there was a relatively even distribution of population throughout the rural areas of the State, with no marked sparseness as yet in the Berkshire area or in the Central Highlands (that hill area drained principally by the Millers, Chicopee, Ware, Swift, and Quaboag Rivers). The metropolitan regions were still relatively small. Boston, Worcester, and

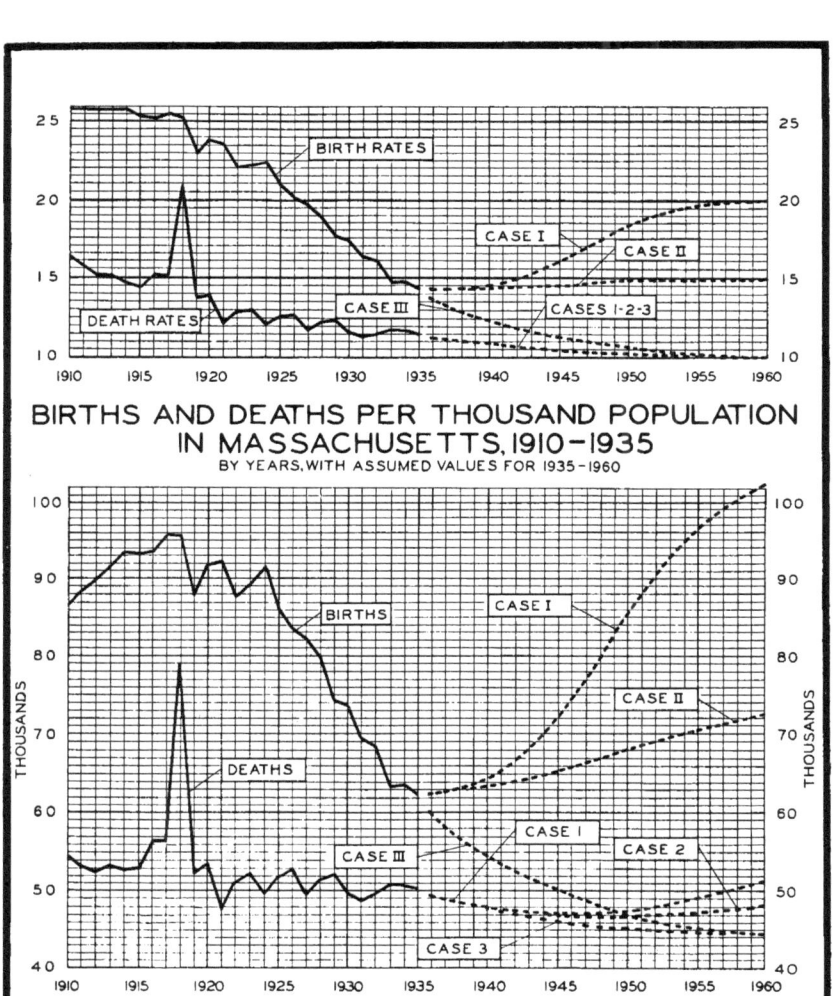

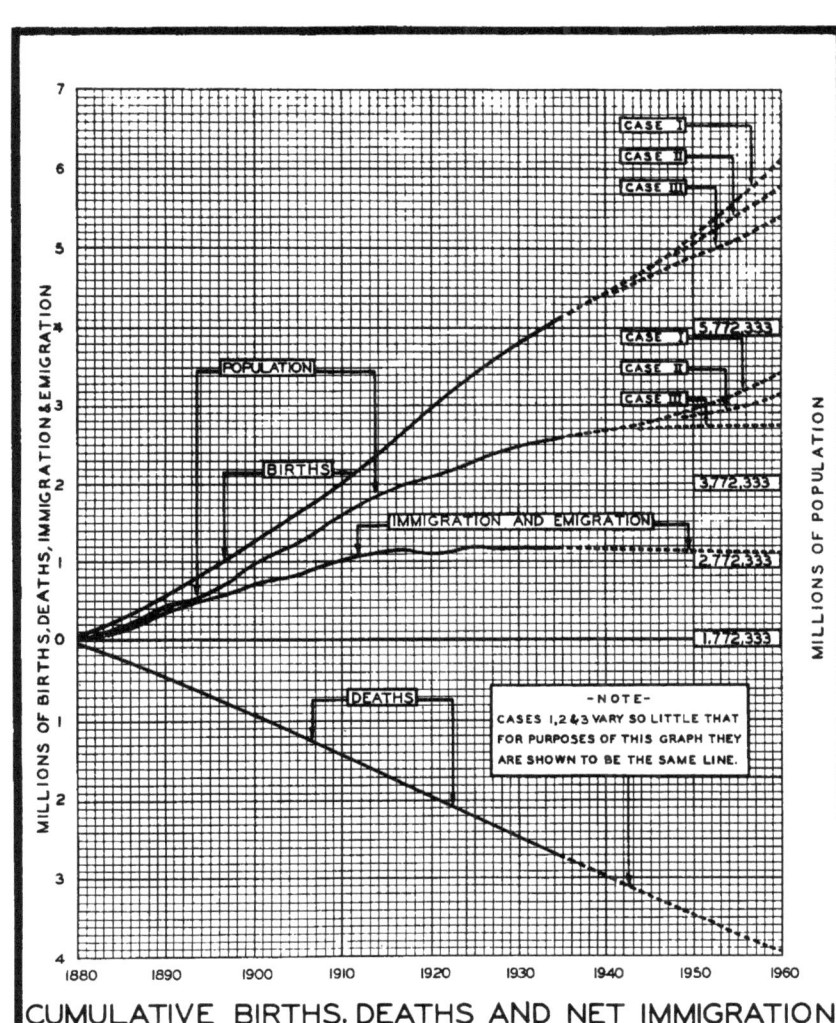

CUMULATIVE BIRTHS, DEATHS AND NET IMMIGRATION
IN MASSACHUSETTS, TOGETHER WITH POPULATION, 1880-1935,
WITH ESTIMATES FOR 1935-1960

MASSACHUSETTS
STATE PLANNING BOARD
OCTOBER 1936

SOURCE: MASS. AND U.S. CENSUSES WITH PROJECTIONS 54A-C5

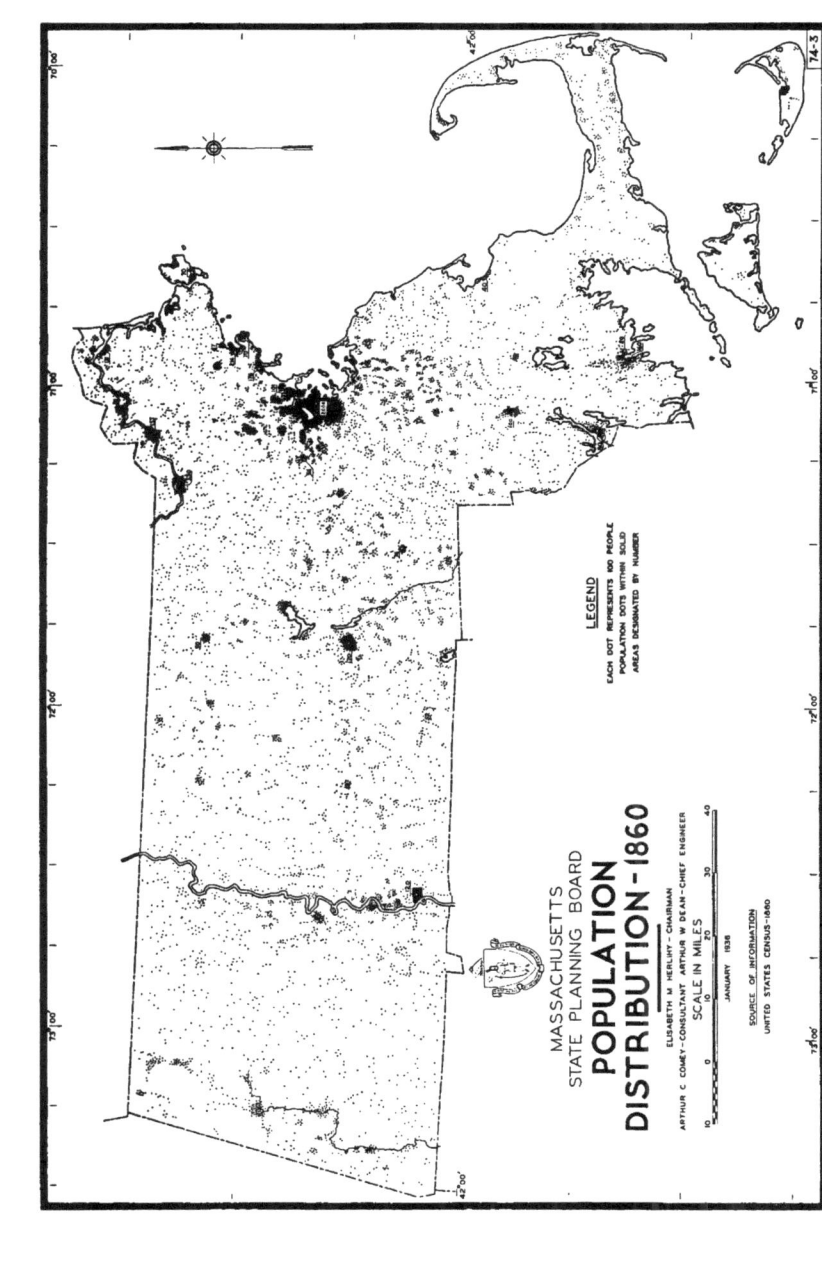

MASSACHUSETTS STATE PLANNING BOARD

Springfield were the largest.

By 1885, this picture had begun to change slightly, with the metropolitan area of Boston considerably extended.

By 1910, as illustrated on Map 74-2, there was an appreciable loss of rural population in the Berkshire Hills and the Central Highlands, and, as was to be expected, a rapid increase of urban population. Metropolitan Boston was growing rapidly and absorbing smaller suburban towns in all directions. The concentration of population into urban centers was marked, as is shown on the map by numerous black areas, indicating rapidly growing small industrial communities. Note also the rapid increase of population in the lower Connecticut Valley, and the increasing density of population throughout the entire eastern part of the State.

Map 74-4 shows that, by 1935, the concentrations of population were even more pronounced, particularly in the metropolitan region of Boston. The metropolitan regions of Worcester, Springfield, Fall River, and New Bedford show similar concentrations. There may be noted a marked decrease in population in the Berkshire Hills and in the Central Highlands. In the Berkshire Hills, population appears to be leaving the entire area, whereas, in the Central Highlands, there appears to be an indication, in the growth of smaller municipalities, that a change from agricultural to industrial occupations is taking place.

Density of Population. Map 74-5 shows the density of population in Massachusetts, in 1935, while Map 74-6 shows the population-density changes in Massachusetts, from 1910 to 1935.

The map depicting density of population in 1935 shows that some of the metropolitan regions have population densities ranging from 10,000 to more than 30,000 persons per square mile. A majority of the towns in the Berkshire Hills have fewer than fifty persons per square mile. Only a few of the towns in the Central Highlands have more than one hundred persons per square mile.

The above-mentioned maps, taken together, illustrate graphically the well-known facts that during the last seventy-five years there has been: (1) a rapid increase in the growth of metropolitan areas throughout the State; (2) a rapid growth in the number of small industrial cities; and (3) a loss of population in the Berkshire and Central-Highland areas. It may well be inferred that the population loss in the Berkshire and Central-Highland areas has been caused by a movement from the rapidly deteriorating agricultural communities to the equally rapidly advancing industrial communities.

MASSACHUSETTS STATE PLANNING BOARD

Distribution in Municipalities of Various Sizes. An effort has been made to determine what size municipalities are growing most rapidly.

The first step in the study was to group into metropolitan districts the cities and towns which are part of these districts, as they are defined by the 1930 Census. The municipalities were then divided into the following population groups: 0-500; 500-2,500; 2,500-10,000; 10,000-25,000; and 25,000-100,000. Metropolitan districts were put together in a separate group.

The study analyzes the growth of these size classes and not the growth of the municipalities which happen to be in them at any one time. A municipality might start in the 2,500-10,000 group, and move through to the 25,000-100,000 group. Its growth would be analyzed not as that of a separate municipality, but as one factor in the growth of a series of population classes, as it passes through them.

The metropolitan regions, as defined in the 1930 Census, have been used throughout this portion of the study. Therefore, the population figures for metropolitan regions represent the population growth of definite geographical units which do not change in physical size or shape throughout the period of study. If the analysis of metropolitan districts were based upon census definitions of them, the apparent population growth of these districts would be distorted by the increases resulting from geographical additions to the territory originally included.

Chart 54A-C14 illustrates the population growth of municipalities in the selected population groups. Contrary to popular opinion, there is a remarkable similarity in rates of growth of municipalities in the different population groups, except the smallest. The curves show, as was suspected, a negative rate of growth throughout almost the entire period of the study for towns with a population of 500 persons or less.

Predictions of Future Distribution

Because of the general character of the considerations involved and the lack of an accurate statistical method for evaluating detailed changes in population distribution, only general predictions of future distribution may be made.

From a study of the maps, general trends in population distribution may be discovered. It seems reasonable, first of all, to assume that the general movement toward concentration of the

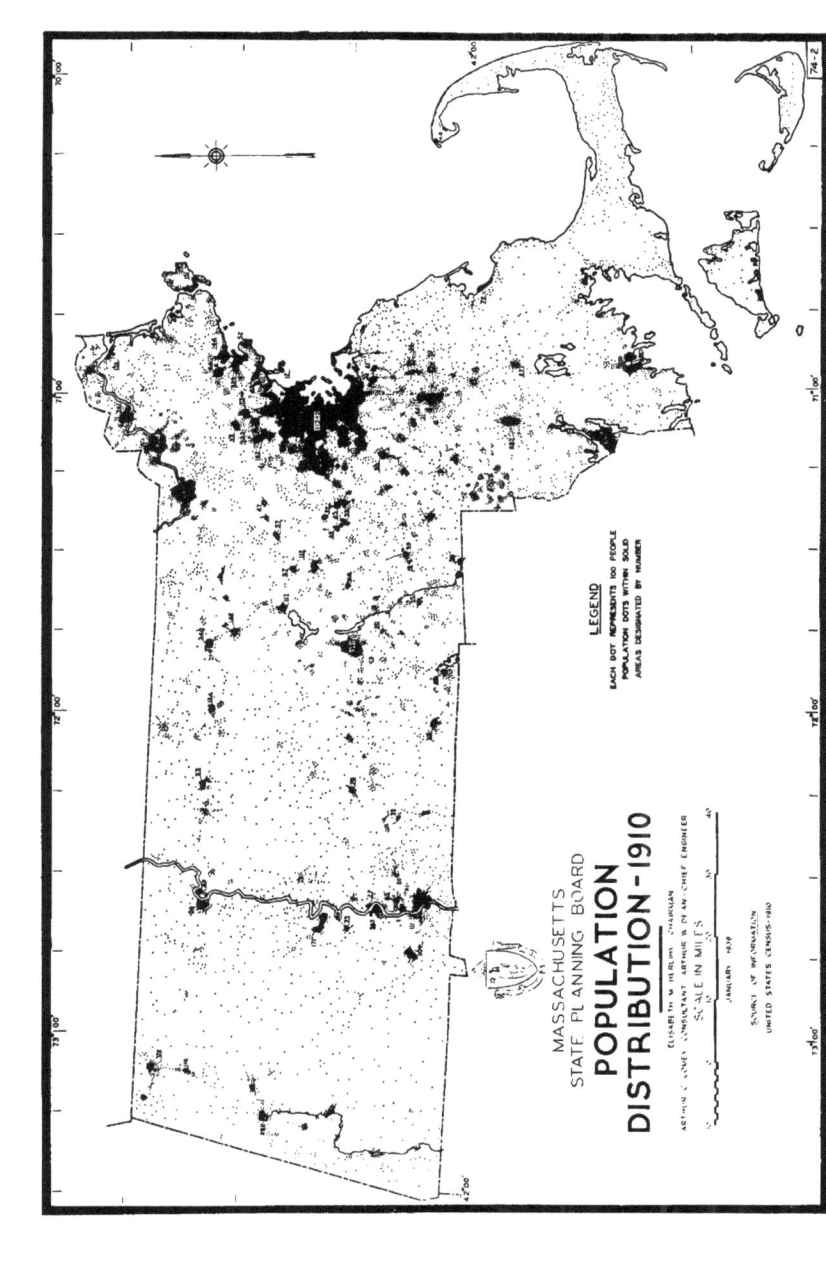

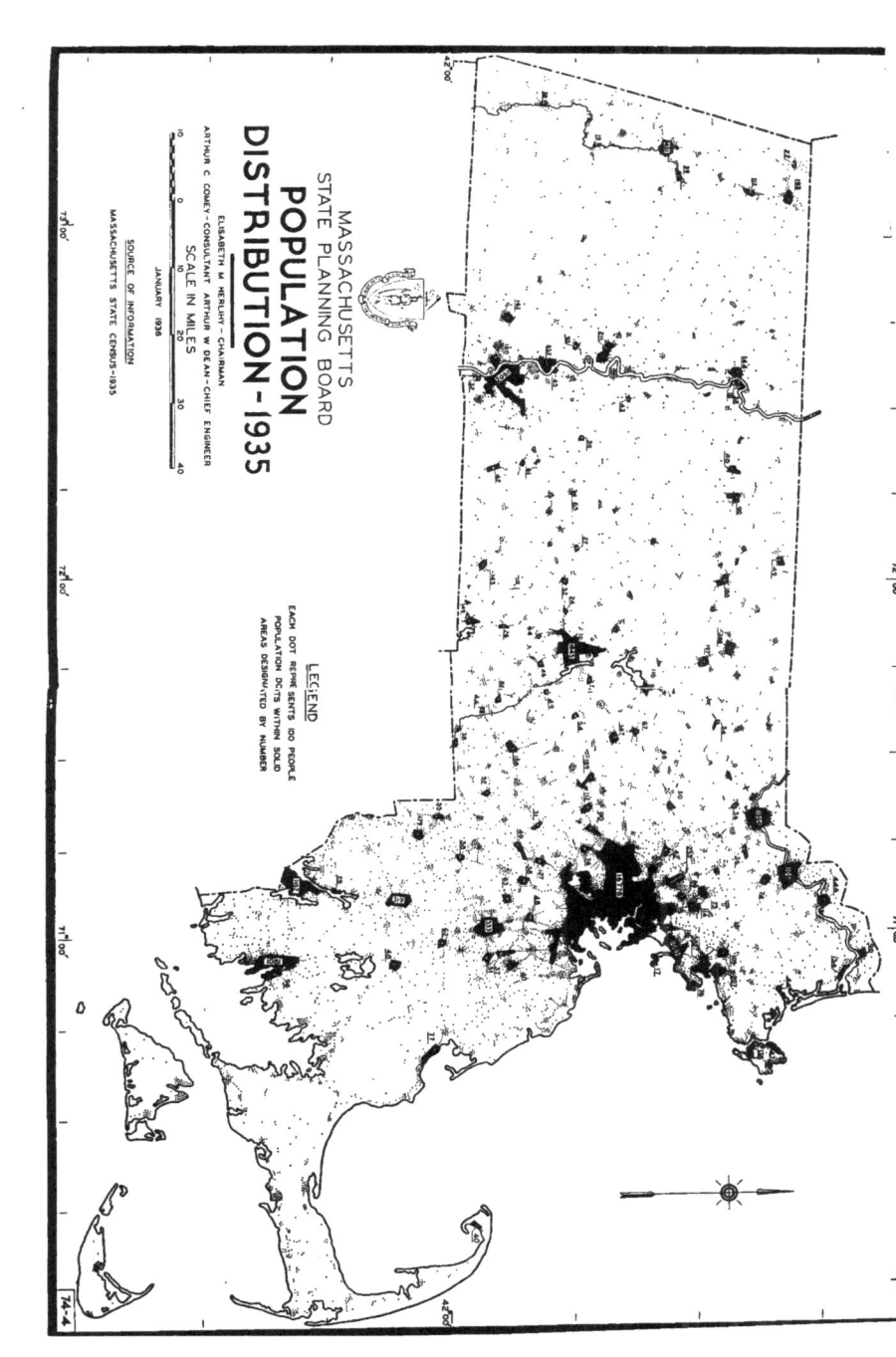

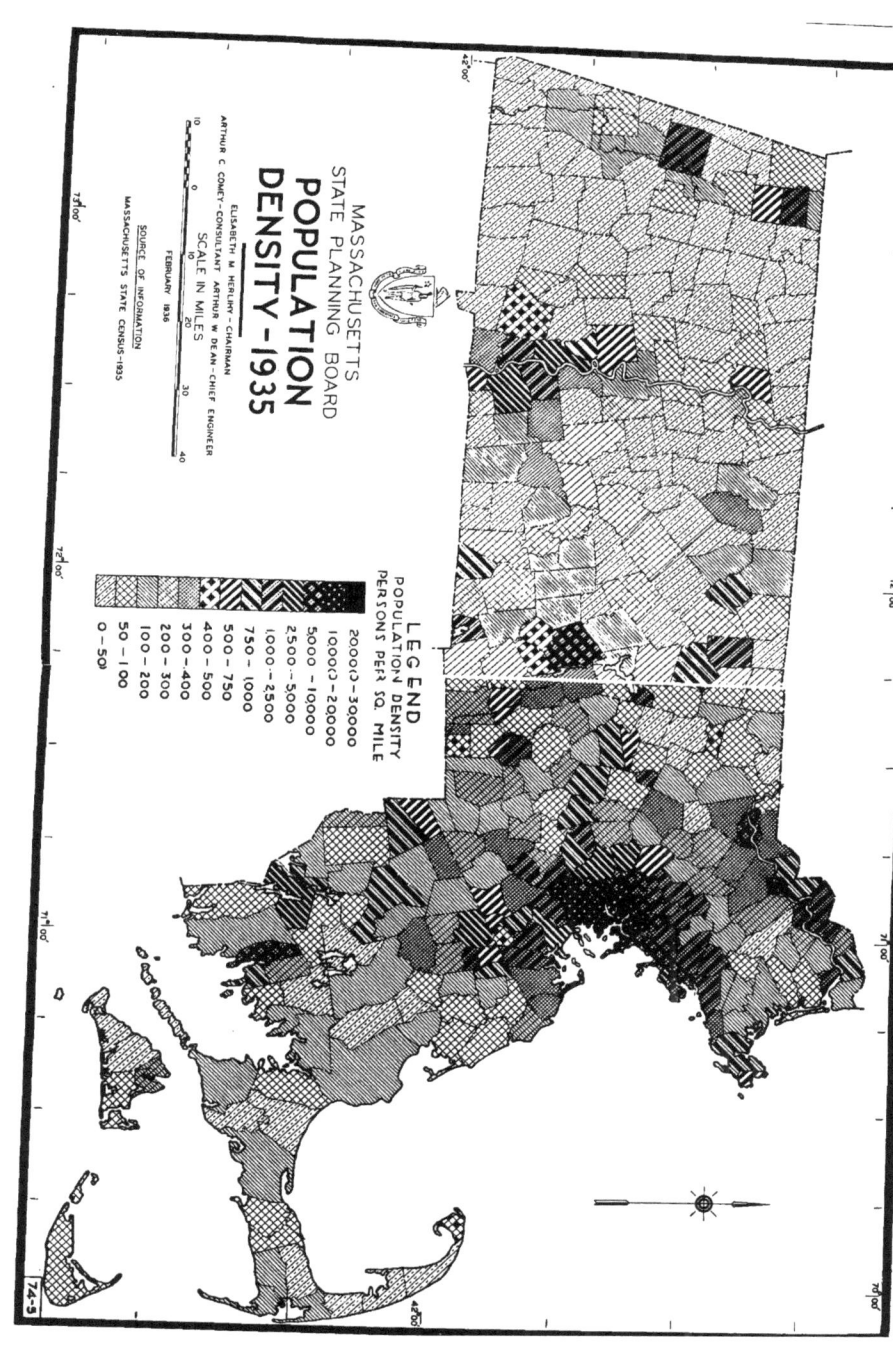

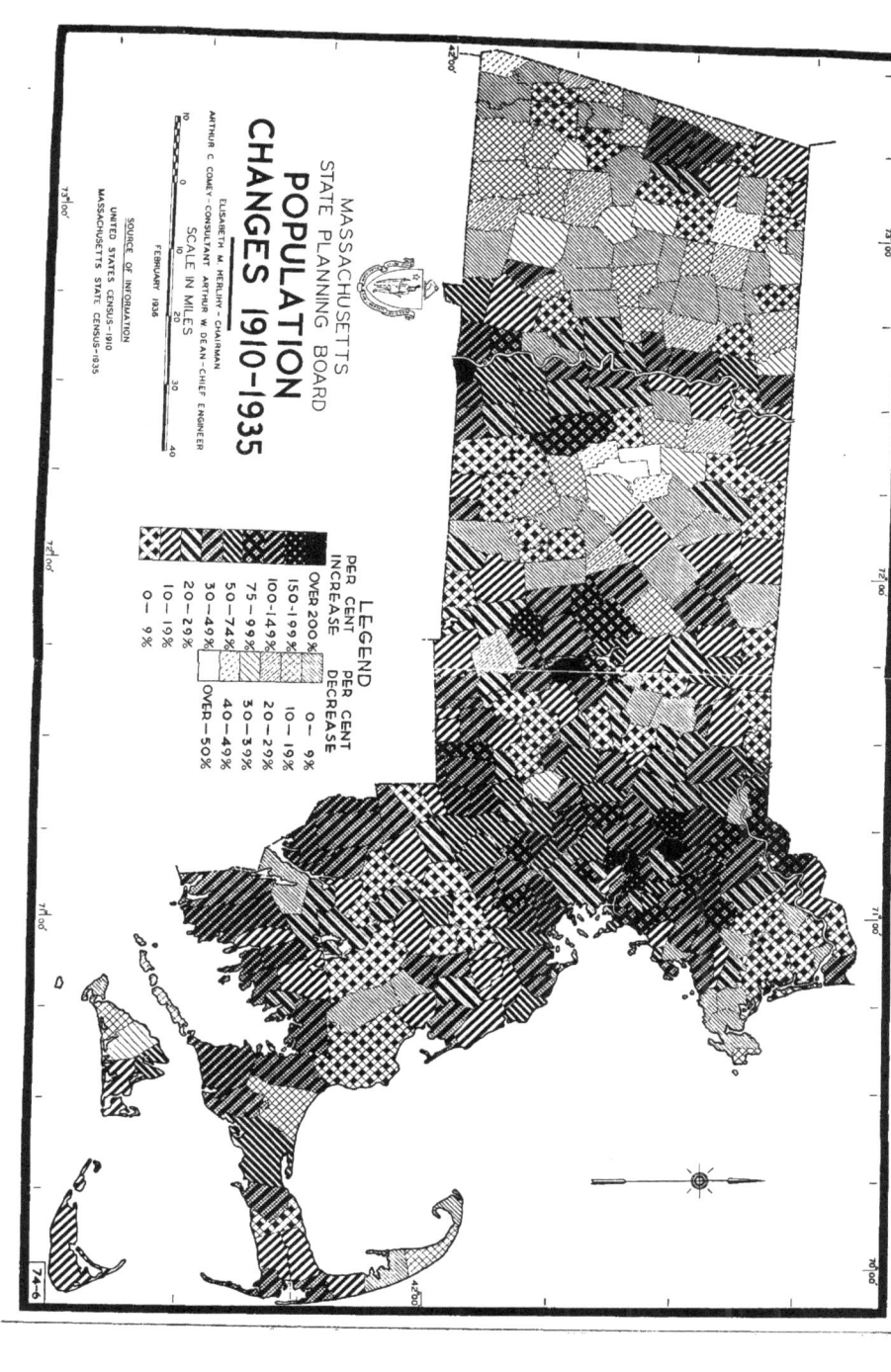

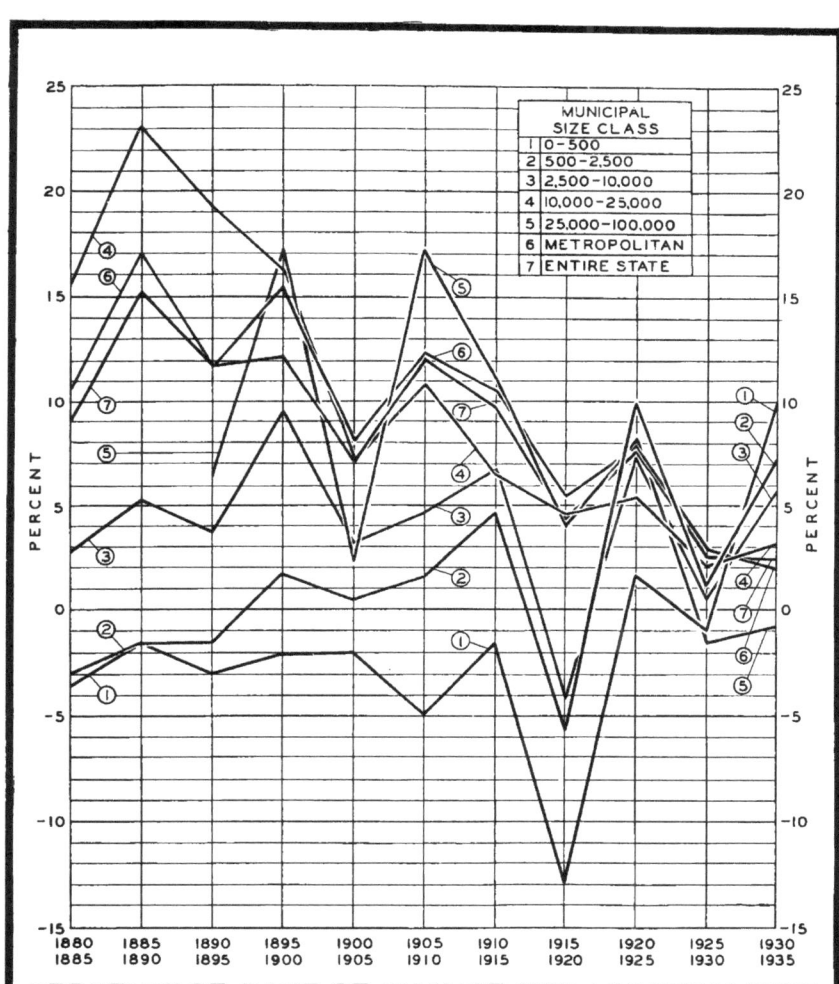

PERCENTAGE RATE OF CHANGE FOR MUNICIPALITIES OF VARIOUS SIZE CLASSES

IN MASSACHUSETTS, 1880-1935, BY FIVE YEAR PERIODS
WITH SAME FOR STATE AND METROPOLITAN DISTRICTS

**MASSACHUSETTS
STATE PLANNING BOARD**
NOVEMBER 1936

SOURCE: MASS. AND U.S. CENSUSES.

54A-C14

population in metropolitan regions will continue although the rate of concentration may be materially lowered. Secondly, unless new or part-time industries are developed in the towns of the Berkshire Hills and Central Highlands, these now sub-marginal agricultural areas will probably continue small in population.

Although no study has been made of the distribution of population within metropolitan areas, there appears to be a tendency toward decentralization. It seems likely, since the principal causes bringing about this pattern are the automobile and rapid transit, that this pattern will be intensified rather than diminished in the future. The amount of future disintegration of the central areas of metropolitan districts will depend, in part, upon the provisions made for low-cost mass transportation. There is no implication that there will be a general exodus of population from the central portions of metropolitan regions.

Population Composition

The present study of population composition is considered from the standpoints of: (1) age groups; (2) sex; (3) nativity; and (4) occupation.

The composition of population from the first three standpoints has significant influences on future population growth. For instance, birth rates vary with different nationalities; death rates are different for the two sexes; and the number of persons in the different age groups is particularly important in determining future birth rates.

Age Groups

There are several methods of studying the age-group composition of population. The first of these is illustrated in Chart 54A-C30, which is developed by graphing the percentage increments of past population according to selected age groups and predicting the future trends by projecting the curves. Although this has been a standard method of procedure, an obvious error in it is the fact that the future size of any particular age group depends, not upon the past experience of that age group, but upon the past experience of those younger age groups from which it has sprung.

On Chart 54A-C12, the data on population age-group composition for 1930 can be read vertically. The male and female composition and the nativity composition of the age groups are presented on this same chart. Chart 54A-C22 also shows the sex composition of the different five-year age groups, from 1880 to 1930.

Age-group studies are particularly useful in predicting the number of children for whom future educational facilities must be provided, and the number of people for whom old-age assistance must be available.

Sex

The charts used to portray age-group composition present sex composition also. Note that, since 1880, Massachusetts has had a relatively well-balanced distribution of males and females in all age groups. Even in periods of high immigration, the normal balance between the two sexes was not appreciably disturbed; that is, the number of immigrants of each sex was about equal. This balance of the sexes still exists today, as indicated for 1930 on Chart 54A-C12. It is likely that this same balance will continue in the future.

Nativity

Nativity composition is interesting and important, particularly from the point of view of birth rates. Population has been divided into three classes according to nativity, as follows: (1) native white; (2) first-generation native white of foreign-born parents; and (3) foreign-born white. The native-white population is derived either from native-white parents or from first-generation native white of foreign-born parents; the later are, of course, derived from foreign-born parents. The last three census periods show, as would be expected, a rapid falling off of foreign-born population, resulting from decreased immigration. For example, in 1910, the number of foreign-born males between twenty and twenty-five years of age was about six thousand, whereas, in 1920, it was only a little over two thousand. The total number of foreign-born is gradually decreasing, as they grow older and die. In 1920, the number of first-generation foreign-born show a decline in the lower age groups, caused by the rapid drop in immigration in the foreign-born of reproductive age and the advancing age of those immigrants already here.

In general, it may be said that of the three nativity groups, the foreign-born has the highest birth rates; the first-generation native white of foreign-born parents, the second highest; and the native white, the lowest. From this it may be inferred that birth rates will continue to drop as these latter two groups become numerically more dominant, unless new factors arise to modify this trend.

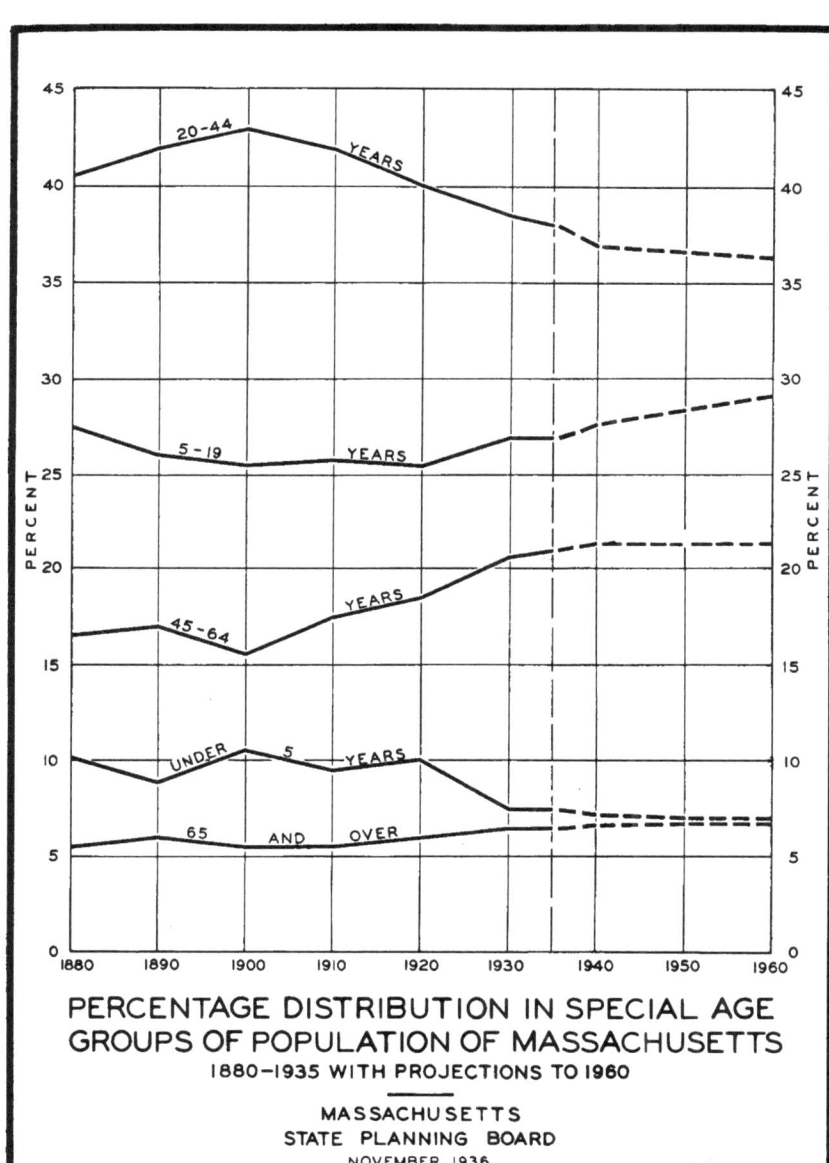

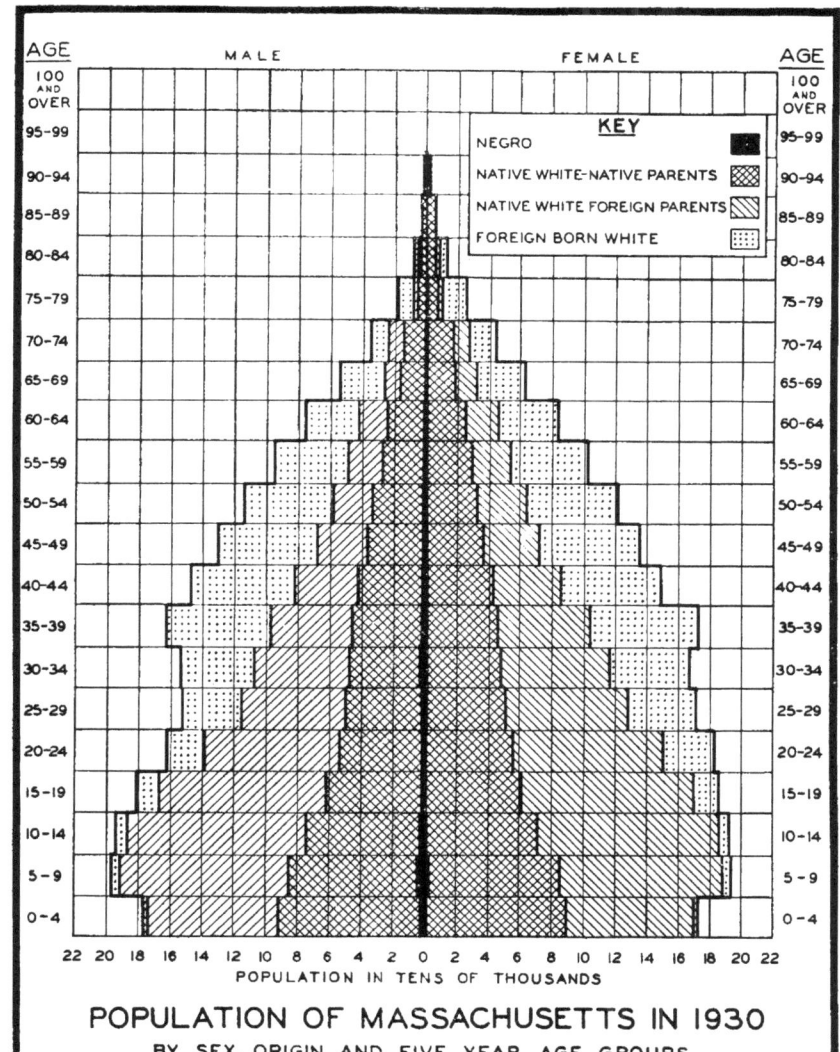

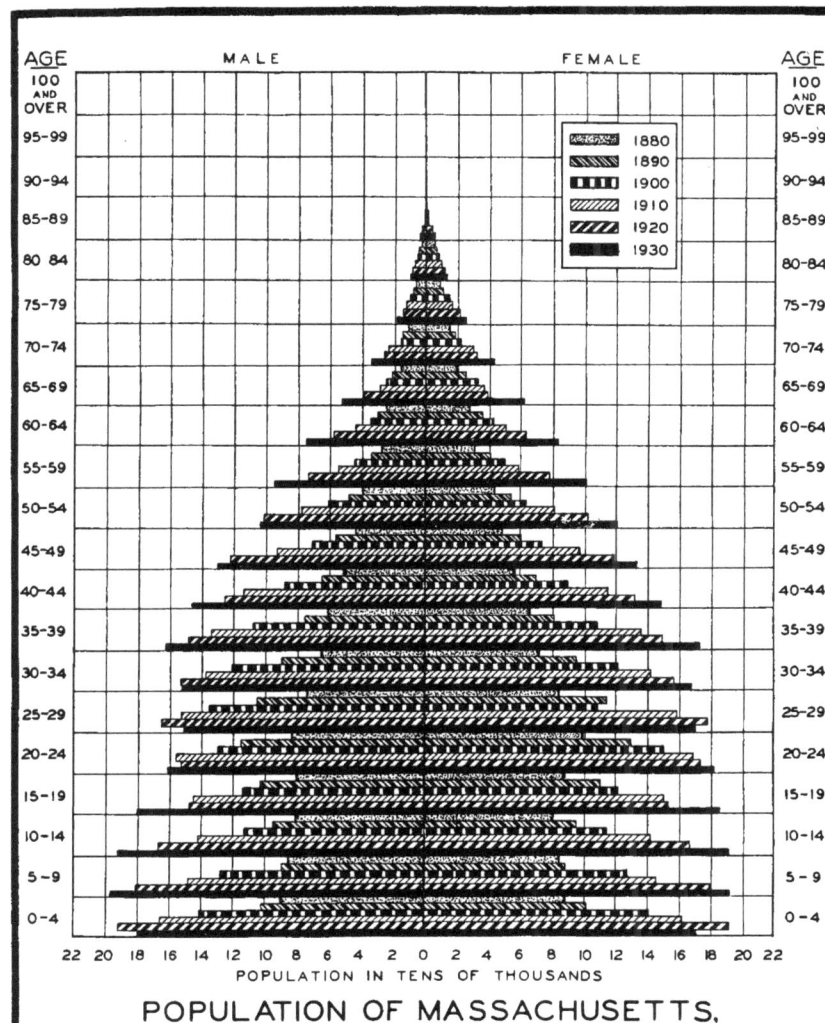

POPULATION OF MASSACHUSETTS,
AT TEN YEAR INTERVALS, 1880-1930
BY SEX, AND FIVE YEAR AGE GROUPS

MASSACHUSETTS
STATE PLANNING BOARD
NOVEMBER 1936

SOURCE U.S CENSUS

54A-C22

MASSACHUSETTS STATE PLANNING BOARD

Occupation

The study of the composition of Massachusetts population from the standpoint of occupation was complicated by the fact that the census occupation classifications have been changed from time to time.

Chart 54A-C32, showing the occupational composition of population from 1880 to 1930, presents the data in varying degrees of detail. For example, it was possible to present the number of manufacturing and mechanical industrial workers and professional workers throughout the entire period covered by the chart, but the number of persons engaged in all other occupations had to be grouped together during the years 1880 to 1900. In 1900, the Bureau of the Census adopted an occupational classification to which it has since adhered, making possible the presentation of uniform data for the subsequent years.

The occupational data show a gradual increase in the number of persons engaged in all commercial activities except the manufacturing and mechanical industries, in which there was a pronounced decrease from 1920 to 1930.

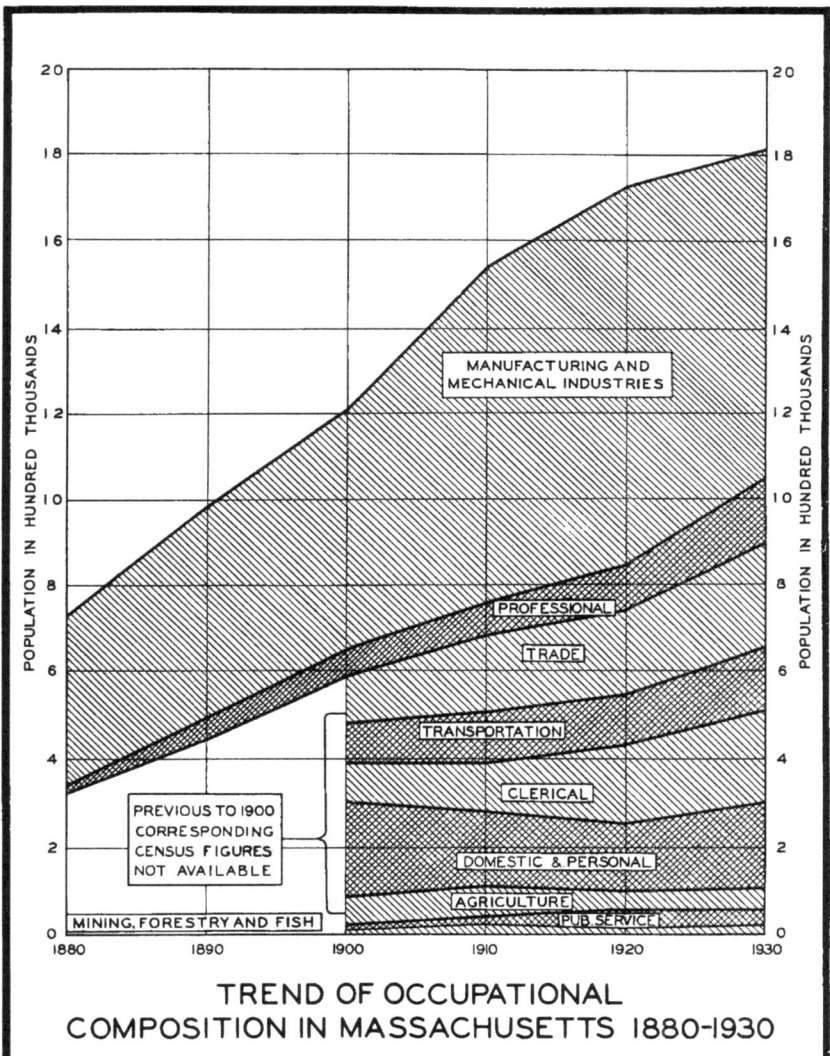

EMPLOYMENT

Summary Outline

I. Two Methods of Determining the Number of Unemployed

II. Employment in All Occupations, 1920-1930

III. Employment in Manufacturing Industries

    A. Employment in Twelve Massachusetts Industries
    B. Manufacturing Employment by Counties

IV. Principal Massachusetts Industries

V. Industrial Condition of the Commonwealth

MASSACHUSETTS STATE PLANNING BOARD

EMPLOYMENT

Massachusetts, like all other States, has problems of technological, cyclical, and seasonal unemployment. But the problem in Massachusetts, and in New England, as a whole, is distinctive in that it is largely the problem of jobs that have vanished, not as a result of increased industrial efficiency, but as a result of the lack of it in certain specific industries.

The study of employment and unemployment in Massachusetts or in the United States as a whole presents difficulties. Reliable unemployment statistics are lacking, and estimates vary widely. The United States Department of Commerce* sets the unemployment figure for the entire country at 9,550,000, as of August 7, 1936. The NEW YORK SUN** estimates it at not over 3,621,000, as of August 8, 1936. The American Federation of Labor has still another figure.

Two Methods of Determining the Number of Unemployed

There are two possible methods of determining the number of unemployed. One is to count the unemployed. The other is to subtract from the total number of employable people the number actually employed at any given date.

Direct Census of Unemployed

The FERA and CWA unemployment census in Massachusetts, as of January 2, 1934, gives the results of a direct counting of the unemployed. Its usefulness is limited by the fact that it covers only one date and that it does not show the number of employables by each type of industry.

According to this census, the total population of the State, on January 2, 1934, was 4,301,931. Of this total, 1,808,840 were employable persons (i.e., persons willing and able to work). Of these latter, 450,855, or 24.9 per cent, were wholly unemployed. A total of 624,526, or 34.5 per cent of the employable persons, were either wholly or partially unemployed.

Employment in All Occupations, 1920-1930

The essential data for employment in all occupations are

---

*Associated Press news release, August 7, 1936.
**The NEW YORK SUN, August 8, 1936.

Table 22

DISTRIBUTION OF EMPLOYMENT IN MASSACHUSETTS, NEW ENGLAND, AND THE UNITED STATES IN 1920 AND 1930*

OCCUPATIONS	UNITED STATES				NEW ENGLAND				MASSACHUSETTS			
	Number Employed in 1930 (thousands)	Per Cent Increase 1920-1930	Per Cent Of All Employment 1930		Number Employed in 1930 (thousands)	Per Cent Increase 1920-1930	Per Cent Of All Employment 1930		Number Employed in 1930 (thousands)	Per Cent Increase 1920-1930	Per Cent Of All Employment 1930	
All Occupations	48,832.6	17.35	100.0		3,431.4	6.09	100.0		1,814.4	4.98	100.0	
Manufacturing and Mechanical Industries	14,317.5	11.69	29.32		1,568.4	-3.91	45.69		837.4	-5.68	46.16	
Trade	7,557.0	77.62	15.44		561.7	70.47	16.37		325.4	67.98	17.94	
Domestic and Personal Service	4,812.1	41.04	9.85		336.5	29.22	9.81		188.9	26.74	10.42	
Transportation	4,498.6	44.87	9.09		274.1	27.37	7.99		148.4	21.71	8.13	
Professional Service	3,425.8	59.8	7.02		267.5	52.6	7.80		153.8	55.69	8.48	
Agriculture	10,432.3	-1.9	21.46		213.3	-4.84	6.22		56.0	8.9	3.09	
Public Service	1,057.9	37.3	2.17		88.4	33.29	2.58		51.4	35.99	2.83	
Forestry	196.0	-9.9	0.40		11.6	-47.98	0.34		1.9	24.68	0.11	
Fishing	74.1	28.8	0.15		11.3	25.2	0.33		5.99	31.2	0.33	
Extraction of Minerals	1,158.1	6.22	2.37		10.2	109.3	0.30		2.9	138.2	0.16	

*Source of information: United States Census of Occupations, 1920 and 1930.
Note: The terms "employed", "employment", and so forth refer to "persons ten years of age or over, engaged in gainful occupations".

summarized in Table 22. During the ten years from 1920 to 1930, total employment increased about 17.4 per cent in the United States, with corresponding increases of 6.1 per cent and 5.0 per cent in New England and Massachusetts, respectively. Conceivably, the difference might be attributed to the fact that the populations of New England and Massachusetts have gained less rapidly than that of the country at large. Yet, even when this allowance is made, employment is seen to have lagged behind in these two units. The increase in population for the United States was 1.9 per cent higher than the increase in employment, indicating a slight relative decrease in the number of jobs, while New England and Massachusetts showed corresponding figures of 6.7 per cent and 7.9 per cent, respectively. The relative number of jobs fell off more in Massachusetts than in New England as a whole.

As might be expected from the above analysis, there was relatively more unemployment in Massachusetts than in New England or in the United States. In 1930, the percentage of unemployed to all employed for Massachusetts was 8.9 per cent; in 1934, the percentage had increased to 19.1 per cent.

During the decade 1920-1930, employment in Massachusetts fell off in mechanical and manufacturing occupations only, and increased in all other occupations. In both 1930 and 1934, there were more unemployed in manufacturing and mechanical industries than in all other occupations. Since, in 1930, manufacturing in Massachusetts supplied the livelihood of about half of the male population and about two fifths of the female population, the conclusion is that the course of employment in manufacturing industries is by far the most important single factor in total employment. It is the key to the fluctuations that have occurred in Massachusetts during the past fifteen years.

Employment in Manufacturing Industries

The following table shows the average number of wage earners employed in manufacturing establishments in Massachusetts from 1925 through 1934. From this table, it is evident that, for the nine-year period from 1925 through 1934, the peak of industrial employment in Massachusetts occurred in 1926. From 1926 to 1929 there was a gradual decrease in employment, although 1929 showed some gain over 1928. There was a rapid decrease in the number of industrial wage earners from 1929 to 1932, when a new low point was reached. The increasing number of wage earners in 1933 and 1934 indicates the beginning of an upward swing in employment. Figures for 1935 are not yet available.

Table 23

MANUFACTURING EMPLOYMENT IN MASSACHUSETTS*

YEAR	AVERAGE NUMBER OF WAGE EARNERS EMPLOYED
1925	591,438
1926	602,343
1927	578,068
1928	540,927
1929	557,494
1930	481,449
1931	434,441
1932	350,521
1933	398,592
1934	423,933
1935	439,449**

*Compiled from the Annual Reports of the Massachusetts Department of Labor and Industries.

**Estimates based on results of "Monthly Surveys of Employment and Earnings in Representative Manufacturing Establishments", by the Division of Statistics, Massachusetts Department of Labor and Industries.

Employment in Twelve Massachusetts Industries

Table 24 shows the trend of employment in twelve important industries from 1925 through 1934. It shows, during this period, a decided loss in the number of persons so employed, although the upward swing in 1933 and 1934 is encouraging. Nevertheless, it is doubtful whether the high point of 1926 will soon be attained again. A comparison between the manufacturing employment figures for United States, New England, and Massachusetts is given in this table. (See also Charts 54D-C3 and 54D-C4.)

Employment in Manufacturing in Ten Massachusetts Cities

Chart 54D-C2 and Table 25 show in ten important cities of Massachusetts, 1925-1934, a similar situation.

Table 24

EMPLOYMENT FOR ALL MANUFACTURING INDUSTRIES IN THE UNITED STATES, NEW ENGLAND, AND MASSACHUSETTS, AND FOR TWELVE IMPORTANT MASSACHUSETTS INDUSTRIES, 1919-1935
(In thousands)

INDUSTRIES	1919	1921	1923	1925	1927	1929	1931	1932	1933	1934	1935	GAINS 1919 1933
United States	9000.1	6946.6	8778.2	8384.3	8349.8	8307.5	6523.0	*	6055.7	*	*	2,944.4**
New England	1351.4	1071.1	1253.9	1122.2	1098.7	1100.0	850.1	*	798.3	*	*	553.1** '19-'35 '32-'35
Massachusetts All Industries	713.8	579.1	667.4	591.4	578.1	557.5	434.4	350.5	398.6	423.9	438.2	275.6 87.7
Cotton Goods	122.5	106.3	113.7	96.2	90.9	70.8	47.0	32.5	45.4	49.3	44.2	78.3** 11.7
Boots and Shoes Other than Rubber	90.7	70.9	76.7	64.4	63.8	62.8	54.1	49.1	53.7	53.0	44.3	46.4** 4.3**
Woolen and Worsted Goods	53.9	56.6	64.8	54.9	51.1	45.7	37.2	28.6	39.3	36.0	54.8	0.9 26.2
Foundries and Machine Shops	27.8	20.1	24.7	19.5	19.9	21.2	14.8	10.2	11.0	12.3	12.5	15.3** 2.3
Electrical Machinery	23.9	17.6	26.4	25.1	24.8	28.8	20.1	13.6	14.3	17.0	17.2	6.7** 3.6
Textile Machinery	17.4	16.5	18.7	13.7	12.0	10.6	7.5	5.2	8.0	8.8	7.2	10.2** 2.0
Leather	15.2	9.0	11.4	10.4	10.8	10.7	8.7	7.9	10.0	10.0	10.2	5.0** 2.3
Printing and Publishing	13.7	12.8	14.2	14.2	14.4	15.2	13.2	12.0	11.4	12.4	11.7	2.0** 0.3**
Rubber Boots and Shoes	13.1	9.4	12.5	11.4	12.1	11.2	6.3	5.1	6.7	6.8	6.0	7.1** 0.9
Paper and Pulp	13.0	12.4	13.3	12.9	12.4	12.4	10.7	9.4	9.5	10.1	9.9	3.1** 0.5
Knit Goods	12.8	10.5	11.7	10.6	9.7	8.3	7.6	6.3	7.7	7.9	6.9	5.9** 0.1
Rubber Goods	9.6	7.8	11.4	10.7	10.4	9.8	6.7	6.4	6.8	6.9	8.0	1.6** 1.6

*Figures not available
**Decrease

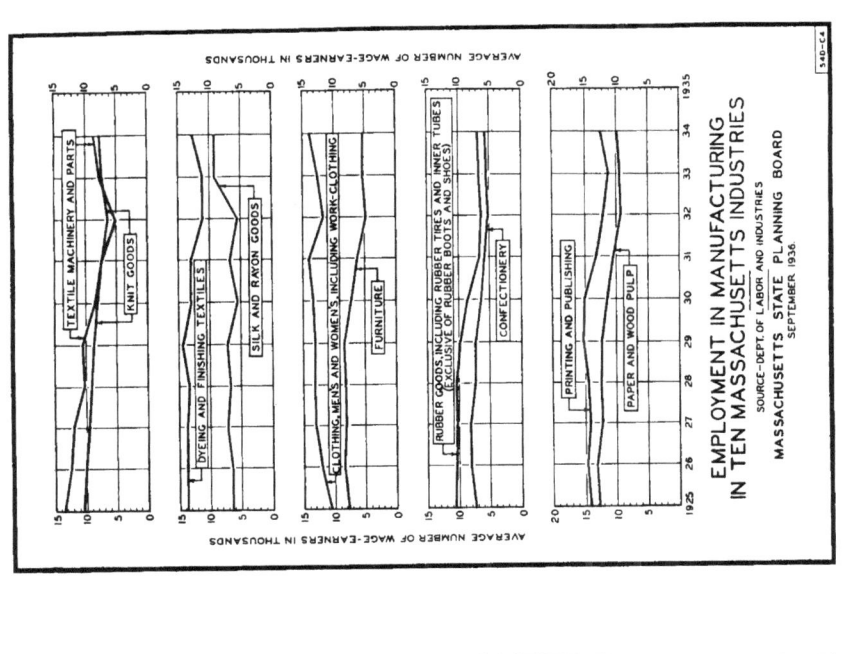

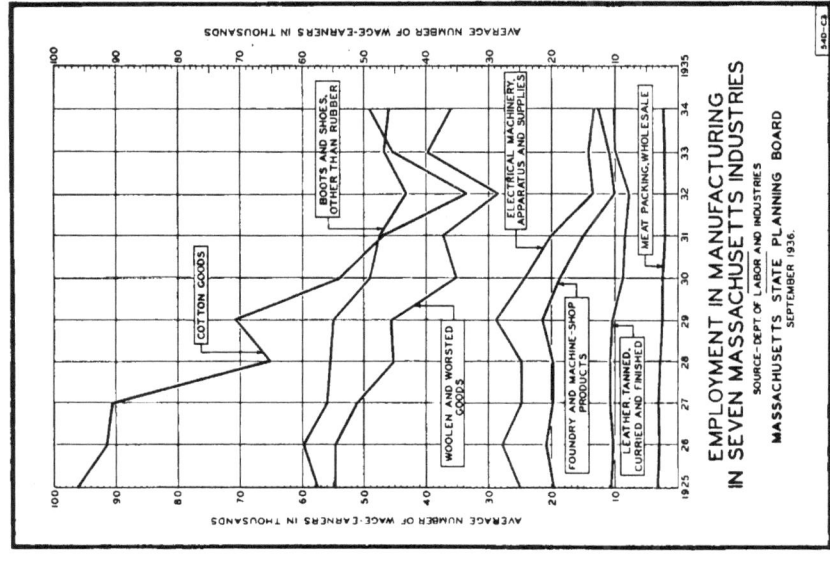

Table 25

AVERAGE NUMBER OF PERSONS EMPLOYED IN MANUFACTURING IN TEN IMPORTANT CITIES OF MASSACHUSETTS, 1925 — 1934*

YEAR	BOSTON	CAMBRIDGE	WORCESTER	LAWRENCE	FALL RIVER	NEW BEDFORD	SPRINGFIELD	SOMERVILLE	LYNN	LOWELL
1925	73,093	21,946	31,563	26,298	30,599	35,756	17,786	5,451	18,968	21,553
1926	90,722	22,705	31,621	26,777	31,353	35,143	19,492	5,316	21,951	20,859
1927	76,876	21,151	30,132	24,893	31,334	35,036	17,109	5,500	20,790	18,818
1928	75,468	21,357	30,091	21,047	25,547	21,249	17,833	5,872	20,076	17,234
1929	76,879	21,857	31,822	23,139	23,977	32,155	19,812	6,701	20,544	16,599
1930	68,516	19,364	27,526	20,582	21,344	25,739	15,613	7,134	17,699	13,981
1931	58,072	16,141	23,955	23,500	22,064	22,533	13,947	5,991	15,675	13,710
1932	46,237	13,875	17,006	17,239	17,326	16,456	11,211	5,317	12,630	12,012
1933	46,823	15,095	23,160	21,469	22,733	23,260	12,490	5,425	12,275	13,308
1934	50,627	15,443	25,109	19,830	24,078	24,631	14,307	5,997	12,251	13,532

*Compiled from the Annual Reports of the Massachusetts Department of Labor and Industries

MASSACHUSETTS STATE PLANNING BOARD

Table 26

EMPLOYMENT IN MANUFACTURING BY COUNTIES*

YEAR	BARNSTABLE	BERKSHIRE	BRISTOL	DUKES	ESSEX	FRANKLIN	HAMPDEN
1927	844	20,251	84,426	9	89,014	5,605	54,301
1928	419	19,131	64,275	8	82,618	5,683	53,993
1931	79	14,552	59,494	10	71,642	4,060	39,010
1932	75	11,697	44,903	6	59,495	3,315	30,953
1933	91	13,514	58,511	**	67,930	3,467	34,845
1934	98	14,791	61,977	**	66,375	4,063	38,232

YEAR	HAMPSHIRE	MIDDLESEX	NANTUCKET	NORFOLK	PLYMOUTH	SUFFOLK	WORCESTER
1927	9,829	99,046	20	22,811	23,200	83,790	84,367
1929	9,401	95,994	20	22,178	22,590	82,080	82,577
1931	6,105	74,929	22	18,919	17,880	62,410	65,076
1932	4,814	63,623	18	15,899	14,179	50,033	51,511
1933	5,376	68,780	26**	15,145	16,452	50,976	63,479
1934	5,868	73,355	31**	18,237	16,843	55,041	69,022

*Compiled from Annual Reports of the Massachusetts Department of Labor and Industries.
**Figures for Dukes County are included with those for Nantucket County to avoid disclosure of operations in the former.

Manufacturing Employment by Counties

The employment situation in the important cities of the State is reflected in the counties. Chart 54D-C1 and Table 26 show employment gains in 1933 and 1934 in all the counties of the State except Essex, where there was a sharp rise in employment from 1932 to 1933 and a decline in 1934.

Principal Massachusetts Industries

The unemployed in Massachusetts, as in many other States, mirror the condition of the State's principal manufacturing industries, which include cotton textiles, boots and shoes, woolens and worsteds, electrical machinery, and foundry and machine-shop products.

Cotton Textile Industry

The condition of the cotton-textile industry, which employs many workers, has important effects upon the employment situation of the State. The industry has declined, and is now increasing production only slowly. Part of the decline has been due to the emigration of cotton mills to the South.

According to the Massachusetts Department of Labor and Industries, in the period between 1921 and 1934, 106 Massachusetts cotton mills went out of business. Of these, thirteen were taken over and operated by other companies in Massachusetts. From the remaining 93 establishments, 22,819 workers were thrown out of employment.

Boot and Shoe Industry

The boot and shoe industry has suffered also. In 1933, 44 establishments ceased operation, and 12 emigrated from the State. In those establishments which went out of business or moved outside the State, 3706 wage earners were employed. But in 1933, new factories were established, employing 3068 persons, so that the net loss in 1933 was 16 establishments and 638 wage earners.*

Other Industries

The same general conditions prevail to a somewhat lesser extent in most of the other major industries of the State.

---

*Data from the Massachusetts Department of Labor and Industries.

MASSACHUSETTS STATE PLANNING BOARD

Industrial Difficulties Capable of Correction

Some of the causes of these industrial difficulties are capable of being corrected. When this is accomplished, employment in Massachusetts will be stimulated. Among the causes amenable to correction are the following:

1. Obsolescence in equipment
2. Seasonal variation
3. Inefficient management
4. Changes in styles
5. Restrictive legislation

Industrial Condition of the Commonwealth

It is difficult to estimate the industrial condition of the Commonwealth. Undoubtedly its industries have recovered from the depths of 1932. In normal times, the four major manufacturing industries, (1) cotton, (2) leather, (3) wool, and (4) metal products, provide employment for more than 40 per cent of the total number of wage earners in all manufacturing industries in the State, but in 1934 the number employed in these major industries was only approximately 28 per cent of the wage earners engaged in manufacturing in the State.

At the present time, in business circles, there is a new note of optimism and hope for the future. There is every indication of improvement in industry, but how far the improvement will extend is still problematical. It is evident that the State has lost its initial advantage of a head start in industry over the rest of the country. It now appears that the development of new industries is essential to the welfare of Massachusetts.

Sources of Information

Cleveland Trust Company Reports
Cotton Textile Industry Report (1935)
FERA and CWA Report on the Census of Unemployment in Massachusetts (1934)
Harvard Undergraduate Studies, by Edward Gay
Industrial Structure of New England, by Charles E. Artman
Industrial Structure of New England, by Whitman
International Labor Reviews
Massachusetts Department of Labor and Industries, Annual Reports
Massachusetts Department of Labor and Industries, Preliminary and Monthly Reports

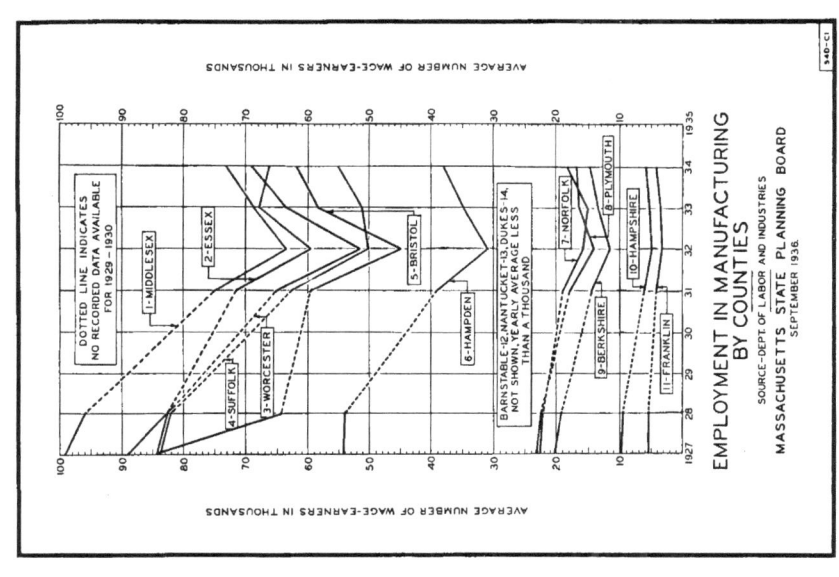
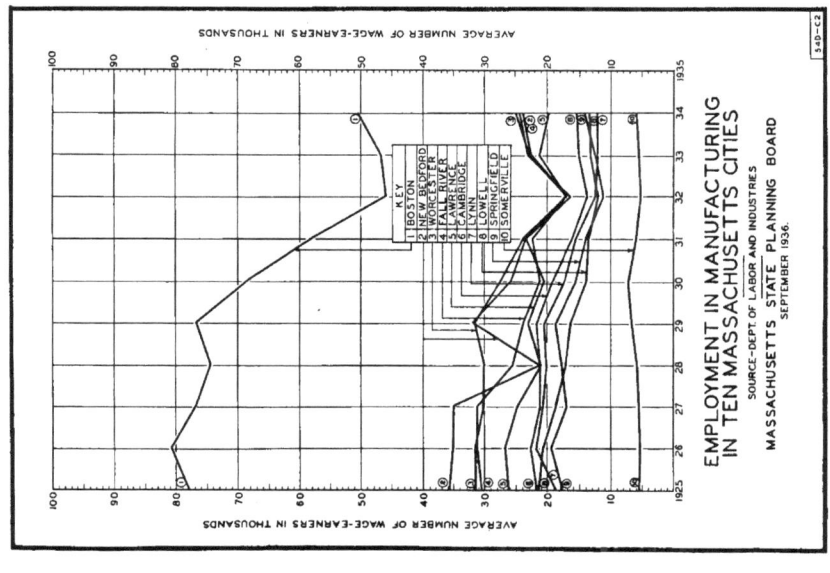

Massachusetts Emergency Commission on Unemployment Reports (October 1931 - April 1932).
Monthly Labor Reviews
National Industrial Conference Board Reports
NEW ENGLAND'S PROSPECT
NEW ENGLAND TODAY, Published by the New England Council
THE FEDERATIONIST (A. F. of L. publication)
THE FLIGHT OF CAPITAL AND INDUSTRY FROM MASSACHUSETTS, by Warren F. Doane
United States Bureau of Labor Statistics (Pamphlets)
UNITED STATES CENSUS (1930)

HOUSING

Summary Outline

I. Pre-War Housing in Massachusetts

II. Post-War Housing in Massachusetts

III. Recent Massachusetts Housing Activities of Public Agencies

IV. Recent Massachusetts Housing Activities of Philanthropic Agencies

V. Statistical Analysis of Housing

VI. Special Aspects of the Housing Problem
    A. Limitations of Private Enterprise
    B. Economics of Low-rental Districts
    C. Coöperation between Federal, State, and Local Authorities
    D. Financing of Public Housing Projects

MASSACHUSETTS STATE PLANNING BOARD

HOUSING

Although much is being done by various agencies, present-day housing fails in many respects to measure up to even minimum standards of health and decency. These unsatisfactory conditions must be remedied; but where, and to what extent? Among the first steps necessary in the search for a solution is a survey of existing conditions and present housing needs.

Pre-War Housing in Massachusetts

Boston Housing Studies

Boston was the first city in Massachusetts to become housing-conscious. In 1891, the Massachusetts Bureau of Statistics of Labor made a monumental census of tenement houses in Boston and published the findings in two volumes. Its investigations included 311,396 persons, comprising 71,665 families; of these families, 12.07 per cent were found to be living under bad or poor conditions. Despite the revelations of this survey, it soon became apparent that little was being done to remedy the conditions.

In 1897, a private civic group, the Twentieth Century Club, appointed a Tenement House Committee. After a thorough investigation of a great number of tenements, a member of this committee, Mr. Harold K. Estabrook, prepared a pamphlet entitled: "Some Slums in Boston."* In 1900, "The Housing Conditions in Boston,"** an article by Mr. Robert T. Paine, of the same organization, revealed results gained from further investigations. These two publications, and other studies, caused so much comment that, in 1903-1904, a commission to investigate tenement-house conditions was appointed by the mayor. As a result of the commission's findings, the Board of Health ordered many houses to be removed or vacated.

The housing committee of the "Boston 1915" movement made a study of ten typical blocks in 1910, revealing information on the number of dark rooms.*** In 1916, the Women's Municipal League, after five years of painstaking investigation, issued a bulletin

---
*A pamphlet (23 pp.), published in 1898 by the Twentieth Century Club.
**ANNALS OF THE AMERICAN ACADEMY OF POLITICAL AND SOCIAL SCIENCE, July 1902, pp. 123-36.
***"Boston 1915", Housing Committee, report (20 pp.) presented to the Board of Directors and accepted by them April 11, 1910.

entitled "Housing Conditions of Today in Boston,"* which disclosed the continued existence of bad housing conditions.

Tenement House Acts

In 1912, a Tenement-House Act for Towns, and, in 1913, a Tenement-House Act for Cities, were enacted. By 1919, twenty-three towns and one city (Revere) had adopted these laws, which were based on the New York law but were more stringent in several particulars. The unsatisfactory feature was that communities were not required to adopt them.

The First Homestead Commission

Organized union labor promoted the First Homestead Commission, established in 1909. It was not until 1917, after the adoption of a constitutional amendment in 1916, that the Commission was given the authority to conduct a careful and conservative experiment in suburban housing, which was the first State housing enterprise in continental North America. The plan was to build fifty houses in a neighborhood-group development, providing decent living accommodations within the reach of men earning from $15 to $25 a week. This plan was not accomplished in its entirety because of post-war conditions, but the twelve houses which were eventually built have proved a financial success. Practically the entire amount of the capital expenditure by the Commonwealth, together with the interest, has already been returned to the State Treasury. The homesteads were an educational demonstration in housing, but not an attempt to supply the housing needs of the Commonwealth.

In 1919, a consolidation act abolished the Homestead Commission, transferring its duties to the Housing and Town Planning Division of the Department of Public Welfare. The housing activities of this organization were in turn assumed by a State Board of Housing, created in 1933.

Creation of Town Planning Boards

Town planning boards in Massachusetts, first authorized in 1913, have greatly aided the cause of housing, for the primary object of the Act authorizing these Boards was better housing.

Post-War Housing in Massachusetts

In 1920, a Special Commission on the Necessaries of Life was

---

*Bulletin of Women's Municipal League, Feb. 1916, Vol. VII, No. 3, 79 pp.

MASSACHUSETTS STATE PLANNING BOARD

created. A law of the same year authorized this Commission to make a survey of housing conditions.

Conditions caused by the war had enabled large groups of people to improve their standard of living, and to demand better living quarters. This demand was, to a great extent, the cause of increased rents. The trend from the poorer class of tenements to better quarters was clearly shown by statistics for Fall River (1920),* where at the peak of the demand for living quarters, 1488 poorer-class tenements were vacant. In Boston, the Mayor's rent committee reported 2000 tenements of the same class vacant.*

Just before the war, there had been a great amount of overbuilding, making loans upon real estate unattractive to bankers and investors. Much property was held under foreclosure, and forced upon the market. The general suspension of building operations during the war changed the situation and, at the close of the war, the inflated cost of labor and material prevented a widespread resumption of building.

Housing Speculation

Landlords were prompt to take advantage of these conditions to increase rents. Properties which for years had been unprofitable were made to pay. Banks and investors were able to transfer their properties, and many men formerly in the business of building dwellings became active in buying and selling. Speculation in houses, due to high rents, created the belief of fear that actual shelter was not available. Dwellings were sold over and over again, each time at an advanced price.

Was There a Housing Shortage?

That the shortage was not so great as generally stated is amply proved by statistics, which show that the building of houses during the ten-year period prior to 1921 had fairly well kept pace with the growth of population, although only in certain classes of housing. That the shortage of houses, alone, did not justify the current high rents was revealed by the fact that in communities where population had actually decreased there had been a general increase in rents; it is probable, however, that some of this increase was due to rising taxes, the cost of repairs, and other factors.

---

*Annual Report, Special Commission on the Necessaries of Life, Jan. 1921, House No. 1260, p. 51.

MASSACHUSETTS STATE PLANNING BOARD

Problems of High Rentals

By 1922, the surplus housing accommodations of five years before were exhausted. Rents were still going up and wages were coming down. The necessary readjustment was the cause of much social unrest. The process of readjusting a scale of living to an increasing income was rapid and pleasant; when the income was decreasing, however, the readjustment was slow and painful. The plight of tenants who, during the housing inflation, had to live upon incomes not increased by war activities was pitiful. Many tried to pay rents entirely out of proportion to their income. They delayed the necessity of moving to cheaper quarters by making economies in other parts of their budget, even to the extent of denying themselves proper food and clothing.

The Resumption of Building

By 1922, building costs were slowly going down. In this year, 6000 to 7000 new houses were constructed. In 1923, in the smaller communities of Massachusetts, new construction was largely of the one-family and two-family type. Builders found it profitable to construct these houses to sell to families whose rent had been excessively raised. In many cases, these costly new houses were poorly constructed. In Boston and in other densely populated districts, the apartment-house or multi-family type of building was predominant. From 1922 to 1926, new dwelling construction continued at a steadily increasing rate. By 1926, the cost of new construction was double that of ten years previous.

However, the number of new dwellings was not yet sufficient to deflate rentals, but new construction was alleviating the acuteness of housing conditions, especially for those who could afford to build their own homes. The drift toward tenantry had apparently been halted, and house ownership was increasing. All the unfortunate accompaniments of a housing shortage were manifest, however, in the low-cost types of rented tenements. These took the form of:

1. Increases in rent, very few of which were justifiable
2. Orders to vacate, subsequent to refusal to pay increases
3. Objections to children
4. Doubling up of families.

By 1927, the situation was less acute, although there was a widespread demand for clean, inexpensive homes. However, there had been practically no dwellings built for families paying rentals of $35 or less per month. The situation was much more serious in urban communities than in rural settlements. An increase in the number of foreclosures was apparent over this period. It represented to a large extent the liquidation of property purchased with insufficient equity and at peak prices. Money for mortgages, a stimulating factor in the construction and sales market, was plentiful and there was a slight decline in interest rates. This led to greater home-building activity.

From 1927 to 1933, real estate was regarded as a desirable investment of savings. Home ownership increased, but there was also an alarming increase in the number of foreclosures. The culmination of the serious effects of the speculative practices, in 1929 and for several years thereafter, resulted in 12,171 foreclosures during 1933 alone.*

Rents

In 1920, rents were rising rapidly, and many local Rent and Housing Committees were created. Their function was to handle housing complaints and arbitrate in landlord and tenant controversies, and to enforce the Emergency Rent Laws.

In 1921, rents had reached the highest point in the history of the State; they had advanced 50 per cent since pre-war times. In rural communities, where the growth of population was very slight, rents had advanced from 10 to 20 per cent; in larger towns and small cities, from 15 to 25 per cent; in attractive residential districts, from 35 to 50 per cent; and in industrial centers, from 25 to 60 per cent.

In 1922, the Special Commission on the Necessaries of Life divided housing accommodations into three groups, for purposes of comparison:

    1. Heated apartments in choice locations, with elevator and janitor service.
    2. Unheated apartments in houses of moderate value.
    3. Heated and unheated tenements without modern conveniences.

During the year 1922, rents in the first class of dwellings declined from 20 per cent to 35 per cent. Economic pressure, forcing people to seek less expensive accommodations, rather than an increase in new building of this type was the cause of the reduction. Consequently, there was a greater demand for the second and third classes of dwellings.

---

*Figures compiled from "The Banker and Tradesman" by the Division of Necessaries of Life, Department of Labor and Industries.

From 1922 to 1925 there was a surplus of the first class of dwellings, and rents decreased slightly; rents in the second class increased until they reached a peak in 1925. The popular reason given for this was the increase of municipal taxes on real estate. Much of the new building was done in this second class in which the most profitable demand for housing existed. Over this period, there was an accentuated demand for the third class of dwellings; factors causing this were business reverses, reduction in wages, and unemployment, with the consequent necessity for rigid economy. Owing to the complete lack of building in this class, rents showed a disproportionate increase.. This unfortunate situation was further aggravated by speculative activity, which had been stimulated in the lower-valued properties by the diminishing opportunity for speculation in the higher-priced types.

From 1926 on, there was a downward trend in rents, the greatest reduction being made in high-rent groups, and the lowest in the low-rent groups. During 1926, landlords of the first class of dwellings gave rent concessions to their tenants to prevent vacancies. Tenants of moderate-priced property frequently sought accommodations at lower rents, even at a loss of some conveniences. This tendency further aggravated the condition of those forced to live in the third class of accommodations, because much of the run-down property was now renovated and leased at a higher rent. Unfortunately, the commercial builder had abandoned the construction of this type of dwelling because such places could not be built to rent for the small amounts the people could pay, and yet give a fair return on the investment.

From 1929 to 1935, rents have remained fairly stationary in all three classes of dwellings.

In 1921, about 33 per cent of the State's population owned and occupied their homes; the remaining 67 per cent lived in rented properties. Philanthropic and State Aid had apparently not greatly increased the desire of people to own their homes. Nevertheless, the growth of the cooperative bank system, savings banks, and thrift organizations under state supervision indicated a trend toward home ownership.

Home Ownership

In 1924, there were about 90,000 homes in Massachusetts. Only about 15 per cent of these homes were owned, without encumbrances, by their occupants; slightly more than 20 per cent were owned, under mortgage, by their occupants; the balance, approximately 565,000, or 65 per cent of the total, were occupied by tenants.

MASSACHUSETTS STATE PLANNING BOARD

Recent Massachusetts Housing Activities of Public Agencies

Massachusetts State Board of Housing

The Massachusetts State Board of Housing was created under the provisions of Chapter 364 of the Acts of 1933. By Chapter 449 of the Acts of 1935, its powers were enlarged.

Since its creation, the Board has been instrumental in obtaining an allocation of Federal funds for housing projects now under construction in Cambridge and South Boston. Attention has been devoted to the laying of the groundwork for future housing by gathering information, making surveys, and investigating housing conditions throughout the State. To date, analyses of sub-standard areas have been made in six different cities: (1) Boston; (2) Cambridge; (3) Chelsea; (4) Fall River; (5) Lowell; and (6) Springfield. These analyses involve a detailed study of land and building value, the income from real-estate and other taxes, and itemized accounts of the various expenditures necessary to maintain and operate the neighborhood for the year.

The Board has also been instrumental in the realization of the rehabilitation project in Chicopee Falls, to be carried out under a limited-dividend company.

The Board has cooperated with local planning boards, and has aided them in the solution of their particular problems.

Local Housing Authorities

Local Housing Authorities, authorized by Chapter 449 of the Acts of 1935, have been organized in the cities of Boston, Cambridge, and Chelsea. They have the authority to undertake slum clearance and low-cost housing projects.

The Cambridge Authority was active in bringing about the acceptance of the Cambridge PWA Housing Project by the local public, which showed considerable opposition. To date, the Authorities have been merely advisory.

Housing Division of the Public Works Administration

The Housing Division of the Public Works Administration was created for the purpose of carrying out housing projects to supplant slums with modern low-rental dwellings.

Two of these projects are at present under construction, in

Cambridge and South Boston, respectively.

In the Cambridge project, there will be provided 294 apartments, of which 92 are three-room, 114 are four-room, and 88 are five-room apartments.

In the South Boston project, there are a total of 1016 apartments, of which 864 are provided in 3-story walk-up apartment houses and 152 in row houses. In the first group, there are 417 three-room, 345 four-room, and 102 five-room apartments. In the second group, there are 44 four-room, 53 five-room, and 55 six-room apartments.

Reconstruction Finance Corporation

The Reconstruction Finance Corporation was organized February 2, 1932, pursuant to the provisions of the Reconstruction Finance Corporation Act of January 22, 1932. It was termed "An Act to provide emergency financing facilities for financial institutions, to aid in financing agriculture, commerce, and industry, and for other purposes."

Under this Act, funds have been made available for the financing of several Federal housing agencies. Section 4 of the National Housing Act provides that the Corporation shall make available to the Federal Housing Administrator such funds as he may deem necessary for the purposes of carrying out the provisions of Titles I, II, and III of that Act. Section 4 (b) of the Home Owners' Loan Act of 1933 authorizes and directs the Reconstruction Finance Corporation to allocate and make available sums of money to the Secretary of the Treasury, to enable him to make payments for the capital stock of the Home Owners' Loan Corporation. The latter functions in Massachusetts, through a loan agency established in Boston.

Home Owners' Loan Corporation

The Home Owners' Loan Corporation was created to prevent the foreclosure of homes. The procedure followed in refinancing was to arrange for the exchange of the mortgage for a bond of the Home Owners' Loan Corporation. That it was of tremendous benefit is shown by the fact that, in 1934, it saved 19,000 homes.

Federal Housing Administration

The Federal Housing Administration offered a new opportunity for people, not only to rehabilitate their present real estate but to construct new buildings to meet current demands. This organization does not loan money, but insures the money loaned by banks.

Recent Massachusetts Housing Activities of Philanthropic Agencies

Philanthropic organizations interested in housing have secured and disseminated knowledge relating to housing, particularly through their studies of the causes of bad housing and of means of promoting good housing; have cooperated with public and private agencies whose work affects housing; have aided in the enactment and enforcement of legislation that will improve housing standards; and have encouraged housing enterprises designed to demonstrate the value of improvement in the planning, construction, financing, or management of dwellings.

Among these agencies, the following have been particularly active in recent years:

1. Housing Association of Metropolitan Boston
2. Massachusetts Housing Association
3. Women's Municipal League
4. Twentieth Century Club
5. Massachusetts Civic League
6. Better Homes in America, Inc.

Statistical Analysis of Housing

Types of Housing

Statistics on the trends in one-family, two-family, and multi-family dwellings are not available for the whole State. The United States Census for 1900 and 1930 reveals changes which took place in ten cities in Massachusetts during this period. (See Table 27.) These figures show a wide divergence in percentages of different types of cities.

One-family Dwellings. The general trend in this type of dwelling was toward a percentage decrease, with several cities showing unusual changes. Fall River showed an increase of 10.8 per cent, while Somerville had a loss of 29.2 per cent.

Two-family Dwellings. The general trend for this type of dwelling was toward a slight percentage increase. Several cities, however, showed percentage increases or decreases above the average. Somerville had the largest increase, of 19.5 per cent, whereas Worcester showed a decrease of 7.6 per cent.

Table 27

PERCENTAGE TRENDS IN THE NUMBER OF ONE-FAMILY, TWO-FAMILY, AND MULTI-FAMILY HOUSES FOR TEN MASSACHUSETTS CITIES, 1900 AND 1930*

CITIES		1900				1930			
		1-Family	2-Family	Multi-Family	Totals	1-Family	2-Family	Multi-Family	Totals
Boston	No.	37,711	15,525	13,246	66,482	44,115	22,681	22,300	89,096
	%	56.7	23.4	19.9	100.0	49.5	25.5	25.0	100.0
Cambridge	No.	9,574	2,633	1,207	13,414	9,156	3,603	2,255	15,014
	%	71.4	19.6	9.0	100.0	61.0	24.0	15.0	100.0
Fall River	No.	3,498	3,045	2,966	9,509	6,771	3,667	3,786	14,224
	%	36.8	32.0	31.2	100.0	47.6	25.8	26.6	100.0
Lawrence	No.	4,353	2,342	918	8,113	5,586	3,263	2,287	11,136
	%	59.8	28.9	11.3	100.0	50.2	29.3	20.5	100.0
Lowell	No.	10,343	2,357	971	13,671	13,197	2,914	1,177	17,288
	%	75.7	17.2	7.1	100.0	76.3	16.9	6.3	100.0
Lynn	No.	7,317	3,127	628	11,072	9,930	3,395	2,078	15,403
	%	66.1	28.2	5.7	100.0	64.5	22.0	13.5	100.0
New Bedford	No.	5,062	2,643	1,039	8,744	10,012	4,284	2,757	17,053
	%	57.9	30.2	11.9	100.0	58.7	25.1	16.2	100.0
Somerville	No.	7,779	2,586	397	10,762	6,139	6,198	1,907	14,244
	%	72.3	24.0	3.7	100.0	43.1	43.5	13.4	100.0
Springfield	No.	7,128	2,583	454	10,165	14,368	5,816	2,372	22,556
	%	70.1	25.4	4.5	100.0	63.7	25.9	10.5	100.0
Worcester	No.	6,298	3,545	3,297	13,130	13,208	4,800	6,716	24,724
	%	47.9	27.0	25.1	100.0	53.4	19.4	27.2	100.0
AVERAGE OF TEN CITIES	No.	9,955	4,039	2,512	16,506	13,248	6,062	4,764	24,074
	%	60.3	24.5	15.2	100.0	55.0	25.2	19.8	100.0
THE STATE	No.	--	--	--	Total	511,051	126,274	65,897	703,222
	%	--	--	--		72.7	18.0	9.4	100.0
	No.	--	--	--	Rural	89,113	5,628	831	95,572
	%	--	--	--		93.2	5.9	0.9	100.0
	No.	--	--	--	Urban	421,938	120,646	65,066	607,650
	%	--	--	--		69.4	19.9	10.7	100.0

*Sources of information: U.S. Census, 1900, 1930

Multi-family Dwellings. The general trend in this type of dwelling was toward a percentage increase which offset the decrease in one-family dwellings. Cities with an unusual percentage increase or decrease were Somerville, with a 9.7 per cent increase, and Fall River, with a 4.6 per cent decrease.

Quantity of Housing

Chart 54B-C1 shows the relative variation in the total population, families, and dwellings in Massachusetts, from 1900 to 1930. The total population is increasing at a decreasing rate while the total families are increasing at only a slightly increasing rate; on the other hand, total dwellings are increasing at an increasing rate. Between the period 1900 and 1910, total population showed a percentage increase slightly in excess of that of total families, while the percentage increase in total dwellings lagged behind; this shows that the supply of dwellings was not sufficient to meet the demand. During the 1910-1920 period, the percentage increase in total dwellings was greater than that in total population; this does not mean that the supply was adequate, because it is evident that the percentage increase in total families was even greater than in total dwellings. The number of families compared with the number of dwellings is a much surer way of measuring surpluses and shortages. (See figures on Chart). From 1920 to 1930, there was perhaps a small surplus of housing, for the percentage increase in total dwellings slightly exceeded the percentage increase in total families. While this is true with regard to certain classes of housing, what this chart does not reveal is that while there was a surplus of high-rent dwellings, there was also a shortage of low-rent units.

Table 28 shows the trends in urban and rural (farm and non-farm) housing for 1910 to 1930. It is interesting to note the small percentage increase in the number of urban dwellings, and the large percentage increase for rural dwellings, between 1920 and 1930. It is probable that the percentage increase has been even greater since 1930.

Costs of Living and Foreclosures

Chart 54B-C2 shows the relative variation in rents and the costs of living and building, from 1916 to 1936. (Index base 1916 = 100.) It reveals that, in the middle of 1920, when the cost of building reached a peak, showing a 169 per cent increase since 1916, rents had increased 43 per cent, as compared with a 96 per cent increase in the cost of living. Since then, although building costs have come down, they still remain at a fairly high level;

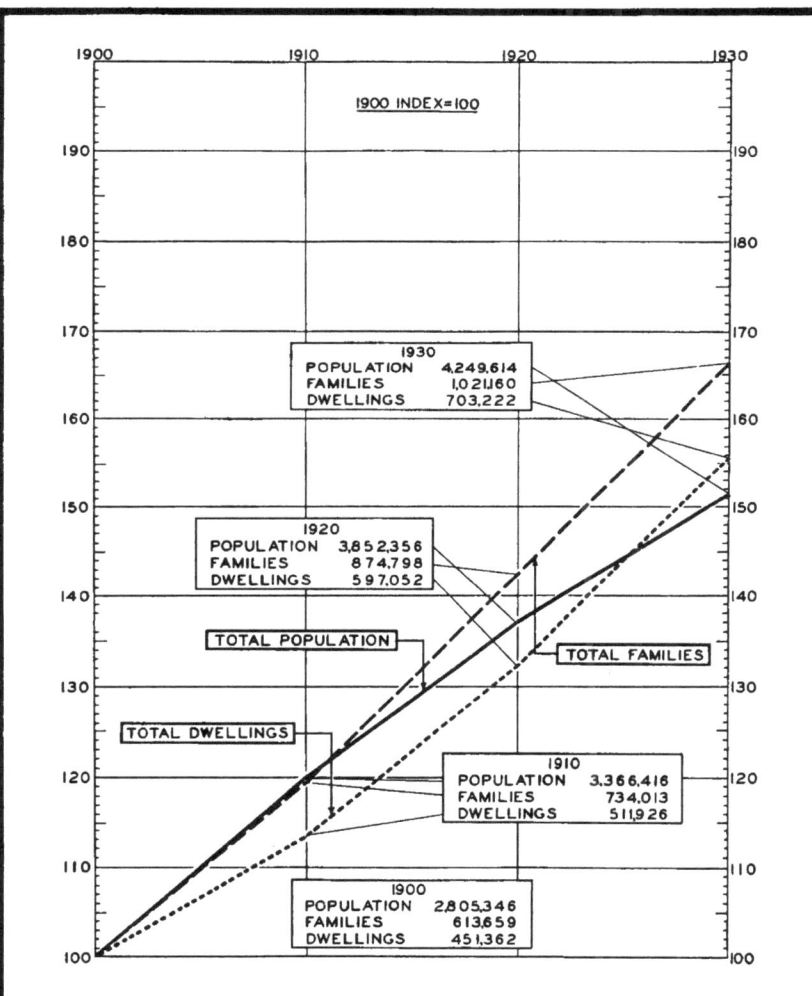

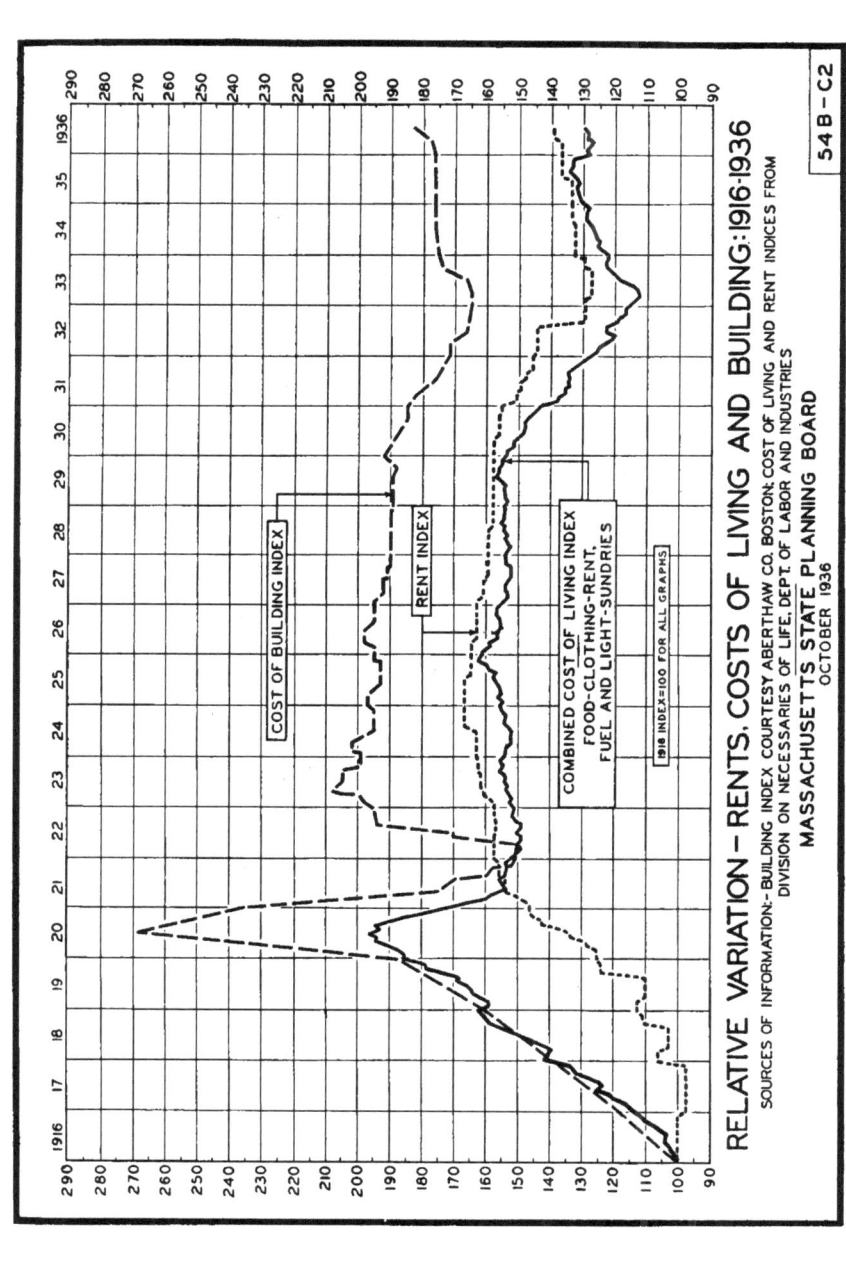

MASSACHUSETTS STATE PLANNING BOARD

Table 28

POPULATION, FAMILIES, AND DWELLINGS
IN MASSACHUSETTS 1910, 1920, 1930*

		1910	1920	1930
Total	Population	3,366,416	3,852,356	4,249,614
	Dwellings	511,926	597,052	703,222
	Families	734,013	874,798	1,021,160
	Persons to a Dwelling	6.6	6.5	3.43
	Persons to a Family	4.6	4.4	4.16
Urban	Population	3,125,367	3,650,248	3,831,426
	Dwellings	455,381	547,896	607,650
	Families	673,167	822,425	917,902
	Persons to a Dwelling	6.9	6.7	3.46
	Persons to a Family	4.6	4.4	4.17
Rural	Population	241,049	202,103	418,188
	Dwellings	56,545	49,156	95,572
	Families	60,846	52,373	103,258
	Persons to a Dwelling	4.3	4.1	3.31
	Persons to a Family	4.0	3.9	4.05

*Sources of information: U.S. Census 1910, 1920, 1930

MASSACHUSETTS STATE PLANNING BOARD

the cost of living index, which in the first years rose above the rent index, has since fallen below it, revealing a disproportionate increase in rents.

Table 29 shows the number of foreclosures in Massachusetts, from 1913 to 1934. The steady increase in the number of these from 1924 through 1933 represents the liquidation of property bought with insufficient equity and at peak prices.

Physical Condition of Urban Houses

No State-wide statistics on this subject are available. However, six Massachusetts cities have taken real property inventories, based on the model set by the Bureau of Foreign and Domestic Commerce of the United States Department of Commerce in its Real Property Inventory Census of 1934 of sixty-four cities throughout the United States, one of which was Worcester, Mass. Figures taken from the Massachusetts inventories of six cities and from the Federal Real Property Inventory of Worcester have been used to obtain a fairly representative picture of urban housing conditions in the State. Table 30 shows the tabulation of these facts, and the average for all seven cities: (1) Boston; (2) Cambridge; (3) Newton; (4) Everett; (5) Springfield; (6) Worcester; and (7) Haverhill.

Table 30 reveals several interesting facts. In interpreting the figures relating to types of structures, it should be remembered that "one-family" structure refers to a type built to house one family. A "dwelling-unit" means a residential unit; that is, the living quarters of a family, commonly called "home". It is apparent, then, that the total number of dwelling-units in one-family structures will be equal to the number of structures. The fact that some of these normally one-family units may have been doubled up at the time of the inventory is taken into account in the "doubling-up" statistics, given separately.

The following interesting conclusions can be drawn from Table 30:

1. By far the greatest percentage of structures are built of wood.
2. Approximately one structure in every hundred is unfit for habitation; over half of the structures are in need of minor repairs, while about one-tenth are in need of major structural repairs.
3. The largest percentage of structures is under 25 years old. Approximately one structure in every twenty is over 80 years

Table 29

NUMBER OF FORECLOSURES, AND PERCENTAGE
INCREASES OR DECREASES IN MASSACHUSETTS, 1913-1934*

YEARS	NUMBER OF FORECLOSURES	PERCENTAGE INCREASE OVER 1913
1913	3,275	-
1914	3,497	6.8
1915	4,275	30.5
1916	4,710	43.8
1917	4,330	32.2
1918	3,783	15.5
1919	2,445	25.3**
1920	1,954	40.3**
1921	1,768	46.0**
1922	2,722	18.9**
1923	1,444	55.9**
1924	1,774	45.8**
1925	2,760	15.7**
1926	4,500	37.4
1927	6,736	105.7
1928	8,239	151.6
1929	9,394	186.8
1930	9,443	188.3
1931	9,498	190.0
1932	12,089	269.1
1933	12,171	271.6
1934	11,049	237.4

*Sources of information: Figures compiled from "The Banker and Tradesman" by the Division of Necessaries of Life, Department of Labor and Industries.
**Decrease.

old; most of the latter are in all probability obsolete, while a great many of those in the 50-80 year group are fast becoming so. The weighted average age is about 34 years.

4. Only one third of the dwelling units are owner-occupied. Of the total number of dwelling units, one out of every twelve is vacant.

5. 2.86 per cent of the total dwelling units contain two families; 23.69 per cent of them are overcrowded. (Springfield reveals the surprising proportion 79.93 per cent of dwelling units having from one to three or more persons per room.)

6. The greatest percentage of rents range from $10 to $50; Newton has the highest rents, while Worcester has the lowest. The weighted average rental is $32.10.

7. Statistics on the facilities available in dwelling units reveal that, for every 100 dwellings, there are 2.5 without any indoor water closets and 11 without tubs or showers.

8. One out of every ten dwellings has neither gas nor electricity for cooking purposes, and one out of every 78 has neither for lighting purposes.

9. One-quarter of one per cent of the total dwelling-units has no type of heating apparatus. The stove is still the most common type used.

10. 1.33 per cent of the dwellings have no running water; less than one quarter of the dwellings are equipped with mechanical refrigeration.

Chart 54B-C3 is a graphic representation of these facts for the average of the seven cities.

Rural Housing

There is, at present, limited information on rural housing. Table 28, showing the trends in urban and rural (farm and non-farm) housing for 1910 to 1930, has already been discussed.

Table 31 shows the trends in the tenure of farm and non-farm homes in Massachusetts, from 1890-1930.

Table 32 shows the trends of various factors related to farms and farm property in Massachusetts for the period 1900-1930. Of great interest is the increase in the average value of land and buildings per farm, accompanied by an increasing average mortgage debt.

A survey carried on by Dr. David Rozman for the Massachusetts State College, in 1930, in two part-time farming areas on the outskirts of Lowell and Taunton brings out interesting facts on

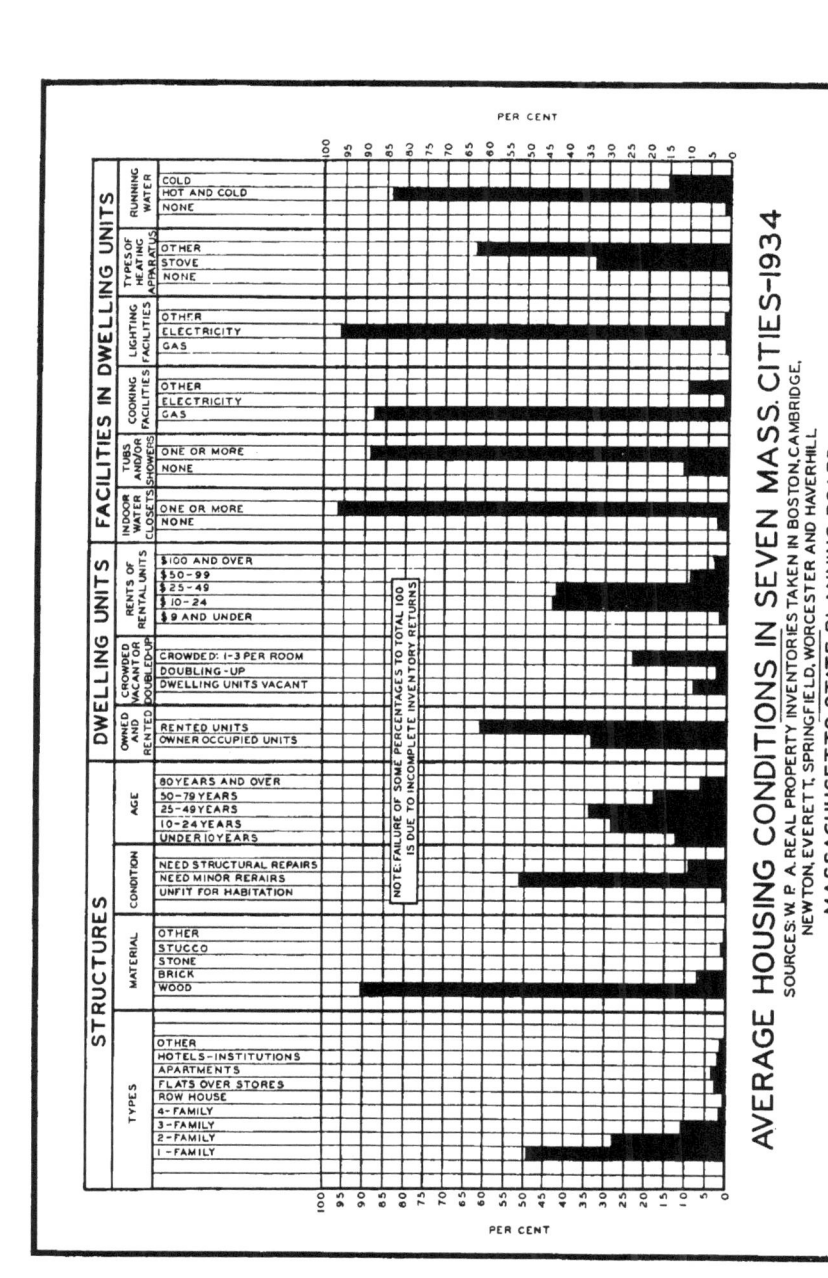

MASSACHUSETTS STATE PLANNING BOARD

Source of Information: Real Property Inventories Taken in Boston, Cambridge, Newton, Everett, Springfield, Worcester, Haverhill, Mass.

Table 30

TABULATION OF FACTS
REVEALED BY REAL PROPERTY INVENTORIES OF SEVEN CITIES IN MASSACHUSETTS, 1934

			BOSTON		CAMBRIDGE		NEWTON		EVERETT		SPRINGFIELD		WORCESTER		HAVERHILL		AVERAGE
			No.	%	No.	%	No.	%	No.	%	No.	%	No.	%	No.	%	%
Structures	Types	One-Family	26,049	30.10	3,648	31.49	10,967	77.86	2,639	40.15	10,400	50.15	21,709	58.63	4,998	58.69	49.30
		Two-Family	20,302	23.43	3,879	33.48	2,705	19.21	2,455	37.35	7,552	36.53	6,950	17.87	2,262	26.55	27.75
		Three-Family	23,331	27.00	1,732	14.95	141	1.00	602	9.16	897	4.53	6,794	17.47	300	3.52	11.05
		Four-Family	456	0.66	394	3.40	53	0.38	126	1.90	363	1.75	513	1.32	199	2.33	1.66
		Row House	140	0.17	129	1.12	35	0.25	-	-	57	0.27	184	0.47	-	-	0.46
		Flats over stores	4,933	5.71	545	4.70	116	0.82	126	1.92	270	1.30	-	-	239	2.80	2.88
		Apartment Houses	7,491	8.67	369	7.42	44	0.23	57	0.87	872	4.21	1,015	2.61	131	1.53	3.65
		Hotels, Institutions	3,829	4.08	295	2.54	24	0.25	-	-	-	-	336	0.86	-	-	1.93
		Other	160	0.20	104	0.90	-	-	569	8.86	343	1.66	1,988	5.57	400	4.68	1.42
		Total	86,391	100.0	11,585	100.0	14,078	100.0	6,573	100.0	20,754	100.0	35,694	100.0	8,529	100.0	100.0
	Materials	Wood	64,234	74.35	10,608	91.60	-	-	6,495	98.81	18,157	87.47	36,588	94.09	8,278	97.02	90.56
		Brick	20,690	23.96	704	6.10	-	-	43	0.66	1,405	6.77	1,286	3.25	164	1.92	7.10
		Stone	681	0.78	66	0.60	-	-	2	0.03	-	-	46	0.12	8	0.09	0.32
		Stucco	434	0.50	122	1.00	-	-	21	0.32	682	3.28	844	2.17	67	0.79	1.34
		Other	329	0.43	66	0.70	-	-	12	0.19	466	2.26	111	0.29	15	0.18	0.68
	Condition	Unfit for Habitation	1,509	1.75	216	1.86	18	0.13	-	-	126	0.61	335	0.86	119	1.39	1.10
		In need of minor repairs	49,031	56.76	5,995	51.75	8,289	58.89	-	-	9,382	45.26	20,684	53.19	3,549	41.63	51.25
		In need of structural repairs	8,671	10.04	1,496	12.91	830	5.90	-	-	1,446	6.97	4,270	10.98	819	9.62	9.40
	Age	0 - 24 Years	22,932	26.54	2,464	21.60	7,498	53.24	2,404	36.57	10,843	52.30	16,845	43.32	4,641	54.63	41.17
		25 - 49 Years	32,247	37.33	5,093	43.90	5,901	27.72	3,466	52.73	6,664	26.28	12,314	31.67	1,518	17.89	34.16
		50 - 80 Years	25,018	28.96	3,138	27.20	2,079	14.77	641	9.75	1,662	7.97	6,752	17.36	1,723	20.30	18.05
		More than 80 Years	5,833	6.75	875	7.60	600	4.26	49	0.75	2,619	7.26	609	1.63	609	7.18	6.62
Dwelling Units	Owner & Tenancy	Owner occupied units	46,278	21.88	6,059	19.84	10,227	57.51	4,349	36.83	12,538	30.26	25,654	36.98	5,516	38.80	34.41
		Rented units	165,250	78.12	21,446	70.24	6,525	36.69	7,088	58.40	28,900	69.74	43,717	63.02	7,418	51.93	61.16
		Total dwelling units	241,528	100.0	30,531	100.0	17,768	100.0	12,157	100.0	41,438	100.0	69,371	100.0	14,287	100.0	100.0
		Total dwelling units vacant	22,567	10.67	3,026	9.92	1,031	5.80	700	5.77	3,895	9.40	5,331	7.64	1,353	9.47	8.37
		Doubling up	7,053	3.33	586	1.90	-	-	380	3.13	-	-	2,948	4.25	216	1.68	2.86
		Overcrowding 1 - 5 or more persons per room	32,795	15.51	7,842	25.69	1,145	15.15	1,757	14.48	33,121	79.93	2,948	4.25	1,395	10.81	23.69
		Weighted average monthly rental	$30.99		$34.44		$51.56		$28.38		$28.52		$24.66		$26.36		$32.10	
Rental Units	Rents	$10 and under	3,152	1.91	221	0.90	176	2.68	15	0.18	202	0.70	2,530	5.79	106	1.46	1.95
		$10 - 25	61,720	37.35	8,744	35.80	1,466	22.46	2,539	33.00	10,938	37.85	31,689	72.49	4,708	63.59	43.22
		$25 - 50	83,315	50.42	11,064	45.30	2,862	33.91	4,651	65.62	14,987	51.86	7,325	16.76	2,499	33.76	42.82
		$50 - 100	12,898	8.41	3,510	14.30	2,140	32.79	21	0.14	904	3.15	1,495	3.58	84	1.14	9.26
		$100 and over	1,318	0.80	331	1.30	533	8.16	0	0.00	21	0.07	92	0.21	6	0.05	3.08
		Rental units	165,250	100.0	21,446	100.0	6,525	100.0	7,088	100.0	28,900	100.0	43,717	100.0	7,418	100.0	100.0
Facilities in Dwelling Units	Indoor Water Closets	None	493	0.23	31	0.10	123	0.69	0	0.00	334	1.57	8,065	7.30	691	4.88	2.46
		One or more	197,410	93.51	30,336	99.63	17,660	99.31	12,157	100.0	20,164	97.25	64,024	92.29	13,472	95.12	96.71
	Tubs and/or Showers	None	34,175	16.19	5,548	18.17	1,516	8.52	139	1.15	850	4.10	10,594	15.27	1,958	13.82	11.03
		One or more	174,229	82.37	24,871	81.46	16,267	91.48	11,998	99.85	19,618	94.62	58,551	84.40	12,208	96.18	88.62
	Cooking Facilities	Gas	200,741	94.90	29,632	97.06	16,213	91.17	11,340	93.43	37,511	90.52	44,274	63.82	11,932	85.43	88.05
		Electricity	670	0.32	31	0.10	422	2.37	0	0.00	825	1.99	950	1.37	82	0.59	1.12
		Other	9,004	4.26	752	2.46	1,100	6.19	88	0.73	2,649	6.39	23,692	34.44	1,953	13.98	9.78
	Lighting Facilities	Gas	2,458	1.16	712	2.33	-	-	3	0.02	250	0.60	24	0.04	342	2.44	1.10
		Electricity	204,842	96.84	29,360	96.17	-	-	11,411	94.02	40,244	97.12	68,179	98.28	13,346	95.29	96.29
		Other	3,149	1.49	343	1.12	-	-	15	0.10	562	1.36	917	1.32	318	2.27	1.28
	Types of Heating Apparatus	None	336	0.15	0	0.00	57	0.32	0	0.00	10	0.03	85	0.12	113	0.80	0.20
		Stove	73,447	34.72	11,072	36.27	1,427	8.02	5,268	43.42	7,653	18.49	35,075	50.54	5,767	40.92	33.20
		Other	134,932	64.73	19,358	63.40	16,299	91.65	6,171	50.85	33,601	81.09	34,036	49.06	5,516	39.15	62.85
	Running Water	None	72	0.03	1	0.00	-	-	-	-	213	0.51	1,656	2.39	340	2.40	1.33
		Hot and Cold	183,843	86.82	25,302	82.87	-	-	12,107	99.75	34,921	84.27	44,998	64.87	-	-	83.72
		Cold	23,770	11.24	5,136	16.83	-	-	30	0.25	6,065	14.64	22,562	32.52	-	-	18.10
Mechanical Refrigeration		Yes	44,892	21.22	7,532	24.67	8,270	46.51	2,008	16.54	11,279	27.22	7,708	11.11	2,136	16.47	23.39
		No	165,692	78.33	22,779	74.61	9,513	53.49	9,416	83.46	28,685	69.22	61,447	88.58	10,843	83.53	75.89
		Weighted Average Age of Structure	41.5 Yrs.		41.47 Yrs.		29.66 Yrs.		33.30 Yrs.		28.44 Yrs.		33.70 Yrs.		33.77 Yrs.		34.12 Yrs.	

Note: Failure of some percentages to total 100 is due to incomplete inventory returns.

207

Table 31

TENURE OF HOMES, FARM AND NON-FARM, FOR MASSACHUSETTS, 1890-1930*

TENURE	1890		1900		1910		1920		1930	
	No.	%	No.	%	No.	%	No.	%	No.	%
All Homes Total	479,790	100.0	504,873	100.0	734,013	100.0	874,798	100.0	1,021,160	100.0
Owned By Occupant	175,053	36.5	206,127	34.1	240,445	32.8	301,245	34.4	439,238	43.0
Rented	304,737	63.5	379,696	62.8	484,932	66.1	564,097	64.5	569,645	55.8
Tenure Unknown	-	-	19,050	3.1	8,636	1.2	9,456	1.1	12,277	1.2
Farm Homes Total	34,576	100.0	36,249	100.0	35,357	100.0	28,653	100.0	27,982	100.0
Owned By Occupant	29,370	84.9	31,587	87.1	31,547	89.2	23,084	80.6	23,619	84.4
Rented	5,206	15.1	4,393	12.1	3,788	10.7	5,059	17.7	3,775	13.5
Tenure Unknown	-	-	269	0.7	22	0.1	510	1.8	588	2.1
Non-Farm Homes Total	445,214	100.0	568,624	100.0	698,656	100.0	846,145	100.0	993,178	100.0
Owned By Occupant	145,683	32.7	174,540	30.7	208,898	29.9	278,161	32.9	415,619	41.8
Rented	299,531	67.3	375,303	66.0	481,144	68.9	559,038	66.1	565,870	57.0
Tenure Unknown	-	-	18,781	3.3	8,614	1.2	8,946	1.1	11,689	1.2

*Sources of information: U.S. Census, 1890, 1900, 1910, 1920, 1930

Table 32

FARMS AND FARM PROPERTY IN MASSACHUSETTS, 1900-1930*

FACTORS		1900	1910	1920	1925	1930
Total Number of Farms		37,715	36,917	32,001	33,454	25,598
Farms Operated by Owners		32,581	32,075	28,087	30,870	23,198
Farms Operated by Managers		1,531	1,863	1,627	979	958
Farms Operated by Tenants	No.	3,603	2,979	2,287	1,605	1,442
	%	9.6	8.1	7.1	4.8	5.6
Owners of Farms Mortgaged**	No.	11,041	13,014	12,632	12,248	12,159
	%	37.8	40.6	45.0	39.7	52.4
Full Owners Mortgaged		—	12,030	11,663	11,660	11,025
Total Value of Farms		$71,093,880	$88,636,149	$119,934,224	$144,165,510	$143,022,570
Average Value, Land & Bldgs.		—	$4,135	$6,066	$6,549	$8,554
Average Amount of Mortgage Debt		—	$1,361	$2,007	$2,436	$3,089

*Sources of information: U.S. Census, 1900, 1910, 1920, 1930
**Includes part-owners

Table 33

RURAL HOUSING CONDITIONS IN PART-TIME FARMING AREAS
NEAR LOWELL AND TAUNTON, MASS., 1930*

CAPACITY OF HOUSES

		Number of Houses	Persons To a House	Rooms To a House
Lowell	Rented	4	6.5	6.3
	Owner-Occupied	111	6.0	6.0
	Total	115	6.0	6.0
Taunton	Rented	14	4.4	6.6
	Owner-Occupied	70	5.8	7.1
	Total	84	5.5	7.0

AVERAGE ANNUAL COST OF THE HOUSE

		Interest	Upkeep	Total Cost for Rent	Light	Heat	Total Cost
Lowell	Rented	-	-	$152	$11	$50	$213
	Owner-Occupied	$118	$85	$203	$19	$57	$279
	Total	-	-	$201	$19	$57	$277
Taunton	Rented	-	-	$160	$13	$57	$230
	Owner-Occupied	$158	$96	$254	$15	$67	$336
	Total	-	-	$239	$15	$65	$319

VALUE OF HOUSES

Value of Houses		Below $1000	$1000-1999	$2000-2999	$3000-3999	$4000-4999	$5000 and Over	Total
Lowell	Number	20	39	33	12	9	2	115
	Percentage	17.4	33.9	28.7	10.4	7.8	1.8	100.0
Taunton	Number	2	22	30	22	6	2	84
	Percentage	2.4	26.2	35.7	26.2	7.1	2.4	100.0

SOURCES AND AMOUNT OF ANNUAL INCOME

	Item	Operator's Non-Farm Labor Income	Farm Income	Income from Roomers and Boarders	Earnings of Wives	Total Income
Lowell	Amount	$1,221	$313	$148	$14	$1,696
	Per cent	72	18.5	8.7	0.8	100
Taunton	Amount	$1,088	$454	$262	$23	$1,827
	Per cent	59.6	24.9	14.3	1.2	100

*Source of information: Bulletin 266, Massachusetts Agricultural Experiment Station

ownership and tenancy, average value of owner-occupied homes, the number of persons per room, and so forth. (See Table 33.)

The Committee on Farm and Village Housing of the President's Conference on Home Building and Home Ownership made a survey, in 1932, of housing conditions on farms and in villages in twenty-eight counties throughout the United States. Ten housing regions were selected, of which one was the New England-New York region. (See Table 34.)

A survey of types of homes, sanitation, and so forth, was made in seventeen mill-towns in Worcester county, in 1934, thirteen of which may be classed as rural; the exceptions are Blackstone, Millbury, Northbridge, and Uxbridge.*

In 1934, in a CWA survey of rural housing in Franklin, Hampshire, and Worcester Counties, 2065 houses were investigated. Table 35 reveals the findings.

The 1930 United States Census gives figures on the facilities to be found in the farms of the State. Of 25,598 farms, 64.7 per cent reported telephones; 74.6 per cent, water piped into the dwelling houses; 42.8 per cent, water piped into bathrooms; and 62.6 per cent, electricity for lighting purposes.

Summary of Statistical Analysis

From the foregoing statistical data the following conclusions may be drawn:

1. Accommodations are sufficient in the best and medium classes of dwellings, but there is still a great lack of family units renting for $35 per month or less, where the demand is greatest. A limited number of accommodations for the low-income groups is being provided in new housing projects.

2. There is a general decrease in the proportion of one-family dwellings to total dwellings in most urban areas. State figures for 1930, however, place the one-family house as still by far the preponderant type.

3. Owner-occupancy of homes is increasing throughout the State (from 34.1 per cent, in 1900, to 43.0 per cent, in 1930). But there is also a steadily mounting number of foreclosures due to

---

*Report on Industrial Rehabilitation, Blackstone Valley Planning ERA-M-Project S-Al-U41, vols. 1-4 (1934-1935).

Table 34

PRESIDENT'S CONFERENCE ON HOME BUILDING AND HOME
OWNERSHIP SURVEY OF RURAL HOUSING IN U.S., 1932*

REGIONS	NO. STORIES IN FARMHOUSE			AVERAGE NUMBER ROOMS AND BEDROOMS			PERCENTAGES HAVING DIFFERENT HEATING EQUIPMENT					
	No. of Houses	One Story	More Than One Story	No. of Houses	All Rooms	Bed Rooms	No. of Houses	Stove Only	Stove & Fire-places	Central System Only	Central System & Fireplaces	Fire-place only
New England - New York	187	8	92	190	8.1	4.3	188	68.6	1.1	25.0	4.8	0.5
Central East	256	4	96	260	7.5	4.0	263	79.3	6.0	12.5	1.2	1.0
Appalachian-Ozark Highlands	181	45	55	192	5.7	3.4	187	36.9	44.4	2.1	1.1	15.5
Tobacco-Blue Grass	143	22	78	127	6.4	3.3	133	46.6	26.3	3.8	2.3	21.0
Cotton Belt	779	81	19	817	5.4	2.7	566	43.9	8.1	1.1	0.4	46.5
Corn Belt	104	8	92	95	7.3	3.8	102	69.6	0.0	29.4	1.0	0.0
Northern Dairy	191	5	95	188	7.8	4.1	189	64.5	3.7	30.7	1.1	0.0
Great Plains	188	78	22	188	5.1	2.6	187	72.7	0.0	27.3	0.0	0.0
Great Basin	58	60	40	58	5.5	2.6	58	79.3	8.6	10.3	1.8	0.0
Pacific Northwest	34	15	85	33	7.3	2.9	-	-	-	-	-	-

*Sources of information: Farm and Village Housing, Vol. VII.

Table 35
RURAL HOUSING CONDITIONS IN FRANKLIN,
HAMPSHIRE, AND WORCESTER COUNTIES*
1934

CONDITION OF HOUSES

Of the 2065 houses surveyed, repairs or replacements were needed as indicated:

	Complete replacement	Repairing
Painting	824	391
Chimneys	96	191
Roofs	181	321
Screens	285	148
Interior Walls and Ceilings	272	575
Exterior Walls	126	286
Doors and Windows	113	285
Floors	234	311

NEED FOR ADDITIONAL SPACE

Space requirements were as follows:

	Present rooms	Additional rooms needed	Per cent of farm houses in which additional rooms are needed
Bathrooms	967	535	25.9
Bedrooms	9212	231	11.1
Front or Side Porch	1480	96	4.6
Work Room	1439	28	1.4

WATER SUPPLY AND SEWAGE DISPOSAL

	Have now	New Installation needed	Per cent of farm houses in which new installation is needed
Water carried by hand	120	-	-
Hand pump in dwelling	547	25	1.2
Running water, cold	1389	221	10.7
Running water, hot	782	399	19.3
Unimproved outdoor toilets	930	-	-
Improved toilets	216	2	.1
Tub or shower bath	961	752	36.4
Kitchen sink with drain	2012	39	1.9

LIGHT AND HEAT

	Have now	New installation needed
Kerosene or gasoline lights	569	1
Gas light	6	1
Electric light	1406	343
Stoves	1442	1
Central heating	983	202

REFRIGERATION

	Have now	Need new	Per cent of farm houses in which new installation is needed
Ice boxes	1194	45	2.1
Mechanical refrigerators	344	95	4.6
Washing machines, hand	69	-	-
Washing machines, power	937	123	5.9

*Source of information: Summary of Federal Rural Housing Survey
Note: These are all preliminary data, subject to change

the active speculation during 1929 and for several years thereafter. The amount of foreclosures has been lessened through the aid given by the Home Owners' Loan Corporation.

4. The cost of building has doubled since the War. The cost of shelter has increased from January 1916 to July 1936, 45 per cent, as compared with a 22.3 per cent increase for food, a 45.6 per cent increase for clothing, a 46.1 per cent increase for fuel and light, and a 52.7 per cent increase for sundries.*

5. There is still much crowding and doubling-up in dwelling units. Necessary facilities are lacking, in sub-standard areas and in outlying rural districts.

Special Aspects of the Housing Problem

Limitations of Private Enterprise

The demand for housing for low-income groups cannot be met by private enterprise alone.

At the date of the 1930 Census, 35.7 per cent of the rented non-farm homes in Massachusetts were renting for less than fifteen dollars per month. In the seven real property inventories of 1934, the average percentage of rented dwelling units renting under fifteen dollars was slightly greater. The figures are not precisely comparable, since the former covered the entire State, and the latter, only seven cities. But in a general way, the apparent difference between the percentage renting for less than fifteen dollars in 1930 and in 1934 represents the fall in rentals due to the depression. In general terms, it is probably true that housing renting under twenty dollars was substandard in 1930, and housing under fifteen dollars, in 1934.

No one will claim that, under the average American construction costs (which have doubled since the war), modern houses of sufficient size to accommodate the average family can be built even on low-cost land to rent, at a profit, at fifteen dollars or even twenty dollars a month. The operative builder will, therefore, make no effort to solve this portion of the problem.

If an enterprising landlord of slum property were to tear down his worn-out tenements and put up new ones, or go to the expense of thoroughly renovating and modernizing his existing buildings, he

---

*Figures supplied by the Division of the Necessaries of Life of the Massachusetts Department of Labor and Industries.

MASSACHUSETTS STATE PLANNING BOARD

would almost certainly lose money. His rents would be too high for tenants in the neighborhood, and better-to-do tenants would be unwilling to move with their families into a neighborhood of slums.

Economics of Low-Rental Districts

In 1935, the Boston City Planning Board published its "Income and Cost Survey of the City of Boston". This study revealed clearly that the costs for municipal services (fire, police, schools, and so forth) in districts of inferior housing far outweighed the costs in better areas. In sixteen different census tracts, where the prevailing rental range per dwelling per month was from ten dollars to thirty-five dollars, and the population density per net acre over two hundred, the maintenance cost to the city was greater than the income derived from the taxes of these districts.

In the analyses of sub-standard areas in six different cities, carried on by the State Board of Housing, it was revealed that the total cost of maintaining these areas was often 300 per cent in excess of the total income derived by the city from these areas.

Cooperation Between Federal, State, and Local Authorities

The State Board of Housing has actively cooperated with the FWA Housing Division of the Federal Government to secure the allocation of funds for housing projects in Massachusetts. The Board has made studies of sub-standard areas in various cities of the State, which would be suitable sites for housing projects; one of these areas, in Cambridge, has been selected by the FWA Housing Division for a project.

Local Housing Authorities are under the supervision of the State Board of Housing, whose duty it is to stimulate and encourage them. The authorities have the power to enter into housing projects which have the approval of the State Board of Housing.

In the near future, it is probable that there will be a more direct contact between Federal agencies and local authorities. Two bills before the State Senate this year proposed that housing authorities be permitted to take over from the Federal government, by lease or otherwise, any project commenced or sponsored by the Federal government, subject to the approval of the State Board of Housing.

Financing of Public-Housing Projects

At present, there are no provisions for State or municipal

financing of housing projects. State and municipal agencies, although having the legal power to engage in housing projects, have had no funds to carry out these powers. Two bills before the State Senate this year would have provided for State and local financial participation in housing projects.

1. Senate Bill No. 265 was an Act providing for State financing of certain projects of the State Board of Housing. It provided that the State Treasurer, upon request of the Housing Board, could borrow on the credit of the Commonwealth up to $500,000 for housing projects, and that the Board could issue bonds and notes in acknowledgement of its debt at interest rates determined by the State Treasurer with the Governor's approval.

2. Senate Bill No. 512 was an Act authorizing cities and towns to finance or assist in financing certain local housing projects. It provided that a town could participate in the cost of a Federal or local housing project by borrowing money equal to not more than one-fifth of one per cent of its assessed valuation; this could not be done, however, unless it were accompanied by a Federal grant of at least 25 per cent of the development or acquisition cost.

Limited Dividend Companies. A limited-dividend company is to be set up in the Chicopee Falls Rehabilitation Project sponsored by the State Board of Housing. The Chicopee Manufacturing Company is giving the land and buildings thereon as equity, the remaining necessary money being loaned by the Reconstruction Finance Corporation.

In the future, if any body of three or more persons, or a limited dividend corporation, is interested in financing a housing project, they must have an equity equal to at least 20 per cent of the total cost; the remaining 80 per cent may be borrowed from insurance companies, banks, or, as in the case of Chicopee Falls, from the Reconstruction Finance Corporation, through the flotation of bonds and issuance of notes.

Sources of Information

Federal Emergency Public Works Administration, Housing Division.
    Housing Digest, Nov. 1935, Jan. 1936

Federal Emergency Relief Administration
    "Standard Procedure for Housing Surveys, 1935"

Federal Housing Administration
    Rules: Circular No. 2; Technical Bulletins Nos. 3, 4, and 5
    Analysis of Housing in Peoria, Illinois

Federal Rural Housing Survey (CWA)
    Franklin, Hampshire, and Worcester Counties, 1934

General Court of Massachusetts

    Acts of 1911, Chapter 607
      "   "   1913,   "   494, 595
      "   "   1917,   "   310
      "   "   1918,   "   204
      "   "   1919,   "   257 (extended to 1927), 341, 365
      "   "   1920,   "   538   855, 577, 578 (all extended to 1927)
      "   "   1933,   "   364
      "   "   1935,   "   449

Income and Cost Survey of the City of Boston, 1935
    City Planning Board, Boston
    ERA Project No. X2235-F2-U46

Industrial Rehabilitation Report, Blackstone River Valley Planning
    ERA Project S-A1-U41, vols. 2 and 3, Oct., Dec., 1935

Massachusetts Agricultural Experiment Station. Massachusetts State
    College Bulletin No. 266, Oct. 1930
    "Part-time Farming in Massachusetts"

Massachusetts Bureau of Statistics of Labor
    Census of Tenement Houses, Boston, 1891

National Association of Housing Officials
    "A Housing Program for the United States, 1934"
    Housing Officials Yearbook, 1935

Necessaries of Life, Special Commission on the
    Annual Reports 1920-1930
    Special Report relative to promoting the financing the construction of apartment houses and maintaining buildings used for living quarters, 1928

Necessaries of Life, Division on the Department of Labor and Industries
    Annual Reports 1930-1934

MASSACHUSETTS STATE PLANNING BOARD

President's Conference on Home Building and Home Ownership
   Washington, D. C. - Vol. VII, Farm and Village Housing

Real Property Inventory for the City of Boston, Mass., 1934
   Boston City Planning Board, Vols. I and II
   ERA Project Nos. 2235-F2-104 and 104A
         X2235-F2-U46, U46A and U46B

Real Property Inventory of Cambridge, Mass.
   ERA Project No. 1849-F2-47, 1934

Real Property Inventory of Everett, Mass.
   ERA, WPA, 1935

Real Property Inventory of Haverhill, Mass.
   WPA, 1934-1935.

Real Property Inventory of Newton, Mass.
   WPA, 1935

Real Property Inventory of Springfield, Mass.
   WPA, 1935

Real Property Inventory of Worcester, Mass.
   Bureau of Foreign and Domestic Commerce
   United States Department of Commerce, 1934

State Board of Housing - Massachusetts Department of Public Welf
   Analyses of Sub-standard Areas in Chelsea, Fall River, Lowe
   and Springfield, 1935-1936
   Annual Reports, 1934-1935

State Planning Board Annual Reports
   Connecticut   1934
   Idaho   1934
   Illinois   1934
   Iowa   1935
   Maine   1935
   Minnesota   1934
   New Jersey   1935
   New York   1935
   Rhode Island   1935
   Iowa, Report on Housing, Sioux City, Iowa, 1935
   Iowa, "The Forgotten House", 1935

Twentieth Century Club, Boston, Mass.
   "Some Slums in Boston", Mr. Harold K. Estabrook, 1897

"Housing Conditions in Boston", Mr. Robert T. Paine, 1900

United States Census Reports
    1890, 1900, 1910, 1920, 1930

Watson, Frank
    "Housing Problems and Possibilities in the United States",
    Harper Bros., N.Y., 1935

Women's Municipal League
    "Housing Conditions of Today in Boston", 1916

Wood, Edith Elmer
    "Recent Trends in American Housing",
    The Macmillan Co., New York, 1931
    "Slums and Blighted Areas in the United States",
    Housing Division Bulletin No. I. Published by Federal Emergency Administration of Public Works Housing Division, 1935

EDUCATION

Summary Outline

I. Existing Massachusetts Educational Institutions

    A. Universities, Colleges, and Professional Schools Granting Degrees

    B. Private Schools of Higher Education Not Granting Degrees

    C. Public Day Schools

    D. Private Schools

    E. Special Types of Schools

II. Effect of Education upon Illiteracy

III. Physical Aspects of the Educational Plant

IV. Cost of Education

MASSACHUSETTS STATE PLANNING BOARD

EDUCATION

Introduction

Since its colonial beginning, Massachusetts has been a leader in the education movement. The first college in the United States was founded at Cambridge, and the first Latin grammar school at Boston. Massachusetts has the first free public high school.

Existing Massachusetts Educational Institutions*

For the purpose of analysis, Massachusetts educational institutions may be divided into the following types: (1) universities, colleges, and professional schools granting degrees; (2) private schools of higher education not granting degrees; (3) public day schools; (4) private schools; and (5) special types of schools.

Universities, Colleges, and Professional Schools Granting Degrees

Massachusetts ranks eleventh among the States in the number of educational institutions granting degrees.** It has fifty-three such institutions, including ten State Teachers' Colleges.

State-Supported Colleges. The State-supported colleges include Massachusetts State College, and ten State Teachers' Colleges (including the Massachusetts School of Art).

Massachusetts State College, at Amherst, was established in 1862 for the promotion of the science of agriculture. On November 1, 1935, it had 1064 students. Its faculty and professional staff, in September 1936, numbered 275.

The Ten State Teachers' Colleges, for the regular session ending June 1935, had a total enrollment of 3,070 students, and a faculty staff of 222. In addition to maintaining the necessary general curriculum for the training of teachers, each of these colleges has specialized in some one branch of education. For example, the college at Framingham is noted for its household-arts course; Salem, for its commercial course; and Lowell, for its music course.

---

*Unless otherwise indicated, the following statistics on Massachusetts educational institutions were obtained from the Massachusetts Department of Education.
**STATISTICAL ABSTRACT OF THE UNITED STATES (1935), p. 113.

Private Schools of Higher Education Not Granting Degrees

According to the latest reports*, Massachusetts has seventeen private schools of higher education which do not grant degrees. These include eight normal schools and nine junior colleges.

Public Day Schools

Good education depends, in the main, upon an adequate public-school system. By far the largest proportion of the school population attends the public schools. In the year 1934-35, the public day schools had an enrollment of 770,653 pupils. There were 26,252 principals and teachers.

Prior to 1929, the statistics on public schools were presented on the basis of eight elementary grades and four high-school grades (the 8-4 system). In 1935, more than half of the public-school pupils in the seventh, eighth, and ninth grades were in towns using the 6-3-3 system (six elementary, three junior high school, and three senior high school grades). The following Table 36 shows the comparative use of the two systems.

Table 36

USE OF TWO EDUCATIONAL SYSTEMS

CLASSIFICATION	NO. USING 8-4 SYSTEM	NO. USING 6-3-3 SYSTEM
Cities	17	22
Towns, 5000 or More Population	53	30
Towns, Less Than 5000 Population	88	20
Towns, Sending Pupils to High Schools in Neighboring Towns	110	14
TOTAL	268	86

During 1934-35, in the towns operating under the 8-4 system, the elementary schools (eight grades) had an enrollment of 197,454 pupils; the high schools (four grades) had 72,396 pupils, a total of 269,850 pupils.

In towns operating, during 1934-35, under the 6-3-3 system, the elementary schools (six grades) had 288,405 pupils; the junior high schools (three grades), 108,295 pupils; and the senior high schools (three grades), 104,103 pupils: — a total of 500,803.

---
*United States Department of the Interior, Office of Education, EDUCATIONAL DIRECTORY (1936), Part III.

The total number of pupils under the two systems, during 1934-35, was 770,653.

In 1935, the average daily attendance was 684,260 out of 833,304 persons between the ages of five and sixteen, inclusive.

Private Schools

During the year 1934-35, 159,044 pupils, or 19 per cent of the 833,304 persons of school age, attended private schools.

Schools Maintained by the Roman Catholic Church. The largest single group of private schools in Massachusetts comprises the schools maintained by the Roman Catholic Church. The following Table 37 gives the data on these schools by dioceses.

Table 37

ROMAN CATHOLIC SCHOOLS - DATA BY DIOCESES*

DIOCESE	NO. OF TEACHERS	NO. OF STUDENTS	NO. OF SCHOOLS
Boston**	3119	93,943	185
Fall River***	534	17,747	57
Springfield****	1142	41,795	94
Total for State	4795	153,485	336

*Figures obtained direct from the dioceses
**As of October 1935
***As of August 1935
****As of June 1936

Special Types of Schools

Textile Schools. Three State textile schools, the Bradford-Durfee Textile School, the New Bedford Textile School, and the Lowell Textile Institute, are maintained at centers of the textile industry, to prepare men for careers as textile specialists. During the school year 1934-35, they had a total enrollment of 451 in the day classes, and 4997 in the evening classes. They had staffs consisting of 61 full-time instructors and 46 part-time. One of these schools, the Lowell Textile Institute, grants a degree.

State Nautical School. The Massachusetts Nautical School had

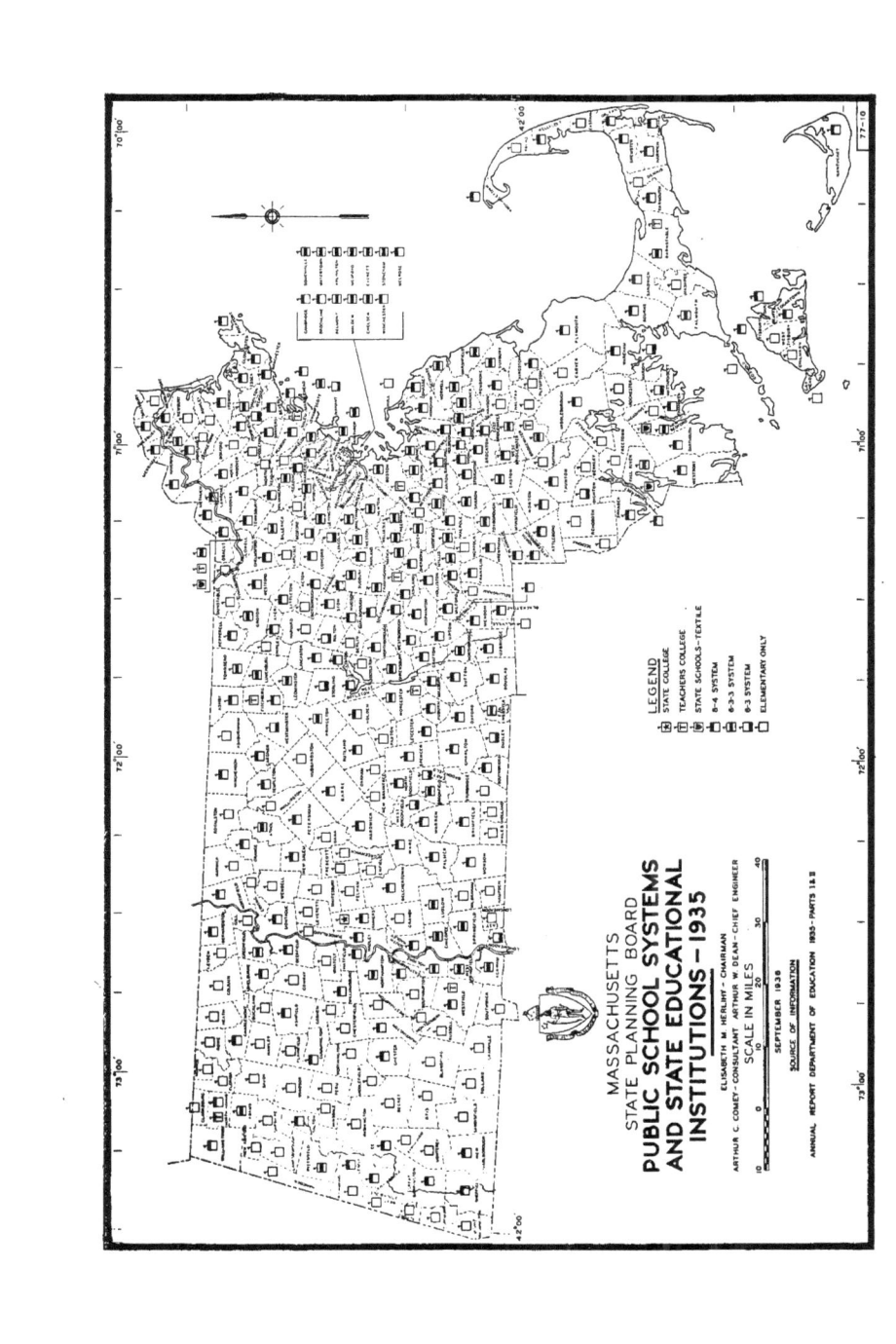

an enrollment in 1935 of 118 cadets, and a staff of 10 instructors.

County Schools. County training schools are established for the instruction and training of children who are habitual truants or school offenders. In 1935, the four county training schools in Massachusetts employed twelve teachers, and had an average attendance of 265.

Schools in State Institutions. Schools in State institutions, on December 1, 1935, employed 59 teachers, and had an enrollment of 792.

Schools for the Blind and Deaf. The State places blind children in Perkins Institution and pays tuition not exceeding the cost of maintenance and instruction. In 1935, 266 pupils received this aid.

A majority of the deaf children of the State are placed in private schools. In 1935, 595 children were so placed in five different schools. Day classes at Lynn, New Bedford, Springfield, and Worcester accommodated 59 more.

There has been an increase in the enrollment of pupils in schools for the blind and deaf, from 768 in 1927 to 920 in 1935.

Schools for Other Handicapped Children. Schools for handicapped children other than the blind and deaf include the Walter E. Fernald State School, Monson State Hospital (epileptic), Wrentham State School, Westfield State Sanitorium (tubercular), Belchertown State School, and the Massachusetts Hospital School (for the crippled).

Vocational Schools. Under the so-called Smith-Hughes Act, the Federal government provides a continuing appropriation from Federal funds for the purpose of cooperating with the States in the establishment and maintenance of programs for vocational education of lower-than-college grades, and for the preparation of teachers to instruct under these plans. On August 31, 1935, the total enrollment in all the vocational, industrial, agricultural, and compulsory continuation schools which are State aided was 35,984, representing a steady decline from the enrollment, in 1929, of 55,800. In 1935, 1818 teachers were employed (148 less than in 1929).

University Extension. In 1916, the State Department of Education established the Division of University Extension. Its enrollments have increased from 3,397 in 1916 to 30,784 in 1935. During the same period, the cost per pupil has decreased from $12.64 to $0.355. This per capita cost only includes the wages of the instructors. Accommodation facilities are supplied free.

Adult Alien Education. In 1919, the Massachusetts Legislature passed an Act (Chapter 295, Acts of 1919) "to promote Americanization through the education of adult persons unable to use the English language". The number of persons enrolled for this adult alien education has declined steadily from a total of 28,903 in 1925 to 11,488 in 1935, owing largely to reduced immigration.

WPA Nursery and Adult-Education Schools. During 1935' 200 nursery schools were operated in different parts of the State. The facilities provided were used by approximately 7000 children of pre-school age, whose parents were on relief or eligible for relief.

Under the adult-education program, more than 30,000 students attended schools distributed all over Massachusetts. Subjects given included courses on arts and crafts, and cultural, avocational, and vocational subjects.

Effect of Education upon Illiteracy

In 1900, 5.9 per cent of the people in Massachusetts, ten years and over in age, were illiterate. By 1930, the percentage of illiteracy was only 3.5, — a decrease of 2.4 per cent (See Chart 54E-C1.) Although the decrease in immigration has held down the amount of illiteracy, the educational system of the State has been an important factor in the progress that has been made. The adult Americanization classes have played an important role in this respect.

Physical Aspects of the Educational Plant

In the period from 1918 to 1933, 490 new school buildings were constructed in the State. The total number of school buildings in use in 1933 was 2724, of which 399 were one-room buildings.

Despite the new buildings, the physical educational plant of the State is still not adequate, according to the State Director of the Federal Emergency Administration of Public Works, who says:

"In many communities the plant was entirely inadequate....
In some cities and towns the school population was nearly twice the preper normal capacity of the buildings".*

---

*Press release No. 255

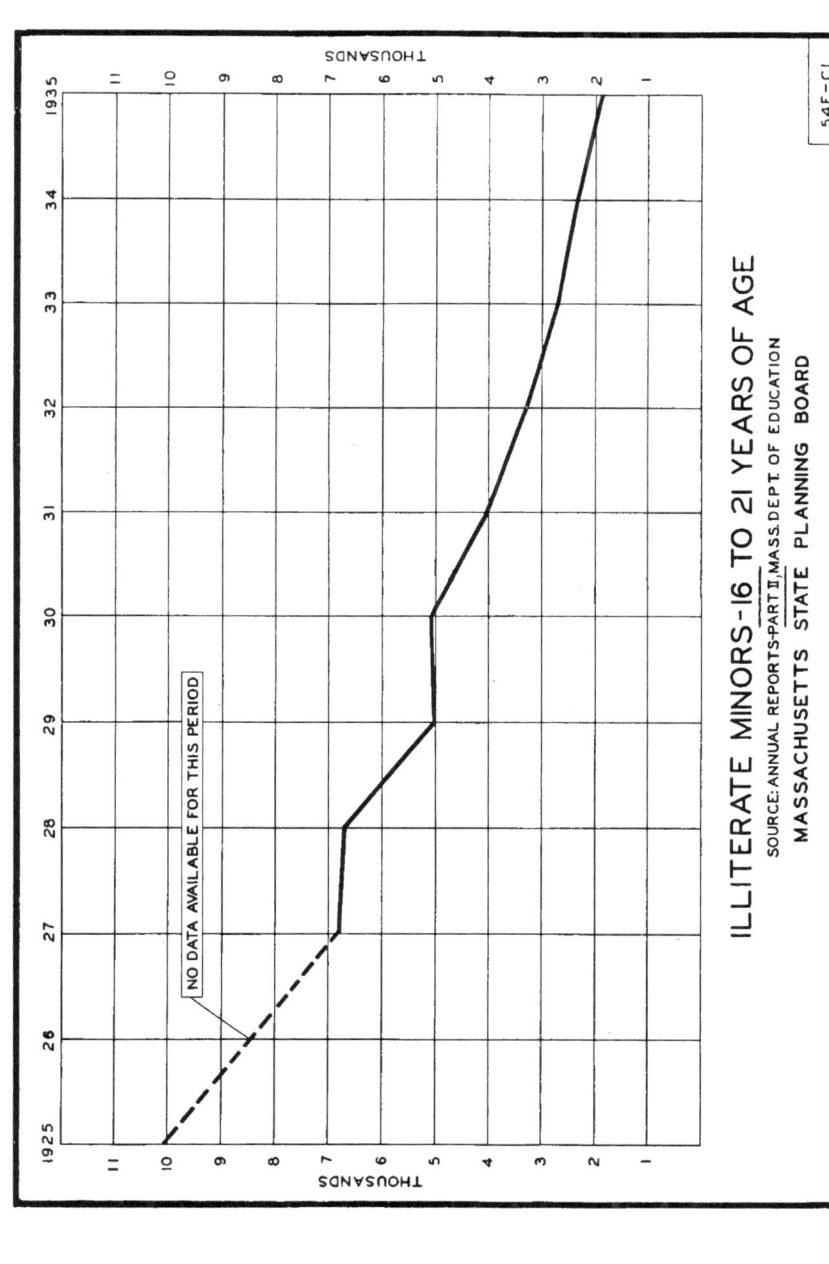

Cost of Education

For the State as a whole, the per capita cost of education has decreased from $107.80 per pupil, in 1925, to $93.74 per pupil, in 1935. (See Chart 54E-C2.) The total expenditures for public schools in Massachusetts, in 1925, were $71,941,985. They increased to $82,593,749, in 1930, and then decreased to $68,661,141, in 1935. The latter decrease is largely the result of curtailments necessitated by the depression.

Conclusions

Important conclusions based on the study of the State Educational system are being reviewed by the State Planning Board with the purpose of making subsequent recommendations.

Sources of Information

ACTIVITIES OF STATE PLANNING BOARDS RELATING TO PUBLIC EDUCATION, National Educational Association
AMERICAN EDUCATIONAL DIRECTORY, by Homer L. Patterson
Annual Education Report, Diocese of Fall River, August 31, 1935
Annual Reports of Massachusetts Department of Education, 1915-35
COMMONWEALTH HISTORY OF MASSACHUSETTS, Vol. V, by A. B. Hard
DIRECTORY OF CATHOLIC COLLEGES AND SCHOOLS (1932-33)
Federal Emergency Administration of Public Works, State Director's Press Release, No. 255
Massachusetts Census of 1905, Vol. I
Massachusetts Department of Education
    Advantages Resulting from a Consolidation of Schools
    Annual Reports of Division of Immigration and Americanization
    Annual Reports on State-Aided Vocational and Part-Time Education in Massachusetts
    Compulsory Laws Relative to Education That Influence the Local School Budget (1932)
    Disadvantages of School Consolidation
    Educational Directory (1936)
    Educational Legislation in 1932, 1933, 1934, 1935
    General Laws Relating to Education
    General Laws Relating to Vocational and Continuation School Education
    High School Requirements for Teachers Certification
    Information Relating to Establishment and Administration of State-Aided Vocational Schools
    Institutions in Massachusetts Having Authority to Confer Degrees, 1926

MASSACHUSETTS STATE PLANNING BOARD

Massachusetts Budget, 1931
Massachusetts Public Schools, 1630-1930
One-Room Schools
Questionnaire to Superintendents - "Improvement of the Teaching Service", 1931
Reports of Board of Free Public Library Commissioners
Salaries of Teachers in Public Day Schools of Massachusetts, 1931
School Buildings Constructed in Massachusetts, 1918-33
State Aid in Financing Education, 1936
The Tax Dollar - Its Source and Expenditure, 1933
Vocational Rehabilitation for Persons Disabled in Industry or Otherwise

Massachusetts House - No. 202, 203, 204, 205, 211, 229, 230, 231, 747
Massachusetts - Its Industrial, Agricultural and Economic Resources
Per Capita Costs in City Schools (1934-35), No. 69, United States Department of Interior, Office of Education

Periodicals

The Nation's Schools, October 1932
School and Society, August 13, 1932, and August 12, 1933
Private Schools, 1935-36. Sargent's Handbook, by Porter Sargent
Proceedings, 1932 and 1933, National Education Association
Report of State Planning Board - WPA Project 4669 - Project No. VII PW. Program - Education
School Committee of City of Boston - Annual Report of Business Manager on Cost of Public School Education, 1934
Selected List of Recent References on Educational Planning National Education Association. United States State College Bulletin, November 30, 1935
United States Census, 13th, 1910, Vol. II
                            14th, 1920, Vol. III
                            15th, 1930, Vol. III, Part I
United States Statistical Abstract, 1916, 1926, 1935

PUBLIC SCHOOL ORGANIZATION AND ADMINISTRATION, Fred Engelhardt
SOCIAL PLANNING AND ADULT EDUCATION, John W. Herring

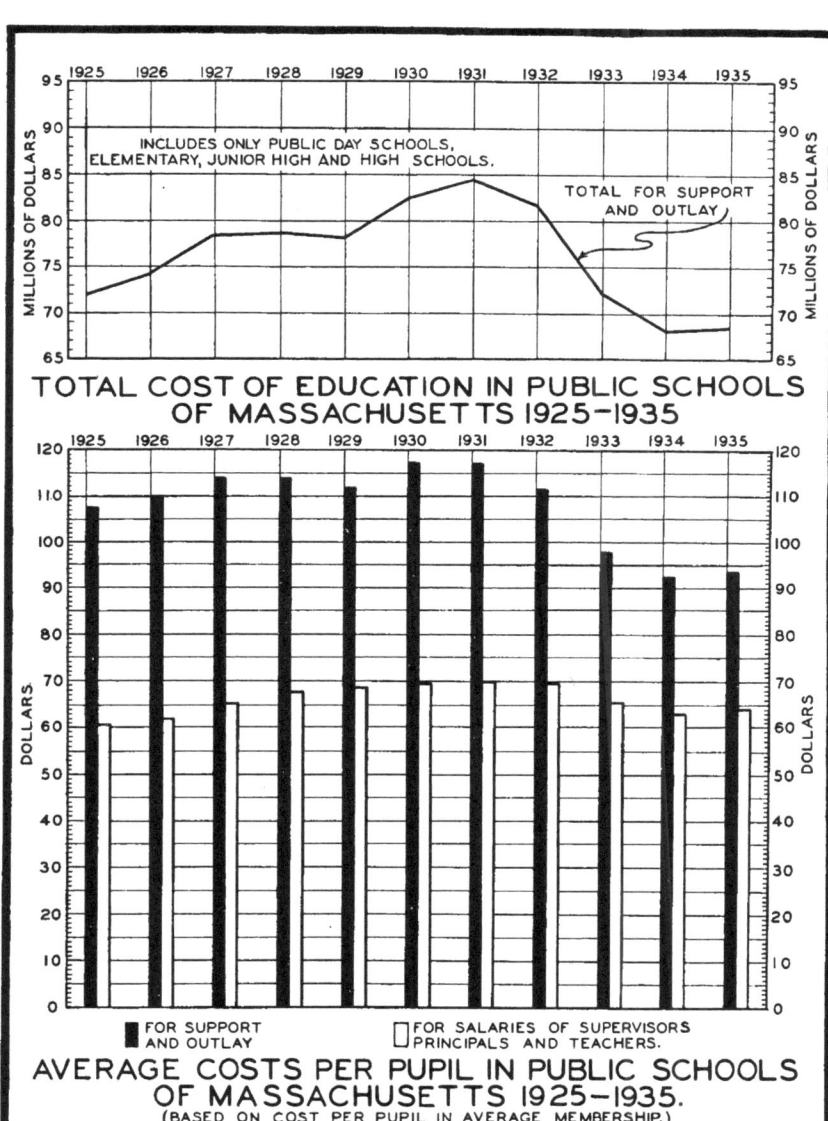

WELFARE

Summary Outline

I. State Welfare System in Massachusetts

    A. Settlement Laws as a Basis for Reimbursement
    B. Department of Public Welfare
    C. Other State Departments and Commissions Rendering Welfare Aid

II. Federal Aid — The Social Security Act

    A. Aid to Dependent Children (Mothers' Aid)
    B. Old-Age Assistance
    C. Child Welfare (Care of Homeless and Neglected Children)
    D. Crippled Children
    E. Maternal and Child-Health Services
    F. Public Health Work
    G. Vocational Rehabilitation
    H. Aid to the Blind
    I. Unemployment Compensation

III. Private Welfare System in Massachusetts

IV. Statistical Analysis of Welfare

    A. Local and State Public Relief
    B. Private Relief

V. Special Aspects of Welfare

    A. Promotion of Welfare Work
    B. Educational Facilities Available in Institutions
    C. Training of Social Workers
    D. Economics of the Welfare System
    E. Coöperation between Public and Private Agencies

MASSACHUSETTS STATE PLANNING BOARD

WELFARE

Massachusetts has long been progressive in public-welfare legislation. As early as 1913, a mothers'-aid law was enacted; later, in 1920 and 1921, respectively, legislation for aid to the blind and aid for vocational rehabilitation was enacted. So enlightened were these and other laws pertaining to welfare, that, upon the passage of the Federal Social Security Act in 1935, few changes were necessary to make them conform to its requirements.

Public-welfare costs have always been high in Massachusetts because of the large amount of aid rendered. Since the depression, however, there has been an abnormal increase in expenditures; from about thirteen million dollars, in 1930, the cost rose to over thirty-seven million dollars, in 1935. In addition, large sums are spent by private relief agencies; their expenditures, in 1935, were more than forty-seven million dollars.

With the additional funds now provided by the Federal Social Security Act, the Commonwealth will be able to expand its welfare activities to the rural sections of the State.

State Welfare System in Massachusetts

The Commonwealth administers public aid through the Department of Public Welfare and its several divisions and subdivisions. Local aid is given through the Town Boards of Public Welfare. The costs of mothers' aid, old-age assistance, and other types of relief are paid by the local boards; the State then reimburses them, in part. The reimbursement is based on the settlement laws* and differs, in amount, for the various types of aid. The costs of relieving needy persons having settlements is borne, in part, by the State and, in part, by the town, whereas the costs of relieving persons lacking a settlement are borne by the State, alone.

Settlement Laws as a Basis for Reimbursement

At present, the Commonwealth is handicapped, in its efforts to improve the relief system, because of the great amount of staff time required to conclude settlement contests between the different

---
*The settlement laws provide that persons twenty-one years of age or over, who have resided in a town for five consecutive years, acquire a settlement therein.

cities and towns. In 1934, the Department recommended legislation to discard the settlement laws as a basis for reimbursement, but this was vigorously opposed by the towns, who wished to retain these laws as a protection against residents of other towns coming to them for relief. The recommendations of the Department were referred to a Recess Commission for study; their recommendations were not supported in the report of the Commission. By legislation passed this year*, however, state reimbursement for Mothers' Aid is made without regard to legal settlement.

Department of Public Welfare

Division of Aid and Relief. This division of the Department of Public Welfare includes five subdivisions, with functions as follows:

1. The Subdivision of Settlements investigates the settlements of patients admitted to the State Infirmary, the State Farm (Infirmary Department), State sanatoria, and the Massachusetts Hospital School.

2. The Subdivision of Relief supervises public relief rendered by local Boards of Public Welfare and Boards of Health to persons who have no settlement. It gives aid to relatives of shipwrecked seamen, sick poor, and persons with dangerous diseases, pays for burials, and supervises wayfarers' lodges and cheap lodging houses.

3. The Subdivision of Mothers' Aid now operates under a recently amended Act* which provides that sufficient aid shall be furnished an indigent parent to bring up properly a dependent child in his or her home. The local board of public welfare must first investigate each case to determine whether the parent is fit to assume the responsibility. Towns are partially reimbursed by the Federal Government, under the provisions of the Federal Social Security Act, and for one-third of the remainder by the Commonwealth; Mothers' Aid is one of the most important and expensive forms of public relief; important, because it provides home life for citizens of tomorrow, under care of their own parents; expensive, because the aid must be adequate to enable the children to be brought up properly.

4. The Subdivision of Social Science serves all patients at the State Infirmary, former patients in need of assistance, and cer-

---

*Chapter 413, Acts of 1936

tain persons referred by other agencies and hospitals. A staff of ten social workers is engaged at the Infirmary and in rendering the important services of supervision and placement after discharge.

The Men's Hospital is badly overcrowded. It now admits men both with and without settlements. It is recommended that those with settlements in the larger towns be cared for in local infirmaries, in order that those without settlements and those in smaller communities where hospitalization opportunities do not exist may have available the Infirmary's facilities. The above-mentioned overcrowding is partly attributable to the renewed presence of transients who were cared for by the Federal Transient Service* until its closing on September 15, 1935. There is need for a special institution to care for these homeless men.

The Women's Hospital, which gives hospital service to married and unmarried mothers, and to delinquent, non-delinquent, and physically handicapped women, is also overcrowded. Mentally defective patients should be cared for in a new and separate institution, and young girls should be segregated from older women.

5. The Bureau of Old Age Assistance, created under Chapter 402 of the Acts of 1930, started operations and began payments to beneficiaries on July 1, 1931. The Act, as since modified*, provides adequate assistance to deserving people sixty-five years of age and over, given, if possible, in the home. Payments are made at the rate of thirty dollars per month to a single person, and fifty dollars per month to a husband and wife. This aid is given through a local Bureau of Old-Age Assistance, established by each local board of public welfare. The number of active old-age assistance cases has increased from 1561, on August 1, 1931, to 30,639, on October 1, 1936.

Towns are partially reimbursed by the Federal Government, and, for two-thirds of the remainder, by the Commonwealth. To provide revenue for this type of aid, a head tax was assessed on every male inhabitant in Massachusetts during the years 1931, 1932, and 1933. Funds are now obtained from the revenues of the Alcoholic Beverages Commission*** and those of the Racing Commission.**

---

*The Federal Transient Service was opened in Massachusetts in 1934. Centers and Camps for housing were set up in different parts of the State. The excellent work of this Service has demonstrated what can be done for the homeless wayfarer.
   **Chapter 436, Acts of 1936
   ***Chapter 120, Acts of 1933

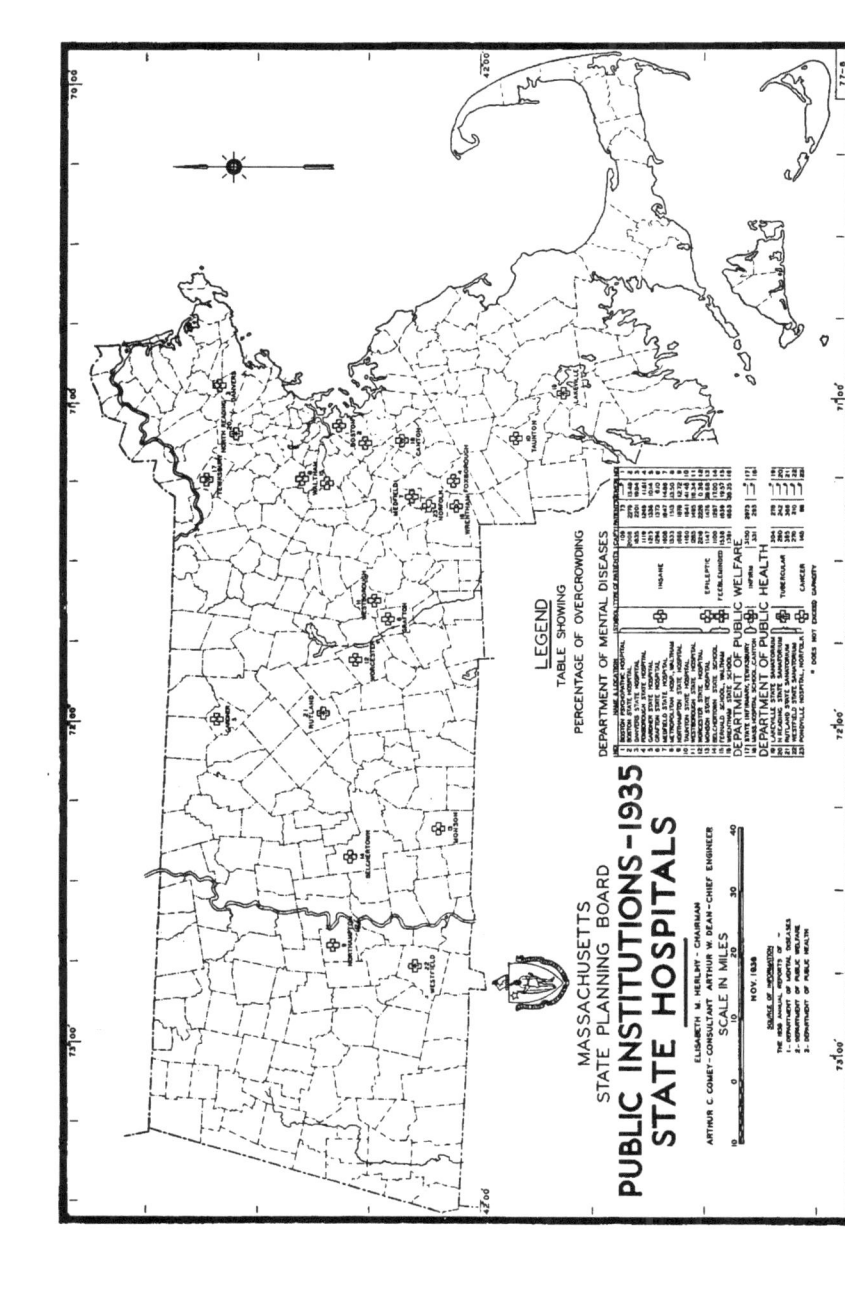

Division of Child Guardianship. The most important function of this division is the care, maintenance, and supervision (in foster homes) of dependent, neglected, wayward, and delinquent children who are wards of the Commonwealth. Delinquents are cared for in the Lyman School for Boys, the Industrial School for Boys, and the Industrial School for Girls; other wards are cared for in the Massachusetts Training Schools, the Massachusetts Hospital School, and the State Infirmary. In addition to caring for these children, the Division has the following responsibilities:

1. Enforcement of laws for the protection of children.
2. Supervision of all infants under two years of age in foster homes, and the licensing of boarding homes for infants.
3. Inspection and supervision required in licensing maternity hospitals.
4. Investigation of proposed adoptions of children under fourteen years of age, referred by the Probate Courts.
5. Annual visitation of all minor children who are placed out and supported at the expense of cities and towns.

Subdivision of Social Service for Crippled Children. This subdivision supervises the annual census of physically handicapped children. It follows up reported cases, and sees that needed treatments are available and are given. Treatments are given in hospitals, institutions, clinics, or privately in the home. The division also supervises the education of these physically handicapped children.

Other State Departments and Commissions Rendering Welfare Aid

Welfare aid of the following types is given by other State agencies:

1. Maternal- and Child-Health Service and Public-Health Work, under the Department of Health.
2. Vocational Rehabilitation and Aid to the Blind, under the Department of Education.
3. Unemployment Compensation, under the Unemployment Compensation Commission.

Federal Aid -- The Social Security Act

State legislation, passed in 1935*, provided for coöperation between the Departments of Public Health, Public Welfare, and Education in the administration of the Federal Social Security Act. The procedure in each form of relief is similar in most respects:

*Chapter 494, Acts of 1935.

MASSACHUSETTS STATE PLANNING BOARD

a State Plan must be drawn up and submitted for approval to the Federal Social Security Board; when the Plan is accepted, Federal funds are made available to the State. In most cases, the State must either match or pay a certain fraction of the Federal contribution. The provisions of the Act deal with a number of distinct, though related, measures, which may be grouped under the following headings:

Aid to Dependent Children (Mothers' Aid)

The State Plan has been submitted and accepted, but Federal funds have not yet been allotted. The Federal grant is equal to one third of the State expenditures; but the Federal Government does not contribute to payments in excess of eighteen dollars a month for the first child, and twelve dollars a month for each additional child. The Federal Government appropriated $8,000,000 for this type of aid throughout the United States for the fiscal year 1935, and $24,750,000, for the fiscal year 1936.

Old-Age Assistance

A State Plan has been accepted, and Federal allotments to Massachusetts to date* have totalled $2,712,109.69. The Federal grant is equal to one-half the State expenditures; but the Federal Government does not contribute to payments to an individual in excess of thirty dollars a month. In addition, the Federal Government pays the State, for administration costs, an amount equal to five per cent of the total Federal grant. The Federal Government appropriated $24,600,000 for this type of aid throughout the United States for the fiscal year 1935, and $49,750,000 for the fiscal year 1936.

Child Welfare (Care of Homeless and Neglected Children)

A State Plan, developed jointly by the Federal Children's Bureau and State public welfare agencies, has been accepted, and Federal allotments to Massachusetts to date* have totalled $3,250. The purpose of this aid is the establishment, in coöperation with the State, of child-welfare services in the predominantly rural areas of the Commonwealth. A rural area in south Worcester County, including twenty-six towns, has been selected for work.

Allotments are made on the basis of the ratio of the rural population of the State to the rural population of the United States. The Federal Government appropriated $625,000 for this type of aid throughout the United States during the fiscal year

*October 10, 1936.

1935, and $1,500,000 for the fiscal year 1936.

Crippled Children

A State Plan has been accepted by the Federal Children's Bureau, and Federal allotments to date* have totalled $21,900.56. The Federal grant matches the State expenditure. The purposes of this type of aid are to extend into the rural areas, and into areas suffering from severe economic distress, services for aiding crippled children. The Federal Government appropriated $1,187,000 for this purpose throughout the United States for the fiscal year 1935, and $2,850,000 for the fiscal year 1936.

Maternal and Child-Health Services

A State Plan has been approved by the Federal Children's Bureau, and Federal allotments to Massachusetts to date* have totalled $44,522.99. Payments are divided into two Funds, A and B. Fund A matches the State expenditure; Fund B is paid to the State after consideration of the number of live births in the State. The Federal Government appropriated $1,580,000 for this type of aid throughout the United States for the fiscal year 1935, and $3,800,000 for the fiscal year 1936.

Public Health Work

A State Plan has been accepted and Federal allotments to Massachusetts to date* have totalled $121,686.62. Allotments to the State are made on the basis of population, and special health problems, and the financial needs of the State. The Federal Government appropriated $3,300,000 for this type of aid throughout the United States for the fiscal year 1935, and $30,000,000 for the fiscal year 1936.

Vocational Rehabilitation

The Federal Vocation Rehabilitation Law** was accepted in Massachusetts in 1921.*** Annual plans were submitted by the States, for approval, to the Federal Board for Vocational Education. The total annual Federal appropriation was allotted to the States in the proportion which their population bore to the total population of the United States. Under the Social Security Act, funds in addition to the amount of existing authorization are

---
*October 10, 1936.
**United States Public Act No. 271 of the 74th Congress.
***Chapter 462, Acts of 1921.

MASSACHUSETTS STATE PLANNING BOARD

available. The total amount expended for this type of aid in Massachusetts for the fiscal year 1935, was $127,604.18, of which $63,802.50 were contributed by the State, and $63,801.68 by the Federal Government.* The Federal Government appropriated $841,000 for this type of aid throughout the United States for the fiscal year. 1936, and in addition to this, $22,000 to pay the costs of administration.

Aid to the Blind

A State Plan has been accepted, and Federal allotments to date** have totalled $50,452.03. Federal grants match the State expenditures. This Federal aid is limited to fifteen dollars per month per person, plus an additional grant of five per cent of the total sum to pay administration costs. The sum of $2,000,000 was appropriated by the Federal Government for the fiscal year 1935, and $3,000,000 for the fiscal year 1936, for this type of aid throughout the United States.

Unemployment Compensation

The Social Security Act does not establish an unemployment-compensation system, but the States are invited to enact laws for the compensation of their unemployed. In 1935, Massachusetts enacted such a law**, which was approved by the Federal Government. Federal allotments to Massachusetts to date***, have totalled $250,499.22. The Federal Government appropriated $4,000,000 for distribution to the States, for administration costs, for the fiscal year 1935, and $49,000,000 for the fiscal year 1936.

Private Welfare System in Massachusetts

The participation of private welfare agencies in the work of relief in Massachusetts has already been indicated. Their contributions exceed governmental allotments for relief.

The Department of Public Welfare is required to investigate all applications for charitable charters, and charitable organizations must report annually, and submit to investigations, if so requested. Of the 1269 charitable corporations which made returns to the Department of Public Welfare in 1935, 122 were organizations maintaining homes for the aged, 150 were child-helping agencies,

---
*Of this latter sum, $34,750 was allotted under the organic Act, and $29,051.68, under the Social Security Act.
**Chapter 471, Acts of 1935, amended by Chapters 12 and 249, Acts of 1936.
***October 10, 1936.

260 were hospitals or other institutions for aiding the sick, 131 were agencies giving family aid, and 206 were organizations doing community or club work. The remaining 400 corporations form a miscellaneous group chiefly civic or eleemosynary in nature.

Statistical Analysis of Welfare

Local and State Public Relief

Table 38 shows the number of persons supported or given relief by the State and by cities and towns in Massachusetts, from 1920 until 1935. The total number given relief increased steadily over 600 per cent from 1924 to 1934, if, to the figures for 1934, as given on the table, are added the number of persons given relief because of unemployment. The figures for 1935 show a slight decline.

This same table shows the relief expenditures of the State and of its cities and towns, from 1920 to 1935.

Table 39 shows the expenditures of the Department of Public Welfare, from 1920 to 1935.

In Massachusetts, in 1935, there were:

    a. 490 licensed public homes, boarding 1007 infants, in 106 towns and cities.
    b. 189 licensed maternity hospitals, in 92 cities and towns.
    c. 306 licensed boarding homes for aged persons, in 98 cities and towns.
    d. 117 infirmaries, caring for 10,701 persons.

Private Relief

Table 40 shows the number of private incorporated charitable organizations reported, year by year, since 1920, the nature of work in which they are engaged, and their current receipts and expenditures. The number of these corporations has grown from 888, in 1920, to 1269, in 1935. Although their current expenditures have fallen from over fifty-two millions, in 1931, to a little more than forty-seven millions, in 1935, the latter expenditures show a great increase over those for 1920.

MASSACHUSETTS STATE PLANNING BOARD

Special Aspects of Welfare

Promotion of Welfare Work

A valuable aid to public and private welfare work is found in the efforts being made to evaluate and improve welfare methods. Two public associations in the State are working on this aspect of the problem. The Massachusetts Relief Officers' Association, composed of members or agents of the local boards of public welfare, in the eastern part of Massachusetts, and the Western Relief Officers' Organization, a similar body in the western portion of the State, hold meetings for the purpose of self-improvement. The Commonwealth coöperates by sending representatives to their meetings, and appointing committees from time to time to recommend new welfare legislation.

Table 38

PERSONS GIVEN RELIEF, AND RELIEF EXPENDITURES BY THE STATE AND BY CITIES AND TOWNS

YEAR	NUMBER OF PERSONS			EXPENDITURES		
	By the State	By Cities and Towns	Total	By the State	By Cities and Towns	Total
1920	19,695	56,173	75,868	1,788,066	5,996,622	7,784,689
1921	25,401	71,333	96,734	1,909,891	5,207,062	7,116,954
1922	35,264	86,172	121,436	2,106,732	6,642,661	8,749,394
1923	35,196	76,370	102,414	2,052,972	6,277,210	8,330,182
1924	25,446	70,404	95,850	2,049,828	6,151,939	8,201,768
1925	29,657	84,764	114,421	2,122,190	7,095,476	9,217,666
1926	27,565	90,081	117,646	2,235,128	7,327,562	9,562,690
1927	28,162	90,503	118,665	1,726,262	7,974,237	9,700,499
1928	32,634	101,238	133,872	1,925,753	9,309,706	11,235,460
1929	34,899	119,309	154,208	2,519,489	11,185,887	13,705,376
1930	39,281	127,867	167,148	2,639,379	10,903,115	13,542,495
1931	65,888	214,364	280,252	2,961,768	13,989,861	16,951,629
1932	96,854	315,779	412,633	3,832,856	23,484,764	27,317,621
1933	---	---	---	6,004,703	36,761,309	42,766,012
1934	*49,561	*134,723	*184,284	5,904,488	38,445,907	44,350,395
1935	*35,402	*128,580	*163,982	5,453,255	32,139,931	37,593,186

*These figures do not include persons given relief because of unemployment.

Table 39

EXPENDITURES OF THE DEPARTMENT OF PUBLIC WELFARE, 1920-1935

YEARS	PERSONAL SERVICES	MAINTENANCE AND OPERATION	NEW CONSTRUCTION, EQUIPMENT, REAL ESTATE, AND FURNISHINGS	TOTAL AID	GROSS TOTAL EXPENDITURES	TOTAL RECEIPTS	NET TOTAL EXPENDITURES
1920	781,031	1,091,725	15,621	2,331,043	4,219,422	253,267	3,966,154
1921	907,125	1,039,956	110,745	2,564,710	4,622,538	261,246	4,361,291
1922	925,541	1,009,590	315,499	2,658,929	4,909,560	215,520	4,684,039
1923	926,096	942,605	255,496	2,657,261	4,803,459	254,469	4,548,990
1924	996,364	901,439	103,836	2,715,772	4,715,463	262,524	4,452,938
1925	1,017,460	978,610	13,207	2,812,641	4,821,920	306,880	4,515,039
1926	1,051,699	970,423	14,401	2,795,202	4,831,726	322,801	4,508,924
1927	1,103,436	1,005,180	54,007	2,246,866	4,409,590	350,860	4,058,730
1928	1,162,146	995,392	77,005	2,565,328	4,799,872	350,905	4,448,967
1929	1,213,568	1,015,212	130,904	3,189,759	5,549,445	371,246	5,178,198
1930	1,275,283	1,041,012	164,633	3,348,190	5,829,120	393,392	5,435,728
1931	1,342,800	959,542	375,779	3,824,187	6,502,303	1,658,208	4,844,100
1932	1,454,474	909,991	316,326	6,617,054	9,297,847	1,590,200	7,707,646
1933	1,370,365	841,977	35,680	9,692,719	10,940,743	1,946,128	8,994,615
1934	1,362,476	956,639	393,282	6,854,750	11,567,148	3,420,613	8,132,930
1935	1,587,636	1,080,530	529,590	8,432,532	11,569,090	4,416,204	7,152,886

Table 40

PRIVATE INCORPORATED CHARITABLE ORGANIZATIONS IN MASSACHUSETTS

YEAR	NUMBER OF ORGANIZATIONS							FINANCES	
	Homes for the Aged	Child-Helping Agencies	Institutions Aiding the Sick	Agencies Giving Family Aid	Agencies Doing Community, Neighborhood, or Club Work	Miscellaneous Agencies	Total	Current Receipts	Current Expenditures
1920	98	114	182	159	115	220	888	27,220,415	25,628,927
1921	107	112	165	160	129	224	917	33,307,933	33,079,681
1922	105	122	186	132	117	260	922	34,278,532	32,131,010
1923	109	118	208	133	134	275	977	39,505,339	32,828,146
1924	112	118	208	137	147	278	1000	40,084,123	23,857,467
1925	112	129	220	128	146	314	1049	44,456,282	36,823,593
1926	113	127	223	128	151	324	1066	41,741,722	38,002,517
1927	115	124	233	127	149	325	1073	44,236,726	40,265,899
1928	114	133	238	129	163	339	1116	48,510,424	44,215,944
1929	121	133	250	124	169	348	1145	52,162,287	49,138,283
1930	120	140	254	131	176	364	1185	52,868,733	49,956,768
1931	123	146	254	133	173	385	1214	55,794,903	52,310,916
1932	126	146	257	135	176	398	1238	53,277,309	50,706,891
1933	123	142	251	135	200	394	1245	48,665,654	46,812,867
1934	126	145	256	137	208	401	1273	48,616,394	45,477,470
1935	122	150	260	131	206	400	1269	48,838,426	47,361,111

MASSACHUSETTS STATE PLANNING BOARD

The Massachusetts Conference of Social Work is one of the most important of the private welfare organizations with similar purposes. It aims to promote knowledge of social conditions, their cause, and measures for their improvement, by the discussion of principles, methods, and results, to the end that preventive, constructive, and curative measures may become more humane, efficient, and permanent.

Educational Facilities Available in Institutions

Children in local public-welfare institutions secure their education at public schools, unless they are physically or mentally incapacitated. Education for the latter is provided in special institutions.* Retarded children attend special classes in the public schools or are placed in the State Schools for the Feeble-minded.**

Training of Social Workers

In-service training and education for social workers is provided at the School of Social Work of Simmons College, in Boston. This school prepares students for professional welfare service in social case work, group work, and social research.

Social workers for towns and cities are required to take civil-service examinations. A recent law*** has abolished educational requirements; this is unfortunate because it may result in a staff of inexperienced workers with little educational background.

Economics of the Welfare System

The 1935 annual per capita cost for public welfare was $8.64. This figure was obtained by dividing the welfare expenditures of the State and cities and towns in 1935, by the 1935 population of Massachusetts. The tremendous increase in welfare expenditures is revealed when this figure is compared with the figures for former years: $2.02, in 1920; $2.22, in 1925; and $3.18, in 1930. These figures do not include the expenditures of either Federal or private relief agencies.

---

*Most important among these institutions are: the Berkshire School for Crippled Children, the Perkins Institute for the Blind, the Massachusetts Hospital School, and State Schools for the Feeble-minded.

**There are three of those: the Belchertown State School, the Walter E. Fernald School, and the Wrentham State School.

***Chapter 228, Acts of 1935.

Cooperation between Public and Private Agencies

From the depression, valuable lessons have been learned. Closer cooperation between public and private relief agencies has grown out of the need for mobilizing all of the community resources to meet the emergency. Private relief agencies have loaned their trained workers to overworked public-relief officials, and pastors of churches of all denominations have undertaken the distribution of Federal surplus supplies.

It is safe to say that boards of public welfare are more experienced in relief administration, and their offices are better equipped than ever before.

CORRECTION

Summary Outline

I. Juvenile Correction Institutions

    A. State Training Schools
    B. County Training Schools

II. Adult Correction Institutions

    A. State Institutions
    B. County Institutions

III. Special Aspects of Correction Institutions

    A. The Plant
    B. Case Work and Medical Work
    C. Educational Facilities
    D. Prison Industries
    E. Coördination of the Correction System

IV. Statistical Analysis of the Correction System

    A. Arrests
    B. Probation
    C. Parole
    D. Social Status of Prisoners
    E. Per Capita Costs of State and County Penal Institutions

V. Proposed Program of the Department of Correction

MASSACHUSETTS STATE PLANNING BOARD

CORRECTION

Massachusetts was a forerunner in many of the correctional practices now in use in the United States. Today, the State is noted for its use of advanced methods of penal administration, and for its complete statistical records of every offender from arrest to post-parole.

Juvenile Correction Institutions

State Training Schools

The State training schools for juvenile delinquents are under the supervision of the Department of Public Welfare. The aim of these schools is to adapt the child to life in the community, with a minimum application of force. The three State juvenile training schools are: (1) the Lyman School for Boys, at Westborough; (2) the Industrial School for Boys, at Shirley; and (3) the Industrial School for Girls, at Lancaster. All three are organized on the cottage system. Only minors are committed or retained in these institutions. After sufficient training, the delinquents may be paroled, at the discretion of the Trustees.

County Training Schools

County training schools aim to reform habitual school truants. There are four such schools in the State: (1) the Essex School, in Lawrence; (2) the Hampden School, in Springfield; (3) the Middlesex School, in North Chelmsford; and (4) the Worcester School, in Oakdale.

Adult-Correction Institutions

State Institutions

State Prison. The State Prison at Charlestown, built in 1805, is a maximum-security prison. It receives men convicted of felonies and given minimum sentences of two and one-half years.

State Prison Colony. The State Prison Colony at Norfolk was built, in 1928, on the cottage plan. All of its prisoners are transferred from other institutions.

Massachusetts Reformatory. The Massachusetts Reformatory at Concord is a maximum-security prison of the cell-block type, in which all State male prisoners under thirty, convicted in either a

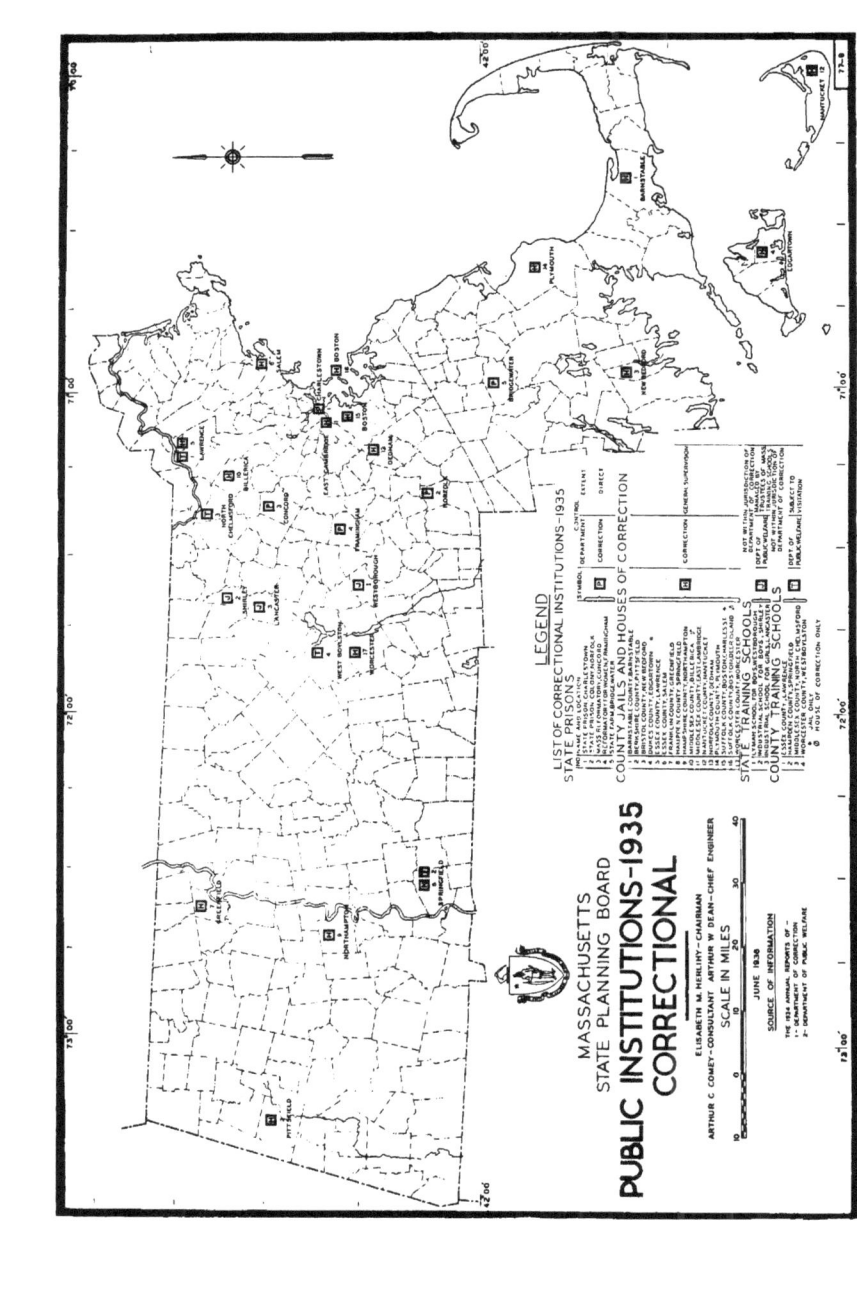

State or Federal court, are confined. It was opened for prisoners in 1884, eight years after the establishment of the pioneer institution of this type at Elmira, New York.

Reformatory for Women. The Reformatory for Women, at Framingham, was opened in 1877. In it are confined all State females convicted of crime in either a State or Federal court. A department for defective delinquents is maintained. There is no maximum or minimum age limit. Women are committed under limited, indefinite sentence.

State Farm. The State Farm at Bridgewater was opened in 1852. It has several departments: a prison department; departments for male and female defective delinquents; and the Bridgewater State Hospital, in which the criminally insane are cared for.

County Institutions

County jails and houses of correction are used for the detention of persons charged with crime and committed for trial, persons committed to assure their attendance as witnesses upon the trial of criminal cases, and persons convicted of crime and awaiting sentence. Offenders may be committed by either State or Federal courts. Jails and houses of correction are under the custody of a sheriff in each county, except in Suffolk County, in which they are under the supervision of the Penal Institutions Commissioner. There are seventeen of these County institutions, two of which (those at Edgartown and Nantucket) are rarely used.

Special Aspects of Correction Institutions

The Plant

Capacity. The capacity and the daily inmate average of juvenile and adult correction institutions in Massachusetts, for 1935, are given in Table 41. From this table, it may be seen that juvenile institutions, both State and county, have adequate capacity. The overcrowding at the Charlestown State Prison is serious, because it makes impossible the segregation of prisoners, based upon classification. Although the figures do not indicate it, there is also overcrowding at the Concord Reformatory. Accommodations there are not sufficient to allow for the segregation of prisoners classified according to offense, recidivism, mental state, and other factors.

Physical Condition. The buildings of the three State Training Schools for juvenile delinquents are in good physical condition.

Table 41

CAPACITY AND DAILY INMATE AVERAGE OF MASSACHUSETTS
CORRECTION INSTITUTIONS, 1935

INSTITUTION	CAPACITY	DAILY INMATE AVERAGE 1935
Juvenile: State		
Lyman School for Boys	480	398
Industrial School for Boys	319	317
Industrial School for Girls	297	274
Juvenile: County		
Essex School, Lawrence	150	103††
Hampden School, Springfield	100	30††
Middlesex School, N. Chelmsford	160	142††
Worcester School, Oakdale	70	31††
Adult: State		
State Prison, Charlestown	700	888
State Prison Colony, Norfolk	1100***	739
Concord Reformatory	1050	936
Reformatory for Women, Framingham	380;60†	296;47†
State Farm*		
Adult: County**		
Charles Street Boston Jail	292	307

*Overcrowding in the female defective delinquent and the prison departments.
**No overcrowding except in the Boston Charles Street Jail.
***Capacity when additional buildings now under construction are completed.
†First figure, capacity for women; second figure, capacity for infants.
††As of December 31, 1935.

MASSACHUSETTS STATE PLANNING BOARD

A Special Recess Commission, created by the Legislature in 1932, found the buildings of the County Training Schools likewise in good physical condition.

Physical conditions in the State adult correction institutions are bad, in most cases. The buildings at the Charlestown State Prison are so antiquated and in such poor repair that the whole plant should be abandoned. The physical plant at the Concord Reformatory is more than fifty years old, and many replacements and renovations are necessary;the situation is identical at the Reformatory for Women. At the State Farm, the buildings of the Insane Department are obsolete. The criminally insane should be placed under the supervision of the Department of Mental Diseases, and a new and separate institution should be built for them. The State Prison Colony at Norfolk is the only State institution in good repair. County jails and houses of correction are, on the whole, in good physical repair.

Building and Repair Programs. Building and repair programs are being carried on at both State and county juvenile and adult correction institutions. Most of these are programs for maintenance and upkeep, and are being accomplished with the aid of WPA allotments.

Case Work and Medical Work

In the solution of correctional problems, case work is important. A complete study of the criminal's life and physical and mental make-up is invaluable for the classification of each prisoner, and for the determination of what treatment he shall receive. Case work is done in State training schools, county training schools, and in State penal institutions, but not in county jails and houses of correction.

Medical work is carried on in every type of institution. In most cases, the medical staff and the equipment provided are adequate. Treatment is given for contagious diseases, operations are performed, and optometrical and dental work are available.

Educational Facilities

Educational facilities are provided in all institutions except county jails and houses of correction; in the latter group, however, inmates may take University Extension courses by correspondence. In the State and county training schools, academic and industrial training is the primary objective. In the State penal institutions, education is voluntary; the program includes academic, commercial, and vocational training. Library facilities, as well as social activities of an educational nature, are provided.

Prison Industries

The problem of finding enough work for prisoners has not been so serious in Massachusetts as in some other parts of the country. According to the report of the Department of Correction for 1935, of a total of 3877 prisoners in State institutions, 1258 were employed on productive industries, 2205 were engaged in miscellaneous work, mostly maintenance, and 414 were either sick or idle.

The State-use system is used; that is, all goods manufactured are intended primarily for use in State, county, and city institutions, although the surplus may be sold in the open market. There is some opposition to this latter practice, because of competition with private enterprise. Industries at State and county institutions consist of automobile repair shops, canning factories, and factories for the manufacture of brushes, boxes, clothing, blankets, foundry products, furniture, mattresses, and so forth.

Coördination of the Correction System

The correctional system in Massachusetts is coördinated through a central authority, the Commissioner of Correction. The Commissioner approves the appointment of heads of the State institutions; appointments of subordinate officers within each institution are made by the head. County jails and houses of correction are under the jurisdiction of the county commissioners. The Commissioner of Correction inspects all State and county penal institutions. He exercises supervision over all prisoners on parole. He has the power to make transfers from one institution to another.

Conferences on various penal problems are held frequently. In 1935, three regional conferences were held at juvenile training schools. A one-day conference on "Crime and the Community," held in November 1935, brought together practically all probation officers in the State, and many judges and workers in allied fields.

Statistical Analysis of the Correction System

Arrests

Massachusetts is the only State in the country which publishes statistics of total arrests. Table 42 shows the total number of arrests, by cities and towns, 1920 to 1935. The arrests are given in three different categories: (1) offenses against the person;

Table 42

TOTAL NUMBER OF ARRESTS, BY CITIES AND TOWNS

1920 - 1935

YEAR	CITIES				TOWNS				AGGREGATE				
	Offenses Against Person	Offenses Against Property	Offenses Against Public Order	Total	Offenses Against Person	Offenses Against Property	Offenses Against Public Order	Total	Offenses Against Person	Offenses Against Property	Offenses Against Public Order	Total	No. Per 1000 Population
1920	6,365	10,599	82,882	99,846	1,374	2,372	12,034	15,780	7,739	12,971	94,916	116,626	30.0
1921	7,559	13,145	107,896	128,600	1,987	3,122	18,357	23,466	9,546	16,267	126,253	152,066	38.9
1922	7,690	11,671	125,004	144,365	1,824	2,733	18,667	23,224	9,514	14,404	143,671	167,589	42.3
1923	7,611	10,539	134,022	152,171	1,837	2,252	21,670	25,759	9,448	12,790	155,692	177,930	44.3
1924	7,535	11,904	147,952	167,391	1,830	2,609	25,265	29,704	9,365	14,513	173,217	197,095	48.4
1925	7,287	12,267	145,609	165,163	1,871	2,812	26,729	31,412	9,158	15,079	172,338	196,575	47.6
1926	6,267	11,805	140,314	159,386	1,747	2,750	27,245	31,742	8,014	14,555	167,559	190,128	45.8
1927	5,908	10,498	151,143	167,549	1,543	2,629	26,783	30,955	7,451	13,127	177,926	198,504	47.5
1928	6,239	11,302	156,949	174,490	1,567	2,926	28,947	33,440	7,806	14,228	185,896	207,930	49.5
1929	5,831	10,924	153,750	170,505	1,677	3,219	30,598	35,494	7,508	14,143	184,348	205,999	48.3
1930	5,950	11,254	161,297	178,501	1,704	3,307	31,553	36,564	7,654	14,561	192,850	215,065	50.7
1931	6,180	12,974	150,529	169,683	2,076	3,745	31,124	36,985	8,256	16,719	181,653	206,668	48.4
1932	6,392	13,441	134,110	153,943	1,701	3,173	31,432	37,306	8,093	17,614	165,542	191,249	44.6
1933	6,272	12,394	127,963	146,629	1,787	4,157	28,244	34,188	8,059	16,551	156,207	180,917	42.0
1934	5,901	11,929	139,923	157,773	1,811	3,820	33,775	39,406	7,712	15,769	173,698	197,179	45.5
1935	5,259	11,366	129,193	145,818	1,837	3,873	36,032	41,742	7,096	15,239	165,225	187,560	43.1

(2) offenses against property; and (3) offenses against public order.

Table 43 shows the total number of arrests and the arrests per 1000 population, for twenty-seven Massachusetts cities of over 25,000 population, during 1935. Crimes have been divided into four groups:

1. Crimes against person and property. These include larceny, assault, murder, and robbery.
2. Drunkenness.
3. Violation of motor-vehicle and traffic laws.
4. All other crimes, including non-support, liquor-law violations, and so forth.

It is to be expected that the number of arrests per thousand population in concentrated areas like Boston and Springfield will be greater than in the more isolated cities. Variations appear, however, when the metropolitan area of Boston is considered. Cambridge has the highest number of arrests per thousand population for offenses against person and property, (8.2), while Medford has a low number (4.8). Boston has the highest number of arrests for drunkenness (48.7), while Somerville shows the low number (15.2). Similar differences are apparent in the other crime groups. These variations are caused by many factors, but a thorough knowledge of conditions in a particular community or city is necessary for conclusions in the interpretation of arrest statistics.

Probation

Massachusetts originated the practice of probation in this country, in 1880. A Board of Probation exercises State supervision; the eighty-eight State courts annually submit total figures on probation to this Board. Probation officers are appointed by the various courts.

The year 1935 showed the largest number of men, women, and children ever placed on probation (35,218). Since there are 195 probation officers, this produces an average of 180 probationers per officer. Several probation offices have been designated as "training stations," at which the newer members of the service spend at least a month observing probation in practice, and receiving instruction.

Table 44 shows, yearly from 1920 through 1935, the total number of male and female adult and juvenile probationers, and the results obtained. The success is shown in the percentage "filed or

Table 43

TOTAL ARRESTS AND NUMBER PER 1000 POPULATION BY CITIES OF
OVER 25,000 POPULATION IN MASSACHUSETTS, 1935

CITY	POPULATION 1935 CENSUS	CRIMES AGAINST PERSON AND PROPERTY		DRUNKENNESS		VIOLATION OF MOTOR-VEHICLE AND TRAFFIC LAWS		ALL OTHER CRIMES	
		Total Arrests	No. Per 1000 Pop.	Total Arrests	No. Per 1000 Pop.	Total Arrests	No. Per 1000 Pop.	Total Arrests	No. Per 1000 Pop.
Beverly	25,671	59	2.3	452	17.5	98	3.8	98	3.8
Boston	817,713	6462	7.9	39,314	43.7	14,446	17.7	8634	10.6
Brockton	62,407	318	5.1	1,399	22.4	401	6.4	526	8.4
Cambridge	118,075	964	8.2	3,249	27.5	1,500	12.7	1553	13.2
Chelsea	42,673	270	6.3	1,079	25.3	100	2.3	186	4.4
Chicopee	41,952	142	3.4	429	10.2	113	2.7	198	4.7
Everett	47,228	238	5.0	917	19.4	443	9.4	177	3.7
Fall River	117,414	646	5.5	1,410	12.0	545	4.6	688	5.9
Fitchburg	41,700	168	4.0	1,321	31.7	262	6.3	111	2.7
Haverhill	49,516	132	2.7	863	17.4	124	2.5	296	6.0
Holyoke	56,139	206	3.7	451	8.0	122	2.2	241	4.3
Lawrence	86,785	227	2.6	2,040	23.5	107	1.2	359	4.1
Lowell	100,114	490	4.9	2,104	21.0	412	4.1	540	6.0
Lynn	100,909	452	4.5	1,768	17.5	549	5.0	603	6.4
Malden	52,277	294	5.6	667	12.8	198	3.8	193	3.7
Medford	61,444	247	4.0	937	15.7	1295	21.1	201	3.3
New Bedford	110,022	496	4.5	1,090	9.9	504	4.6	1295	11.8
Newton	66,144	252	3.8	733	11.8	497	7.5	205	3.1
Pittsfield	47,516	355	7.5	696	14.6	1029	21.7	334	7.0
Quincy	76,929	301	3.9	1,397	19.1	1035	13.5	301	3.9
Revere	35,319	213	6.0	478	13.5	377	10.7	176	5.0
Salem	43,472	120	2.8	739	17.0	66	1.5	110	2.5
Somerville	100,773	500	5.0	1,533	15.2	227	2.3	314	3.1
Springfield	149,642	749	5.0	3,686	24.6	1997	13.3	902	6.0
Taunton	37,431	115	3.1	424	11.3	129	3.4	86	2.3
Waltham	40,557	231	5.7	781	19.2	175	4.3	252	6.2
Worcester	190,471	819	4.3	4,050	20.8	619	3.2	656	3.5
TOTAL	2,720,473	15,476	5.7	74,587	27.2	27,370	10.1	19,345	7.1

Table 44

PROBATION FIGURES FOR MASSACHUSETTS, 1920 - 1935

YEAR	PROBATION POPULATION AT END OF YEAR	JUVENILES		ADULTS		SUCCESSFUL CASES FILED OR DISCHARGED		CASES PLACED ON PROBATION	EXPENDITURES	
		Boys	Girls	Men	Women	Number	Percentage		Total Cost of Probation Service	Per Capita Cost
1920	13,925	2572	318	9,299	1736	14,263	54.37	18,209	$311,636	$22.30
1921	16,182	2684	303	11,326	1842	15,654	82.4	23,845	339,890	21.00
1922	16,472	2284	289	12,176	1723	16,924		28,177	345,319	20.90
1923	17,838	2365	272	13,446	1755	19,552	83.4	29,767	367,206	20.60
1924	17,562	2415	314	14,925	1908	18,906	80.7	33,544	384,447	19.60
1925	19,215	2678	307	14,254	1976	19,208		32,881	430,545	22.50
1926	19,702	2803	392	14,575	1932	20,559	79.2	30,934	474,438	24.10
1927	19,735	2822	344	14,469	2100	21,496	80.3	31,368	498,171	25.30
1928	21,145	*	*	*	*	21,694	85.7	33,163	536,794	25.50
1929	20,676	*	*	*	*	23,791	84.7	32,809	590,016	28.60
1930	22,444	3462	419	16,535	2028	23,130	82.5	34,304	614,480	27.40
1931	24,347	3383	465	18,249	2250	26,031	85.8	34,922	664,758	27.40
1932	24,638	3004	504	18,963	2167	26,483	85.8	33,981	679,819	27.62
1933	26,066	3172	381	20,532	1981	19,181	71.6	32,009	632,978	24.28
1934	26,948	3289	356	21,397	1906	22,409	76.8	34,880	609,909	22.63
1935	26,097	3129	416	20,650	1902	23,792	77.2	35,218	693,195	26.56

*Figures not given separately

discharged." The years 1931 and 1932 seem to have been the most successful (85.8 per cent of the probation cases were "filed or discharged"). The ratio of the number sentenced to the number placed on probation has been slowly rising over the past few years. At present, the ratio is approximately one person sentenced to every two placed on probation.

Probation cannot be applied in all cases, but it is especially applicable to family desertion, non-support, and certain forms of crime against property. These represent the largest proportion of crimes. The above-mentioned table shows per capita cost of probation, yearly from 1920 to 1935, obtained by dividing the number of probationers at the end of each year by the total cost of the probation service for that year. The per capita cost of probation is only a small fraction of the cost of keeping offenders in institutions.

Parole

Parole is given by a Board of Parole, created in 1919, as a division of the Department of Correction. Table 45 shows parole statistics for Massachusetts from 1922 to 1935. A tentative idea of the value and success of parole may be gained by considering the percentage of permits revoked. In 1930, 32.3 per cent, and, in 1935, 31.96 per cent, of the permits were revoked, indicating apparently that 67.7 per cent and 68.04 per cent, respectively, were successful. These figures cannot be taken at their face value, for many of the released prisoners cannot be traced, and the figures issued by the institutions are based only upon the information at hand.

Many meetings for the discussion of parole work are held each year throughout the State; 417 such meetings were held in 1935.

The great weakness in the parole system of Massachusetts is the lack of a sufficient number of parole officers to supervise properly the paroled. In 1935, the thirteen parole officers, covering the entire Commonwealth, had an average of 158 paroled persons. The number which may be supervised by one officer should be limited by statute, as is done in some other States; in New York, the limit is 75, and in New Jersey, 50.

Social Status of Prisoners

Table 46 shows the social status of prisoners sentenced to county and State penal institutions, from 1920 to 1935. "Social Status" includes the number and percentage of recidivists, married persons, native-born, foreign-born, and illiterates.

Table 45

PAROLE STATISTICS FOR MASSACHUSETTS

1922 - 1935

YEAR	NUMBER OF CASES CONSIDERED EACH YEAR				UNDER ACTIVE PAROLE SUPERVISION			REVOKED CASES NOT RETURNED			AVERAGE CASE LOAD PER AGENT		NUMBER OF AGENTS	
	Considered for Release	Permits Granted	Per Cent of Cases Granted Permits	Per Cent of Permits Revoked	Total	Males	Females	Total	Males	Females	Total Males	Total Females	Males	Females
1922	2730	2056	75.3	28.7	1045	860	185	378	310	68	149	110	6	2
1923	3081	2415	78.3	21.5	1060	908	152	337	289	48	155	86	6	2
1924	3569	2784	64.3	14.2	1024	909	115	394	350	44	160	70	6	2
1925	3683	3052	82.8	26.0	1078	951	127	435	404	31	151	71	7	2
1926	4223	2943	69.6	28.6	1097	975	122	546	505	41	169	72	7	2
1927	4913	3476	70.7	29.5	1178	1030	148	670	625	45	194	83	7	2
1928	4677	3259	69.6	34.3	1391	1226	165	716	665	51	221	95	7	2
1929	4861	3644	74.9	30.8	1582	1412	170	733	671	62	241	104	7	2
1930	4343	3073	70.7	32.3	1532	1351	181	532	487	45	167	99	9	2
1931	4351	3192	73.0	34.0	1598	1400	198	457	418	39	152	104	12	3
1932	4357	3268	75.6	38.7	1540	1347	193	293	254	39	122	77	13	3
1933	4475	3385	75.6	30.0	1689	1421	268	254	207	47	125	105	13	3
1934	5136	3882	75.6	32.7	2047	1677	370	283	247	36	159	150	12	3
1935	5297	3670	69.23	31.9	2350	2052	288	377	326	51	178	76	12	3

254

Table 46

SOCIAL STATUS OF PRISONERS SENTENCED TO STATE ADULT PENAL INSTITUTIONS AND COUNTY JAILS AND HOUSES OF CORRECTION, 1920-1935

YEAR	TOTAL NUMBER SENTENCED	RECIDIVISTS		MARRIED PERSONS		NATIVITY				ILLITERACY	
		Number	Percentage	Number	Percentage	Native Born	Percentage	Foreign Born	Percentage	Number	Percentage
1920	4,377	2,358	53.9	1532	35.0	2,919	66.7	1458	33.3	424	9.7
1921	7,567	3,890	51.4	2697	35.6	4,863	64.3	2704	35.7	740	9.8
1922	10,745	5,926	55.2	4280	39.2	6,603	61.5	4142	39.5	1064	9.9
1923	11,691	6,305	53.9	4321	41.2	6,996	59.8	4695	40.2	1025	8.8
1924	15,945	8,175	51.3	6285	39.4	9,816	61.6	6129	38.4	1418	8.9
1925	17,429	9,217	52.9	7800	44.8	10,751	61.7	6678	38.3	1098	6.3
1926	17,611	9,673	54.9	7313	41.5	11,067	62.8	6544	37.2	1090	7.2
1927	18,204	10,852	59.6	7823	43.0	11,665	64.1	6539	35.9	1303	7.2
1928	20,059	11,246	56.1	8881	44.3	12,838	64.0	7212	36.0	1050	5.2
1929	18,770	9,774	52.1	8194	43.7	12,298	65.5	6472	34.5	1120	6.0
1930	18,803	10,368	55.1	8163	43.4	12,613	67.1	6190	32.9	941	5.0
1931	19,551	11,201	57.3	8952	45.8	13,464	68.9	6087	31.1	958	4.9
1932	18,476	10,444	56.5	6614	35.8	12,890	69.8	5586	30.2	858	4.6
1933	17,770	10,590	59.6	6580	37.0	13,046	73.4	4724	26.6	661	3.7
1934	19,048	11,217	58.9	7392	38.8	14,024	73.6	5024	26.4	546	2.9
1935	16,591	11,039	66.5	7066	42.6	13,577	81.8	4550	18.2	569	3.4

MASSACHUSETTS STATE PLANNING BOARD

The determination of recidivism has always been a difficult task, because information as to previous commitments is exactly what most offenders wish to conceal. Particular care is now taken, however, in ascertaining the number of repeaters. It is safe to assume that the figures given materially understate the facts. It will be seen that, until 1935, when the figure rose to 66.5 per cent, the percentage of recidivists varied between 50 and 60 per cent.

The percentage of married prisoners gives some indication of their stability in society. According to the statistics shown, the percentage of married prisoners is always less than the percentage of single.

Per Capita Costs of State and County Penal Institutions

Table 47 shows the gross per capita cost of the State and county adult penal institutions and the net per capita cost of the juvenile training schools. Gross per capita cost is the total cost of maintenance of an institution for the year, divided by the average population of that institution during that year. Net per capita cost is the total cost of maintaining the institution minus the receipts of prison industries, rentals, and so forth, divided by the average yearly population.

The most important factor in per capita cost is the average number of inmates. When the population of a penal institution is small, the institution is likely to have a high per capita cost. There has been a net increase in the number of inmates in the State Prison, Concord Reformatory, Reformatory for Women, State Farm, and Jails and Houses of Correction (taken as a whole), from 1920 to 1935, and of the State Prison Colony, from 1928 to 1935, and a corresponding decrease in per capita costs.

Proposed Program of the Department of Correction

The Department of Correction submitted to the State Planning Board a program which the Department would like to accomplish during the next twenty-five years. The suggestions in this program are incorporated herein.

Institution for First Offenders

An institution for first offenders, which could be constructed at a cost of $1,500,000, is urgently needed. All first offenders would be committed there in the future, and first offenders, now placed in other institutions, would be transferred there. The

256

Table 47

ANNUAL PER CAPITA COSTS OF STATE AND COUNTY PENAL INSTITUTIONS*

1920 - 1935

YEAR	STATE PRISON		MASS. REFORMATORY		REFORMATORY FOR WOMEN		STATE PRISON COLONY		STATE FARM		JAILS & HOUSES OF CORRECTION		AVERAGE FOR THREE MASS. TRAINING SCHOOLS	
	Av. No. Inmates	Gross Cost Per Capita	Av. No. Inmates	Gross Cost Per Capita	Av. No. Inmates	Gross Cost Per Capita	Av. No. Inmates	Gross Cost Per Capita	Av. No. Inmates	Gross Cost Per Capita	Av. No. Inmates	Gross Cost Per Capita	Av. No. Inmates	Net Cost Per Capita
1920	501	$599.06	388	$736.14	168	$953.32			1345	$320.32	1016	$952.59	332	$557.
1921	517	562.91	462	566.99	162	987.67			1457	271.01	1305	708.32	353	511.
1922	580	475.53	584	537.80	196	772.49			1663	242.00	1639	568.16	337	501.
1923	627	464.23	486	605.19	193	824.13			1793	239.76	1557	665.94	294	591.
1924	651	434.14	534	601.79	199	769.00			2072	201.27	1935	548.75	329	500.
1925	735	408.42	705	518.02	212	701.04			2213	215.67	2294	530.72	337	512.
1926	852	407.75	312	446.94	227	649.93			2234	216.02	2427	539.12	329	478.
1927	890	416.04	755	513.21	241	673.91			2364	234.48	2348	574.63	361	515.
1928	923	392.82	765	435.33	259	629.85	92	742.81	2517	237.28	2548	576.69	357	498.
1929	925	431.76	840	463.11	289	571.34	118	713.72	2494	258.84	2512	619.92	375	502.
1930	972	483.09	211	477.72	261	575.60	159	672.02	2467	275.23	2478	673.81	367	488.
1931	963	460.33	858	456.23	257	650.63	244	811.57	2507	256.02	2653	601.76	373	468.
1932	892	441.04	993	404.80	295	535.77	358	665.28	2419	264.55	2843	540.35	377	451.
1933	898	406.19	996	393.07	341	482.67	492	547.56	2379	251.26	2982	502.62	371	454.
1934	905	417.85	838	461.86	367	502.36	590	535.31	2450	257.37	3025	502.26	331	473.
1935	889	469.12	935	502.49	357	587.59	735	549.30	2357	239.89	2851	581.65	329	555.

*Source of Information: Annual Reports of the Commissioner of Correction and Annual Reports of Trustees of Massachusetts Training Schools.

State Prison would be abandoned, and all recidivists would be housed at the Concord Reformatory. The State Prison Colony would be used for only the less vicious type of criminal. The erection of this institution for first offenders would render unnecessary a new maximum-security prison, the cost of which would be $5,000,000.

Institution for Criminally Insane

An institution for the criminally insane should be erected at once. Under the provisions of Chapter 421 of the Acts of 1935, the Department of Mental Diseases was ordered to erect, on land controlled by the State Prison Colony, an institution with accommodations for 500 criminally insane persons. The act stipulated that Federal money be used.

Receiving Building

A Receiving Building with accommodations for 300 persons should be erected. The present site of the State Prison could be used for this building. All convicted offenders would be committed here. A centralized bureau in the Receiving Building would make psychological studies, and compile case histories, and so forth, for classification purposes. Each person committed would be under examination for thirty days. The cost of this building would be about $750,000.

Housing Facilities for Officers

A complete survey should be made to determine which penal institutions need modern housing facilities for officers. A preliminary estimate places the cost of providing the necessary facilities, about $1,000,000.

Capital Expenditure Needs at Existing Penal Institutions

The Capital expenditure needs at existing penal institutions have been estimated as follows:

    State Farm, Bridgewater--------------- $ 750,000
    Massachusetts Reformatory, Concord - $ 497,300
    Reformatory for Women, Framingham -- $ 625,000
    State Prison Colony, Norfolk -------- $ 101,500

                            TOTAL $1,973,800

MASSACHUSETTS STATE PLANNING BOARD

Additional Recommendations

1. That a statutory limit, preferably fifty, be placed on the number of paroled persons assigned to each officer.

2. That the Essex and Worcester County Training Schools be closed, in accordance with the recommendations contained in House Bill No. 230, of 1933. Only the Middlesex and Hampden Schools are needed.

RECREATION

Courtesy of Secretary of the Commonwealth

CHAPTER VII

R E C R E A T I O N

PART I - VACATIONAL SHELTER

    A. Public Shelter
    B. Private Shelter

PART II - RECREATION ACTIVITIES

    A. Games
    B. Water Sports
    C. Picnicking
    D. Amusements
    E. Winter Sports
    F. Hiking
    G. Riding
    H. Bicycling
    I. Touring
    J. Recreational Access
    K. Aviation
    L. Scenic Interest
    M. Scientific Interest
    N. Wildlife Interest
    O. Historic and Archeologic Interest

PART III - RECREATION AREAS

    A. State Forests, Parks, and Reservations
    B. Metropolitan Reservations
    C. Municipal Forests and Parks
    D. Quasi-public Reservations

PART IV - SOCIAL ASPECTS

    A. Recreational Organizations
    B. Social Values

PART V - THE RECREATION INDUSTRY

    A. Income from Recreation
    B. Publicity for the Recreation Industry
    C. Trends in Recreation Activities

MASSACHUSETTS STATE PLANNING BOARD

RECREATION

The central theme of a recreation plan is a study of activities. In a state-wide plan, such of these as are ordinarily provided locally, for example, playground games and indoor activities generally, may be passed over. Having determined the appropriate character and degree of participation for each activity, the areas and facilities for it can be effectively planned. In a state-wide plan, those activities, in particular, which are remote from the homes of the people involve a study of overnight shelter. This vacational aspect of recreation is particularly important economically in a state which attracts people from other states.

Primary Objective

The objective of the recreational studies is the preparation of a comprehensive state-wide plan on a two-fold basis:

1. To provide an ample, well-planned, coordinated, well-developed, and diversified program of activities, areas, and facilities, which will operate economically and efficiently to the maximum benefit of the greatest number, preserving the natural attractions as well as providing for intensive recreation.

2. To promote the recreational industry in Massachusetts to the end that this State may enjoy more of the financial benefits that may accrue through such recreation developments and an increased number of tourists.

A Recreation Inventory

Accordingly, the first year of activity has been concerned mainly with the first step in the attainment of this plan, an inventory of the existing activities, areas, and facilities, and a partial analysis of the findings. This inventory records basic data for the determination of the recreational needs of the citizens of Massachusetts and of the people from other states who come here as vacationists, and of the extent to which these needs are fulfilled by existing facilities.

The social importance of recreation to the residents, rather than the economic value, has been stressed principally because there has been insufficient opportunity for an accurate and complete economic survey. However, the economic aspect has not been disregarded and throughout the report its importance has been care-

fully considered, since it entails an important source of income to
the State, its political subdivisions, and its residents. Massachusetts is primarily an industrial State and, as such, houses a dense
population within its boundaries,concentrated in several urban centers. The provision of adequate recreational advantages for these
urban residents is the foremost consideration. The economic phase
of recreation relates primarily only to certain sections of the
State, and thus may receive secondary consideration.

Principal Aspects

The present recreation study has been conducted under five
broad aspects: (1) vacational shelter; (2) State-wide recreational activities; (3) State-wide public recreation areas; (4) social
values; and (5) financial (monetary) values. Of these five aspects,
satisfactory progress has been made on the first four, while the
fifth has received little study,for the reasons previously mentioned. Further information, resulting from the compilation of the
data of research and field surveys, conducted by the State Planning Board WPA Land (Conservation) Field Staff, and covering the
entire State, will be available at a future date. These data, it
is expected, will render present studies more complete, and test
the accuracy of existing research statistics. The present study,
while incomplete, indicates conclusively that further research,
augmented by field surveys, is necessary to complete the necessary
information as to the existing conditions of certain activities,
and particularly as to the economic situation of all activities.
The study has already brought to light some of the weak spots in
the existing recreational developments, but further field study and
research are necessary before any definite comprehensive plan for
future development may be made.

PART I

VACATIONAL SHELTER

An essential factor in a State-wide recreation plan for a State
with such attractions for the vacationist as Massachusetts possesses is the provision of overnight accommodations. The question of
where to go for a vacation is based first on the accommodations that
are available. Therefore, the State should not attempt to promote
itself recreationally without some knowledge of the types and number of shelter accommodations which it has to offer to vacationists,
be they resident or non-resident.Vacational shelters may be classified broadly into two categories: (1) those which are open to the
public and (2) those which are private. Each type may be subdivided into several different classifications. For the purpose of

MASSACHUSETTS STATE PLANNING BOARD

this analysis, a sub-classification of public and private types of shelter has been made as follows:

1. Public

    a. Hotels and private-residence tourist homes

    b. Overnight tourist cabins

    c. Campgrounds, tent and trailer sites, and open shelters and cabins on public land

2. Private

    a. Juvenile and adult camps

    b. Youth hostels

    c. Clubs

    d. Dwellings used for vacation only (rented or owned houses, cottages, and camps)

A brief discussion of each type follows, with all pertinent data obtained. Table 48 is a resumé of the statistical data relative to vacational shelters by counties, while Map 75-4 shows the capacity distribution.

Data on Vacational Shelter Not Complete

It must be borne in mind that the present tabulations relative to shelter facilities are probably not more than 75 per cent complete, owing to the lack of sources of information, and to the lack of cooperation of certain city and town officials, who would not give information as to hotels, tourist homes, and other forms of shelter, unless the law specified that they should. The results obtained, however, are sufficient to prove that Massachusetts may easily house a large vacation population. Nevertheless, the conclusions may be drawn, with safety, that additional shelter accommodations, to fulfill the ever increasing demand, are warranted.

Public Shelter

Hotels, Boarding Houses, and Private-Residence Tourist Homes

These three types of vacational shelter provide a majority of the accommodations in Massachusetts. They are well distributed

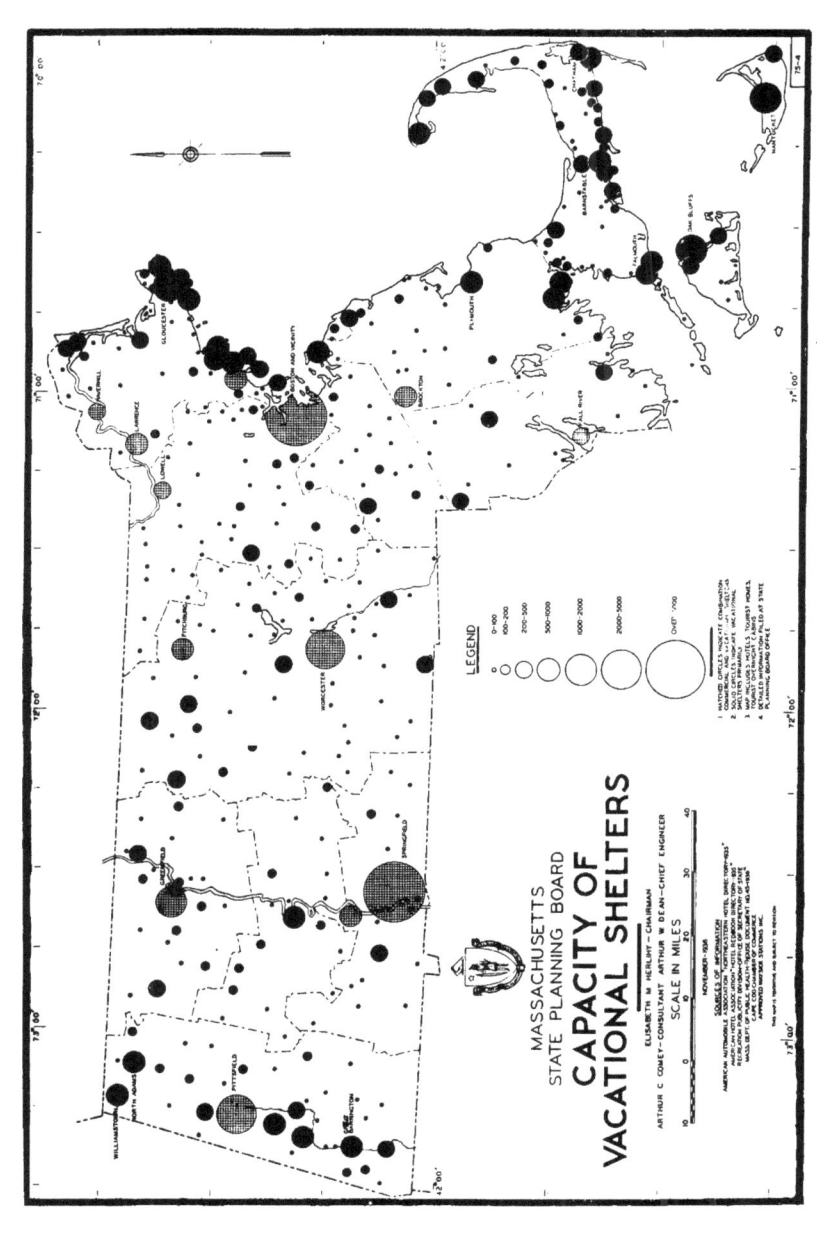

Table 48

REPORTED NUMBER OF PEOPLE WHO CAN BE SERVED BY
VACATIONAL SHELTERS IN MASSACHUSETTS, 1936.

COUNTY	HOTELS	PRIVATE-RESIDENCE TOURIST HOMES	OVERNIGHT TOURIST CABINS	CAMPGROUNDS			CAMPS			YOUTH HOSTELS	TOTAL ACCOMMODATIONS
				Camp-grounds	Tent & Trailer Sites	Cabins & Open Shelters	Juvenile	Adult			
Barnstable	6080	1065	1519	-	-	-	2292	-	-	10956
Berkshire	6306	840	714	250	246	42	2684	-	50	11132
Bristol	1508	21	252	-	-	-	472	59	-	2322
Dukes	2289	6	-	-	-	-	67	-	-	2342
Essex	10114	480	854	25	-	-	258	133	-	11864
Franklin	1878	375	398	125	474	12	90	30	184	3566
Hampden	5925	144	271	125	216	3	760	-	10	7454
Hampshire	1422	261	112	25	33	-	470	-	80	2403
Middlesex	4348	267	459	50	48	15	1125	214	20	6546
Nantucket	1400	46	-	-	-	-	-	-	-	1446
Norfolk	4256	69	114	-	-	-	629	529	20	5627
Plymouth	4226	393	365	100	135	15	1220	243	-	6697
Suffolk	18751	33	-	-	-	-	100	50	-	18934
Worcester	6634	466	484	75	96	12	1338	270	40	9415
TOTALS	75527	4466	5552	775	1248	99	11505	1528	404	101104

over the State, but naturally show more concentration in the few prominent vacational centers, such as Cape Cod, Northeastern Massachusetts, and the Berkshire Hills. Hotels are more permanent institutions than are the other types, and the number of available accommodations in the hotels varies less from year to year. What percentage of the available accommodations, of the types we are considering, should be classed as vacational or recreational is difficult to determine and, as no information was available on this point, total available accommodations have been used. Table 49 sets forth, by counties, the findings of the shelter survey relative to these types. While the survey covered all sources available, it is at best incomplete. Further data will be available, it is hoped, from the State Planning Board WPA Staff Field Survey. The results obtained present a definite indication, however, of the extent of these types of shelter. They show that Massachusetts has some 1400 units, with over 50,000 rooms, and with accommodations for approximately 80,000 people.

Hotel Accommodations. The figures for hotel accommodations are equally impressive. The 903 hotels reported offer approximately 47,000 rooms, and accommodations for 75,000 people. It appears that Massachusetts is well favored with hotel accommodations, and has adequate facilities.

Private-Residence Tourist Homes. Private-residence tourist homes, primarily used for overnight or week-end shelter, are numerous in Massachusetts. The survey disclosed 497 tourist homes, providing approximately 2800 rooms, and accommodations for 4500 people. This type of shelter has increased rapidly during the last few years because it is convenient and inexpensive for tourists, and provides an additional source of income to residents. The number operating and, consequently, the number of accommodations offered are extremely variable. Residents open their homes one year, and not the next. Thus, any data obtained are an approximation, at best, and will not be reliable for any length of time. Massachusetts has numerous, but not enough, tourist home accommodations, especially in the primarily vacation centers, if the 1936 season may be used as an indication. It is believed that additional homes could be opened to vacationists, to advantage, and local civic organizations might well foster their growth, under appropriate safeguards.

Overnight Cabins

Overnight cabins provide a form of shelter which is inexpensive, convenient, and popular with the motoring public. These cabins are well distributed throughout the State, primarily on major

Table 49
CAPACITY OF HOTELS, BOARDING HOUSES, AND TOURIST HOMES IN MASSACHUSETTS

COUNTY	HOTELS			TOURIST HOMES-BOARDING HOUSES			TOTAL PERSONS ACCOMMODATED IN COUNTY
	Approximate Number			Approximate Number			
	Hotels	Rooms	Persons Accommodated	Houses	Rooms	Persons Accommodated	
Barnstable	125	3988	6080	121	683	1065	7145
Berkshire	110	4114	6306	68	529	840	7146
Bristol	22	995	1508	4	13	21	1529
Dukes	36	1472	2269	1	4	6	2275
Essex	135	6574	10,114	55	303	480	10,594
Franklin	33	1246	1878	46	228	375	2253
Hampden	49	4193	6325	20	90	144	6469
Hampshire	32	941	1422	28	167	261	1683
Middlesex	59	2094	4348	32	167	267	4622
Nantucket	20	929	1400	7	28	46	1446
Norfolk	39	1534	4266	7	46	69	4335
Plymouth	88	2799	4226	48	262	393	4619
Suffolk	61	12,407	18,751	2	22	33	18,784
Worcester	94	4170	6634	58	251	466	7100
TOTALS	903	47,453	75,527	497	2793	4466	80,000

MASSACHUSETTS STATE PLANNING BOARD

highways and in groups of from one to twenty, the average being about twelve cabins to a site. Table 50 presents statistics on this type of shelter. Data were obtained from an investigation made jointly by the Departments of Public Safety and Public Health, during 1935, and incorporated in Senate Document No. 45, 1936. This study disclosed 368 sites in Massachusetts, with a total of 1990 cabins, furnishing accommodations for 5552 persons. From these figures, it is readily seen that overnight cabins are an important factor in the vacational-shelter field.

There is ample room for expansion of this type of facility in the vacation regions and elsewhere, but any new cabins should be strictly regulated to assure satisfactory types which will produce lasting benefits.

Water Supply and Sanitation. Because of doubts as to the quality of water supplies and sewage-disposal facilities at overnight cabins, there is some question whether they are liabilities or assets to the State, and to the health and well-being of the people using them. The investigation by the Departments of Public Safety and Public Health showed that 15.5 per cent of the cabin colonies were served by unsafe water supplies; 19.2 per cent, with questionable water supplies; and 65.3 per cent, with safe water supplies. Of the total, 20.4 per cent had sewage-disposal arrangements which endangered their water supplies; 4.6 per cent had sewage-disposal facilities which were unsatisfactory in other respects; and 75 per cent had a satisfactory means of sewage disposal. The large percentages of cabin colonies with questionable water supplies or unsatisfactory sewage disposal facilities demonstrate that some adequate control over the operation of overnight cabins should be exercised, to prevent the possible occurrence and spread of contagious diseases. Such control should be exercised by the local health boards. Effective control would assure better accommodations, assist in the permanent growth of patronage, and make the cabins assets to the communities and to the State.

Campgrounds, Tent and Trailer Sites, and Open Shelters and Cabins on Public Land

Campgrounds, providing tent and trailer sites and open shelters and cabins, supply accommodations for more than 2000 people in Massachusetts. These types of vacational shelter are popular because they afford opportunities to "rough it", are inexpensive, and afford more peace and quiet than do the usual summer resorts. Since the number of people who enjoy "roughing it" is limited,

Table 50*

OVERNIGHT TOURIST CABINS
IN MASSACHUSETTS

COUNTY	NO. OF SITES	NO. OF CABINS	NO. OF PERSONS ACCOMMODATED
Barnstable	73	461	1519
Berkshire	50	245	714
Bristol	19	97	262
Dukes	-	-	-
Essex	50	288	854
Franklin	27	139	398
Hampden	11	108	271
Hampshire	23	45	112
Middlesex	28	233	459
Nantucket	-	-	-
Norfolk	8	51	114
Plymouth	32	138	365
Suffolk	-	-	-
Worcester	47	185	484
TOTAL	368	1990	5552

*Statistics obtained from Senate Document No. 45, 1936, and from the Massachusetts Department of Public Health.

MASSACHUSETTS STATE PLANNING BOARD

these facilities need not be so extensive as the other types. The survey took into consideration only campgrounds situated on State and certain quasi-public recreational lands, and therefore is only a partial indication of the extent of the accommodations available. There are numerous other campgrounds throughout the State with tent and trailer sites and cabins, which would possibly increase the total several hundred per cent. A few of these are on municipal recreational lands, the rest on private lands, and it has been possible to determine but few of these with any degree of accuracy.

Sites Not Well Distributed. The sites reported are poorly distributed, with the majority in the four western counties. The State Department of Conservation, in conjunction with the National Park Service and the CCC is providing additional facilities in some of the less developed State forests and reservations. Table 51 gives the statistics relative to campgrounds in Massachusetts.

Recommendations. With the increasing use of tents and trailers by vacationists, it is highly desirable for Massachusetts to provide facilities comparable to those found in other States. Near every large center of population, there should be adequate campgrounds with tent and trailer sites and cabins and open shelters for transients or residents. It is expected that private operators will provide adequate overnight accommodations in most sections of the State, but, in addition to these, and not competing directly with them, it is recommended that the Department of Conservation develop more extensive campgrounds on State forests and reservations in central, southern, and southeastern Massachusetts, and on Cape Cod.

Private Shelter

Juvenile and Adult Camps

The first private summer camp in Massachusetts was "Camp Harvard", established at Stow in 1882 by William Ford Nichols. Ten years later, "Camp Idlewild" was established at Silver Lake, Wilmington, by John M. Dick of Yale University. "Camp Becket-in-the-Berkshires", a Y.M.C.A. camp, established in 1903, was the first organization camp established in Massachusetts. These older camps were for boys. The pioneer camp for girls was "Camp Quanset", established in 1905 at Orleans. In 1930, there were about 180 camps in Massachusetts. Owing to the economic situation prevailing throughout the country, there has been little increase since then.

Number, Distribution, and Capacity of Camps. The 1935 records show approximately 211 camps. The distribution of these camps,

Table 51

PUBLIC CAMPGROUNDS, TENT AND TRAILER SITES, AND CABINS AND OPEN SHELTERS IN MASSACHUSETTS

COUNTY	CAMPGROUNDS		TENT AND TRAILER SITES		CABINS AND OPEN SHELTERS		TOTAL CAPACITY IN PERSONS
	Number	Capacity in Persons	Number	Capacity in Persons	Number	Capacity in Persons	
Barnstable	-	-	-	-	-	-	-
Berkshire	10	250	82	246	14	42	538
Bristol	-	-	-	-	-	-	-
Dukes	-	-	-	-	-	-	-
Essex	1	25	-	-	-	-	25
Franklin	5	125	158	474	4	12	611
Hampden	5	125	72	216	1	3	344
Hampshire	1	25	11	33	-	-	58
Middlesex	2	50	16	48	5	15	113
Nantucket	-	-	-	-	-	-	-
Norfolk	-	-	-	-	-	-	-
Plymouth	4	100	45	135	5	15	250
Suffolk	-	-	-	-	-	-	-
Worcester	3	75	32	96	4	12	183
TOTALS	31	775	416	1248	33	99	2122

their classification, and their capacities are presented on Table 52 and on Map 75-1.

The metropolitan Boston region is well represented by organization and charitable camps, maintained by social welfare agencies and settlement houses. Private camps and the camps of national organizations have tended to establish themselves in the wilder summer-resort areas, such as the Cape, the central lake region of Massachusetts, and the Berkshire Hills.

The survey disclosed that 89.1 per cent of the camps in the State are intended primarily for juveniles, while 10.9 per cent for adults. Organization support 56.4 per cent of the camps, while 43.6 per cent are private. Barnstable County has the largest number of camps (forty) but Berkshire County can accommodate the largest number of persons in camps (2684 persons).

Massachusetts camps accommodate, at one time, approximately 13,000 juvenile and adult campers. Assuming each camp accommodation serves two different persons each season, Massachusetts camps annually provide for over 25,000 campers, making the State a leader in this phase of recreation.

Youth Hostels

A new form of vacational or recreational shelter in Massachusetts to the youth hostel, conducted under the auspices of American Youth Hostel, Inc.

Purpose. The purpose of the organization is "to help all, especially young people, to a greater knowledge, understanding, and love of the world by providing for them youth hostels, bicycle trails, and foot paths in America; and by assisting them here and abroad. Youth hostels are primarily for those who travel by foot or bicycle, who like to live ruggedly and simply, who enjoy cooking their own meals, and who wish to or must travel economically. The age limits are 4 to 94."

In Massachusetts, there are already 22 hostels, with an approximate capacity of 404 persons. Table 53 sets forth youth hostel statistics by counties. Each hostel is required to furnish accommodations for at least five girls and five boys, but many have a larger capacity. To use these facilities, one has to be a member of the American International Conference. In Massachusetts, the membership is over 500, at the present time, and is increasing rapidly each year. Fees for accommodations and supplies are very reasonable.

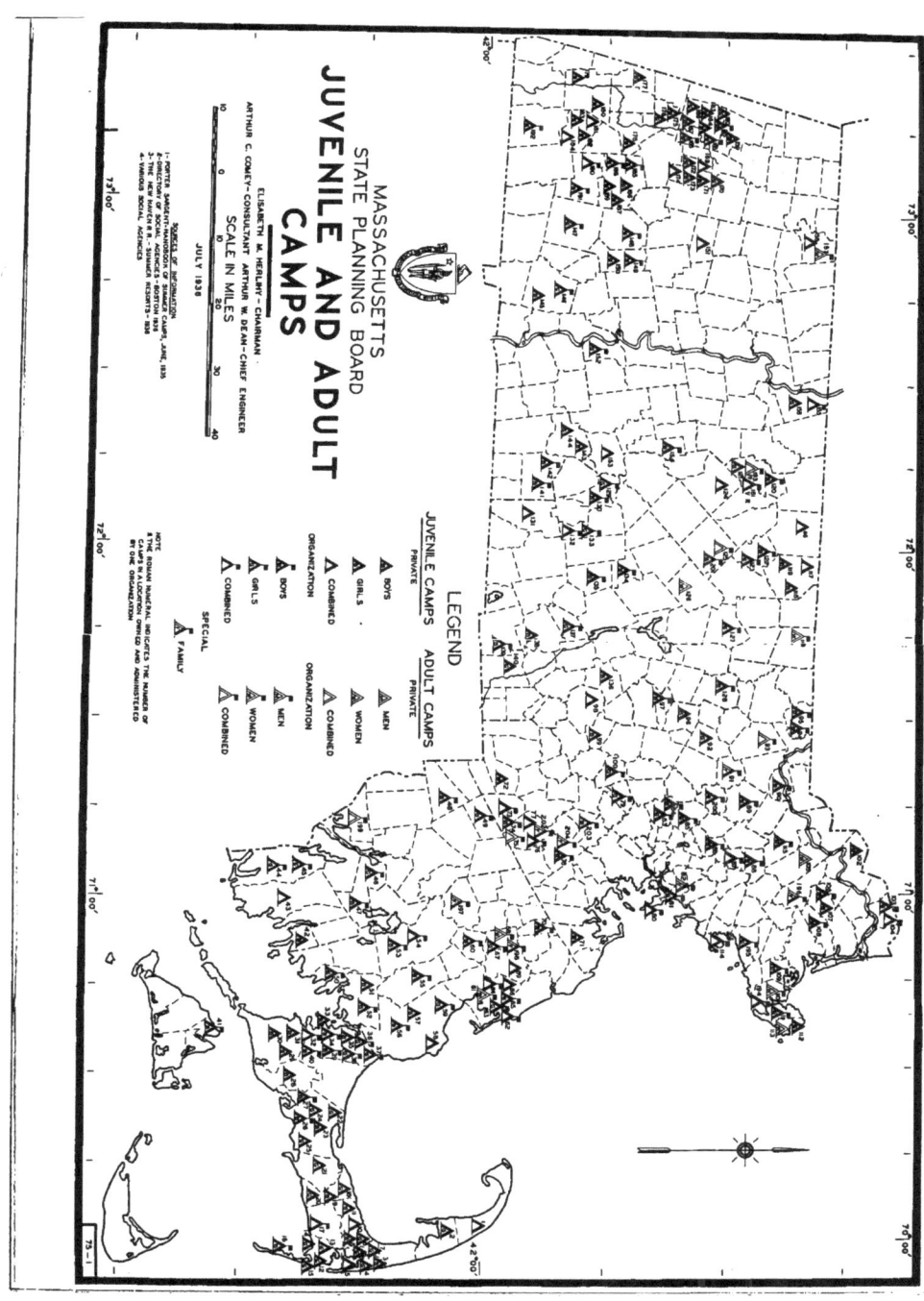

Table 52
JUVENILE AND ADULT CAMPS
IN MASSACHUSETTS

COUNTY	TOTAL NUMBER CAMPS	NUMBER JUVENILE CAMPS	PERSONS* ACCOMMODATED JUVENILE CAMPS	NUMBER ADULT CAMPS	PERSONS* ACCOMMODATED ADULT CAMPS	TOTAL NUMBER PERSONS* ACCOMMODATED
Barnstable	40	40	2292	--	--	2292
Berkshire	33	33	2684	--	--	2684
Bristol	9	8	472	1	59	531
Dukes	1	1	67	--	--	67
Essex	17	13	258	4	133	391
Franklin	4	3	90	1	30	120
Hampden	8	8	760	--	--	760
Hampshire	6	6	470	--	--	470
Middlesex	20	17	1125	3	214	1339
Nantucket	--	--	--	--	--	--
Norfolk	11	8	629	3	529	1158
Plymouth	24	20	1220	4	243	1463
Suffolk	3	2	100	1	50	150
Worcester	35	29	1338	6	270	1608
TOTAL	211	188	11505	23	1528	13033

*Figures are approximate only

Table 53

YOUTH HOSTELS IN MASSACHUSETTS

COUNTY	NUMBER OF HOSTELS	LISTED ACCOMMODATIONS		ESTIMATED ACCOMMODATIONS		TOTAL ACCOMMODATIONS
		Boys	Girls	Boys	Girls	
Barnstable						
Berkshire	5			25	25	50
Bristol						
Dukes						
Essex						
Franklin	6	82	82	10	10	184
Hampden	1			5	5	10
Hampshire	2	40	40			80
Middlesex	2			10	10	20
Nantucket						
Norfolk	2			10	10	20
Plymouth						
Suffolk						
Worcester	4			20	20	40
TOTALS	22	122	122	80	80	404

MASSACHUSETTS STATE PLANNING BOARD

Extent of Use. The average length of stay is from one to three nights. Since the start of the organization in Massachusetts in 1935, there have been some 9000 overnight accommodations furnished by the hostels, and the 1936 season has seen a great advance in their use. The hostels in Massachusetts are open during the winter to furnish inexpensive accommodations for hostelers who enjoy winter sports. At the Northfield hostel, during the first three winter months of 1935-36, 1100 overnight accommodations were provided, thus showing that the use is an all-season one.

Clubs

Clubs providing recreational shelter include golf clubs that have sleeping rooms, private sporting, vacation, and other clubs. Data on the shelter facilities of clubs can be obtained only by a field study. The present field-survey forces were unable to investigate this phase. It was felt that a questionnaire would bring in such meager information that no definite conclusions could be drawn. Clubs are not particularly important in the provision of recreational shelter since they cater only to members and their guests, and these include only a small fraction of the seekers of vacational shelter.

Vacation Houses, Cottages, and Farms

This phase of shelter is, without question, great in number and capacity. Many thousands of dwellings throughout the State are used primarily for recreational purposes, and for only short periods of time. The WPA Field Survey Staff has had neither time nor personnel to investigate vacation houses. Data are difficult to secure. About the only possible method is to contact the proper local officials (Selectmen or Clerks) and to examine the town assessment records, in conjunction with these officials. This involves a lengthy field survey, impossible at the present time. However, this method or, as a second and last choice, a questionnaire, should eventually be resorted to, as this information is needed in developing a program of utilizing all of Massachusetts' recreational resources to the best advantage.

Vacation Farms. Abandoned farms, or farms for sale for vacation homes deserve special mention. The utilization of these farms for recreational purposes has been fostered elsewhere in New England with gratifying results. In Massachusetts, the Department of Agriculture Bulletin: "Massachusetts Farms for Sale - 1936" lists some 350 farms situated in all sections of the State, ranging in size from 5 to 300 acres, usually well-developed and readily accessible to major transportation routes. The utilization of these

MASSACHUSETTS STATE PLANNING BOARD

farms, if the proper publicity and other methods of inducement are developed, might well be the means of building up certain parts of Massachusetts, both recreationally and agriculturally. It is a matter well worth the attention of the Recreation Publicity Division of the Secretary of State's office, with whom the State Planning Board will gladly cooperate.

PART II

RECREATION ACTIVITIES

Recreation comprises a wide variety of activities and interests. These may be grouped, according to participation in them, as active or passive (for example, playing games, on the one hand, and contemplation of scenery, on the other), or according to the degree of concentration of use, whether intensive or extensive (for example, bathing, on the one hand, and hiking, on the other).

For the purposes of the State planning program, recreation activities have been arranged according to a classification covering certain elements of each of these approaches with a view to facilitating an understanding of the factors involved, as given below.

There are many minor activities, such as archery, skeet shooting, and figure skating, which have not been included in the recreation survey. These activities attract comparatively small and specialized groups. They usually require only small areas and few facilities.

1. Games
    a. Golf
    b. Baseball, Tennis, and Other Local Activities
2. Water Sports
    a. Boating
    b. Bathing
3. Picnicking
4. Amusements
    a. Fairgrounds
    b. Racetracks
    c. Amusement Parks
5. Winter Sports
    a. Skiing
    b. Skating, Tobogganing, and Snowshoeing
6. Hiking
7. Riding

MASSACHUSETTS STATE PLANNING BOARD

    8. Bicycling
    9. Touring
  10. Access
  11. Aviation
  12. Scenic Interest
  13. Scientific Interest
      a. Geologic
      b. Botanic
  14. Wildlife Interest
      a. Bird Sanctuaries
      b. Hunting
      c. Fishing
  15. Historic and Archeologic Interest

These headings, with one or two exceptions, are self-explanatory. Games, water sports, picnicking, amusements, and winter sports constitute those activities, intensive in character, which in general, are concentrated within the limits of recreational areas. Hiking, riding, and bicycling comprise those activities, extensive in character, which may transcend the boundaries of recreational areas, and often connect one area to another. Access does not, of course, primarily supply an element of recreation, itself, but constitutes a means of reaching a recreation spot. It should not be confused with touring, which is a recreational activity in itself, the points reached being more or less incidental to the pleasure in the tour. Scenic, scientific, historic, and wildlife interest, with the exception of hunting and fishing, comprise those activities which are passive in character, with the degree of participation limited to contemplation of natural scenery or historic objects.

While the activities are the main theme of the following paragraphs, some discussion of the areas and facilities is necessarily included, particularly under the headings of amusements and wildlife interest. It must be realized that the study of activities is incomplete, and that further research is essential.

Games

Golf

Golf is one of the oldest and most popular of recreational activities. Massachusetts had the first golf club in America, the Country Club, of Brookline, founded in 1882. Massachusetts is bountifully supplied with fine courses well distributed throughout the State. On Cape Cod, the adjacent islands of Nantucket and

MASSACHUSETTS STATE PLANNING BOARD

Marthas Vineyard, and the several other ocean-front cities and towns, are many courses overlooking the sea. The eastern and central portions of the State provide numerous sporty courses on typical rolling or more variable topography. The courses of western Massachusetts or the Berkshire Hills have a setting of rugged hills and valleys.

Distributed throughout the State are approximately 215 courses, varying in size from 6 to 36 holes. The majority of these courses are open to the general public. Tournament and special matches, both amateur and professional, held during the golfing season on representative courses, serve as added attractions.

Classification of Courses. For the purpose of the present study, golf courses were classified into three categories:

1. Private courses-open; guests welcome at fee.
2. Private courses-restricted; guests welcome under restrictions.
3. Public courses-guests welcome at fee (municipal-or State-owned).

Of the total number of courses in Massachusetts, 40 per cent are private courses open to the public for a fee; 44.2 per cent are restricted private courses; 9.8 per cent are public courses. Of the total number of cities and towns in the State, 41.2 per cent have courses, while 58.8 per cent have none. A statistical analysis of golf courses in Massachusetts is presented in Table 64. (See also Map 75-3.)

Baseball, Tennis, and Other Local Activities

Baseball. Baseball, the American sport of sports, is fully as popular in Massachusetts as in other States. Complete statistics on the number of baseball fields in the State will be available when the Staff Project Field Survey data are received. However, the 1934 and 1935 municipal recreation surveys for Massachusetts, prepared by the National Recreation Association, show that 57 Massachusetts cities and towns have a total of 350 baseball fields. The selected cities and towns, of widely varied population, are well distributed throughout the State.

Baseball is primarily a local recreation problem and, as such, needs little actual development or planning by the State. However, the State might provide criterea for minimum standards and assist, where possible, in the attaining of those minimum standards.

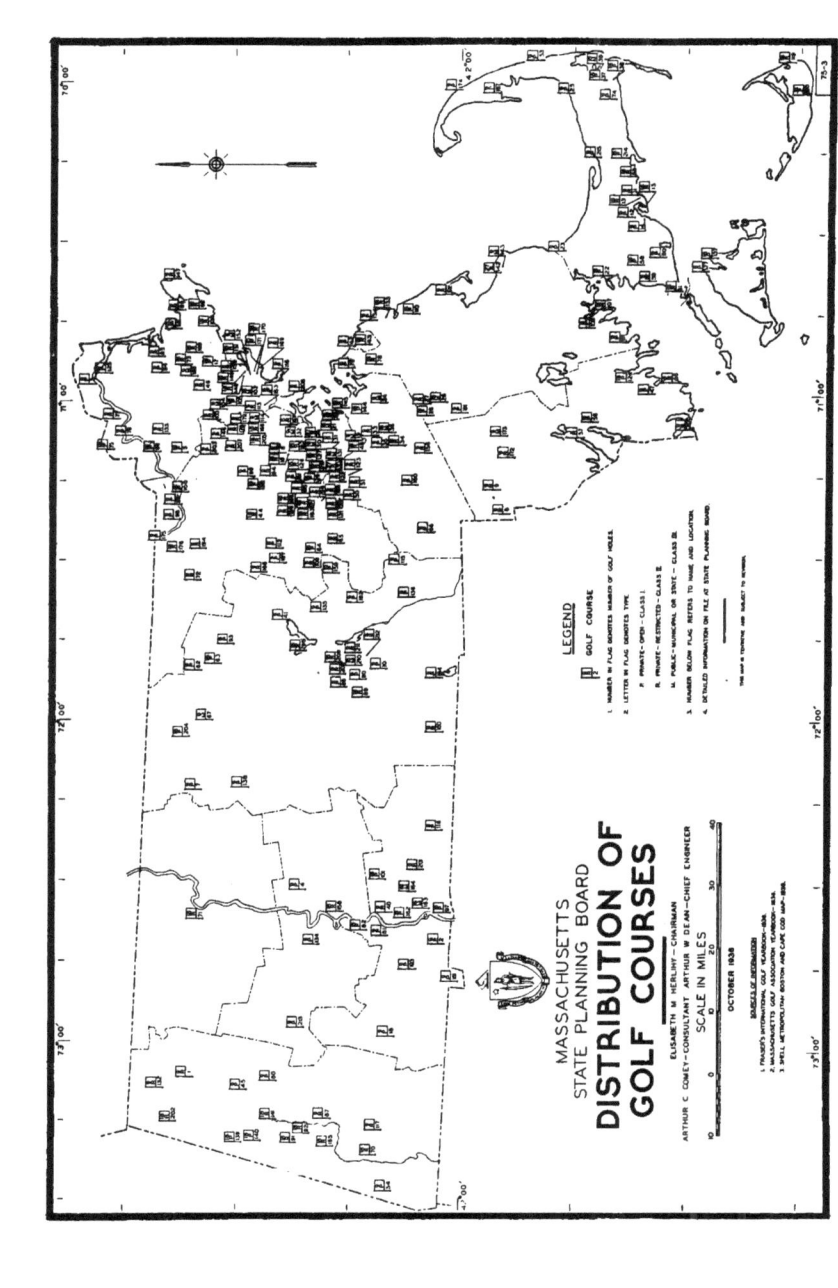

Table 54

CLASSIFICATION OF GOLF COURSES IN MASSACHUSETTS

COUNTY	CLASS I - PRIVATE - OPEN				CLASS II - PRIVATE - RESTRICTED					CLASS III - PUBLIC			COUNTY TOTALS
	No. of Holes				No. of Holes					No. of Holes			
	9	10	18	Total	6	9	18	27	36	Total	9	18	Total	
Barnstable	11		4	15		1	5			6		1	1	22
Berkshire	3		2	5		3	5			8				13
Bristol	3		1	4		5				5	1		1	10
Dukes	1		1	2										2
Essex	7	1	5	13		10	7		1	18	3	1	4	35
Franklin							1			1				1
Hampden	5		4	9		2				2		2	2	13
Hampshire	3		1	4			1			1				5
Middlesex	10		3	13	1	15	12	1		29	2	1	3	45
Nantucket			1	1		1	1			1				2
Norfolk	4		1	5		7	5	1		13	1	1	2	20
Plymouth	7		2	9		2	3	1		6	1	1	2	17
Suffolk	1			1							1	2	3	4
Worcester	13	2	3	18		3	2			5	2	1	3	26
TOTALS	68	3	28	99	1	48	42	3	1	95	11	10	21	215

Tennis. In Massachusetts are many hundreds of tennis courts, established under a variety of governmental, quasi-public, and private agencies. Complete statistics on the number of courts are not available, and no intensive research has been carried on, since the provision of such facilities is more a local-community than State problem. The National Recreation Association Annual Survey volumes for 1934 and 1935 show that a total of 57 cities and towns have 450 tennis courts. Tennis courts are provided as part of the recreational development of the Myles Standish State Forest in Plymouth, and on certain Metropolitan District Commission reservations. Therefore, it is evident that, while the problem is chiefly local in character, some State-wide aspects are involved.

Many courts available for public use for a fee, at specified times, are under the administration of colleges, private schools, and private organizations. From a cursory study, Massachusetts seems to have adequate facilities in certain sections, but should have a more complete quota in others. The Department of Conservation and other commissions empowered with care and development of State recreation lands should provide an adequate number of tennis courts to serve the demand that exists where any intensive development attracts large numbers from near-by centers of population.

Every city and town in Massachusetts should have minimum standards for all recreational facilities, including tennis courts, and where they do not now exist, definite plans should be made for attaining them.

A coördinating committee, composed of representatives from the State Planning Board, National Recreation Association, and others, might well be established to conduct a survey of all local recreation facilities, to fix desirable minimum standards, and to assist local authorities to attain these standards.

Water Sports

Boating

Under the general title of boating occur a variety of activities such as yachting, canoeing, and rowboating.

Yachting. Massachusetts nautical history is a tradition, and her hundreds of miles of coastline offer untold opportunity for yachting. Large fleets of yachts and boats annually dot Massachusetts waters, engaging in races, regattas, and general cruising.

National and international yachting competitions take place off her shores. As becomes such a nautically-minded State, Massachusetts is well represented by yacht and boat clubs, not only on coastal waters, but on the many inland lakes and rivers.

In Massachusetts, there are approximately one hundred and thirty yacht and boat clubs (which include motorboat and dory clubs), distributed among the nine eastern and southern counties. In the central and western part of the State, there are four such clubs, the primary interest of which is undoubtedly motor or speed boating. Table 55 and Map 75-2 show the distribution of these facilities, by counties. These yacht and boat clubs are quite evenly distributed along the coast, with the major concentration in Essex County on the north shore, Suffolk County on the central shore, and Barnstable County on the south shore. Essex and Barnstable Counties serve primarily the non-resident yachtsman, while Suffolk County serves the resident yachtsman. There are clubs representative of all classes of people. Growth in the number of yacht and boat clubs should result from the efforts of private individuals or agencies, but Massachusetts may well publicize her advantages to the end that non-residents establish Massachusetts as their base of operations. Such publicity should be carried on by the Recreation Publicity Division of the Secretary of State's office, the local Chambers of Commerce, and civic organizations.

Canoeing. Canoe trips in Massachusetts are many, and varied as to type and length. Most of the trips offer distinct natural scenic beauty and ample opportunity for camping out-of-doors overnight during the trip. The following information concerning canoeing trips is based on the booklet, "Quick Water and Smooth," by John C. Phillips and Thomas D. Cabot, members of the Appalachian Mountain Club. Of the trips recorded, those set forth by Map 75-2 comprise a selected list which were most highly recommended and which offer primarily smooth-water canoeing and attractive natural scenic beauty. The map does not purport to contain a complete recording of possible canoe trips in Massachusetts. Ample opportunity exists on many other streams for seasonal canoeing or for fast-water canoeing.

Canoes are available on nearly all the larger lakes and ponds and along many of the rivers, at very reasonable cost. Any growth in the facilities must necessarily be accomplished through the efforts of private organizations or agencies, except that the State and local public organizations may well publicize the existing favorable opportunities.

Canoe clubs in Massachusetts probably exist in large numbers, but such research as has been possible has divulged only eight such clubs, all located in or near Metropolitan Boston. Table 55 and Map 75-2 show the distribution of such clubs, by counties. Many interesting regattas are held each season, by these clubs, and they are very active in furthering interest in canoeing.

Boating in General. Rowboating in Massachusetts is an activity for which there exist sufficient opportunities and facilities. The many lakes, ponds, and rivers provide ample space. On the majority of water bodies boats may be rented at small cost. Table 55 presents a partial list, by counties, of the number of water bodies on which boats are available. Unless specifically prohibited by local or State regulations, all great ponds in Massachusetts are available for boating purposes.

Other forms of boating in which considerable interest is shown are skulling, kayaking, and motorboating (particularly outboard). Groups in various parts of the State foster these activities. Any further growth should be dependent on local boating clubs or organizations, with some publicizing, by the proper State Department, of the opportunities Massachusetts affords.

Most of the Massachusetts rivers should be further developed and protected for boating and other water sports. However, before any such development is planned, comprehensive surveys, such as have recently been made by the Staff Project in Berkshire County, should be conducted. These surveys will determine the extent of pollution and debris that must be eliminated, the possibilities for developing campgrounds and other facilities for canoeists, the most favorable locations for water sports and swimming, and the extent of landscaping necessary to reclaim the distinctive vistas. From the results of these surveys, a comprehensive program for the development of our inland waterways for boating and other water sports should be formulated.

Bathing

Ocean Beaches. One of the most valuable assets of the Commonwealth is its ocean front, of which there are over 1000 miles, but to only a small mileage of which the public has right of access, as the shore frontage is owned only to a limited extent by the State, by cities, and by towns. Private owners control a major portion of the shore. Many towns which have acquired and have developed ocean shores have restricted their use to their own residents. With a population of over four million people, and a transient population of approximately three million people annually, Massachusetts has not yet fully realized her obligation to her

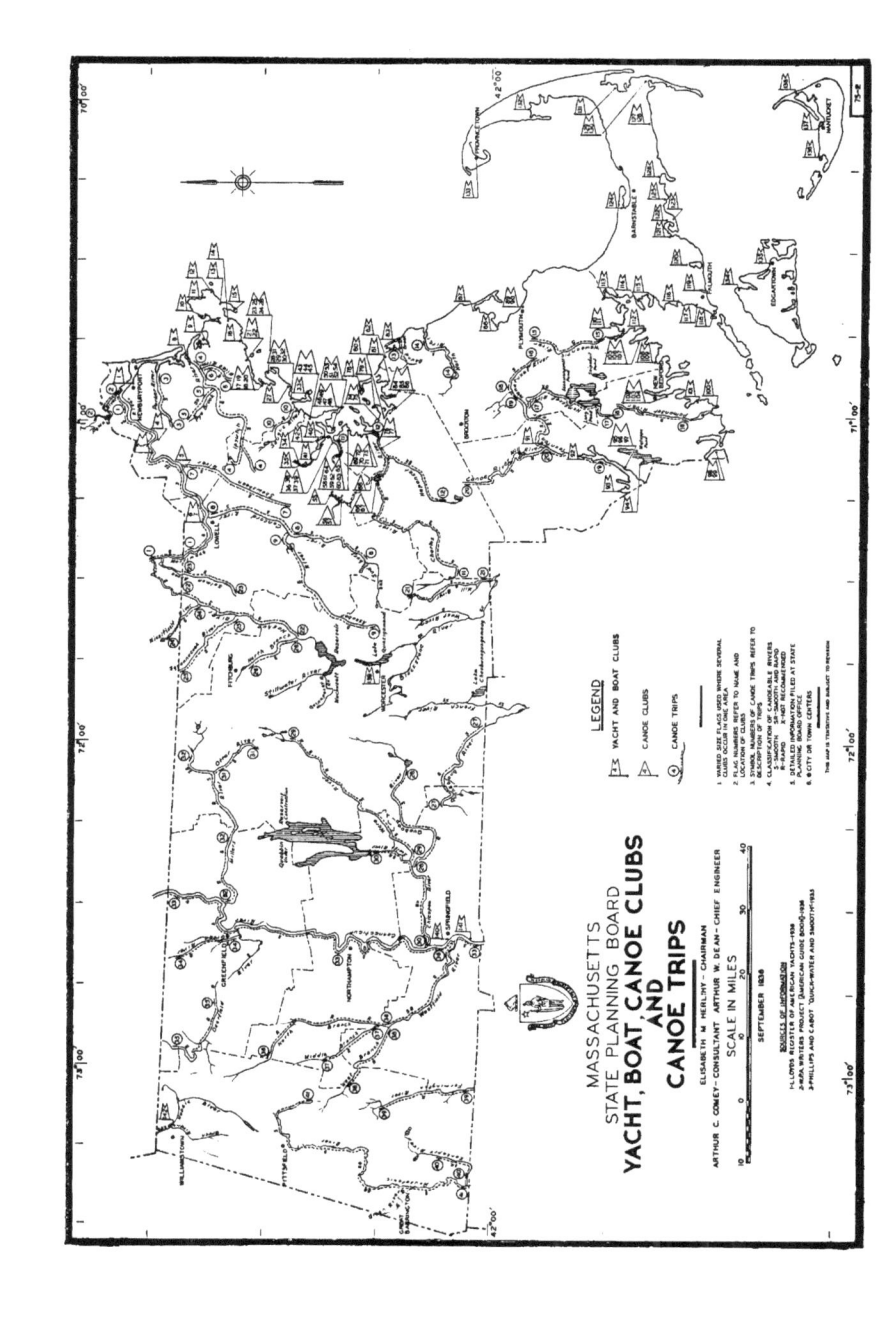

Table 55

YACHT, BOAT, AND CANOE CLUBS, CANOE TRIPS,
AND BOAT LIVERIES IN MASSACHUSETTS

COUNTY	YACHT AND BOAT CLUBS	CANOE CLUBS	BOAT LIVERIES			Canoe Trips
			No. Towns Supplies	No. of Water Bodies	Number of Liveries	
Barnstable	21		10	19	22	-
Berkshire	1		17	22	36	4
Bristol	14		11	12	19	5
Dukes	2		-	-	-	-
Essex	30	1	19	23	25	8
Franklin	-		5	5	5	3
Hampden	2		11	18	36	3
Hampshire	-		10	12	15	-
Middlesex	9	3	27	37	42	3
Nantucket	3		-	-	-	-
Norfolk	9	2	14	16	24	3
Plymouth	14		13	23	32	2
Suffolk	28	1	1	1	1	-
Worcester	1		35	56	71	10
TOTAL	134	8	174	244	343	41

MASSACHUSETTS STATE PLANNING BOARD

citizens, and the potentialities of these shores. True, the State has acquired and is developing Salisbury Beach; also, the Metropolitan District Commission has acquired five ocean and seven inland beaches and provided accompanying facilities; yet these shore reservations are far from adequate to serve the existing and potential demands. It must be realized that the centers of population are many, and that Metropolitan Boston alone houses nearly one-half the total population of the State.

State-owned beach reservations are necessary and should be acquired as rapidly as possible:

1. To relieve other beaches, both State and local, of the heavy burden which they are now called upon to bear, but for which they are inadequate.
2. To lessen the difficulties local governments face in maintaining local-resident restrictions on their local beaches.
3. To lessen the amount of trespass and destruction of private property by a careless and inconsiderate general public.
4. To fulfil the demand for outdoor recreation activities and facilities of this type, which is steadily becoming greater owing to the increased leisure made possible by modern machinery, changing economic conditions, and the ever-increasing population.
5. To help increase the tourist trade in Massachusetts, thus adding a new source of income to the State, its political sub-divisions, and its citizens.
6. To escape the steadily rising land costs and to secure the sites while they are available, making possible the development of the sites as fast as they are needed.
7. To furnish employment to many people in the development of the reservations.

The acquisition of ocean-beach reservations has been studied many times in years past. In 1924, a Joint Special Committee was appointed by the Governor to investigate the question of the establishment of public reservations, particularly ocean-beach reservations, for recreational purposes. In 1925, this Committee, reporting the results of its investigation (House Document 1080), cited the need of more beach properties. It recommended further study by an unpaid commission. Such a Commission was set up (Chap. 26, Resolves of 1925) consisting of the Commissioners of Public Works, Public Safety, Public Health, and Conservation. Its findings were reported to the Legislature in 1926 (Senate Document 25, 1926). It recommended that the towns acquire, develop, and maintain beach reservations, with the State assisting (by developing roads, primarily), and that the State should not acquire or develop such reservations unless the towns failed to do so. It further stated that by statute (Chap. 45, General Laws) the towns were legally entitled to establish such reservations, as the town of Scituate had done in the establishment of Peggory Beach. As a result of this investigation, an attempt was made to stimulate the acquisition of beaches by the passage of a law (Chap. 387, Acts of 1926) authorizing towns to petition the County Commissioners to lay out reservations within their town. To date no town, so far as is known, has taken advantage of this statute.

In 1927, Governor Alvan T. Fuller appointed "The Governor's Committee on Needs and Uses of Open Spaces" to investigate and determine the needs of Massachusetts relative to State forests, parks, and reservations. This survey resulted, in 1929, in the presentation of a plan of existing and proposed open spaces for the Commonwealth. Among the proposals were several highly recommended beach sites, further evidence and recognition of the need of State acquisition of ocean beaches. In accordance with House Order 1222 of 1923, a special "Salisbury Beach and Duxbury Beach Reservations Commission" was appointed by the Governor to report on the advisability of these two sites for public beaches. The Commission reported in 1929 (House Document 1011), and advocated the acquisition of both sites. Some years later, the Salisbury Beach Reservation was acquired.

Many investigations have been made since, and annually bills are submitted to the Legislature either for acquisition of beaches or for further investigation of possible sites. In 1935, the then Commissioner of Conservation, Samuel A. York, in his "Massachusetts Plan", stressed the necessity of acquiring ocean beaches, and advances six specific sites that should be obtained by 1940. The 1936 Legislature has also shown interest in this subject by providing for a further beach investigation.*

Thus, over a period of ten years, the acquisition of ocean beaches has been advocated, many investigations carried on, and as a direct result of it all, Salisbury Beach has been acquired and is being developed. This is only a beginning. Several additional beach reservations are needed.

There are now eight State-owned ocean beaches: one administered by the Department of Conservation; one in charge of the De-

---

*An investigation relative to the acquisition and maintenance of Horse Neck Beach in the town of Westport as a state reservation (Resolve No. 52, 1936; House Document 1000, 1936).

MASSACHUSETTS STATE PLANNING BOARD

partment of Public Works; and six controlled by the Metropolitan District Commission. Salisbury Beach serves the Merrimack Valley region; and the beach at Provincetown is far from centers of population, while the other six beaches inadequately serve the Metropolitan Boston region. (See Map 55-1.)

The needs of the population from both the larger cities and small communities throughout the State may be met by providing a system of State-owned beaches, spaced at intervals of approximately twenty-five miles, supplementing the existing State and local beaches, and relieving their overcrowded condition.

Technically, a sea beach consists of that strip of land between mean-high water and mean-low water. It has been the general practice to include some upland, as the use of the beach without such upland is manifestly impossible, at least for recreation purposes. Thus, in the discussion of each proposed beach, the addition of upland area is taken into consideration.

For the purpose of the study, the proposed system of beaches has been arranged in a suggested general order of priority of acquisition, as follows:

1. Duxbury Beach-Duxbury
   (Alternatives, White Horse and Long Beaches-Plymouth)
2. Wingaersheek Beach-Gloucester
3. Horse Neck (Westport) Beach-Westport
4. Cape Cod Beaches in addition to Provincetown(Province Land) Beach already owned by the State, at least three beaches from the sites available, herein listed in order of apparent suitability
   (a) Preferred list:
      1. Poponesset Beach-Mashpee
      2. Scusset Beach-Bourne
      3. Harding Beach-Chatham
   (b) Alternatives:
      1. Monomoy Beach-Chatham
      2. Nauset Beach-Orleans and Eastham
      3. Sandy Neck Beach-Barnstable

Duxbury Beach is a six-mile sand spit located in Duxbury and Marshfield in Plymouth County. The proposed beach reservation* is

*Massachusetts House Document 1011, January 1929, "Report of the Joint Special Recess Commission(known as the Salisbury Beach and Duxbury Beach Reservation Commission) established to consider the maintaining of ample spaces for the public at Salisbury Beach and at Duxbury Beach".

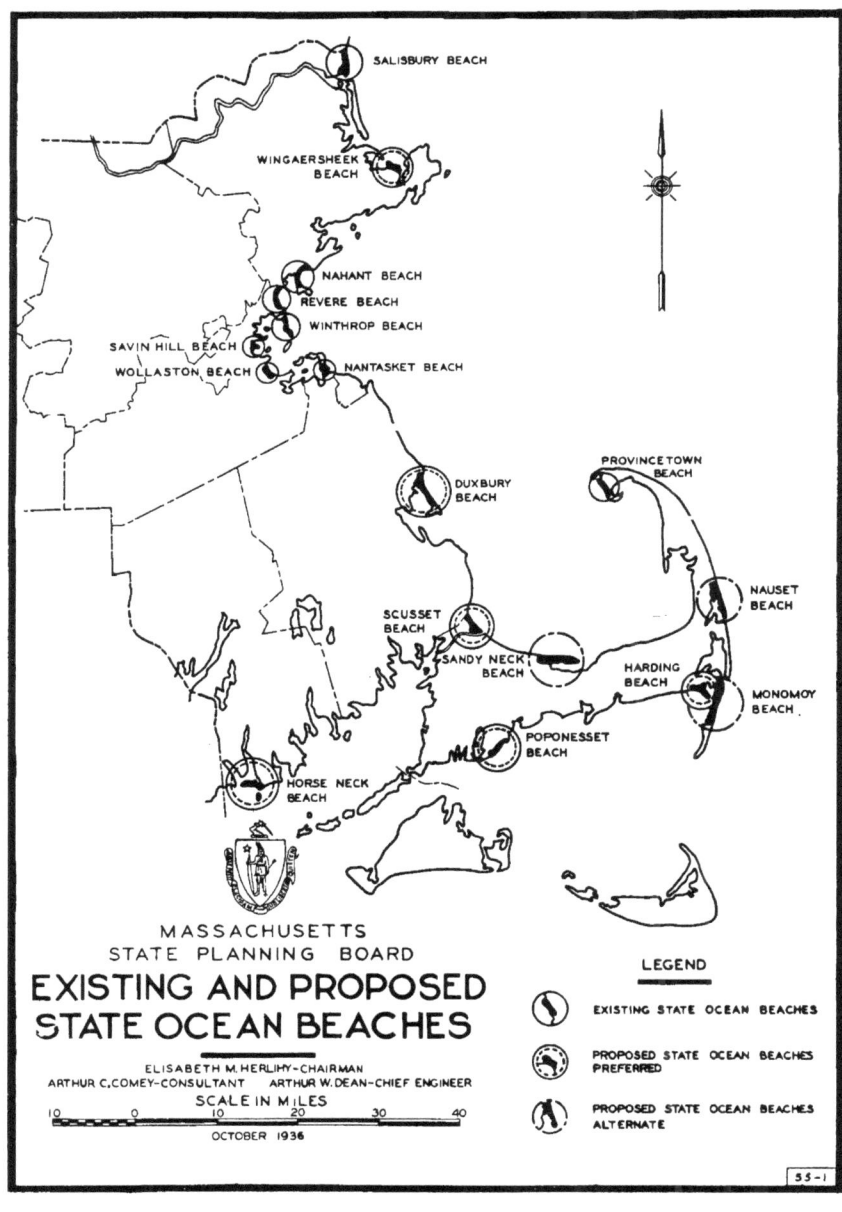

MASSACHUSETTS STATE PLANNING BOARD

a tract of about 782 acres of beach and salt meadow, of which 730 acres lie in Duxbury, and the balance, a narrow strip, in Marshfield. Approximately 242 acres are covered with sparse grass and some small scrub growth. The remainder is salt marsh and meadow, submerged by high-course tides. At the northern end is a low drumlin, about 30 feet high, covered with scrub growth, called the "Hummock". On the southern end is a range of high sand dunes called Plum Hills. The balance of the beach varies between 6 and 10 feet above high water, with an average width of 100 yards at low water. At high tide, the beach ridge is 25 to 30 yards from the water line. An outstanding feature is the fact that high-tide bathing may be enjoyed in either the ocean or the warmer waters of Duxbury Bay, as the average width of beach between high water lines is only 100 yards. The topography and shape of the proposed reservation give a maximum amount of unexcelled beach for bathing and recreational purposes for a minimum taking.

While the beach itself is not a particularly stable location for permanent improvements, there is ample space on the marsh behind it, which could be filled in, a little at a time, as needed. There are two approaches to the beach at present, neither of which is really good nor would serve any great concentration of people. The first approach, at the northern end of the beach near the United States cable station, is from State Route 3A at Green Harbor, about two miles. This leaves the people to the land end of the peninsula, with parking facilities for 700 to 1000 cars. The second approach, farther south, is through the Powder Point summer residential section of Duxbury, over the half-mile wooden Powder Point Bridge, at the end of which is a small parking space intended primarily for residents. There is no road over the four-mile stretch south to Gurnet Light. These two approaches, with no road to connect them, give the public an opportunity to use but a small portion of this beach. A new approach from Route 3A could easily be laid out, and would form the terminal section of the long-projected Bay Circuit, giving adequate and attractive access from the interior cities. On the bay-side (west), Beach Channel provides a good approach to the shore, for boats, and offers excellent facilities for the future development of this proposed beach section for various water activities.

This proposed beach reservation is owned by the Duxbury Beach Associates, and, as far as is known, the public has never been denied the use of it. There are about thirty houses, the light station at Gurnet Light, and a few buildings at the northern end, including the United States cable station.

MASSACHUSETTS STATE PLANNING BOARD

Duxbury Beach would serve as a public bathing beach for:

1. Brockton, with a population of 62,407
2. Whitman, " " " " 7,591
3. Rockland, " " " " 7,890
4. Taunton, " " " " 37,431
5. The majority of Plymouth, Eastern Bristol, and Southern Norfolk Counties.
6. Less frequent patronage from Metropolitan Boston and the rest of the State.

Wingaersheek or Coffin's Beach is located to the west of the mouth of the Annisquam River in Gloucester, Essex County. It comprises approximately 1000 acres, including beach, upland, and salt-marsh. There are about 1 1/2 miles of ocean shore with an additional 1/2 mile of bathing beach on the river side. The beach has apparently been stable over a long period of years. There is sufficient adjacent upland for intensive recreational activities and facilities. There is no undertow at this beach, due to its sheltered location and gradual slope for several hundred feet, even at low tide. The beach is composed of an extremely fine white sand, and is entirely unspoiled.

The beach is located within about two miles of the projected extension of Route 128, which extends around Boston and through the middle of the Cape Ann peninsula to West Gloucester. At present, the last mile or two of beach approach is over narrow woods and marshland roads from surfaced town roads. These roads are being reconditioned by the State under the "Farm-to-Market" roads project. However, there is need for a more suitable entrance road to the beach.

The property, with the exception of a few sections, is owned by one family, and public use is forbidden, except for the small area at the east end owned and operated by the City of Gloucester. This site has been offered to the State. Action should be taken before private interests intervene and make acquisition too expensive or entirely impossible. The former Commissioner of Conservation, Mr. Samuel A. York, stated* that, in the opinion of the Department of Conservation, Wingaersheek is one of the two beaches most desirable for acquisition by the Commonwealth. Its need is second only to an acquisition on the south shore, but it might be considered first, owing to the favorable opportunity for purchase.

---

*Letter of November 12, 1935 to Miss Elisabeth M. Herlihy, Chairman, State Planning Board.

MASSACHUSETTS STATE PLANNING BOARD

Wingaersheek Beach would afford relief to smaller beaches in the vicinity, as well as partial relief to the crowded metropolitan beaches north of Boston. It would serve the tributary area of central and northern Essex County, a large portion of northeastern and central Middlesex County, and, for less frequent patronage, the rest of the Metropolitan District and the State in general.

Horse Neck (Westport) Beach is a most suitable site for an ocean beach, as will be discovered from a brief study of the southwestern region of the Massachusetts shore. There are no other beaches with sufficient length and area to provide efficiently the necessary bathing-beach facilities and intensive recreation development in this southwestern section.

Horse Neck Beach is located in the extreme southeastern section of the town of Westport, in Bristol County. It is a tract of about 850 acres, with two and three-quarters miles of shore, located at the mouth of the Westport River. The area consists of beach, dunes (a part of which are covered with pine growth), and marshland. There is access by road at both the eastern and western ends. At the western end, the approach is by a paved road to within a short distance of the beach, and thence by cart path over cinders and sand along the northern shore. From the eastern end, the beach is reached by a surfaced road along the northern shore and by two surfaced roads extending from the beach marshland south to the ocean beach. Inadequate parking spaces are provided, at fee, on private land, or free, on a narrow public road.

Horse Neck Beach has been partly pre-empted already by the general public, certain portions of the beach being rather intensively developed by private owners. The ownership of the land is primarily in large tracts, which makes acquisition a relatively easy problem. In view of the existing development, certain portions are deemed unsuited for acquisition.

At present, the beach is used by nearly 40,000 people on a peak-load summer Sunday. The tributary area served consists of New Bedford, Fall River, and adjacent towns in both Massachusetts and Rhode Island. The dunes, which have been platted for subdivision, are used for picnicking. The beach needs more adequate accommodations, as well as suitable restrictions. The property should be secured in advance of further private developments. It is now owned by a small group, mostly non-resident locally. Horse Neck Beach, with proper development for bathing and intensive recreation, would serve:

MASSACHUSETTS STATE PLANNING BOARD

    1. Bristol County
       (a) Fall River, with a population of 117,414
       (b) New Bedford, "   "   "   " 110,022
       (c) Taunton,   "   ".   "   " 37,431
       (d) Attleboro,   " . "   "   " 21,835
    2. Southwestern Plymouth County
    3. Southeastern Rhode Island

On the basis of the present extensive use of this beach, the revenue accruing to the State (if the beach were State-owned) might easily be sufficient to make the beach self-sustaining.

Gooseberry Neck, a 100-acre island at the southeastern tip of Horse Neck Beach, accessible by means of a jetty, should be included in the acquisition. It is a barren moor, in private ownership, open to the sweep of the sea, and at present used as a picnic ground for the overflow from the beach, at a fee. The area should be preserved for picnicking and enjoyment of the ocean view, as an adjunct of Horse Neck Beach, at no fee.

Poponesset Beach (one of the preferred Cape Cod beaches) is situated in the extreme southern part of the town of Mashpee, in Barnstable County. The site comprises about five miles of shore and approximately 4000 acres of beach, upland, and marshland. The entire area, with the exception of the beach proper, is well wooded with pine and oak growth, which is ideal for picnic and camp grounds. There is sufficient upland for all types of recreational development. The beach is good-grade sand with little gravel and few stones, with the exception of a strip four to six feet in width between high and low water levels. This element is now detrimental, but, undoubtedly, might be overcome by a system of jetties. The water, typical of the south side of the Cape, is warm, as a rule. There is no extreme amount of erosion or shifting of sand. The varied topography is ideal for an extensive beach development. There are several moderately high bluffs and low-lying level areas, all of which are wooded and ideal for camping and picnicking.

Access to the beach is secured by means of a road leading directly off the southerly side of Route 28, two and one-half miles southwest of Santuit, and approximately midway between Falmouth and Hyannis. The beach is located about five miles from this State route. This access road is paved for the first two and one-half miles, the remainder being a wide dirt road. This dirt road parallels the beach for some two to three miles northeasterly.

The beach and adjacent lands are under one ownership, so far as is known. At present, the area is being operated, on a small scale, as a private commercial enterprise, at reasonable fees. There are a small store, to serve tent and trailer campers, and several small cottages, which are rented. The area is well-patronized, primarily by tent and trailer campers and Sunday bathing and picnicking parties. This site is the Cape beach most highly recommended. It would serve the largest number of people readily, and should be easy and inexpensive to develop, while providing the most favorable topography for all recreational activities. It should be acquired as soon as possible, with the development following as needed. The beach, with the necessary accompanying facilities, should prove self-sustaining. Its development would in no way disturb existing residential developments on the south side of the Cape.

While this beach would have the Cape and southeastern Massachusetts for a natural tributary area, it would also serve other sections of the State, since it could readily provide excellent facilities for week-end trips. In addition to sites for tents and trailers, many cabins or small cottages might easily be provided, thus enlarging the use and tributary area as well as the income to the State.

Scusset Beach is located in the Sagamore section of the town of Bourne, in Barnstable County, and extends from the Cape Cod Canal northwesterly to the Bourne-Plymouth town boundary. The beach is approximately one and one-half miles long. The tract comprises about 700 acres, including beach, dunes, upland, and marshland. There is little upland adjacent to the beach except at the northwesterly end, which, with the exception of a small section, is given over to a summer residential development. However, there is sufficient upland to provide space for buildings and other necessary appurtenances. There are many acres of dunes and marshland. It is possible that these marshlands might be filled in conjunction with the dredging of the Cape Cod Canal, which would provide additional area suitable for development. Across the marshes some distance to the east of the beach, the land rises sharply, thus providing extensive upland, which is sparsely developed at present. The disadvantage to this land is its distance from the beach proper, and the lack of access to it.

The beach can be reached from Route 3, about three miles north of the Sagamore-Canal Bridge. The access road is paved, for the most part, is three to four miles long, and passes through a good summer-cottage development. It would be desirable to provide another access route which would be more direct and would carry the traffic around the summer-cottage colony. A new access road could be built from Route 3 directly to the northern extremity of the beach.

MASSACHUSETTS STATE PLANNING BOARD

The beach is covered with gravel and stones, a condition which it is possible to alleviate by proper jetties and filling. Sufficient land could be obtained for the necessary accompanying facilities, such as bathhouses, parking areas, and space for recreational activities. Campgrounds and picnic sites might be provided, thus attracting people from a larger area. The site would serve eastern Bristol, southern Plymouth, and western Barnstable counties, in addition to Sunday and week-end bathing and picnicking parties from all sections of the State. It would provide an alternative beach for those not desiring to travel the additional twenty to twenty-five miles to Poponesset Beach. Early acquisition is desirable.

Harding Beach is located at Stage Harbor, West Chatham, in Barnstable County. There are about two miles of shore, with nearly 400 acres of beach, upland, and saltmarsh. In general, the land is undeveloped, although there are a few houses at the northwestern end of the site. The area is zoned for general residence at present. The northwestern upland, well-wooded, rises higher than fifty feet. The northeastern side of the beach, abutting Oyster Creek, is primarily low-lying saltmarsh. Thus, the site provides all of the prerequisites of an ideal beach development, with sufficient upland for structures, recreational activities, and parking. On the creek side, facilities for boating and water sports might easily be developed.

At present, an unimproved dirt road leading directly from Route 28, one mile east of the junction of Routes 28 and 137, provides the only approach. However, the location of the beach is so close to the junction of these two State routes that a suitable approach can easily be developed, making it thereby readily accessible from all sections of the Cape. The present unimproved access road extends to the southeastern tip of the peninsula, a distance of approximately two and one-half miles from Route 28. If improved, it would make the entire area accessible by automobile.

While this beach is situated near the southeasterly tip of the Cape, it is a desirable unit in the proposed system. It would adequately serve the resident and non-resident population of Barnstable County, as well as the many Sunday and week-end tourists, thus relieving other local beaches of much of their out-of-town patronage.

The land is owned, in large tracts, by local residents, which should simplify the problem of acquisition. The present undeveloped condition should further facilitate the acquisition. Serious consideration should be given to the procuring of this site within a few years, before extensive private developments or intervention prevent State Acquisition.

Since, for various reasons, one or more of the preferred Cape Cod beaches may not be possible, a supplementary list of alternate sites has been included in this report. This supplementary list consists of those beaches which offer certain of the necessary prerequisites, but, in general, because of their location or lack of sufficient upland for structures and recreational activities, become secondary in value, and should be acquired only if the others are unobtainable. The following brief discussion of these beach sites sets forth their principal characteristics.

Monomoy Beach lies on Monomoy Island, an eight-mile sand bar in the southeastern section of Chatham, in Barnstable County, extending into Nantucket Sound. The island consists of approximately 2500 acres of barren sand dunes and salt marshes, the former subject to erosion and extensive shifting. At the northern end, two sections rising to a maximum height of perhaps forty feet might be used for structures, parking spaces, and so forth, if, upon further investigation, the land is proven stable. The site is used primarily for gunning stands and blinds, and should entail no complex problems of acquisition.

The Island is not conveniently accessible. Two unimproved roads, leading from Route 28, provide access to the northern end, but the rest of the island is inaccessible by automobile, except by driving over the sands as the tides permit. Owing to the unstable conditions, it might be inadvisable to attempt to construct roads. Thus, this location is less favorable, and should be acquired only in the event of failure to obtain others.

Nauset Beach is a six-mile beach located in the towns of Orleans and Eastham, in Barnstable County. Three miles of the beach are in the form of a sand spit, extending to the mouth of Nauset Harbor. The site has an area of approximately 1200 acres composed of beach, dunes, salt marsh, and upland. At the northern end of the beach, there is sufficient upland, in an undeveloped condition, for structures and other appurtenances. A paved road just north of the center of North Eastham and a short stretch of unimproved road south of this center provide access from Route 6 to the beach, located approximately two and one-half miles to the east. These access roads provide approaches to the Nauset Beach Light section and to the northern end of the peninsula.

This beach would be similar in character to Harding Beach in that it would serve the Barnstable County region, primarily, but would involve traveling a longer distance and would be closer to the present State-owned but undeveloped beach at Provincetown. Therefore, this beach assumes secondary importance as an alternative choice.

Sandy Neck Beach is a six-mile strip in the northwestern section of the town of Barnstable, in Barnstable County. It comprises approximately 3000 acres of beach, sand dunes, and marshland. The beach, from the Sandwich-Barnstable town boundary to the eastern tip, has an average maximum height of a little over 100 feet above mean-high tide, with sand dunes varying in width from one-quarter to one-half mile. There is little upland other than the dunes, except at the western end, which is covered with scrub oak and pine. The beach is gravelly, a detrimental factor which may be overcome by pumping on a considerable quantity of sand. There are few developments here, and the land is, for the most part, held in large parcels by private individuals, which should facilitate acquisition.

Access to this beach from Route 6, one-quarter mile northwest of the Sandwich-Barnstable town line, may be had over a road one mile long, partly paved, partly dirt, leading to a small parking space. It is then necessary to walk approximately one-quarter of a mile to reach the beach proper. More adequate access is needed. The eastern end of the area is accessible only by boat.

It is the opinion of the Trustees of Public Reservations* that the area is best suited for a wildlife sanctuary and scenic reserve. However, it seems more reasonable to acquire and develop the site in accordance with the two-fold purposes of a beach and scenic reserve, at the western end, and a wildlife sanctuary, at the eastern end. The area is of secondary importance as a beach, being an alternative to Scusset Beach, but should be acquired in the near future and used as a wildlife sanctuary unless, or until, needed as a beach, at which time the two uses could take place in segregated sections. Sandy Neck would serve the same tributary area as Scusset Beach, namely Bristol County, southern Plymouth County, and Barnstable County.

Inland Beaches. While this report is devoted principally to a study of ocean beaches, inland beaches merit similar consideration. Because of a limited staff, it has been impossible to investigate inland bathing beaches. The problem is one worthy of investigation, and is State-wide in aspect. A field study is nec-

---

*Annual Report, Trustees of Public Reservations, 1933, p. 34.

essary to determine the available facilities, the needs of the people, and the location of potential sites.

Conclusion. From investigations made it has been ascertained that there are insufficient opportunities for the public use of ocean beaches. The six beach sites, Duxbury, Wingaersheek, Horse Neck, Poponesset, Scusset, and Harding, being situated conveniently to the major centers of population within their respective districts and being approximately equidistant one from another, are considered the most suitable locations for the establishment of State-owned beach reservations for public use and enjoyment.

The demand for, the value of, and the success of State beach reservations are demonstrated by the present extensive use of such sites.

It is the undeniable duty of the State to provide public recreational opportunities which are of State-wide interest and benefit. The authority for the acquisition, development, and maintenance of beach reservations may well be granted to the Department of Conservation, for the purpose of facilitating administrative problems. Not more than five years should be consumed in acquiring the system of six beaches. A Bill, suggested for Legislative enactment to carry out these recommendations, follows:

An Act Providing for the Acquisition by the Commonwealth of Certain Ocean Beaches and the Maintenance thereof as State Reservations

Be it enacted, etc., as follows:

The Commissioner of Conservation, on behalf of the Commonwealth, may acquire by purchase or gift, or may take by eminent domain under Chapter 79 of the General Laws, and thereafter improve and maintain as State reservations the whole or any portion of the properties comprising Duxbury Beach in the towns of Duxbury and Marshfield; Wingaersheek Beach, also known as Coffin's Beach, in the Town of Gloucester; Horse Neck Beach, also known as Westport Beach, in the Town of Westport; Poponesset Beach, in the Town of Mashpee; Scusset Beach, in the Town of Bourne; and Harding Beach, in the Town of Chatham; together with marshes or upland adjacent to any of said beaches. For said purposes there may be expended such sums, not exceeding _____ dollars, as the General Court may from time to time appropriate. Such land shall be acquired before December 1, 1942.

MASSACHUSETTS STATE PLANNING BOARD

Picnicking

Massachusetts is a leader in providing opportunities for picnicking, enjoyed alike by young and old from the first warm spring days of May to the colorful autumnal days of October.

The State forests, which have been considerable expanded both in size and facilities during the past four years, offer the most elaborate and convenient provisions for picnicking. Of the 69 State forests, approximately 39 have one or more developed picnic areas equipped with numerous tables, benches, fireplaces, sanitary facilities, and often additional facilities for camping, such as tent sites, trailer sites, and cabins, as well as facilities for swimming. In the remaining 30 State forests, picnicking is allowed, but there are few or no tables and benches, and fires are prohibited.

There are numerous other opportunities for picnicking in the two State parks, eleven State reservations, eight quasi-public reservations owned by the Trustees of Public Reservations, and fourteen reservations controlled by the Metropolitan District Commission, all of which permit picnicking, in some form, and provide, as a rule, some of the necessary facilities, such as table and benches. Table 56 contains a brief and partial resumé of available information relative to picnic areas and facilities, showing the extent to which Massachusetts has made provision for this activity.

Opportunity for picnicking is not limited to the State-provided facilities heretofore mentioned. Many cities and towns have large parks or lakeside reservations where non-residents, as well as residents, may picnic. Too, there are many commercial picnic grounds, campgrounds, and beaches where, at very reasonable fees, the public may picnic, swim, camp, or just relax. A majority of these facilities for picnicking, distributed throughout the State as shown by Map 75-7, are easily and readily accessible from major highways or improved secondary roads.

Conclusions and Recommendations

1. Massachusetts has a large number of well-developed picnic areas, but they are concentrated in certain sections, not in relation to the centers of population.
2. More adequate picnic sites are needed in the central part of the State, to serve the concentration of population in and about Worcester. More areas are needed to serve the population of the eastern and east-central part of the State, which contains approximately one-half of the total State population.

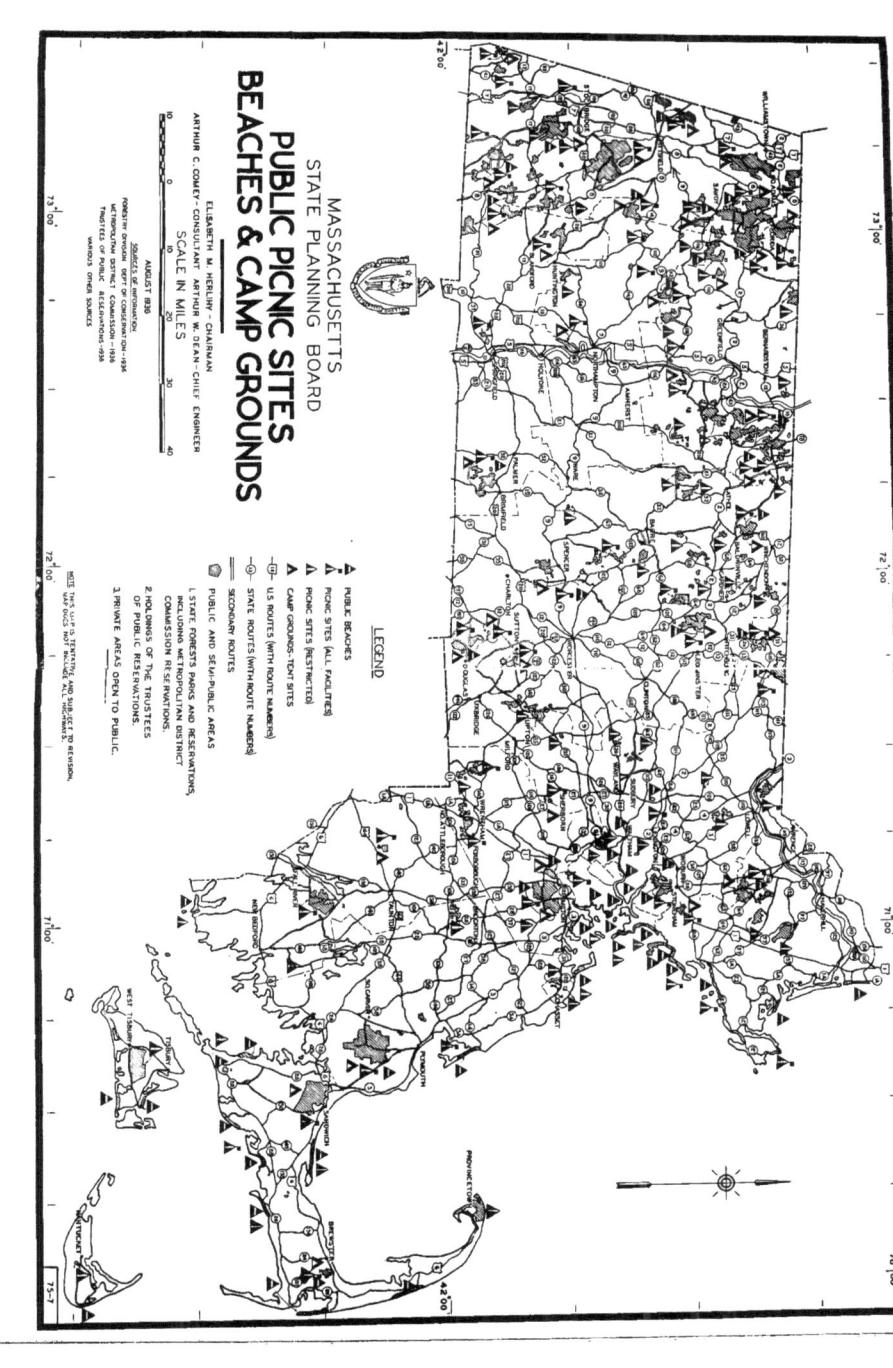

Table 56

PICNIC GROUNDS AND FACILITIES IN MASSACHUSETTS, 1936

TYPE OF AREA	ADMINISTRATION	TOTAL ACREAGE	NUMBER WITH ALL PICNIC FACILITIES	NUMBER WITH PARTIAL FACILITIES	NUMBER OF PICNIC SITES	TABLES	BENCHES	FIREPLACES
State Forests	Department of Conservation	164,596.16	39	30	117	903	72	699
State Parks	Department of Conservation	2,382.37	2	-	5			
State Reservations	Department of Conservation Special Commissioners County Commissioners	13,169.97	9	3	15	73		79
Metropolitan Reservations	Metropolitan District Commission	11,044.53	8	6				
Quasi-Public Reservations	Trustees of Public Reservations	1,177.50	6	2				
TOTAL		192,370.53	64	41	137	976	72	778

3. For the benefit of those who desire to picnic while traveling by automobile, small roadside picnic sites should be developed. As has been the practice in other States, these sites could be developed within the right-of-way of the highway if sufficient land is available. Sites should be chosen for their landscape beauty and convenience in preference to a regular spacing every mile or five miles. They should have such facilities as tables, benches, and a fire place, should be suitable landscaped, and properly marked so that they may be readily located. They will provide a desirable adjunct to the more extensive existing picnic grounds, and meet the needs of the "short-order" picnicker.

Amusements

Fairs

Fairs, in Massachusetts, are institutions of long-standing importance. Each year, fairs are held in various parts of the State from late August until early October. Fairs have great drawing power, are an important source of revenue to the recreation industry, and are an influential factor in the recreational life of at least the rural population.

In 1935, approximately 20 outstanding fairs held throughout the State, attracted an attendance of some 750,000 people. Over 50 per cent of the attendance was at the two major fairs: the Brockton Fair and the Eastern States Exposition. These fairs represent an investment of over $4,000,000. Thus, it is readily seen how important a position fairs and fairgrounds command in the more commercial recreation field. Massachusetts has sufficient fairs, which should continue to be held, and on the same high level.

Racing

Horse and Dog Racing. Horse and dog racing in Massachusetts, under the pari-mutual system of betting, while a form of commercial recreation, must not go unrecognized in the general survey of recreation, primarily because of the financial aspect, which involves the State and every city and town therein. In 1935, the first year of operation of horse and dog racing under the pari-mutual system of betting, four flat running horse tracks, four harness horse tracks, and three dog tracks were licensed. The State received over $115,000 in license and registration fees, and over $1,000,000 in percentages of the pari-mutual betting. Of the net receipts to the State, 75 per cent reverted to the General Fund of the Commonwealth and 25 per cent was returned proportionately to the cities and towns. Table 57 sets forth detailed statistics.

Table 57

HORSE AND DOG RACE TRACK ACTIVITIES IN MASSACHUSETTS, 1935

CLASS	TOTAL NO. OF DAYS	TOTAL ATTENDANCE	AVERAGE DAILY ATTENDANCE	AVERAGE WAGER	STATE REVENUE FROM PARI-MUTUEL HANDLE @ 3 1/2%	STATE REVENUE FROM BREAKS @ 50%	STATE REVENUE FROM ASSOCIATION LICENSE FEES	STATE REVENUE FROM REGISTRATION AND LICENSE FEES	TOTAL STATE REVENUE
Running Horse Meets	73	876,967	10,275	$17.29	$666,007.87	$160,214.95	$70,200	$8,766	$905,188.82
Harness Horse Meets	17	6,165	705	$10.54	$ 3,239.44	$ 925.40	$ 1,475	----	$ 5,639.84
Dog Meets	200	1,252,671	6,401	$12.43	$541,032.70	$117,816.03	$40,000	$ 5,308	$704,156.73
	290	2,135,803	5,760	$13.42	$1,210,280.01	$278,956.38	$111,675	$14,074	$1,614,985.39

Horse and dog racing are important sources of revenue, and increase tremendously any estimate of the total income derived from recreational sources.

In 1935, there was a combined total of 290 days of horse and dog racing, which attracted over two million people, or an average daily attendance of 5760. Massachusetts offers suitable provisions for horse and dog racing, but should exercise due caution in their control, lest they prove detrimental even though they are an important source of revenue.

Auto Racing. In Massachusetts, auto racing is engaged in primarily as amateur competition and as a feature event at certain of the major fairs. For amateur competition for midget cars, two dirt tracks have been built, one at Wayland and one at Marstons Mills on Cape Cod. On these tracks, several races are scheduled during the summer and early fall. All types of cars are used, and the usual length of race is fifty miles. These races attract large crowds, are interesting, exciting, and seldom dangerous. The season of 1936 is the third of competition, and a national association has been formed to foster interest in the sport in other sections. Professional and semi-professional auto racing is limited to the major fairs, at which it is popular and well-received. Except for these latter races, professional auto racing is nonexistent in Massachusetts. Both amateur and professional auto racing are minor recreational activities.

Amusement Parks

Any study of amusements would be incomplete without mention of amusement parks, commercial enterprises that attract thousands of people throughout the summer months. Massachusetts has 24 of these parks distributed principally throughout the central and eastern parts of the State. They usually are located at ocean-beach resorts or next to some inland lake. Indirectly, these commercial enterprises contribute to the recreational income of the State. While amusement parks may be a doubtful asset to the State or to a community, nevertheless, they furnish recreation for certain types and classes of people, and are almost certain to continue their existence. State supervision is necessary to protect the health and morals of the people who are attracted to them.

Winter Sports

Winter sports, especially skiing, have come into their own during the past four years. The untiring interest of the many winter sports, ski, and outing clubs in the construction of trails, in

MASSACHUSETTS STATE PLANNING BOARD

the holding of competitions, and the conducting of publicity; the efforts of private individuals who have constructed special facilities, held meets, and publicized them both for and in the interest of the sport; and, lastly, the Snow Trains have all contributed to the phenomenal growth of interest in winter sports. With the entire State winter-sports conscious, the State Department of Conservation, in cooperation with the National Park Service and the CCC has extended the winter-sports facilities in the State Forests and reservations, and is still developing them to the point where Massachusetts may compete on an equal basis with other winter-sports States.

Climatic conditions and natural topography make certain sections of the State ideal for extensive winter-sports developments. Other regions, while not so favorably endowed, are nevertheless suitable for a certain amount of development. Massachusetts has two major regions which are most favorable for winter sports: the Berkshire Hills and the Wachusett region of central Massachusetts. At the present time, the Berkshire region is the best developed section, but new trails have been constructed in the Wachusett region of central Massachusetts, which now make it a winter-sports center, more favorable located in relation to principal centers of population than are the Berkshires. They need not compete for patronage, however, for they serve different centers of population within the State, and should draw from entirely separate regions outside Massachusetts. In addition to these regions, several smaller centers, under public or private auspices, serve local or special groups. Massachusetts has ample winter-sports facilities in certain sections, but inadequate facilities in many others. The Department of Conservation and the Metropolitan District Commission should establish more facilities on the recreational areas under their control in the central and eastern part of the State, in which one-half of the entire population is concentrated.

Skiing

Skiing, the outstanding winter-sports activity, may be classified into the following main types: (1) Downhill, including "Slalom"; (2) Cross-country, including "langlauf"; and (3) Jumping. Skiing is indulged in, both as a competitive and as a noncompetitive sport. At present, downhill racing enjoys the most prominent vogue. Jumping competitions continue to attract many spectators. But langlauf racing is seldom done. However, recreational skiers far outnumber the racers, on both open slopes and downhill trails. A more limited number enjoy cross-country skiing.

In Massachusetts, there are approximately 75 areas devoted to skiing in its many forms, with many miles of trails and acres of open slopes. Jumps are few in number, only thirteen being recorded, ranging from small natural to large professional jumps. Probably more than 75 per cent of the skiing facilities are concentrated in the four western counties, primarily because of the more favorable climatic conditions. The major portion of this 75 per cent is located in Berkshire County alone. On the Mt. Wachusett State Reservation, two downhill trails have been developed or improved during the past year. In the eastern part of the State are few facilities. Mt. Hood Memorial Park, Melrose, the two trails on the Metropolitan District Commission's Blue Hills Reservation, and a few small municipal or private open slopes and jumps complete the list. Table 58 and Map 75-10 show the distribution of skiing and related winter sports facilities in Massachusetts. In the 1935-36 season, many golf clubs allowed the use of open slopes on the courses for skiing, primarily for the novice. This enabled many people to enjoy the activity without traveling long distances to slopes used largely by more expert skiers.

Skiing facilities in western Massachusetts are adequate for the present demand except that more open slopes for the novice skier are needed. Central and eastern Massachusetts are decidedly lacking in adequate facilities. A good beginning has been made in both regions, the two new Wachusett trails, in the former, and the two Blue Hills trails, in the latter, partially fulfilling the demands. The Department of Conservation and the Metropolitan District Commission should establish more ski trails, particularly of the novice class, on the existing recreation lands, and acquire suitable land for the same purpose, in the future, in central and eastern Massachusetts.

Research has brought to light seventeen Ski and Outing Clubs, primarily located in central and western Massachusetts, which actively engage in and promote skiing and related winter sports. The Western Massachusetts Winter Sports Council is the largest combined organization actively promoting winter sports in the State. The Berkshire Hills Conference is also actively engaged in winter sports publicity. There is need for more promotional work by the local civic organizations and the Recreation Publicity Division of the Secretary of State's office, in addition to the publicity the State receives through the Governor's Fund of the New England Council.

Recommendations. The more important of the above recommendations may be summarized as follows:

1. More attention should be given to the development of ski-

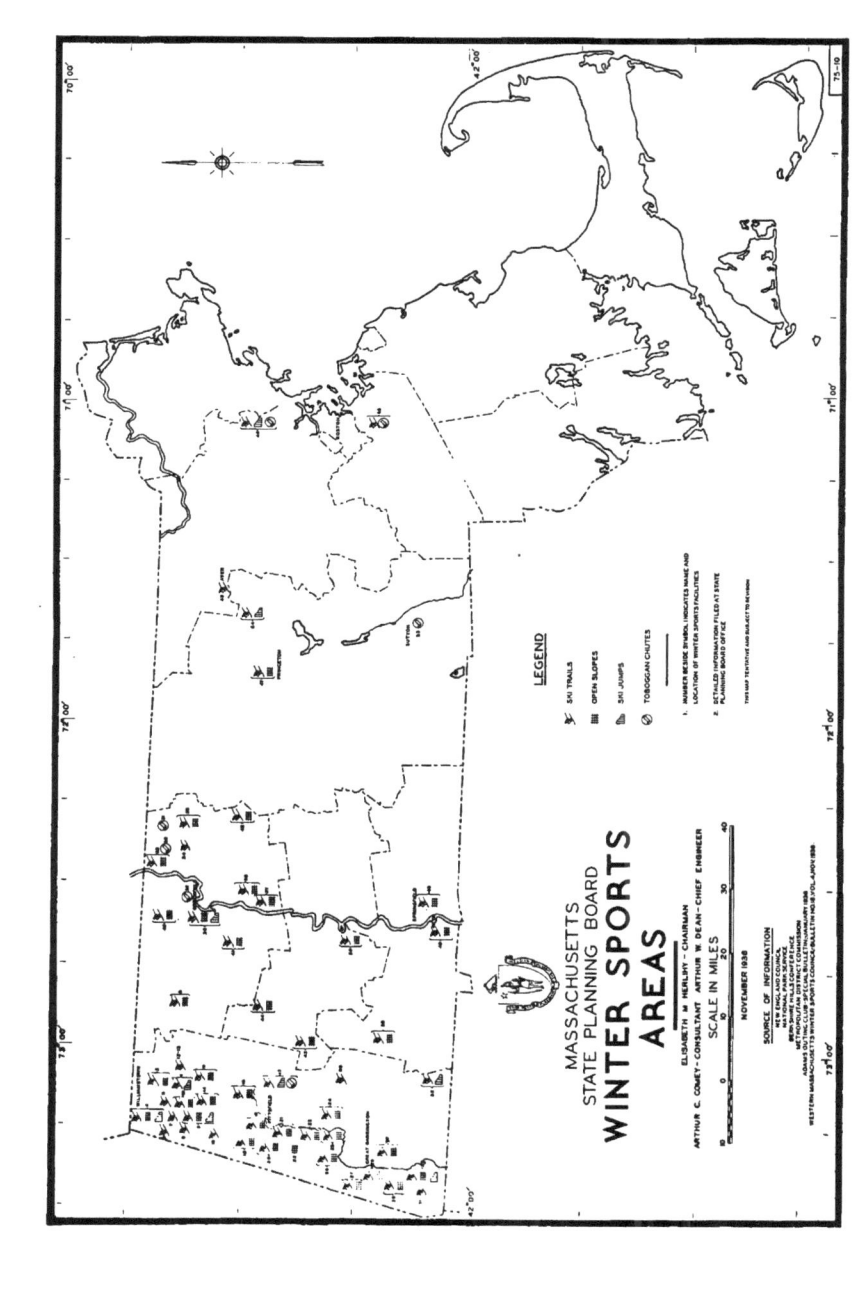

ing facilities in central and eastern Massachusetts, by the Department of Conservation and Metropolitan District Commission, on the recreational lands under their supervision.

2. A survey should be made of possible additional locations, such as drumlin hills (if suitable ones do not exist on present State lands), that may be acquired for winter-sports purposes, particularly skiing. Although these drumlin hills are small, and afford no great drops, they are suitable skiing hills for the majority of skiers, who are novices.

Skating

Practically every city and town in Massachusetts has sufficient water area on which skating may take place. However, many have failed to make the proper provision by keeping these areas cleared during the winter months. Likewise, most State recreation lands provide skiing areas, but few or no skating areas. It may be argued that provisions for skating are a local municipal problem and, in general, such is the case. Interest in skating has, for a time, been eclipsed by skiing, but, through the activity of local recreation leaders and clubs, is increasing. This fact has been recognized, in a small way, by the State, for several of the ponds or lakes on State reservations and forests have been kept cleared during the period of best ice conditions. While no survey has been made of the number of areas available for skating throughout the winter in Massachusetts, it is safe to draw the conclusion that facilities, both local and State-owned, are inadequate in most regions. Therefore, it is recommended that each city and town make proper provision, through utilization of either natural or artificial areas, for skating for its population. It is further recommended that the State, through the Department of Conservation and Metropolitan District Commission, make more adequate provision for skating on natural or artificial water bodies. In both cases, it is recommended that proper shelters be provided.

Tobogganing

Tobogganing, in Massachusetts, is primarily a local or commercial problem, and needs little if any State-wide consideration. There are a few facilities widely scattered over the State. Those which were ascertained through office research have been included in Table 58. On most State reservation lands, no constructed chutes are necessary because natural conditions, dependent on suitable snow cover, are sufficient. The same is true for most municipal parks. There are apparently ample opportunities and facilities for tobogganing, in every section of the State.

MASSACHUSETTS STATE PLANNING BOARD

Table 58

MASSACHUSETTS WINTER SPORTS, 1935 - 1936*

COUNTY	NO. OF SKI TRAILS	MILES OF SKI TRAILS**	NO. OF OPEN SLOPES	NO. OF JUMPS	NO. OF TOBOGGAN CHUTES
Barnstable	-	-	-	-	-
Berkshire	23	76.23	21	8	1
Bristol	-	-	1	-	1
Dukes	-	-	-	-	-
Essex	-	-	-	-	1
Franklin	8	10.87	5	1	3
Hampden	2	8.80	4	-	-
Hampshire	1	-	1	-	-
Middlesex	-	-	-	3	3
Nantucket	-	-	-	-	-
Norfolk	1	.05	-	-	-
Plymouth	-	-	-	-	-
Suffolk	-	-	-	-	2
Worcester	3	-	-	1	1
TOTAL	38	95.95	32	13	12

　*There are 75 "Winter Sport" sites in the State, some having more than one type of activity.
　**Miles of ski trails, shown on this table, are only a small part of the total miles of ski trails in Massachusetts. Figures on the additional mileage were not available.

Snowshoeing

Snowshoeing is dependent on the quantity and condition of snow. Since it requires no special areas or trails, there are adequate opportunities for it in every section of the State when there is ample snow. If trails are desired, existing foot trails or minor back roads may be used.

Hiking

Foot Trails

Foot trails, numerous and widely distributed throughout Massachusetts, may be classified as through trails and local trails.

Perhaps the best known trail is the Appalachian Trail (Massachusetts section), extending from the Connecticut boundary to the Vermont line and forming a link in the route from Georgia to Maine. It is 86 miles long, and passes through two State reservations and two State forests. Then there is the Wachusett-Watatic Trail covering a distance of over 20 miles from the Mt. Wachusett Reservation to a point near the New Hampshire line, where it connects with the Wapack Trail. The State forests and reservations provide a total of 225 miles of local trails, constructed by the Department of Conservation in cooperation with the National Park Service and the CCC during the past four years. The Metropolitan District Commission has developed a considerable number of trails on its reservation, particularly the Blue Hills and Middlesex Fells. Thus, it is safe to say that over 400 miles of foot trails are available in Massachusetts for either the experienced or novice hiker, and in every section of the State.

While there exist in Massachusetts hundreds of miles of foot trails, of one type or another, it is doubtful whether the facilities are adequate. At the present time, the newly formed Connecticut Valley Trails Conference is endeavoring to establish the "Rim Trail", extending from the Connecticut line to the Vermont line and back to the central part of the State. This will make another through trail of some hundred odd miles, more or less parallel to the Appalachian Trail, but many miles east of it. If the Berkshire-Cape Bridle Trail may be considered a foot trail also, then the adequacy of trails is considerably increased. The conclusion may be drawn, then, that there are sufficient and adequate foot trails in certain sections of the State. More local trails are necessary within the State forests and other State reservations, and within the environs of the larger centers of population, to provide opportunities for hiking without traveling excessive

MASSACHUSETTS STATE PLANNING BOARD

distances. Further studies should be made to determine the advisability of through trails extending from Metropolitan Boston to the western part of the State, one across the central part, and another across the southern part, connecting where possible with State forests and reservations. These trails could be located near the proposed Massachusetts Bridle Trail System. Enabling power to make possible the taking of easements and construction of State trails is given by Chapter 132, Sections 35, 36, General Laws, Tercentenary Edition 1932.

Several organizations are actively engaged in the promotion and construction of foot trails, preparation of guide books, and the establishment of trail shelters. Prominent among these are the Berkshire Chapter, Appalachian Mountain Club, the Connecticut Valley Trails Conference, the Massachusetts Forest and Park Association, the Outing Clubs of several colleges and preparatory schools, the American Youth Hostel.Inc., the New England Trails Conference, and the Massachusetts Department of Conservation.

Mountain Climbing

While Massachusetts has no mountains comparable to the White or Green Mountains, there are several peaks from which distinctive vistas may be obtained. The outstanding elevations in Massachusetts range from 650 to 3500 feet above sea level. The following description* is of interest:

"The Hoosac Hills, which divide the Connecticut River from the Housatonic River, are 1200 to 1600 feet high. The western and midwestern parts of the State are mountainous, the principal peaks being Mt. Tom, near Holyoke, 1214 feet; Mt. Holyoke, near South Hadley, 954 feet; Mt. Toby, near Leverett and Sunderland, 1275 feet; Mt. Williams, near North Adams, 3040 feet; and Mt. Greylock, near Adams, the highest elevation in the State, 3535 feet. The central and eastern parts of the State have such elevations as Mt. Wachusett, near Princeton, 2108 feet; Mt. Lincoln, near Pelham, 1246 feet; and the Blue Hills, near Boston, which rise to 650 feet."

All these mountains have trails which make them readily accessible. The various outing clubs and trails conferences promote trails, and assist in the construction and maintenance of them. Mountain climbing in Massachusetts is primarily a more vigorous form of hiking, owing to the comparative low altitudes encountered, and the excellent condition of the trails.

*Daniel Rockford. "Massachusetts, the Sportsman's Paradise." Recreation Publicity Department, Secretary of State's Office.

Riding

Bridle trails in Massachusetts consist of several local municipal units, some few miles developed on the State forests and reservations, a few miles developed by the Metropolitan District Commission on their reservations and parkways, and the Berkshires to the Cape Trail, a through trail 450 miles in length.

The Berkshires to the Cape Trail is the first completed unit in the proposed Massachusetts Bridle Trails System, sponsored by the Massachusetts Forest and Park Association. It is the only through bridle trail in the State, is well marked, and is so developed that shelter for both horse and rider is available. The trail was laid out to increase the recreation use of State forests and reservations, to serve as an added attraction to tourists, to increase the income of residents on the route through provision of shelter accommodations, and lastly to increase the use of horses for recreation.

Throughout the State, there are many miles of old wood roads and minor back roads which might well serve as bridle paths. Excluding these roads, there are over 500 miles of existing bridle trails in Massachusetts, and a proposed network of many more miles which will cover the entire State.

The Massachusetts Forest and Park Association is the principal organization promoting interest in bridle trails. However, there are 86 riding academies and many local outing clubs distributed throughout the State, which also sponsor and promote interest in riding. Many of these riding clubs are located on or near the Berkshires-to-the-Cape Trail, and offer shelter to horse and rider.

It is fairly obvious that, at the present time, Massachusetts has sufficient bridle trails or a State-wide character, and that any additional facilities should be more local in character, to provide riding facilities in and about the larger centers of population.

Bicycling

During the past two years, there has been a revival of interest in bicycling, accompanied by a demand for bicycle trails. Since bicycle trails require hard-surfacing and low grades, they are neither easy nor inexpensive to provide. At present, there are no bicycle trails, as such, in Massachusetts. The American Youth Hostel Inc., has laid out a bicycle loop trip through New

MASSACHUSETTS STATE PLANNING BOARD

England, utilizing back roads and portions of the Berkshires-to-the-Cape Trail, in Massachusetts. If interest in bicycling is permanent and not a passing fad, then, some system of trails may be necessary. At the present time, interest in bicycling is increasing, as shown by the upward trend of bicycle sales, the increase in the number of rental agencies, and the innovations of the "Bike and Hike" trains and the "Relay Rental System." The American Youth Hostel Inc., considers* that "the revival of interest particularly in biking is not in any sense a fad, but a definite expression of a need long felt for a simple, almost universal sport available to individuals of almost any age which enables them to see new pastures inexpensively and simply." They state that 80 per cent of the hostelers are now using bikes. Various other groups in the State, such as the Connecticut Valley Trails Conference, are promoting interest in the acquisition of abandoned trolley lines, and the establishment of a combination bicycle-bridle trail which will give both types of riders an opportunity to be off main-traveled highways. There is also a demand for bicycle paths in parks or reservations within the incorporated limits of cities and towns. This need can be readily observed in Metropolitan Boston in which the bicycle popularity is probably no greater than in any other section of the State. Thus, a twofold problem presents itself: (1) the need for a system of State-wide bicycle trails; and (2) the need for some effective method of providing bicycling facilities within the municipalities.

It is recommended that a survey be made to determine the possibility of establishing a combination bicycle and bridle trail along the proposed Massachusetts Bridle Trail System, this trail to connect and pass through State forests and reservations, where possible, since these areas are objectives of the riders in many cases. It is also recommended that a survey be made to determine the feasibility of controlling the location of bike rental agencies, within population centers, to locations where definite paths or trails have been developed for bicycling, thus decreasing the hazard to motorists, which exists, at present, with so many cyclists on main arteries of traffic. It is also necessary to determine how best to get cyclists from the city proper to a State-wide trail system, readily and safely. In conducting a survey for a State-wide system of bicycle trails, consideration should be given to the provision of shelter along the trails. The survey should determine whether private residences, open shelters, or cabins should be utilized, and the distance apart these accommodations should be located.

―――――
*Letter of September 18, 1936, to Mr. Karl M. Tomfohrde from Isabel and Monroe Smith, National Directors, American Youth Hostels, Inc.

MASSACHUSETTS STATE PLANNING BOARD

Touring

Automobile touring routes demand special treatment to a greater degree than do ordinary trunk highways. They should be scenic routes leading tourists through the favorite scenic and historic areas, covering all the more attractive sections of the State, bypassing centers of population, and connecting with touring routes in the adjoining States.

Before selecting routes for touring, studies should be undertaken to determine the amount of recreation travel on the highways, at present, the directions of flow, the principal resort areas, the number of out-of-State cars on Sundays and week-ends, their destinations, and other pertinent facts. This work should be carried on by the Department of Public Works in cooperation with the State Planning Board. Further information on touring and the adequacy of touring routes will be found in Chapter VIII; Transport.

Recreational Access

Various types of access routes, such as highways, foot, horse, and ski trails, are necessary to make recreational lands available for public use and to provide easy communication within the areas. Access within the recreational areas is fully as necessary as access to the area from the centers of population. These internal-access routes make for greater utilization and enjoyment of the areas by opening up scenic-interest sites, favorable places for swimming, picnicking, camping, and, in the winter, skiing and other winter sports.

Access to and within the various public recreational lands in Massachusetts is good, but not always excellent. All sites are on, or close to, major or secondary State routes. Within the areas that have received some recreational development are many miles of foot, horse, and ski trails, and old wood roads, all of which may be utilized for access to the sites of major interest, be they picnicking, camping, beach, scenic, or some other special interest. Some recreational lands lack adequate trails to open up the special-interest sites within their boundaries, and to provide better circulation of the people using the areas. Trails, paths, and secondary access roads are not always clearly marked, thus leading to confusion in reaching the recreational areas. The establishment of a standard method for marking trails and other access routes within the borders of public recreational lands is recommended. It is further suggested that more adequate highway markers be erected to advise tourists and others of their approach to public recreational lands, as is the practice in other States. Access to recreational regions is treated further in Chapter VIII.

Aviation

Aviation has two cardinal relationships to recreation: first, as a method of transportation to recreational centers; and second, as a recreational facility. For those who must, or desire to, commute from long distances to the resort areas in Massachusetts in a minimum of time, the airplane is the solution. There are many airports near the principal recreation centers, and others are contemplated, as part of the State plan for Massachusetts. It is possible that more use of inland Massachusetts waters might be made for hydroplane transportation. Also, the provision of landing strips in certain State forests, for both winter and summer patrons, might be feasible and is worth further study.

Aviation, as a recreational activity, requires the provision of adequate airports near population and recreation centers. Aviation country clubs are a possible development of the future.

Scenic Interest

Sites of scenic interest may be classified into eleven types, for the purpose of the study, as follows: (1) ocean; (2) lakes; (3) marshes; (4) rivers; (5) waterfalls; (6) gorges; (7) valleys; (8) wilderness; (9) viewpoint; (10) cliffs; and (11) mountains. To attempt to list all the examples under each type would involve a lengthy survey. Therefore, a statement only will be made on the subject.

Massachusetts is bountifully supplied with examples of every type of scenic site, some of which have already been acquired by the public but the majority of which are still in private hands. Many of these scenic sites should be acquired and preserved, for the following purposes:

1. To keep the amount of open spaces comparable to the growth of the use of open spaces.

2. To prevent the loss of the economic and recreation values which might be destroyed under private ownership.

3. To prevent the destruction of natural landscape by distributing the increased wear otherwise caused by excessive use by crowds of people.

MASSACHUSETTS STATE PLANNING BOARD

4. To make available for posterity typical and outstanding examples of our natural inheritance, before they are lost forever by destruction or private acquisition.

The Massachusetts Landscape Survey, conducted by the Trustees of Public Reservations, in 1933, listed and similarly classified outstanding examples of scenic interest in the State. These data form the basis of this study.

It is recommended that further field surveys and coöperative action with the Trustees of Public Reservation be carried on for the purpose of preparing a plan and program for the acquisition of scenic sites, based on the results of the above-mentioned Massachusetts Landscape Survey.

Scientific Interest

Geologic

Little reliable information as to sites of geologic interest is available, except for the data compiled by the Trustees of Public Reservations, in their Massachusetts Landscape Survey. Isolated examples of kettle holes, glacial drumlins, and rock formation of certain types have been recorded. The Staff Field Survey will secure additional information, but these data are not yet available. From a comprehensive field study, a program for acquisition may be drawn. It is desirable to preserve, for future generations, type examples of geologic formations while they are yet available.

Botanic

Botanic-site preservation has received some attention in Massachusetts, as well it should. Certain types of wild flowers and shrubs that enhance the beauty of the landscape (such as ferns, laurels, native orchids, cardinal flowers, and trailing arbutus) are rapidly approaching extinction, owing to continual picking by motorists and others. This is particularly true with regard to the laurel and arbutus. Thus, the principal reason for establishing Wild-Flower Sanctuaries is to prevent this extinction. Among the organizations actively promoting the preservation of wild flowers in Massachusetts are the New England Wild Flower Preservation Society, Inc., the Trustees of Public Reservations, the Massachusetts Audubon Society, the Mt. Everett Reservation Commission, the Greylock Reservation Commission, and a private Berkshire group. These organizations not only discourage the picking of wild flowers, but attempt to increase the growth and distribution of them by planting and transplanting. The New England Wild Flower Preservation Society is the most active of these groups in the dissemination of printed leaflets, through which they are trying to instill, in an unresponsive public, the necessity of preserving flowers.

There were listed a few good examples of botanic preserves in Massachusetts, owned by various organizations previously mentioned. These preserves are widely spaced over the State, with three in Berkshire County, and two in Norfolk County. These five botanic sites, with the organizations responsible for them, are:

1. Pleasant Valley Bird and Wild-Flower Sanctuary-Private Berkshire group.
2. Mt. Everett State Reservation-Mt. Everett Reservation Commission.
3. Mt. Greylock State Reservation-Mt. Greylock State Reservation Commission.
4. Rhododendron Swamp-Trustee of Public Reservations.
5. Moose Hill Bird Sanctuary-Massachusetts Audubon Society.

While Massachusetts has only a few areas devoted to the preservation of plants, a genuine interest exists. There are undoubtedly many more sites and botanic types worthy of preservation, which are determinable only through an adequate field survey. It is therefore recommended that a comprehensive field survey be made to determine sites of botanic interest worthy of preservation, and to prepare a program for their future acquisition.

Wildlife Interest*

Bird Sanctuaries

Massachusetts has made extensive efforts to protect bird life by the provision of ample sanctuaries. Nine of the fourteen counties have sanctuaries within their boundaries. In Essex County, alone, there are six bird sanctuaries. In all, Massachusetts has nineteen sanctuaries, ranging in size from one acre to twelve hundred acres. In addition to these areas, there are eight State reservations under the supervision of County or Special Commissioners and many State institutions, comprising approximately 121,000 acres, on which no hunting at all is allowed. Thus, these areas might be classed as Bird Sanctuaries. In addition to these larger sanctuaries, there are numerous small home-lot sanctuaries maintained by private parties.

*For the distribution of Wildlife Areas in the State, see Map 75-8.

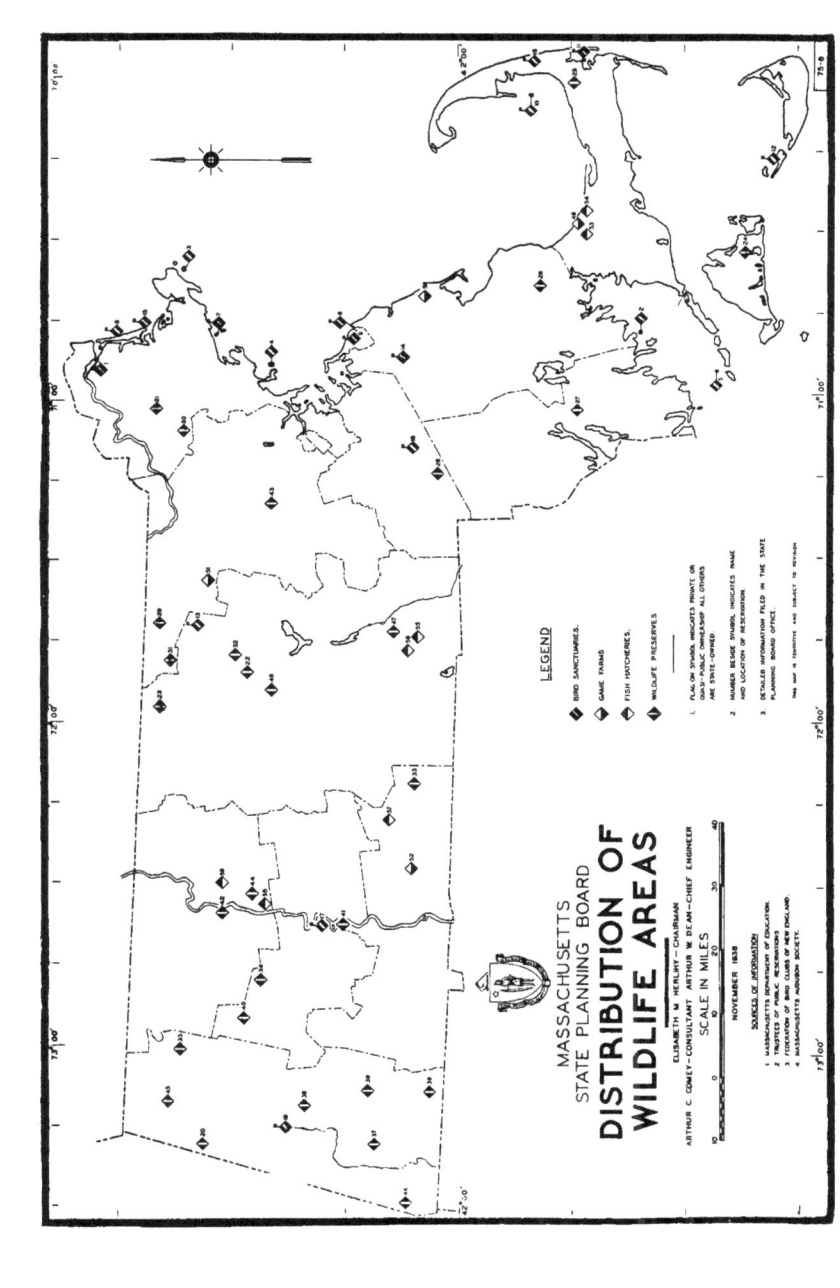

The principal reasons for setting up bird sanctuaries are to protect and study birds and to interest people in the welfare of birds and in all useful and beautiful wildlife.

Organizations in the State, actively engaged in the establishment of bird sanctuaries, include the Massachusetts Department of Conservation, Division of Fisheries and Game, the Trustees of Public Reservations, and the New England Federation of Bird Clubs, now merged with the Massachusetts Audubon Society. These organizations, in addition to maintaining sanctuaries, promote the study and protection of birds through printed matter, nature talks, and the encouragement of appropriate State and Federal laws. They assist in the establishment and maintenance of private sanctuaries, and foster the forming and carrying on of bird clubs. The Audubon Society carries its educational programs into the schools throughout the State. Massachusetts is earnestly doing all in its power to protect and foster bird life, and to prevent the extinction of any native species. Additional areas well suited for bird sanctuaries, are available in the State. The Department of Conservation should acquire these lands as fast as possible, following a definite program.

Hunting

Shooting Grounds. Under the General Laws of Massachusetts (Section 114, Chapter 131) public hunting is allowed on all State forest lands acquired under Sections 30 and 33 of Chapter 132, subject to the regulations and rules established by the State Forester (Chapter 132, Section 34). Hunting, except at the discretion of the administrative authorities upon written license and subject to the limitations of Sections 77 and 97 of Chapter 131 specifying types of game, is strictly prohibited on all State reservations, parks, commons, or any land owned or leased by the Commonwealth or any political subdivision thereof. Thus, the State forests are the only lands open to the public shooting, and these are regulated by the State Forester. Of the sixty-nine State forests, sixty-four were primarily purchased under Chapter 132, Sections 30 and 33, while the other five are now partly available for public shooting, since additional land has been acquired under the more liberal clauses. These 64 State forests comprise more than 150,000 acres. On thirty of these forests, hunting is strictly regulated by permit, and portions of ten forests, comprising approximately 3200 acres, are set aside for game preserves on which no hunting is allowed. Public shooting grounds are permissible in Massachusetts under Chapter 131, Section 116A. However, there are no such shooting grounds in Massachusetts at present. Public lands available for public hunting (State Forest lands) are widely distributed throughout the State, with the largest percentage, both in number and acreage, in the central and western portions.

The Division of Fisheries and Game carries on extensive stocking of covers, particularly with quail, pheasants, hares, and rabbits. A brief examination of the 1935 records (Table 59) show 730 quail and 1859 pheasant covers stocked. These stocked covers are quite evenly distributed, with the greater number in central and eastern Massachusetts.

Facilities for public shooting, and the amount of stocking, while inadequate in proportion to the number of hunters, are all the Division of Fisheries and Game is able to furnish with the appropriations granted. It is felt by the Division that, to carry on their work effectively, the minimum appropriation which should be made available is the total amount received from the hunting and fishing licenses issued each year. In 1935, this amounted to nearly $300,000. As previously mentioned, stocked areas exist in every county, and in approximately 85 per cent of the cities and towns. In 1935, a combined total of over 36,600 quail, pheasant, hares, and rabbits were distributed in covers throughout the State, of which some 32,000 were products of the State game farms, and 4500 were imported stock. The Division of Fisheries and Game is meeting the increasing demand for adequate hunting grounds and quantities of game to the best of its ability. In the work, it is actively cooperating with more than 250 fish and game clubs throughout the State. These clubs assist in breeding, raising, and distributing various types of game, particularly pheasant, to covers in their vicinity.

No reasonably accurate estimate of the quantities of game in the State is possible, for no accurate method has yet been devised for making such a game census. One method, which, at best, gives only a meager clue to whether the quantity of game is decreasing or increasing, is to study the records of the annual kills, and of the number of licensed hunters. This method would give only an indication based on many assumptions.

There are apparently insufficient public shooting grounds in Massachusetts. Although Chapter 131, Section 116A, authorizes the acquisition of more areas, possibly other means are more practical. The best remedy would be to have suitable appropriations given to the Department of Conservation to acquire the additional 500,000 acres of State Forest land, allowed by the statutes of 1936. Thus, the State would have public shooting lands for all time rather than for five-year periods, the expense would be less, and the threefold policy of the Department, namely, the development of forestry, recreation, and wildlife management, could be carried on. With its

Table 59

HUNTING IN MASSACHUSETTS, 1935*

COUNTY	NO. OF FORESTS OPEN TO PUBLIC HUNTING	SITES STOCKED WITH QUAIL		NO. OF CITIES AND TOWNS	SITES STOCKED WITH PHEASANTS		NO. OF FISH AND GAME CLUBS IN MASS., 1936
		No. of Stocked Areas	No. of Cities and Towns with Stocked areas		No. of Cities and Towns with Stocked Areas	No. of Stocked Areas	
Barnstable	1	50	14	15	15	45	6
Berkshire	14	---	---	32	24	179	23
Bristol	2	106	17	20	18	127	16
Dukes	1	17	---	7	6	13	1
Essex	2	---	---	34	33	193	24
Franklin	9	---	---	25	21	110	16
Hampden	2	---	---	23	17	122	32
Hampshire	4	---	---	23	17	99	20
Middlesex	9	102	32	54	41	236	26
Nantucket	1	---	---	1	1	16	1
Norfolk	3	---	24	28	24	109	21
Plymouth	1	203	25	27	25	218	19
Suffolk	---	---	---	4	---	---	3
Worcester	16	159	51	61	60	392	49
TOTALS	65	730	168	355	302	1859	257

*Data from the Division of Fisheries and Game of the Department of Conservation

released appropriations, the Division of Fisheries and Game could do more effective work in wildlife conservation and restocking.

At present, a very large part of all hunting is done on private land not posted against trespass. With the increasing diffusion of population, particularly near large cities, this opportunity seems destined to shrink. The acquisition of public shooting grounds should keep pace with the demand thus created.

Game Preserves and Farms

Game Preserves. Game Preserves, under a variety of classifications and organizations, are numerous in Massachusetts. The State contains thirty-three or more preserves, varying in size from 12 to 8600 acres and representing a total of approximately 21,300 acres. Included in the total are the various State reservations, under the control of County and Special Commissioners, which, under Statute, unless otherwise specified, are closed to hunting. This tabulation also includes areas within State forests, concerning which the 1935 Annual Report of the Division of Fisheries and Game says:

"For the purpose of establishing wildlife refuges on certain of the State Forests, areas approximating 10 per cent of the total forest area have been set aside, as such, and are closed to all activities except those pertaining to the development of the area as a wildlife habitat."

The distribution of game preserves in twelve of the fourteen counties of the State is satisfactory, but the preserves are inadequate in number and acreage. With the continual depletion of game stock through increased hunting, insufficient cover, lack of food, and various other natural or artificial courses, more extensive game preserves are necessary, together with a more extensive fish-and game-restoration program.

Game preserves are for the most part under the administrative authority of one of four agencies: (1) the Department of Conservation, Division of Fisheries and Game; (2) Department of Conservation, Division of Forestry; (3) Various County Commissioners; (4) Various Special Commissioners.

Thus, all preserves mentioned are under State ownership. There are various other areas, classified as bird sanctuaries, which, in reality, are set aside for the preservation of all wildlife, and which have been discussed elsewhere in the report.

Game Farms. Massachusetts has four game farms, in widely separated counties, varying in size from 23 to 132 acres, and comprising a total of 364 acres. All are under the direct control of the Division of Fisheries and Game of the Department of Conservation. While this Division lacks acreage, equipment, and other facilities for breeding and raising of game, it has done very effective work. It has coöperated with the Massachusetts State College, Department of Poultry Husbandry, on research and experimental breeding of certain types of game birds. Annually, many hundred heads of game are raised and distributed directly or through coöperating clubs. Intense census work has been accomplished by the State Ornithologist and Biologist, coöperating with all Division of the Department of Conservation, and effective and extensive programs have been prepared for preserving, raising, and distributing game stock. Insufficient space, equipment, and personnel are available for this important phase of wildlife conservation. Table 60 shows the game distribution in Massachusetts during 1934-35.

Fishing

Fishing Grounds. While a large part of the brook fishing is still on private lands not posted against it, more and more streams seem destined to be closed to the public by individuals and private clubs who fish them. However, opportunity for public fishing in Massachusetts is fairly extensive and liberal. Under the General Laws of Massachusetts (Chapter 131, Section 25, and Chapter 436, Section 5), the Director of the Division of Fisheries and Game is permitted to acquire, by gift or lease, fishing rights and privileges in any brook or stream in the Commonwealth, with rights of ingress and egress, unless it is a source of, or tributary to, a public water supply. Under Chapter 30, Section 37, he has the right to prescribe rules and regulations for these public fishing areas. According to Division records, there are eleven such areas in the State, comprising some eighty miles of stream. In addition to these streams, the great ponds in the State, with the exception of those used for water supply, are public for the purpose of fishing, hunting, and boating (Chapter 131, Section 36). Distributed throughout the State, are 1302 great ponds, of which approximately 200 are used for water-supply purposes, and certain others are controlled either by the Division of Fisheries and Game, for breeding purposes, or by cities and towns, under direct authority granted by the Legislature (See Table 61). Marine fishing areas off the coast of Massachusetts are too numerous for classification.

Stocking activities, on the limited appropriations granted, have been carried on throughout the State. More than 1300 ponds and streams were stocked, from 1933 to 1935. Fifty-two water bodies in 25 of the 69 State forests were stocked with trout and pond fish.

Table 60

GAME DISTRIBUTION IN MASSACHUSETTS*

1924 - 1935

TYPE OF GAME STOCK		PRODUCT OF STATE GAME FARMS				NOT PRODUCT OF STATE GAME FARMS		TOTALS
		Direct to Covers	To Clubs for Winter-Liberation, Spring of 1936	Day-old Stock to State Forests for Rearing and Liberation	For Exhibit and Experiment	Direct to Covers	To Clubs for Winter Liberation, Spring of 1936	
Pheasants	Young	19400	2805	2000	6	1488	504	26203
	Adult	1117	-	-	6	-	-	1123
Quail	Young	5350	-	-	20	-	-	5370
	Adult	1026	-	-	-	-	-	1026
Cottontail Rabbits	Adult	334	-	-	-	1889	-	2223
White Hares	Adult	-	-	-	-	707	-	707
TOTALS		27227	2805	2000	32	4084	504	36652

*Data from the Division of Fisheries and Game of the Department of Conservation

Table 61

FISHING FACILITIES IN MASSACHUSETTS, 1936

COUNTY	LEASED PUBLIC FISHING AREAS*		GREAT PONDS (HOUSE NO. 1300 - 1934)			INLAND BOAT FACILITIES FOR FISHING*			MARINE FISHING FACILITIES*	
	Number	Miles	Total Number	Used for Water Supply	Available for Fishing	Number of Towns with Boat Liveries	Number of Ponds with Boat Liveries	Number of Liveries	Number of Liveries	No. of Boats
Barnstable	1	1	164	1	163	10	19	22	29	29
Berkshire	3	12	73	10	63	17	22	36		
Bristol	2	10	82	3	79	11	12	19	5	5
Dukes			26	1	25				15	15
Essex			79	31	48	19	23	25	38	151
Franklin	1	10	27	3	24	5	5	5		
Hampden			60	15	45	11	18	36		
Hampshire	3	37	36	5	31	10	12	15		
Middlesex	1	10	149	32	117	27	37	42		
Nantucket			6		6				5	5
Norfolk			75	5	70	14	16	24	8	30
Plymouth			178	15	163	13	23	32	26	26
Suffolk			5	1	4	1	1	1	9	50
Worcester			342	74	268	35	56	71		
TOTALS	11	80	1,302	196	1,106	174	244	343	135	311

*Data from the Division of Fisheries and Game of the Department of Conservation

MASSACHUSETTS STATE PLANNING BOARD

Tables 62 and 63 show, in more detail, the stocking activities of the Division of Fisheries and Game. Greater production and distribution, combined with more rigid closing of ponds to give time for natural and artificial propagation to work together to bring depleted stock back to normal, are necessary. The method devised by the Division of Fisheries and Game, of closing great ponds in rotation, is worthy of careful consideration and the ultimate development of a program for its fulfilment. The plan is to close against winter fishing two-thirds of the ponds in each county for a period of two years, the plan to be carried out in the different counties in rotation.

The fact that breeding, raising, and stocking facilities are inadequate is due primarily to the lack of adequate funds. Greater funds should be made available to the Division of Fisheries and Game.

Fish Preserves and Hatcheries. The seven hatcheries in Massachusetts, under the administration of the Division of Fisheries and Game, range in size from 20 to 316 acres, and comprise a total 679 acres. At these hatcheries, fish are raised for distribution, and experimental work on diseases of fish, methods of propagation, and foods is carried on under the direction of expert biologists.

Historic and Archeologic Interest

Massachusetts has many sites of historic and archeologic interest. For the purpose of this study, the sites have been classified into the following types: forts, churches, houses, Indian relics, gardens, and sites of historic events. These sites are found in all parts of the State, with the eastern region the most generously favored. Limited time precluded the completion of two important studies in this field: first, the compilation of a list of historic sites which are marked, and available for public inspection; and second, the determination of those sites which are not available for public inspection, and which should be acquired by some protective organization, before they are destroyed.

The Society for the Preservation of New England Antiquities, active since 1910, owns some twenty historical houses in Massachusetts, alone, and there are more than one hundred local and family historical societies which are members of the Bay State Historical League. A recent survey, made by the New England Council and the Art Committee of the New England Conference of the Federation of Women's Clubs (1936), lists, as open to the public, 132 historic houses in Massachusetts. Although this is a splendid showing, it is evident that there is need for the preservation of many more ex-

Table 62

STOCKED WATERS IN MASSACHUSETTS, 1933-1935*

COUNTY	TROUT		POND FISH		SALMON		STATE FORESTS		FISH AND GAME CLUBS
	No. Towns	No. Sites	No. Towns	No. Sites	No. Towns	No. Sites	Number Forests Stocked	No. Sites	
Barnstable	7	14	13	38	9	9	1	4	6
Berkshire	29	130	20	36	-	-	8	14	23
Bristol	12	26	13	17	-	-	-	-	16
Dukes	3	3	2	2	-	-	-	-	1
Essex	20	45	21	39	-	-	1	8	24
Franklin	26	93	14	19	-	-	5	7	16
Hampden	22	65	15	29	-	-	3	4	32
Hampshire	23	93	13	30	1	1	1	3	20
Middlesex	33	62	36	70	-	-	1	1	26
Nantucket	-	-	-	-	-	-	-	-	1
Norfolk	20	41	17	33	1	1	-	-	21
Plymouth	21	58	16	54	1	1	1	7	19
Suffolk	1	1	1	1	1	1	-	-	3
Worcester	56	196	50	132	-	-	4	4	49
TOTALS	273	819	231	500	12	12	25	52	257

*Data from the Division of Fisheries and Game of the Department of Conservation

Table 63

STOCKED FISH DISTRIBUTION IN MASSACHUSETTS, 1934-1935*

TYPE OF FISH	PRODUCT OF STATE HATCHERIES			NOT PRODUCT OF STATE HATCHERIES		GRAND TOTAL
	Direct to Public Waters	To Clubs for Later Distribution When Larger	Study and Exhibit	Direct to Public Waters	For Rearing to Larger Size Before Liberation	
Brook Trout	621,927	29,505	1,979	73	--	653,484
Brown Trout	203,395	1,200	481	600	--	205,676
Rainbow Trout	136,306	5,000	100	107	--	141,513
Small-Mouth Black Bass	9,550	10,000	--	40,485	--	60,035
Large-Mouth Black Bass	8	--	--	48	--	56
Rock Bass	--	--	--	2,698	--	2,698
Chinook Salmon	39,000	--	--	--	--	39,000
Crappie	100	175	--	1,406	15	1,696
Horned Pout	34,955	5,300	150	101,354	50	141,809
Blue Gills	50,200	--	--	4,231	--	54,431
Pickerel	1,718	--	--	3,486	12	5,216
Yellow Perch	142,377	1,300	--	110,630	--	254,307
White Perch	--	--	--	383,915	200	384,115
Pike Perch	--	--	--	250,014	250,000	500,014
Muskellunge	--	--	--	--	20,000	20,000
TOTAL TROUT AND POND FISH	1,239,536	52,480	2,710	899,047	270,277	2,464,050

*Data from the Division of Fisheries and Game of the Department of Conservation

amples of the different types classified. The principal cause for the failure to make more adequate preservation has been the lack of finances. Important sites have been lost forever. A study of the best examples of each type and the preparation of a program for their acquisition, over a period of years, should be undertaken by the State Planning Board in close cooperation with the interested societies. Under such a program,emphasis should be placed on those types which at present are least well represented in order that a well-balanced plan may result.

PART III

RECREATION AREAS

In this study, areas devoted to recreation are considered primarily in their capacity to serve activities. Many types of these areas have already been discussed, in conjunction with specific activities. However, certain areas, including some of the most important ones, need separate consideration, chiefly due to the fact that they have multiple recreation purposes. (See Map 75-6.)These may be grouped under four main heads:

1. State forests, parks, and reservations
2. Metropolitan reservations
3. Municipal forests and parks
4. Quasi-public reservations

State Forests, Parks, and Reservations

The history of the acquisition and development of State forests, parks, and reservations in Massachusetts is unique,and extends over a period of nearly fifty years.

Probably the first lands acquired as a public open space were the Province Lands, situated at the extreme tip of Cape Cod. A Legislative enactment in 1893 gave to the citizens of Provincetown the occupied portions of the tract, and set aside the remainder as a permanent public open space of approximately 3810 acres,now under the control of the Department of Public Works.

State Forests

State Forests are now being acquired in accordance with the Massachusetts Plan, evolved, in 1934, and designating 26 tentative purchase areas. When completed,these areas will provide State Forest Lands within fifteen miles of all centers of population. The forests are being developed in accordance with a master plan prepared by Landscape Architects of the Department, under a three-point program of forestry, wildlife management, and recreation. At the present time, 21 of the 26 areas are being acquired, and a 1936 Legislative Act, subject to suitable appropriations, will complete the program.

State Parks

Massachusetts has placed little emphasis on the acquisition and development of State Parks, as such. There are but two in the State. They are areas devoted entirely to recreation, rather than to the joint uses of forestry, recreation, and wildlife.

State Reservations

There are virtually State Parks, usually placed, by special Act, under a special or county commission. The first reservation, created in 1898, was Mt. Greylock. Others followed in succession until, at the present time, there are eleven.

Summary

State recreation lands in Massachusetts, in 1936, comprised eighty-two sites, with a total area of approximately 182,000 acres, apportioned among the fourteen counties as shown on Table 64. In brief, the distribution among the three types is as follows:

1.	State Forests	69	165,596.16 acres
2.	State Reservations	11	14,359.97 acres
3.	State Parks	2	2,382.37 acres

Of the State land utilized for public recreation, approximately 37 per cent is located in Berkshire County. This concentration in one county calls attention to the desirability of locating future acquisitions in relation to population.

Metropolitan Reservations

The Metropolitan Park Commission, now the Park Division of the Metropolitan District Commission, was founded in 1893, by Act of the General Court, for the purpose of acquiring, maintaining, and making available to the inhabitants of thirty-seven cities and towns in the vicinity of Boston open spaces for exercise and recreation, to be known as reservations.

In the forty-three years since its creation, this Division has established a notable system of reservation and parkways in

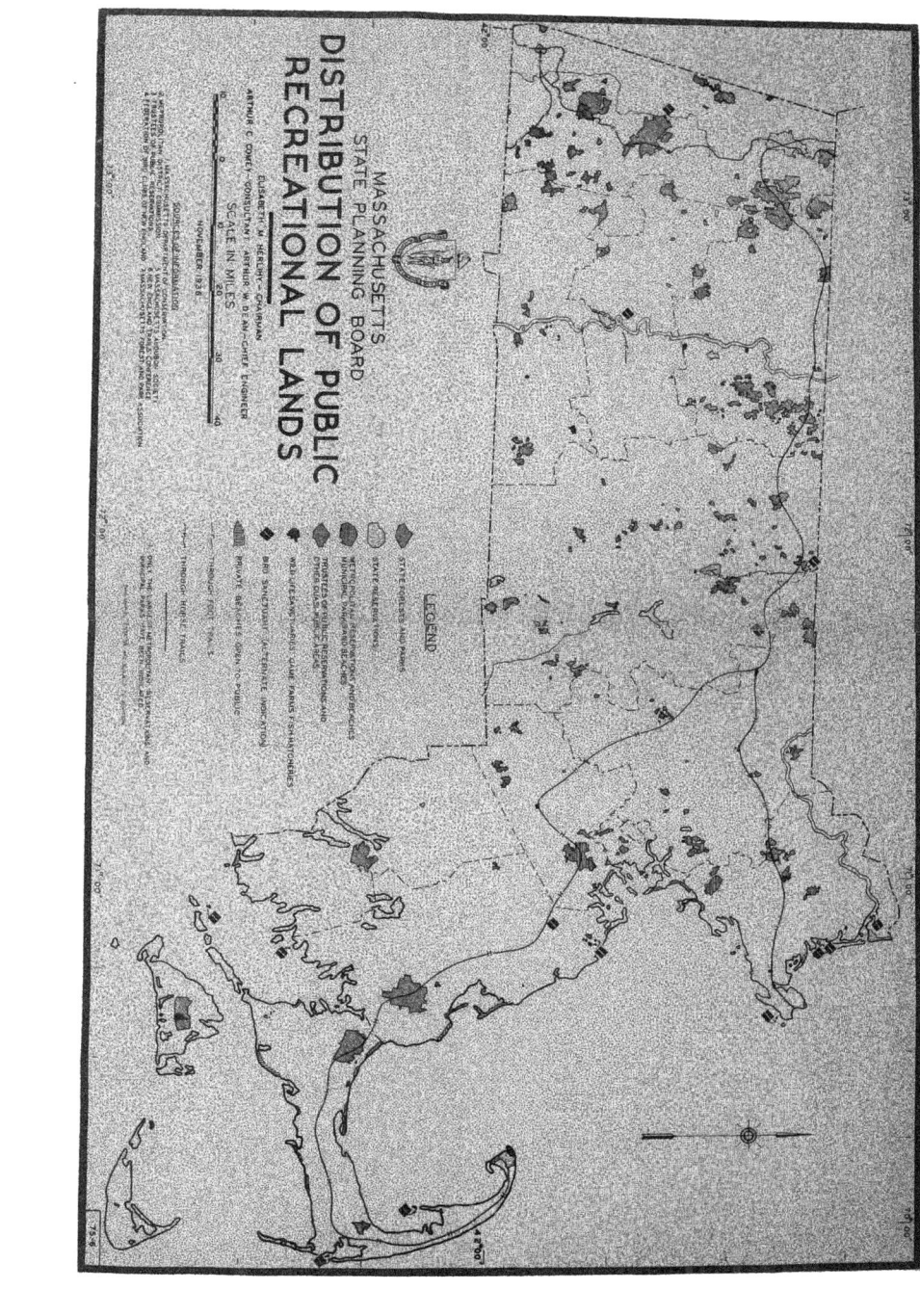

Table 64

OPEN SPACE LANDS IN MASSACHUSETTS, 1936

COUNTY	STATE FORESTS, PARKS, AND RESERVATIONS, DEPARTMENT OF CONSERVATION	SPECIAL COMMISSIONERS	COUNTY COMMISSIONERS	METROPOLITAN DISTRICT COMMISSION RESERVATIONS AND PARKWAYS	TRUSTEES OF PUBLIC RESERVATIONS LANDS	DEPARTMENT OF PUBLIC WORKS	CITY AND TOWN FORESTS	COUNTY TOTALS
Barnstable	10205.6				149.00	3810	781	14945.6
Berkshire	58776.67	9415.30			260.00		7912	76363.97
Bristol	6541.02						-707	7248.02
Dukes	4472.75							4472.75
Essex	4043.06			392.30	178.00		750	5363.36
Franklin	28434.21	755.60	89.29				976	30255.10
Hampden	9893.37		.559.60		7.50		8266	18731.47
Hampshire	5270.59		1378.40		313.00		252	7213.99
Middlesex	7730.87			3995.01	21.00		2005	13751.88
Nantucket	133.							133.
Norfolk	2563.41			7063.77	691.00		716	11034.18
Plymouth	10884.41			25.59			650	11560.
Suffolk				1130.77				1130.77
Worcester	19462.36	1580.00					4553	25595.36
TOTALS	168416.32	11750.9	2027.29	12607.44	1619.50	3810	27568	227799.45

325

the Boston region. On December 1, 1935, the Metropolitan District Commission held 15 reservations with a total area of 11,044.5 acres, and 19 parkways, with an area of 1,563 acres, distributed among the 14 cities and 23 towns comprising the Parks District. Included in this total are nine inland and five ocean bathing beaches and two eighteen-hole golf courses. These reservations, particularly the Middlesex Fells and Blue Hills, furnish extensive recreation areas readily accessible to the large population of Metropolitan Boston. In addition to the reservations are 113 miles of beautiful parkways.

The Metropolitan District Commission has discharged its duties admirably and made as adequate provision for recreation on its reservations as its funds permit. However, there is still opportunity on many reservations for additional recreational facilities, especially winter-sports facilities to provide recreational opportunities for those unable to travel to the more distant areas.

Municipal Forests and Parks

Municipal Forests

The Town Forest Act of 1913 authorizes cities and towns to set aside lands for the growing of timber. When the forest is established, the State Department of Conservation will supply trees for reforestation purposes. These town forests offer excellent opportunities for a three-point program of forestry, recreation, and wildlife development.

Distributed throughout Massachusetts are approximately one hundred city and town forests, ranging in size from 15 to more than 6000 acres, with a total of about 27,500 acres. Many serve as watershed areas for local water supply. Thus, they are often utilized for a fourth purpose. Town forests, now established by less than one-third of the cities and towns in the State, should be created by many more towns, as a means of adding to their income through timber production, of utilizing idle land, and of providing recreational areas and wildlife sanctuaries.

Municipal Parks

Nearly every city and town in the State has one or more parks, but little information has yet been obtained as to their number and acreage. A report compiled by the U. S. Department of Labor, Bureau of Labor Statistics, in 1930, showed that 73 municipalities in Massachusetts with a population of 5,000 and over had 1314 parks, with a total area of 14,637.6 acres. These figures indicate the

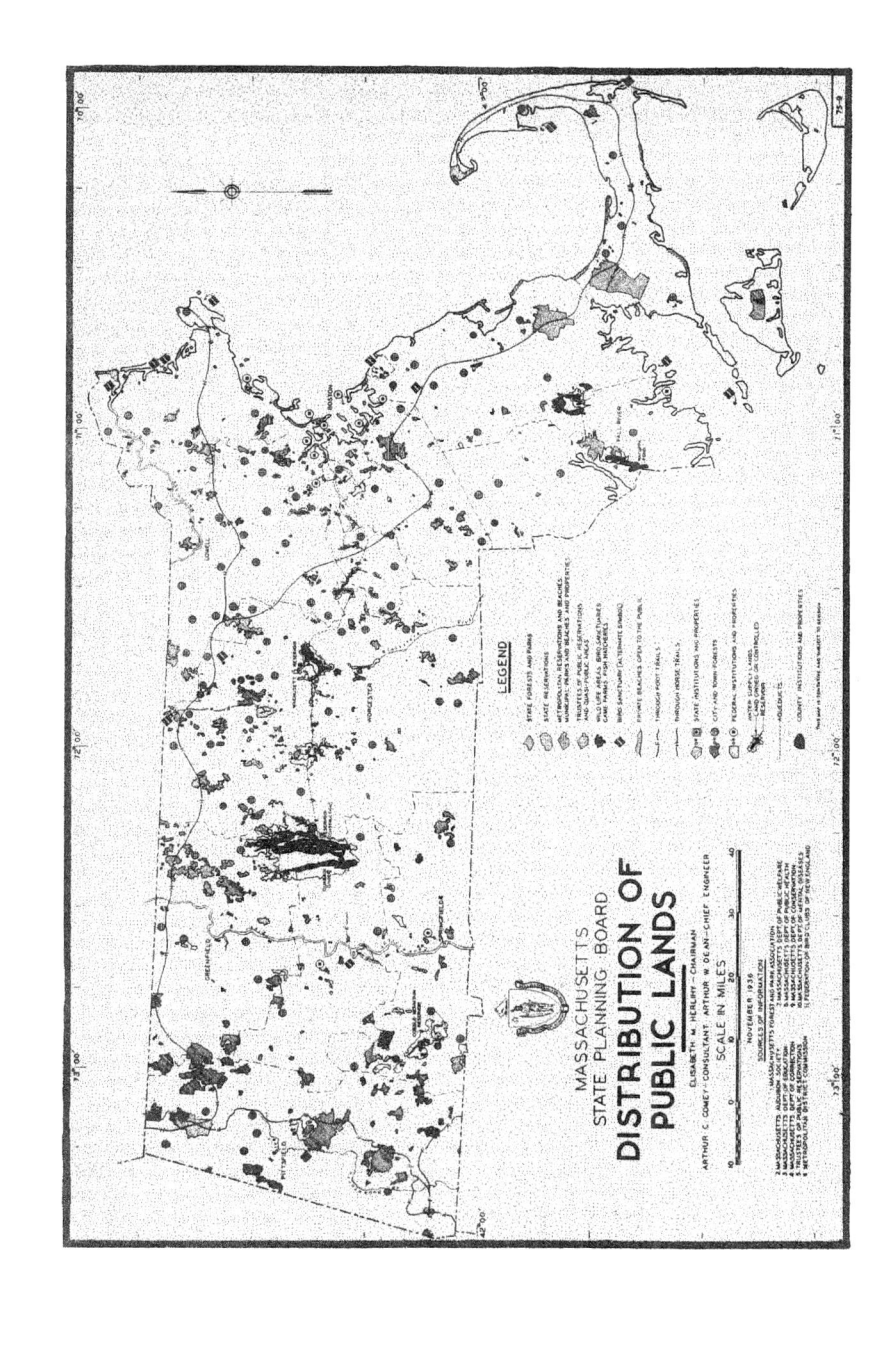

extent of municipal parks, but they are far from complete. Further investigation is necessary before complete figures can be given.

Quasi-public Reservations

The principal quasi-public organization maintaining public lands in Massachusetts is the Trustees of Public Reservations. The purpose of this organization is to acquire, maintain, and open to the public, under suitable regulations, beautiful and historic places within the Commonwealth. It is a corporation, established in 1891, by the General Court, with authority to acquire beautiful and historic places by gift, devise, or purchase, and to hold such lands, open to the public and exempt from taxation. In addition to its work of acquiring and developing public lands or assisting in this work, the corporation has conducted surveys, notably the Massachusetts Landscape Survey of 1933, and coöperated whole-heartedly with various other organizations, Commissions, and Departments in making surveys and formulating plans and programs for future acquisitions.

In its forty-five years of activity, the Trustees of Public Reservations has assisted in securing 28 sites, comprising a total of 9883 acres. Of these sites, the Corporation owns and administers fifteen, varying in size from 10 to 640 acres, with a total area of 1619 acres. Included in the list of their holdings are a historic house, wildlife sanctuaries, sites of botanic, geologic, and archeologic interest, and sites primarily noted for their scenic value. These reservations have been developed to a limited extent for recreational activities, such as picnicking, camping, hiking, and riding. They serve as valuable supplements to the public lands provided by the State.

PART IV

SOCIAL ASPECTS

Recreational Organizations

There are approximately 200 quasi-public and private organizations, in various parts of the State, which publicize recreational activities, acquire and develop recreation areas, or promote legislation for the extension of recreation. Most of the organizations depend on public subscriptions or membership fees for funds with which to carry on their work. Many are associations of several groups with similar interests, such as the Western Massachusetts Winter Sports Council, an allied group of outing and ski clubs, laymen, and professional men interested in the promotion of winter sports activities.

An inventory of such organizations is going forward, and a card index is being prepared. When complete, it will briefly summarize the phase of recreation the group is primarily interested in, the lands owned or controlled, the purposes of the group, and any definite programs being undertaken.

Social Values

The social importance of recreation is steadily increasing. The leisure time of people has been increased by the development of labor-saving devices and machinery; and the economic crisis has produced additional leisure time resulting from unemployment. People turn to recreation as a means of utilizing leisure hours, of preventing physical and mental breakdowns, of curbing anti-social characteristics, and of reducing juvenile or adult delinquency.

The social values of recreation are receiving continued study and action from the many public and private social agencies in the State. The Boston Council of Social Agencies, comprising approximately 450 public and private social agencies functioning in Boston, and the Massachusetts Conference on Social Work are examples of these agencies.

PART V

THE RECREATION INDUSTRY

In the study of recreation activities, areas, and facilities, due cognizance must be given to the "recreation industry". By many authorities it is regarded as the second largest industry in the State, second only to textiles.

Income from Recreation

According to many estimates, recreation produces a $200,000,000 annual income to the governments and people of Massachusetts. This income is derived from taxes on recreational property, from gasoline taxes in connection with recreational uses of automobiles, and from hunting and fishing licenses, shelter accommodations, retail stores, amusements, and other sources too numerous to mention.

The State Planning Board has not yet attempted to make a determination of the amount of annual income from the State recreation industry. The following fragmentary information on recreational income of two types is set down merely as an example of the financial importance of recreation.

MASSACHUSETTS STATE PLANNING BOARD

Taxation of Recreation Property

The Massachusetts Industrial Commission Recreation Survey of 1929-1930 indicated that, in at least 20 towns of the State, more then 50 per cent of the total assessed valuation was on recreational land. The total valuation of recreation land in the State was approximately $190,000,000, from which the State, cities, and towns received nearly $5,000,000 annually in taxes.

Sale of Hunting and Fishing Licenses

In 1935, 140,543 resident and 1835 non-resident hunting and fishing licenses were issued. Over a period of 12 years, the average of non-resident licenses has been only 1.9 per cent of the total. This is extremely low; and indicates that Massachusetts is not attracting as many non-resident hunters and fishermen as are some other States. The net income from resident hunting and fishing licenses, in 1935, was $260,290, and from non-resident licenses, $8035. Over a period of twelve years, the income from non-resident licenses has averaged 4.2 per cent of the total.

The foregoing figures demonstrate that Massachusetts is not receiving the amount of income from hunting and fishing licenses that might reasonably be anticipated. The opportunities for hunting and fishing in the State are more favorable than the income from licenses would indicate. It is probable that, through the continuance of stocking activities and the policy of maintaining reasonable license fees, plus more generous advertising, greater income could be obtained.

Publicity for the Recreation Industry

Publicity for the recreation industry in Massachusetts is carried on by the New England Council, the Recreation Publicity Division of the office of the Secretary of State, and by many local civic organizations.

Activities of the New England Council

The broadest program under which Massachusetts recreational attractions are publicized is that of the New England Council, known as the "The New England Governors' Joint New England Recreational Advertising Campaign", now in its second year. To advertise the recreational opportunities of the New England States, a sum of $100,000 is appropriated annually by the six New England States. The contribution of each State is Based on its percentage of the total taxable valuation of property used for recreational purposes

MASSACHUSETTS STATE PLANNING BOARD

in New England. The amounts contributed for 1935-36 were as follows: Connecticut, $9,500; Maine, $20,000; Massachusetts, $34,500; New Hampshire, $17,800; and Rhode Island, $11,500. The plan and budget were laid out by the Council and approved by the Governors.

Activities of the State Recreation Publicity Division

The program under which Massachusetts publicizes her attractions, recreationally and otherwise, is formulated by the Recreation Publicity Division of the office of the Secretary of State. Annual appropriations were granted for 1935 and 1936.

In 1935, $100,000 was appropriated. Of this sum, $34,500 was expended, under the direction of the New England Council, as Massachusetts' share of the Governor's Fund. The remainder was utilized by the Division on a three-fold basis, approximately as follows:

1. $30,000 for advertising copy in newspaper and magazines
2. $ 4,900 for outdoor advertising
3. $20,600 for direct mail, printing, and mailing

The appropriation for 1936 was reduced to $75,000, of which $35,000 is to be expended by the New England Council. Thus, the State will expend for direct advertising of the State only $40,000.

The extent of the recreational publicity campaign carried on under the direction of the Recreation Publicity Division of the office of the Secretary of State may be grasped from the following brief summary of its first year's activity.

Advertisements. Newspapers advertising included 200 line advertisements in 35 daily newspapers east of the Mississippi, and full-page rotogravures in seven large newspapers. Magazine advertisements appeared in the Sportsman and the American Legion Monthly. Newspaper and magazine advertisements had a circulation of 19,500,000. Responses from these advertisements were received from 48 states and 15 foreign countries.

Special Articles and Photographs. Special articles and photographs featuring Massachusetts were carried in 112 publications. Six pamphlets were published and distributed.

Outdoor Advertising. Twenty-nine outdoor painted advertising signs were utilized.

Miscellaneous. The Division cooperated with 115 Chambers of Commerce and civic and hotel organizations in Massachusetts and answered more than 2800 special inquiries.

Local Publicity Campaigns

In addition to the extensive publicity campaigns conducted by the State and by the New England Council, the Chambers of Commerce, civic, and hotel organizations of many of the more prominent recreational centers are actively engaged in recreational publicity. Their appropriations are usually obtained from dues or subscriptions from local business groups who participate in the added revenue resulting from this publicity.

Trends in Recreation Activities

Summer Recreational Activities

Summer recreational activities show two definite trends: first, an increase in the popularity of touring with trailers and other paraphenalia for camping out; and second, an increase in the establishment of summer homes or camps in the principal recreational areas. Both increases are more or less concentrated in certain sections of the State. Touring occurs all over the State, with many opportunities to pitch a tent or park a trailer at little expense. The objectives of a majority of the tourists, however, are either the Cape or the Berkshire Hills. In both regions, there are many campgrounds which have been well occupied all summer. The establishment of new summer homes has taken place primarily on the Cape and on the adjacent islands of Marthas Vineyard and Nantucket, in the towns adjacent to the ocean along the entire length of the Massachusetts Coast, in the Berkshire Hills, and, to a limited extent, in the central Massachusetts lake region.

Winter Recreational Activities

Winter recreational activities show an increasing growth, especially in the field of skiing. The growth has taken place largely in the four western counties of Berkshire, Hampden, Hampshire, and Franklin, although some growth has been noted in central and eastern Massachusetts. While the winter activity trend is predominantly towards skiing, skating and snowshoeing have shown some growth, primarily in the Berkshire region, owing to the more favorable climatic conditions there.

All-Season Activities

All-season activities, such as touring, fishing, and many passive forms of recreation, show upward trends resulting from the general increase of leisure time and the lessening of the economic crisis. An increase in the number of fishing licenses is one of

MASSACHUSETTS STATE PLANNING BOARD

the favorable signs of better times. Hotels have experienced a sharp increase in activity.

Thus, it may be concluded that there is a definite trend upward in participation in all recreational activities. The demand for facilities has been fully as extensive as the supply. Future seasons will see a further increase in the use of outdoor recreational activities, areas, and facilities, and the supply must keep pace with the demand. Thus, further acquisition of public lands and the development of them for recreational purposes should be made, annually, on the basis of a comprehensive State plan.

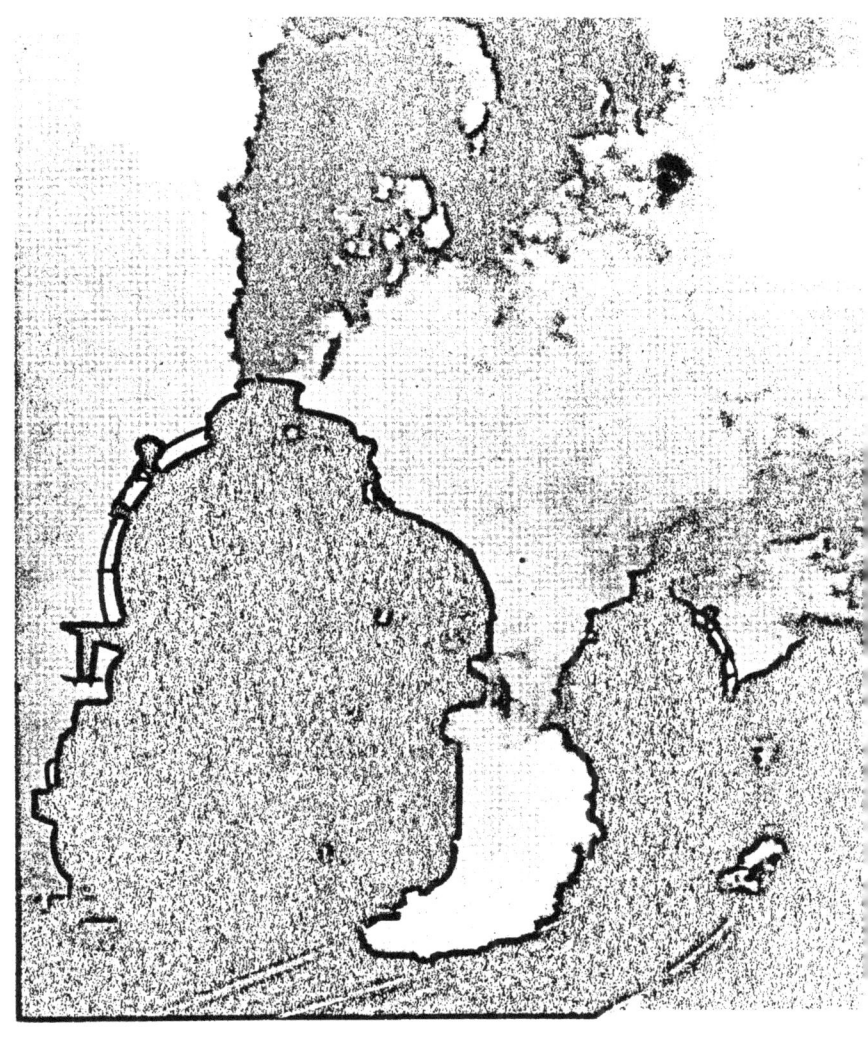

TRANSPORT

Courtesy of TECHNOLOGY REVIEW

CHAPTER VIII

T R A N S P O R T

Summary Outline

I. Highways

    A. Highway Transportation
    B. State Highway System
    C. Highway Legislation

II. Railroads

    A. Value of Railroads to the Commonwealth
    B. Special Railroad Problems

III. Water Transport

    A. Value of Seaports to Massachusetts
    B. Methods of Increasing Port Business
    C. Free Port
    D. Ports of Massachusetts
    E. Port Administration

IV. Aviation

    A. Use of and Need for Aviation in Massachusetts
    B. Essential Physical Developments

MASSACHUSETTS STATE PLANNING BOARD

HIGHWAYS

The highway pattern of the State has developed in a piecemeal manner over a long period of years. There have been few comprehensive studies of the highway needs of the State, particularly as they are related to land uses, commerce, and industry. The undertaking of such a study, and the development of a plan for a complete highway system for the State are functions of the State Planning Board.

The following report presents a brief summary of the highway studies to date.

Highway Transportation

The automobile, as everyone knows, has been the important factor in producing a demand for improved highways. The present-day machine, with its improved operating characteristics, such as rapid acceleration, great power, and speed, demands new types of highways over which it can operate efficiently and safely.

The highway system of the future must be built to meet future highway transportation needs. To determine these, the staff of the State Planning Board has studied the present and probable future uses of private passenger cars, motor trucks, and busses. Brief discussions of those studies follow.

Private Passenger Cars

The 680,537 passenger cars registered in Massachusetts in 1935 constituted 87 per cent of the total motor-vehicle registration in the State.* For every six persons, there is one private passenger automobile. Each individual automobile acts as a highly flexible transportation unit of definite economic value to its owner. Passenger-car owners have shown themselves willing and able to pay the maintenance and the capital costs of both the vehicle and the highways which it uses.

Business Uses. Undoubtedly, the great majority of automobiles has been purchased because the business advantages of owning a car has outweighted the disadvantages of its cost. There is, of course, a limit to the number of additional cars that will be purchased because their economic advantages outweight the disadvantages, but the number is not easily estimated.

---

*Figures from the Registry of Motor Vehicles, not including passenger- or commercial-car reissues.

MASSACHUSETTS STATE PLANNING BOARD

Recreational Uses. The passenger car has two primary recreational uses: (1) it provides access to recreational areas; and (2) it provides opportunities for pleasure driving. It is necessary to plan for both of these uses.

The problem of facilitating access to recreational areas may be solved by developing and supplementing the major-highway system with access roads which provide attractive introductions to the recreational areas.

There are natural tourist routes which are used by those traveling to recreation areas. The establishment of more efficient and pleasant through routes in Massachusetts would attract larger numbers of those seeking recreation, with consequent benefit to the State. Massachusetts recreational areas are the termini of a large proportion of the out-of-State vehicles which travel over Massachusetts highways during the summer. Most of the balance are cars of tourists traveling to recreational areas elsewhere in New England. No adequate survey has ever been made of the routes used, or the number of out-of-State tourists cars on Massachusetts highways. From the limited data available, the following appear to be the principal out-of-State tourist movements in Massachusetts:

1. North and south in the Berkshires.
2. North and south in the Connecticut River valley, in larger quantities than in the Berkshires.
3. North and south in the eastern part of the State, over several routes. There is some concentration on Route U.S. 1, between Providence and Boston.
4. East and west along Route 2, in the northern part of the State.
5. East and west along Route U. S. 20, in the southern part of the State.
6. East and west in great numbers through the Buzzards Bay and Cape Cod Canal district.

The provision of opportunities for pleasure driving is more difficult than that of providing access to recreational areas. In only a few areas will it be economically feasible to build pleasure drives. In most regions, pleasure driving will take place over ordinary highways, which may, however, be made much more attractive than most of them now are.

This problem has been well solved by the parkways of Westchester County, New York, which are not only attractive routes for passenger vehicles, but are also safe routes with a large capacity.

335

MASSACHUSETTS STATE PLANNING BOARD

Up to the present time, the State has not completely developed the recreational possibilities of the highways of the State. Substantial commercial advantages to the Commonwealth would result from a sweeping attack upon this problem.

Future Passenger-Car Traffic. The usual indices for determining trends in passenger-car traffic are motor-vehicle registrations, gasoline sales, and volume of traffic on the highways. All of these, at present, appear to indicate that the use of passenger automobiles is still increasing but at a decreasing rate. The point at which the number of passenger automobiles will become stabilized and cease to increase, except in proportion as the population increases, cannot be accurately determined; but, barring any revolutionary new invention to improve, radically, automobile transportation, the saturation point may be reached within the next twenty years. Marked increases or decreases in real incomes are also important factors in the number of passenger automobiles.

For a number of years, studies have been made, by the State Department of Public Works, of the distribution of traffic on the highways. A series of their maps showing a large part of the results of these studies is on file at the State Planning Board offices. Further studies need to be made of the probable amount of future traffic, its origin and destination, and its probable distribution over the highway system of the State.

Motor Trucks

The use of motor trucks has been steadily increasing since 1905. Approximately 100,000 are now registered in Massachusetts, of which number about 80 per cent are privately owned, 15 per cent are contract carriers, and 5 per cent are common carriers.* Governmental attempts to bring about direct coördination between railroads and motor trucks cannot readily be effective except with the latter 20 per cent. The three groups are highly competitive.

The ease with which the trucking business may be entered has produced some poorly trained, inadequately financed, and irresponsible operators. Reasonable public control over motor-truck operators is essential.

Advantages of Motor Trucks. Motor trucks have a number of advantages over railroads. Because of the lower costs of their terminal operations, they can perform short hauls at less cost than can the railroads. They render complete door-to-door service, which is often more personalized, flexible, and rapid than the

---

*Harold G. Moulton and Associates,"The American Transportation Problem", The Brookings Institution, Washington, D.C., 1933, pp.519-20.

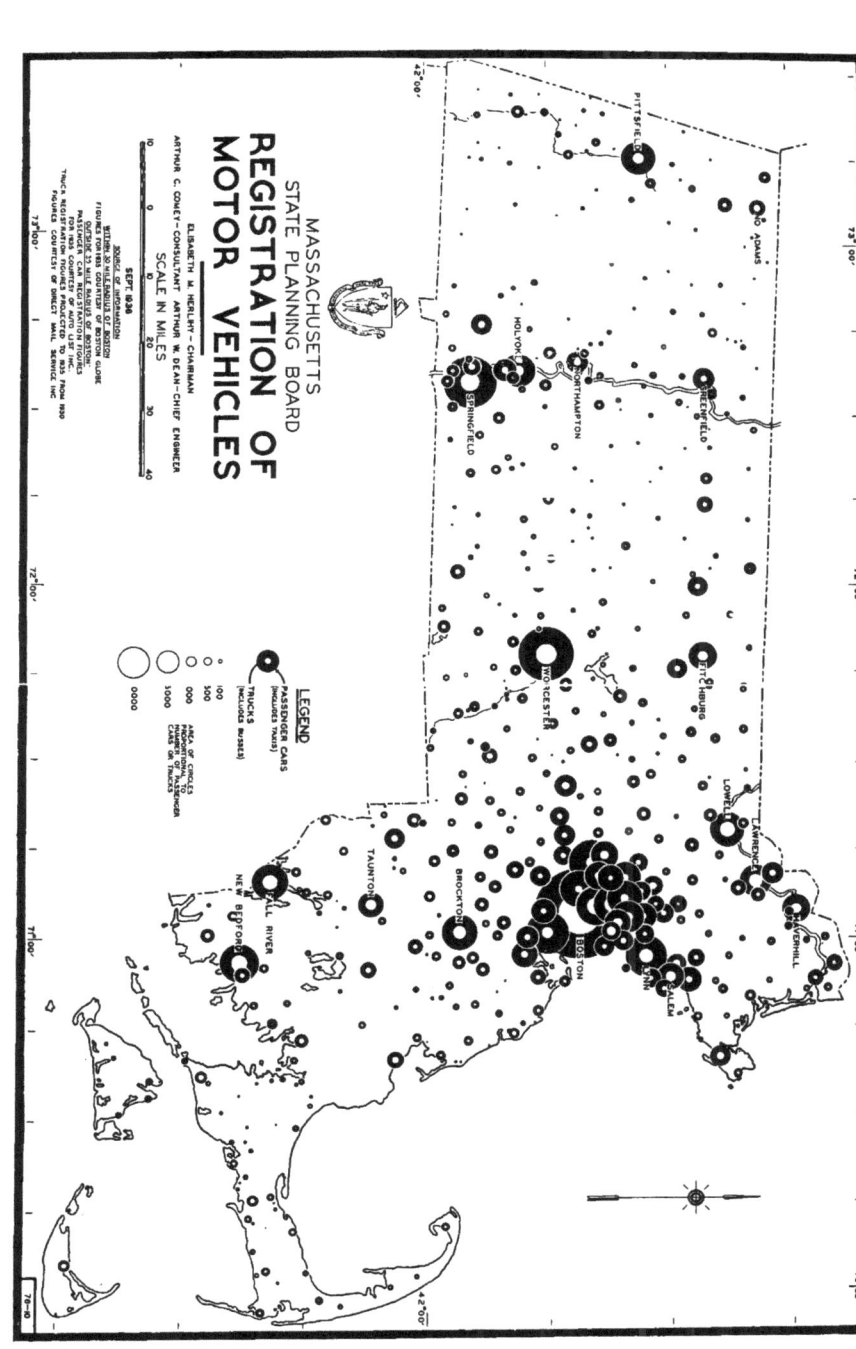

service rendered by the railroads. They avoid excessive handling of household goods, livestock, and perishable fruits and vegetables.

Truck and Railroad Coordination. New England railroads carry a larger percentage of high-grade manufactured products than do railroads in other parts of the country, and a large percentage of the total New England railroad traffic is in less than carlots. The railroads serving New England manufacturing districts have a large number of junction points per hundred miles of railroad, and a short average haul, resulting in terminal charges which are comparatively high. These traffic characteristics give the truck an advantage which was early recognized by New England railroads. Trucks are used by them for terminal service and, to some extent, for line haul. Because the railroads are operating trucks through subsidiary companies, the problem of coordinating truck and railroad services in Massachusetts is not acute. (See Map 76-11.)

Motor-truck traffic is concentrated much more in the vicinity of urban centers than is passenger-car and bus traffic. This fact gives weight to the contention that the economics of truck transportation establishes a limiting beyond which successful operation cannot go.

The most important intercity trucking routes in the State lie between the following regions:

1. Boston and the Lowell, Lawrence, and Haverhill area
2. Boston and the Fitchburg-Gardner area
3. Boston and Providence
4. Boston and the Fall River-New Bedford area
5. North and south along the Connecticut River Valley

Busses

It is estimated that only 1200 busses, representing 1.5 per cent of the total number of motor vehicles, are registered in Massachusetts. Will the bus increasingly compete with and eventually supplant railroads and street railways, or does it offer services which are supplementary to them?

In many cases, busses perform valuable supplementary services. Between many cities, the small amount of local traffic does not justify railroad services but is sufficient to support comparatively frequent bus service. (See Map 76-1.) In the larger cities, busses may supplement street railway lines by serving as feeders in outlying sections, and so on; but, in the smaller cities, it appears likely that they will eventually supplant surface street cars.

MASSACHUSETTS STATE PLANNING BOARD

Comparative Advantages and Limitations of Busses. The advantages and limitations of bus service, as compared with railroad and private-automobile transportation, have been concisely stated as follows:

"The bus offers advantages which in many respects equal those of the private car. There is, to be sure, less flexibility of routing and of schedules. There is a generally greater convenience as to points of departure and arrival than in the case of rail travel, although there is no advantage in this respect over interurbans and a disadvantage with respect to the private car; schedules are generally more frequent then by rail and are more easily understood through being spaced at regular intervals; the scenic advantages of the highways are brought within reach; and off-rail points are served, though of course such points are relatively few compared with those which can be reached by the private car. The novelty of bus travel for many people also continues to be a factor. On the other hand, railroads exceed motor-bus carriers in safety and responsibility; there are opportunities to read and work on trains which are generally lacking on buses; dining and sleeping facilities on buses have proved unsatisfactory; and lavatory accommodations are generally lacking. The time in transit is frequently materially greater than by rail, though this depends on the distance, the sections served, and the relative mileage by rail and highway. Buses carry less baggage than do trains. Much rail equipment, except that used in solely local service, has been modernized to a degree comparable with and in some respects superior to the facilities offered by the modern parlor coach."*

State Highway System

Brief History of Highway Development

The "good roads" movement started about 1890 but gained its first real impetus at the introduction of the "gasoline buggy."

At first, there were only disconnected pieces of good roads, which were not very satisfactory for long-distance travel. To connect these many bits of improved roads into continuous routes, State Highway Commissions were created. In 1921, the Federal Aid Act stipulated that Federal Aid funds should be spent only on a limited articulated system of highways. This required that less

---

*"Coordination of Motor Transportation", 182 I.C.C. 263, p.315. Quoted in Report of the Federal Coordinator of Transportation, 1934, 74th Congress, First Session, House Document 89, Government Printing Office, Washington, D.C., 1935, pp. 117-18.

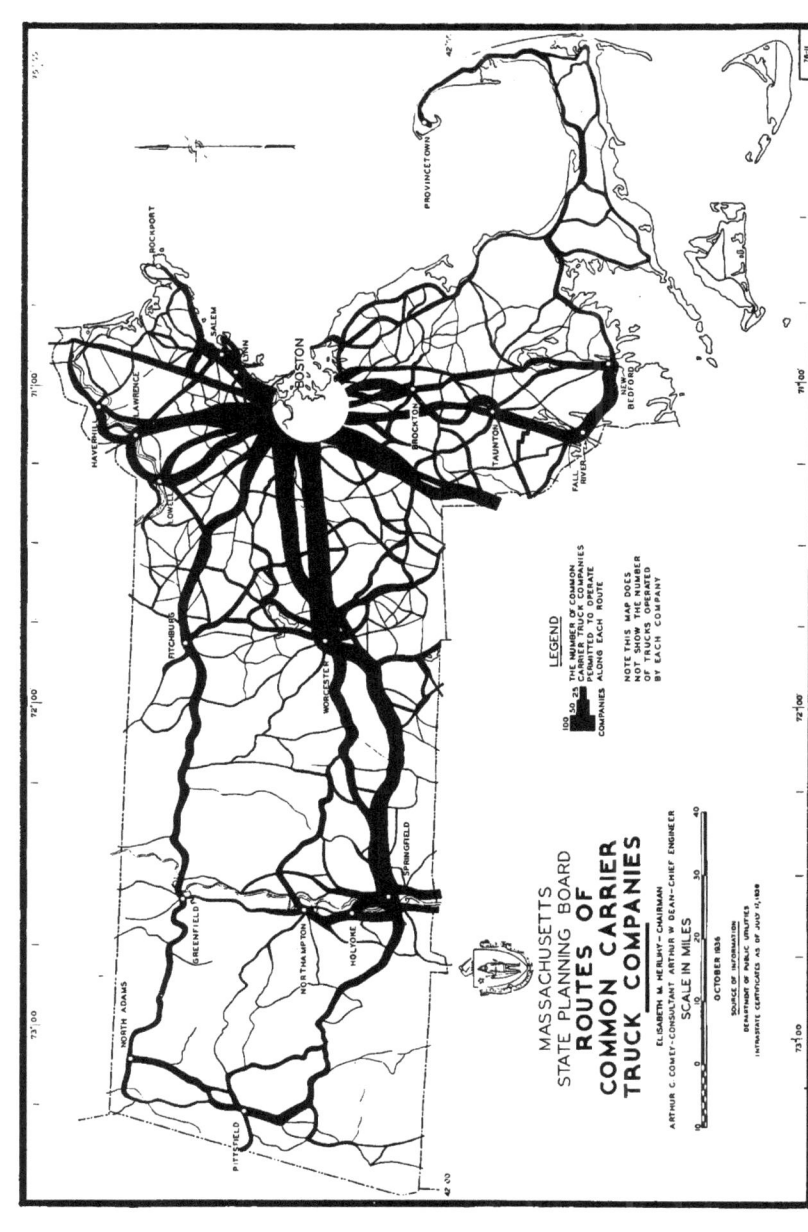

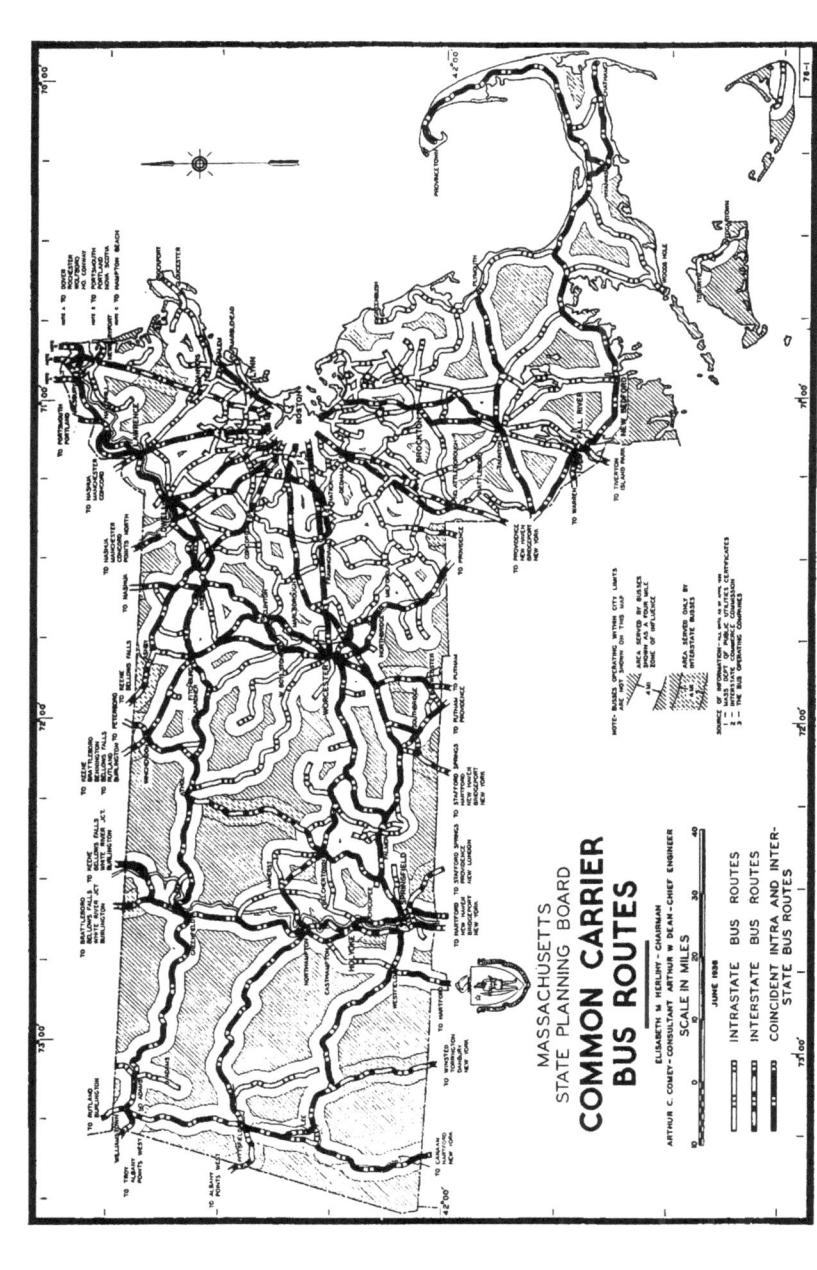

than seven per cent of the rural road mileage in the State be selected and mapped to show a net of connected routes that would allow ready travel between the most important centers of population, and would give access to the most important rural districts. This system, which was set as a goal fifteen years ago, is essentially completed.

However, the task of building an adequate system of routes for highway transportation is far from complete. A rational plan for future highway development requires three distinct steps: first, an inventory or survey of relevant factors; second, a proper plan and program, based upon the information gathered in the surveys; and third, a determination of methods, policies, and legislation necessary to carry out the plan.

Highway Surveys

Among the general surveys needed are analyses of the character, distribution, and number of motor vehicles, consumer activity and trade centers, industries that originate traffic, the recreational use of the highways, and the classification of agricultural areas and their likely future traffic demands. Surveys are needed to appraise the usefulness and capital value of each unit of the existing physical plant. They would include: the location, type, condition, width, proper load, and value of highways and bridges, the width of the right-of-way of highways and their approximate land value; and standards of design, such as radius of curvature, super-elevation, grades, and sight distances.

Two problems that most emphatically demand attention today are highway accidents and highway congestion.

Highway Accidents. The extent of the highway-accident problem is well known and need not be set forth here. The general program for an attack on it takes three main lines: (1) More thorough education of the public; (2) more complete enforcement of traffic regulations; and (3) improvement and refinement of the highway system in line with better engineering standards.

In order to carry out the second two parts of this program, every accident should be classified and plotted on a detailed map of the highway. These detailed surveys should then be digested and summed up on maps showing the whole State highway system so that one could see at a glance where most of the accidents are occurring, what is causing them, and where to spend money to correct the situation. Such an exhaustive study and analysis of the detailed causes of accidents have been begun by the Public Works

339

Department. Pending this study, accident problems can only be dealt with piecemeal.

Highway Congestion. Highway congestion occurs where two streams of traffic cross each other, where local and through traffic are mixed, where the highway is used as a walk by pedestrians, where an excessive number of entrances and side streets border a through highway, where there are too short sight distances, and wherever something distracts the driver's attention from the road ahead. Congestion may result from a too narrow piece of road or bridge. In these cases, the cause for congestion is readily discovered.

Comprehensive traffic surveys are the essential preface to analyzing the causes of congestion and establishing a plan for their removal. The Public Works Department regularly makes traffic surveys, and is completing this year a very extensive survey, the results of which will have great value. In the past, no origin and destination surveys have been made. Such surveys are difficult to make accurately, but the facts obtained from them are extremely valuable, for they make it possible to determine whether traffic is going out of its way and could be rerouted with advantage, and to determine the amount of through traffic and of local traffic.

A Trunk-Highway System for Through Travel

To cope successfully with accident and congestion problems, a trunk-highway system should be planned. This plan will indicate a limited mileage of highways to carry the heavy through traffic of the State. Traffic studies show that most of the major streams of quasi-local traffic (between points from ten to fifty miles apart) follow the same lines as the streams of through traffic. It is believed that, with proper design and selection, a broadly spaced network of highways, comprising perhaps a little over 1000 miles, or about 6 per cent of the total road mileage in the State, can be developed to carry over 50 per cent of the vehicle-miles of traffic that move outside of metropolitan and similar urban areas. Such a system, in addition to serving as the basic network for the majority of travel within the State, should also be so designed on a regional and national basis as to tap most efficiently the natural trade routes along which move commerce and tourists attracted to Massachusetts.

Standards of Design. Certain standards of design are essential if the system of major trunk highways for through travel is to be effective. The ordinary narrow right-of-way with its strip of hard surface may still be sufficient for city and village streets and ordinary access highways. For arterial thoroughfares, such a highway is dangerous, subject to congestion, and in many cases, responsible to a large degree, for the depreciation of abutting property values. To assure that whatever money is invested in these special routes will give proper returns in transportation values, several objectives must be attained:

1. Removal of causes of highway accidents
2. Removal of obstacles to the free flow of traffic and prevention of congestion
3. Preservation of the natural beauty of the countryside and the highways

As these three are all interrelated, improvements to serve one of these ends may serve all three.

One great obstacle to going from place to place in reasonable time is the present necessity of traveling through populated areas on comparatively narrow streets, often with parking on both sides of the street, and with pedestrians constantly crossing from one side to the other. The built-up area is detrimental to the movement of traffic, and the heavy flow of passenger cars, trucks, and busses may ruin the charm and lower the values of the abutting property. Measures to remedy this situation by widening and straightening local highways have been costly and only temporary. Trunk highways for through travel should pass near to but not through the built-up parts of cities and towns.

A condition similar to that which arises in urban areas occurs along many of the highways. They have deteriorated because they are flanked by a double row of hot-dog stands, gas stations, billboards, ice-cream parlors, and every other conceivable nuisance to distract the driver from the business of driving, into the business of spending. The resulting innumerable possibilities that the driver in front will jam on his brakes to make a turn off the highway or that a car will dart unexpectedly onto the highway from the side creates a situation that is far too hazardous to be tolerated on any highway in which the State invests money, ostensibly for the purpose of carrying a heavy load of traffic. It is obvious that this condition markedly increases the time required to go safely from place to place and, by its unsightly, disorderly, and tawdry character, in some places lowers abutting land values and certainly creates a very bad impression on the State's extremely valuable tourist trade. The resulting economic losses make it imperative that this situation be anticipated and prevented from springing up along future trunk highways for through travel. A large mileage of such highways will be constructed over new land acquired at agricultural-land prices. Their transportation values can be conserved by taking additional land or easements to prevent access to the roadway from abutting property. This is no unprecedented policy. It has been carried out along the nationally famous parkway system of Westchester County, New York, and along the new Merritt Parkway in Connecticut, and has been done to some degree by the Metropolitan District Commission and by municipal governments. The legislation necessary to carry out such a policy is discussed in detail below. Sound policy requires that the improvement of any read or highway be carried out in stages; hence, the first thing to be provided for is the acquisition, while the land is still cheap, of all the right-of-way and easements that will be needed.

Several important features must be built into a trunk highway for through travel, whenever the traffic becomes heavy. A center reservation is extremely important; for, by confining traffic movements along a pavement strip to one direction, the liability to accidents is very much reduced. The necessary intersections must be protected either by a separation of grades or by the construction of circles of sufficient diameter to permit fairly free passage around the circle and weaving into proper lanes to make the desired movements to and from the intersecting streets.

Modern highway lighting systems will prevent many serious accidents on thoroughfares that have a heavy, fast-moving night traffic. Regulatory methods, such as warning signs, painted centerlines at hazardous points, well-designed shoulders, and safety fences, improve the safety of highways.

All of these features have their proper place on trunk highways. The time of their installation will depend upon the volume of traffic and the State's ability to pay for them. The Public Works Department highway engineers are well acquainted with these features and, given a stabilized budget to work with, could install them where and when they are most needed.

Primary Intrastate and Secondary Highways

Under this classification falls the extensive highway network connecting cities and towns with one another. On the whole, Massachusetts has a satisfactory system of primary intrastate and secondary highways.

Local Service Roads

Many settled rural areas and centers with small population depend upon highway transportation for their contacts with the outside world. In many cases, the highway facilities are inadequate. Individually, most of these roads are primarily of local interest; only a few of them will be incorporated into the major highway system. Nevertheless, it is important, to everyone in the State, that people from every part of Massachusetts have adequate year-round highway access. Justification for expenditures for the development of local roads will increase and decrease in different areas in relation to the changing rural development. Two surveys that are now being carried on will provide the bases for classifying local service roads in order of their importance: (1) the traffic census, sponsored by the Public Works Department, which will indicate the roads that should be included in the major highway system, and (2) the land-use survey, sponsored by the State Planning Board, which will indicate the areas of stable or expanding rural developments which require improved local-service roads. When this information is assembled, a program for the improvement of local-service roads can be developed.

Economic Aspects

Further study should be given to several important problems in the development of a long-term highway-construction program, such as the determination of the economic benefits resulting from any particular piece of construction and the determination of whether each group of taxpayers is receiving an equitable share of the benefits of highway building.

Valuable results have been obtained in other States from studies of this nature. Such studies are being pursued to serve as guides for highway development in Massachusetts.

Highway Legislation

The most-needed new legislation for better highway practice is that authorizing the construction of freeways.

All of the practices and inferences that are wrapped up in current definitions of a highway are the product of pre-automobile history. The legal definition of a highway needs to be liberalized and changed,to make the highway suitable for present-day automobile traffic. Mr. Edward M. Bassett, a lawyer and expert on planning legislation, has defined a highway, in the old sense, as a "strip of public land, dedicated to movement,over which the owner of abutting property has the right of light, air, and access." A parkway has been defined by him as a "strip of public land dedicated to recreation, over which the owner of abutting property has no right of light, air, or access."

MASSACHUSETTS STATE PLANNING BOARD

The efficiency of the parkway in handling traffic suggested the idea of a highway of the parkway type, but serving other purposes than recreation. This he called a "freeway" and defined it as "a strip of public land, dedicated to movement, over which the owner of abutting property has no right of light, air, or access."

Three bills are proposed for submission to the legislature, covering the various situations to be met, as follows:

1. A bill, hereto appended, defining a freeway and giving the Public Works Department the authority to build such freeways.

2. A bill, hereto appended, giving the Public Works Department the right to buy reservation strips at the sides of highways which are either existing or to be laid out. These reservations would serve the purpose of denying abutters the right of access to the highway and would, in addition, provide land for such accessories as bridle paths and sidewalks, and would permit widening or changing the alignment of the highway within the limits of the reservation.

3. A bill to give the Public Works Department the right to establish set-backs or building-lines similar to those established by municipalities for many years and to a certain extent by counties. The prepared bill is the one introduced by the Public Works Department in 1932 (House 149).

A BILL RELATIVE TO THE LAYING OUT AND CARE BY THE COMMONWEALTH OF FREEWAYS, AND MAKING CERTAIN LAWS APPLICABLE TO SUCH WAYS

Be it enacted, etc., as follows:

Section four of chapter eighty-one of the General Laws (Tercentenary Edition) is hereby amended by inserting in the third line, after the word "highway", the words: - "or freeway", - and adding to the end of said section the following: - "All the provisions herein and of existing laws relating to State highways shall apply to freeways, except that access to such freeways shall be had only over public ways existing or over such public ways thereafter laid out connecting with such freeways as may be approved in writing for such purpose by the Department of Public Works."

MASSACHUSETTS STATE PLANNING BOARD

A BILL TO PERMIT THE PUBLIC WORKS DEPARTMENT TO ESTABLISH
RESERVATIONS ALONG STATE HIGHWAYS

Be it enacted, etc., as follows:

Chapter 81 of the General Laws is hereby amended by adding to the end thereof, under the caption "HIGHWAY RESERVATIONS", the following new section:

Section 32. If the department determines that, in order to preserve the usefulness of a highway for purposes of transportation or to preserve the amenities of travel on a highway, it is necessary to acquire reservations, not exceeding 100 feet in width, abutting said highway, the department may acquire the same by purchase or gift or may take the same by eminent domain on behalf of the Commonwealth under Chapter Seventy-Nine. No owner of land abutting such a reservation shall have any right of access to such highway over such reservation or any right to construct any driveway or other means of access across or in such reservation.

The department shall have the exclusive right and power to lay out, alter or discontinue any or all streets, highways and bridges within the border of such reservations; to landscape the land and rearrange its contours; to embellish such reservations so as to make them available for the use and attractive to the sight of travelers; to grant to any governmental agency licenses or easements for any purpose that does not unduly interfere with the initial purpose of the highway and the reservation; to grant to individuals or corporations licenses or easements to enter upon at designated points or to construct sewers, lay water and gas mains and electric conduits within and across such reservations.

For the purpose of this section the department may expend any money that is appropriated for this purpose or that is not specifically set aside for some other purpose.

MASSACHUSETTS STATE PLANNING BOARD

RAILROADS

Value of Railroads to the Commonwealth

Railroads are still the backbone of the entire transportation system, despite the fact that their former transportation monopoly has been partially taken from them by the automobile.

The long-haul movement of freight and passengers can be accomplished most efficiently by the railroads. Massachusetts' industries import raw materials and coal from comparatively distant points and export high-grade manufactured articles to all parts of the United States via rail. Curtailment of cheap railway transportation, upon which Massachusetts industries have always been dependent, might easily force many industrial plants and workers to move elsewhere. The preservation and strengthening of the railroad system is very important to the State.

The railroads operate under heavy debt burdens and complex financial structures. Only increased traffic will solve many of these financial problems, which were accentuated by the depression. Rail service and rates advantageous to commerce and industry will insure continued growth of traffic.

New England railroads are alive to the situation and are taking measures to revive their former traffic. The recent inauguration of fast streamline trains and other improvements of service are indications of progress. A good line of attack has been indicated by Colonel Charles D. Young.*

"Ships, trucks, buses, private automobiles and airplanes have their places and the effort of railway management now is to determine the place the railway best fits in the transportation body; then to concentrate on making that part function in the best possible manner. This will not only require the joint efforts of the scientist, the engineer and the economist to find the possibilities, and managerial ability of a high order to convert those possibilities into useful functions in the public interest, but also a like attitude on the part of competitive transportation so that the two may be coördinated to give the best service at the lowest possible cost."

---

*Colonel Charles D. Young, "The Railway Outlook", News Service, the Massachusetts Institute of Technology, June 8, 1936.

Special Railroad Problems

Freight Service

The railroads which operate in Massachusetts serve in New England a densely populated coastal belt about seventy-five miles wide, extending from the Hudson River in New York to Portland, Maine. The major portion of traffic on these railroads originates and terminates in New England. The railroads are dependent upon connections with other railroads serving the rest of the country, and with steamship lines.

Railroads are still the most important carriers of freight, especially long-haul imported bulk freight such as cotton, wool, iron, and other raw materials, and coal. Rail exports consist of products of the forests and the quarries, and manufactured products. It has been estimated that for every three carloads of manufactured products moving westward from New England, five carloads of raw materials move eastward into New England.*

Short-haul freight is comparatively unprofitable to the railroads, and much of this tonnage, especially less-than-car load lots, has been taken over by motor trucks, which can, on the average, carry freight up to a distance of about seventy-five miles more economically than can the railroads. It would seem to be advantageous for the railroads to abandon all short-haul operations, and utilize their equipment for the more profitable long-haul freight. Long-haul railroad service might be supplemented by railroad-owned trucks for short-haul service.

Present freight services in Massachusetts are shown on Map 76-2.

Passenger Service

Railroads are still the most important transportation agency in long-distance passenger travel and in outer suburban commuting service. Traffic is growing in these two fields. Although the private automobile and the bus have permanently diverted much passenger traffic from the railroads this loss is largely local passenger traffic between adjacent cities and small towns, over relatively short distances. The New Haven and the Boston and Maine Railroads have met this motor-coach competition by operating their own motor-coaches. Highway congestion, especially during rush hours, at present tends to prevent serious inroads on railroad commuting services, which are superior in convenience and speed to highway travel.

---

*Interstate Commerce Commission Reports, Vol.49 (1918), p.421.

MASSACHUSETTS STATE PLANNING BOARD

Present passenger services in Massachusetts are shown on Map 76-4.

Railroad Lines with Light Traffic

Approximately 30 per cent of the railroad truckage in Massachusetts has less traffic moving over it than is economically required to pay the costs of the services provided. There are two possible solutions of this problem.

First, rail traffic may be increased. This may possibly be accomplished by the utilization of new types of equipment, such as smaller train units using motive power other than steam (gas, diesel, or electric), and light-weight and air-conditioned passenger cars.

Second, lines bearing light traffic might be abandoned in favor of truck and bus services.

Terminals

The costs of terminal operations of New England railroads are very high, in proportion to income, owing to the shorter average haul. Over four-fifths of the time required for typical completed car movement is spent in terminals. The costs of terminal services and the time required for them indicate a need for improvements and readjustments in this department of railroad operations.

There is a general tendency to move terminals from intown locations to the outskirts of cities. These changes will probably continue, although they usually involve throwing more traffic on the streets. On the outskirts, sufficiently large areas are usually available to permit future expansion and to facilitate coordination with motor trucks, thus facilitating freight transfer. Circumferential truck routes and other highway improvements may be needed between terminals.

Coordinated Railroad Services

The possibilities of developing coordinated railroad services have been studied. Joint freight and passenger terminals at junction points, joint use of shops, pooling of freight cars and trains, standardization of equipment by a centralized research bureau, reduction of interline transfers of cars, simplification of accounting, and revision of rate differentials to meet present competitive conditions are a few of the improvements which may be accomplished.

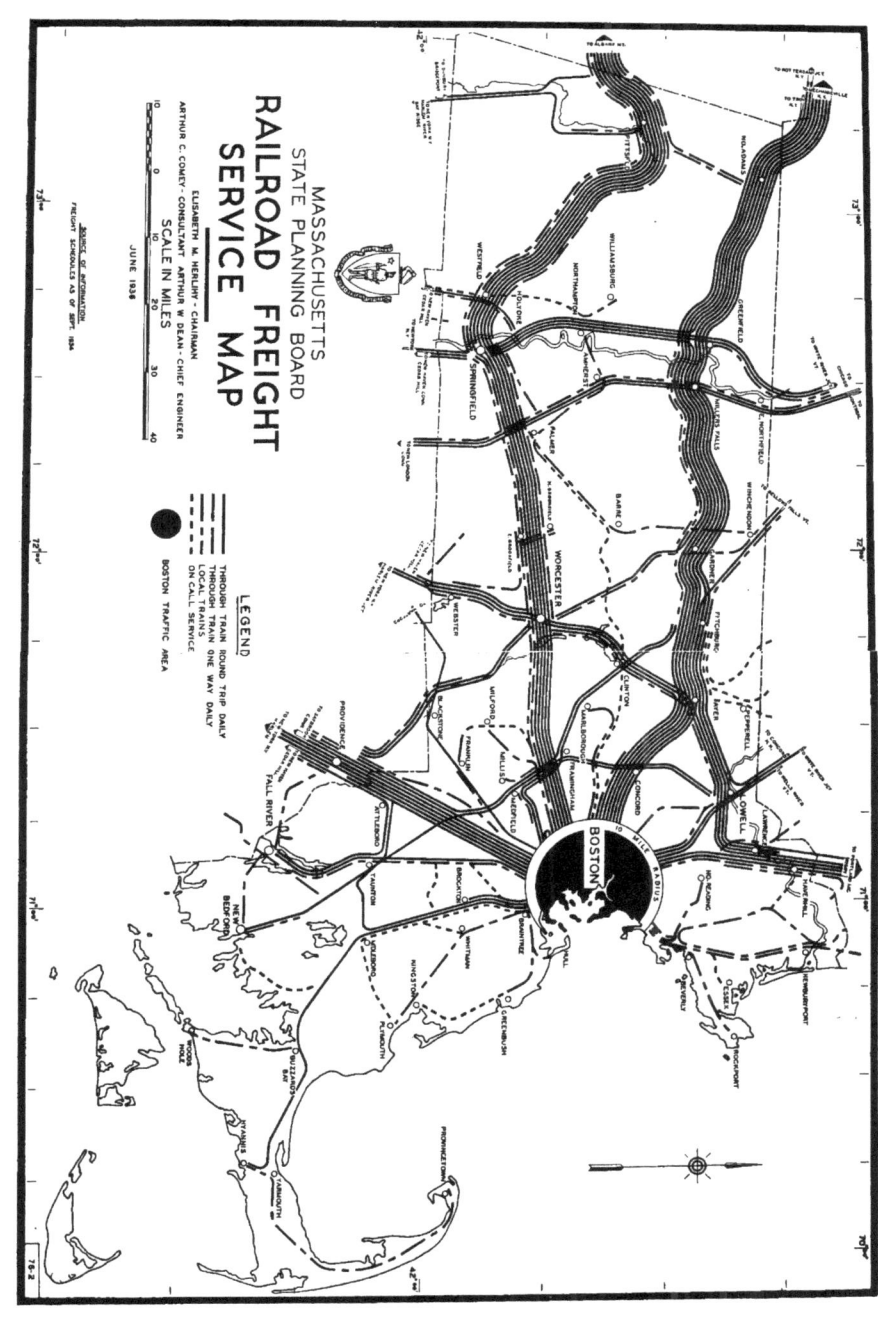

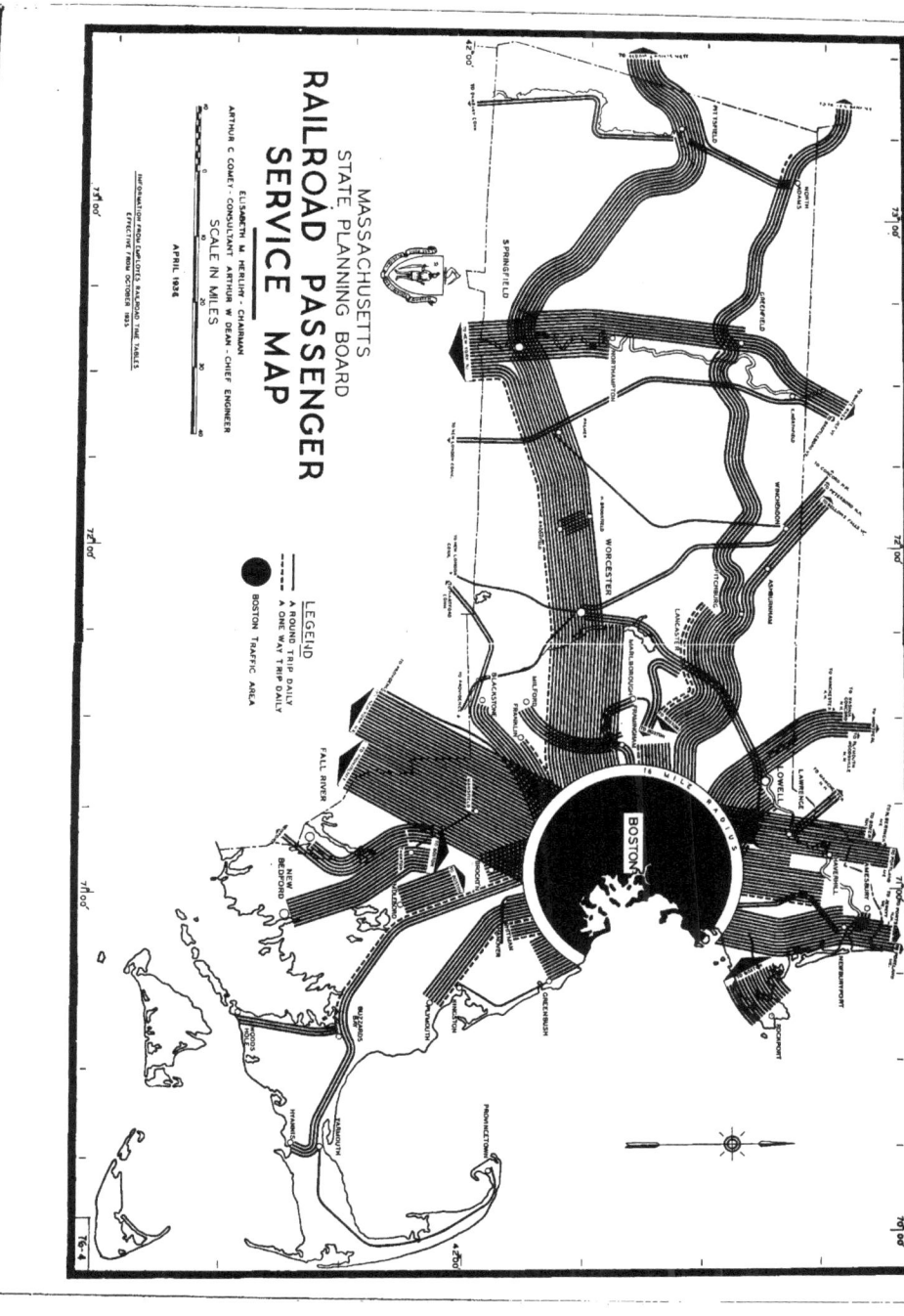

Government restrictions should not prohibit the railroads from operating subsidiary truck, bus, air, and steamboat companies. When two or more forms of transportation are operated by a single company, advantageous coordinations which will promote public interest may be effected. As fast as the railroads are able to establish such lines they should be permitted so to do, under appropriate control.

Store-Door Collection and Delivery Service

Of much importance to shippers is store-door collection and delivery service. The extra expense of this service to the railroads will probably be off-set by increased traffic.

MASSACHUSETTS STATE PLANNING BOARD

WATER TRANSPORT

Transport by water in Massachusetts is practically confined to ocean waterways, as there are no inland waterways of importance in the State. The three major ports of Massachusetts are at Boston, Fall River, and New Bedford; Boston is one of the principal seaports of the United States. Minor ports, used largely by local shipping, such as those at Gloucester, Lynn, and Beverly, are not specifically considered in this report. The harbors and facilities of the three major ports, especially those of Boston, are excellent, and are adequate for present traffic. Indeed, the problem, well recognized, is to provide more complete utilization of present facilities. The causes for the comparatively small port business are: (1) lack of bulk cargoes; (2) diversion of port traffic to the port of New York; and (3) unfavorable rail differentials. Certain recommendations for developing the commerce of Massachusetts ports are here considered, but no definite plan is presented, pending a forthcoming report of a special recess commission of the General Court, which has been making an exhaustive study of the port situation in the State.

Value of Seaports to Massachusetts

Water transportation is as important as railroad service to many of the industries of the State, which depend upon efficient and low-cost transportation of incoming raw materials and outgoing manufactures. Bulk imports of raw materials, such as coal, fuel oil, and other commodities, enter the State through Massachusetts ports and the port of New York; while manufactured exports of small bulk and high value are shipped out of Massachusetts ports, or are sent overland to the port of New York or to ports in Canada.

Foreign trade is an important item of commerce for Massachusetts and for New England. Three ports -- Boston, Mass., Portland, Maine, and Providence, R.I., -- handle 86 per cent of the foreign traffic of New England. The port of Boston handles 55 per cent, Portland, 17 per cent, and Providence 14 per cent.*

Imports

Among the imported raw materials are wool, cotton, timber,

---
*Edward F. Gerish, "Commercial Structure of New England"(1929), p. 264.

hides and skins, iron and steel, and chemicals. Boston is the largest wool market in the world and figures largely in the distribution of this commodity, as well as of hides and skins, to other parts of the United States. With these exceptions, the port of Boston serves chiefly the New England territory. Coal and fuel oil are bulk commodities imported in large quantities.

Imports have been steadily increasing in both volume and value over a thirty-year period to 1930. A preponderance of the shipping consists of coastwise receipts and imports. In 1930, the value of imports at the port of Boston was more than five times the value of exports; while the import tonnage was eleven times the export tonnage. The total annual tonnage of imports and exports, passing through the port, increased 40 per cent during the thirty-year period.

Boston has been unable to compete successfully with New York for imports destined for points west of New England. Although the port of Boston is nearer to Europe, a mountainous hinterland and longer rail haul, coupled with the fact that the port is off the main through continental routes of travel, which terminate at New York, have been handicaps.

Exports

While imports have been increasing, exports have been declining. Since the turn of the century, Massachusetts ports have lost a large part of their export trade to the port of New York. A survey of New England's foreign trade disclosed that, in 1928, 60 million dollars worth of Massachusetts' manufactured exports, or 56 per cent of the total value, were exported through the port of New York; whereas but 23 per cent were handled by the port of Boston. The chief reasons for this condition are the more frequent sailings from New York to all parts of the world and a lack, at Boston, of bulk cargoes which are attractive to shipping. Since New York is geographically the gateway to much of the United States, it has become the world's greatest seaport. It is natural that some Massachusetts trade should be attracted to this great port because of close proximity.

This situation seems to support the contention that the larger the port, the less its percentage loss in trade has been. The larger ports show a better balance between import and export tonnage, and have the advantage of more frequent sailings.

MASSACHUSETTS STATE PLANNING BOARD

Methods of Increasing Port Business

Increasing the Frequency of Sailings

If a way could be found to attract ballast cargoes from the interior of the country, present empty out-going bottoms could be filled, and the tonnage and frequency of shipping would increase. Railroad connections and rates between Oswego, New York, on Lake Ontario, and Boston are favorable to ex-lake grain shipments, and it is hoped that some trade can be attracted via this route.

Port facilities for general merchandise should be concentrated at as few ports as possible in order to increase export shipping at these terminals. This principle does not apply particularly to facilities designed especially for bulk cargoes, such as coal and oil, for it is expected that there will always be an unbalanced import-to-export movement in such commodities. The concentration of port facilities at a few locations where rail heads and other transportation lines can be tapped most readily will tend to encourage more frequent sailings at such ports.

Development of Fast European Service

The development of fast passenger, mail, and express service to and from Europe has been pointed out, as follows, as another way of increasing traffic through the port of Boston.

"The advantage of Boston over New York in distance to Europe combined with the ease of access of this port to the open sea, and the freedom of the port from congestion of traffic, would make possible a saving in time of about a day for the North Atlantic crossing if fast passenger and mail trains from New York, Chicago, Montreal, and other interior cities were made to connect with fast steamships at Boston."*

Express air lines from Boston to the interior would be an important adjunct to such a plan.

Free Port

In a report to the Boston Port Authority,** in 1935, Mr. H.

---
*G. B. Roorback, "The Importance of Foreign Trade to New England," NEW ENGLAND'S PROSPECT, 1933, New York, American Geographical Society, 1933, p. 384
**House Document 1950 (1935).

MASSACHUSETTS STATE PLANNING BOARD

Fugl-Meyer, an expert on free ports, advised against the establishment of a free port at Boston. He declared that the present system of bonded warehouses meets commercial needs in a more economical manner; that no part of the present port is technically suitable for conversion to a free zone; and that the geographical location of Boston appears unfavorable to the development of a free port. It is uncertain how well a North Atlantic free port in the United States would function, since all past experience with free ports has been European.

Ports of Massachusetts

Harbors and Channels

Boston. The outer harbor of Boston has three main channels 40 feet, 30 feet, and 27 feet deep, and 1,000 to 1,500 feet wide. They are well marked with lighted buoys, and are navigable throughout the year. The main ship channel of the inner harbor is 35 feet deep (now being dredged to 40 feet), and has a width of 1,200 feet. Several navigable rivers and creeks empty into the harbor. Dorchester Bay, Neponset River, and Weymouth Fore River have channels 15 to 24 feet deep. Boston Harbor has a total waterfrontage of over 140 miles, of which 7 miles has a depth of 35 feet or more. There are approximately 1,500 acres of anchorage.

Fall River. Fall River Harbor is about 2 miles long, and one-fourth to one mile wide. Narragansett Bay, a wide and deep natural waterway, affords an approach to the harbor and an excellent, protected anchorage. The major portion of the approach channel is 30 feet deep and 300 feet wide, and is navigable throughout the year. The total frontage is about 10 miles. The main harbor has about 195 acres of anchorage.

New Bedford. The outer harbor of New Bedford is approached, from the sea, through Buzzards Bay, and is 2 miles wide and 2 miles long. A 30-foot channel extends to the New Bedford and Fairhaven bridge, and continues north to Belleville, a distance of about 2 miles, with a width of 100 feet and a depth of 18 to 25 feet. Protected anchorages are available in Buzzards Bay. The inner harbor anchorage has an area of 114 acres.

Terminal Facilities

Boston. In East Boston there are 51 wharves, all of which have good highway connections. Of these, 10 are used for public purposes and have rail connections. Three are used by regular overseas steamship lines. The most important terminal is the Grand

MASSACHUSETTS STATE PLANNING BOARD

Junction Wharves of the Boston and Albany Railroad.

There are 28 wharves on the Mystic River, including the largest lumber terminal and one of the most modern coal-discharging plants on the Atlantic seaboard. There are 37 wharves on Chelsea Creek, Chelsea waterfront, Island End River, and Malden River.

The Charlestown waterfront has 23 wharves, including 10 used by important overseas steamship lines, the Boston and Maine terminal known as "Mystic Wharves", and the Hoosac Tunnel Docks. There are 35 wharves on Charles River, Millers River, and Lechmere and Broad Canals.

On the city waterfront, there are 28 wharves and piers devoted to coastwise and local traffic. On Fort Point Channel and South Bay, there are 22 wharves. There are 11 wharves on the South Boston waterfront, including four piers owned by the Commonwealth of Massachusetts. Commonwealth Pier No. 5 is a modern two-story structure with berthing spaces for five or more ocean steamships, and facilities for passenger and freight traffic. Commonwealth Pier No. 6, known as the Fish Pier, is highly efficient for its specialized purpose.

There are 15 wharves on the Reserved Channel. The immense Army supply base has a landing platform extending for three-quarters of a mile along this channel. There are more than 60 acres of floor space within the buildings, and many additional acres in open storage platforms, paved roadways, and open tracks.

Dorchester Bay and Neponset River have 13 wharves; Weymouth Fore River, 14 wharves; and Weymouth Back River, 2 wharves.

There are three grain elevators at the port; two have a storage capacity of 1,000,000 bushels, and one has a storage capacity of 420,000 bushels.

Boston is well equipped with warehouses suitable for handling a large foreign and domestic business. The terminal facilities at Boston are capable of accommodating more than the volume of traffic which passed through the port in any year prior to 1935. The majority of the modern piers, docks, and warehouses are connected with the three trunk railroads. The Commonwealth Pier and Army supply base provide unusual facilities for storage, with modern equipment which makes possible exceptional rapidity in the handling of shipments, yet they were used to only a small part of their capacity prior to 1936. At times, during the past year, many of the docks have been crowded.

Fall River. The port of Fall River has 36 wharves. Of these, 3 are used by steamship and railroad lines for public transportation, and 2 are public wharves owned by the City of Fall River. Thirteen warehouses are used principally for the storage of cotton. In addition, there are privately owned facilities for the storage of coal, lumber, and oil.

New Bedford. There are 29 wharves on the New Bedford waterfront, and 8 wharves on the Fairhaven side of the harbor. Of these wharves, 4 are used exclusively by regular transportation lines, 7 are used for coal, 3 for oil, and the remainder for miscellaneous purposes. There is a State Pier and a City Pier. There are private storage facilities for coal, oil, and lumber. The greater part of the storage-warehouse space is used for raw cotton and cotton goods.

Port Administration

The subject of port administration will be dealt with in a forthcoming report by a special recess commission of the General Court. This commission was authorized, by Resolve 66 of the Acts of 1936, to make a comprehensive study of "the functions and problems of the Boston Port Authority, and other related matters, with a view to facilitating the production and development of the commerce of the port of Boston and other ports in the Commonwealth." Among other things, the advisability of transferring the administration of the waterfront terminals of the Commonwealth to the Boston Port Authority is being considered. Decisions relative to improvements in port administration should await the findings of this commission.

Sources of Information

Artman, C.E., and S.H. Reed, "Foreign Trade Survey of New England." Bureau of Foreign and Domestic Commerce (Domestic Commerce Series, No. 40), Washington, Government Printing Office, 1931.

Clapp, Edwin J., "The Port of Boston," New Haven, Yale University Press, 1916.

Corps of Engineers (U.S. Army) and the United States Shipping Board, "The Port of Boston" (Revised, 1929) (Port Series No. 2) and "The Ports of Southern New England" (Port Series No. 18, 1928), Washington, Government Printing Office.

MASSACHUSETTS STATE PLANNING BOARD

Fugl-Meyer, H., "Report to the Boston Port Authority on the Fracticability of Establishing a Free Port at Boston, Mass.", The Commonwealth of Massachusetts, 1935. House Document No. 1950.

Gerish, Edward F., "Commercial Structure of New England," Part II of the Commercial Survey of New England, Bureau of Foreign and Domestic Commerce (Domestic Commerce Series No. 26), Washington, Government Printing Office, 1929.

Jones, Grosvenor M., "The Ports of the United States," Bureau of Foreign and Domestic Commerce (Miscellaneous Series No. 33), Washington, Government Printing Office, 1916.

Roorback, G. B., "The Importance of Foreign Trade to New England," NEW ENGLAND'S PROSPECT, 1933, American Geographical Society, New York, 1933.

MASSACHUSETTS STATE PLANNING BOARD

AVIATION

Introduction

Aviation is becoming a commonplace as people are discovering in their everyday lives the tremendous value of flying. Air transportation companies now furnish regular scheduled services, which are probably the most important uses of our present-day air facilities, but are by no means the only ones. Aviation renders a variety of services.

PART I. THE USE AND NEED FOR AVIATION IN MASSACHUSETTS

As the ocean is free for sailing, so the air is free for flying, and, for the same reason that it is a wise policy to furnish light houses and serviceable harbors for ocean traffic, it is expedient to furnish certain public aids to aviation. In order to plan the extent and time of construction of these public aids to air navigation, it is necessary to consider the uses which aviation serves, at present, in Massachusetts and the prospects for increased usefulness.

Commercial Aviation

Scheduled Common-Carrier Air Transport Operations

Growth. The tremendous and phenomenal growth which air transport has enjoyed since its beginning ten years ago is shown on Chart 56-C1.

Operations in Massachusetts. Three air transport companies connect Massachusetts with all parts of North America by air. American Air Lines, Inc. flies scheduled trips from Boston to Providence, Hartford, New Haven, and New York City; connecting in New York (Newark Airport) with major airlines. This company also flies scheduled trips via Springfield to Albany, Buffalo, Cleveland, Detroit, and Chicago; again connecting with major airlines. National Airways, Inc. operates between Boston and Burlington, Vermont, with stops at Manchester and Concord, New Hampshire, and White River Junction and Montpelier, Vermont. It also has scheduled flights between Boston and Bar Harbor, Maine, with stops at Portland, Augusta, Waterville, and Bangor, Maine. Mayflower Airlines, Inc. has this summer provided service between Boston, Provincetown, Hyannis, Marthas Vineyard, and Nantucket. "Cape Cod Seaplanes, Inc." provided service between New Bedford, Marthas Vineyard, and Nantucket. Map 56-1 shows the relation of these scheduled flights to the scheduled services being flown over the eastern United States, as of May 1936.

357

MASSACHUSETTS STATE PLANNING BOARD

Tests for Value of Scheduled Air Transport to Business Men. The value of scheduled common-carrier air transportation to business men can be compared with that of other methods of transportation in the light of speed, cost, safety, reliability, and convenience.*

Speed. Persons engaged in all types of commercial enterprises need the fast transportation that airlines provide. Light merchandise of high value, requiring rapid delivery, is now regularly sent by airplane. Speed is an important asset of air transportation, but, unless air terminals are located reasonably close to community centers, much of this advantage is lost in the time taken in getting to and from the airport.

Cost. Reasonableness of fare is another factor which influences the amount of use. Not until fares were considerably reduced (in 1929) did air transportation come into vogue. The rate of fares, in some instances, is now less than first-class railroad accommodations and averages $5\frac{1}{2}¢$ per mile.** The reduction in travel time frequently brings about sufficient savings in incidental expenses to counterbalance any differences in fare.

Safety. The hazards of travel by scheduled air transport are, most unfortunately, exaggerated in the minds of the public. Travel over a well-organized airline is now considered safer than travel in a private passenger automobile. However, air travel has not approached the safety offered by railroad transportation.***

Reliability. The ratio of miles actually flown to scheduled miles is the most commonly used index of reliability of service. The reliability figures for United States and New England in 1935 are shown in the following table:

---

*Cf Harold G. Moulton and Associates, "The American Transportation Problem", Washington, D.C., The Brookings Institute, 1933, pp. 725-33.
  **Colonel Edgar S. Gorrell, "Current Trends in Air Transportation", News Service of the Massachusetts Institute of Technology, June 8, 1936, p. 9.
  ***Harold G. Moulton, "The American Transportation Problem", p. 730.

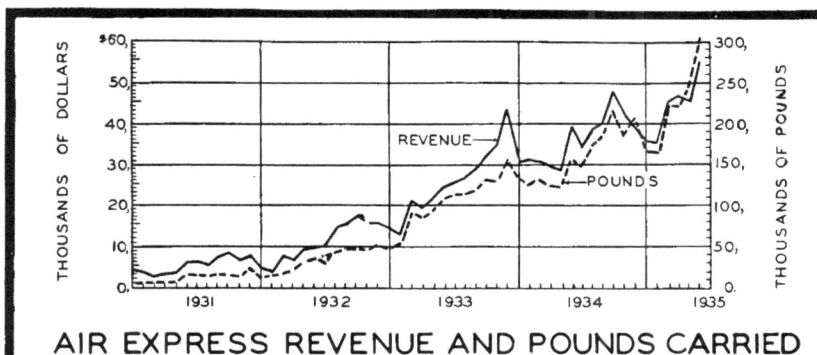

AIR EXPRESS REVENUE AND POUNDS CARRIED

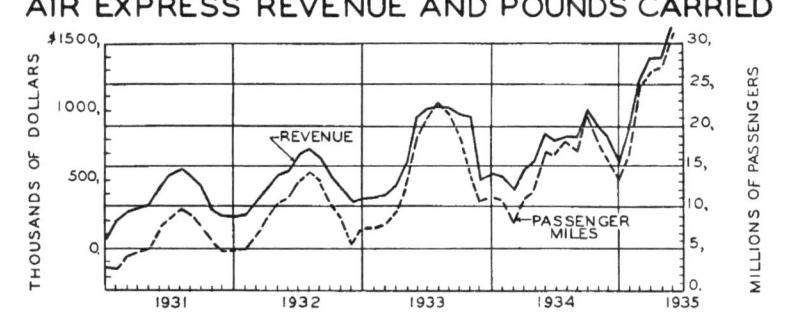

PASSENGER REVENUE AND PASSENGER MILES

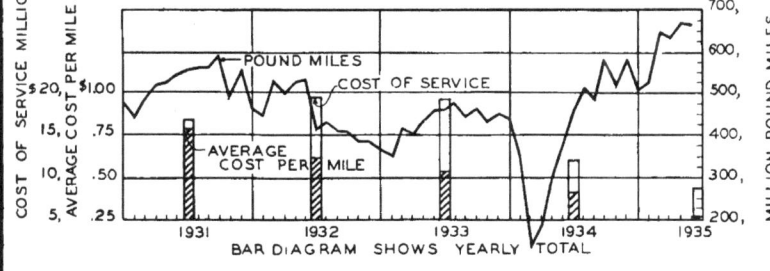

POUND MILES OF MAIL,
TOTAL COST OF MAIL AND AVERAGE COST PER MILE
AIR MAIL CONTRACTORS—FOR THE UNITED STATES
SOURCE—1935 ANNUAL REPORT OF POSTMASTER GENERAL.

MASSACHUSETTS STATE PLANNING BOARD
NOVEMBER—1935

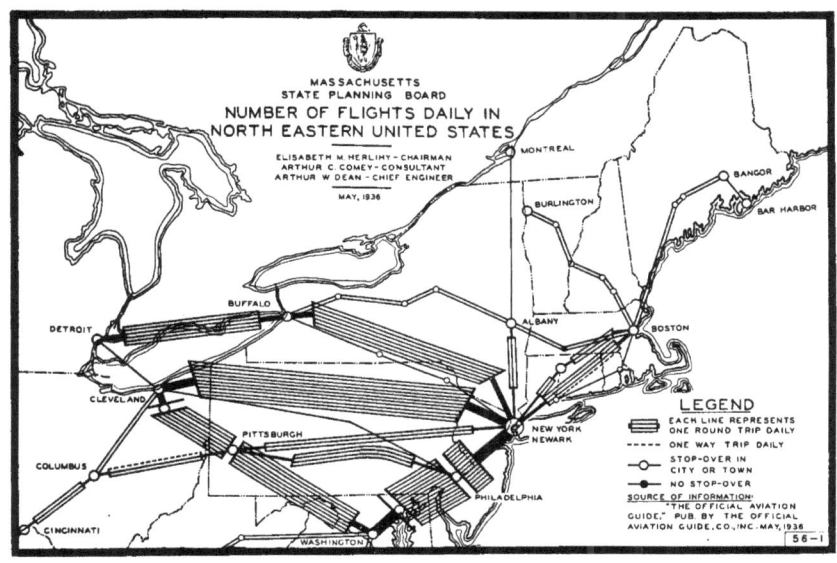

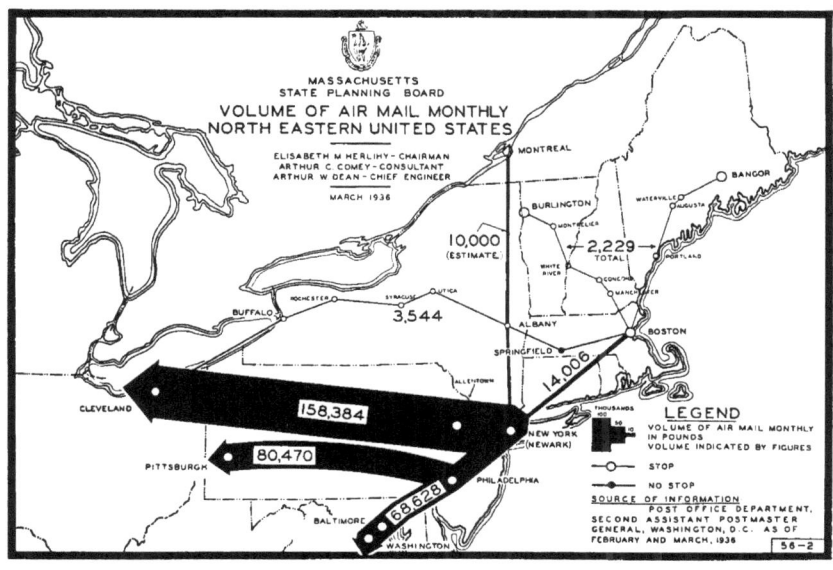

MASSACHUSETTS STATE PLANNING BOARD

Table 65

RELIABILITY OF AIR TRANSPORTATION SERVICE, 1935*

LOCATION	MILES OF SERVICE		
	Scheduled	Actually Flown	Percentage Flown
U. S. total	33,770,091	31,143,853	92.22
Boston-Bangor			
Boston-Burlington	292,790	252,154	86.12
Boston-Albany-Cleveland	447,906	379,065	84.63
Boston-New York (Newark)	417,166	340,279	81.57
New England total	1,157,862	971,498	84.11

*Annual Report of the Postmaster General for the Fiscal Year ended June 30, 1935, Washington, D.C., Government Printing Office, p. 123.

Convenience. Airline passenger tickets are now readily obtainable. Every post office accepts air mail, and the Railway Express Agency, as well as the Postal Telegraph Company, picks up parcels to be sent to all points reached by scheduled airlines. Terminal facilities are reasonably satisfactory. Airsickness is being reduced by improved ventilation and greater stability in flight. Noise is appreciably reduced in the new transport planes. Air conditioning on sleeper planes is a development that may be expected in the very near future.

Transportation facilities between airports and business centers are usually provided, but they are not always satisfactory. As Mr. Harold G. Moulton points out:*

"Transfer of passengers from one form of transportation to another can be made much more convenient as soon as the volume of traffic warrants it. A cheap, rapid, and convenient form of transportation between airports and metropolitan centers is much to be desired, but present traffic levels do not warrant even the regular scheduling of small motor buses in most cases. Taxis are usually pressed into service, to be followed by small buses with growth in traffic, and possibly by rapid transit extensions to exceptionally busy airports."

Possible Summer Tourist Services. Persons having but two weeks vacation, who otherwise would stay at home or drive their automobiles to some near-by resort, may fly to distant home towns, resorts, and national parks within the two weeks allotted. The

*"The American Transportation Problem", p. 730

MASSACHUSETTS STATE PLANNING BOARD

recreational areas in the Berkshires and on Cape Cod, for instance, are only an overnight's journey by air from Chicago. The summer tourist business is increasing in importance in New England, and air transport can contribute to this growth. The Federal Aviation Commission made a recommendation* for national policy that might wisely be considered in terms of State policy.

"It should be the policy of the Federal agencies concerned to provide airports and glider sites in or adjacent to recreational areas under Federal control, such as national parks and monuments....The national parks and monuments are perfect cases in point. Almost without exception they include an elaborate provision for the comfort and safety of the visitor by motor. It seems to us thoroughly appropriate that some modest attention should be given to the visitor by air. There need be no great elaboration of airport facility, but there should be a landing strip of some kind".

Contract-Carrier Air Transport Operations

Air Mail. The use of air mail and its influence on the development of air transportation are so important as to require special attention here. The Federal Aviation Commission has stated:**

"The Government has spent, and is spending, very considerable amounts of money on civil aviation....The beginning of the record slightly antedated the end of the World War. The establishment of regular air mail service by the United States Post Office Department in the summer of 1918 was in strict accord with an American tradition of taking full and early advantage of new forms of transport and of using the postal service as the instrument to insure their rapid development. For more than sixteen years airlines, at first carrying mail alone and subsequently passengers and express as well, have been maintained within our borders upon a generally expanding scale".

In 1935, approximately $55,500 was paid by the United States Post Office Department to air-mail contractors for flights within the borders of Massachusetts and $294,207 for flights that directly

---

*Federal Aviation Commission. Message from the President of the United States transmitting, pursuant to law, a report of the Federal Aviation Commission containing its recommendations of a broad policy covering all phases of aviation and the relation of the United States thereto. 74th Congress, 1st Session. Document No. 15, Washington. Government Printing Office, 1935. p. 115.
　**Ibid. p. 43

serve Massachusetts.* The ability to get an air-mail contract has, in the past, been a most important factor in deciding where an airline company may operate. The advantages of an air-mail contract have been well set forth in "The American Transportation Problem"** as follows:

"The air mail carriers as a group are older, larger, and more stable than the non-mail carriers. Air mail route certificates are much in the nature of franchises; they confer a limited monopoly, security of tenure, and a reasonably assured income. These advantages account for the fact that no air mail route has been abandoned by the carrier since 1927; since that date, air mail carriers passed out of existence only through mergers, of these there have been many....The passenger air mail operators with no mail contracts persist as a group but the existence of the individual members of the group has been precarious".

Express. The volume of air express carried by American air mail contractors is growing rapidly. Starting in 1926, it has increased to one hundred and fifty thousand pounds in 1931. During the first six months of 1935 the average monthly volume was more than two hundred and twenty thousand pounds.***

Miscellaneous Commercial Operations

Included under this heading are taxi flying, pleasure trips, training of airmen, aerial advertising, photography and aerial surveying, exhibition flying, crop dusting, and other activities generally carried on by fixed-base operators and flying services. Taxi flying meets many of the emergencies arising in business and personal affairs that require rapid transportation. Some aviation companies have expensive equipment and highly trained personnel for specialized types of work, such as aerial photography, crop dusting, and mosquito extermination. Aerial photography and mapping are steadily increasing in use. The importance of miscellaneous flying operations may be gathered from the following Table 66, in which they are statistically contrasted with scheduled airline operations.

---

*Derived from figures contained in the Annual Report of the Postmaster General for the Fiscal Year ended June 30, 1935, p. 123.
**Page 720.
***Derived from figures contained in the Annual Report of the Postmaster General for the Fiscal Year ending June 30, 1935, p.128.

Table 66

STATISTICS OF SCHEDULED AND MISCELLANEOUS FLYING OPERATIONS*

	DOMESTIC MILES FLOWN, 1935	DOMESTIC MILES FLOWN, 1929-1935	PASSENGERS CARRIED (DOMESTIC), 1935	PASSENGERS CARRIED (DOMESTIC), 1929-1935
Scheduled Air Lines	55,380,353	287,841,727	746,946	3,180,776
Miscellaneous Flying	84,755,630	622,372,202	For Hire 1,014,957 For Pleasure 272,418 1,287,375	8,848,527 2,693,368 11,541,895

*Letter from Charles L. Morris to Victor M. Cutter, July 17, 1936.

Governmental Use of Aircraft

There are many ways in which aircraft serve the people and their government; among them are military defense, coast patrol, and miscellaneous uses in such public emergencies as floods.

Private Use of Aircraft

While private flying has not yet reached imposing proportions, efforts are being made to stimulate it by the Bureau of Air Commerce in the development of low-cost planes with high factors of safety.* The amount of time needed to learn to fly and to keep in training, the scarcity of suitable landing places, and the high operating costs account largely for the dearth of private operations. The governmental and private uses of aviation do not greatly influence the layout of airways and airports.

PART II. ESSENTIAL PHYSICAL DEVELOPMENTS

In contradistinction to the first section, which dealt with the subject of how aviation serves the Commonwealth of Massachusetts, this second section will consider the extent and kinds of physical works required for the development of aviation in the State.

*Aeronautics Bulletin No. 1, "Civil Aeronautics in the United States", Aug. 1, 1935, Government Printing Office, Washington, D.C., 1935, p. 51.

MASSACHUSETTS STATE PLANNING BOARD

The Development of Airways

Suitable economic conditions, as well as physical structures, are essential to the successful operation of scheduled air transport over an airway. It is the purpose of this section to ascertain locations at which the economic conditions are such that scheduled air transport is likely to develop, and then, along that geographical line, to determine what basic physical facilities are required. These facilities would not be built simply for the use of air transport companies. The line along which scheduled transport service is likely to develop is also the line along which a developed airway would be most valuable to all other forms of flying service and the general public.

Airway Development More Than a State Problem

In order to establish a plan for the development of airways, the State will find it necessary to work in close cooperation with regional and national organizations and with the representatives of the scheduled air-transport lines. The length of a typical flight precludes the possibility of attempting to decide the lines along which airways should be developed by studying Massachusetts alone. To date, the establishment and development of airways have been functions of the Bureau of Air Commerce of the Federal Government. This is proper and desirable, for practically all airways extend beyond State boundary lines.

Existing Airways in Massachusetts

There are already existing in Massachusetts well-established airways over which scheduled air-transportation service is being flown. Some of these airways need additional facilities. The existing airways, as shown on Map 76-12 are as follows:

1. Boston-New York, serving Providence, Hartford, and New Haven. This route is furnished with light beacons, at approximately fifteen-mile intervals, and with radio beams of sufficient power to cover the entire airway.

2. Boston-Albany, via Springfield. This route is furnished with light beacons for the entire distance, and with radio beams to cover the Albany-Springfield leg.

3. Boston-Burlington and Montreal, via Concord, White River Junction, and Montpelier. This route is furnished with light beacons as far as Concord, New Hampshire, and with a high-power radio beam as far as White River Junction, Vermont, and low-power radio beams at Concord, New Hampshire, and Burlington, Vermont.

MASSACHUSETTS STATE PLANNING BOARD

4. Boston-Bangor, via Portland and Augusta. This route is furnished with light beacons and a high-power radio beam as far as Portland, Maine, and low-power radio beams at Portland, Augusta, and Bangor, Maine.

5. Boston-Providence. This route is furnished with light beacons and a radio beam.

Proposed Airways in Massachusetts

As a result of studies and consultations with aviation experts, it has been possible to determine new airway routes along which regular flight services will probably be established in the future. The study and analysis of the need for developing each of these airways are too extensive for inclusion in this report, but the desirable new airways, in order of their probable priority, are:

1. East-West across Massachusetts, via Greenfield. This is part of a straight line drawn between Boston, Mass., and Buffalo, N. Y. This will be the natural express through route west from Boston. Local service via Worcester and Springfield would be continued.

2. Between Boston and some centrally located point on Cape Cod. One leg of the Boston radio beam is available for this route, which will be used mainly by summer traffic, and is being flown at present by Mayflower Airlines, Inc.

3, or 4. Between Providence, via Fall River and New Bedford, to some centrally located point on Cape Cod. This route would be used mainly for summer traffic.

4, or 3. North-South along the Connecticut Valley.

5. A local airway along the west escarpment of the Berkshires for New Yorkers vacationing in New England.

Navigation Aids Along Airways

The additional equipment needed on existing airways can be definitely determined, since the needs are readily checked by the everyday experience of airmen. A determination of the equipment needed on proposed airways cannot be easily made. The essential navigation equipment along an airway consists of radio beams, beacon lights, airway markers, intermediate landing fields, and airports. The details of the location and type of proposed additional navigation aids will naturally be decided by the United States Bureau of Air Commerce.

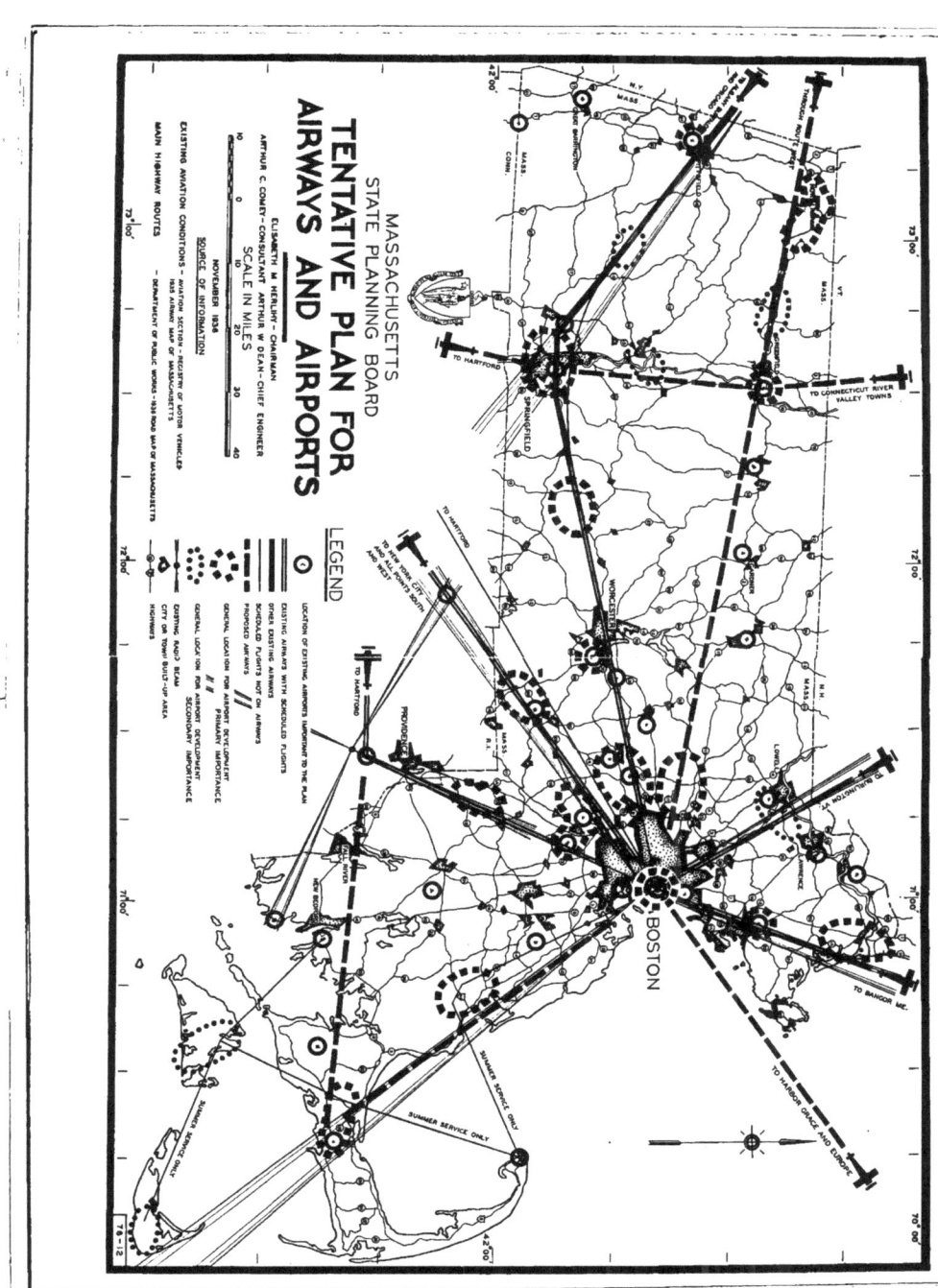

MASSACHUSETTS STATE PLANNING BOARD

Radio Beams. Radio beams should cover the entire length of every regularly flown airway. They are as serviceable and effective in foggy weather as in clear weather. This radio facility, as well as indicating to the airman the direction to port, once every hour broadcasts the weather conditions.

Beacon Lights. Beacon lights have been installed along air routes to guide the flyers. They are effective at night in clear weather, but are of little service in bad weather. Nevertheless, they are essential to the safe night operation of planes without radio equipment.

Airway Markers. Along the airways, conspicuous signs are painted on the roofs of buildings and sometimes on highways to give pilots their location and to guide them to intermediate landing fields and airports.

Intermediate Landing Fields. Intermediate landing fields, located at approximately twenty-mile intervals along an airway, may serve as both local and emergency landing fields. If their sites are judiciously chosen, these intermediate landing fields may serve most of the local aviation needs of the State.

The Development of Airports

Airports, properly located in relation to city areas and to means of transportation and adequately developed, are essential to the progress of air transportation. We shall first consider some of the principal considerations which determine the selection of a proper airport site, a matter of fundamental importance.

Selection of an Airport Site

No simple set of rules will suffice in choosing an airport site, for the many factors will have a different relative importance in each case. Each community presents a different problem. The following discussion will present some of the more important considerations.*

Type of District in Which Airport Should Be Located. Like the railroad or bus station, the airport is a terminal of transportation lines. An early recognition of this fact may enable cities to avoid a recurrence of the blighted residential and commercial

---

*Cf. Hubbard, H. V., M. McClintock, and F. B. Williams. "Airports: Their Location, Administration, and Legal Basis".

districts which have frequently surrounded railroad stations.

The airport frontage is hardly commercial in character, for commerce refuses locations which do not attract many potential buyers. In spite of the open land, the airport frontage can hardly be called <u>residential</u>, because the landing and departure of planes, the movement of searchlights, and the noise and commotion are objectionable to most people. The airport is essentially <u>industrial</u> in character.

<u>Accessibility</u>. This is a most important factor, especially to an airport that may serve scheduled airline operations. The transport of passengers and freight from plane to train is not at present of very great importance. However, an airport that has a spurline railroad connection for the delivery of fuel and other materials has a definite advantage. The relation that should exist between an airport and rapid transit facilities and highways has been well summed up as follows:*

"We are seeking proximity in time rather than proximity in space between the airport and the center of the city. The better the transit facilities, the farther away may the airport be. In each case, it must be determined whether the most per dollar can be obtained by providing physical nearness or by paying for transit facilities. A surface car line is an advantage, but a line of busses is just as good, and busses can operate over any sufficient street....Elevated lines and subways give the most rapid transit, but where they already exist, the land valued near their termini reflect their advantages, and these high values will sometimes be better borne by some more intensive use than that of an airport".

"The master consideration determining the effective nearness of the airport to the center of the city is likely to be good highway connection for use by busses. Separating grades at the principal intersections, eliminating railroad grade crossings, adequate width and proper pavement of highway, proper control of traffic, especially at street intersections, and avoidance of existing developments which cause traffic congestion will be the natural things to be sought in facilitating traffic".

<u>Possibility of Expansion</u>. It should be remembered that an airport must be planned for the future and not for present use only and, therefore, the sound procedure is to acquire more land than is

---

*Hubbard, H. V. and H. K. Menhinick, "The Airport in City Planning", Proceedings of the National Conference on City Planning, 1930, pp. 122-23.

immediately needed in order to avoid the higher price that would have to be paid after the airport has been developed. Furthermore, advance buying precludes the possibility of the surrounding land becoming intensively developed and unavailable for airport purposes.

Miscellaneous Considerations. Freedom from dangerous adjacent obstructions, such as power lines and tall structures, is essential. A site with high buildings or hills to the windward, which might cause hazardous air currents, should be avoided. The direction and velocity of prevailing winds, precipitation, and the presence of fog or smoke all need to be considered in the selection of an airport site.

Favorable soil characteristics include ease of excavation, porosity, firmness, and fertility of top soil for areas to be kept in turf. Natural or artificial drainage must take care of the disposal of storm torrents quickly.

Acquisition of Airport Sites

Airports may be constructed and maintained on any land owned or controlled by the Commonwealth, a city, town, or district by the appropriate public officials or by the Department of Public Works.* A site which is not public property must be purchased or taken by eminent domain. Only towns and cities, at present, are authorized to take land by eminent domain for airport purposes. If the town or city is unwilling to purchase or take the land by eminent domain proceedings, a State or regional plan for aviation is stalemated in its execution. If the proposed airport is of State-wide interest, the State legislature might be justified in passing a special act enabling the Commonwealth to purchase or take the land by eminent domain.

Protection of the Surroundings of the Airport

The subject of protecting the surroundings of the airport has been authoritatively discussed in the Report of the Committee on Airport Zoning and Eminent Domain of the Aeronautics Branch of the United States Department of Commerce.** The following excerpts from that report are of special interest:

"Briefly, the airport should be free from the encroachment of

---
*See Chapter 90, Section 43, General Laws of the Commonwealth of Massachusetts (Tercentenary Edition).
**Report of December 18, 1930, pp. 3-4.

obstructions that impede the ready access to, and departure from, the landing area; it should have the power, particularly if it is a terminal airport, to condemn the additional area that may be required to meet the changing demands of larger flying equipment, where the tendency is toward heavier wing and power loadings, consequent faster landing speeds, and increased runs for take-off. It needs the power to condemn air easements over surrounding land and the power to condemn the right to air mark neighboring structures of a hazardous nature. Also, it should have and would have under existing laws, the right, as a landowner, to appear in court in opposition to condemnation proceedings of other interests and urge that the preservation of the field is for the greater public interest.

"To the air traveler while in the upper air, structures below him are not a menace. In landing and taking off, however, aircraft approach and leave the airport at approximately a 7 to 1 angle (seven feet of horizontal distance for each foot of height); in some instances, particularly in the case of heavily loaded transport planes, this angle may be as flat as 10 to 1. Therefore, structures in the neighborhood of the port constitute a peril. These obstacles may be overcome, of course, by increasing the size of the airport and thus increasing the distance from the point of landing or take-off in which there are no structures to jeopardize the safety of operations. To do this completely is obviously impracticable, and to do it at all increases the cost of the landing area. The requirements for the airport ratings granted by the Federal Government -calculate that for conditions up to 1,000 above sea level a structure 100 feet high at the end of a runway or landing strip reduces the effective length of that runway or landing strip by 700 feet. It is, therefore, expedient to analyze the various obstacles to be found in the immediate vicinity of airports to see to what extent they may be eliminated or rendered less dangerous to flying operations.

"These obstacles have been found to be buildings, especially tall buildings; towers on buildings or tower buildings; smokestacks, radio towers, flagpoles and similar structures; telephone and telegraph lines; and, especially, high-tension transmission lines. In addition, smoke and gases may interfere with the operation of the port by reducing visibility. Not only does the smoke itself produce a condition of poor visibility, but the smoke particles themselves serve as condensation nuclei and materially increase fog frequency. Certain industrial plants give off vapors having a corrosive action on the materials used in aircraft construction, and while the plant structures may not constitute physical obstacles yet the port should be free from the harmful action of such gases.

"In general, it has been found that the air traveler needs protection from obstacles, such as indicated, in leaving or approaching an airport, for a distance of about 1,500 feet in all directions from the outer. boundaries of the port. So far as is reasonably possible, this protection should take the form of prevention of the construction of such structures in the future, and either the removal or the day and night marking of existing hazards, as conditions may dictate. High-tension transmission lines, however, are such a great danger in aviation that removal of existing lines of this nature from the surface should, if possible, be compelled".

Special State Airport Problems

Transatlantic Air Terminal. Consideration should be given to the possibility of establishing a transatlantic air base in Massachusetts. The desirability of such a base is apparent. The most direct air route from the eastern United States to Europe lies along the New England coast, and Boston is the first major transportation terminal encountered in a voyage from Europe over this route. The disembarking in Massachusetts of European travelers to the United States would give these visitors an opportunity to become acquainted at once with historical landmarks that epitomize America, and it would make available to them the best transportation facilities in New England, any point of which would be but a few hours journey by land or water or an hour or two by air.

The Boston Airport would be a logical air terminal for transatlantic planes. Congestion at this port, however, would undoubtedly prove disadvantageous in the future unless the airport is substantially enlarged. It is hoped that the levelling of Governor's Island, now going forward, and the filling of the intervening mud flats will accomplish the desired result. However, this project, as now planned, has serious disadvantages. It will provide the longest runway across the prevailing winds rather than with them. Modifications which would correct this situation are possible.

An extension of rapid-transit facilities, a most desirable improvement, might be accomplished by extending to the airport the East Boston tunnel, which now ends at Maverick Square.

Dirigible Base. A mooring mast and hangar for airships are not of immediate importance in Massachusetts. When they are needed, they should certainly not be located at the Boston Airport, since the presence of a dirigible like the Hindenburg would render the

MASSACHUSETTS STATE PLANNING BOARD

port unfit for use by other aircraft. It is estimated that these great dirigibles require a minimum landing area four thousand feet in diameter, in the center of which the mooring mast is located. Obviously, the place for such a base is somewhere outside of Boston at a location where rapid transportation to the city is available.

Integration of Ocean Lines to Airplane Service. A study should be made to determine the economics of a regularly scheduled seaplane service from the Boston Airport to incoming and outgoing ocean liners for the purpose of expediting passengers, mail, and express.

PART III. PERTINENT QUESTIONS AND ANSWERS ON MASSACHUSETTS AVIATION LAW

References to the Tercentenary Edition

Regulatory Matters

Ch. 90, Sec. 38 to 46

1. Q: What State agency holds the regulatory power over air matters?
   A: The Aviation Section of the Registry of Motor Vehicles.

Sec. 49

2. Q: In general, what regulatory powers are exercised?

Sec. 38

   A: Rules and regulations pertaining to airports and air traffic are made by the registrar and approved by the Commissioner of public works. The Superior Court has jurisdiction in equity to enforce the rules. The licenses of airmen and aircraft issued by the United States Department of Commerce must be registered with the registrar.

3. Q: What is the relation between the Federal regulatory agency and the State regulatory agency?
   A: They are complementary and closely cooperative. In general, the Federal agency enforces rules and regulations relating to interstate flying, while the State agency applies similar restrictions so far as they apply to intrastate operation. The Bureau of Air Commerce also acts in an advisory ca-

pacity in matters of local authority, such as the standardization of airports and their equipment.

4. Q: Is there any legal limitation upon the growth of air transport?
   A: There is no limitation in Massachusetts. The United States air mail law does, however, place restrictions on air transport.

5. Q: Are municipalities expressly relieved, by statute, of liability for negligence in the operation of municipal airports?
   A: No.

Ch. 90, Sec. 42

6. Q: Who has the right to build and maintain an airport or landing field?
   A: 1st, any private individual, corporation, or municipality, provided that the rules and regulations of the registrar are followed.
   2nd, any district of the commonwealth that holds public land (e.g., the Metropolitan District Commission).
   3rd, the State itself (i.e. any department having jurisdiction over State lands).

Land Acquisition

References to the Tercentenary Edition

1. Q: Can a State agency acquire land on which to establish an airport?
   A: Not without express permission of the legislature.

Ch. 40, Sec. 14

2. Q: Can a town or city take land by eminent domain within its boundaries for airport purposes?
   A: Yes, provided the land is not already appropriated to other public use.

Ch. 40, Sec. 5 (35)
Ch. 44, Sec. 7 (12)

3. Q: Can a town or city acquire land outside its boundaries for airport purposes?
   A: It may appropriate or borrow money for the purchase of land within or without

371

MASSACHUSETTS STATE PLANNING BOARD

its boundaries. It may also act jointly with another town or city.

4. Q: Can a municipality acquire land by eminent domain outside its own boundaries?
   A: Only with the express permission of the State Legislature.

5. Q: Can an airport management company be considered as a public utility and acquire land for an airport by eminent domain?
   A: No. The only public utility companies that may acquire land under eminent domain are railroads and electric-power companies, and then only under certain conditions. Under present law, air transport companies are not defined either as public utilities or common carriers.

Air Rights

270 Mass. 511

1. Q: How definitely has the ownership of air rights over private land been established?
   A: Aircraft have an undisputed right to fly over all land or buildings at a minimum altitude of 500 feet. Flights as low as 100 feet constitute trespass. The zone between 100 and 500 feet is problematical, and rights to it would depend on particular circumstances. A landowner has the right to erect a building to any height not limited by zoning or other building restrictions.

270 Mass. 530

2. Q: Can air rights be acquired by eminent domain (a) for public airports: (b) for private airports)?
   A: (a) They may be so acquired by a city or town.
   (b) They must be purchased or leased, if flights as low as 100 feet are necessary.

372

MASSACHUSETTS STATE PLANNING BOARD

Reference to the
Tercentenary Edition

3. Q: Have public airports and commercial airports of the public-utility class power to take by eminent domain:
   (a) air rights over contiguous property in order to insure safe approaches to the landing area?
   (b) easements for the air marking of obstructions jeopardizing the safety of the public in its use of the port?
   (c) contiguous property necessary for expansion of the port to meet public needs?

   A: (a) No.
      (b) No.
      (c) No.

Prevention and Elimination of Hazards

Ch. 143,
Sec. 2, 3
Ch. 40,
Sec. 25

1. Q: Is it possible to height zone the property surrounding public or private airports in the interests of safer and more convenient air navigation?

   A: A municipality may height zone the property adjacent to either publicly-owned airports or privately-owned airports. However, owing to the uncertainty of obtaining effective zoning, it is necessary at present to buy up extensive land or air rights surrounding an airport in order to insure its protection. At present there is no law permitting a Department of the Commonwealth to do any zoning.

2. Q: Does the public utility commission protect airports against the hazards of electrical supply and communication lines?

   A: The commission has no direct power. Public utility companies may take land by eminent domain for transmission lines only with the commission's approval, which might be withheld. Other lines must be given a location by municipal authorities which might be specified underground. The removal of existing lines would require special action in each case.

SOURCES OF INFORMATION

Reports

"Current Trends in Air Transportation," by Col. Edgar S. Gorrell, Report to the National Conference of Transportation held at M.I.T., June 8, 1936.

Federal Aviation Commission, 1935.

National Association of State Aviation Officials, 1934.

"New England Airways," New England Regional Planning Commission, 1935.

1934 Regional Plan Report for the State of Wisconsin, p. 425.

North Dakota State Planning Board Report.

Report of the Postmaster General, 1935.

Proceedings of the First Pacific Northwest Regional Planning Conference, 1934, p. 51.

Proceedings of the Second Pacific Northwest Regional Planning Conference, 1934, p. 96.

Progress Report of the Pacific Northwest Regional Planning Commission, 1935, pp. 110-111.

"Proposed 10-year Plan of Aviation Development," for the State of Florida.

Books and Pamphlets

AIRPORTS: THEIR LOCATION, ADMINISTRATION, AND LEGAL BASIS, H.V.Hubbard, M. McClintock, and F.B.Williams, Harvard University Press, 1930.

AIRPORTS AND LANDING FIELDS IN MASSACHUSETTS. Registry of Motor Vehicles, Aviation Section.

JOURNAL OF THE ROYAL AERONAUTICAL SOCIETY, January 1933.

MASSACHUSETTS STATE PLANNING BOARD

OFFICIAL AVIATION GUIDE, May 1936.

PLANNING PROBLEMS OF TOWN, CITY, AND REGION, 1930.

THE AMERICAN TRANSPORTATION PROBLEM, by H.G.Moulton, Brookings Institute, 1933, Chap. 31.

THE MODERN AIRPORT, by Sterling R. Wagner, 1931.

TRANSPORT AIRPLANES, 1934.

Bureau of Air Commerce Bulletins

Air Commerce Bulletins. Published Monthly.

Air Commerce Regulations, 1934.

Airport Bulletin No. 1, "Airport Grading and Drainage," 1935.

"Airport Design and Construction."

"Airport Management."

"Airport Rating Regulations," 1932.

Airway Bulletin No. 2, "Descriptions of Airports," 1936.

Airway Map of the United States, 1932.

Airway Map of the United States, 1933, 1934.

Airway Map of the United States, 1935. (In No. 1).

"Civil Aeronautics in the United States," 1935, Government Printing Office, Washington, D.C.

Domestic Scheduled Air Line Operations Statistics for the months of January to May, 1936.

"Outstanding Features of Current Types of Radio Facilities." Special No. 794.

Report of Committee on Airport Traffic Control, 1933.

Report of Committee on Airport Zoning and Eminent Domain.

The Federal Airways System, 1932-1935.

MASSACHUSETTS STATE PLANNING BOARD

Miscellaneous

Airway Map of Massachusetts Department of Public Works.

American Society of Municipal Engineers, Proceedings of the 36th Convention, 1931: "Airports and Landing Fields," pp. 75-153 (Drainage and surfacing).

Massachusetts Air Terminal and Arena, Inc. (A Metropolitan Airport at Canton).

Legal References

Acts and Resolves of the General Court. Published yearly.

Air Commerce Act, 1926.

Air Mail Acts of 1934 and 1935.

Corpus Juris, Vol. 20.

General Laws of Massachusetts (Tercentenary Edition).

Massachusetts Uniform Aeronautical Code, 1935, Chap. 418.

Nichols, Eminent Doman, 2 Vols.

Report of Committee on Airport Zoning and Eminent Domain.

Report of Special Commission: Massachusetts Aviation Policy, 1927.

Report of Massachusetts Commissioners to Consolidate and Arrange the General Laws, 1916-1920.

Rules and Regulations Relating to Aircraft. Department of Public Works.

Rules and Regulations Relating to Airports. Department of Public Works.

"The Law of Airports," AIRPORTS: THEIR LOCATION, ADMINISTRATION, AND LEGAL BASIS, Williams, Hubbard, and McClintock.

"The Uniform State Aeronautical Regulation Act," Report of the National Association of State Aviation Officials.

PUBLIC WORKS

Courtesy of Secretary of the Commonwealth

CHARTER IX

P U B L I C   W O R K S

Summary Outline

I. Introduction

II. Federal Agencies

    A. Bureau of Public Roads of the Department of Agriculture
    B. Federal Emergency Administration of Public Works
    C. Corps of Engineers of the War Department
    D. Works Progress Administration

III. State Agencies

    A. Department of Public Works
    B. Department of Mental Diseases
    C. Department of Correction
    D. Metropolitan District Commission
    E. Department of Public Health
    F. Department of Public Welfare
    G. Department of Education

IV. District Agencies

    A. Metropolitan District Commission
    B. Metropolitan District Water Supply Commission

V. County Agencies

VI. Municipal Agencies

MASSACHUSETTS STATE PLANNING BOARD

PUBLIC WORKS

Introduction

In setting up a division for the study of public works, it was recognized that public works, in the final analysis, are an end product of planning; they accomplish the translation of plans into their physical counterparts and, as such, should logically be sequential, rather than parallel, to the other studies. The public-works program of a State consists of a comprehensive plan for the expenditure of public money within the State on Federal, State, district, county, and municipal projects. The public-works program can be prepared only after detailed study and analysis of the plans for the public works of these various political subdivisions.

Public Works Are Essential

Public works, covering as they do all fields of activity of the various political subdivisions, are wide in scope. They touch every division for which capital expenditures are made. Without highways, waterways, public buildings, and water-supply and sewage-disposal systems, our present-day manner of living could not continue. Education, public health, transportation, and so on are all dependent upon physical equipment to accomplish their functions.

Flexibility Is Important

Since conditions are not static but are changing constantly from day to day, that which we plan for today may be obsolete in a few years. No plans for the future can be considered final. In order to be of real value, a plan must be so flexible that it may be changed from time to time to meet new conditions.

Cooperative Method of Program Preparation

In order to obtain the greatest amount of good from every dollar spent, every piece of construction undertaken should be a part of a comprehensive plan for the development of the entire State. This means that the future plans and requirements of each public agency operating in the State must be studied.

Since it has been impossible for the limited staff of the State Planning Board to make a personal study of the requirements and plans of all the different agencies in the State, the Staff has asked each of the different agencies concerned with public works

MASSACHUSETTS STATE PLANNING BOARD

in the State to submit its proposed future program. Most of these advance programs cover a period of six years: The agencies that have been contacted have proved most coöperative.

Organization of Study

In the following study, the public-works requirements of the State have been classified under the principal headings of Federal, State, district, county, and municipal agencies. The public works of each agency have been studied from the standpoints both of past expenditures and of future program.

The following report summarizes a more complete report which is now being prepared by the staff of the State Planning Board.

Federal Agencies

The following Federal agencies are making expenditures for public works in Massachusetts:

Bureau of Public Roads of the Department of Agriculture
Bureau of Lighthouses of the Department of Commerce
Civilian Conservation Corps
Bureau of Yards and Docks of the Navy Department
Post Office Department
United States Coast Guard of the Department of the Treasury
Federal Emergency Administration of Public Works
Veterans' Administration Facility
Corps of Engineers, War Department
Quartermaster Corps, War Department
Works Progress Administration

The Bureau of Lighthouses of the Department of Commerce, the Civilian Conservation Corps, the Bureau of Yards and Docks of the Navy Department, the United States Coast Guard of the Department of the Treasury, the Veterans' Administration Facility, and the Quartermaster Corps of the War Department do not generally make large expenditures for new construction. The Post Office Department has made some large expenditures within the State in the last few years. An analysis of the public-works programs of the other Federal agencies making expenditures within the State follows.

Bureau of Public Roads of the Department of Agriculture

The Federal Bureau of Public Roads of the Department of Agri-

MASSACHUSETTS STATE PLANNING BOARD

culture makes allotments to the State of Massachusetts for highways and bridges, elimination of grade crossings, and landscape development along highways.

The Bureau was established, in its present form, by Act of Congress, approved July 11, 1916. The Federal Highway Act, approved November 9, 1921, amended and supplemented the original act, and forms the basis of nearly all the subsequent acts.

The current activities of the Bureau are authorized under the following Acts of Congress:

National Industry Recovery Act--Approved June 16, 1933 (100 per cent grant).

Hayden-Cartwright Act--Approved June 18, 1934 (50 per cent grant).

Emergency Relief Appropriation Act of 1935--Approved April 8, 1935 (100 per cent grant).

Hayden-Cartwright Act--Approved June 16, 1935 (50 per cent grant).

The State Department of Public Works furnishes plans, specifications, and estimates for projects, subject to the Bureau's approval. The Department of Public Works then carries out the work in accordance with regulations issued by the Bureau.

Total appropriations to Massachusetts, from 1917 through the fiscal year 1937, amount to $42,288,168. A normal annual appropriation for this State is approximately $1,750,000, the State supplying an equal amount.

Outstanding examples of projects in the State, accomplished under the supervision of the Bureau, are the Worcester Turnpike, the Providence Turnpike, the French King Bridge, and the Fore River Bridge. The widening of the Newburyport Turnpike has recently been started.

Under the allotment for the elimination of railroad grade crossings, plans have been approved for twenty-three projects, with three more still pending. Three projects have been completed, and sixteen are under construction.

Future Program. The allotment of funds under each Act of Congress is programmed for the future, and the program is submitted to the Washington authorities for approval. Total appropriations of $125,000,000 for each year have been made by Congress for the fiscal years 1938 and 1939, but allotments have not yet been made to the various States. Massachusetts' share would be approximately $1,750,000 for each fiscal year.

Federal Emergency Administration of Public Works

The Federal Emergency Administration of Public Works was authorized under the National Industrial Recovery Act of 1933, and extended by the Emergency Relief Appropriation Act of 1935 and the First Deficiency Appropriation Act of 1936. The Massachusetts Division was organized in August 1933.

These Acts of Congress aimed to create useful work to relieve unemployment and to construct permanent public improvements that are urgently needed. They allow the Federal Government to make grants to the States, municipalities, and other political subdivisions for the construction of permanent public improvements under regulations regarding labor, material, and the awarding of contracts. It is the function of the State PWA Director to recommend projects to Washington for approval, and to see that all regulations are carried out after a project has been approved.

Under the National Recovery Act of 1933, the Public Works Administration was allowed to grant to public agencies approximately 30 per cent of the estimated cost of the labor and material required by approved projects. Under this Act, as of February 6, 1936, Washington approved projects in this State amounting to a total estimated cost of approximately $42,000,000, of which $12,000,000 was a Federal grant.

Under the Emergency Relief Appropriation Act of 1935, the Public Works Administration was allowed to make grants to public agencies of approximately 45 per cent of the total cost of approved projects. Under this Act, project applications, amounting to a total of approximately $77,000,000, were received from nearly every municipality in the State and from the State itself. As of February 6, 1936, projects amounting to approximately $30,000,000 were approved. Of this amount, approximately $12,500,000 was a Federal grant.

Under the 1936 program, the grant basis is the same as under the 1935 Act. As of November 20, 1936, the program under development includes projects amounting to approximately $10,000,000, with a total Federal grant of over $4,300,000.

Taking the 1935 program as an example, the types of construc-

MASSACHUSETTS STATE PLANNING BOARD

tion carried on under the Public Works Administration are as follows:

Table 67

PUBLIC WORKS ADMINISTRATION 1935 PROJECTS

TYPE OF CONSTRUCTION	PERCENTAGE OF TOTAL PROJECTS
Schools	40
Hospitals	14
Sewerage Systems and Sewage-Treatment Plants	19
Waterworks Systems	9
Highway Bridges	4
Streets	2
Miscellaneous Public Buildings	9
Piling Protection	3

Housing Division. The Housing Division of the Federal Emergency Administration of Public Works has charge of the construction of large housing developments in South Boston and Cambridge. There will be 1,016 apartments with a total of 3,912 rooms in the South Boston development, for which approximately $6,500,000 has been allocated. The Cambridge development will contain 294 apartments, with a total of 1172 rooms. Approximately $2,500,000 has been allocated for this project. From nine months' to one year's employment will be given to about 2,500 building mechanics.

Corps of Engineers of the War Department

The War Department, through the Corps of Engineers of the United States Army, has supervision of river and harbor improvements in Massachusetts. The District Engineer has charge of carrying out Federal improvements, and has supervision, within his district, over all structures built by the State, cities, towns, or private parties in or over the navigable waters of the United States.

Massachusetts comes under three districts. The office of the U.S. Army Engineer, Boston District, has control of the Massachusetts coast as far south as Chatham on Cape Cod, including the Cape Cod Canal and all rivers entering Massachusetts Bay; the Providence District, in Massachusetts, comprises the coast of Massachusetts south of Chatham, and the rivers in Massachusetts draining into the ocean between Chatham and the New York-Connecticut State line;

the New York District, in Massachusetts, comprises the streams in Massachusetts which empty into the Hudson River.

A large project in the Boston District, for which $900,000 of Emergency Relief funds have been provided for the start, is that of deepening the main ship channel in Boston Harbor, from President Roads to a point opposite Commonwealth Pier No. 1, East Boston, to a depth of forty feet over a width of six hundred feet. In addition, FWA funds of $1,000,000 have been provided for dredging, to a depth of 40 feet at mean-low water, a large anchorage area to the north of President Roads in Boston Harbor.

ERA funds of $475,000 are being used to dredge the Mystic River, from the mouth of Island End River upstream to the Charlestown playground, to a depth of thirty feet at mean-low water over a width of five hundred feet.

The largest project now in progress in the Boston District, and one for which $6,115,000 FWA funds and $5,000,000 ERA funds have been allocated, is the enlargement of the Cape Cod Canal to a depth of thirty-two feet and a bottom width of five hundred and forty feet in the land cut, 500 feet in a straight channel in Buzzards Bay to Wings Neck, and 700 feet beyond Wings Neck. In addition to the above funds, $3,214,000 from Regular Funds of a War Department appropriation are being used in the enlargement of the Canal. The estimated cost of this project, which includes two fixed highway bridges with a clear span of 550 feet and a vertical clearance of 135 feet above high water, and a railroad bridge with a vertical lift with a span of 500 feet, affording a clearance of 135 feet above high water, is $27,000,000. The bridges have already been constructed.

The Corps of Engineers in the Boston District is also actively engaged in an extensive flood-control project on the Nashua River in the vicinity of Fitchburg, and on the Merrimack River at Haverhill, with allotments of $1,800,000 and $1,020,000, respectively, from the Emergency Relief Appropriation Act of 1936.

Under the District Engineer, Providence District, dikes and riprap for flood prevention are being constructed at several points on the Connecticut River in Massachusetts.

Future Programs. At the present time, the Corps of Engineers is making extensive surveys of the flood of March, 1936, and preparing plans to coördinate navigation, power, and flood control on the principal navigable streams of Massachusetts.

MASSACHUSETTS STATE PLANNING BOARD

Works Progress Administration

The Works Progress Administration was created under the Emergency Relief Appropriation Act of 1935, approved April 8, 1935, and the Emergency Relief Appropriation Act of 1936, approved June 22, 1936. Its purpose is to take persons off the relief roll and to put them to useful work at their usual occupations, so far as is possible. The projects undertaken must be useful, and a considerable portion of the money spent on a project must be for wages.

There are two classes of projects: first, Federal projects which originate in departments and agencies of the Federal Government and are conducted entirely by the Federal Government; and second, non-Federal projects which a State, municipality, or other public agency initiates and conducts, and which the Federal Government finances entirely or in part, by loan or grant.

A major part of the work carried on by the Works Progress Administration is construction. Up to September 30, 1936, approximately $44,000,000 of Federal funds had been expended in Massachusetts on construction projects for labor and material, excluding services and rentals. Following is a table showing the percentage distributions of expenditures for construction projects by specified types.

Table 68

WORKS PROGRESS ADMINISTRATION PROJECTS

TYPE OF CONSTRUCTION	PERCENTAGE OF TOTAL PROJECTS
Highways, Roads, and Streets	35.1
Public Buildings	20.3
Housing	*
Recreational Facilities	11.2
Flood Control and Conservation	7.0
Sewerage Systems and Other Utilities (Excluding Electric)	15.4
Electric Utilities	*
Airports and Other Transportation Projects	1.9
Sanitation and Health	2.8
Projects not Elsewhere Classified	6.3

*Less than 0.5 per cent

MASSACHUSETTS STATE PLANNING BOARD

State Agencies

The State makes large expenditures for public works in the form of buildings, land, and equipment necessary for the different State departments to carry on their work. In nearly all cases, the needs of a department increase from year to year. It is essential that there be an advance program showing the requirements of the departments, and the estimated expenditures necessary to meet them. In order to be financed and executed properly, the advance program for each department should be considered in relation to the programs of other departments.

Of the twenty State departments, only the following seven spend substantial amounts on capital improvements. These departments, in order of the size of their expenditures, are listed in the accompanying table.

Table 69

STATE DEPARTMENTS MAKING SUBSTANTIAL CAPITAL
IMPROVEMENT EXPENDITURES

DEPARTMENT	PERCENTAGE OF TOTAL CAPITAL EXPENDITURES BY STATE DEPARTMENTS, 1925-1935, INCLUSIVE
Department of Public Works	64.5
Department of Mental Diseases	21.4
Department of Correction	4.9
Metropolitan District Commission	2.8 (Boulevards)
Department of Public Health	2.3
Department of Public Welfare	2.1
Department of Education	2.0

As can be seen from this table, the Department of Public Works spends more on new construction than all other departments combined. The Department of Mental Diseases spends the next largest amount, but its expenditures are only one third those of the Department of Public Works.

Department of Public Works

The Department of Public Works has charge of the construction, maintenance, and repair of all State-owned highways and bridges,

MASSACHUSETTS STATE PLANNING BOARD

including the removal of snow and ice from them, and has jurisdiction over certain waterways and public lands.

When a petition is submitted to the Department by County Commissioners, Aldermen, or Selectmen, stating that public conveniences and necessity require that the Commonwealth lay out and take charge of a new or existing highway in their county, city, or town, the Department may, after due process of law, take over the highway as a State highway.

Under the provisions of Chapter 90, Section 34 of the General Laws, the Department may pay the whole or part of the expense of building or rebuilding a highway (or a part thereof), which is not a State highway, but which is an important link in the highway system of the State. The Department may enter into an agreement with the County Commissioners and/or Aldermen of a city or Selectmen of a town whereby the county, municipality or both may pay part of this cost.

The Department spends considerable sums yearly for the repair and improvement of public ways other than State ways, in towns which have a valuation of less than five million dollars and which need financial assistance.

Under Chapter 81 of the General Laws, as amended, the Department is authorized to construct sidewalks along such parts of State highways as public necessity and convenience require. This year, the Department is constructing several miles of sidewalks, taking advantage of Federal funds.

The Department has charge of all lands, rights, and interests owned by the Commonwealth upon or adjacent to the Boston harbor front, except lands under control of the Metropolitan District Commission, and has charge of the construction and maintenance of piers and other public works in the harbor, and administers all terminal facilities under control of the Department. The Department secures information as to the present and probable future requirements of steamships and shipping, railroads, warehouses, and industrial establishments. It has general care and supervision of all harbors and tidal waters within the Commonwealth, and the flats and lands flooded thereby, and maintains, protects, and makes such improvements in and along the harbor, rivers, and foreshores as it deems proper and necessary, when funds are appropriated therefore. The Department also controls the waters and banks of the Connectiout River and the waters and banks of the non-tidal portion of the Merrimack River, and all structures therein, and also parts of the Westfield River in the towns of West Springfield and Agawam.

The Department controls the great ponds within the Commonwealth (that is, all natural ponds having area of ten acres or more) and such smaller ponds as the Commonwealth may own.

The dredging of channels in the harbors and principal rivers of Massachusetts is done by both the Corps of Engineers of the United States Army and by the State. In general, the Federal Government does all such work on projects regarded as affecting interstate commerce and the general public.

The State may extend such a project upstream in a river, or may extend such a project in a harbor when, from the point of view of the State, it is deemed necessary in order to give access to the channel dredged by the Government. In certain of the smaller harbors, an arbitrary boundary has been set up between work by the Corps of Engineers and by the State. This may be a bridge at the mouth of the river which empties into a harbor, the Corps of Engineers taking care of the necessary dredging on the downstream side of the bridge, and the State, on the upstream side.

Following are the expenditures by the Department of Public Works for new construction from 1925 to 1935, inclusive:

1925	$2,421,526.54	1931	$10,176,195.16
1926	2,245,807.61	1932	7,046,878.10
1927	3,419,368.82	1933	7,393,371.92
1928	2,742,475.40	1934	9,934,848.90
1929	3,624,606.88	1935	10,535,201.66
1930	4,823,392.36		

It was not practicable at this time to secure a program of future construction from the Department of Public Works.

Department of Mental Diseases

The Department of Mental Diseases prepares plans and controls the construction, under special appropriations, of new buildings and unusual repairs, and the expenditure of money for such purposes, at the following State hospitals and State schools. It also selects land to be taken by the Commonwealth for new or existing institutions that come under its supervision.

State Hospitals

Boston Psychopathic Hospital
Boston State Hospital
Danvers State Hospital

Metropolitan State Hospital
Monson State Hospital
Northampton State Hospital

MASSACHUSETTS STATE PLANNING BOARD

Foxborough State Hospital
Gardner State Hospital
Grafton State Hospital
Medfield State Hospital

Taunton State Hospital
Westborough State Hospital
Worcester State Hospital

State Schools

Belchertown State School   Walter E. Fernald State School
Wrentham State School

Following are the expenditures by the Department of Mental Diseases for new construction and permanent improvements from 1925 to 1935, inclusive:

1925	$ 522,057.55	1931	$2,629,307.51
1926	689,070.24	1932	2,682,155.90
1927	1,058,923.85	1933	882,149.71
1928	1,810,012.38	1934	1,762,034.62
1929	2,570,620.74	1935	3,917,852.47
1930	2,866,642.71		

With such large amounts expended annually for new construction, it is evident that the careful expenditure of this money should be planned as far as possible in advance.

A program of public works, covering the years 1936 to 1940, inclusive, has been outlined by the Department of Mental Diseases, and a chart covering this program has been completed (See Chart 77-C1).

This program covers construction, at thirteen State hospitals and three State schools, with an estimated cost of $4,891,515 for the first year, $5,252,485 for the second year, $3,583,200 for the third year, $2,026,000 for the fourth year, and $2,065,000 for the fifth year, or a total estimated cost for the five-year period of $17,818,200. This proposed new construction would give the State hospitals an additional 3,442 beds for patients and 1,866 beds for employees, at an estimated cost of $15,025,015. It would give the State schools an additional 1,152 beds for patients and 277 beds for employees, at an estimated cost of $2,793,185.

Department of Correction

The Department of Correction handles all new construction work for the State Prison, State Prison Colony, Massachusetts Reformatory, Reformatory for Women, and State Farm.

S.P.B.-W.P.A.-FORM 8

AGENCY **DEPARTMENT OF MENTAL DISEASES**
 DEPARTMENT OF REVIEW
REPORT ON CONSTRUCTION YEARS **1936-1940 INCLUSIVE**
APPROVED BY **WALTER E. BOYD, ENGINEER IN CHARGE**
 DIVISION OR DIVISION IN CHARGE
DATE **JULY 8, 1936**
PAGE   OF   SHEETS

ADVANCE PLANNING - PROGRAMMING OF PUBLIC WORKS
MASSACHUSETTS STATE PLANNING BOARD

KEY Ⓐ TO METHOD OF FINANCING

O.B. Ordinary Revenue
S.R. Sinking Fund Revenue
L Loan
L(R) Loan (Revenue)
C Contributed
H.R. Highway Revenue
F.A. Federal Aid
P.W.A. Public Works Admin. (Part)
F.L.D. Federal Land Development (Loan)

KEY Ⓑ TO STATUS OF LAND

A Site or Site Acquired
B Site Taken
C Title Pending
D Condemnation Pending
E Condemnation Proceedings Started
F Title Action Completed
G Option in Consideration
H Land Owned by Dept. of Public Works
I Land Owned by State
J Land Privately Owned by State

KEY Ⓒ TO STATUS OF PLANS

K Preliminary Surveys Started
L Preliminary Surveys Completed
M Preliminary Plans Started
N Preliminary Plans Completed
O Final Plans Started
P Final Plans in Preparation
Q Final Plans Completed
R Specifications & Estimates
S Contracts Ready
T Contract Signed
U Work Started

Following are the expenditures by the Department of Correction for new construction, equipment, real estate, and furnishings, from 1925 to 1935, inclusive:

1925	$ 49,773.24	1931	$ 568,224.31
1926	74,262.37	1932	954,600.13
1927	84,146.11	1933	357,067.38
1928	117,386.76	1934	789,759.11
1929	146,990.65	1935	1,486,672.44
1930	266,388.83		

From these figures, it is obvious that the substantial amounts spent on capital outlay make it worth while to have a plan of future construction, if the ultimate objective of the Department of Correction, the protection of the public, is to be attained in the most efficient manner.

The Department of Correction has submitted an advance program of construction covering twenty-five years, which they consider to cover the absolute needs of the Department, as follows:

An Institution for First Offenders--$1,500,000. This will permit abandonment of the present State Prison at Charlestown. If a new maximum-security institution were to be built, it would cost approximately $5,000 per unit; or, in other words, for 1000 capacity, the cost would be $5,000,000. It is the opinion of the Department that it is not necessary nor wise to spend the additional $3,500,000, as there are now available 1,050 maximum-security cells which will be sufficient for the needs of this department for some time to come, if the first offenders are lodged elsewhere. There are approximately 450 first offenders at the Massachusetts Reformatory. With these and others recruited from various institutions housed in the new institution, the Charlestown State Prison may be done away with by the transfer of the more serious offenders to the Concord prison, which is the most modern maximum-security institution in the State. If the Charlestown State Prison is to be retained, an expenditure of approximately $750,000 will be necessary to put this institution in repair.

An Institution for the Criminally Insane. Under the provisions of Chapter 421 of the Acts of 1935, the Department of Mental Diseases was ordered to erect, on land controlled by the State Prison Colony at Norfolk, an institution housing approximately 500 criminally insane. There was a stipulation that Federal money must be used. The criminally insane are now housed on the State Farm at Bridgewater, under the supervision of the Department of Correction.

A Receiving Building--$750,000. It is necessary, with the addition of a First-Offenders' Institution, to have a receiving building with a capacity for 300 persons, into which all commitments would be made, in which they would be classified, and from which they would then be sent to the proper institution. Here, psychological analyses, case histories, and so forth would be studied for each individual over a period of thirty days. This receiving building would be equipped for medical treatment for those in need of it. The present site of the Charlestown State Prison could be used for this proposed building.

Housing Facilities for Officers--$1,000,000. At the present time, officers' quarters in certain institutions are not the modern, up-to-date buildings they should be. The necessary funds to provide proper housing facilities for officers would be allocated after a survey, by the department, of the institutions, and a determination of which ones need these facilities the most.

State Farm, Bridgewater

Funds, as indicated, are needed for the following purposes:

Service Building	$ 150,000
Employees Building	250,000
Electrical wiring of entire institution (Survey has been made)	50,000
Re-piping for both plumbing and heating (Survey has been made)	200,000
Renovation of hospital buildings	100,000

The renovation of hospital buildings is greatly needed. The criminal insane should be placed in the care of the Department of Mental Diseases. The space now occupied by the criminal insane could be utilized for housing the 350 male defective delinquents, and also for classifying and segregating many border-line feeble-minded cases now in other prisons. The capacity of approximately 1,000 persons would be utilized. The first offender unit of 500, plus the additional space made available by a new institution for the criminal insane, would give a slightly larger capacity than there is at present.

New buildings for female defective delinquents....... $100,000

At the present time, one building is available for this particular type. This is filled, and there is no room for admissions. This institution is receiving requests every day from various institutions under the Department of Mental Diseases for transfers to

MASSACHUSETTS STATE PLANNING BOARD

this institution at the State Farm.

Sewerage .... $ 5,000

This amount will complete all the sewerage projects which have been initiated under CWA, ERA, and now WPA.

Hot- and cold-water lines .... $ 90,000

This item is for the replacement of hot- and cold-water lines. The piping on both hot- and cold-water lines is on the verge of breaking through the gathering of scale and other materials on the interior of the pipes. The pressure has been reduced considerably because of the collection of this material. From the standpoint of health of those committed to this institution, the complete replacement of hot- and cold-water lines should be accomplished at the earliest possible time.

Farm buildings .... $ 25,000

This money will be used in the re-roofing, re-painting, and repairing of the group of farm buildings, which is in fairly good condition except for a very poor roof and some clapboards which have become loosened.

Gas installation .... $ 12,000

The authorities have studied this particular proposal extensively. There has also been made a survey by the Brockton Gas Light Company.

Renovation of the Women's Prison .... $ 50,000

This is contingent upon the allowance of items 1 and 2. The department would then tear down the infirmary building which houses old, infirm men, and transfer them to the Women's Prison. The new buildings would be erected on the site of the present infirmary building. There are about 75 to 100 of the above-mentioned men at this institution all the time. They are not custodial risks, and can be given the freedom of the yard and the benefits resulting from fresh air and sunshine.

Enlarging present poultry plant .... $ 6,000
Piggery 10,000
Cannery 20,000

A modern, up-to-date cannery is an absolute necessity at this institution, because the farm production is much greater than can be currently consumed. The produce over and above the amount needed for consumption at this institution could be canned and sold to other institutions.

Massachusetts Reformatory, West Concord

Funds, as indicated, are needed for the following purposes:

Additional sprinkler system	$ 11,000
Farm-building group	149,300
Assembly and recreational building	150,000
Tear-gas installation	25,000
New steel stairways for factory buildings	7,000
Roads, sidewalks, etc.	20,000
Modernization of present hospital equipment	15,000
Purchase of land	10,000
Repairs and renewals	$110,000

The latter appropriation is for such items as wall extension, replacing old brick floor and heavily traveled corridors, plumbing repairs, and an entirely new electrical wiring system throughout, for radio reception. This institution has no individual radio headpiece sets, and it is deemed essential that this installation be made.

Reformatory for Women, Framingham

Over the period prescribed at the beginning of this report, a new institution of the cottage type should be erected, at a cost of $1,250,000. This institution could be built as accommodations are needed. There are now two cottages which house the mothers and babies in one, and the junior inmates in another. It is hoped that cottages can be added, and that the construction of an Administration, Receiving, and Hospital Building can proceed as soon as money is appropriated. If these funds are not forthcoming, immediately, the following are most necessary:

New staff house	$125,000
New hospital-unit equipment	150,000
Renovation of power house, and addition of new equipment	150,000
Repairs to present institution	200,000

The latter item includes plumbing, heating, re-painting of

walls, new roofing, repairs to farm group, and the building of two new duplex houses, and so forth.

Purchase of land $12,000

State Prison Colony, Norfolk

Additional sewage-treatment plant $53,000
Power-house protection 10,000
Purchase of land 15,000
Roads, sidewalks, grading, etc. 10,000
Additional wooden silo 1,500

The total estimated cost of this twenty-five year program is over $6,000,000, and demonstrates by its size that careful planning will be necessary in order to receive the greatest value from money spent, and to coordinate the building programs of other departments. The over-lapping of the programs of two departments is shown by the proposal to erect at the State Prison Colony at Norfolk an institution to house 500 criminally insane. Although the institutions will be situated on land now controlled by the State Prison Colony, it would be erected and supervised by the Department of Mental Diseases.

Metropolitan District Commission

This department is treated later under the heading of District Agencies, because of the nature of its organization and functions. The only expenditures of State funds for construction by the Metropolitan District Commission are those for Metropolitan District boulevards.

Department of Public Health

The Department of Public Health administers the following five institutions:

Lakeville State Sanatorium   Westfield State Sanatorium
North Reading State Sanatorium   Pondville Cancer Hospital
                Rutland State Sanatorium

The Division of Sanitary Engineering of the Department of Public Health, which acts in a consulting and advisory capacity to cities, towns, and other agencies of the Commonwealth, lays out sewer and water-supply systems for these institutions. The Division of Tuberculosis of the Department of Public Health is directly in charge of these institutions.

MASSACHUSETTS STATE PLANNING BOARD

Following are the expenditures for new construction and alteration from 1925 to 1935, inclusive:

1925	$ 76,705.16	1931	$ 265,644.86
1926	270,984.86	1932	108,249.50
1927	260,559.41	1933	8,778.40
1928	149,320.18	1934	121,316.93
1929	275,996.75	1935	281,453.96
1930	496,272.92		

A cancer and tuberculosis unit is now under construction at the Westfield State Sanatorium. It will furnish 50 beds for cancer patients and 150 beds for tuberculosis patients.

The Department of Public Health has given the State Planning Board the following advance program of construction for the institutions in that department.

<u>Lakeville State Sanatorium</u>. The following improvements should be accomplished during 1937:

Pool building for treatment of convalescent cases of poliomyelitis (infantile paralysis) in children and adults, to include physiotheraphy equipment for treatment of out-patients and house cases. Estimate not yet prepared.

Infirmary Building, two stories, fire-proof construction, with 76 beds for men and women convalescent from infantile paralysis. To include treatment rooms, equipment and furnishings. $200,000

Steam mains and electric lines for above two buildings. 18,000

Renovation of the present power plant, with extensive changes in building, and three new boilers. 75,000

An enlargement of the present power plant will be necessary to take care of the proposed new buildings.

Construction of the proposed buildings at Lakeville is necessitated by the transfer of responsibility for the care of crippled children from the State Department of Public Welfare to the State Department of Public Health, under Chapter 347 of the Acts of 1936, and by the permission given the department to admit convalescent cases of infantile paralysis to the Lakeville State Sanatorium, under Chapter 346 of the Acts of 1936.

MASSACHUSETTS STATE PLANNING BOARD

In 1938, a male employees' dormitory, 100 beds, with garage in basement, including furnishings and equipment $155,000

In 1939, a female employees' dormitory, 50 beds, including furnishings and equipment 32,500

North Reading State Sanatorium.
1939, Superintendent's house, including furnishings 25,000

This is the only institution in the Department of Public Health which does not provide a house for the Superintendent. One should be provided to allow the Superintendent to live outside the administration building, and to make the present Superintendent's quarters available for other staff physicians.

In 1940, an infirmary building, of first-class construction, to provide 40 beds for girls with pulmonary tuberculosis. Estimate not yet prepared.

As the North Reading State Sanatorium is constantly getting a large proportion of patients with pulmonary tuberculosis, it is necessary to provide a modern type of infirmary building to replace the antiquated wooden shacks.

Rutland State Sanatorium, 1937-38-39. Complete reconstruction of the Rutland State Sanatorium, to accommodate 310 patients, is needed. The first State sanatorium in the country, Rutland is still using buildings erected thirty-five to forty years ago, which are entirely inadequate for the modern treatment of tuberculosis, and whose wooden construction constitutes a serious fire hazard to patients and employees. The rebuilding program contemplates the replacing of existing wooden-frame buildings with first-class fireproof structures, making use of the present power plant and such other existing facilities as are suitable. It is proposed that the new construction be carried out in three units to insure a minimum loss of patient and employee beds at any one time. The following estimates show the approximate cost of the units:

1937--Unit I: A three-story building, with two-story wings, with a total of 134 beds, including furnishings. (Estimate includes $9,000 for moving a building) $335,375

Female employees' dormitory, 34 rooms, including furnishings 62,100

Male employees' dormitory, 50 rooms, with furnishings 74,900

Change in sewers and extension of steam and water
lines under ground $10,600

Miscellaneous, in connection with above 26,350

1938--Unit II: Contains administration wing, out-
patient department, medical library, staff conference
rooms, and 42 patient beds, including furnishings and
equipment 198,432

Superintendent's house, including furnishings 18,400

Service building, including fixed kitchen equipment 100,700

Connecting corridors 7,420

Furnishing and equipment for hospital building and
service building 20,000

Miscellaneous, in connection with above 19,322

1939--Unit III: This unit is a duplicate of Unit I,
including furnishings and equipment 326,331

Recreation building, including furnishings 62,284

Miscellaneous, in connection with above 22,730

Westfield State Sanatorium, 1939.
Addition to the present male employees' building,
with 70 beds, first-class construction, including
furnishings and equipment 81,000

   This is to provide housing for additional employees needed in
the new Cancer and Tuberculosis unit; the basement will provide garage space for employees' cars.

Pondville Cancer Hospital, 1937.
Administration Building, first-class construction, to
house the business offices of the institution, and to
include offices for the superintendent and assistant
superintendent, the pathological laboratories and
morgue, bacteriological and biological laboratories,
small-animal quarters, auditorium, pathological mu-
seum, and staff library. It should be connected by
tunnel with Ward A of the present hospital building.
Estimated cost, including furnishings and equipment $130,000

   This building is necessitated by the rapid growth of the work

MASSACHUSETTS STATE PLANNING BOARD

ᴊf the hospital and the necessity of providing more space for record offices and an auditorium, and additional space for laboratories.

In 1938, a women employees' building, 100 rooms, first-class construction, to provide additional housing facilities for nurses and other women employees. This is needed because of recent additions to the hospital. It should be connected by tunnel with Ward A of the present hospital building. Estimated cost, including furnishings and equipment $185,000

Remodeling present administration wing of hospital building, including beds for 15 patients on the second floor. Estimated cost, including furnishings and equipment .... $ 4,500

This is to utilize the space made available by the new Administration Building, for enlargement of medical-record offices, and for additional patient rooms.

Remodel power plant to include three new boilers .... $ 35,000

Steam turbine and new engine 30,000

New steam lines 20,000

This enlargement is necessary to provide for the new women employees' building.

1939, a cement-block garage for 40 employees' cars .... $ 10,000

The total estimated cost of this advance program, by institutions is:

Lakeville State Sanatorium .... $ 540,500
North Reading State Sanatorium 25,000
Rutland State Sanatorium 1,284,944
Westfield State Sanatorium 81,000
Pondville Cancer Hospital 414,500
Total $2,345,944

Department of Public Welfare

The five institutions which come under the supervision of the Department of Public Welfare, and for which expenditures for new construction are made are:

State Infirmary, Tewksbury
Massachusetts Hospital School, Canton
Lyman School for Boys, Westborough
Industrial School for Boys, Shirley
Industrial School for Girls, Lancaster

The expenditure of funds for new construction at these institutions is made not directly under the Department of Public Welfare but under the trustees of the institutions. The Department of Public Welfare has general supervision over these institutions.

The following are the expenditures for new construction, equipment, real estate, and furnishings from 1925 to 1935, inclusive:

1925	$ 13,207.31	1931	$375,779.37
1926	14,401.04	1932	316,326.69
1927	54,007.51	1933	35,680.89
1928	77,005.30	1934	393,282.20
1929	130,904.95	1935	528,590.06
1930	164,633.92		

The Department of Public Welfare submitted to the State Planning Board the following six-year program of capital improvements which they consider necessary.

State Infirmary, Tewksbury.
A new building to provide 400 beds for male patients, with recreational room. This would make unnecessary the use of double-decker beds at Stonecroft. The estimated cost is $160,640

New quarters for 100 female employees for whom there are not suitable accommodations at present. Estimated cost 135,000

New quarters for male employees, to replace those which are most suitable at the present time. Also, there is a shortage of rooms, making it necessary for 150 employees to live outside the institution and receive money in lieu of maintenance. Estimated cost 75,000

Modern construction to accommodate 100 beds is urgently needed to replace the Fiske, the present Women's Tubercular Hospital, which is old. Estimated cost 135,000

A new medical and surgical center of 150-bed capacity, exclusive of corridors, bathrooms, linen rooms, sterilizer rooms, utility rooms, closets, and so forth, at an estimated cost of 300,000

A new,300-bed women's hospital, estimated to cost $300,000

The reconstruction of steam and hot-water systems, including a new engine, is a vital need. Estimated cost   82,000

A new fireproof cattle barn to care for 200 cows and 20 horses. The present barn, of wooden construction, is a fire hazard. Estimated cost   225,000

The roads and sidewalks of the institution are in poor shape, and 19 miles of new 16-foot macadam road are essential. Estimated cost   37,240

Of 940,213 square feet of roof area at the institutions, 300,000 square feet need immediate repair. Estimated cost   21,200

Massachusetts Hospital School, Canton.
Two 30-bed cottages to replace an old wooden dormitory, at an estimated cost of   125,000

A new nurses' home to replace old, inadequate two-story wooden building originally used as an infirmary, at an estimated cost of   95,000

A new industrial building to replace an old, cheaply constructed wooden building, including a new cold-storage plant in the basement to replace ice boxes which have been in use nearly thirty years. The estimated cost of these replacements is   45,000

Lyman School for Boys, Westborough.
Three new brick cottages of fireproof construction, with heating and service connections, similar to the brick cottages erected during the last four years, to replace three old cottages. Estimated cost   225,000

A new fireproof school infirmary, including heating connections, with provision for isolation of all incoming commitments. Estimated cost   100,000

New institution school building, at an estimated cost of $150,000; sewage-disposal system with sanitary filtration, at $50,000; and reconstruction and re-equipment of the central heating and power plant.   200,000

Industrial School for Boys, Shirley.
A boys' double, brick cottage of first-class construction, with furnishings, equipment, and subway connection to Administration Building, similar to one built two years ago. Approximate cost   130,000

MASSACHUSETTS STATE PLANNING BOARD

A boys' single, brick cottage of first-class construction, with furnishings, equipment, and service connections, at an approximate cost of .... $ 75,000

An officers' building of brick, containing dining and recreation rooms and living quarters, with furnishings, equipment, connections to heating plant and to kitchen, and basement for cannery. Estimated cost........... 97,000

A heated garage of masonry construction, to hold eight cars, ... 10,000

Industrial School for Girls, Lancaster.
Extension of sewage-disposal system by construction of additional filter beds, estimated to cost. 7,500

A new girls' cottage of brick, fireproof construction, with furnishings, equipment, and service connections similar to the one constructed two years ago. Estimated cost 100,000

Construction of central-heating unit in new location, with provisions for storage of coal, with connections to additional buildings. Estimated cost 125,000

Laundry building of one story with basement and sewage, water, and service connections. Estimated cost 7,500

The total estimated cost of this six-year program amounts to $3,013,080, divided as follows:

State Infirmary, Tewksbury	$1,471,080
Massachusetts Hospital School, Canton...............	265,000
Lyman School for Boys, Westborough..................	725,000
Industrial School for Boys, Shirley	312,000
Industrial School for Girls, Lancaster	240,000

The State Board of Housing, a division of the Department of Public Welfare, has submitted a program of better housing for those citizens living under sub-standard conditions in different parts of the State. The program for the years 1937 and 1938, including the estimated cost of the work, follows:

Boston, South End, rehabilitation of densely populated area	$1,500,000
Bristol, reconstruction of slum area	1,500,000
Chicopee, reconstruction of slum area	250,000
Lowell, reconstruction of overcrowded area	1,500,000

New Bedford, reconstruction of overcrowded area ...... $ 500,000
Springfield, reconstruction of slum area 2,000,000
Worcester, reconstruction of overcrowded area 2,000,000
The total of this two-year program amounts to $9,250,000

Department of Education

The Department of Education controls all new construction at the State Teachers Colleges at Bridgewater, Fitchburg, Framingham, Hyannis, Lowell, North Adams, Salem, Westfield, Worcester, the Massachusetts School of Arts at Boston, and the State Textile Schools at Bradford, Lowell, and New Bedford.

New construction at Massachusetts State College at Amherst, Massachusetts, is under the control of the board of trustees, appointed by the governor, which manages the college.

The amounts spent by the Department of Education on capital outlay at those institutions over which it has control of construction, is as follows for the years 1925 to 1935, inclusive:

Year	Amount	Year	Amount
1925	$230,976.87	1931	$292,593.99
1926	334,850.27	1932	106,428.26
1927	93,587.42	1933	7,177.82
1928	122,213.02	1934	56,193.80
1929	258,104.86	1935	103,455.02
1930	401,571.14		

The building program which the Department would like to accomplish in the next six years is as follows:

State Teachers College, Bridgewater.
Construction of an athletic field, at an estimated cost of .... $ 7,000

State Teachers College, Fitchburg.
Construction of a gymnasium and recreation building, at an estimated cost of 200,000
Grading of the athletic field, at an estimated cost of .. 7,000

State Teachers College, Framingham.
An addition of an auditorium and gymnasium building to the new classroom building, at an estimated cost of .. 146,000
The remodeling of May and Wells Halls, at an estimated cost of 50,000
The razing of Crocker Hall, at an estimated cost of 5,000

State Teachers College, Hyannis.
A gymnasium building, at an estimated cost of 150,000
Completion of the athletic field at an estimated cost of 5,000

MASSACHUSETTS STATE PLANNING BOARD

State Teachers College, North Adams
Construction of a coal pocket, at an estimated cost $ 3,500

Lowell Textile Institute
An addition to the Colonial Avenue Building, at an
estimated cost of 150,000
A gymnasium and social hall, at an estimated cost of   200,000
The total estimated cost of this building program is $923,500

District Agencies

Metropolitan District Commission

The Metropolitan District Commission is composed of three divisions: The Metropolitan Parks Division, the Metropolitan Water Division, and the Metropolitan Sewerage Division.

The following table shows the total expenditures for capital outlay by the three divisions of the Metropolitan District Commission for the years 1925 to 1935, inclusive:

1925	$3,219,269.82	1931	$2,875,185.59
1926	3,776,967.12	1932	2,063,408.04
1927	2,542,857.51	1933	1,992,261.11
1928	2,312,304.56	1934	1,826,217.73
1929	1,695,710.66	1935	1,371,547.24
1930	1,915,728.61		

The following list of construction projects has been submitted by the Metropolitan District Commission to the Public Works Administration, in the hope of obtaining grants:

Metropolitan Park Division projects for the construction and reconstruction of parkways. Estimated cost $7,104,011
Metropolitan Water Division projects for water supply, at an estimated cost of 1,150,000
(This does not include the cost of a water-supply pressure tunnel from Wachusett Reservoir to Boston, which is awaiting the report in 1937 of the Metropolitan District Water Supply Commission and the State Department of Health).
Sewerage Division projects for the construction of sewers and pumping stations, at an estimated cost of   9,487,000
The total of this program amounts to.. $17,741,011

Metropolitan District Water Supply Commission

The Metropolitan District Water Supply Commission was established by Chapter 375 of the Acts of 1926, and additional appropriations were authorized under Chapters 111 and 321 of the Acts of 1927.

This Commission is charged with the development of a portion of the watersheds of the Ware and Swift Rivers for additional water supply for the Metropolitan District. When these works are completed, they will be turned over to the Metropolitan District Commission. The Metropolitan District Water Supply Commission has also developed a portion of the southern Sudbury water supply.

Following is a statement of the capital expenditures of the Metropolitan District Water-Supply Commission for the years 1926 to 1935 inclusive:

1926	$ 22,960.50	1931	$2,760,414.22
1927	2,496,208.28	1932	3,619,871.89
1928	3,503,726.49	1933	4,229,608.16
1929	5,204,827.06	1934	3,413,275.85
1930	4,513,897.61	1935	3,712,520.66

The total capital expenditures over this period amount to $33,477,310.72.

The aqueduct from Wachusett Reservoir to Quabbin Reservoir is complete. The portion between the Ware River intake at Colebrook and Wachusett Reservoir has been in use since 1931. Quabbin Reservoir, which is on the east, middle, and west branches of the Swift River, is now under construction.

The future program of the Metropolitan District Water Supply Commission is to complete the main dam, the dike, reservoir, and appurtenant works, which will require four years or more.

County Agencies

The most important item of capital expenditure by the county is for inter-town improvement. The County Commissioners cooperate with the State authorities in this work, the State obtaining its share of the necessary funds from the gasoline tax and automobile fees of the highway fund, under the provisions of Chapter 90, Section 34, of the General Laws. Under this Act, the State ordinarily pays 50 per cent, the county 25 per cent, and the town 25 per cent of the costs. The sums granted by the State, county, and towns for inter-town roads are usually added together, to be expended on a comprehensive plan of road improvement, rather than having the three agencies work by themselves. Better results in planning and

MASSACHUSETTS STATE PLANNING BOARD

construction have resulted from this cooperation.

The cooperation between the State, county, and town is accomplished through a petition for relocation and specific repairs. The State makes a contract with the town to perform work that meets with the acceptance of the Department of Public Works. The county order for repairs follows Department of Public Work specifications. The work is performed, in certain instances, by the town, through its highway department; and, in certain instances, by contract, through a general contractor. Some counties maintain engineering departments; others rely on the State Department of Public Works for engineering services.

Under the provisions of Chapter 81, Section 26A, of the General Laws; small towns may be aided by the county in road repair and improvements; and, under the provisions of Chapter 84, Section 11A, of the General Laws, small towns may be aided by the county in repairs to roads on which State and county funds have been expended. Usually, under these provisions, the State, county, and town contribute.

The counties also make expenditures for the construction and repair of certain bridges. Bridges are built, in certain instances, by county and State and local participation, and, in other cases, by the State without the county or local participation.

The county makes capital expenditures for county buildings, including county courts, prisons, hospitals, and training schools. However, the expenditures by the county for highways and bridges are usually considerably larger than are the expenditures on county buildings.

For purposes of illustration of the amounts the counties spend for capital improvements on highways and bridges, and on county buildings, the following table of expenditures for the year 1935 is given:

Table 70

COUNTY EXPENDITURES FOR CAPITAL IMPROVEMENTS IN 1935

COUNTY	HIGHWAYS AND BRIDGES	COUNTY BUILDINGS NEW CONSTRUCTION
Essex	$ 235,474.10	
Middlesex	281,326.03	$ 463.90
Suffolk	*	*
Norfolk	37,996.02	27,199.66
Plymouth	129,895.31	
Bristol	8,407.97	
Barnstable	94,136.80	
Dukes	55,295.52	
Nantucket	283.14	
Worcester	249,802.50	3,078.16
Franklin	39,126.78	
Hampshire	40,356.62	
Hampden	111,777.47	
Berkshire	113,753.02	

*No expenditures by the county for new construction during 1935

Under the heading of repairs, furnishings, and improvements to county buildings, as shown in the reports of the county treasurers, certain items are probably chargeable to capital outlay, but the major portion of the charges under that heading are chargeable to maintenance. Consequently, only those items which are actually new construction of county buildings are shown in the previous table.

Although the counties do not usually publish in their reports an advance program of construction for more than one year, all counties have future programs of work which they desire to accomplish as fast as funds become available. These programs may cover five years or more, depending on the amount of work.

A factor which limits the counties in outlining a future program is that it is not always possible to determine in advance the advance program of the State and municipalities in a given area. The programs of these other agencies, of course, have a large bearing on any program that the county may desire to carry out.

Municipal Agencies

The municipalities of the State make capital expenditures which vary according to the size of the municipality, but which amount to

MASSACHUSETTS STATE PLANNING BOARD

a large total each year. These outlays are made on municipally owned buildings, such as schools, libraries, and buildings necessary to the various municipal departments, roads and sidewalks, water-supply and sewerage systems, and parks and playgrounds.

Following are the total capital expenditures, by years, for all the municipalities of the State, from 1925 to 1934, inclusive:

1925	$ 60,133,887.70		1930	$ 67,857,331.45
1926	61,250,512.97		1931	72,919,122.68
1927	59,751,429.88		1932	45,654,050.74
1928	59,847,338.85		1933	26,113,089.74
1929	59,045,358.30		1934	31,753,087.33

Taking into consideration the outlay for this ten-year period, it is evident that the municipalities, together, spend a large amount, and that it would be of great benefit to have a future program of municipal construction harmonized with the Federal, State, district, and county programs.

In order to formulate a future municipal program, a survey of the public-works requirements of all the municipalities is necessary. Without such a survey it is impossible to create a master program, and without a master program, the work undertaken will not be a part of a general scheme. If requirements are understood and planned for, cooperation between municipalities can be secured and public works carried out in a manner beneficial to all concerned. Also, a survey should result in a list of projects which can be undertaken at the preper time to maintain a more constant level of labor employment and to obtain better financing.

With the idea of promoting a planned and integrated program of public works over a period of years, the National Resources Committee suggested that the State Planning Board extend its help to State and local governmental agencies in making inventories of public construction requirements, and prepare a six-year program from these inventories.

At the end of August of this year, a letter was sent by the Chairman of the State Planning Board to the Mayors of all cities, Chairmen of Boards of Selectmen of all towns, Chairmen of County Commissioners, and Chairmen of Planning Boards of Municipalities, requesting that they cooperate with the State Planning Board by listing and describing public construction projects that they recommended for construction during the six-year period beginning January 1, 1937. Project reporting forms, together with detailed instruction for filling out, were also sent.

MASSACHUSETTS STATE PLANNING BOARD

The agency was asked to indicate the order in which the projects reported should be constructed. This information assists the State Planning Board in reviewing the projects and in transmitting the agencies' recommendations to the Resources Committee in Washington, which will use them as a basis for determining National public-construction needs.

The replies to this survey have been coming in extremely slowly, to date. Certain municipalities have requested more copies of the questionnaire; others have advised the State Planning Board that they could not fill out the questionnaire, owing to different difficulties. One was that, while they had work that they would like to plan for, the town was small and had no one competent to estimate the cost of the work. Another reason was that those now holding the executive positions in certain of the municipalities did not believe that they should try to line up a program of work that they might not be able to carry out in the future, because of changes in administration. Another was that no funds were available to acquire the information necessary for the questionnaire. Still another reason was that the voters of the town, in recent town meetings, had voted down projects that required either local or Federal funds. Probably the most important reason was that the various agencies wished more time in which to decide upon a program of future construction.

To date, thirty-one agencies have replied to the survey questionnaires, but only seven have filled out the forms and returned them. In order not to bother the municipalities any more than necessary and to give them plenty of time to outline their programs and make their returns, nothing further in the matter has been done by the State Planning Board, except to answer any questions that have arisen. It seems now as though it would be necessary to make personal contact with the different municipalities, assisting them in filling out their returns, in order to achieve the desired goal of a comprehensive, six-year advance program of public works.

COMMUNITY PLANNING

Courtesy of Institute of Geographical Exploration,
Harvard University.
Photographed by Bradford Washburn.

CHAPTER X

COMMUNITY PLANNING

Summary Outline

I. History of Community Planning in Massachusetts

    A. Early Examples
    B. Early Planning Legislation
    C. The Homestead Commission, 1911-1919
    D. Development of Planning Boards since 1913
    E. Planning Board Activities

II. How Planning Boards are Functioning

    A. Budget Appropriations
    B. Personnel
    C. Standing in Community
    D. Zoning Law Administration
    E. CWA, ERA, and WPA Projects
    F. New Town Planning Act
    G. Practical Results of Planning Board Activity
    H. Relation to State Planning Board

III. Conclusions

    A. General Appraisal of Local Planning Activities
    B. What the State Planning Board Can Do

MASSACHUSETTS STATE PLANNING BOARD

COMMUNITY PLANNING*

History of Community Planning in Massachusetts

A real history of community planning should be an attempt to trace the forces that were working towards a correlating of municipal activities affecting the physical environment of cities and towns. The following pages present the results of such an attempt.

Early Examples

Characteristics of Early Planning. Some of the best traditions of town and village planning are found in New England. The town common, around which were grouped the meeting house, churches, and other community buildings, was the focal point in an otherwise informal design. Many of these town centers, such as that of Lexington, Massachusetts, have survived the years with little physical change.

Until the early part of the nineteenth century, the towns were generally developed in an informal manner. Streets necessarily followed the contours of the land, in most cases, although with the subdivision of farms that had already been laid out in squares, the rectangular or gridiron street systems became more common. A burying ground and a common field for pasturage were the only public open spaces needed in these communities, in which every inhabitant had ample land for his own use and the open country at his doorstep.

Thomas Graves' Plan for Charlestown. One of the earliest Massachusetts town plans is that prepared by a skilled engineer, Thomas Graves, of Kent, England, for the Massachusetts Company. He was engaged, in March, 1629, to lay out the town of Charlestown with streets about the hill, providing a two-acre plot for each inhabitant. The original settlement was soon abandoned, and the inhabitants moved to what is now Boston.

Plan Proposals of Robert Gourlay. Seventy years before the Massachusetts Legislature passed the bill requiring all towns of over 10,000 inhabitants to have planning boards, a Scotsman, Robert Fleming Gourlay, published a pamphlet entitled "Plan for Beautifying New York and Enlarging the City of Boston, being Studies to Illustrate the Science of City Building." Mr. Frederic H. Fay has de-

---

*Abridged from a report prepared by Mr. William Stanley Parker for the Urbanism Committee of the National Resources Committee. Published by permission.

scribed Gourlay's main proposals as follows:

"At first glance Gourlay's plan might appear wholly fantastic, but a certain significance is to be found among other proposals in his forecast of our subway system. In connection with his project for 'sub-urban railways,' the ultimate need of which he emphasized some ten years before Boston had ever seen a horse car, upon grounds which later proved wholly valid, Gourlay declared that the better to avoid congestion in our streets it would be well to carry the suburban and distributing railways through the City Proper by means of tunnels. One of these tunnels he projected from the West Boston Bridge to a point very near the South Boston of today, a plan which took shape seventy years later in our Dorchester-Cambridge Tunnel. Gourlay's subway from the Lowell Railroad, now the North Station, is an almost equally close parallel to the present Tremont Street Subway.

"His Beacon Street Subway has become our Boylston Street Subway, with the same destination in view, while the route from the State House to the South Ferry is a very fair prototype of the East Boston Tunnel. Finally, Gourlay expressed the belief that motive power would be provided for his city railways, not by steam but by compress-air, distributed from a central station as electricity is today.

"Speaking from a city of 100,000 persons in 1844, Gourlay declared that Boston fifty years thereafter would contain 500,000 souls. The actual number was 496,920; and within a century he prophesied a million at least, a rate of increase which we are closely approximating today".

Robert Copeland's Community Plans. In 1872, Robert Morris Copeland, a landscape architect, published a volume entitled "Essay and Plan for the Improvement of the City of Boston".* Although his proposals were confined largely to streets and open spaces, the area covered extended from the Charles River to the Neponset River and his study had almost the scope of what today would be called a regional plan. He said in part:**

"How best to use Boston's area must be a problem which he admits of division into parts, of discussion and measurement, and a plan can be as well digested for its future progress so as to do full justice to the wants of a future population as for the laying out and construction of a building for public or domestic use.

*Lee and Shepard, Boston, 1872
**Ibid., p. 10

MASSACHUSETTS STATE PLANNING BOARD

"The sole difference, or hindrance to such planning, is that we have not been accustomed to plan in this way. We have supposed that, for some unnamed reason, planning for a city's growth and progress could only be done as it grows; that no one can foresee sufficiently the future requirements of business to wisely provide for them. This is a fallacious belief".

"We have not been accustomed to plan in this way". In this short sentence is contained a truism that is even more self-evident today than it could possibly have been in 1872.

Copeland may have been the first in America to use the words "city plan". "When a man or company wish to begin a new or valuable business", he writes, "they can adapt their wants to the city plan".

Previous to his plan for Boston, Copeland had prepared a number of plans for subdivisions, including a plan for laying out the Village of Oak Bluffs, Marthas Vineyard, in 1866. An interesting feature of the latter was the use of culs-de-sac, or dead-end streets, and small parks in the interior of blocks.

Planning of Industrial Villages. At the beginning of the twentieth century, a number of large industrial concerns were turning to the problem of providing adequate housing accommodations for their workers. The population of the industrial communities in Massachusetts was increasing at a rapid rate, and few towns were provided with a sufficient number of dwellings to house the factory employees.

Referring to "Model Factories and Villages",* by an English social investigator, Budgett Meakin, Mr. Thomas Adams states:**

"It was in New England, however, that Mr. Meakin found the most attractive industrial villages. Of these, Hopedale, adjoining Milford in Massachusetts, was given the credit of being America's best model village. Established in 1841 as a Christian socialist community, it was taken over and extended in 1856 by a firm of cotton machinery makers. The streets and dwellings were pleasantly laid out, a special feature being the appearance of the rear yards......

---
*Published by T. Fisher Unwin, London, 1905.
**In his "Outline of Town and City Planning", New York, Russell Sage Foundation, 1935, p. 177.

MASSACHUSETTS STATE PLANNING BOARD

"Other examples mentioned were Whitinsville, Massachusetts, housing 2,500 workers; Ludlow, near Springfield, begun in 1868 and developed after 1890 on 1,500 acres, housing 1,200 employees".

In 1632, the citizens of Cambridge agreed "by a joynt consent" that the "Towne shall not be Inlarged until all the place be filled with houses". They also required that the "houses shall range even and stand just six feet in their owne ground from the street".

In 1694, Malden voted that the village common be divided, and ordered commissioners making the division to "employ an artist to layout ye lands".

Important Planning Developments. Despite early trials and difficulties, Massachusetts was finally to point the way in the attack on problems in the field of planning and housing, by the establishment of the Metropolitan Park Commission and the Water Supply and Sewerage Board of 1890, and the Homestead Commission in 1911, and by the enactment of the planning laws of 1913 and 1936.

Early Planning Legislation

Until comparatively recent years, there was practically no legislation that could be designated as "planning" legislation. However, since the early colonial days a great variety of acts and ordinances have imposed various restrictions on privately owned land and buildings. Although these restrictions might be considered as the fore-runner of what we now call "zoning", most of them were more comparable to provisions of building roads. The protection of health and the elimination of fire risks were the paramount objectives of most of these regulations.

In 1872, Massachusetts passed legislation permitting municipalities to regulate the inspection, materials, construction, alteration, and safe use of buildings. It was passed primarily as a law for the prevention of fire and the protection of life and property from fire hazards. In 1912, an amendment, Chapter 334, adding the words "health and morals" and "height, area, and location" made the law comprehensive enough to justify the title of "zoning". Thus since 1912, Massachusetts has had a law which may be called a zoning enabling law, because permission was given to regulate the use, height, area, and location of buildings for the prevention of fire, the preservation of life, the protection of health and morals, and the general welfare.

In 1898, there were enacted for Boston special eminent domain

MASSACHUSETTS STATE PLANNING BOARD

provisions limiting the height of buildings in and around Copley Square; and in 1904, by special statute, the principle of districting or zoning for height, under the police power, was applied to Boston. These Acts formed a basis for the zoning enabling Acts of 1920 and 1935.

The Homestead Commission, 1911 - 1919

No better example can be found of the initial willingness of the General Court to pass progressive legislation, coupled with the unwillingness, or inability, of the citizens of the Commonwealth to take full advantage of the opportunities thus offered, than that furnished by the history of low-rental housing in Massachusetts. More than twenty years before the United States Government embarked on a Federal housing program, and twenty-five years before the erection of the first PWA housing projects in South Boston and Cambridge, the State of Massachusetts had created a Homestead Commission to investigate methods of providing surburban cottages for families in the lower-income groups.

By the terms of Chapter 607 of the Acts of 1911, the Homestead Commission was instructed to report "a bill or bills embodying a plan and the method of carrying out, whereby, with the assistance of the Commonwealth, homesteads or small houses and plots of ground may be acquired by mechanics, laborers, and others in the suburbs of cities and towns".

In pursuance of these instructions, the Commission reported a Bill (H. 442, 1912), accompanied by a brief report (H. 441, 1912), in January, 1912. At about the same time, the Massachusetts Bureau of Statistics issued a review of housing activities in other countries (Labor Bulletin, No. 88).

The Bill provided that part of the unclaimed deposits in saving banks, which had been called into the State treasury, should be loaned to the Commission to undertake the work proposed in Chapter 607, Acts of 1911. The constitutionality of this proposition was questioned during the passage of the measure through the Legislature, and the Bill was submitted to the Supreme Court for an opinion. On May 28, 1912, the court made answer (H.2339,1912) that such use of those funds or any public funds would be a private and not a public use, and, therefore, it would be contrary to the provisions of the constitution. More than twenty years later, the Federal government was to meet with the same obstacle in its attempt to purchase land for public housing by exercise of the right of Eminent Domain.

MASSACHUSETTS STATE PLANNING BOARD

On June 4, 1912, the General Court passed the following Act (Chapter 714, Acts of 1912):

<u>Section 1.</u> The commission established by chapter six hundred and seven of the Acts of the year nineteen hundred and eleven shall continue its investigations of the need of providing homesteads for the people of the Commonwealth and its study of plans already in operation or contemplated elsewhere for housing wage-earners, and shall report to the legislature not later than the first Wednesday in January nineteen hundred and thirteen, and may recommend such legislation as in its judgment will tend to increase the supply of wholesome homes for the people. The commission may expend in prosecution of its work such sums, not exceeding in the aggregate two thousand dollars, as the governor and council may approve.

<u>Section 2.</u> This act shall take effect upon its passage.

The report called for by the above Act was carefully prepared (H. 2000, 1913). It presented a comprehensive picture of housing conditions in the State, with particular emphasis on the situation in Boston. However, the report is chiefly noteworthy for the grasp shown by the Commission of the relation of housing to city planning, and for its proposal that planning boards be set up in all towns and cities with a population of more than 10,000.

That the obstacles to adequate low-rent housing were as clearly recognized a quarter of a century ago as they are today is indicated by the following quotation from the report:*

"The problem is one of proper distribution of population. The principal obstacles to its solution are low wages, the high cost of land, difficulty of obtaining funds, inadequate transportation. Yet it is imperative that this problem be solved, not only on account of obligations to humanity, but because the stability of the State is involved. The physical condition of the home is so vitally related to morals, health, and the well-being of the family and the individual that the welfare of the State depends upon it".

After stressing the need for comprehensive planning in order that the housing program might be effective, the report ended with the following conclusions:**

"This Commission was created in response to an earnest desire

---

*Page 36
**Pages 41-42

MASSACHUSETTS STATE PLANNING BOARD

to bring healthful suburban homes within the reach of the poor. Its recommendation that the uncalled for savings banks deposit be used for that purpose having been rejected by the Supreme Court as unconstitutional, and the Legislature having authorized the continuation of its investigations, the foregoing is set forth as a brief summary of the information it has gathered as to the need of a larger supply of wholesome homes".

The Commission's conclusions are:

"1. That present conditions are not only unjust to the laboring classes but seem to be detrimental to the general health and may be a contributory cause of unnecessary deaths, breeding disease, poverty, ignorance, vice and crime, and blighting the lives of thousands who might otherwise have been good and useful citizens.

"2. That these conditions are to some extent the result of the haphazard, unsystematic development of our cities, and the selfish utilization of their natural resources, and the resultant conditions of lack of room, air and sunlight in congested tenement districts undoubtedly tend to increase infantile mortality.

"3. That each city and large town should make at once a thorough study of its resources and possibilities, what ills in housing and development now exist, and how they can be remedied and their growth prevented".

These conclusions impel the Commission to recommend:

"1. <u>That planning boards be instituted in each city and town of more than 10,000 inhabitants.</u> The work of such boards would show what the actual local conditions are and would disclose the resources at hand to better them. The spread of bad conditions would be stopped and means found gradually to abolish slums now existing.

"2. <u>That the Commonwealth and community encourage and promote the formation of associations to plan and construct low-cost suburban homes.</u>

"Bills in support of these recommendations are presented herewith".

What more comprehensive or far-sighted program than this could have been conceived by a commission appointed to investigate housing conditions? Unfortunately most of the planning boards which owed their very existence to the above recommendation of the Homestead Commission rapidly proceeded to forget the primary object for which they were appointed, and to expend most of their energy on traffic problems, billboard regulation, and zoning. A few cities, like Boston and Haverhill, made surveys of housing conditions within their borders; but, in general, those planning boards which have made any attempt at all to carry out the objects stated in the Act establishing them have confined themselves to indirect attacks on the housing problem.

In 1913, Acts were passed by the legislature providing for the establishment of planning boards in cities and towns, and further enlarging and defining the duties of the Homestead Commission. The Commission was enlarged by the addition of two members, one of whom was to be an attorney-at-law, and the other a recognized expert in the planning of cities and towns.

The Commission took an active part in the promotion of city planning and housing betterment, and, with the exception of the war period, during which the Commission was partly disorganized by reason of the activity of its members in war work, annual conferences on city planning and housing were held.

At the instigation of the Commission, the following amendment to the State constitution was approved by the legislature and ratified in 1915 by a referendum vote of 284,568 to 95,148:

"The General Court shall have power to authorize the Commonwealth to take land and to hold, improve, sub-divide, build upon and sell the same, for the purpose of relieving congestion of population and providing homes for citizens; provided, however, that this amendment shall not be deemed to authorize the sale of such land or buildings at less than the cost thereof".

A Bill was presented to the General Court, in 1915, requesting authority to build homesteads for wage earners, laborers, and others, and asking for a preliminary appropriation of $50,000. This was rejected, and in 1916 the Commission renewed its request and presented detailed plans for typical housing projects. Finally, on May 26, 1917, the Bill was passed, and signed by Governor Samuel W. McCall. This Act authorized probably the first governmental appropriation in the United States to aid workers in acquiring "small houses and plots of ground".

About seven acres of land in the City of Lowell were subsequently purchased by the Commission, and plans were made for the development of the tract in 33 house lots. Under the direction of the Commission, twelve houses were completed at an average cost per room of $500 for five-room houses, and less, for semi-detached four-room houses. These twelve houses were sold to workers for a small down-payment and a long-term mortgage. The project developed no further because the legislature refrained from adding to the original grant of $50,000.

The Homestead Commission published its last annual report in December 1919, and in the following year its activities were taken over by the Division of Housing and Town Planning of the Department of Public Welfare.

Development of Planning Boards since 1913

The years since 1913 have shown increasing activity in the preparation of planning and zoning studies, broken only during the period, 1917 to 1920, following America's entrance into the World War, and the current period of depression. The Planning Board Act was passed in April, 1913, and, by the end of that year, 45 municipalities had established Boards. In 1914, an Act (Chapter 283) authorized towns with a population of less than 10,000 to establish planning boards. The increase in the number of boards established is indicated in the following table:

Table 71

PLANNING BOARDS IN MASSACHUSETTS

YEAR	ACTIVE BOARDS	INACTIVE BOARDS	NO. BOARDS APPOINTED
1915	50	15	-
1920	36	17	13
1925	77	4	7
1930	115	-	3
1935	123	-	4

Conferences of the city and town planning boards with the Homestead Commission were held in 1913 and 1914, and on November 12, 1915, at the third annual conference, steps were taken to organize the Massachusetts Federation of Planning Boards, the first meeting of which was held the following week. Twenty-three members, representing twelve planning boards, were present, and a constitution was adopted, in which the purpose of the Federation was set forth as follows:

"Article 2. The purpose of the Federation is to promote city and town planning in Massachusetts; to suggest fields of usefulness and to aid and perfect the work of planning boards; to encourage the organization of planning boards in other localities; to collect and publish facts regarding the economic, industrial, and moral values to be secured by wise planning; and to affiliate

MASSACHUSETTS STATE PLANNING BOARD

organizations and individuals interested in the scientific study and development of city and town planning in its largest aspects".

Planning Board Activities

The work of the planning boards since 1913 has been extremely varied both in character and accomplishment. Any survey of their activities, in order to come within the confines of this report, must necessarily be limited to a chronological list of some of the major accomplishments in comprehensive planning.

Activity in the year 1914 was mostly confined to outlining the objects and scope of the individual planning boards. The year 1915 found Springfield preparing a topographical map, and working on a plan for the undeveloped portions of the city. Winchester was also making plans for future development.

In 1916, Salem, which had organized the first board in the State, in 1912, was drafting a housing code, developing plans for its water-front, and carrying on a lecture campaign to educate the public in the value of city planning. In 1917, Boston was working on surveys of East Boston and the North End, and making studies of passenger transportation, parks, and playgrounds.

Haverhill started on housing study, in 1918, and was investigating problems of land and water conservation. Newton had employed an expert to study the future needs of the town, and Quincy was making plans for the Pilgrim Parkway. In 1919, a comprehensive plan and zoning ordinance for Newton were started.

Boston was investigating housing conditions, in 1920, its bills for housing measures having been defeated in 1919. In 1920, Walpole accepted the comprehensive plan made by its Town Planning Committee. In 1921, Newton's plan was completed and published, and Springfield and Worcester were having comprehensive plans prepared.

Norwood completed its comprehensive plan in 1922, and, in 1923, Boston took the first step in the preparation of a thoroughfare plan for the city. In 1924, Arlington started on a comprehensive plan, which was published in 1926. Wakefield completed its plan and zoning by-law in 1924, and, in the same year, Springfield's plan was completed and accepted by the city government.

The year 1925 found Newton developing its town square in accordance with its planning studies, and Springfield, Walpole, and Winchester carrying out improvements, such as schools, fire houses, parks, playgrounds, and streets, in accordance with the recommen-

MASSACHUSETTS STATE PLANNING BOARD

dations of their city and town planning boards.

Worcester's plan was completed in 1925, and, in the following year, the planning board was considering measures for controlling land development in its open areas. Springfield had the distinction of having its plan adopted as an official document by the city, and it was decreed that all future development would be required to conform to this plan.

Boston completed and published a thoroughfare plan in 1930. Melrose was making basic studies, in 1928, preparatory to making a master plan, and, from 1928 to 1930, Newton, Springfield, Melrose, and Worcester were reporting improvements that were taking place in accordance with their plans.

Since 1930 there has been a universal lessening in the amount of municipal construction, and planning boards have either been inactive or have been engaged in the sponsoring of projects under CWA, ERA, or WPA auspices, the City of Boston being particularly active in this type of work. A number of cities and towns, such as Lynn, Gloucester, and Reading, have undertaken planning projects which have provided them with much valuable information concerning their social, economic, and physical resources. Gloucester and Reading are using this information as the basis for comprehensive master plans which they are now developing.

How Planning Boards Are Functioning

A statistical investigation indicated wide variance in the degree of success or failure being experienced by local planning boards. Many boards, optional as well as required, were clearly inactive. Required boards were appointed to conform to the law but given no funds with which to work, and no incentive to function. Similarly, even in towns that were not required to appoint a planning board at all, boards had sometimes been created under some impulse and had then been allowed to lapse into uselessness.

Yet there were obvious cases of small communities with active planning boards and with budgets far in excess of those provided by many of the larger cities. What were the underlying causes of these different conditions? It was evident they could not be discovered from questionnaires. Only local contacts with the members of the planning boards could bring forth the reasons for success here and failure there, reasons likely to be related in varying degrees to the character of the community, the personnel of the planning boards, and the local political situation.

MASSACHUSETTS STATE PLANNING BOARD

Since there are more than 130 planning boards, time did not permit, at first, separate interviews, although this direct contact between the State Planning Board and the local planning boards is a necessary procedure if the State Board is to succeed in stimulating and coordinating the activities of the local boards, as the Act creating it clearly contemplates (See Map 58-2). Twelve regional meetings were therefore arranged to include all the boards in the State, grouped as seemed most expedient, in some cases by county lines, in others by river valleys, and in still others by general interests.

The meager attendance indicates an unfortunate lack of interest in planning board activities. In spite of this, those who did attend maintained a concentrated discussion of the problems of the local boards for two hours and a half and provided a good cross-section of the opinions, procedures, and progress of the average local planning board.

In addition to these regional meetings, letters were written to thirty individuals closely associated with local planning board activity, in most cases either as chairman or member of a local board, asking for an expression of personal opinion on the following four points:

1. Has your community been importantly affected in its physical development by the plans prepared by the Planning Board?
2. What developments have been brought about by and carried out in accordance with such plans?
3. What developments have been carried out against the advice of the Planning Board?
4. What is the attitude of local officials and citizens towards the Planning Board?

The regional meetings considered various essential matters, as indicated by the following headings. The results of the discussions, as well as the comments received in answer to the letters noted above, are included in the following summary:

Budget Appropriations

One of the clear indications of the questionnaires was the paucity of funds generally provided for the local planning boards. Many boards have no appropriation. Most of those that have appropriations have $100 or less. Only eighteen boards are known to have $250 or more and only thirteen, $500 or more.

A comparison of 1936 and 1934 questionnaires discloses that

MASSACHUSETTS STATE PLANNING BOARD

thirty-three boards report appropriations in 1936 that reported no appropriations in 1934, and fourteen additional boards reported increased appropriations. The total of these new appropriations, plus the increases, total $50,208. On the other side of the ledger, fourteen boards reduced their appropriations, in whole or in part, by a total of $2,235. Cities and towns of the Commonwealth, in 1936, appropriated for planning board activities $47,973 more than was appropriated in 1934. It is in the natural order of things that Boston should provide a large share of the increase, $36,640, on account of its substantial program of WPA activity. Various reasons doubtless account for the increased appropriations. The contacts made by the New England Regional Planning Commission when securing information for the questionnaires, in 1934, evidently stimulated new activity and appropriations. Improved business conditions may have eased the tax situation and permitted new or increased budget items for planning. The opportunities offered by the CWA, ERA, and WPA programs have resulted in appropriations to take care of incidental expenses of projects or for other planning work.

The meetings disclosed the fact that in many cases all drafting needed by the planning board was done by the City or Town Engineer, under his department's appropriation. In one case expenses are defrayed from the Mayor's special funds. Thus, the budget item is not always a true indication of the planning board's activity and influence.

It was pointed out that a planning board with an appropriation of $25 a year might be considered by the community, for that reason, of little importance, although the City Engineer might be spending from his budget $1,000 for drafting on work required by the planning board. The practical, political value of having the planning board's budget tell the true story of its activities was emphasized. It was also pointed out that the city engineer's office is concerned with the day-to-day engineering problems of the city, and that a staff under the direction of the planning board was better adapted to the broader study of the future development of the city.

Minimum budget items to cover a technically trained draftsman to act also as secretary to the board, a part-time or full-time stenographer, and miscellaneous expenses, and totaling from $2,250 to $3,500 were outlined. While many looked upon such an appropriation as hopeless, others indicated a belief in the desirability of a permanent staff to carry on consistent studies.

In some cases the City Engineer, ex-officio, may be the active, technically-trained member of the board. In this case the mainte-

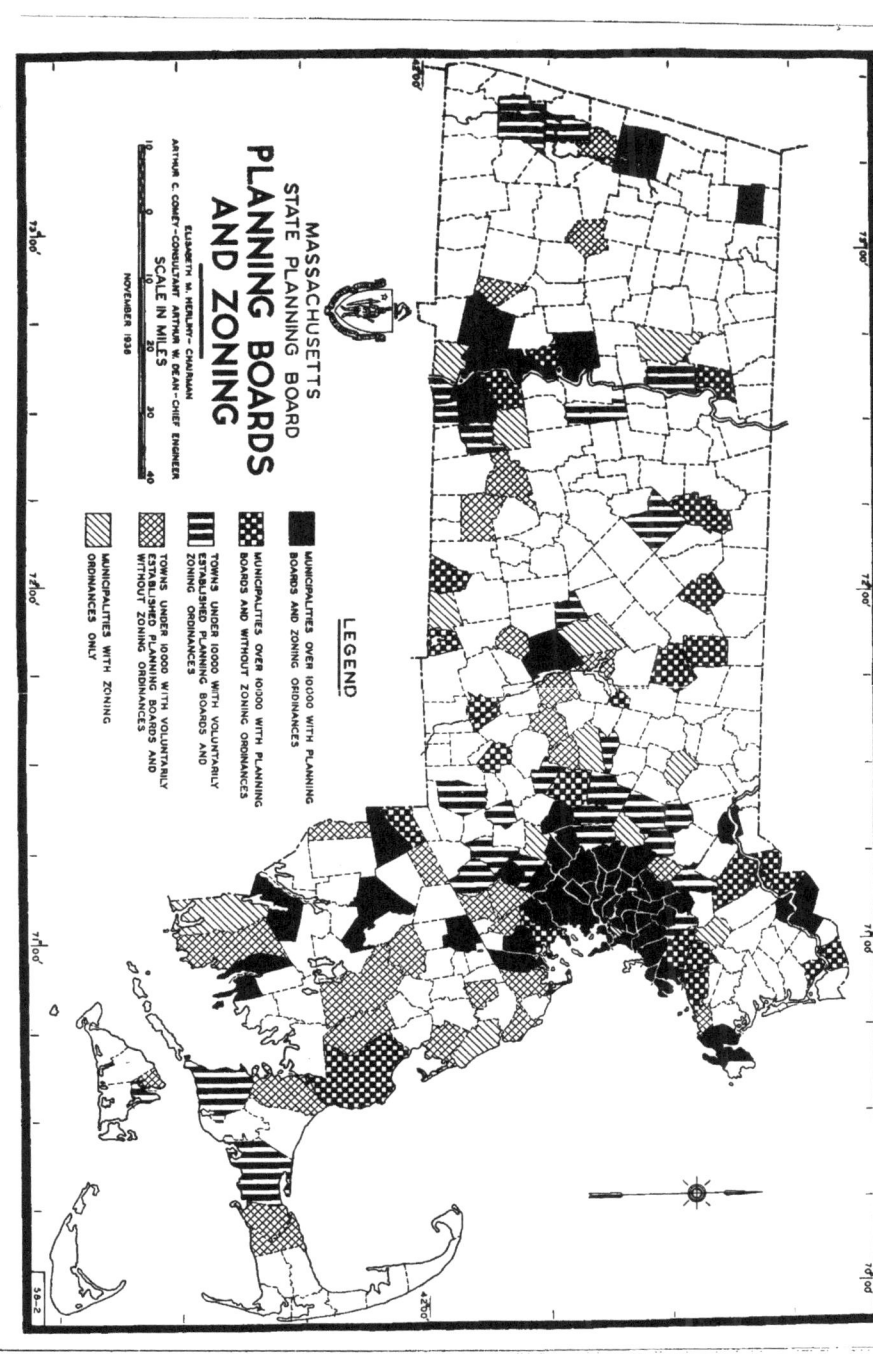

nance of a double staff would hardly be feasible or necessary. It may be questioned whether, as a general principle, this is as good a scheme of organization as one which sets up a planning board independent of all administrative boards.

At several of the regional meetings, the need of regional coöperation by certain groups of planning boards was stressed by members of the local boards. It was pointed out that this was doubtless in many cases valuable, but that such coöperation must spring from a clear local conviction of the need and a definite local desire to develop such coöperative measures. The local planning boards were assured of the coöperation of the State Planning Board in such undertakings, and it was suggested that at such regional conferences it would probably be desirable for a representative of the State Planning Board to be present. The larger the area involved, the more likely that local plans will involve some phase of a State-wide program. The presence of a representative of the State Planning Board would tend to prevent any conflict between local and State plans.

In this connection, there was made a suggestion, bearing upon local appropriations, that seemed of real significance. This suggestion was that regional coöperation might well involve the joint employment by a group of boards of a single planning consultant for part-time service to each, permitting him to give each community advice as to its local problems and to the group of communities advice as to their common problems. This raises the further possibility that such boards, none of which alone could afford a permanent staff, might coöperatively employ a minimum permanent staff, such as already been suggested, to serve the group. If this were found to be feasible, the technical details of allocating the necessary appropriations for such a joint staff would seem possible of solution.

Personnel

The personnel of the planning boards show a wide variety of occupations, including engineers, architects, landscape architects, merchants, lawyers, physicians, professors, editors, statistical clerks, builders, farmers, food brokers, bankers, a minister, funeral director, cotton broker, foreman, paymaster, textile designer, and insurance man.

In a large majority of the boards so far interviewed, at least one member is an engineer, architect, or landscape architect. There is warrant for feeling that their technical training is of definite value to their board, permitting a readier understanding by the

MASSACHUSETTS STATE PLANNING BOARD

board of the problems involved, as well as the procedure needed for their investigation. The boards that are composed wholly of persons without technical design training, especially those that have no permanent technical staff, are inevitably less effective.

It is held by some that planning boards might better be lay boards and employ technicians. This would no doubt be agreeable to the technicians. It appears to be a fact, however, that engineers, architects, and landscape architects accept positions on planning boards, and find in their appointments opportunities to render valuable public service. Such service, although occasionally intensive and involving almost complete professional service of great value, is necessarily, as a rule, intermittent, and its value can be greatly magnified where there is a permanent staff carrying on the routine work.

Only the occasional professional man can afford to give a substantial portion of his time to planning board activities. His services, at best, are bound to be intermittent. What is needed is consistent progress along carefully defined lines of study. This can be secured only by means of a permanent staff working under competent guidance.

Standing in Community

Recognition by Public Officials. One board pointed out that it is desirable for a planning board to be "politically minded", which, however, was not intended to be synonymous with "playing politics". A planning board, to be effective, must be respected and must gain the cooperation of other public officials. Its personnel should carry weight in the community not only for technical competence, but also for soundness of judgment on matters of local policy and finance. It is of interest that the board referred to is one of those having no appropriation in its own name. Some fifteen years ago, a comprehensive town plan was laid out and a zoning law adopted, and these form the background for present activities. The board is called in on all zoning matters and on new street layouts by the Board of Survey. Its advice is asked and taken. Any plans the board needs are made by the town engineer. Light is shed on the reason for the satisfactory existing conditions by the fact that appointees to the planning board are apt to be ex-chairmen of the selectmen. Thus, the board membership is thoroughly informed on town affairs and its opinions command the respect of the citizens and town officials. There is food for thought in the success of this board.

The above situation is far from general. Some boards are

MASSACHUSETTS STATE PLANNING BOARD

appointed by Mayors merely to conform to the law requiring all cities to have planning boards, but with no intention that the appointees shall become active. This is due, in my opinion, largely to a lack of clear conception of what a planning board's function is and its relation to the administration of the city's affairs. Whenever a Mayor passes upon problems concerned with the physical development of the city, his decision is related to considerations involving, inevitably, the function of the planning board. He must form an opinion of what the city should do in the light of existing conditions and observed needs.

A planning board, competently staffed, can collect the facts, present them graphically and statistically, and indicate what action will be best for the future needs of the city in the light of existing conditions. Without a planning board, the Mayor must act as one, collecting the facts as best he can from various city officials and other sources, analyzing them, and deciding what actions to take. This will inevitably require more of the Mayor's time, produce a less competent and complete presentation of the facts, and frequently involve, as a result, a less desirable decision and a more expensive one. The Mayor is elected to perform the duties of his office. If he assumes in his own person the duties of subordinate city departments, he cannot exercise his own function so well and the subordinate function will also be less well administered. It is to his own advantage, as well as to that of the city, to delegate subordinate functions to the appropriate competent agencies.

It is stated by some that certain planning boards are kept inactive because other local officials wish to be free to make their own expedient decisions, which it might be embarrassing to make against the counter advice of the planning board. I believe this is more likely to be true of other department heads than of the Mayor. There appears to be a definite indication that the Town or County Engineer feels competent to perform this function of the planning board and that his professional pride is hurt at any suggestion of the need of a full-time staff for the planning board.

It is probable that, so far as this feeling exists, it is in the smaller communities rather than the larger. In the former, the planning problems are less obvious being less intense and complex and the day-to-day engineering problems equally so. The danger of this situation lies in the fact that, if the community is growing, the time to prevent future difficulties arising out of congestion is while the community is still relatively small. Later, when congestion has developed, many a desirable improvement will be impossible because of its cost.

MASSACHUSETTS STATE PLANNING BOARD

Benjamin Franklin, while his printing shop was at the corner of Washington and State Streets in Boston, urged the city to widen that narrow stretch of Washington Street at a cost of some thirty thousand dollars, and warned that if this were not done promptly the day would come when property values would have so increased as to make the cost of this improvement prohibitive. Several generations of Bostonians have already borne testimony to the soundness of his advice and the accuracy of his prognostication. A current statement recites that the Planning Board had early made a comprehensive report on street improvements to which little attention had been paid. One of its suggestions could then have been carried out with land damages of about $200,000, that would now involve over $2,000,000.

It would seem that there have been a sufficient number of examples of failure to act in time, to warn our smaller communities to arm themselves against a similar fate. The only arms that will be effective are those that involve analysis of the present and imagination as to the future. These are the two arms of a planning board.

Recognition by the Public. Securing the support of the public is as vital as that of gaining the cooperation of public officials. Evidence will be cited later in this report of the value of standing up for one's convictions and fighting it out in town meetings. When a planning board can do this so effectively that it can subsequently fight for and secure an appropriation over the opposition of the Finance Committee, as one board reports, it can properly claim that it has won public support. The evidence received indicates that the public can be convinced of a planning board's usefulness by practical results and by soundly conceived projects ably presented and lying within the town's financial ability. Plans out of scale with the community's present pocket book or too far ahead of the current needs, are likely to bring the planning board into disrepute.

Public support can be planned for just as well as a street improvement, and an essential element of success in securing public approval and appropriations for projects is a carefully-thought-out program of public information about the needs of the community and the improvements required to meet the needs. Well-devised newspaper publicity is important, and other methods of informing the public can be made effective.

The support of local civic bodies is essential. This can be gained more easily if some form of regular contact can be established, as through the agency of an officially recognized advisory

MASSACHUSETTS STATE PLANNING BOARD

Without the first, an understanding of how to attack the problems will be difficult. Without the second, the problems cannot be effectively studied, even if understood. Without the third, friction and lost motion will constantly obstruct progress. Without the fourth, a popular conviction of the need of suggested improvements will be difficult to obtain, and favorable action on appropriations correspondingly unlikely.

What the State Planning Board Can Do

From the experiences gained at the regional meetings already held, opportunities for useful action by the State Planning Board appear to lie along the following lines:

a. By general counsel and technical advice assist inexpert local boards to understand their local planning problems and opportunities and how to study them.

b. Assist local boards, through conferences with local public officials and otherwise, to secure proper recognition and adequate appropriations so that they can perform the functions they are intended to perform by the Act under which they are established.

c. Assist local boards in the development of appropriate methods of organized coöperation with the public so that their work will be understood, and so that soundly devised public improvements will be more likely to receive practical support through appropriations.

d. Develop an adequate method for contact with local boards, at regular intervals, for the distribution of current information about the development of the program of the State Planning Board, significant activities of local boards, and other matters calculated to be helpful to the local boards in the solution of their own local problems.

e. Assist, where problems of a regional nature make desirable and where the local boards desire such action, in the development of regional meetings of local boards, and be represented at such meetings in order to assist with information about the State program as it may bear upon the regional problems under consideration and to keep the State Planning Board fully advised as to the progress of all such regional discussion.

f. Provide, so far as may be feasible, when requested or at other reasonable intervals, personal consultations with local boards in their own communities, to assist in the general development of the local program in such ways as may be most appropriate to the local situation; but in all cases in a purely advisory capacity, leaving with the local board full responsibility for action.

MASSACHUSETTS STATE PLANNING BOARD

committee made up of delegated representatives of civic organizations, improvement associations, professional bodies, and other groups interested in public affairs. If such advisory groups can be kept in close contact with the development of the planning board's ideas, their members will be effective agents in securing the endorsement of the bodies they represent. These bodies will rightly feel that they have been consulted in advance and have had a part in devising the solution. They will tend to support it if it is wisely conceived.

In a larger community with subordinate districts having definite social and geographical characteristics, this idea can be extended to the creation of district advisory committees similarly constituted of representatives of all the interested local groups. These local committees create recognized points of contact with the planning board and permit it to obtain adequate local consideration of projects as they develop, and local support for them later.

The development of these committees will depend on the circumstances and personalities in each community. Generalizations beyond the underlying idea are futile, as the precise methods to be used should not be imposed but should develop naturally from the local conditions. Organized contacts between the planning board and the public, however, can be accepted quite definitely as valuable, and the idea left in the hands of each planning board to develop in such form as best suits its own community.

The reaction of the members of local planning boards to this procedure was uniformly favorable and in some cases indicative of its value, as evidenced by the following incident. A member of one Board reported that in his community an individual interested in securing a change in the zoning law, in order to obtain a filling station permit on an important corner lot in a residence district, carried the matter on appeal to special town meetings six times. The Planning Board consistently opposed the zoning law change and five times the town meeting supported their action. On the sixth appeal, the applicant succeeded in gaining enough votes to obtain favorable action. The member of the Planning Board reporting this incident stated emphatically that, in his judgment, if the Planning Board had organized an Advisory Committee as suggested herein, it would have been able to develop an informed public opinion on the matter and the appeal would never have been granted.

Several planning boards apparently involved in the development of zoning ordinances indicated an intention to take immediate steps to develop advisory committees as a means of assisting in the development and adoption of a zoning ordinance.

MASSACHUSETTS STATE PLANNING BOARD

Zoning Law Administration

    A study of Community Planning would not be complete without some investigation of zoning administration. Unfortunately the zoning of American cities has frequently preceded their planning. This constitutes an inherent weakness in the administration of the zoning law, since modifications, ill-considered and unwarranted, do not appear to disrupt the orderly and sequential development of the community along pre-arranged lines. It is appropriate, therefore, that the State Planning Board should inaugurate a series of studies of zoning administration in the towns and cities in this State. The methodology, as well as the related problems involved in such a comprehensive survey, were explored in connection with a study of the Board of Zoning Adjustment and the Board of Zoning Appeals of the City of Boston.

    An extensive (in contra-distinction to intensive) survey of the actions of the Boards of Zoning Adjustment and Zoning Appeals of the City of Boston, revealed evidence that might lead one to widely different conclusions as to the operations of the two Boards. The fact that the former Board granted only 37.2 per cent of the petitions it heard, while the Appeal Board granted 64.0 per cent of the cases brought before it, would suggest, at least from the petitioners' standpoint, a greater harshness on the part of the one Board and a "reasonableness" on the part of the other. However, from the standpoint of Zoning Administrator, interested in the preservation of the essential integrity of the ordinance and believing in the probable validity of the zoning plan as it stands, it might appear that the Board of Zoning Adjustment was more conscientious and cautious in granting pleas for the variation of existing zones, whereas the Board of Appeals was too lenient and rash in granting nearly two-thirds of all the requests made to it for individual changes. Still another possibility is that the original zoning ordinance and plan is working an undue hardship in so many individual cases that two-thirds of all appeals are justifiable and legitimate.

    A careful examination of the verbatim records available in each case, for the purpose of evaluating the evidence as presented and debated, would be the only scientific method of arriving at a sound conclusion. Furthermore, whether a two-thirds grant of all appeal cases in unusual or not (regardless of justification under the unnecessary hardship clause), cannot be determined until the performance of other cities in this regard has been studied. A similar study of eight years of operation of the Board of Appeals at Columbus, Ohio, revealed that 59.5 per cent of all appeals were granted, but, correlated with that, was evidence that the Board had

MASSACHUSETTS STATE PLANNING BOARD

responded to group and individual pressures of one sort or another.

Because of the limitation of time, it was impossible to go back to the original case records, as was done in the Columbus study. For the Boston study, the investigators had to rely on the published annual reports and summaries of the Board of Zoning Adjustment, on the one hand, and on the meagre case summaries of over 1,400 Board of Appeals cases, on the other. It would be highly desirable to go back to the verbatim reports of these two Boards, either on the basis of a complete enumeration or on a sampling basis. However, the conclusions and recommendations appended to the investigators' report, based on generalizations from statistical material from these secondary sources, are probably valid and sufficient for the purpose in hand.

The Board of Appeal in the twelve years of its existence has heard 1427 cases, involving 1665 requested variations of the zoning law. Of this number, 49.2 per cent were sustained outright, an additional 14.9 per cent sustained with proviso, 29.7 per cent were dismissed, and 6.3 per cent were withdrawn. In general, the trend has been toward an increasing number of appeals each year. The percentage of appeals sustained shows also a definite tendency to increase with the years. In 1935, 76.4 per cent of requested variations were sustained, a higher percentage than in any other year since the Board was established.

No really intensive investigation into the true nature of the working of such legislation can or should be attempted without first carrying through an extensive exploratory survey. The fact that the Board of Appeals has never filed a comprehensive annual report or even made an annual summary of its operations for its own information and guidance is, in itself, a justification for the State Planning Board to sponsor this preliminary survey. On the other hand, the excellent annual reports of the Board of Zoning Adjustment leave little to be improved upon or added to.

However, this preliminary survey of zoning administration in the City of Boston, does seem to suggest a step that the State Planning Board might reasonably take in the near future. That is, the inauguration for the cities and towns of Massachusetts of a uniform system for the reporting of all cases currently to the State Planning Board, suggested forms for which are indicated on the accompanying table. The collecting, by the State Planning Board, of a single file of all decisions would be a valuable reference file for the Board in giving publicity to current actions for the benefit of the various local planning boards.

MASSACHUSETTS STATE PLANNING BOARD

CWA, ERA, and WPA Projects

One of the best indications of the inactivity of planning boards is the extraordinarily slight advantage taken by them of the emergency relief programs. The best measure of the failure is the substantial and valuable progress made by those communities that did set up planning projects. One small community, with a normal appropriation of $100, had projects in all three relief programs, with total allotments of $14,513, with which they carried out a general survey of one section of the town, a survey of public property, and a traffic survey. These funds represented $1.00 per capita of population.

Another town has been developing a master plan, the three projects furnishing employment equivalent to the work of fifteen men for a period of two and one-half years, the total allotment being $24,397, or $2.25 per capita of population.

A larger city likewise carried out projects in all three programs, at a total cost of $52,891, representing $0.35 per capita of population.

These are not all the cases, but they represent the more successful activities in the smaller communities.

The opportunities offered in a city the size of Boston, having a larger list of unemployed and more extended studies that could be made to advantage, provided the largest single field for planning projects, which were carried on through all three relief programs. The maps of the city were corrected, a use map of the city was brought up to date, housing studies in the inner congested areas, a real property inventory, an alley survey, and an income and cost survey were made. These projects involved total allocations of approximately $450,000 (or $0.58 per capita). A current project for the completion of the engineering survey of the city, left partially complete for the past forty years, involves the use of over 400 persons for several years, and a total allocation of nearly $900,000 (or $1.10 per capita). The fact that only a handful of Massachusetts cities and towns have reported such projects is a sign of a wasted opportunity. If, as seems likely, the need for similar unemployment relief is destined to continue for some time, it may not be too late for other communities to take advantage of these most valuable types of work relief.

New Town Planning Act

The 1936 legislature passed a law (Chapter 211) "providing an

MASSACHUSETTS STATE PLANNING BOARD

Table 72

SUGGESTED FORMS FOR CURRENT REPORTS OF ACTION
BY ZONING APPEAL BOARDS AND FOR ZONING DISTRICT CHANGES
(addressed post card forms)

1. Suggested Form for Reporting Actions of Boards of Appeal

```
City or Town _____ Your Case No. _____
Street and No. _____
Premises are in a _____ zone.
Reason for Refusal of Permit by Bldg. Dept. _____

Reasons offered by Appellant _____

Decision of Board    Date _____
    Granted      Granted-Proviso          Denied      Withdrawn
Comment _____
```

2. Suggested Form for Reporting Re-zoning Cases

```
City or Town _____ Your Case No. _____
Location of Property _____
From _____ zone to _____ zone.
Recommendation of Planning Board _____
Date _____
Action by Council or Town Meeting _____
Date _____
Comment _____
```

MASSACHUSETTS STATE PLANNING BOARD

improved method of municipal planning". The Act goes into effect January, 1937, after which time all new planning boards must be organized in accordance with its provisions. The Act, however, does not require existing boards to reorganize. Inquiry at the regional meetings disclosed considerable unfamiliarity with the Act. Copies were distributed and discussion was had as to the wisdom of reergonizing under the Act, and appropriate methods of so doing. A considerable number of boards indicated an intention of taking such action, and no general opposition to such action appeared to exist in the minds of selectmen and mayors, some of whom were represented on the planning boards. The town of Saugus has already voted to adopt the provisions of the Act and to appoint a planning board thereunder. It intends to elect the Board members at the annual town meeting in 1937, after the Act has gone into effect. Another planning board has indicated its intention to act at a similar special town meeting prior to December 31.

In some cases, a distinct disinclination to reorganize the planning board in accordance with the new Act was found. In one case, the reason given for not acting was the completely satisfactory coöperation now existing between the Planning Board and the town officials. In another case, the reason for not opening up the question was the very unsatisfactory local political situation.

The local boards were unanimous in asking the State Planning Board to issue a document explaining the provisions of the Act, and the methods to be adopted in creating a planning board under its provisions. Decision as to any action to be taken obviously rests with the local communities but a clearer understanding of the provisions of the Act is obviously desirable.

Practical Results of Planning Board Activity

It is often difficult to appraise the value of the results of planning board activity. Long-range plans, in the nature of things, are principally on paper, their value largely potential. The actual value of projects planned and constructed is not a matter of precise figures. Members of planning boards are likely to be prejudiced in favor of the value contributed by their work, but nevertheless are better informed on the facts than is the average citizen.

Feeling that a more detached point of view would be desirable, inquiry was made of an architect prominent in his community and his profession, as to the work of his local Planning Board. His reply in substance was that he really didn't know much about it, had never heard anything about it, and suspected it wasn't very active

MASSACHUSETTS STATE PLANNING BOARD

or effective, but that he would investigate and report further. A week or so later, a report was received outlining the situation and ending with the following sentence: "Although one does not hear very much of the activities of the Planning Board, it seems to be a fact that all the changes, modifications, and developments of the city plan are under its control and that a real public service is being rendered in a thoroughly efficient manner".

It seemed unwise to rely generally on such outside investigations, and, therefore, letters were sent to a selected list of chairmen and members of local boards, as already noted. The discriminating character of the replies, often frankly pessimistic and reporting negative results, gives credibility to the opinions stated and suggests that where assertions of substantial results are emphatically made that they may be taken at their face value.

The following summary of the twenty statements, so far received, as to the effectiveness of planning board activity is, therefore, of interest:

10 replied emphatically "yes".
4 replied with a qualified "yes" indicating that the values largely related to zoning.
3 replied "no, except for zoning".
3 replied "no", for the past but one of these reported current work on a master plan, including revision of the zoning law, with a substantial appropriation.

This last statement also included the information that another town board had been forced by the Planning Board to adhere to plans for a public improvement that had been developed by a special committee in consultation with the Planning Board. The statement adds "A by-product of this episode was a very apparent general increase in respect for the Planning Board". An exactly parallel episode and result were reported at one of the regional meetings. It would seem, therefore, that at least one of the two negative votes should be accepted with substantial reservations, as being too modest a statement.

It is not strange that the practical values should appear to relate largely to zoning matters, as these are the current adjustments of business needs or desires, and are more continuous and obvious than matters involving the larger elements of the city plan and its gradual development. It also appears in these reports that, in various cases, a master plan had been made ten or fifteen years ago, at which time a substantial appropriation had been made for this purpose, and that, since then, this plan had been used

MASSACHUSETTS STATE PLANNING BOARD

steadily as a general guide in laying out new public ways.

The list of public improvements cited as having resulted from planning board activity need not be quoted at length. It includes: street improvements, parkways, location of new subdivision layouts, improved design of stores and filling stations, and the protection of new highways from undesirable developments. On this score, one statement concludes as follows: "All important physical developments since 1923, have been influenced in detail by the work of the City Planning Commission".

Relation to State Planning Board

The creation of a State Planning Board in a State in which local planning boards have long existed makes it desirable to establish clearly the limits within which the State Board is intended to function. It is as undesirable for the local boards to expect too much of the State Board as it would be for the agency of planning on a State-wide basis to fail in providing adequate support, encouragement, and coördination to the work of the local boards. With this in mind, the legitimate fields of activity of the local and State Beards were discussed at the regional meetings and a tentative outline of the functions appropriate to each was submitted.

This outline was the result of an analysis of the answers by local boards to a previous inquiry from the State Board as to the kinds of assistance the local boards would like to receive. Some of these were clearly beyond the proper scope of action by the State Board, involving support of purely local projects. Such requests made doubly clear the need of establishing promptly in the minds of the local boards the limits within which the State Board should appropriately function.

A regular bulletin of some form, to be issued by the State Planning Board and sent to all the members of the local planning boards at stated intervals, monthly or otherwise, was suggested as a means of accomplishing effectively the distribution of information of various kinds. Some such instrument seems necessary if the State Board is to keep in constant touch with the more than 130 local planning boards throughout the Commonwealth.

The following outline, as presented at the regional meetings, is recorded here as a tentative draft that should be perfected and then distributed to the various local boards.

MASSACHUSETTS STATE PLANNING BOARD

Elements of a State Program

1. Action by State Planning Board

    a. Clearing house of information for local Boards on:
        1. Action of other boards;
        2. Legislation;
        3. Court decisions;
    b. Support for local projects involving State-wide factors
    c. Regular contact with representatives of local boards
    d. General technical advice as to:
        1. Developing a master plan
        2. Zoning
    e. Developing the support of officials and public by:
        1. State publicity releases
        2. Regional and local meetings as feasible
        3. Speakers at local meetings
        4. Conferences with local officials and citizens

2. Action by Local Boards

    a. Maintain contact with State Planning Board
    b. Inform it of local developments of importance
    c. Demand recognition by adequate appropriations
    d. Secure local technical advice as needed
    e. Secure public support by effective actions
    f. Develop desirable local publicity program

Conclusions

General Appraisal of Local Planning Activities

From the facts presented in this report it seems proper to draw up the following general conclusions. A local planning board is likely to be effective, if:

    a. Its personnel includes some members technically trained in one or more of the techniques involved in community planning.
    b. It is given an adequate appropriation with which to carry on a consistent program in scale with the needs of the community.
    c. It is able to secure adequate cooperation from other public officials.
    d. It is able to develop public understanding of the problems involved in the community's plan and to secure cooperation of civic leaders in the study of its problems.

APPENDIX

MAPS AND CHARTS
(Prepared, but Not Presented in This Report)

File
Number

Miscellaneous

50-2	Standard Gradation Symbols
50-3	Standard State Outline (1 in. = 8 mi.)
50-8	Standard Symbols for Watershed Maps (Revision)
50-11	Sample Precipitation Chart
50-14	Sample Damage Graph and Flood-Loss Profile
50-C1	Standard Alphabet
50-C2	Standard Outline for Charts and Graphs
Atlas 50-3 (1-54)	Corrected Town-Boundary Atlas
70-1	Physical Changes Authorized by the Legislature, 1935
70-2	Physical Changes Proposed by the Legislature, 1935
70-4	Standard Town-Boundary Map with Town Names
70-5	Standard Town-Boundary Map without Town Names
70-6	Standard State Outline (1 in. = 4 mi.)
70-7	Standard State Outline, Legend, and Lettering

Land

51-1	Average Value per Acre of Farm Land in Massachusetts by Towns and Cities, 1930
51-2	Percentages of Town and City Areas in Farms in Massachusetts, 1930
51-3	Percentages of Improved Land in Farms by Cities and Towns, 1930
51-4	Equalization of Property as Used in Determining State Tax, 1935
51-10	Average Annual Temperature
51-11	Average Summer Temperature
51-13	Average Maximum Temperature
51-14	Average Minimum Summer Temperature
51-15	Average Minimum Winter Temperature
51-16	Average Maximum Winter Temperature
51-17	Average Length of Growing Season
51-23	Average Date of First Killing Frost in Autumn
51-24	Average Date of Last Killing Frost in Spring
Atlas 51-1 (1-54)	Land-Ownership Atlas
51-C2	Land Utilization in Massachusetts

MASSACHUSETTS STATE PLANNING BOARD

File
Number

71-1	*Topography of Massachusetts (ERA State Planning Board Freject)
71-4	*Geology of Massachusetts (B.K. Emerson)
71-5	*Land Classification of Massachusetts (Dr. Rozman)
71-21	Physiographic Regions

Water

52-1	Deerfield Watershed
52-2	Housatonic River Watershed
52-3	Millers River Watershed
52-4	Chicopee River Watershed
52-5	Westfield River Watershed
52-6	Connecticut River Watershed
52-7	Taunton River Watershed
52-8	Blackstone River Watershed
52-9	Merrimack River Watershed
52-10	Farmington River Watershed
52-11	Nashua River Watershed
52-12	Hoosic River Watershed
52-13	Neponset River Watershed
52-14	Charles River Watershed
52-15	Concord River Watershed
52-16	North Shore Rivers Watersheds
52-17	Quinebaug and French Rivers Watersheds
52-C1	Deerfield River Profile
52-C2	Housatonic River Profile
52-C3	Millers River and Other Creek Profiles
52-C4	Chicopee River, Swift, Ware, and Quaboag Branches, Profiles
52-C5	Westfield River, Main, East, and West Branches, Profiles
52-C6	Connecticut River Profile
52-C7	Taunton River Profile
52-C8	Blackstone River Profile
52-C9	Merrimack River Profile
52-C10	Farmington River Profile
52-C11	Nashua River, North and South Branches, Profiles
52-C19	Precipitation Chart -- Farmington River Watershed at Otis Station
Atlas 52-1	(1-38) Flood-Control Atlas
Atlas 52-2	Connecticut Valley Flood Control.
Atlas 52-3	Connecticut River Flood-Inundation Data Sheets

*Maps from outside sources, which are pertinent to State Planning Board Studies

MASSACHUSETTS STATE PLANNING BOARD

File
Number

72-1   Watersheds and Stream-Gaging Stations
72-4   Municipalities Without Sewage-Disposal Works

Industry and Social Conditions

54-C16   Massachusetts Business Index -- Volume of New Home Building
54-C17   Massachusetts Business Index -- Department Store Sales
54-C18   Massachusetts Business Index -- Cotton Textile Production
54-C33   Comparison of Per Capita Assessed Values for Various Uses and Residential Types, City of Boston, 1934
54-C34   Comparison of Per Capita Net Cost and Per Capita Net Income for Various Residential Rental Ranges, City of Boston, 1934
54-C35   Comparison of Per Capita Net Cost or Per Capita Net Income for Various Residential Rental Ranges and Fine Residential Types, Boston, 1934
54-C37   Comparison of Per Capita Income or Per Capita Expenditures for Various Rental Ranges
54-C38   Effect of Increased Federal Spending on Total Spendable Incomes 1934, 1935, 1936 (Diagram #1)
54-C39   Effect of Increased Federal Spending on Total Spendable Incomes 1934, 1935, 1936 (Diagram #2)
54-C40   Effect of Increased Federal Spending on Total Spendable Incomes 1934, 1935, 1936 (Diagram #3)
54-C41   Effect of Increased Federal Spending on Total Spendable Incomes 1934, 1935, 1936 (Diagram #4)
54-C42   Effect of Increased Federal Spending on Total Spendable Incomes 1934, 1935, 1936 (Diagram #6)
54-C43   Effect of Increased Federal Spending on Total Spendable Incomes 1934, 1935, 1936 (Diagram #7)
54-C44   Effect of Increased Federal Spending on Total Spendable Incomes 1934, 1935, 1936 (Diagram #8)
54-C45   Relation of Federal Primary and Secondary Spending to Total National Income (Diagram #5)
54-C46   Comparison of Per Capita Net Cost or Per Capita Net Income for Various Residential Rental Ranges for Other Cities and Towns, 1934

Transport

76-3   Safety Ratio of Certain State Routes

MASSACHUSETTS STATE PLANNING BOARD

File
Number

Public Works

57-C1	State Operating Costs by Departments, 1925-1935. Financial Table #1
57-C2	Total State Revenue by Sources, 1925-1935. Financial Table #2
57-C3	State Expenditures According to Subdivisions (Personal Services, State Aid, State Debt, Capital Outlay, and Other Expenses), 1925-1935, Inclusive. Financial Table #3
57-C4	Graph of Receipts and Expenditures, 1925-1935, of the State Department of Public Works
57-C5	Graph of Expenditures, 1925-1935, of the State Department of Mental Diseases
57-C6	Graph of Expenditures, 1925-1935, of the State Department of Public Health
57-C7	Graph Showing Portion of Every State Dollar Expended by Department, 1925-1935
57-C8	Graph of Construction Status of All Approved PWA Projects, as of Feb. 6, 1936
57-C9	Graph of Estimated Cost and Federal Allotment of All Approved PWA Projects, as of Feb. 6, 1936
57-C10	Percentage Graph of Construction Status of All PWA Projects, as of Feb. 6, 1936
77-1	PWA Education Projects
77-2	PWA Projects -- Hospital Improvements
77-3	PWA Projects -- Waterworks
77-4	PWA Streets, Sidewalks, and Drainage Projects
77-5	PWA Bridges, Canal, and Dredging Projects
77-6	PWA Sewers and Sewage -- Treatment Works Projects
77-7	Miscellaneous PWA Projects

Community Planning

58-C1	Disposition of all Appeals by Type of Appeals
58-C2	Percentage of Use, Height, and Coverage Appeals Sustained
58-C3	Distribution of Board of Adjustment Petitions
58-C4	Board of Adjustment Petitions and Numbers Sustained
58-C5	Percentage Disposition of Appeals, by Sections of Zoning Law Involved
58-C6	Relation of Annual Expenditures to Number of Petitions Filed
58-C7	Number and Disposition of Appeals
58-C8	Percentage of All Appeals Sustained, by Years, 1924-1934
58-C9	Appeals, by Wards, 1926-1935

MASSACHUSETTS STATE PLANNING BOARD

File
Number

58-C10 Ratio of Appeal Cases to Building. Permit Applications
58-C11 Seasonal Variations in Number of Appeal Cases and Building. Permit Applications
58-C12 Percentage of Rezoning Petitions Recommended Granted by Planning Boards and Percentage Granted by Council, 1927-1935
58-C13 Planning Board Recommendations on Rezoning Cases Accepted by the City Council, 1927-1935
58-C14 Number of Rezoning Petitions and Number Granted, 1927-1935
58-C15 Number and Disposition of Appeals, Lynn, Mass., 1926-1935
58-C16 Trend of Percentage of All Appeals Granted, Lynn, Mass., 1924-1935
58-C17 Seasonal Trends in Appeal Cases and Building Permits, Lynn, Mass.
58-C18 Relation of Appeal Cases to Building Permits, Lynn, Mass., 1926-1935

Lightning Source UK Ltd.
Milton Keynes UK
UKHW012307140219
337323UK00011B/379/P